ONE, TWO, THREE... PIZZAZZ!

My Forty Years In Competitive Show Choir

(1977-2016)

By

Dave Willert

"One, Two, Three ... Pizzazz" by Dave Willert. ISBN 978-1-947532-71-7 (hardcover).

Published 2018 by Virtualbookworm.com Publishing Inc., P.O. Box 9949, College Station, TX 77842, US.

Table of Contents

INTRODUCTION

"*One, two, three... Pizzazz*!" I've shared those exciting words with the members of just about every show choir I have ever taught, for as long as I can remember! Did it help them learn to instantly *pour on the passion* or to have more *exciting facial expressions*? Well, I have no proof that would hold up in court… but, *yes*, I strongly believe that it did! More importantly, it gave my groups a special *mantra, to unite us*! The truth is, it was always a big part of each of my show choir's improvement and road to confidence! In fact, "*One, Two, Three... Pizzazz*," has been one of the hallmarks of almost every successful group I have ever directed, along with, "Success Finds a Way, Failure Finds an Excuse!" But, I thought the former sounded more like a show choir, so I chose it to be the title of this *show choir* book! Maybe the latter can be the title of the sequel?

To begin with, I think generally speaking, when an adult tells another adult that they were in *show choir*, while in high school, or junior high, the other person simply smiles and says something encouraging like, "I'll bet that was fun!" But show choir, at least the type of show choir that Margaret, Doug and I have been a party to, was a lot more than that! Learning to work together for the common goal of *winning*, while singing, dancing and performing is *so much more than just fun*! In fact, sometimes it wasn't *fun at all*, being yelled at or criticized… but we all learned to handle those days that *always* seemed to happen when we least expected them. Sometimes it was a student who was frustrated and decided to vent… but more often than not, it was Doug or me sharing our thoughts and demanding that the students in question get their acts together! Wow! Those were some pretty passionate times. But I don't believe that our groups would have been nearly as competitive as they were, if not for *timely, honest and passionate critique*. It's definitely a huge part of the process that leads us all to getting better at what we do.

But, before going any further, I had best explain that I was actually only a *high school and junior high, show choir director* for *39 years…* and a *student teacher* at West Covina High School, under Tom Kessler, for part of *another year…* well, *actually closer to ten weeks*. I added them together to make forty years, because I thought it was important to make my wonderful *West Covina High School student teaching* experience, part of my story… and besides, *I felt that the number, "forty," just sounded better than the number, "thirty-nine," when talking about anything*, except perhaps a person's age. In short, I spent those *forty* years, working with choir kids, teaching them about singing and performing, while Doug simultaneously taught them all kinds of choreography. In addition, Margaret and Doug designed the costumes, and the three of us, *together*, built an attitude throughout every single group of every single year, that winning a show choir competition… *really meant something!* Without the students *absolutely* buying into that premise… *this book would have had absolutely no reason to be written*! But they did buy into it, and so did Doug and I, and the parents and the principals and the school boards, and the communities! Every time the students competed as a group at a competition, against groups from other schools, they felt united! Furthermore, by winning or even by just *competing together…* they felt a part of something special… *something that really mattered*! People, who have never competed with groups, probably cannot understand the joy, the excitement and the sense of belonging to something, that is such an inherent part of the experience! We were all trying so hard to win, so many hundreds of times! But many times… *we didn't win.* However, we kept trying, always trying… until hopefully… we did! So you see? That's why I had to write this book. It is so important to recount those forty exciting years of singing and dancing together on the stage, hoping for a trophy, but getting so much more! I wrote this book especially for *everyone who was there*, performing on stage, helping off-stage or supporting us from the audience. May these brief recollections give you exciting and permanent memories of those forever frustrating, but exciting days of past… when you, Doug, Margaret and I, *first came to love show choir*!

Unlike what many people, outside of show choir, believe… the competition results *really weren't* the crowning achievement of each competition year! That's because show choir competitions, like most competitions, are judged *subjectively*, and not *always* according to the score-sheet, similar to competitive ice-skating in the *Olympics* or the method of having a small group of voters select the *Academy Awards*. No matter how educated and qualified the judges may be, they are always open to subconscious or even conscious *bias*. I don't think as a rule they are doing anything dishonest, it's just that when you know the background and the track record of an adjudicator, you will very seldom see them change. *They believe what they believe*. Adjudicator bias has worked both ways for us over the past forty years. Sometimes an adjudicator just loves our style, or our choreography. Sometimes, he or she might even be a professional friend who may score us a couple of points higher than we deserve. But at other times, they may have never heard of us, we are not like what they are used to, or as a former show choir competitor, they are now given the perfect opportunity to get back at us for beating them in the past, by scoring us a bit more harshly. For these reasons, when going into a competition, I always had some idea of how we would, or would not place. So, the competition results *aren't the most important* part of competitive show choir, but on the other hand, they *are the part* that drives your groups to work harder, they get you valuable accolades from the school and community and keep your program running at a high level! Actually, my earliest groups at Nogales High School, from 1979-1982, were definitely some of my hardest workers, with a very clear vision of what they wanted. W*hat they wanted*, no show choir from Nogales High School had ever earned before! They wanted to *place, and earn a trophy* at a competition… but sadly, for whatever the reasons, *they never did*. However, the passionate work ethic they left behind, for the next group… earned them a couple of trophies in

1983! Do you see? We're talking about hard work, faith, and the ability to deal with frustration while simultaneously continuing to try your hardest! There are no trophies for those attributes, but if there were… my early Chamber Singers at Nogales High School would have certainly won them every year!

When I decided to undertake this massive project, just after retiring, I immediately realized that I was *unprepared to do it.* My memories were all so recent, and there was still a lot of *ancient* show choir history that I had yet to uncover! So, I set-up individual sites on Facebook for each school I had previously taught at. Next, I proceeded to track down my former students from those schools, and I invited them to become members. Fortunately for me, the initial members of each group did most of the work recruiting *other members*. Next, I picked everyone's brain about each year in choir, including festivals, trips, competition sets, competition results, the colors of costumes and student officers. But what I learned was *extraordinary.* Although many students shared performance programs and candid pictures… most of them *could not remember* exactly *where we had competed* or *what places we had come in*, much less the *color of our costumes* or who the *student officers* were? The funny thing about this is that while they were in choir, *where* the groups placed and *whom* they beat, was a matter of life and death! But many years later, it's those wonderful things that we all took for granted at the time, like *friendship, memorable experiences and fun,* that everyone remembers. Who knew? I guess, for some odd reason, I was sort of expecting some of these "kids" (some of them over 50 years old) to think and behave *just like they did back in high school*! But, of course, they had matured and most had families of their own. Even their furthest thoughts were not on show choir, anymore! So, I decided to make the second half of this book, the thoughts and memories of my former students, containing what they *remembered most* about their years in show choir. In direct contrast, the first part of this book would be a mosaic of *factual information* I would collect from a variety of sources, that would briefly, but unfortunately, *incompletely*, describe each show choir year. This overview would hopefully include, at the very least, *the songs we competed with, the basic colors of our costumes, the results of how we did in some competitions, what Doug and I were thinking at the time* and *who the student officers were*, if that information became available to me.

There have certainly been a lot of changes in California show choir since it's beginning, in the early 1970s. Studying *my* show choirs, throughout the years, is a perfect way to see the evolution of show choir in California, and how *some of those changes* affected us. We did go through *a lot of changes*, but even so, I don't think that the *positive essence* of our show choirs ever changed! While the media was fixating on one terrible thing after another… show choir was always there, as a friendly and exciting alternative for the kids and me to get lost in. In show choir, my kids and I always felt motivated and powerful with the ability to create or do, *just about anything*! Beginning in 1977, singing, dancing, costumes, props, concerts, competitions, tours and writing musical arrangements became my *normal* for the next forty years! I am not shy to admit that the groups Doug and I led, have certainly been some of the most successful competing high school show choirs in the country! As evidence, they were generally winning or placing, for *four decades*! But it was never easy.

I will say that running top show choir programs for so many years got to be a little hectic at times and I did suffer a debilitating stroke in 2012, purportedly from overwork. But I am grateful for *every bit of time* I was privileged to spend in show choir, and I don't regret a single moment! I guess to a large extent, you could say that show choir had *become my life*! Along with my talented and understanding wife, Margaret, my terrific son, Alex and my genius choreographer and set designer, Doug Kuhl… it proved to be an exciting and never-ending adventure in high school, junior high school and even college show choir, for forty years!

But it wasn't just show choir. I loved working with the kids, developing their skills and attitudes that would eventually (if they were willing to work hard enough) lead them to become motivated and successful people throughout their lives! Skills like, *being goal oriented* and *learning to get along with all types of people*, are attributes that never go out of style! I am proud to say that throughout my career, no matter how young or inexperienced my top groups were, we *always competed at the top level*. Due, in large part, to my first five frustrating years of high school show choir, when my groups *never won one single award*, I learned patience and perseverance. I also learned that if my groups kept working hard enough, it would eventually lead them to success! I didn't believe my groups would develop a consistent hard working attitude in singing and performing (which they would need to win), unless they were regularly competing against the best of the best… so, they did! Although in the early years, that often meant *being blown out of the water*, and I'll be honest, *that never felt very good, at the time*! However, as a consequence of losing, we always seemed to improve at our very next competition… and eventually, *we learned to win*!

The purpose of this book is definitely *not* to pat myself on the back for surviving forty years of competing and working with countless numbers of wonderful and talented students, all exceptional in their own ways. I loved every minute of it, and I've received countless accolades for my trouble! No, I wrote this book, with the help of many former students, parents and associates, *to share my incredible experiences in show choir over the past forty years*! To tell you the truth, in some ways, I guess I am actually writing this book *for myself*, and for the opportunity to *make those very special memories permanent*! However, if anyone else cares to read it… *please be my guest*! I have written the first half of this book, the historical part, in chronological order, so that any readers, who were in my show choirs, may find *their years* without much trouble. But I also did this, so that anyone *wishing to read the entire book* might experience, as Doug, Margaret and I did, *the successes and the rebuilding of our groups throughout our entire thirty-nine year teaching span*, or within the years that we taught at each school. For us, *rebuilding* was actually much more prevalent than *prolonged winning streaks,* but *both experiences proved invaluable* to our staff and students, in learning how to cope effectively, with any situation… and still maintain a "*winning*" attitude! Handling both *winning* and *losing* well, are essential to good character building. We always stressed that there was as much to gain from a loss as a win… although, it didn't always feel as good!

I don't pretend that every one of my former choir students, throughout the years, *felt the same positive way* about my program. That component varied from year to year, from group to group, from person to person and sometimes even *from day to day*! However, I do believe that *most of my students*, throughout the years, probably rated their choir experiences in a positive way, with a small group having more *negative* opinions, while another select group most assuredly, *absolutely loved being in choir above all else at school*! To many of these former students, who found choir to be *fun and worthwhile*, being in choir meant being completely immersed in this exciting and fulfilling school activity! To them, choir was a funhouse, complete with friends, music, dance, rehearsals, performances, trips and the opportunity to excel and improve their dance spots and solos, through hard work! They may have even thought of the choir room as being their second homes! I *sentimentally* refer to these students as being my "*choir kids*!" But what I truly loved most about working with *all of my students from my different show choir programs*, was that even though everyone joined for different reasons and came in with different attitudes toward singing and performing… in the end, we all *grew together as one family*! You can see *exactly what I'm talking about*, when you watch the video recordings of our competitions and home concerts! *Those groups were tight*!

For those of you who were choir students of mine at some point, thank you, for the inspiration you gave me, resulting in the writing of this book! Some of you also shared memories of *your own years in show choir*, for me to use, and I would especially like to thank you for your contributions! Your names should appear at the end of this book, under, **Acknowledgements**, as my token of thanks! I'd also like to thank all of my former *Norco students* on the Facebook page, who have helped immensely in bringing those *very early years of show choir* to light again. From Nogales, I would like to thank *Gabriel Lomeli, Ruben Hoyos, Margaux Yap, Jeanette Zapata* and many others for helping me to find a lot of the Nogales choir history, which I had almost given up on. From Diamond Bar I would like to especially thank *Caroline Yenydunyeyan, Janae West, Julia Weil, Letty Garcia and Catherine Larson* for all of their help in remembering costume colors, and *Jessica Jones* for her help in figuring out the year of our Disneyland competition. I also wish to thank *Spike Abeyta,* for providing the programs from three different Diamond Bar musicals that he participated in, during my years there, giving me a wealth of information, for this book! From Brea, a great big thank you to *Charisse Green Groh, Terry Dopson, Sean Barba, Ally Catanesi, Kayla Camacho & Kristen Webster* for tracking down the different colors of each group's costumes. I would also like to offer a very special thanks to *Charisse Green Groh* for sharing her highly detailed memories of life in the choir room immediately after I had my stroke, as well as to *Jennifer Eckels Winters,* for her vivid memories of that first turbulent year at Brea Olinda. Finally, a huge thank you to *Andrea Strom*, for all of her help gathering dates and specifics on important Brea choir history! From Show Choir Express, thanks to *Allie Mayer, Hailey Leeann Johnson and Ayla Golshan for* their big help with the costume colors, and to *Kayla Camacho*, for playing a vital role in collecting the names of Brea Junior High's very first *Show Choir Express*. Also, a very special thanks to *Ayla Golshan* for finding so many former students and their dates of attendance at Brea Junior High! Last, but not least, a warm thanks to *Paula Crowley Hanson*, a student of *Tom Kessler's*, while I did my student teaching at West Covina High School, in 1977. She provided me with a plethora of wonderful memories and insights about being in choir with Tom, which I am very grateful for!

This book is in no way designed to be *all-inclusive*, regarding my forty years in show choir. As I already mentioned, it only *briefly chronicles* each show choir year, *mentioning only some of the competitions*, and a few other select activities, according to the information that I was able to collect. For example, I will mention in greater detail, the *musicals* that *choir produced* at both Nogales and Brea Olinda, because *I have more information on those*. I will also recognize the Diamond Bar musicals, but since the drama department handled most of the work, my information on those is understandably, more sketchy, although fortunately, *I do have the cast lists for three of those shows*! The most important thing to remember, however, is that what is written, in this book, is completely true, *to the best of my knowledge*. I sincerely hope that you enjoy reliving this wonderful time again!

If you picked-up this book by mistake, you are probably wondering, *what exactly is show choir?* Well, there are a number of fine books written on the historical beginnings of show choir, but the most thorough one I have read is, ***Sweat, Tears and Jazz Hands: The Official History of Show Choir from Vaudeville to Glee,*** written by Mike Weaver and Coleen Hart and published by Hal Leonard in 2011**.** There is even a paragraph in the book about the Nogales High School Chamber Singers, Doug Kuhl and myself, and how we were all a *force in developing early show choirs in California*! Very cool! In addition, this is a well-documented reference on show choir history, including the west coast, mid-west and east coast styles, which all began from *diversely different influences*. As I have said, my book *does not* deal with the history of show choir. It deals with *my personal story, in show choir*, for forty years, as I remember it, and then backed-up by as many facts as I could find. High school music teachers and show choir directors will surely find something of interest here. However, as I told you, I have really written this book *for myself and for all of the people who were involved with me…* students, parents, family and associates. The result, is my memoirs of forty years in show choir, *exciting memories*, which I wanted to chronicle while they were still fresh in my mind, *or at least in somebody's*! I never want to forget this fantastic journey or the wonderful people who I worked with and was inspired by, for a lifetime!

I would especially like to thank my wonderful wife, Margaret, who made *beautiful and very complete concert programs for almost every home concert, banquet and festival my choirs ever hosted.* She then had the smarts to *save a copy of each*, through all of these years. I used the information on these programs, including song lists, competition results and names of group members *almost exclusively*, along with my personal memories, to write the first draft of this book. In addition, these programs helped me to make sure that dates, events, songs performed, band members, and group names were all accurate. These programs turned out to be my personal *Dead Sea Scrolls*! When I had *absolutely nothing* for Brea Junior High, she also came up with the idea of checking the trophies at the junior high to see how and where each year's group or groups placed! My Margaret is and has always been… *my better half*!

Apparently, an apology seems to be in order, for *not including pictures* in this book. I am fully aware that a lot of people are very disappointed and I understand completely. However, *since I am assuming all responsibility and expense for the publishing of this book*, adding pictures would have just made the *cost too prohibitive* for me. Also, the resulting book with the addition of pictures (to what is already over six hundred pages long without them) would have resulted in an even *more astronomical price tag for you,* than this book already has! Besides, I would be hard-pressed to decide *which pictures*, representing the *160 different competing show choirs* I have taught, over the years, should be used? In breaking them down, I had two groups at Norco over a period of two years, fifty-eight groups at Nogales over a period of nineteen years, forty-one groups at Diamond Bar over a period of seven years, forty-six groups at Brea Olinda over a period of eleven years and thirteen groups at Brea Junior High over a period of eleven years. The number of pictures I would have wanted to use, *representing every group,* would have surely made-up an entire book, all by themselves! However, all of the pictures *I would have used*, are available to you, either on my personal website, davewillert.com, or on the separate Facebook pages, for each school, where many of you have shared pictures, and I hope will *continue sharing pictures*, including, *Dave & Doug Choir Alumni Group, Brea Junior High Show Choirs with Dave & Doug, Brea Show Choirs with Dave & Doug, Diamond Bar Show Choirs with Dave & Doug, Nogales Show Choirs with Dave and Doug, and Norco Show Choirs with Dave.* With the purpose of celebrating our very memorable show choir years together, I hope this book proves to be as much fun for you to read… as it was for me to research and to write!

ONE, TWO, THREE, PIZZAZZ!

My Forty Years In Competitive Show Choir

(1977-2016)

CHAPTER I

West Covina High School... 1977...
The Seed of Show Choir Takes Root!

Long before I had become obsessed with show choir, and even a few years before the first *Star Wars* movie was released… I fell in love with musical theatre. After performing the role of *Fagin* in *Oliver*, in the spring of 1972, my senior year of high school, I was hooked! I went on to perform a number of other *amateur* musical theatre roles in college and community theatre productions, over the next decade or so, simply because I loved doing it so much! During my childhood, I credit my mother, Ruth, for my initial love of music through the weekly piano lessons she gave me, as well as encouraging me to sing in the youth choir, for a time, at the church she played organ for. I credit my initial love for the theatre to my father, Oriel, who directed a youth musical theatre group, in Glendora, for a short time, while I was too young to participate, but was still *completely enthralled by the magic going on, on the stage*! Disneyland was also an early source of inspiration, during my childhood. We didn't go there very often, but when we did, it was as if I had just stepped inside a *fantastic land full of fun and imagination, that always included music and shows… my favorites*! I am not ashamed to admit that I have had a lifelong love affair with Disneyland! In addition, I took up the guitar, at twelve, and sang for fun with my talented brothers and sisters and close friends, well beyond my college years. I had some *exceptional* teachers at Glendora High School, the place where I first formally began learning the arts of singing and performing, but *Thomas Timm Brucks*, my drama teacher, during my junior year, probably inspired me the most! He is the teacher who first introduced me to *professionalism,* as well as trusting me enough, *even as an inexperienced young actor*, to cast me in my first lead role, in the play, *A Thurber Carnival*. I was also influenced heavily by the *beautiful and creative harmonies* the Beatles always featured on their albums (usually attributed to the arranging of George Martin). I have to admit, that during my forty years of arranging music for my own groups, I have always used *the Beatles as my inspiration and model* for writing many of my own harmonies. In addition, I credit God with always being an inspiration and a comfort to me, even as I made some "*questionable*" decisions, like leaving Norco for Nogales and Diamond Bar for Brea. In both of those instances, I felt *certain* (for no apparent reason), that these moves, regardless of their inherent challenges, were right for me, at the time… *and they were*! While in college, at the University of Redlands, I received a very good *traditional* music education, with inspiring teachers such as *Professor Jeff Rickard*, my choir director during my senior year. In theory, this education prepared me to teach choirs in schools, although even after graduation, I still felt as if *I had a lot to learn*! I minored in theatre arts, at the U. of R., with the thought that I could possibly put that to use someday, as well. I was torn at this time; because I really did not love the idea of teaching only traditional choirs… my true love was still *musical theatre*! Once I graduated, in 1976, I moved back home, to Glendora, and immediately enrolled in a student teaching program at Cal Poly, Pomona.

While at Cal Poly, I received some excellent vocal training from their choir director, at the time, *Dr. Charles Lindsley*. The concept of breathing for singers was made much simpler for me, as he taught it using the names of the actual muscles involved. This proved to be a fundamental learning in my own teaching for years to come. Dr. Lindsley also treated each note created by a singer, as special, and requiring the *necessary polish before being ready for an audience*. His *attention to detail* also proved to become a cornerstone of my own teaching. But, this *music education enrichment* only lasted for a quarter, as I soon began my student teaching, during the second and third quarters of the 1976-77 school year.

For the second quarter, I was placed at *Ganesha High School*, to work with both the choir and drama programs. Ganesha High School boasted a predominantly black student body, and it was located in the heart of Pomona. Although I grew to love my beginning drama class, where the students were involved with every lesson, and participated fully, every day… unfortunately, my experience with the choirs was far different. My master teacher graciously allowed me to fully teach two separate choir classes of beginners, *everyday*, but unfortunately, I proved to be woefully unprepared for the challenge! I wielded no real authority, to speak of and basically both choirs were energetic, but undisciplined. As a result, my first real experience in teaching high school choirs was difficult and consequently… unsatisfying… *for everyone*! I had no problem getting the kids *initially motivated*, as motivating people seemed to be one of my early strengths… but as soon as we began singing the traditional choir pieces, the fidgeting began and the learning ended. It probably did not help that I was a *barely proficient pianist* and the choirs did not have an accompanist to assist me, in holding the singers together.

I was soon convinced, albeit disappointed, that I did not possess what it took to be a successful choir director. At the conclusion of the second quarter, I went to my advisor at Cal Poly and shared with him what an unfulfilling experience I had received at Ganesha High School, mostly because *I felt unqualified*. I told him, that for obvious reasons… *I was considering dropping out of the teaching program altogether*. He laughed, and told me that I should not rush to judgment, merely because of one *less than perfect experience*. He shared with me that he knew I would love the next program he was sending me to… *West Covina High School and Mr. Tom Kessler*. Over the years, I have forgotten the name of my student teaching advisor at Cal Poly, Pomona. But I wish now that I could thank him!

Tom Kessler, had actually served as a very successful band and orchestra director at local Virgil Junior High School, in West Covina, for a number of years, when the choir opening came up at West Covina High School, I believe in 1974. He was asked to take the job and to revive the stagnant choral program. He was obviously up to the task! He immediately developed two fine Bel Canto choirs, one women's choir and a beginning choir to anchor the program… but he also transformed the school's small and elite, Chamber Singers into a *nationally known show choir*! At that time, show choir was still in its infancy in California. By 1977, when I did my student teaching with him, the West Covina High School Chamber Singers were already the group to beat, in any California competition!

I met Tom Kessler, an unassuming, but very energetic man, in the main office of *West Covina High School*, in early March of 1977. He went over the daily choir schedule with me and then smiling, he told me that he would see me in class on Monday. I walked out, feeling rather curious and excited about his choral program. He was a very friendly man, very approachable… but beneath all of that, he was also *very driven!* This is what excited me most about learning his teaching methods and especially all about his show choir!

Over the next ten glorious weeks, I learned what Tom did to develop and to maintain a high school choral program, which featured the hardest working kids (up to this point) that I had ever had the privilege of working with! He was a *demanding director* but also a father figure to all of his kids… and consequently… they *wanted* to work hard for him. But when I reached the final period of each school day, *I was truly amazed.* This was when Tom's *Chamber Singers* would rehearse, and they were something special to behold, especially for a choir class. They sang well… but performed flawless choreography at the same time! They also exhibited phenomenal *facial expressions* and *energy*, while performing. That's when I knew! This is what I wanted to spend my life doing. More than anything, I wanted to be a *show choir director!* I had finally discovered a genre that was both musical and included all of the excitement of a Broadway show! *Show choir was perfect*!

In 1977, competing show choirs were mostly small. The West Covina High School Chamber Singers, for example, featured only ten couples… ten boys and ten girls. They would sing and dance in class almost every day, and bring a smile to my face for the entire time. I was in awe! If I had been fortunate enough to begin my teaching career with *them*, I would have felt like I had *died and gone to heaven*! Although he played piano well, Tom *chose to have* an *excellent* full-time accompanist (who also happened to be his daughter, Karen), to free him up to be a director. Not being much of a pianist, myself, *I loved that idea*, and insisted on having an accompanist at every school I taught at, throughout my entire career!

Unexpectedly, I discovered a *forty year-old journal* where I had described my experiences (along with the emotions I was feeling at the time) as a student teacher at West Covina High School, in 1977. I remember that I had kept that journal at the request of my master teacher, Tom Kessler, to hopefully make my student teaching thoughts and experiences beneficial to me in the future, as a *real teacher*. Among other things, he also asked me to learn all of his students' names within the first two weeks that I was there, to choreograph his show choir, Chamber Singers, on a song, to direct several pieces for the Bel Canto choirs to perform, to pick up his mail everyday, so that I could get to know the office staff and to see what kind of mail a choral director gets, and finally, to give voice lessons after school each week to all of his interested students, for $3.00 per half hour lesson! Those experiences all proved to be very advantageous for me, once I began teaching. I am awed by how well Tom Kessler realized this, and how *smoothly he blended all of that* into my student teaching! About five weeks into my time at West Covina High School, Tom brought to my attention, in his normal easy-going manner, that if I wanted to excel as a teacher I would have to improve my *class discipline, control the class talking*, and *have a point* to everything that I told the class. In other words, I had to *focus the class and focus myself* on what it was I was trying to accomplish. Although at the time, I was a little disappointed to hear this (it was *as if I had failed the test)*, I had to admit that *his critique was spot-on* and immediately made me aware of these personal shortcomings, which enabled me to immediately work on them… and in time… I was able to conquer them… *mostly*! Part of the problem was that I had always been a very mild-mannered person, who had hardly talked at school until I got involved in the performing arts (drama and choir) beginning with the second semester of my sophomore year of high school. So being "in charge" and "taking control" of five classes full of teenagers, on a daily basis actually sounded very challenging to the person I had spent my first 23 years of life being. From that standpoint, I can't thank Tom enough for making it clear to me that as a teacher I had to be more focused and assertive! His critique actually changed my life! Finally, if there was one thing that completely permeated every lesson that Tom Kessler taught, it was his *gentle demand* that his students always give him the very best they had! No sluffing off! Thanks to Tom, that became my attitude, as well, almost from the very beginning of my teaching career!

On a fun note, at the end of the year's, *West Covina High School Chamber Singers Banquet*, Tom Kessler honored me for, "*Directing the choirs like I was karate chopping*!" I never lost that 'special raw technique,' either! Earlier in the year, at the end of the Spring Concert, I was also presented with a *pair of scissors*, in order to help *improve my cut-offs*! I loved how Tom Kessler always wove humor into his lessons. Very effective! Looking back now, there is no doubt in my mind that Tom Kessler was not only *the father of Southern California competitive show choir*, but also an exceptionally good teacher! I will always honor him for being both!

I would just like to add, that *Nia Peeples*, of television, recording and movie fame, was a freshman in Tom's Chamber Singers when I worked with them in 1977. She went on to choreograph Tom's Chamber Singers, for several years, after she graduated. In 1990, while she was hosting *The Party Machine with Nia Peeples*, a thirty-minute nightly variety show, on television, she graciously agreed to serve as an adjudicator for me, at the NDSCC (Nogales Divisional Show Choir Competition) at Citrus College. She was so wonderful. At the end, she stayed and signed autographs for all of the very excited show choir kids, until long after the festival had ended!

Paula (Crowley) Hanson, a student of Tom's, while I was *student teaching* at West Covina High School, had this to say about Tom Kessler's Chamber Singers and how working with him, affected her:

As a freshman at West Covina High School, I found Tom Kessler (the choir director from my junior high) again directing a show choir, only bigger and better than the junior high version. I watched and dreamed of becoming a part of the WCHS Chamber Singers (which wasn't a chamber choir at all, but a show choir). I attended and enjoyed all of their competitions, discovering performers from other schools with whom I would later perform, in college. Meanwhile, in summer school, I enrolled in Chamber Singer Workshop, and obtained some dance instruction. I rehearsed with our band department's dance team, in preparation for auditions, so that I would gain that experience. Meanwhile, I sang with the choirs and took voice lessons, and when, as a sophomore, I auditioned for Chamber Singers, I was accepted into the group, where I practiced and performed for my junior and senior years.

As an introvert, who loved to sing, having the opportunity to shine in an award-winning show choir was a wonderful experience for me. We rehearsed (seemingly forever) and all our hard work paid-off, as we were frequently the winners of the show choir competitions in which we competed. It wasn't all about winning, however. Equally rewarding, perhaps more so, was the experience of our local performances for women's clubs, luncheons, civic groups, and a school auditorium filled with children who had Down syndrome. This was perhaps the most rewarding performance and appreciative audience.

I am a stronger and better person, because Mr. Kessler taught me to work hard, make no excuses and get the job done. Along the way, he also taught me to make and appreciate beautiful music, to focus on making someone else's day better and even to dance! He was a strict taskmaster, and yet, he had a goofy sense of humor. Mr. Kessler wasn't a big man, and sometimes his bluster, intended to intimidate unruly kids into submission, came off slightly comedic... and yet, no one ever thought to laugh, but was motivated to strive harder to make our beloved director happy!

It really helped us to grow when we had "Open Mic Fridays" (Friday Solo Days), and anybody who had prepared a song, had the opportunity to sing for the rest of the class. We learned mic technique, stage presence, confidence and so much more. The singers had all levels of ability (or seemingly lack, thereof), but all improved and were affirmed on these days. Just as we closed each road performance with, "The Lord Bless You And Keep You," may the Lord bless and keep Tom Kessler (& Dona Kessler, too), in the palm of His hand.

~Paula (Crowley) Hansen, WCHS Class of 1980~

CHAPTER 2

Norco High School... 1977-1979... Norco, I Hardly Knew Ye!

Have you ever considered the possibility that things *happen*, or *don't happen* to you, *for a good reason*? The older I get, the more I believe this! Upon receiving my teaching credential from Cal Poly Pomona, I applied for *every choir opening in California,* from San Diego to Sacramento. I received a number of interviews, but with the exception of one, where the principal called to say that *I didn't get the job*, but I was his *second choice*... they were all very *unsuccessful*. By the end of the summer, the magic and awe of watching the *West Covina High School Chamber Singers* rehearsing each day, had completely worn off! This was because I found myself still living at home and working at a local liquor store... with no teaching job in sight! Frankly, *this was not at all what I had envisioned*! Then, one day, out of nowhere, I received a phone call from the personnel director of Corona Norco Unified, who proceeded to offer me a job at *Norco High School*! The previous choir director had resigned late in the summer to take a job elsewhere. I was apparently the only person in the world, who had recently applied for a choral job in their district (I had applied for a middle school opening in March, but had not been hired), who was still available... *so they gave it to me*. *Not necessarily great for my ego*, but I was eternally grateful for the job, nonetheless! Upon signing the contract, which was for a stunning *$10,000.00 a year* and finding an apartment in nearby Corona, for an equally stunning $275.00 a month, my longtime girlfriend, *Margaret*

Walter, and I, were finally able to set our wedding date for November 19, 1977.

In hindsight, when you were raised in Glendora, California, during the 1960s and 70s, as I was, you sometimes felt that you were actually in a small town, in a less crowded state, where everyone knew one another, and the term *lazy day* applied to almost every day! This is not to say that I did not enjoy living in Glendora, because I certainly did! In fact, at the time of this writing, some of my family, including my 96 year-old-mother, Ruth, still lives there. She actually lives in the same house I was raised in, *beginning in 1960*! I am just making the point that growing up in Glendora felt very *comfortable and predictable* while working in Norco felt anything but! The city was designed to feel rural, with no sidewalks, and with many people possessing animals, that you could see in their yards, such as pigs, chickens and goats, as you drove by. Many people also had stables and owned horses. Although the picture of Norco, that I've described, actually sounds quite charming… the truth of the matter is, that *I was a city slicker at heart*, so all of that *small town rural reality* that Norco quickly made me aware of, *was like nothing I had ever experienced before…* and I wasn't exactly sure how I felt about it?

I began teaching at Norco High School in the fall of 1977. The former choir director, Chet Farmer, appeared to leave me a solid program of five classes, which I was certainly grateful for. He had been very popular with the kids, I am told, but late in the summer (as I previously mentioned), he decided to accept a teaching position in San Diego. The classes I was assigned to teach, to the best of my memory, were Guitar, Music Appreciation, Concert Choir, Madrigals and… *New Generation…* ***The choral program had a show choir!*** I was so excited! I visited my new classroom about two weeks before school started. At first glance, I thought the room was very neat, *but sterile*. I had never seriously considered decorating a classroom before, and had shown no talent in decorating anything, in my life, including myself! *'Decorating Your Classroom,'* probably should have been a required course for teachers-in-training… but it wasn't. So, I did the best I could, which wasn't much. In later years I learned to let other people with some *artistic* flair, like Margaret or Doug, do my decorating for me… but I hadn't grown *smart enough* yet to realize that asking for help, *was not* a sign of weakness! Next, I went through the choir's music library (consisting of a few file cabinets). Unfortunately, I did not find a lot of popular or musical theatre pieces to build a show from in there, so I perused through a couple of music catalogues and eventually ordered a few pieces from an Anaheim store, called National Music. We were still many years away from the use of computers in the classroom. At that time, even simple things like ordering music, were very time consuming, being done entirely on the phone or through a school purchase order.

I came to class that first day of school with visions of recreating *Tom Kessler's Chamber Singers, dancing through my head,* right here at Norco High School! But, I soon learned that Norco's *New Generation* had apparently been, for a number of years, a *rock and roll show, thinly disguised as a traditional show choir…* or at least that's what the students told me. As the year went on, I found myself in a *civil war of sorts*, with a small group of students, mostly veterans, from New Generation, the last year. This "*war*" came to a head, one day, when they spoke to me in my office. Without beating around the bush, they declared that *New Gen* was a group that had always been run by the students! They went on to add that the students also selected their own music. My job, as director, they told me, was simply to *schedule their performances*. There were just over twenty students in the group, in total, so they probably felt confident that I needed them and would probably succumb to their demands. A few moments later, *after I got past my initial shock*, I politely let them know that I had a *different vision* of where I wanted New Generation to go. I wanted a show choir, like Tom Kessler's at West Covina High School. I wanted the group to be determined, high energy, musical and most of all, competitive! In addition, I insisted on being the one to select their repertoire, although I did offer to listen to any of my students' ideas. In defense of those unhappy kids, I know that they were only saying the things, that they felt were right! They clearly liked the way the group had been before

I had arrived and saw *no good reason to change it*! But, as the semester moved on, the harder I pushed, *the harder they pushed back*! Consequently, at the end of the first semester, a number of the unhappy students dropped the class, not in anger, but citing *scheduling conflicts*. I responded by adding students from the Concert Choir to take their places. This wasn't an immediately popular move to some students, who felt that the new kids *did not deserve* to be in New Generation. However, by the time they began rehearsing together, all of that animosity seemed to be forgotten.

The competition set I had chosen for the year… *actually changed from show to show*, depending upon what sounded the best to me at the time. I was a rookie show choir director, in my first year of teaching, and just like the students, I was learning a lot of new things! Unfortunately, this was just a natural part of my evolution that the group and I had to endure. Put yourself in my shoes for a moment. I was leading a group through a genre (show choir), which I had *not known existed* six months before! I was learning on the fly as well as leaning on the performance genres I knew best, which were pop and musical theatre! The songs that New Generation learned throughout the year were:

New Generation 1977-78

Costume Colors: *Royal Blue*

Competition Set

Magic To Do
With You
Free Ride
Fun, Fun, Fun
Don't Stop
I Got The Music In Me
Celebrate
Like To Sing About Sunshine
Lucy In The Sky With Diamonds

As soon as the second semester began, we had a little trouble because the former New Generation choreographer, who had already taught a lot of the choreography, had to abruptly quit for some reason. Our show was mostly learned by then, but I actually had to create and teach the choreography for *Like To Sing About Sunshine*, myself, because there *didn't seem to be anyone else who wanted to do it*! I apologize profusely to any members of the group, who may be reading this, for being subjected to my "*so called*" choreography! The talented student choreographers, in choir, we used during that first year, included *Kathy Briggs* and *Mary Leonti*, but they didn't know the song well enough to teach it. Luckily, the choreography turned out okay in the end, but I made a vow to get a full time choreographer next year, to avoid repeating this problem. As luck would have it, I actually found her sometime during the second semester. Her name was *Jani Eubanks*. She worked as a checker at a nearby Stater Brothers Market and shared with me one day that she was also a choreographer, for a local dance studio! I hired her on the spot! She helped put together the Spring Concert and then became our regular choreographer for the next year. We were also very fortunate to have an excellent, unpaid student accompanist, named *Carol Mount*, in the group, to accompany us at our concerts, while later we added *Charles Shealey*, on guitar. *Kathy Whitescarver*, another talented pianist, was the president of Concert Choir, and their excellent accompanist as well. I believe that she too *may have* accompanied New Generation at times. I was fortunate enough to follow her as the choir director at Diamond Bar High School, many years later.

With the students added, to take the place of those who had dropped, I finally felt like New Generation was mine! At least the civil war was over! The group was still on the smaller side, seven boys and fourteen girls, but we did our best to create a fun atmosphere and a competitive show. I remember on the first Saturday of the second semester, two of my "unofficial" choir leaders, *Mary Leonti* and *Jim Thatcher* and I led the group in a series of bonding exercises. I don't know if that actually helped bring the group closer together, but we sure had fun!

Our performances were generally held in the little theatre, with the option of using the gym, for the Spring Concert, at the end of the year, because it seated more people. Besides performing at our Christmas and Spring Concerts, our Madrigals also combined with the Drama department on a fun presentation called *Comedy Tonight*! Many of the New Generation members were also in Madrigals, and I heard that they had the most amazing time performing! The songs they performed included *Nothing Can Stop Me Now, Camelot, Corner Of The Sky, Beautiful City, Comedy Tonight* and *No Time At All.* At that time, *all of those songs* were some of my musical-theatre favorites!

In other areas, our costumes, as I recall, were blue and white, and parents or family members took care of making them. Evening rehearsals, for choreography, were tough that first year, as kids would miss for any number of reasons, including taking care of their animals. *Dedication was quite a problem.*

Speaking of problems, I remember setting-up a trip to Riverside City College to join other area schools in the joint rehearsing of Handel's *Hallelujah Chorus*, which we planned to use for our Christmas Concert. That sounded fun… but regardless of announcing this to my classes… *only three people showed up to the bus*! Everyone else, I discovered, had "*good excuses"* why they could not go. The problem was… they felt no sense of commitment to the choir, or to me… and they felt *no responsibility* to let me know in advance! The same thing happened at the end of the year for Senior Baccalaureate. I told all of my underclass choir students that I could not force them to show up and sing, because it fell on a Sunday morning… but *I expected them to be there*. Many kids confirmed. On the morning of the event, exactly *one* singer showed up to sing… *Karen Marian.* I was very proud of her, but once again… the rest of the choir felt no responsibility to show up at all… even after confirming! I'm almost *embarrassed to mention* this next experience, but in my guitar class, one day, probably during the first week of school, *my entire class left the classroom, en masse*, after I had walked into the choir office, out of sight, for a moment, to get some guitar worksheets! When I returned, I was *shocked and flabbergasted* as I looked around my classroom to see absolutely nobody there! It was like an episode from the *Twilight Zone*! I decided to *hunt for them all over campus*, because I was too embarrassed to admit to the principal that I apparently had *no class control*! I did eventually find them…

hiding in the "*smokers field*," (legal area for students to smoke on campus), and brought them back to class as they all laughed! Thankfully, I learned from all of this, to give my students consequences for missed rehearsals and performances… and for *leaving my classroom as a group, without permission*! I had expected everyone to *just do the right thing* without any prodding, but I was a bit naïve. Sadly, most people don't work that way, and my students at Norco High School, during that first year, *definitely did not*! It all seems so funny now, when I look back at it. I was just not prepared for all of that *anarchy and antagonism.* But, I don't blame the kids. I suppose I learned, what *every new teacher learns,* during the course of their first year of teaching… "*Teacher respect must be earned*!"

As far back as show choir goes, in those early years, there were very few rules. In fact, the *Aztec Sing*, our very first competition, hosted by John Wilson and the Azusa High School Aztec Singers, didn't even have categories for choreography, because it was *optional*! Tom Kessler's *Chamber Singers*, from West Covina High School, however, with *amazing choreography*, were influencing directors to do more dancing if they wanted a chance to win, categories or no categories! In those early years, every group competed together, advanced, intermediate and novice. Divisions didn't appear in show choir festivals until much later. Single gender groups were *unheard of* and would not be introduced into the competition circuit for many years yet. Trophies were also skimpy in those early competitions. Usually *only three places* were awarded (like in the Olympics), plus plaques for *Best Musicianship* and *Best Showmanship* of the night. This left the other seven to nine groups (the losers) to take a silent, depressing walk, out of the auditorium and back to their buses… *because they did not get their names called during the awards ceremony*! The show choirs that generally *earned trophies* at competitions during those early years included *West Covina HS* (directed by Tom Kessler), *Redlands HS* (directed by Roger Duffer), *Edgewood HS* (directed by Dick Kinzler), *Arcadia HS* (directed by Rollie Maxson) and *Los Altos HS* (directed by Dwight Fichtner). In my opinion, all five of those schools sang exceptionally well and had clean choreography… but I believe Tom Kessler's *West Covina High School Chamber Singers* continued to be the most stunning group to watch! I still wanted my group to be just like them!

We only competed twice during that initial year. Our first competition was the *Aztec Sing* at Citrus College, at the end of January. The night of the event, I was very excited. This was my *first* of what would ultimately be *hundreds* of show choir competitions in my career! I stood at the back of the house and proudly watched my group perform, ending with a rousing production of the Beach Boys' *Fun, Fun, Fun!* A cappella pieces were not mandatory yet, but we did sing, *With You*, a very pretty ballad from the Broadway show, *Pippin*, to contrast our up-tempo pieces. A few bars of the song were too high for the tenors to sing in rehearsal… and unfortunately, they were *still too high for them to sing in performance*! Still, once our performance was over, several parents from West Covina High School, whom I had met the previous year, were kind enough to congratulate me on how well *New Generation* had performed. That felt good. However, at the end of the night, when the awards were announced… *we did not have our name called*! *That did not feel good*! I discovered, after reading the score sheets, that we did beat somebody… but disappointingly, still *placed ninth out of ten groups*! I was still new at this game, but that was no excuse! It was obvious that we needed to improve our *singing* as well as making our *choreography* sharper and more interesting! The kids had fun, however and actually did not seem at all fazed, by our final ranking. I was crushed, embarrassed and felt *inept* at preparing a competing show choir! But, I was not about to give up!

When we returned to class, on Monday, I explained to the group what I believed the scores and comments from each adjudicator meant. We played a cassette tape of one adjudicator's comments of our group's performance, and his positive spin, made everyone feel better about not placing. Unfortunately, videotaping was very rare back then, so the kids *never did get the opportunity to watch themselves, singing and performing*.

I knew that our next competition, *Tops 'n Pops*, in Chula Vista, wasn't for a couple of months, but I began having the kids run-through their show daily, with the intent of developing more stamina and consistency. In addition, after not placing at the Aztec Sing, I was more determined than ever to give a better showing at Chula Vista. So, I added my own arrangement of the Beatle song, *Lucy In The Sky With Diamonds,* as our new ender, in hopes of spicing things up! *Tops 'n Pops*, arrived, before we knew it. To make the end of the year, *even more fun for the kids,* I decided to transform the competition into an overnight trip! We were graciously hosted and housed by the Mount Miguel choirs of Chet Farmer, *Norco's former choir director*. He and his students even attended the competition to cheer us on! Our presentation was much tighter than our first effort at the Aztec Sing, and *Lucy In The Sky With Diamonds* was very well received… but as usual… *Tom Kessler and the West Covina Chamber Singers* were victorious! I believe that we came in seventh, at this one, which was at least an improvement! I was heartened by this performance and I think things went very well for our first overnight choir trip, too. I must admit, that I was very proud of the group's performance, even though they didn't place. Those kids *sang and performed their hearts out*, and I began to realize that *there is not much more, in competitive show choir, that the kids in any group can control*!

Our "official" hardworking officers for that first year, to the best of my knowledge, included *Guy Wessell* (president), *Jeff Crawford* (vice-president), *Kathy Briggs* (secretary) and *Lyle Allen* (treasurer). "Unofficially," I also worked with *Mary Leonti* and *Jim Thatcher*, as assistants. I think the highlight of the year, for a lot of the kids, was performing a thirty-minute set for the *Fireman's Benefit* at the Long Beach Arena. Everyone seemed to love the show and the kids had a great time. I was especially jazzed, that our choir actually got paid a monetary stipend, for performing. I'm sure that this was the *first paid choir performance* of my career!

Another important memory I have, was my *very first* fieldtrip with Norco, which was a trip, with our Madrigals, to sing Christmas songs at Knott's Berry Farm, in December of 1977. I had never taken a group *anywhere*, nor had I traveled to an amusement park with my own choir while attending Glendora High School. Consequently, this trip represented entirely *uncharted waters*! When it came time to meet for the performance, the park's instructions were a little vague, only telling me the *basic area* for the kids and I to meet. I arrived there, ahead of the group, and looked around. Finally, thinking we would be performing in a theatre, I saw an open stage door, leading into the *Knott's Goodtime Theatre*! I walked inside, to a barely lit stage, with only the emergency lights turned on, to find my way. I saw a grand piano on the stage, so *naturally,* I sat down and began playing it for about five or ten minutes, to check the tuning. But after a while, I looked at my watch, and noticed that it was only fifteen minutes before our scheduled performance time and *absolutely no one* from Knott's had come in to greet me or to lead my students inside the theatre? Hmm? *Could this be the wrong performance location*? I quickly jumped up and *briskly walked* through the stage door (being careful to look like I knew what I was doing), and proceeded back into the park. There, outside, about fifty feet away, stood a set of choral risers with an upright piano, and my Madrigals, standing around it, waiting for further instructions. *It was right then, out of necessity that I grew to take responsibility for being Norco's high school music director*. I didn't know a lot, but I knew we were *performing right here* and it was my job to be my choir's leader! So, pretending that I had known this was the spot, *all along*, and that I had *not spent the past five or ten minutes inside a dark Goodtime Theatre playing the piano…* I organized the kids. *Kathy Whitescarver*, my student accompanist, took her seat behind the piano, and soon we began our thirty-minute performance. Although I felt that the choir sang pretty well, I also remember that *almost no one* came over to hear us. The park was pretty barren on that Wednesday morning, which was unfortunate for us and for them. But, we had successfully performed at Knott's Berry Farm, and for me, that was a *great relief*! As I alluded to before, that day was a major turning point in my career. I abruptly realized that on all fieldtrips, *I was the man*, and *I had to know exactly what to do, in advance, all of the time... and if I didn't... I had to act like I did*! After that experience, I became much more deft at leading students on fieldtrips and I asked many pertinent questions regarding every trip we took… *in advance*!

In May, we held auditions for the next year's New Generation, and there was a good turnout. Qualified boys were hard to find, but I think we accepted eleven of them along with twenty girls *to make up next year's group*! By and large, most of the kids who auditioned were already in the choral program, so they already had a year's experience working with me in one of our groups! Getting to initially know and to trust each other is the prerequisite for any effective group, so I was hopeful that next year would be a lot easier than this year… *for everyone*!

How about a story? It's either one of my most *frightening* or *funniest,* memories from the 1977-78 school year, depending on how you view it! *How you view it*, will depend *entirely* on whether or not you're a choir director, *who wanted to keep his job!* This happened during the evening of our Spring Concert, the *very first* Spring Concert of my career, in May of 1978! One of my most helpful seniors, Chris Breyer, had arranged for flash pots to go off at the high point of our New Generation performance. Flash pots are basically vessels for gunpowder to burn quickly, causing an exciting flash effect, mainly for outdoor rock concerts. This method was used prior to the age of high tech lighting. We even put tarps on the gym floor to make sure that we didn't burn it. Well, the big moment came and the flashes were huge and blinding from both pots! *Too blinding*! Chris had apparently *overfilled them with too much gunpowder*! Soon, the entire gym was full of smoke! Billows and billows of thick, white smoke! We finished performing the set and *quickly exited the gym* along with the entire audience! I was certain I would be fired, *right then and there, and never teach again* for using gunpowder in the gymnasium! But the vice-principal on duty, casually walked over to me, and just laughed. He told me, "Maybe next time you ought to use a little less powder?" You have no idea how relieved I felt at that moment! In any case, my first year of teaching ended *dramatically… but with me still employed*!

At the beginning of my second year of teaching, in September of 1978, due to the surprising power of *Proposition 13 (which lowered property taxes and severely cut state funding to California schools),* the school district changed my teaching position. It went from the *five-period-day* at Norco High School, that I'd enjoyed the previous year, to a *two-period-day* at the high school with an added *three periods* at Auburndale Intermediate School, only one of which was a choir! At no point during the summer, had anyone given me the heads up regarding this major change in my assignment. I had only known of this major change to my teaching schedule, for about a week! Subsequently, *I was not happy*! Madrigals, Guitar and Music Appreciation had been tragically *erased from my schedule*! Only New Generation and Concert Choir remained. At this point, I really began to question the noble career I'd chosen? I realized, that with this new age of Proposition 13, not leaving anytime soon… building a solid, quality show choir program at Norco High School was going to be harder than ever! Remember, at the beginning of this chapter when I asked, "*Have you ever considered that things happen, or don't happen to you for a good reason*?" Well, here I was, still at Norco High School, with my professional life in a shambles… but I *had* auditioned a talented young man, whom I accepted into New Generation, for the 1978-79 school year. He was destined to play a *huge role in my future show choir journey…* his name was *Doug Kuhl.*

I began my second year at Norco High School, and although I had a difficult schedule, high school Concert Choir in the morning followed by three periods at the intermediate school and ending with New Generation at the high school, I felt more confident as a teacher, at the high school, anyway. It's amazing how just one tumultuous year of teaching can really *toughen* a guy up, to handle almost anything. Another problem was that the high school *took away the choir room,* from me, and turned it into a social studies classroom. They apparently had decided (although they had never even mentioned this to me) that it was a *good idea* to have the choir and band classes *share* a room! The band director and I *made it work,* although neither of us was exceptionally happy about it! In truth, that second year at Norco was already beginning to feel like *the school didn't care about either one of our programs!* This belief would play a major influence on what I would do at the end of the year.

Meanwhile, back at school, I was determined to continue making New Generation a show choir in the West Covina image, with more and better choreography, a wider variety of songs and a striking costume! Well, the group voted for the costume (such was the tradition at Norco), and they chose to go to an *Angel Flight* discount store in Pomona to dress the boys. The boys costume ended up consisting of tan pants (tight), a tan shirt, a tan vest and black platform shoes. The girls purchased matching tan skirts and leotards and then wore matching black character shoes. The result… *a lot of tan!* To be fair, the seventies were the age of earth tones, so we probably fit right in. Although, I have no fashion sense, even *I could see* that something was missing? So, to salvage the girls' costumes, my wife, Margaret, made some tan scarves to add to each girl's neck. It was an improvement… albeit *tan*. Our new weekly rehearsals with choreographer, Jani Eubanks, assisted by Mary Leonti, were also a great improvement over the last year when a series of students taught most of the choreography and did not always get the respect they deserved from their peers. My outstanding student accompanist for New Generation from 1977-78, Carol Mount had graduated, but I was lucky enough to pick up another talented student to accompany for the year, named *Kathleen Scott*. She had actually accompanied the group in 1976-77, the year before I had arrived, so a lot of the kids already knew her. Student, *Julie Potter*, also accompanied choirs for me, and as luck would have it, we were fortunate enough to add talented musicians and students, *Steve Hauser* and *Scott Chapman* to our band as drummer and bass player!

The year started out pretty well for New Generation. We experienced a little *carryover dissension* from the previous year, but overall, everything progressed smoothly. Janie did a marvelous job of rehearsing the kids every week at a local multipurpose room that we affectionately called, *The Tin Palace* (after it's roof) and we had the show choreographed and learned in record time! Our competition set, was much more *concise* this year, and consisted of:

New Generation 1978-79

Costume Colors: *Brown & Tan & more Tan*

Competition Set

Travelin' Freedom's Road
Corner of the Sky
I Return To Music
Short People
Celebrate

In my opinion, these songs were a good fit for New Generation, complementing the talents of this group. We learned a series of songs from Grease, later in the year, *Summer Nights, Hopelessly Devoted To You and You're The One That I Want*, but these were never used in competition, only for home concerts and community performances.

We competed at The *Aztec Sing*, in January, and since a number of the students in the group had competed with me last year, they knew *exactly what to expect* and just how hard they would have to work in order to *even be considered* for winning a trophy! In the end, they came in a little better than the year before… I think it was eighth place. But, the important thing was the positive impression they had left with the judges, as expressed through the comments they had written on our score-sheets, involving our *improved vocals and choreography*! We also competed at a new competition at *Colton High School, later in the year,* and although we did not place, we all felt that we had delivered our best performance in two years!

One of the best memories I have, from the 1978-79 school year, is about *Doug Kuhl*, and the night that we were presenting the Christmas Concert. It so happened that he had been absent from school that day. Being one of our *only basses* in Concert Choir and arguably our *strongest bass* in New Generation, I was greatly concerned! I called him, and he told me that he had the flu, and *would regrettably have to miss the concert*. I pleaded my case… and Doug, *sick and all*, showed up that night to perform in the concert! I know that encouraging a sick student to come back to school to perform in a concert, *may not sound like appropriate behavior for a teacher*, but it seemed *positively essential* at the time, and Doug *showed up willingly*, because he knew that the groups *needed him, and his personal integrity obviously agreed*! Doug did a great job that night (especially considering that he was sick), and I couldn't have been prouder of him, while the other choir kids were also very grateful. By this time, Doug, had pretty much established himself as an integral part of the New Generation. His work ethic was terrific and everyone in the group concurred as they elected him *president,* for the following year! I recall that Doug also "directed" our choir men, in a song called, *To The Sea*, at our Spring Concert, while *Kathy Scott*, directed our women in *Three Precious Gifts*. I was beginning to trust certain students with more responsibility, when they proved worthy, as Doug and Kathy had, throughout the year. So, aside from the obvious negative effects left by *Proposition 13,* musical life was beginning to feel right at Norco High School.

The New Generation students and I took a bus tour to San Francisco at the end of the year to celebrate all of our hard work. Being a young and inexperienced teacher, I hired a travel company to arrange everything, leaving me to handle only the fundraising. In hindsight, I realize that I needed help arranging this trip, but the travel company I chose, gave us an old and dilapidated hotel, that has since been remodeled, called the *Yerba Buena*, that appeared to be deep in the heart of Chinatown. They told us to *never turn left out of the hotel for safety reasons*. In addition, we were instructed to *walk as a group* from the hotel to a local Chinese café for breakfast every morning... *also, for safety reasons*. I was already thinking about putting together my own tour packages, with no middleman, where I could select a better hotel in a safer location for the kids, but this was not destined to happen for a few more years yet. Everything else was satisfactory, although the kids had to pay for most of their own meals. We visited *Hearst Castle* and *Alcatraz* as well as exploring the city! The hotel situation was all right, after all, as we spent very little time there. New Generation performed in San Francisco both at a retirement home and outside on Pier 39!

Overall, the trip went great! One of the kids' favorite memories was a group dinner at the San Franciscan on Fisherman's Wharf!

My second year of teaching at Norco High School was thankfully, *relatively free of drama* and a lot more fun for everyone, because of it! What I remember most fondly about that year was the *fun* we had putting on concerts and going to competitions. My toughest memory is telling *Doug Kuhl* and *Karen Marion*, during the summer, that I was leaving and was accepting a position somewhere else… for their senior years! The "official" officers for that year included *Jeff Crawford* (president), *Mary Leonti* and *Teri Patterson* (vice-president), *Jonnie Hall* (secretary) and *Lyle Allen* (Treasurer). "Unofficially" I also worked with *Kathy Scott*, *Karen Marian* and *Doug Kuhl*, as assistants. As a second year teacher, *at the same school*, I was beginning to feel encouraged that *we had the talent to build a pretty good choral program here at Norco High School*, and over time… we could even win a few trophies! I would like to recognize all of those hard-working members of my 1978-79 New Generation:

Norco High School New Generation 1978-1979

Lyle Allen • Annie Billenstein • Julie Potter
Lisa Gamboa • Mike Harris • Kathleen Scott
Heidi Hoganson • Mary Leonti • Steve Hauser
Karen Marion • Terri Patterson • Tim Steele
Steve Scalisi • Debra Williams • Scott Chapman
Gwen Benner • Julie Cahill • Laura Luchtiker
Kim Gibson • Michelle Harris • Kevin Moss
Ron Hughes • Paula Leonti • Cheryl Hartwell
Cindy Melendez • Steve Perkio • **Doug Kuhl**
Karen Smith • Lori Bird • Jeff Crawford
Jonnie Hall

I soon auditioned the group for the following year, and for the first time, we had over 35 members! Things were certainly looking up for Norco High School's New Generation, and everyone seemed to be excitedly looking forward to next year! By the beginning of summer, however, I could not get the

Corona-Norco USD to improve my situation at Norco High School by adding another period of choir, even though I had the students to fill the class! So, determined to quit, I began looking for schools near West Covina and Glendora, where I had grown up, thinking that they probably cared more about choral programs there than Corona-Norco did. On the one hand, I hated the idea of having put all of this work into the Norco High School choral program and connecting with all of these students, in the process, only to throw it all away… but on the other hand, I couldn't bear the thought of working here for another year, without the opportunity to improve my situation! For me, Norco High School had become a *teaching dead end*! The other reason, a much more personal one, was that over the past two years, I had not acclimated to living in Norco. I was very homesick for life closer to Orange County… *closer to Disneyland*! Toward the end of the summer, my search was rewarded. I resigned from Corona-Norco USD and accepted a job at Nogales High School in the Rowland USD. The pay scale was slightly higher than Norco High School's, and I didn't have to teach at two different schools… but that is where the improvement ended.

As a new and inexperienced teacher, I was very fortunate (in the right place at the right time) to get the Norco High School choral job, and I will *always be thankful* for the opportunity to begin learning my craft there. Granted, I did feel a little disrespected for part of my first year and Proposition 13 severely diminished my program in the second year… but I still secured countless fond memories from the program and the students I was lucky enough to work with. Under all of the debilitating circumstances, as well as my *rookie status*, I was just not there long enough to figure out a way to *build New Generation into an award-winning show choir!* But, I got *my start* at Norco High School and I will be forever grateful for that, as well as for getting to know the terrific kids whom I shared this wonderful learning experience with! I learned on the job how to take a fieldtrip and an overnight trip, how to arrange a song (beginning stages), how to put on an end of the year banquet, how to put on a concert and how to select a competition show, among other things… and although all of these skills *got better with each year of teaching*, it was here, at Norco High School… that I first learned how to be a *show choir director*!

CHAPTER 3

Nogales High School... 1979-1983... Building From Scratch!

Nogales High School was known in the area, as a *tough or "gang" school*, located on the border, between West Covina and La Puente. Whereas most of the students had been of the same racial background, white, at Norco High School, Nogales was a true melting pot of Hispanics, Filipinos, blacks, whites and a spattering of everything else. The school featured a full-time security staff and about 2,000 kids. The choral program was nearly non-existent, but to the school's credit, they were still attempting to keep it alive. The school *did supply* a part-time accompanist and a *little theatre*, for performances. My schedule consisted of *Guitar, Consumer Math, Concert Choir, Consumer Math* and *Treble Choir.* Why they would give me math, when I had never taken a single math class in college, I'm not sure? But the worst part was… there was no show choir or *even a history of one*, at the school! Even so, I was here now… determined to make it work!

I remember my first day of school, 1979-80, so vividly. I walked into my third period class, which was Concert Choir, to see about twenty kids in the room. The *white students* sat on one side of the room, while the *black students* sat on the other, with every other race of students mixed-in. They were all perfectly polite, quiet, in fact, but their actions spoke louder than words! Looking at this *student-initiated segregation* was almost comical if it hadn't been true. So, the first thing I did was to introduce myself and make a seating chart that was *not segregated by race*.

Next, I proceeded to explain what a show choir was, and I asked the class how many of them would be interested in joining one for second semester? I suppose I should have checked on the possibility of this happening with the principal or counselors, first? But, I am a spontaneous person, and I was determined to *find out immediately* if these kids were willing to build a show choir here! So, I asked, the students on the *unfounded premise* that I *would be* granted the class! But, I had faith the school would support me on this. As it turned out, the school *was happy* to add another class for me, at semester. Since I wanted to model it after West Covina High School's group, I called it *Chamber Singers*, just as they were called. I was thrilled when I was able to enroll thirty kids into that first group! Unfortunately, they were not even remotely auditioned. I basically accepted *anyone who agreed to enroll in the class.* Since most of the new members were already in a choir class, in order to keep the other choir classes from getting too small, many of these kids agreed to take both classes. There weren't nearly the number of requirements in those days, and in fact, students were even *encouraged by their counselors to take multiple electives.* As excited as I was initially, this group had *no training, no experience and no idea what show choir was really all about*!

Meanwhile, now in his senior year, Doug Kuhl, had surprisingly quit choir at Norco High School, after the first semester, due to some disagreements with the new teacher, and he went on to join the prestigious, *Young Americans*. Unaware of any choreographers in the area, but knowing how talented and easy to work with, Doug was, one day, I came up with the brilliant idea of having him choreograph my Chamber Singers this semester! After giving him a call, he agreed to choreograph the Chamber Singers on the song, *Summer Nights* from *Grease* as well as to set the kids in their other numbers, assisted by Mary Leonti and Lysa Gamboa, from New Generation, at Norco High School. A couple of months after second semester began, *Summer Nights* was choreographed, and it became a big part of our very first Nogales Chamber Singers show! Our non-competing competition set included:

Chamber Singers 1980

Costume Colors: *Red*

Competition Set (non-competing)

Nothing Can Stop Me Now
Summer Nights
Don't Cry Out Loud
Everybody Rejoice

We didn't actually have an accompanying band, but we did have *Rita Denholtz*, the talented school accompanist. I don't think she was enamored with show choir the way that I was, but she still gave it her best shot, every day she was there! We didn't officially start the "*Chamber Singers*" choir class until February, when second semester started, but I tried to have as many lunch rehearsals as possible, during that first semester, in hopes of preparing the kids for what was coming. However, by late January, as much as it hurt me, I knew that we were *not even close* to being ready to compete against any other groups. So, we all attended the *Aztec Sing* to watch the other competing show choirs, and to learn, by listening and observing, what we needed to do to improve. That experience was certainly an eye-opener for the kids… *and for me*! But sadly, *we ended up not competing at all for that entire year*. We did take an overnight trip to San Diego, however, and just like Norco's trip to San Francisco, the year prior, I hired the same travel company, out of convenience, to set it up. *Shame on me*! Once again, we got an old hotel deep in the heart of downtown San Diego. The kids, of course, handled it beautifully, but now I was determined, more than ever, to plan our next trip by myself! Chamber Singers performed (unaccompanied) at an amphitheater, in a large park, near Old Town. They tried very hard to sing the songs they had learned and to dance the choreography in *Summer Nights*… unfortunately, it was painfully clear… we had a *whole lot* of work ahead of us, if we were ever to become an award winning show choir! This beginning level of singing and performing, *initially* seemed to represent a step *backward* for me, professionally, as I was completing my third year of teaching, albeit my first year at Nogales. However, the kids were great! They had the potential, and it was just going to take some time for them to learn the skills necessary to compete in show choir! I believe that the first president of the Nogales Chamber Singers was senior, R.E. Fort, who along with the other officers, really tried, *against all odds*, to make that group of kids, into a show choir! I felt it was a very positive beginning. I believe that the kids were excited about it, too!

I want to honor that first group of Chamber Singers, in 1980, right here! Nineteen wonderful years of show choir at Nogales… and it all started with them!

The Original Non-Competing 1980 Nogales Chamber Singers

Kim Benton • Manuel Aranda • Tami Nash
Jennell Fort • Ralph Contreras • Beatrice Rubio
Pat Gallegos • Kit Downing • Kris Wells
Vicky Melhuish • R.E. Fort • Angel Santiago
Kim Johnson • Larry Green • Connie Stamm
Mandy Linnartz • Steve Stone • Celeste Wentworth
Grace Mendoza • Mike Holguin • Catherine Myer
Ellen Murray • Richard Kemper • Ray Janeway
Charlene Zimmerman • Keith Fort • Mary Prosser
Lynn Romanofsky • Robert Prosser • Gabriel Sinohoui

On an unrelated topic, choir combined with drama that year to put on the classic musical, *The King and I.* I had actually never produced full-lengthed musicals before, only performed in them. So, working with the director, Craig Faire, and serving as music director, really prepared me for producing them in the future. I want to congratulate one of our seniors, *Gabe Sinohoui*, who was the only choir kid cast in a lead role, amongst many drama students. I would also like to mention that *Lori Halopoff*, one of the young children cast in the show in 1980, later became an important member of Chamber Singers during our *six year winning streak*, between 1988 and 1993.

Over the summer of 1980, I did a lot of soul searching. Why had I moved from Norco High School, where they had a *history of show choir*, to Nogales High School… where they *did not*! The truth? I had moved because of the *potential for growth*, I saw here. I knew that I had to teach the kids everything, from the ground up, about a genre *I didn't even know existed* before 1977, but I also believed that they were anxious to learn! Since I was *obviously not gifted* at dancing or choreography, I would need help, however, to make this show choir transformation work! My short list of people who could help me train these kids was limited and I didn't have much money to spend, either. So, once again, I called upon my former student, and current friend, Doug Kuhl, and asked him if he was interested in taking on the challenge of choreographing my Chamber Singers… *full time*! Doug had graduated from high school, the past June, and as I previously mentioned, was currently very active with the *Young Americans* (which I guess could be best explained as a professional show choir, where no one got paid), but he agreed to do it. We decided to really emulate the West Covina High School Chamber Singers as closely as we could. So, we included one of the songs that they had recently performed, *Travelin' Freedom's Road*, which Doug had also performed with New Generation, two years before! To the best of my memory, in it's entirety, our 1981 competition show consisted of:

Chamber Singers 1980-81

Costume Colors: *Lavender (Purple)*

Competition Set

Travelin' Freedom's Road

Corner of the Sky

Ricky Tick Sound

I Sing The Body Electric

The 1980-81 school year felt vastly different to me than 1979-80 did at Nogales High School. Rita Denholtz, our accompanist from last year, had resigned and taken a job in the Walnut District, so we hired *Kathleen Scott*, my former *student accompanist* at Norco High School and current music student at

Fullerton College, as our accompanist for the Fall semester, and *Karen Thune* (a local teacher on temporary maternity leave), for the spring. We still didn't have a regular drummer, but we did have our Chamber Singers meeting *every day*, we already had a taste of *show choir experience* from last year and we had a *weekly choreographer* coming in to help us build the competition show! If memory serves, the group had 20 girls and 8 boys. Boys were especially difficult to recruit for choir, as they always are, but we had enough male singers to hold one part... and occasionally two. The girls were decent vocally, too. I was actually very pleased with their vocal sound over the first couple of weeks. If there was one weakness that stood out to me, it was the students' *lack of a consistently energized work ethic*. In truth, whatever they felt like, each day... energetic or dull... was evident in the way that they rehearsed, causing them to be *wildly inconsistent*. Of course, they could not be faulted for this weakness, because none of them really understood that *consistency* was a major part of being an award winning show choir, and each of them had to give 100% at all times! So, Doug and I developed the *'Pizzazz!' exercise* to help them create a plethora of energy on demand. The way this exercise works, is someone counts to three and then *everyone in the group shouts "Pizzazz,"* while simultaneously striking *an* energetic pose of their choice, with an insanely happy facial expression. Before long, in addition to Doug or I leading it at the beginning of every class period or rehearsal, the kids enjoyed this exercise so much that *they practiced it on their own*! In fact, we found this energy exercise to be so effective that we *have used it with every group we have worked with ever since*... and it also made *a pretty nifty title for this book*!

When the second semester rolled around, at the end of January 1981, I think our Chamber Singers were beginning to believe that as soon as they started competing, they could *beat somebody*. They knew, that being a first-time competing group, they dared not embrace any higher aspirations. I had called John Wilson at Azusa High School in September, inquiring about bringing our Chamber Singers to the Aztec Sing this year, but he told me that *unfortunately*, his festival was full. So, although we now had a competition show, that was basically learned, *we had absolutely no place to take it*! I believe that's why we had been dragging our feet, insofar as getting a costume for the group. But really, our first competition would not be for over a month, so there really seemed to be no hurry. That is, until John Wilson called me one day, out of the blue, to ask me if my group would like to compete in the Aztec Sing, *next week*? Apparently, he had a group drop out at the last minute. I didn't know how to answer him at first? The Aztec Sing was *next week*? We still had *no costumes, no drummer* and we certainly had not been preparing for this? I replied, "Sure!" Since I still lived just outside of Norco, Margaret and I drove all over Riverside, that weekend, looking for dresses… and we finally found them at a local department store. The men's shirts, pants and shoes came soon afterwards. So, we had found costumes and by the skin of our teeth, even someone to drum for us! We ran the show as often as we could, in preparation for the competition… and soon it was off to the *Aztec Sing*! I remember clearly, that our kids were *noticeably scared that night*, as they watched the other groups perform. I suppose reality may have finally set-in, as they realized that soon they would be on stage, *actually competing too*! Before long, it came time for us to go into warm-up. As soon as I had gotten them assembled, in "top of the show" formation, I told them that *I knew we were not ready for this*, but that when opportunity knocks, like it had last week, *we had no choice, but to answer it*! Looking around, I saw frightened kids, but I knew in my heart, that they would all do their best tonight! We were shortly called on to the stage… *and we performed*! I was, of course, very proud of the kids' efforts, but I also knew that they looked amateur up there, and the boys' sound was lacking. The awards came… and we had placed *dead last*! To add insult to injury, Norco High School, my previous program, had *beaten us*, placing ninth to our tenth place! The kids on the bus ride home were quiet, seemingly quite dejected, and humbled. In contrast, Doug and I sat on the bus intently discussing the scores and comments the adjudicators had given us. We planned out, in detail, like a couple of generals planning out their next battle, how to make our group better in time for our next competition in a few weeks.

On Monday, we went over our scores with the group and explained why we had been marked down in each category. I also reiterated that *we really didn't have much time to prepare for the Aztec Sing*, and I expected that our next competition would *surely be much better*! Our kids didn't respond much, but continued to look both somber and dejected. Doug and I outlined, in detail, what we believed needed to happen, in order for us to seriously improve.

1. *Students needed to learn the choreography* and perform it consistently with the most skill, energy and desire possible.
2. *Students needed to learn their vocal parts* in each song and sing them consistently with confidence and musicality.
3. *Students needed to learn and understand the ten categories on the score sheet*, including: *Tone Quality, Intonation, Balance, Blend, Dynamics, Diction, Musicality, Musical and Visual Interpretation, and Showmanship*, and rehearse to that score sheet!

As you can plainly see, back in those days, show choir adjudication was quite simple to understand, compared to the much more elaborate score sheets of today, and was probably just as simple to adjudicate! There were eight distinctly different vocal categories followed by two *very nebulous* performance ones. This meant, that no matter how entertaining a group was, if they didn't sing well, they were *never going to place*, much less win a competition! Our three-step plan certainly put a lot of responsibility on the students… but we knew that until they embraced their duties, *no amount of rehearsal would lead them to placing*! From that day on, we rehearsed Chamber Singers hard, with these three areas in mind, *correct singing, correct performing* and *understanding the score-sheet*. However, being that some of the students in Chamber Singers had poor grades or a poor work ethic, some kids continued to be inconsistent and even missed local performances. Still, we did not let up. We rehearsed the kids as if they were a contender, when in reality… *we just hoped to beat someone in competition*!

On the day of our second competition, the kids were truly ready to perform, unlike the slightly frightened tepidness they had displayed on stage at the Aztec Sing, a few weeks earlier. This competition was hosted by *Walnut High School*, in a small local theatre. This was quite a switch from the 1400 seat auditorium at Citrus College we had just competed in! Our competitors were slightly different, although West Covina, Redlands and Arcadia were all in attendance, so there was not much hope of placing. A funny memory I have of that day, was when prior to the performance, Doug and I walked over to a convenience store to get a snack. The man behind the counter kept smiling at us, and finally asked, if we were going to a Sadie Hawkins Dance? We looked back at him, baffled… and then we looked at each other, and *shockingly realized*, for the first time, that *we were wearing the exact same red and white striped long-sleeved shirt,* with blue jeans! Margaret had bought one for each of us, and apparently, without collaborating with one another, *we had both elected to wear the same shirt today*! There was a moment of silence, as we comprehended the situation, before both Doug and I *burst out laughing*! Momentarily, we both returned to our group, but we were careful… *not to stand side by side*! Meanwhile, back to the competition. When it came our turn to perform, the kids seemed like a completely different group! They had fun on stage singing and performing! The Awards Ceremony came, and West Covina won, but was *penalized* and placed second for going *under-time,* by performing a show that lasted *less than ten minutes*! That was the news of the day! Redlands and Arcadia, I believe, took the other two awards… and in the end… *we beat one group*! The kids were thrilled! This was the first group a Nogales Show Choir had ever beaten! I believe our kids even *celebrated* after they got home from that competition!

This limited "success" led us to have some very productive rehearsals, as we prepared for our final competition, at Colton High School, in April. As the competition date drew closer, surprisingly, we lost our part-time drummer. Or to be clearer… he quit! We were frantic to find somebody to drum for us! A few days before the competition, during school, a young man named *Bo Eder*, confidently walked into the choir room. He introduced himself as a freshman in the school band and told me that his director had told him that we were looking for a drummer. He agreed to do the Colton performance for $100.00, "No more and no less." Well, I was so relieved to find a drummer that I didn't even *quibble about the price*! Bo rehearsed with us a couple of times, and before we knew it, the big day was upon us!

When we arrived at *Colton High School*, I think that our kids believed we had a real chance of placing. Looking back at this situation now, with decades of experience behind me, since many of the groups in attendance had already beaten us *twice this year…* I would have to say we were a *long shot to place* at best. But I agreed with the students that night. I suppose the adrenaline was kicking-in, and we were all feeling very excited! When it came our turn to perform, we headed out to the stage like champions! Our performance was great except for one thing… *the microphones had been accidentally turned off during our entire show*! I immediately went to see Rick Solano, the host of the competition, to plead our case. He checked with the adjudicators, who agreed that the microphones had been turned off, but due to the hour of the event, they urged him to deny our request to perform again. Regardless, Rick agreed with me that under the circumstances, a second performance was warranted, and we were slotted to perform, *once again*, following the last group.

Unfortunately, Bo had to leave with his parents, following our first performance, so we would have to go on, that second time, *without drums*! We heard our introduction and our group entered the stage determined to give their all! When they were done performing, I thought the second show was good, but I missed the drums and *the kids looked a little bit tired up there*, probably because it was close to midnight. The Awards Ceremony came very quickly. The normal winners were victorious once again, while Nogales ended up coming in seventh place, *having beaten three groups* this time! The funny thing was that the scores of our first performance, without the microphones, were slightly higher than the scores of our second performance, with no drums! But, the lower score did not change our placement, and I would attribute our lower scored second performance to fatigue. I never requested a second performance again, throughout my entire career. But I was very proud of our kids for *taking that chance*, anyway!

The school year meant more than just competitions. We had begun presenting a *Pop Music Revue*, in April, where many of the Chamber Singers could "show off" their talents, that weren't normally displayed at our other concerts. As part of the Pop Music Revue, the Chamber Singers sang their competition show as well as other songs they had learned. In 1981, our *additional songs* included, *Summer Nights, Fun Fun Fun* and *Nothing Can Stop Me Now,* all songs I had used at Norco. Even then, I thought that *good songs* should be sung often! I believe that 1981 was also the beginning of our tradition of *traveling to "Disneyland."* Although we performed at *Knott's Berry Farm, Universal Studios* and *Magic Mountain*, a number of times, over the years, *Disneyland* was always our most popular theme park to visit! Between 1981 and 1998, I believe that Nogales choirs performed on the famed *Carnation Plaza* stage, nearly every year! When we didn't, it was usually because we were competing in Showstoppers at the *Fantasyland Theatre*, or participating, backstage, in a *Magic Music Days* workshop, complete with a *special tee shirt*, a *commemorative Disneyland pin*, and some years, each student even received a *lunch voucher*!

Graduation and then summer came quickly upon us. Doug and I both felt the same way. Something drastic had to happen in order for our group to place in this competitive circuit. *That's when I had an epiphany*. Dick Kinzler, the well-respected choral director at local Edgewood High School in the West Covina school district, did something that I really admired. Unlike the vast majority of choirs who sang music that was *in print*, he chose, instead, to *arrange his own shows*, allowing him to use *any music he wanted to*, regardless of whether or not it was arranged and available to purchase! His groups didn't always win, but they were always in contention and they were so much fun to watch... *like a breath of fresh air*! That summer, the summer of 1981, I was determined *to arrange our entire show*! I had a few years of experience arranging a couple of pieces, but this would be a major undertaking for me. I really looked forward to having complete control of which songs we sang, and through arranging them myself, I had the ability to feature our strongest choral sections! Our only other option was to be *limited by whatever arrangements were in print* and running the risk of not having the right mix of voices to sing them well. *It was no contest*! I also wanted to avoid choosing the same songs as multiple other show choirs were performing, simply because they were available. That happened a lot, in those days, especially with the arrangements for *Eli's Coming*, *The Rose* and *Wake Me Up Before You Go Go*. It's either funny or irritating, when you hear multiple choirs singing the same song and arrangement as you, in a competition. But I prefer my groups to be more original. To finish up, let me just say that *Lynn Romanofsky Hurd* was the president of Chamber Singers, for 1980-81, and she and the rest of the choir officers, *did a simply marvelous job*!

So, during the summer of 1981, Doug and I carefully selected the songs for the 1982 competition show that we wanted to see our Chamber Singers perform. If memory serves, the show went like this:

Chamber Singers 1981-82

Costume Colors: *Burgundy*

Competition Set

Send In The Clowns
On Broadway/Celebrate
Jump Down Spin Around
Morning Glow
Singing In The Rain

There were a number of differences in our show, this year, compared to the shows performed by my Norco groups and Chamber Singers from last year. For one thing, we added a *large lamppost prop* that Doug's dad had built for us, complete with a light, to sit on the center of the stage throughout the show. We also added an a cappella song (*Send In The Clowns*) since by this point in time, every group that placed seemed to have one. It was even a requirement at some festivals to sing one within your show. We also added hand lights to turn on during a blackout in *Morning Glow*. But the biggest change was developing large and exciting solos for our strongest soloists: *Jump Down Spin Around,* sung by *Jim Mills* and *Morning Glow*, sung by *Tamara Wells*! For us, this was the beginning of using full-length solos and power ballads, in our shows. Their use was actually pretty new to the competition circuit, and even *discouraged* at some festivals, because they felt that having a great soloist in your show could enhance your adjudicators' scores. In truth, *this was sometimes the case*, but the full-length ballad also made the shows much more fun for the audience… so they continued to grow in popularity. When fall came around, we handled Chamber Singers as if they were a contender already. The group was pretty talented but they didn't have the confidence that placing in a competition brings you… *not yet*. So, we rehearsed the group very hard. By the time competition season arrived, Doug and I felt almost *giddy* at how entertaining our show was! We compared this show to last year's, and it was so obvious to us that we had reached a *new high*! Over the summer, we had hired *Francine Stewart*, a very talented, young accompanist, to replace Karen Thune, as well as making *Bo Eder*, our first permanent drummer!

The evening of the *Aztec Sing* arrived, and we were waiting impatiently in the warm-up room to begin our set-up on stage. Finally, we were called, to enter the stage. After a quick set-up (we only had drums and the lamp post), we were introduced, and the curtains opened. Most shows weren't videotaped in those days, but I did receive a cassette recording of the show. The only problem was that there was so *much screaming from the audience,* that it was often difficult, if not impossible, *to hear our group singing at all*! The audience was going crazy throughout our entire show, and the ending applause went on forever! Even to this day, I have never heard anything like it! The show looked and sounded great to me, and the kids agreed. If this had been a movie, we would have defied the odds and won! But, alas, the awards, which had been expanded to five this year, were announced… and once again, *our name was not called*. We had placed *sixth*! Although we had beaten four other groups for the first time in our existence, we took this defeat very hard. We already felt as if we had done everything right, so what should we do now? Our choices were to go back to rehearsing and hope for a break-through at a later event… or to give up. Of course we weren't going to give up, but this loss really hurt. *No one was happy on the bus ride back home*.

The remainder of the competition season was exciting, as we competed all over Southern California! Unfortunately, we continued to come in *one place short of earning a trophy*, every time. It was very disheartening for the kids in Chamber Singers who really believed, as Doug and I did, that this show *deserved* to place! To most groups, this would have been the signal to quit! But, our Chamber Singers, predominantly juniors, some of whom, had been with me since my arrival to Nogales, two years before, griped a little… but never lost hope that we would place, eventually!

During the 1981-82 school year, I began to strongly encourage my students to get their parents to attend our local competitions, and actually *purchase their tickets presale*, from me! I knew that we needed a cheering section, like all of the major groups had, just to be competitive, and actually, some of these events *sold out in advance*! Our sale of presale tickets got better and better, especially as we became increasingly more successful in competition.

All year, I had taken the time to carefully watch all of the competing groups' performances and try to pick the winning three. Interestingly, I found that *certain adjudicators seemed to always favor certain groups*, and when they adjudicated, those results came in, very consistently. I also saw that many of the adjudicators judged multiple events throughout the year. So, I studied those groups that placed a lot, mainly West Covina, Redlands, Arcadia, Los Altos and Edgewood to look for things they had in common. I found them. They all sang with a *very blended tone* and many of their songs (especially their a cappellas) were from the 1940s and 1950s musicals. Bingo! We were going to change our style once again, at least for this next year. We were going to create a medley of songs, *predominantly from old musicals*!

Although these kids never placed at a competition in 1982, they lifted our bar *way up*, and set the table for Chamber Singers to place, the following year, in 1983. I'm not sure who the exact officers were, but *Vicky Melhuish, Keith Fort, Della Longnecker* and *Anna Rosselli* did an awful lot of work that year! In addition, I wouldn't feel right, if I didn't post *everyone's name in the group*, as a great big thank you from me, from Doug, and from all of our future Nogales groups for establishing the Nogales Chamber Singers as a contender!

"Almost" Award Winning Nogales Chamber Singers 1981-82

Kim Benton • Chrissie Casey • Val Greer • Mary Grubb
Barbara Hardie • Josie Harris • Anita Hasten • Norma Jeffries
Jodie Johnson • Sophie Kovacs • Mandy Linnartz
Vicky Melhuish • Janet Prosser • Veronica Tucker
Jamie Jamieson • Della Longnecker • Gina Pinedo
Sheila Rantz • Anna Rosselli • Ana Trujillo• Kris Wells
Tamara Wells • Virgil Advincula • Danny Copeland
Kit Downing • Dwayne Ganier • Andy LaBarbera • Rudy Medina
Steve Stone • Ernie Tovar • Michael Vergara • Tim Clark
Keith Fort • Jim Mills • Tom Murray • Troy Peace
John Short • Mark Stevens

During the summer of 1982, I was once again, very busy arranging music for our upcoming show in 1983! The core of the group was made-up of incoming seniors whom I had worked with since they were freshman. This would be *their last chance to place in a high school show choir competition.* The Chamber Singers had started from scratch three years before, and had improved so very fast in that time. Surely this would be their year?

The school year began and the Chamber Singers felt strangely mature? They radiated a confidence, which I had never felt before from any of my groups at either school I had taught at. But of course, I had never had so many of the same kids for *four years* before, either! In fact, I had *never taught* at the same school for *four years* before! The women's performance outfits featured a long gray dress with a small black and white checkered coat that they took off during one part of the show. Years later, Doug and I would joke that this was probably the *first show choir costume change in the west coast circuit*! Whether it was or not, it certainly added another dimension to our show. The men wore white pants, black shoes, a red shirt and a long black tie. Our performance set included:

Chamber Singers 1982-83

Costume Colors:

Gray, Red, Black & White

Competition Set

All That Jazz/ Razzle Dazzle

The Hills of Shilo

Beaucatcher Mountain

MGM Medley

Our band, in 1983, consisted of Francine Stewart, on piano, Bo Eder on drums, and his brother, Chuck Eder, on stand-up bass. Our selection of songs made for a very long performance set. Not that the songs didn't look and sound great, but the average performance time by show choirs at that time, was somewhere between ten and twelve minutes. Tom Kessler, of West Covina High School, had once told me that the most successful show choirs do *just enough* material, leaving the audience wanting more. A performance time of ten to twelve minutes seemed to be his idea of perfection. Most festivals at that time had a fifteen to twenty minute performance allotment for each performing group, *including* set-up and tear down! This allowed each group to have an upbeat opener, followed by a beautiful a cappella or ballad, a character piece came next and the show ended with another up-tempo piece. Some groups moved the order of their songs around... but nearly everyone kept to this formula. I knew that our show was too long, *according to those standards*, but I had *never seen any group penalized for an overtime violation*, and I really didn't want to cut anything from our show. We discussed this in Chamber Singers and the kids agreed, that performing our show in its entirety, as it had been envisioned, was far more important than cutting it down, in order to adhere to the rules. Did I mention that I have *a stubborn nonconformist streak*? Well, I do. I was so excited about sharing our *artistic creation*, that I didn't think that a "one size fits all" time limit was fair to those groups who wanted to perform more than 12 or 15 minutes. *Actually, our show ran 22 minutes*, not even close to conforming, but who's counting. So, we ventured into the competition season, knowing in the back of our minds, that *there could be a problem*, wearing our black, white, red and gray costumes, and prepared to sing and perform our hearts out!

Our first competition of 1983 was a brand new festival, hosted by the late television personality and music director, *Johnny Mann*. John Wilson, of Azusa High School, actually ran the event. Mr. Mann served as the Master of Ceremonies and producer. I think that the event was called, *Johnny Mann's Great American Show Choir Festival*! In any case, the festival only gave out three trophies, so we knew that we would have to be at our best. When it came our turn to perform, the kids were very excited. The seniors had waited for this moment for *four long years*, hoping that this would be the one where they would finally win a trophy! Their performance was impressive and garnered a lot of well-deserved applause. At the Awards Ceremony, all of the directors were asked to take the stage. I stood beside Tom Kessler, who didn't seem particularly confident about West Covina's chances. I, on the other hand, felt *very confident* that we would finally place this time! I had watched all of our competitors perform, and I felt that we were just a tad stronger than most of them. I would have been ecstatic about a *third place* trophy… but it was not to be. The awards were announced and the *Azusa High School Aztec Singers*, directed by John Wilson, the host of the event, received the *Third Place* trophy, because Mr. Mann said that even though they weren't entered, the adjudicators felt that 'their performance was so good that it deserved to be recognized.' I don't remember who placed second, but of course, the West Covina Chamber Singers won. Tom Kessler's parting words to me were something to the effect that they had 'gotten lucky this time, but they'd be sure to learn their vocal parts correctly for the next competition.' Tom was always honest in his assessments, which made him an excellent adjudicator for many years after he retired from teaching, following the 1985 school year. I was very honest, as well, when I went up to John Wilson and asked him, in no uncertain terms, how we had been scored? Unlike every other show choir event at the time, *this festival didn't provide the individual adjudicator comments and scores* at the end, for the director to peruse, so I really didn't know? John was friendly as he shared that our Chamber Singers had actually *placed third*, but with our *overtime penalty*, the adjudicators had voted to award the trophy to Azusa instead. *This was to be the first of quite a few overtime penalties that my groups would receive throughout the years.* Still, we actually were *scored in third place* by the adjudicators, and even though it wasn't announced, the kids, after initially being angry about the penalty, grew more confident about their chances at the Aztec Sing next week... also hosted by *John Wilson and the Aztec Singers*.

The day of the *Aztec Sing*, at Citrus College came quickly. Acoustics in the Citrus College auditorium, as I had learned over the years, were pretty much dead. So, performing groups depended greatly on the microphones, in order to be heard. The adjudicators sat in the middle, of an ocean of seats, about twelve rows back. Our group was probably about thirty in size. We had a good sound, this year, but we had to pray that the microphone coverage was ample. Our show still ran 22 minutes, although the rules at the Aztec Sing were really *guidelines,* so we hoped that our show's overtime would not be a problem.

The Aztec Sing began. I think our performance slot was either third or fourth out of ten. When our time came to perform, the kids seemed really nervous. What happened to us at the Johnny Mann event had apparently eroded much of their early confidence. Fortunately, by the time they hit the stage, they looked and sounded as determined as I'd ever seen them. The curtain opened, and the show began. The *Chicago* songs went well. The audience seemed to enjoy them very much. Next came our, a cappella, *In The Hills Of Shilo*. I stood up from the front row of seats to direct it. The choir began to sing… *and the sound was beautiful*! *Vincent Washington*, our soloist, was perfect too. This song received an abundance of heartfelt applause that seemed to go on for almost a minute after the song was done! The rest of the show was clean and well blended. I think this show lacked a little of last year's theatrics, but made up for it with a very good, clean, choral sound throughout. Finally, the awards ceremony began. My Chamber Singers had been coming to this event for three years now, without ever experiencing the joy of having their name called and winning a trophy. Could this really be our year? John Wilson strode to the lectern, on the far right side of the stage, and began to read the award winners. "And in fifth place," he began, "we present the trophy to, the ***Nogales High School Chamber Singers!***"

I don't have a clue which other groups placed that night. *My group was screaming so loud that I couldn't hear anything else*! My kids were hugging each other, while most of the seniors were sobbing for joy. We had done it! We had finally done it! The curse was broken. ***We had placed!*** Now I realize that to most people, placing fifth out of ten in a show choir competition probably does not seem like much of an achievement… but to us… *it meant everything*! As I recall, we came in only 1 point ahead of another up and coming group that night, the *Burroughs Chamber Choir*, who years later, changed their name to *Powerhouse*. We would see a lot of them in the future! As you already know, that fifth place was the first trophy ever earned by the Nogales Chamber Singers, and it completely validated them and all of the hard work and determination it had taken them to earn it. But, that fifth place award was also *the first trophy I had ever won* in six years of teaching. I felt validated that night, as well. Maybe I *could* lead a group to become award winning, after all? When I left Nogales High School in 1998, I took that single trophy with me. To this day, it sits in my den, in a place of honor.

Following that victory, I realized that if Nogales High School wanted to be taken seriously by the other groups, we would have to host our own festival to put ourselves permanently on the map. That next week, I arranged to meet Tom Kessler for lunch, where I proceeded to pick his brain about the inner workings of hosting your own show choir festival. He graciously shared his experiences of the past five years, when he had hosted an event and answered every question I had. When I left, I had ten pages of very precious notes that would help me bring the *first annual Nogales Divisional Show Choir Competition* to life! I'll say more about that, later.

Well, as you have probably guessed, the kids were absolutely thrilled about winning their trophy, and we lost little time advertising it in the school bulletin and the local papers! Our next competition was the *West Covina High School Show Choir Invitational*, where the only groups invited were *groups who had placed in a competition this year or last*, of which we were now one of them! I'll save you the drama. *We didn't place*, but we did put on a good show and we were not last! The kids took it well, as they were still savoring their victory at the Aztec Sing.

Finally, we competed at the *Colton High School festival*. It was just like the others we had competed in this year, with the exception of having *different adjudicators*, from the ones we were used to seeing. To make a long story short, our performance was great, probably the best, of the year! When the awards were read, Colton High School's director, Rick Solano, announced, "In fourth place, the *Nogales High School Chamber Singers*!" Once again, our kids were ecstatic! West Covina, won, of course, but I couldn't help noticing that we were *inching closer to them* with every competition! Now, I began dreaming of *beating them*!

But, our year was not done! Not quite. We had yet to host the final competition of the year! Citrus College was not available, so we settled on Whittier Union High School as our location. *The Nogales Divisional Show Choir Competition*, or NDSCC, as we called it, as far as I know, was the *very first show choir competition to offer divisions*! After spending six long years trying to beat quality groups, before finally earning a couple of trophies, I *felt*, for every new director and group out there! I believed that offering them an Intermediate Division, would give them a much better chance of placing for the first time. The more experienced groups would compete in the Advanced Division, as usual. I followed Tom Kessler's notes to a tee, and the festival went off without a hitch. The "*intermediate*" groups seemed to appreciate the more reasonable opportunity to place, while the "*advanced*" groups found it to be more competitive to compete in a division of their own. As for my Chamber Singers… they did a great job of hosting groups and running the festival under Doug and Margaret's tutelage. We also made a bit of money for the choir, so we decided to do it again next year!

Toward the end of the year, as I mentioned earlier in this chapter, we had started the tradition of putting on a *Pop Music Revue,* designed after Tom Kessler's *All Choral Revue*, where the students could perform all sorts of acts, like singing, dancing or skits, that wouldn't normally fit into the regular choir concerts. We had a very experienced and talented group in 1983 that Doug and I felt could pull off and *appreciate* performing a skit, poking fun at ourselves for *never winning*, no matter how much we tried! Our skit was greatly influenced by the sketch on an early episode of Saturday Night Live, about the *killer landshark*. In our skit, the landshark humorously and in good taste (?), *eats all of the Nogales competitors*, including Bonita Vista, Redlands and West Covina, so that our Chamber Singers would *finally win a competition*! Unfortunately, it was all for naught, as in our skit, the *combined elementary school choirs of West Covina* took the top prize! Although, the playful sarcasm in this skit was not really appreciated much by the audience (at least one parent told me that it was in poor taste), to me, *it perfectly captured the frustration the kids, Doug and I had felt as we attempted to win a competition, and were thwarted at every turn*! At least this year, we had actually placed a couple of times! After tasting that… we were all ready to win! I believe that *Keith Fort* was the president of Chamber Singers for this historical year, and he and the other officers, including *Anna Rosselli, Della Longnecker* and *Kris Wells*, were simply awesome!

Listed below, are members of the Nogales Chamber Singers, from 1983, who were the first show choir, from Nogales High School, to ever **win a trophy!**

The Award Winning 1982-83 Nogales Chamber Singers

Marylen Ayash • Carl Quadro • Kris Wells • Veronica Tucker
Tori Bosinski • Joey Enriquez • Sheila Rantz • Sheryl Poremba
Chrissie Casey • Keith Fort • Phong Ly • Nicole Love
Teresa Cimino • Dwayne Ganier • Vincent Washington
Anna Rosselli • Mary Grubb • Glen Jimenez • Janet Prosser
Marsh Pennington • Jodi Johnson • Edward Lee • Suzette Love
Nanette Varela • Jamie Jamieson • Troy Peace • Lupe Orozco
Robert Zurrica • Della Longnecker • James Mills • Ernie Tovar
Kenny Johnson • Tamara Wells

Shortly, thereafter, we held the auditions for the 1983-84 group. We were losing our wonderful core of seniors, and the kids coming in were basically young and inexperienced… but we hoped that our *new seniors* could teach them the ropes… and in record time!

CHAPTER 4

Nogales High School... 1983-1988... Building A Winner!

Now that our kids had *finally* felt the joy of placing in competitions, no one wanted to go back to the frustrating years of 1980-82! But as the year began, we found that our *new group* was very small and unfortunately, *they sang like it*. They weren't bad… they just lacked the tools and experience to compete at the high level that last year's group did! As I mentioned in the previous chapter, a whole slew of talented and experienced seniors had graduated the year before. We had arranged the show for this group, over the summer… but now *we weren't so sure that they could handle it*? In the first place, the group was not well balanced with only eight boys compared to eighteen girls. But I loved those kids. I knew they would work as hard as they could… they would just need a lot of rehearsal and a little luck! Once again, our accompanist quit, and we hired *Marge Penner*, to replace her. Our drummer, *Bo Eder*, also quit, late in the season, so we hired two very talented Nogales Chamber Singer graduates, *Keith Fort* and *Vincent Washington*, to share the jobs of drummer and bass player. *Della Long* (formerly Longnecker), another exceptional Nogales Chamber Singer graduate, became a valuable staff member at this time, working with Doug during performances and me in the choir office, during some school days, doing whatever needed to be done, while simultaneously going to school at Cal Poly Pomona, until she began a teaching career of her own, in the early 1990s!

Our show was a lot of fun, on paper, featuring many Broadway songs. Our plan was to have a lot of "*pizzazzy*" numbers in this show to allow the kids to exert their playful personalities. Every song was especially selected to demonstrate a different style, keeping the show interesting.

Chamber Singers 1983-84

Costume Colors: *Silver & Burgundy*

Competition Set

Hit Me With A Hot Note
Grant Avenue
There but For You Go I
Memory
Sit Down You're Rocking The Boat!

The group certainly looked Snazzy! The girls wore gray dresses with spaghetti straps and a sequined torso, while the boys wore white shoes, pants and shirt with a long black tie and a red vest. We also added silver sequined derbies for part of the show. Unlike the previous year, this show was short and easily fit into most competitions' time limits. We did, however, have another issue that would prove to be quite a problem at most of our festivals.

Troy Peace, one of our longtime members, brought a young girl to rehearsal one night, named LuAnne Ponce. He told me that she wanted to audition for Chamber Singers. Doug and I agreed to hear her, and wow! The girl was a fabulous belter! She had one of the best show choir voices, I had ever heard! She would make an amazing soloist! When we told her she was in, she broke the news, that there was a problem. We asked her what it was, and she replied that she was only an *eighth grader*! *Disappointment* is a mild way of expressing my feelings at hearing that. Still, we asked her to stay for the rehearsal and I would check out the possibility of her joining the group with our principal. The next day, I asked our principal if using this girl in our group was a possibility, since she was obviously qualified! He responded, "Yes, it was." He compared it to a great junior high math student, taking math at the high school, because they exceeded every class the junior high offered. She would not be allowed to attend choir classes, at the high school, however, only after-school rehearsals and performances. Well, that news was all right by me, and I told Troy to pass it on to LuAnne as soon as he could. This meant that we now had the *'belting soloist'* we needed to sing, *Memory*, from *Cats*! Life was good!

But, nothing always goes according to plan in life or show choir, now does it? I asked the other directors who hosted festivals if they would allow an 8th grader to perform with our group.... and they unanimously said, *"No!"* The Johnny Mann festival was okay with it, but that appeared to be it. So, LuAnne would be allowed to perform at the Johnny Mann event, but would *not be allowed* to perform at the Aztec Sing, West Covina, Colton or Fullerton events. She could, however, perform at all home concerts and at local performances, so for her it wasn't a total loss, but for the choirs, it was a *major disappointment*!

Our competition season, once again, opened with *Johnny Mann's Great American Show Choir Festival!* There weren't a lot of competitors that year, due to the expensive entry fee and the early date of it in January. Usually no one competed before the *Aztec Sing at the end* of January. Our group went on stage, a little green, but tried very hard. When it came time for LuAnne's solo in *Memory*, her voice sounded full and confident like a Broadway star (which she was destined to become later), and the audience went nuts! The awards were announced following the last performance, and by the time they had reached the final award, our name had still not been called! Johnny Mann finally read, "Our first place award goes to...***The Nogales High School Chamber Singers!***"

Need I say more? The kids went bonkers! They *excitedly accepted the award* and then sang all the way back to Nogales High School! This award represented the very first, **1st Place** that the Nogales Chamber Singers had ever received! Again, we bragged to the school and to all of the local papers about our magnificent achievement... yet I knew that we had not gone up against the "big boys" yet, and when we did, we would not be allowed to use LuAnne and her Broadway voice for the *Memory* solo! The Aztec Sing would be coming up in a few weeks, so we rehearsed the show without LuAnne, which made everybody a little sad.

Well, the *Aztec Sing* was here, before we knew it. We were finally returning to Citrus College, the place where we had earned that glorious *Fifth Place* trophy, last year! But this year felt completely different. Whereas last year had featured a group made up predominantly of seniors, who had spent *four years working hard, for that moment…* this group was mostly new and inexperienced. Don't get me wrong, we still had a strong core of experienced singers and performers like *Tamara Wells, Chrissie Casey, Troy Peace and Dwayne Ganier…* but even though our kids already had a big win under their belts… they had not yet faced *Arcadia, Redlands, Los Alamitos, Edgewood or West Covina*, to name a few!

The night of the *Aztec Sing* arrived, and our Chamber Singers performed with energy and confidence! They sang well too, with Tamara Wells effectively singing the *Memory* solo. To tell you the truth, I was pretty impressed with them when I recently watched the video on YouTube. Doug had a number of props he used in the show including tambourines, fans and a Chinese hat for Grant Avenue, which all worked well. But, we were young sounding, the boys had a very light tone quality, and our performance could have been more energetic… especially facially. Our band, consisting of a piano and light drums, was effective, but the tempos seemed a bit slow. So, for these reasons, I believe, when the awards were announced, we were not last… *but we were not among the winners*, either! It was predictably, a quiet bus ride home.

We also competed at the *West Covina, Fullerton* and *Colton festivals*, that year. But, if memory serves, the Johnny Mann Competition, remained the *only one we placed at all year*. But there was *much more* than the plight of our Chamber Singers' competition season going on in the *amazing* Nogales High School choral program! Margaret, Doug and I had been very impressed with a musical we had seen at the now extinct, *Sands Hotel*, in *Las Vegas*, over the past summer. That show was called *Dream Street*! It was an eclectic collection of pop songs, sung by a group of young people, as they hung-out in the street one night and shared their dreams with one another. We were so impressed with it, that we were inspired to do two major things. First, we created a new all-girls show choir called, *The Dream Street Singers*! It was made into a class by the spring of 1984. They would be only the *second all-girls competing show choir on the west coast*! Arcadia's *New Spirit* had already burst on to the scene a year earlier, to rave reviews! But while New Spirit was a traditional 50's/ 60's group… Dream Street, in theory, was to be *whatever we felt like they should be* each year. In that spring semester, I don't believe that they ever competed, but we did prepare a show to sing at the Spring Concert. Listed below are the members of the original, non-competing Dream Street Singers in the spring of 1984, and the titles of their songs:

<u>Dream Street Singers-1984</u>

Costume Colors: *Lavender*

<u>Competition Set (non-competing)</u>

Please Mr. Postman

Morning Glow (sung, once again, by Tamara Wells)

Boogie Woogie Bugle Boy

<u>Dream Street Singers 1984</u>

Joyce Allgood • Sabrina Dacumos • Carol Meyer
Teresa Cimino • Tammy Barber • Claudia Gamboa • Kim Nall
Nancy Mendoza • Carol Bemis • Rosa Grimes • Colleen Ory
Amy Chan • Heather Bruce • Marnie Hazleton • Tameka Scott
Michelle Terrazas • Chrissi Casey • Donna Jackson
Marilyn Tambio • Chris LaBarbera • Tamara Wells

The second thing inspired by the musical, *Dream Street*, was for us to produce and perform *our own musical*, with our own story, loosely based on the original musical that Doug, Margaret and I had been so impressed with! We would call this show, *Living On Dream Street*, and the actors would *make up the story as they went along*, and also be assigned solos that fit their characters and enhanced the story! This seemed to be a very experimental way to put a musical together, but it forced each actor to be very *hands-on,* in order for it to work. I loved the concept! Doug and I auditioned *Living On Dream Street* in March, with May performance dates in mind! We opened it up to all Chamber Singers. There wound up being 24 of them who were ultimately cast. The entire rehearsal and performance experience was awesome! The band was made up of Marge Penner, Doug and me on the piano, Keith Fort on bass, Bo Eder and Keith Fort on drums and 1980 Nogales graduate, Gabriel Sinhoui, on lead guitar. The ensemble cast included*: Marylen Ayash, Tori Bosinski, Chrissie Casey, Lisa Castilleja, Teresa Cimino, Tracy Fair, Dwayne Ganier, Glen Jimenez, Kenny Johnson, Mona Lewis, Gabriel Lomeli, Nicole Love, Kim Nall, Troy Peace, LuAnne Ponce, Robyn Price, Anna Rosselli, Lori Strait, Ernie Tovar, Selly Tsui, Laura Washington, Greg Wells, Tamara Wells and Chris Whitmire.* Those kids learned a lot about performing from the heart, in that show. Needless to say, it was a hit!

I would like to end this year by thanking Chrissie Casey Brockman, the president of Chamber Singers, and all of the other choir officers, including Laura Washington and Tamara Wells, for working so hard for the group. They succeeded, as winners always do! In 1984, the Nogales Chamber Singers won their very first *1st Place* in competition and the choir put on their first musical, *Living On Dream Street*! Congratulations to everyone who was a part of this very special year!

The summer of 1984-85 was busier for Margaret, Doug and I than ever before! We had a very good audition for show choir at the end of the previous year, ending up with 47 members in Chamber Singers and 25 members in Dream Street Singers. As for our band, once again, *our accompanist quit*, so I hired a good piano player who had accompanied me for a church choir, I had directed in Riverside, named *Kathy Keith*. In all, there were now five members in our accompanying band, including, Kathy Keith on piano, Bo Eder on drums, Keith Fort on bass, Dwayne Ganier on guitar and Nicole Chain (student) on flute. Our *Dream Street Singers* were competing for the first time, so we chose their songs very carefully. Chamber Singers were coming off a *rebuilding year*, so we had to change that perception of them through our careful choice of songs and choreography… and I believe we did a *great* job of it! In the fall of 1984, Chamber Singers began working on their show, which consisted of:

Chamber Singers 1984-85

Costume Colors: *Burgundy*

Competition Set

On Broadway/ Celebration

O My Luve's Like A Red Red Rose

Don't Cry Out

The Best Little Whorehouse In Texas (highlights)

This was indeed a very ambitious show for us to undertake. The two most difficult songs were, *O My Luve's Like A Red Red Rose,* a beautiful a cappella piece that would take many hours of work to perfect, and a medley of songs from *The Best Little Whorehouse In Texas*. It wasn't that the latter was difficult to learn… it was the subject matter! Anyone who had watched the movie or seen the live theatrical presentation of *The Best Little Whorehouse in Texas* knew that the singers' emphasis was on *disgust and the desire to close the place down*! But, as soon as anyone hears the word, ***whorehouse…*** they seem to automatically assume that you are singing inappropriate lyrics! So, Doug and I decided to *err on the side of caution* by having the kids sing, "uh oh," instead of *whorehouse*, to alleviate any potential problems… *at least at first*.

Dream Street was another story. This was their premiere year! They needed to perform songs that were both *memorable and fun*, if they wanted to make the proper impression! But, at the same time, Dream Street was a *very small* group with little experience, so we couldn't really be too challenging in that first year. Ultimately, we selected:

Dream Street Singers 1984-85

Costume Colors: *White*

Competition Set

Tell Him
Scarborough Fair
Second Hand Rose
Won't You Come Home Bill Bailey!

This show was designed to be fun, with *Tell Him*, providing a moment of sweetness, *Scarborough Fair*, providing beauty and wonder, *Second Hand Rose, providing a bit of wacky humor* and *Won't You Come Home Bill Bailey* showcasing our best choreography! Would this show be effective? We had no idea, until we performed it in front of adjudicators!

When competition season was finally here, come January, Chamber Singers traveled to the *Aztec Sing,* full of confidence. We had a very good series of rehearsals, over the past few weeks, leading up to this first competition, and now it was up to us to prove, once again, that we had what it takes to beat groups of this caliber! Once we had taken the stage, and the curtain opened, that exciting riff from *On Broadway,* began from the piano, and the show was off and running! On a side note, this was the first year we had ever repeated a song in a Chamber Singer competition set (we had previously performed *On Broadway/ Celebrate*, in 1982). Our feeling was that this arrangement was special, and since it hadn't been part of a show that had placed before… we'd give it another try! Our Aztec Sing performance was very good! Our a cappella piece was also very sensitively sung and LuAnne Ponce (who was now a freshman, and able to perform here *legally*) sang *Don't Cry Out Loud,* to a standing ovation! *The Best Little Whorehouse In Texas* medley was a blast to watch, and cleanly performed with tambourines. All in all, the kids and I felt that we had hit the bull's eye! When it came time for the awards, everyone in the group excitedly held hands and waited for our name to be called… *But, it never was*. Apparently, we had gone overtime, so once again, we were disqualified. I can't remember the exact placement where we *would have* come in… I think it was *fourth.* Regardless, the kids went home completely disappointed. But, we had traveled this disappointing road before. Perhaps, I thought, the problem was that we were being *too safe,* and not free to be ourselves? It was right then and there, that I decided to *be a little more risky* and allow our group to sing, the word, ***whorehouse,*** in their very next performance!

The next big competition was the *Fullerton College Jazz Festival.* The Chamber Singers had rehearsed very hard for this one, hoping to put what happened to them at the Aztec Sing, behind them. Our Dream Street Singers, meanwhile, were scared to death! The group had never competed before, although luckily we had a few Chamber Singers' girls in that group, pulling double duty, to help give them some experience. In addition, somehow Dream Street had shrunk to only 17 girls from the beginning of the year, when they had boasted 25! But still, they were more determined than ever, to make their first competition memorable! So, win or lose, *everyone* was ready to perform his or her heart out! As I mentioned before, in those days, *every group, regardless of their level or gender*, competed together in one big division. Aside from the Nogales competition, the *NDSCC*, where we offered *two different divisions, consisting of intermediate and advanced*, every other event competed everyone together. Fullerton had increased their awards to five, this year, so everyone had a little better chance of placing, out of the fifteen competing show choirs! The festival began. Dream Street performed second, and although their sound was light, I heard the adjudicators laughing at the humorous parts we had put in! That seemed like a good sign, didn't it? The Chamber Singers performed fifth. We received such an excited reaction from the audience, but also the adjudicators, especially when we began to sing, *"Texas has a whorehouse in it!"* Well, at the conclusion of that show, the kids couldn't have felt any more pumped! This festival was designed to give the performance categories about twice the value that the Aztec Sing offered, so we felt our chances of placing today were particularly good, considering all of our energy! As an aside, early on, in my career, I had learned that competitions usually placed the younger or unproven groups *toward the beginning of the performance order* and the older or more successful groups, *toward the end.* I suppose they thought that this would make a better show for the audience? You know, *saving the best for last*? I don't know if the staff at Fullerton College knew enough about the show choir competing groups in their festival to do this, but since both Nogales groups competed in the *first five slots out of fifteen*… I would suspect they might have. At long last, it was time for the awards to be announced! "In fifth place… *Burroughs High School Chamber Choir*!" This was a group we had always scored close to at the Aztec Sing. "In fourth place… *Act One*!" This was an *independent show choir*, lacking any school affiliation, directed by a very young Mark Henson, who later directed award winning show choirs at Canyon, Brea and Troy high schools. Now my students were *really* getting nervous. "In third place… the *Nogales High School Dream Street Singers*!" Wow! In their first competition! The girls were going crazy! Meanwhile, my Chamber Singers were tightly holding hands hoping for a miracle. "In second place… the *West Covina High School Chamber Singers*!" *Instant surprise and silence gripped the theatre,* before everyone finally began to applaud. No one knew what to think? If West Covina had come in second… that meant that there were still eleven groups left *who could win*? My Chamber Singers were almost in tears as they clung to each other with hope beyond hope that somehow they would be the final group to have their name called! "And In first place, the winner of the 1985 Fullerton College Jazz Festival is… *the Nogales High School Chamber Singers!" Tears were instantly pouring down my kids' faces*! My group was screaming and everyone in the building was applauding! Yes, the Nogales Chamber Singers had won the Fullerton College Jazz Festival! But, more important than that, to both the kids and me… *we had finally beaten West Covina*!

Well, to say that the confidence in both groups had grown, would be a major understatement! I think that winning at Fullerton and beating West Covina were both gigantic achievements, but to have the adjudicators finally appreciate our energy, hard work and artistry, along with our singing, gave everyone, the feeling that even if we were disqualified at the Aztec Sing for the next *one hundred years*… there was still life after that… *and we had just proven it at Fullerton*!

Our next competition for the Chamber Singers was at *Colton High School.* We were meeting West Covina for the last time this year. I think the kids were more interested in beating them again, than in winning the competition… although winning the whole thing, *would certainly not be bad.* My Chamber Singers seemed different than before, as they performed that night on the stage. They seemed to be even more animated than they had been at Fullerton! They believed in themselves… it was obvious! The awards were read at the conclusion of the festival. First they announced fifth place, and it was a shocker. They announced the *West Covina Chamber Singers*! Just like at Fullerton, there was a moment of stunned silence in the audience before they began applauding for them. I saw West Covina perform that night and they *were every bit as good as they had ever been*! Perhaps that was the problem? Perhaps West Covina was *not evolving*, as other groups were? Perhaps their proud brand was finally looking passé to the more progressive adjudicators? In any case, the Nogales Chamber Singers were announced *fourth place*, and I can't remember who placed first, second or third, *nor did it matter to me, or to the kids*. We had just beaten *the West Covina High School Chamber Singers* for the second consecutive time! Later that year, Tom Kessler announced his retirement from teaching choir at West Covina High School.

Besides hosting the third annual *NDSCC*, at Whittier Union High School, we still had one competition left. That would be *Tops 'n Pops* in Chula Vista. We had entered both Chamber Singers and Dream Street to compete in it. This year, because they had so many groups entered (18), *they were giving awards to the top ten scoring groups*! We had never placed here before, so it was clear we would have to impress the adjudicators, all over again, just like we had at Fullerton. This competition began in the morning, had lunch and dinner breaks, and then ran until it was over… which proved to be *very late at night*! Dream Street was once again, one of the first groups on. They performed well, but we were acutely aware that every other competing group was *mixed,* with a bigger sound and stage picture! We only hoped that Dream Street had made a big enough impression to be remembered at the end! Chamber Singers performed somewhere in the middle, and were also well received. But, frankly, by the time they were ready to announce the awards, my kids were starting to fall asleep and *didn't seem to care whether they placed in this competition or not*! That mindset quickly changed, however, as the Dream Street Singers were announced in *10th Place*! I know that winning tenth place doesn't compare to the third place trophy they had won at Fullerton… but the girls were excited just the same. After all, they had their name called, while there would be *eight groups* tonight who would not! They were already learning that every competition is different and to appreciate whatever they received. Our Chamber Singers ultimately earned *3rd Place* at that San Diego marathon, only two points out of second place! Consequently, our Chamber kids were very excited. They were at last establishing themselves as a group that always places… one of the "big boys… and girls!" Teresa Cimino was president while Colleen Ory Caron was vice-president of Dream Street during the 1984-85 school year. They, along with the other choir officers, including, Gabriel Lomeli, Laura Washington and Chris LaMantia, were outstanding leaders all year!

One "special" extracurricular activity that select singers from Nogales shared with select singers from Rowland and Los Altos High Schools in November and December of 1984, was performing a holiday show at *Bullwinkle's* (similar to Chuck E. Cheese), in Montclair, probably called, "*Bullwinkle's Christmas*!" To get there, our students carpooled to Bullwinkle's, for about twelve performances. It was actually kind of *fun and grueling* at the same time. The Nogales cast included Teresa Cimino, Tori Bosinski, LuAnne Ponce, Laura Washington, Lori Strait, Glen Jimenez, Jeff Crouch, Chris LaMantia, Gabriel Lomeli, Kenny Johnson and Ernie Tovar. I apologize for not listing anyone else who participated in this. There was no list, and *these are the only students who shared their names*. I believe they wore their Chamber Singers outfits as costumes. My favorite song they sang was, "We need a little *ChrisMoose*, right this very minute!" I was very proud of our kids' for the professionalism they demonstrated in their performances and for their dedication and responsibility in seeing this *entire performing obligation* through! However, this was *so time consuming*, that after one year, I opted to *never do it again*!

The year was fast approaching the end, and then one day, out of the blue, Tom Kessler called me on the phone. He asked me if I was interested in the West Covina job he was vacating? After a lot of thought… *I decided that I was*! It seemed as if ever since I had begun teaching, all I could ever think about was building a program, *just like Tom Kessler's at West Covina High School*! I wondered if following Tom Kessler at West Covina was to be my destiny? That summer of 1985, I interviewed with the principal of West Covina High School and was ultimately offered the job. I very excitedly visited the choir room I had loved so well as a student teacher… but upon closer examination… I realized that the Nogales choir room was actually larger and in better condition. I asked about pay, and found out that West Covina paid almost $5,000.00 *less per year* than Nogales High School did. I asked about an accompanist and learned that West Covina High School didn't provide one… the choir boosters paid a person to come in as needed. At that moment, I thought about my own students at Nogales High School, how hard they worked and how far they'd come! I realized that *it was not West Covina High School that was so special to me… but the incredible show choir program that Tom Kessler had created*! As my wife, Margaret, told me, *there was really no question that the Nogales job was a better fit for me.* I agreed. So, I immediately called the principal of West Covina High School, and told him that regrettably, *I could not accept the position.* That was it. I would not ever be teaching at West Covina High School… but I would continue to be motivated by Tom Kessler's brilliance and hopefully build a show choir dynasty, myself, someday, with my students, staff and parents at *Nogales High School*!

As great a year as 1985 had turned out to be, Doug and I were determined to make 1986 even better! One of the first things we did, once we had our costumes, was to take the Chamber Singers' officers to the gardens of the Sheraton Hotel, in the city of Industry, to take some classy photos in a classy place to use in some *classy looking pamphlets* we intended to create and distribute to anyone who would take them! This was our *not so subtle way* of announcing that *we were, an award winning show choir*! This, of course, wasn't my idea… I had "borrowed" it from something similar that the West Covina Chamber Singers had done, while I was student teaching, back in 1977! By this time, our accompanying band began to solidify. Once again, we had Mrs. Kathi Boothby (formerly Kathi Keith) on piano, Keith Fort on Bass, Dwayne Ganier on guitar, and Bo Eder on drums. I also had a student teacher for part of the year, Tim Bullara, who had been a member of the Cal Poly Chamber Singers, at the same time as I was, in 1976-77.

We had a lot of the same kids in Chamber Singers this year, as we did last year. They were also, a year more experienced, so we felt good about whatever music we chose! We decided to change gears completely and have a set featuring *jazz and country*! The show went as follows:

Chamber Singers 1985-86

Costume Colors: *Blue*

Competition Set

Java Jive/ The Joint Is Jumpin'
Send in the Clowns (a cappella)
Morning Glow (a repeat from the 1982 show)
Country Style
Beaucatcher Mountain

With this show, we went back to focusing more on the vocals while making the choreography more stylized and fun. Our power ballad, *Morning Glow*, would most likely feature *LuAnne Ponce,* as the soloist, which was certainly reassuring.

The Dream Street Singers, now in their second full year, were given a show that once again, *would show off their dazzling personalities*!

Dream Street Singers 1985-86

Costume Colors: *Red*

Competition Set

Ma, He's Making Eyes At Me
My Favorite Things
Leader Of The Pack
Material Girl

Unlike the Chamber Singers, Dream Street wasn't given an a cappella, because most of the group was made up of freshman girls, and we didn't think they were ready to sing one yet. Additionally, in those days, most choir directors made their music choices based on what the publishers were offering that year. While I had largely arranged the Chamber Singer's show for the past few years now, the Dream Street show was comprised of four pieces I could order from a catalogue. The problem was that lots of groups ordered the same music. Luckily, there were very few all-girls show choirs competing at that time, so most of these choices were not duplicated by anyone else in our competition circuit.

As usual, the year began with the Chamber Singers performing at the *Aztec Sing*. There was no chance of us going overtime, this year, and we had worked extensively on our vocals, based on the score sheet… so we were *cautiously optimistic* that our show would please these adjudicators. Actually, part of the ending medley, *Country Style*, was a song I had heard West Covina sing while student teaching in 1977. We were performing it in honor of Tom Kessler, who had just retired, but now worked as an adjudicator for many of these compctitions.

The night of The *Aztec Sing* arrived and we all felt pretty confident that we would place. This good feeling was probably due, for the most part, to all of the success we had experienced in the competition circuit, last season. Our performance went very well, and everyone came off stage feeling triumphant! When it came time for the awards, everyone in Chamber Singers held hands, not in desperation, like last year… but rather as a *show of unity*. When the smoke had cleared… we had won the trophy for

3rd *Place*! This trophy represented *our highest placing ever* at the Aztec Sing, and it gave us hope for the rest of the year!

Meanwhile, the Young Americans were hosting a national competition, for the second consecutive year, in late March, where they selected one show choir from each state to compete together in Pasadena. The top five finishers would then travel to NBC studios, the next day and tape the Finals competition, which would be aired to the public, at a later date! One day, following the Aztec Sing, I received a packet in the mail, from the Young Americans, *congratulating our Chamber Singers* on being selected *to represent California, and to compete in their national competition*! I was shocked that *we were the choir they had selected,* because we were not nearly as *successful, as* a handful of other groups, I could name… but I was very excited, all the same! I showed the invitation to our principal, who was instantly ecstatic that we had received this *great honor*, and proceeded to authorize the buses needed for our trips to Pasadena and the time off school required, for us to attend a number of mandatory workshops. He also granted a waiver to a number of our boys (who were academically ineligible at the time) so that they could participate. To explain this inexplicable behavior by our principal, you need to understand that Nogales High School *did not often* receive accolades, such as this invitation, for our programs. We were a poor and gang-infested school, where something like this would *undoubtedly create a positive buzz* about the school, *which was badly needed*!

So, the Chamber Singers prepared to compete in our first national competition! We worked very hard at every rehearsal. The group knew they were representing California, so they especially felt the need to not let anyone down. We were able to see the tape of the 1985 event and took note that *California did not make the Finals in that one*. The Nogales Chamber Singers were determined to make the Finals, and then give *that* performance *everything they had*! We even had a reporter from KABC Television, interview us, at school, and film us rehearsing. This clip, lasting a minute or so, was later shown on KABC News, multiple times, with newscaster, *Jerry Dunphy*, congratulating us, on the air! Being on television meant a lot, in those days, and our parents and school administration were thrilled!

To be honest, at first, to me, this experience seemed a *little surreal*. We would drive into Pasadena and share performance workshops with choir members from some really talented groups that hailed from all over the country... *some of the best show choirs of the day*! I don't think we were unconfident about ourselves... we were just in awe of so much talent around us! The other obvious thing was that the only two groups that appeared to be of mixed races were a group from Georgia... *and us*. The rest of the competing groups were *overwhelmingly white*. Our group definitely displayed a multiple-raced flair, and to be honest, *we took pride in it*! Sometimes we would catch some of the kids from the other groups staring at us, in curiosity? Not in a bad way, but probably because they hadn't seen a mixture of races like ours, in their own choirs. But after a day or so of working with each other, everything seemed pretty normal.

We would perform in the Pasadena Civic Auditorium. It was a beautiful old theatre with plenty of seats for anyone who wanted to attend. If memory serves, there were *eighteen* groups competing, represented by *eighteen* different states. The competition began early on a Saturday morning and ended by late afternoon. That evening, at an awards ceremony, after *every participating group* had been honored, then the *five finalists* would be announced to compete at NBC studios on Sunday... *the very next morning*!

The day of the *Young Americans' National Show Choir Competition* arrived and our Chamber Singers were more than ready to perform! I think our slot was somewhere in the middle. Doug and I had already decided to take out our a cappella, *Send In The Clowns*, because as a result, it made our show more *fast paced and exciting*. We felt that since most of these groups didn't do *full length a cappellas*, dropping ours, and singing the first verse of "Java Jive," a cappella, would meet the competition's a cappella requirement, and would probably make us *more competitive*! Without the a cappella, our show ran just over ten minutes! We certainly didn't need to worry about going overtime today! After we were announced, there was a large cheer from the audience. Many local competitors had come to watch. This might be the only time we would ever see our competitors *cheering for us*... but after all, we were all rooting for the same state! We began our performance and it seemed as if everything was clicking. From *Java Jive* to *The Joint is Jumpin'* to the inspirational, *Morning Glow*, with LuAnne Ponce nailing the solo and ending with *Country Style/Beaucatcher Mountain*! Everyone felt wonderful coming off stage, but we quickly raced out into the house, following our performance, to watch the rest of the competition. Because of our being backstage during our warm-up, there was only one group we weren't able to watch. After "unofficially" scoring everyone else, I had us figured for fourth or fifth. But I had not seen one group, so if they were really good, that could place us at fifth or sixth. There were at least three or four groups I saw that day, that were *so exciting to watch*, that I *knew* they were very likely to make the Finals! We would basically be fighting it out for that fifth Finals spot, if my calculations were correct! Fortunately... or unfortunately, *we'd find out tonight at the Awards Ceremony*!

The Awards Ceremony was very exciting and suspenseful. After thanking every group for being a part of this wonderful sharing experience, and giving each of us a parting gift, the awards were announced. They were grouped into three categories. The first was for **Choreography and Showmanship**. The trophies were attractive brass bowls with the placement it represented, engraved on it. They awarded Fourth Runner Up, first, which was actually fifth place, but sounded better the way they said it. We won the next award, **Third Runner-Up**, to a combination of shock and excitement, not because we hadn't placed higher, but because *we had placed at all*! The next category was **Vocals**. We earned **Second Runner-Up**, on that one, and our kids were just thrilled! (Actually, Margaret, Doug and I were too!) Finally, the awards everyone was waiting for... the announcement of the *five groups that would move on to the Finals* at NBC studios tomorrow! Even though we had earned awards in both *Choreography & Showmanship* and *Vocals*, we knew that *anything could happen* in a competition! So, we anxiously waited for them to announce the **Overall Winners**!

We all sat quietly in anticipation, until finally we were announced, **Third Runner-Up,** and the world stopped for just a few moments as everyone screamed and hugged. It was a remarkable achievement to be placed alongside the four other very talented groups in the Finals. I had to pinch myself, but tomorrow, *we were going to perform at NBC Studios*!

After arriving on our bus, back at Nogales High School, at midnight, we all rushed home and returned to school the next morning, at 6:00 am, for the long bus ride to NBC Studios! Most of us probably got *four hours of sleep*, if we were lucky. I imagine the other finalists found themselves in the same boat, so at least we were all going to NBC Studios, *equally tired*! The Finals were not set-up *anything* like the preliminary competition. As you know, we were told to arrive early in the morning (7:30 am) with the other groups… and then, *we all sat around and waited to find out what would happen next*? Everyone got hungry, but I think, eventually, a parent went out to pick-up something for our kids to eat and drink. We all found out that preparing for this television special was *nothing* like performing for a live audience. Each group took turns recording 30 seconds of each song they were singing today: one for choreography, one for vocals (a cappella) and one for overall. Since we had not used our regular a cappella in this competition, we opted to record 30 seconds of *Java Jive* without piano, the same way we had sung it for last night's competition. We used *The Joint Is Jumpin'* for the choreography and *Beaucatcher Mountain* for overall. When our turn came to perform, we would sing the song without microphones, because the recording of our voices would cover them, anyway! Our band would just pretend they were playing, because they too would be taped. Using this method we would be immediately scored by the adjudicators (who were hidden from view), after each segment, and those scores would be *shown* to the television audience as they happened. So in essence, we were being scored on our recordings! Some of the groups, like the one from Wisconsin, were playing hacky sack and running around, during those extremely long stretches of having nothing to do, but I insisted that our kids *sit and rest*. The group from Wisconsin had *won everything* the night before, and they were *understandably excited…* but if their lack of sleep was anything like our lack of sleep… I was afraid that all of their playfulness backstage, might cause them to poop-out when the competition began. I believed this was probably a once in a lifetime experience for all of us, so I wanted our group to feel, no matter how it turned out, *that they had given it their best effort*!

After all of the groups had successfully recorded their three songs, they changed into their respective performance costumes… and the Finals began! Our *Master of Ceremonies* was *Army Archerd*, a famous columnist for *Variety*, who welcomed the television audience to the event. Following this, a member of Young Americans introduced each one of the finalists, who would then *compete* in each individual category along with their thirty second recording. To be honest, this whole *prerecorded Finals thing* was very anticlimactic as compared to the excitement of the preliminary competition the day before, where we had performed before a *live audience*! Here, there was *no audience reaction at all. Zero*! The process was extremely clinical. *Welcome to television*! Still, the kids performed well, and scored well. In the end, we placed as *Third Runner-up*, the same as we had in the preliminaries. The biggest surprise of the Finals was that the group from Wisconsin, who had *won everything* at the preliminary competition the night before… *placed last*. That's show biz! Regardless of how long and tedious the day was, everyone felt very proud of themselves for enduring it and performing at their best. It was a very special experience!

There were a number of other competitions we went to, including the *Fullerton College Jazz Festival*, where we placed *3rd*, *Burroughs*, where we placed *4th*, and possibly *Tops 'n Pops* and *West Covina*. But to my recollection, Chamber Singers found it very difficult to top the excitement they had generated the previous year! Don't get me wrong… they placed at nearly every festival they competed in, for the first time in our history! I believe that for the festivals I don't have results for, they probably earned *3rds* or *4ths*. The highlight of the year, and perhaps of the decade so far, however, was the brilliant performance of Chamber Singers in the *Young Americans'*

National Show Choir Competition! We were now a school and a group that would be known all over the country!

1986 was also a great time for the Dream Street Singers! They didn't compete a lot, but everywhere they went, they were noticed... and they placed! They were one of only two girls groups competing in the Southern California Circuit. Their breakout year appeared to be coming, in the not too distant future! We had been experimenting with their set the past couple years, to find out what type of songs would be most effective for them in competition? In general, the results were fuzzy. Audiences seemed to like everything they sang, but the judges were still holding off that love on the score sheets!

The only other important thing I would like to mention about 1986 is that we moved from Whittier Union High School, and began hosting our competition, the NDSCC, at beautiful Citrus College, in Glendora. This is where the Aztec Sing and West Covina Festival had been taking place, for quite a while now. This was also the auditorium where I had *personally performed in plays and musicals*, a number of times during both high school and college. This had always been my preference, but Whittier Union High School was much cheaper in 1983, when we began. By the end of 1985, they had raised their rates so much, that Citrus became the better bargain.

1986 was the first year that the Nogales Chamber Singers had *ever competed* in a national competition and for good measure, *placed*! The officers for that group, included, *Colleen Ory (President), Nicole Chain (Vice-President), Jennifer Dunigan (Secretary), Maritza Gonzales & Tracy Fair (Treasurer) and Rod Chandler (Historian)*. The entire group is listed on the following page:

The 1985-86 Nogales High School Chamber Singers

Michelle Brown • Lisa Castilleja • Nicole Chain
Jennifer Dunigan • Tracy Fair • Maritza Gonzales
Rosa Grimes • Madeline Hsuing • Mindy Inman
Michelle Maxwell • Shirline McMurray • LuAnne Ponce
Lori Strait • Nannette Varela • Jonnetta Thomas
Sabrina Ganier • Gloria Hernandez • Nancy Mendoza
Lila Orozco • Colleen Ory • Claudia Saenz • Michelle Terrazas
Caroline Vergara • Rod Chandler •Jeff Crouch • Mike Gash
Shun Griffin • Chris LaMantia • Art Lucero • Lawrence Fitz
Kevin Pinedo • Vincent Dacumos • Art Farias • James Fox
Dale Hersh • Glen Jimenez • Kenny Johnson
Robert LaBarbera • Gabriel Lomeli • Brian Nunn
Robert Sanchez • Robert Zurrica

When the fall of 1986 rolled around, we presented both Chamber Singers and Dream Street with their 1987 competition shows! Doug and I felt very strongly that after the huge successes of the past two years, we had to challenge the groups a little more to ultimately reach the top. We had 40 talented kids enrolled in Chamber Singers and a whopping 51 in Dream Street! We intended to be in the thick of every festival we competed in! A very important change, this year, was that we were now using a local company, *Hollywood Babe*, owned by a former choir parent, *Yolanda Romero*, to make custom outfits (especially dresses and vests) for our groups! Doug and Margaret worked closely with her to design the styles and colors they wanted. Our look immediately went up ten notches! Our costumes *popped,* and looked completely original! No more looking through department stores for *generic mass quantities* for us! I continued using Hollywood Babe, up until I retired in 2016, at which point, Alex, the next director at Brea Olinda High School, also continued to use them! Our Chamber Singers, group, in particularly, was just loaded with talent! It seemed to be improving in a natural progression from 1994 to 1995 to 1996 to 1997, as our groups became more confident, more musical and more energized! Dream Street, was huge! But, most of those 51 girls were either freshmen or brand-new to Dream Street! Our competition sets were:

Chamber Singers 1986-87
Costume Colors: *Burgundy*
Competition Set
A Quiet Place
Cotton Fields
Brother Love's
Traveling Salvation Show
Bridge Over Troubled Water
Shine Down (added later)
Who Put The Bomp?

Dream Street Singers 1986-87
Costume Colors: *Pink*
Competition Set
Please Mister Postman
The Fawn's Lullaby
Don't Sit Under The Apple Tree

To tell you the truth, since we had worked with the Chamber Singers a lot longer than we had Dream Street, and most of the girls in that group were new every year, we did not yet challenge them nearly as much as we did our mixed group. This statement is evidenced by the fact that their show still did not include an a cappella piece and by the *obvious simplicity of their show design.* But in defense, we were not looking to have *two hard-hitting shows* like Chamber Singers.' Our girls' group was still fairly new and we didn't want to push them too hard as they progressed. We wanted Dream Street to be more of a *retro-show* that was effectively charming and sweet and could show-off their femininity, in direct contrast to the more dynamic style of the Chamber Singers show.

Chamber Singers performed a number of local shows for community events, at the end of 1986 and beginning of 1987, which, believe it or not, was quite unusual for us. Apparently, our success at the Young Americans' national festival had been spread around quite effectively. We even performed a thirty-minute set for a local convention in Los Angeles, held in a gigantic convention hall! With each performance, the group grew stronger, after exhibiting disturbing signs of '*breaking of character*' during some of our early shows. To explain, *breaking of character,* is when a performer *laughs or smiles inappropriately*, telling the audience that they are no longer focused on the character required for their song or play. This behavior can be compared to moving, when the leader ***does not say***, "Simon says move." So, Doug and I were encouraged that this Chamber Singers group, loaded with talent and improving in showmanship, could be the one we had been building for seven years now, to permanently place us at the top, with the other consistently tough competitors!

One very big addition to our family of performing groups this year were the *Silhouette Singers*, an intermediate level show choir, that depending upon the year, could be mixed or all-girls! I believe, they were added in the spring, and didn't begin competing until the next full school year. Unfortunately, our choir shirts had the group's name misspelled as Silhoute (we pronounced it, Sil- how-dy). The group laughed, but no one felt the problem was worth redoing the shirts over. In fact, they felt proud to wear the shirt of a brand new group... even if it was spelled wrong! I had a number of student teachers throughout the years, but this year, I was fortunate enough to have my sister, *Linda Willert Atherton*, who worked with the Dream Street Singers for nine weeks, on the way to her teaching credential! She was a great student teacher! We had fun!

The *Aztec Sing* came around, as it always did, and I felt strangely calm. That's because I had so much faith and expectations for Chamber Singers this year! Our performance there was very good. The trophies were announced, and we were awarded, according to my sources, *Second Place*! This was our *new highest placing* ever, at the Aztec Sing! We hadn't won, but this made the second year in a row that we had improved our placing here! Things were changing in the competition circuit. After West Covina's director, Tom Kessler, had resigned at the end of the 1984-1985 school year, their Chamber Singers got a director from the mid-west, who led them to one first place, at their final competition of the year, in San Diego. This year, they had *another new director*, and I don't believe they placed at all at the Aztec Sing! This huge void left by the departure of West Covina's former domination, was up for grabs. Of the former "big boys" of the circuit, only Arcadia High School, under the direction of Rollie Maxson, and Los Altos High School, directed by Dwight Fichtner, remained dominant! Redlands and Edgewood were still competitive, but *new groups* were quickly challenging them. These groups included, the *Nogales High School Chamber Singers*, the *Burroughs High School Chamber Choir* (later changed to Powerhouse) and the *Bonita Vista High School Music Machine*.

Soon after the Aztec Sing, I received a call from Bill Brawley of the Young Americans. He asked me if the Chamber Singers and I would like to co-host their newest venture, the *Young Americans' Southern California Show Choir Competition*, open to every California show choir who wanted to participate! He told me that my job would be to gather a list of active California show choirs who might like to compete in their event, and then be available as an advisor to them. According to Bill, my Chamber Singer students would host the selected groups, the night of the event and perform at the conclusion of the program. I took a day to talk to my students about it, and soon called him back to accept his offer. To be honest, I felt like after competing at the Young Americans national event, last year, this would be the *perfect follow-up* to further solidify our reputation as an exceptional show choir! *Another step toward the top*!

Our Chamber Singers' competition season turned out to be the most successful, so far! We placed *2nd* at our next two competitions, *Fullerton College Jazz Festival* and *Colton High School* and *3rd Place* with *Best Showmanship*, at the *West Covina* event. In all, our Chamber Singers had come in *second to Los Altos High School* in three of our first four competitions! On the bus ride to our final competition of the year, *Burroughs*, our kids began chanting, "We're number two!" I laughed. They knew, as I did, that we had already been beaten four other times by the same group, with similar judges, and that this festival *probably wouldn't go any differently*! But, as always, we gave it our best shot! However, Los Altos had a new song in their arsenal… *I Heard It Through The Grapevine*, complete with boys in trash bags, representing raisons, like the song was performed in a recent television commercial! Apparently, that song clinched the deal! The year belonged to Los Altos High School, who did indeed win the Burroughs High School Competition, for their *fifth consecutive win of the year,* while we came in second, right behind them, *four of those times*! Their director, Dwight Fichtner, was a very kind and friendly person, and to tell you the truth… I was very happy for his group and for him. Those were the days, before social media, when directors were friendly with the other competing directors, and bad-mouthing by students or directors was not instantly posted all over the universe, like it is through the Internet today. Our kids didn't feel too bad either! Coming in second, *four times,* behind a group that goes undefeated on the year? Not too shabby!

The Dream Street Singers also competed, and although there are no memories of *exact placements*, it is commonly agreed that they won their fair share of awards. The group, being so large, was a problem on small stages, but their show was very entertaining, both vocally and choreographically!

The *Young Americans Southern California Show Choir Competition,* arrived, and my students were ready to host! The event took place in the Ballroom of the Disneyland Hotel in Anaheim! There is really not a lot to say about this event, other than it went very smoothly and at the end, no groups seemed overly upset by their outcomes. At my suggestion, they embraced the divisional competition concept, and allowed groups to enter either the advanced or intermediate divisions. There was one little problem I might mention, however. The West Covina Chamber Singers were now under the direction of another new director. On the day of the festival, before the competition began, he asked if his group could move from the advanced division to the intermediate. He felt this change should be made because, as a first year director, he entered the advanced division, without understanding how tough it was. Since his group had not placed all year… he felt that his students would be better served competing with other young groups. I told Bill Brawley (the general manager), who then told Milton Anderson (the founder of Young Americans), and in a few minutes we all had a meeting. Ultimately, after a whole lot of questions and answers, West Covina was allowed to compete in the Intermediate Division. That change worked out well for them, as they came in *2nd place that night*! However, after that incident, I never heard of any group being allowed to change divisions on the day of the festival, ever again, *at any festival*! Situations like this were usually preempted in everyone's competition guidelines.

One major, non-competing piece of news in 1987 was that Nogales High School finally approved "earned" *letters* for their choir students, so they would be on par with student athletes! The choir letter was expertly designed by two of our officers, *Tracy Fair Fort and Gabriel Lomeli*. We used that same design through my final year of teaching (1998) at Nogales High School! This just proves, once again, that if you stubbornly, *refuse to give up on a worthwhile cause*, no matter how many times you are denied… *success will find a way*! Our kids proved that every time!

I had always loved visiting, the Hotel del Coronado on Coronado Island! So, for a couple of years, probably in 1985 and 1986, I brought the Chamber Singers and Dream Street Singers across the street from the Hotel del Coronado, to an inexpensive motel (nicknamed the Motel Del) to stay, while we competed in San Diego. We were close enough to visit the hotel, even if we could not afford to stay there. But then, in 1987, I was able to get some decent rates for the actual *Hotel Del Coronado*, and we stayed there! I've got pictures to prove it! The rooms cost a lot less than they do today. I think the average cost per room was only about $60.00 per night compared to today when the average Hotel Del room rents for over $500.00 a night! Inflation or not, those were darn good rates! *Tracy Fair* was president, *Gabriel Lomeli* was vice-president, *Jennifer Dunigan* was secretary, *Michelle Maxwell* was Treasurer and *Moni Grzesczak* was historian of Chamber Singers, during the 1986-87 school year. They, and all of the other choir officers, including Jeanette Zapata, did an amazing job!

Summer came to a close, and suddenly it was fall of 1987, and we were once again, preparing for the competition year. Over the summer, Kathi Boothby had resigned from her role as accompanist, and as luck would have it, we were able to rehire *Francine Stewart*. *Dan Rojas* also filled in for Keith Fort, from time to time, on bass. The biggest change to our shows, however, was the use of *performance boxes*. Using these, allowed our students to stand or sit, in any number of *formations,* according to Doug's visions! We "*borrowed*" this idea from Bonita Vista, who had been using them for years. Doug and I felt that they made the stage picture cleaner and more symmetrical. The only differences between our boxes and Bonita Vista's, were that where Bonita Vista's had small tops and were painted white, ours were almost square and painted black, to blend-in with the stage better. We had performed on a blank stage since the beginning, but we felt we could elevate the back rows and change the stage pictures, throughout the show, with boxes. They instantly made our groups look neater, better organized on stage and provided us with different height levels, for the first time, which we both agreed, was a very good thing! It wasn't long before we were announcing the *1988 competition sets* to each of our competing groups, which now numbered four! The sets included:

Chamber Singers 1987-88
Costume Colors: *White & Red*
Competition Set
Singing In The Rain
The Search
Celebrate America
Sixties Medley
Operator

Silhouette Singers 1987-88
Costume Colors: *Black*
Competition Set
Tear Them Down
I Dreamed A Dream
Bye Bye Love

Dream Street Singers 1987-88
Costume Colors: *Pink & Gray*
Competition Set
Why Do Fools Fall In Love?
Always On My Mind
Mr. Sandman
Golden Oldies

Uptown Girls 1987-88
Costume Colors: *Pink*
Competition Set
The Supremes Medley
Danny Boy
Splish Splash

I would like to talk a little bit about each of the Chamber and Dream Street sets, because this (spoiler alert) was a *very special year* for us! Although every year for the Nogales Choirs had been fun and eventful, up to this point, I guess you could call this year, *the beginning of the golden years!* I'll explain more about that later. The Chamber Singers set opened with yet another song from the fabled 1982 show, *Singing In The Rain.* Second, came the a cappella piece, which I wrote and arranged, called *The Search.* Our third song had been performed by one of the mid-west groups we had competed with in The Young Americans' Nationals in 1986, called, *Celebrate America!* It was catchy and patriotic… and featured *flag props*! What's not to like? In our fourth slot was a driving and fun medley of songs containing *Thank The Lord For The Night Time, La Bamba* and *Twist and Shout.* This is where the majority of our fast and furious choreography went. To end the show, we chose an unusual power ballad. I had first heard this song in the early eighties performed by *Roger Duffer's Redlands High School Chamber Singers*, on their way to a first place. The title was, *Operator*, originally performed and recorded by Manhattan Transfer. We were taking a risk, because a song like this required a passionate gospel performance from the soloist. We had several girls in the group we thought would be effective on this, but we ultimately chose, *Jenifer Dunigan*!

In the Dream Street set, we selected a more sophisticated show, although we still didn't allow the group to sing an a cappella piece. Their first song was *Why Do Fools Fall In Love?* This is a great fifties tune with tight harmonies. Since the group was wearing poodle skirts this year, it seemed like an ideal opener! Their second song was a gentle ballad we had heard *Arcadia New Spirit*, sing several years ago, called, *Always On My Mind.* The song was lovely, but when we put the warm and harmonic voices of *Lila and Loretta Orozco* on a solo verse… wow! Next we had another fifties song with smooth and beautiful harmonies called, *Mister Sandman*! We ended the set with an exciting medley called *Golden Oldies*, which included a number of great "girl" songs from the late fifties and early sixties!

Something just felt very different about this year, and I mean that in a good way. To begin with, it felt a lot like 1983, when the core of Chamber Singers had been made-up of motivated four-year choir seniors! We did have that in common, of course, but where in 1983, we were just trying to place, I think, after experiencing our rapid progress over the past few years, *this group was ready to consistently win against anybody and everybody*! As for Dream Street, they had been thrust into competition in 1985, and now, three years later, I think they were ready to let everyone know that they had finally arrived! Many of the key singers in Chamber Singers were also in Dream Street Singers, so the prognosis for both groups entering competition, seemed good!

Our Chamber Singers *did not* actually begin their competition year at the Aztec Sing, as was usually the case. They had been invited to participate in Bonita Vista High School's *Fantasy Festival 1988*! This unique "festival" took place exactly one week prior to the Aztec Sing! This was a very exclusive event that director Ron Bolles and his group, *Music Machine*, hosted every year. The way it worked was that each year, *one show choir* from outside of San Diego was invited to perform for one selected adjudicator, followed with a performance by the Bonita Vista *Music Machine*! Following those performances, the adjudicator would share his comments with both groups. This was meant to be a "scrimmage," prior to the first competition, for both of the groups, prior to entering the *real* competition season. I was intrigued!

We arrived at Bonita Vista High School on a Friday evening. Mr. Bolles welcomed us, and the event began! I was very pleased with our performance. It sounded good and it was energetic, just as we'd rehearsed. Next, the Bonita Vista Music Machine performed! I had first seen them perform at the West Covina competition, in 1982, and remembered being very impressed with their solid sound, stage presence and energy! Reina Bolles, Ron's wife, was their very creative choreographer. Their group's performance did not disappoint, as they powerfully presented their trademark style of choreography and vocals for us to enjoy! As an aside, over the next few years, our two groups competed a lot together, often coming in first and second, in either order. I truly believe that our groups fed off each other's energy, and ultimately, it made both of us better! We left Bonita Vista High School, following the performances and if memory serves, spent the night in a local motel, perhaps a La Quinta. The next morning, we returned to Bonita Vista High School, about 9:00 am, to hear the adjudicator's comments.

We were met in the parking lot by a student and led into a multipurpose room. Mr. Bolles welcomed us, once again, and after we sat, he introduced the adjudicator to us, Mr. *John Jacobson*, a popular choreographer and clinician for show choirs all over the country! He was all charm and smiles as he told the kids a little about his impressive resume. I didn't quite know what to expect? I had never met the man, although I had been reading about him for a number of years now, through the Hal Leonard (publisher) brochures that advertised his upcoming clinics and workshops! I knew that he hailed from the mid-west, so neither Doug nor I were sure he would like our *California show choir style*? But, he seemed nice. Then, he proceeded to share his comments about the prior evening's performances. First, he commented on us.

To put his comments in a nutshell... *he loved us*! He commented on the musicality of our a cappella piece, our exceptional choreography, our wonderful soloists and the overall energy and professionalism of our group! When he was done speaking, our kids were beaming! Next, he commented on the Music Machine's performance. He was also very positive in his remarks toward them, although he had a few *helpful suggestions* for their a cappella piece.

When we left for home, that day, our kids were sky high. We hadn't really competed... but still... it felt as if *we had won a competition*! Mr. Jacobson's positive comments were enough to make us feel more than ready for next week's Aztec Sing!

The evening of the *Aztec Sing* arrived, and for the first time both Chamber Singers and Dream Street were competing in it together! The Aztec Sing 1988, appeared to have a stellar line-up of show choirs! Something I had learned, over the years, about the Aztec Sing, was that with 80% of the score sheet dealing with singing and only 20% dealing with choreography and performance categories, a group that didn't sing well, *could never win this competition*! However, after our apparently stellar vocal performance at Bonita Vista High School, last week, we really felt encouraged! When it came time for Dream Street to perform, the girls felt very special. To my knowledge, *they were the very first girls group to compete at the Aztec Sing*, since the beginning in 1974! They were aware that they represented girls groups everywhere, and they didn't want to disappoint. They certainly didn't! When the curtain opened, I can recall the enormous applause that they received. More than simply being a novelty at the Aztec Sing, the girls were very entertaining and *so musical*! At the end of their performance, everyone in the group felt very good about their performance, and like we always said, win or lose, *nothing could take that wonderful feeling away*! Chamber Singers performed an hour later, and they also felt great after their performance! They showed a great deal of confidence in this performance! At the end of the competition, if memory serves, Dream Street, earned *5th Place*, while Chamber Singers earned *3rd Place* and won the plaque for *Best Showmanship*! It was quite interesting to watch, as Dream Street was *ecstatic* after winning their fifth place, while many of the Chamber Singers were actually a little disappointed, after having *placed third*! But, regardless, we could proudly stand up and brag to anyone who would listen, that we were the *first school* to have two groups *place* during the same year, at the Aztec Sing! I think that was the *greatest thing* we took away from that competition!

Regrettably, no one, including myself, seems to remember *all* of the competitions we participated in for 1988, after all, it was over thirty years ago! But, I do remember that we won a lot! This was indeed the year that belonged to Nogales, either through Chamber Singers or Dream Street! After the Aztec Sing, I remember going to the *West Covina* competition, being held in Downey, for some unknown reason? To the best of my recollections, Chamber Singers won that one and Dream Street came in, right behind them, in *2nd Place*! And happily, we experienced the exact same outcome at *Fullerton College*! In the Novice Division, Silhouette also won at Fullerton and I believe that Uptown Girls placed in the top five!

However, at the *Act One competition* (also held at Fullerton College), we encountered a *big surprise*! Both Chamber and Dream Street performed very well that night. Chamber, in fact, felt pretty confident that they would win, while Dream Street, just hoped to place. When Mark Henson announced the winners, *Dream Street had earned 1st Place and Chamber Singers had earned 2nd Place*! Wow! The girls in Dream Street, who were not also in Chamber, were ecstatic! The Dream Street girls, who were also in Chamber, were conflicted… and the people only in Chamber Singers were 100% in shock, which changed abruptly to denial about ten seconds later! This was the *very first time* Dream Street had placed first, or beaten Chamber Singers! To this day, there are mixed feelings about this one, when you talk to former choir members of that time. I say, *hurray*! It marked another big win for the evolution of the Nogales Choirs!

Our final competition of the year, for Chamber Singers, was *Burroughs*. It looked tough, as usual, with all of the regular players participating. Doug and I felt that we needed to add something dynamic and musical… perhaps something from a Broadway show that would really get the audience's emotions going? Well, it just so happened that we were performing highlights from *Les Miserables,* for our District Festival. Lila Orozco sounded sensational singing the solo for *I Dreamed A Dream*… so… we added it to the set! Just like that! When we arrived at the Burroughs competition… I immediately felt very strange. I suppose I felt like Dwight Fichtner and the Los Altos High School *Production Choir* must have felt the year before… *like the favorite that everyone was gunning for*! The only director to talk to me, besides Mary Rago, of Burroughs, was Ron Bolles, of Bonita Vista. There was no friendly atmosphere here at all… at least not for me. I could feel the tension all afternoon! When our group was finally in warm-up, that night, preparing to go on, I shared my feelings with them and they shared their similar feelings with me. We had never really been in this situation prior to this year. That feeling, you get, when you win enough competitions to know you are the best… *and every other competing group knows it too*! You know that every group wants to beat you, and nothing would bring them greater pleasure! We were discovering, that night, what it felt like to be on top. It was truly, *very lonely*! I asked the kids if they would like to lose tonight, and probably not feel so alienated… or to win? There was no discussion, as they all yelled, "Win!"

I never wanted to win a competition so badly in my life! I wanted it for all of those talented and hardworking kids we had in Chamber Singers, since their beginning in 1980! This competition was definitely against the "big boys!" If we won this one, I had no doubt we could do it again and again! We went on stage, receiving a warm welcome. By the end of our show, with Lila Orozco singing, *I Dreamed A Dream* and Jennifer Dunigan singing, *Operator*, the audience was standing up for us! No matter what the outcome, our kids were exhausted! They could not have worked any harder! We returned to our seats, pumped, but not overconfident about the outcome. Soon, Burroughs' director, Mary Rago, was on stage announcing the awards. By the time she had reached 1st place, our name had still not been announced! I could see some of our kids growing a little nervous. But, they all held hands before the final awards were called. Mrs. Rago smiled, "In *First Place*, with both plaques for *Best Musicianship* and *Best Showmanship*… **the Nogales Chamber Singers**! Yes, our group screamed and hugged for the longest time. You would think they had never won a competition before? But they certainly had… this marked their *third win this year*! Through this win, I think all of that tension, we had felt earlier in the day, when groups and directors weren't talking to us… was permanently eliminated! When I received our score sheets, from the judges, a little while later… I found that we had won in all ten categories of the score sheet, and by a total of *100 points*! This closed the curtain on a wonderful year of competing! It seemed very doubtful that anything could beat this feeling! For Margaret, Doug and I, this represented the culmination of eight years of competing with the Chamber Singers of Nogales High School! For our kids in the group… I'm sure this felt *as good as it gets*!

Besides competitions, Chamber Singers and Dream Street also traveled to the Hotel del Coronado, as they had last year, only this year was the hotel's *one hundred year birthday celebration*! We performed in the lobby for the guests in the hotel, and also competed at Chula Vista. In any case, we all loved the hotel… and apparently the hotel loved us! On another topic, Chamber Singers was invited by the Disney Company to perform for Governor Deukmejian, in the ballroom of a downtown L.A. hotel! That was fun, and the group sounded great!

To top the whole year off, most of the members of Chamber Singers, participated in a new and updated version of, *Living On Dream Street,* the musical, we had performed, so successfully, in 1984. It was the same basic story as last time, but with new characters and songs, to reflect our talent. We also rented and used cordless microphones for our two performances of this musical. The show was directed and produced by the team of Doug, Margaret, Della and me. The band consisted of Francine Stewart on the piano, Bo Eder on the drums, Keith Fort on the bass and Dwayne Ganier on guitar. The very talented ensemble cast of 22 students included: *Carrie Acosta, Lettie Burciaga, Jennifer Dunigan, Lawrence Fitz, Sabrina Ganier, Shun Griffin, Moni Grzeszczak, Lizsa Halopoff, Lori Halopoff, Suzan Hernandez, Dale Hersh, Erin Lindsay, Michelle Maxwell, Sergio Mejia, Carlos Morales, Lila Orozco, Loretta Orozco, Kevin Pinedo, Brad Salsman, Heather Tjaden, Blandina Vergara and Jaime Zavala*. I believe that this was the only time in my career that we included an individual picture of every performer, above their names and individual write-ups, in the program! Okay, I'm looking at a copy of the program right now, and since it was copied in black and white, *the pictures aren't of the clearest variety*… but at that time, *considering our very limited budget*, that was already stretched, due to renting five cordless microphones and a soundboard to run it, as I honestly told the kids, "This event was the most *professional thing* any of *my choirs*, had ever done!" It was a great swan song for the Chamber Singers of 1988... *especially for our very talented and dedicated seniors*!

On a related topic, I had been writing songs for many years, and beginning in 1986 until 1991, I turned some of these songs into *choral arrangements* for high school choirs to sing! Margaret and I developed our own publishing company, *Damar,* and we recorded demos of these songs, using many of these 1988 choir students to sing on them, along with Doug, my sister, Linda and myself. You can hear the recordings online at *davewillert.com*! I sold a few copies, but no major publisher would pick up my arrangements. It turns out the music publishing business can be *pretty tough*! I had over 50 rejection letters! So, we decided to fold in 1991. Still, I used many of these arrangements for my own choirs to sing, over the years, including, *Take My Hand, There Is A New Day A Comin,' Happy Folk, Heart Of America, The Search, Just Love Me, A Kinder And Gentler Me, My First Love and Run To The River!* It was a great experience! Like I have always told my students, *When you do something from the heart, you don't need others to verify its worth... you are already successful!*

Our president of Chamber Singers was Jennifer Dunigan-Zamora, while Dream Street president was Shauna Bragg, assisted by Sabrina Ganier, and I believe, Lawrence Fitz was vice-president of the Silhouette Singers! What a great job all of the choir officers did! I have listed the names of both the 1988 Chamber Singers and Dream Street Singers, below. They deserve to be acknowledged, because they represent the beginning of our *six-year winning streak* for *Chamber Singers*, and because there were very few women's divisions, the consistent *winning and seconds (behind Chamber)* that Dream Street achieved over that same period! From time to time, you will hear me refer to this era as the "*golden years*" for the Nogales show choirs. This statement has absolutely nothing to do with the talent or effort of these groups being better than other years… *all of our Nogales groups* were talented and dedicated! The term *golden years*, simply applies to the *great success we experienced in competitions* over those six years. In many ways, I feel as if the 1987-88 Chamber Singers and Dream Street Singers represented what Doug and I had been trying to achieve at Nogales since the beginning! They were *perfect*! Great singing, performing and dancing groups with exceptional soloists, accompanied by an exciting band! Our decision to use boxes for the first time, only made their performances that much more exciting for the audiences. Although the boxes *technically limited* our dancing potential, they more than made up for that by providing us with levels and stage pictures that had never before been possible for us! Undoubtedly, many of our four-year seniors were the main catalysts for us finally reaching the top! Their hard work and leadership, beginning with the school year 1984-85, following a massive rebuilding year in 1983-84, led to stronger and stronger groups between the 1985 school year, and ending with 1988! I will list some of these remarkable leaders and performers, as best I can remember them. Please forgive me if I inadvertently leave off your name. It doesn't mean I don't appreciate your efforts it's just that I have no comprehensive list to work from! A special thanks to *Jennifer Dunigan, Sabrina Ganier, Vincent Dacumos, Lizsa Halopoff, Michelle Maxwell, Lila Orozco, Kevin Pinedo, Amy Brazil, Art Farias, Barbara Kovacs, Lilia Barragan, James Minatogawa, Jeanette Zapata and Christine Terrazas.*

1987-88 Chamber Singers

Carrie Acosta • Michelle Alcantara • Paul Alley • Scott Arnold
Beverly Boceta • Lettie Burciaga • Latanya Burnett
David Chavez • Mike Chavez • Melynie Coates • Lucy Cordero
Vincent Dacumos • Fred Dew • Jennifer Dunigan (president)
Art Farias • Lawrence Fitz • Alfred Flores • Sabrina Ganier
Vanessa Gonzalez • Shun Griffin • Moni Grzeszczak • Dale Hersh
Lizsa Halopoff • Lori Halopoff • Susan Hernandez • Chris Mejia
Chrystal Inman • Erin Lindsay • Michelle Maxwell • Lila Orozco
Sergio Mejia • James Minatogawa • Carlos Morales
Loretta Orozco • Kevin Pinedo • Jaime Polanco • Yolanda Ruiz
Brad Salsman • Jonnetta Thomas • Heather Tjaden
Teresa Trejo • Blandina Vergara • Jaime Zavala

1987-88 Dream Street Singers

Carrie Acosta • Angie Avila • Lupe Baldonado • Amy Brazil
Lilia Barrangan • Beverly Boceta • Shauna Bragg (president)
Veronica Bruny • Lettie Burciaga • Brenda Burt • Betsy Chavez
Charmetra Chatmon • Sonia Contreras • Michelle Dahlstrom
Jennifer Dunigan • Bernadette Escaro • Melissa Fabros
Sabrina Ganier • Christina Gardea • Betty Gardea
Jeanette Zapata • Anel Herrera • Catherine Gill
Melinda Gonzalez • Vanessa Gonzalez • Moni Grzeszczak
Lori Halopoff • Brenda Horton • Torrie Johnson • Janette Kater
Lila Orozco • Barbara Kovacs • Ellen Lindsay • Erin Lindsay
Miriam Mata • Griselda Macias • Julie Martinez
Michelle Maxwell • Susie Medina • Mona Moore
Patrice Moore • Loretta Orozco • Marynie Patnugo
Melanie Randle • Marie Rey • Kristina Roach
Denise Rogoff • Jenifer Stockton • Christine Terrazas
Heather Tjaden • Keisha Walker • Monique Walton

CHAPTER 5

Nogales High School... 1988-1993... Maintaining A Winner!

Well, with all of the success we had experienced from 1988's group, the pressure really hit the 1989 Chamber Singers, since they had an *incredibly tough act to follow*! Once again, we lost a slew of talented seniors to graduation, including many of our soloists… but the kids who remained, were hard-working and experienced, so, at least we were not starting over from square one! We were once again, accompanied by the same band… Francine, Bo, Dwayne and Keith! Della Long was still with us too, doing whatever was needed to help keep the program running smoothly.

Our competition sets were both fun and musical, and, looking back, we seemed to be getting a bit more sophisticated and a tad longer with our shows.

Chamber Singers 1988-89
Colors: *Blue & White*
Competition Set
Songs of The South
The Hills Of Shiloh
Take My Hand
Steam Heat
Summertime Fifties
Rockin' Pneumonia

Dream Street Singers 1988-89
Colors: *Silver, White & Blue*
Competition Set
Downtown
Take These Wings
My Boyfriend's Back
Do You Wanna Dance?
Sincerely

<u>**Silhouette Singers 1988-89**</u>

Costume Colors: *Gold & Black*

<u>**Competition Set**</u>

Puttin' On The Ritz
Don't Cry Out Loud
Got My Mind Set On You
Brand New Day

To begin with, I felt early on, that Chamber Singers were not rehearsing as hard as I would have liked. So, in the beginning of the year, I found myself *very uncharacteristically, yelling at them*, as they rehearsed, as if they were in boot camp! To be honest, it wasn't *them* that I was worried about… it was, *me*! They were all great kids, albeit not as experienced, as the choir members had been the year before, when everything seemed to fall so perfectly into place! I think I was just afraid of losing our competitive edge. Having *never been in this situation before*, I wasn't sure of what I should do in order to avoid that? So, I did what I have always done when I wanted to get ahead, or at least not fall behind… *I worked harder*! And that meant… *I worked my groups harder too!*

Well, when competition season rolled around, the Chamber Singers were about as well rehearsed as is humanly possible! I mean it! Every musical chord, every dance step and every facial expression, had been rehearsed at least a hundred times! As usual, the *Aztec Sing* started our competition season off. We were excited to be there and anxious to prove that we belonged with the other elite show choirs who regularly placed. But after the awards had been announced… our name was not among the winners! Upon my review of the score sheet, I discovered that we had once again been disqualified for *going overtime about 25 seconds*! We would have placed third, I believe. My young group was a mess! I tried to explain that these things happen, and some competitions give no leniency to groups who go over their imposed time limits! Chamber Singers had been disqualified from placing *quite a few times now*, usually at the Aztec Sing, so I seriously began thinking about *NOT attending the Aztec Sing*, next year, for the first time in 13 years! It was beginning to feel as if I was purposely leading my group into an ambush, by bringing them here! It was a very long bus ride home, and seeing all of those shattered faces after we had left the auditorium, was not something I wanted to see again, if I could help it!

Our next competition was at *Monrovia High School*, where my sister, *Linda Atherton*, was now the director! Her score sheet was a lot like mine, which had the performance and show categories at about 35% while music was at 65%. The Aztec Sing was still at 80% music and only 20% show, which made the Monrovia festival much better suited to our heavy show style! That evening our show appeared flawless to me, the kids were working so hard. When the awards were announced, Chamber Singers had won *1st Place*, along with the plaques for *Best Showmanship* and *Best Musicianship*, with Dream Street, placing *2nd*, right behind them! That was more like it, as Doug and I let out a *combined sigh of relief*, following those awards.

Meanwhile, apparently, Bonita Vista's Music Machine was preparing to challenge us for *domination of the show choir circuit!* I was told, they were adding *props* to their shows, and making their choreography even *more incredible than it already was*! I think some of our kids had spoken with a number of their kids at the Aztec Sing, and *a new rivalry was born!* To be honest, it had actually begun last year, when Chamber Singers surprised everyone by how *impressive and effective* they were! To add to that, we had beaten Bonita Vista several times last year, so, knowing how *competitive we both were…* I believed that this new rivalry would be an *incredible dogfight*. I guess for the time being, anyway, the two of us represented the *new West Covina, atop the heap*! I had waited a long time for this!

For the first time, we took an overnight trip to *Cuesta College*, in *San Luis Obispo*, on Highway One, not far from the Pacific Ocean. The scenery was breathtaking, with the college, near hills, that were covered in dense, billowy fog on the day we arrived. The competition, designed after Fullerton College's, was actually a jazz festival that included show choirs to fill-up the daylong event. If memory serves, we only took Chamber and Dream Street to compete. There were a number of show choirs entered, but *no other groups* from our regular circuit were there.

Many of our competitors sang well, and had clean choreography… but honestly, and I'm not bragging here, I didn't watch a single performance *that came close* to our level of performance energy! At the end of the day, Chamber Singers placed *1st* and Dream Street Singers placed *2nd*, right behind them. Although some festivals featured multiple divisions at this time, Cuesta only had one for show choir. To be fair, that area of California was not big on show choir. Most of that area's high school choirs, I'm told, focused on *vocal jazz*. Even though I really didn't know much about vocal jazz, I decided then and there, that next year we would bring a group to compete in that division!

It seemed lately, as if every year or so I was contacted by somebody inviting us to participate in something very special! This year was no exception. John Jacobson, the popular choreographer and clinician from the mid-west (remember, he had adjudicated us at the Bonita Vista event last year), called to encourage us to participate in his brand new event called, *America Sings*! This was to be an event where 10,000 choir kids from all over the country would join together to sing a selection of patriotic songs on the lawn, in front of the *Washington Monument* to raise money for the homeless children of America! My students in Chamber Singers were wildly in favor! We even raised the necessary money without too much trouble! As part of the celebration, John Jacobson selected my song, *Just Love Me* (a song about homeless children seeking love), to be performed by our Chamber Singers and by the other California group that was participating, on the main stage, to open the event there!

We were thrilled! My biggest problem would be *deciding who would sing the prominent solo* in *Just Love Me*? As expected, a number of our singers *really wanted to be the soloist on this*. However, it was becoming quite a problem choosing, as we had so many qualified singers! So, Doug and I ultimately decided that it would be more exciting for the crowd (and none of our kids would be terribly disappointed), if we had a person, currently *in a Broadway show* sing it! That would solve the problem! I called, former student, *LuAnne Ponce*, who was currently playing the role of *Little Red Riding Hood*, in Stephen

Sondheim's, *Into The Woods*, at the Martin Beck Theatre in New York City! She graciously agreed to sing!

We arrived in Washington D.C., for *America Sings*, and stayed in a downtown hotel. *I could write a book about this trip, alone*, as we explored so much exciting American history on guided tours, caught a couple of musical theatre productions and had a million individual adventures! It was a very exciting trip! When the time came to join the other groups at the Washington Monument, it was thrilling! The sky was overcast, but no rain. The view of all of the singers, on the lawn, was incredible! There were estimated to be 10,000 of them, along with their chaperones! Soon, we were scheduled to begin! Incidentally, I had been asked by John Jacobson several months before to prerecord all of the background voices along with the accompaniment, to be played, while we sang, *Just Love Me*. He believed this would allow everyone in this massive outdoor venue to hear us! I was skeptical about that, at first... but when I heard that beautiful wall of sound backing up LuAnne on the solo, *I understood*! I know that this event happened nearly thirty years ago, but I'm certain that everyone who was there participating, *still gets goose bumps* when they remember that performance of *Just Love Me*! We were on a portable stage with all of the dignitaries, facing the lawn, which, as I mentioned, was filled with a projected *ten thousand high school singers*, all there to support homeless children! Wow!

The rest of the trip went very well. It rained, the next day, so the scheduled performances of each individual choir were done under the protection of a whole lot of large tents, with portable stages. The kids enjoyed performing, although the audience size could not compare to the night before. Still, that was a trip to remember!

The *Fullerton College Jazz Festival* was next. It was very exciting as all of our groups competed there, as usual. I believe that Silhouette Singers won their division, and celebrated the entire bus ride back! Bonita Vista and our Chamber Singers, faced off together, and although both of us put on stellar shows... in the end... *our Chamber Singers won*, and Bonita Vista came in second! Dream Street, however, did not fare as well... I believe they came in 4th that day. The group was very large, but apparently not as impressive on stage as we'd hoped, because, unfortunately, they were cramped... *there were just too many bodies performing to make any of their moves clean!* But we did receive compliments from the adjudicators *for fitting 55 girls on the small stage they provided us*! Show choirs of that size were unheard of in that time. Today, it's much more common. That was a very exciting time for all of us, and I think one could make a strong case that, as mentioned, *Nogales was definitely one of the leaders of the Southern California show choir circuit*! Now, the problem with being a leader *in anything* is that every other group is trying their best to beat you! The kids felt the pressure, but it dwarfed next to their pride!

At the end of the year, we decided to take only Dream Street to compete in *Tops 'n Pops*, in San Diego, since Chamber had gone to Washington D.C.! It was probably their best show of the year, but once again, they were hampered by a small stage. They again came in 4th! They won a trophy, but 4th *Place* was certainly not what they had experienced last year! Doug and I went into the summer intent on finding a solution to Dream Street's problem.

Lawrence Fitz was the president of Silhouette Singers in 1988-89, and both he and the other officers, including Lori Halopoff, Heather Tjaden and Sergio Mejia, were just terrific leaders! Their dedication and drive had a lot to do with their groups' successes!

On another topic, after the successes of 1988 with Nogales, I decided to look into the possibility of teaching in college! I sent letters out to all of the local junior colleges and universities, around Christmas time, of the 1988-89 school year. I especially pushed my recent success in show choir. There were a few nibbles, but only one bite, as a result. *Mount San Antonio College* (Mt. SAC) contacted me about the possibility of directing a show choir program there, but they wanted to see my product, first! So, I invited the head of their Music Department to come to our 1989 NDSCC, at Citrus College, in early February, where he would have the opportunity to hear my Chamber Singers perform! The Citrus College Auditorium was packed, and all of the approximately 1440 seats were occupied! In those days, show choir in Southern California was electric and virtually every event that the major groups attended was just like this! The next day, the man called me and offered me the job, for the next school year! However, I was a little disappointed to learn that *the job* only entailed one class, which would meet twice a week for two hours! The pay, as I remember, was only $22.00 an hour, which was considerably less than I earned teaching at Nogales, but I decided to give it a try! Mt. SAC also hired Doug, with a similar contract, to do the choreography! That summer, I sent letters to every high school director I knew from the Southern California Vocal Association's directory! I introduced myself, as the new director of the *Mt. SAC Singers*! The name we chose was a bit generic, but it seemed to fit. When Doug and I attended that first session, we were *amazed* to see that most of the roster consisted of *featured Nogales High School alumni!* The choir included:

The 1989-90 Mt. SAC Singers!

Sopranos	**Altos**	**Baritones**
Charmetra Chatmon	*Michelle Dahlstrom*	*Dan Copeland*
Sabrina Ganier	*Jewel Barnes*	*Jeff Crouch*
Dierdre Lauder	*Karri Knight*	*Lawrence Fitz*
Della Long	*Lila Orozco*	*Carlos Morales*
Julie Martinez	*Loretta Orozco*	*Lee Nyman*
Kimberly Quist	*Ana Trujillo*	*Brad Salsman*
Marie Rey	*Monica Castro*	
Lisa Rubi		
Jennifer Dunigan		

There were only a handful of these terrific 22 students who were *not* alumni from our Nogales program! We took the music, mostly from fifties and sixties standards, like the music the Silhouette Singers had been singing, because we expected a beginning group. Nonetheless, we spent the next four months of class meetings, singing, dancing and auditioning for solos, as we prepared for our major end of the semester concert in January of 1990! We did have a few local concerts, but **Mt SAC Singers In Concert**, in Mt. SAC's Little Theatre, accompanied by our own

Nogales Choir band, was the big one for the semester. It was a wonderful bit of nostalgia, as Doug and I had the unexpected delight of working with many of these kids again, and they with us. But, at the end of the semester, both the kids and staff agreed that for this class to be more than a trip down memory lane, it had to be part of the *main* music program here at Mt. SAC, and the curriculum had to be *college level* and rehearsed more than twice a week! Well, the only way these changes could occur would be if I, or someone else, were hired as a full-time employee of Mt. SAC, and in charge of the show choir division. I discussed this possibility with the head of the music department, who *very graciously explained to me* that the Mt. SAC Music Department's teaching staff was already full, and until the older teachers began to retire, the best I could hope for would be this single class. Consequently, Doug and I *both resigned at the end of the first semester*. It was a fun diversion, but there was *no hope for growth*, and neither Doug nor I wanted to waste any of our students' time, if we were not able to bring them to a higher level than a few hours a week allowed! *Mark Henson* took over the position that Doug and I had vacated, and stayed a few years until Mt. SAC finally hired *Bruce Rogers* as their full time choral director in the mid-nineties. The Mt SAC Singers class was dissolved at that time and replaced by an adjunct vocal jazz group. I have always been grateful to those students who took the time to be part of this adventure with Doug and I. However, I ultimately decided to *continue teaching in high school*. I never again applied for a college teaching job.

The 1989-90 school year brought us hope and a *whole lot of kids*! For the first time, my choral program had grown at Nogales High School to the point where I was finally able to offer *five choral classes during the day* and a sixth that met after school, that we'll talk about soon, called *Renegade*. *The Uptown Singers and Madrigal Singers* were the only two groups in our program, not expected to compete this year! We had lost a number of seniors, from last year, but having survived, and even thrived last year, we felt prepared to do it again! Fortunately, our accompanying band was exactly the same with Francine Stewart on piano, Keith Fort on bass, Dwayne Ganier on guitar and Bo Eder on drums. Our competition sets included:

Chamber Singers 1989-90
Colors: *Red & White*
Competition Set
On Broadway/ Celebrate
There But For You Go I/ Memory
New Day
Hernando's Hideaway
Proud Mary/ Good Lovin'

Silhouette Singers 1989-90
Colors: *Black & Gold*
Competition Set
Jump Shout Boogie
Moonglow
Salvation Train
Trickle Trickle

Dream Street Singers 1989-90
Costume Colors:
Silver
Competition Set
I've Got The Music In Me
My First Love
Shuffle Off To Buffalo
Get Ready
Great Balls Of Fire
Footloose

Renegade 1989-90
Costume Colors:
Silver Jacket
Competition Set
Born To Be Wild
Da Doo Run Run
I Can't Help Falling
The Great Pretender
You're Sixteen
R.O.C.K. in the U.S.A.

The most important addition to our family of choirs, in the 1990 competition year, was our brand new all boys group, *Renegade!* To my knowledge, *we were the first competing boys' group* in Southern California, as we did not see or hear about any others for another year or so. This group of very talented and passionate performers was an instant hit with all of their audiences, *especially, the girls*! Renegade's show was comprised of mostly fifties and sixties rock songs. If you looked very carefully at the competition sets of our other groups, you probably noticed a few changes that are well worth noting. First of all, the Chamber Singers set was very dance heavy, to accommodate the strong dancing group we had. The power of their vocals was still in question. Dream Street changed drastically from the past few years, by dumping the "cutesy girl" music and substituting it for a more masculine set of famous feel-good rock tunes on testosterone! They still did not sing an a cappella piece, but they did sing a sweet ballad, called *My First Love*. Finally, Silhouette Singers were having a tough time *finding themselves*, with another mixed show choir, Chamber Singers, already in the program… so I made their entire set *vocal jazz*! Probably not *real* vocal jazz, but since I had never sung it or taught it before, this set was just jazzy enough! We planned to test their set out at both the Cuesta and Fullerton Jazz Competitions, later in the school year.

This was going to be a busy year, perhaps not quite so busy as last year, but we had a lot of competitions scheduled and Renegade was going all out, and competing *three times*! In addition, we were planning *two overnight trips*, one to Cuesta College and one to San Diego.

True to my feelings about how we had been treated during the past year, we *did not attend the Aztec Sing* this year. Instead, I believe that our first competition was *Monrovia*. We took both Chamber Singers and Dream Street, with both of them competing together in the same division. Well, our new "rocking" Dream Street *beat* Chamber Singers by one point for *1st Place*! Dream Street, also won the plaque for *Best Musicianship* while Chamber Singers won the plaque for *Best Showmanship* along with *2nd Place*! Looking back, I believe that this was an important *turning point*! Not only for the success of Dream Street… but for *all of our girls' groups in the future, too*. This was the year that we made Dream Street more masculine… and they beat Chamber Singers in their first competition! *We would remember that*!

Our next competition was an encore, overnight trip to *Cuesta College*, to compete in their Jazz Festival. If there was one thing we had learned by attending the Fullerton Jazz Festival, it was to *bring as many different groups to the event, as possible*. Although they may not all win, this always gave our program a chance to give every group some performing experience, as well as the opportunity to cheer on our other Nogales groups, when not performing! Well, we arrived at Cuesta College, in the morning, and the surrounding area was even *more stunning* than it had looked last year! Our first group to compete was Renegade, whom was entered in the Novice Division. They were all that they were supposed to be! They were hard driving, cute, energetic and fun. When the Novice awards were announced, they had captured *2nd Place*! Our next group to perform was the Silhouette Singers. They were competing in the novice vocal jazz category. Doug had also included some *simple* choreography in their set to make them more interesting, although there was *no actual category* for it in this vocal jazz competition. I'm very glad we competed novice, because our competitors *were just learning the style too*. So, although we seemed very different from everybody else, *we didn't stand out as badly* as I feared we might, for not embracing the full vocal jazz style, whatever that was. However, we wore black and white with matching gold jackets, which made us *stand out*, to some extent, since every other group wore very simple, non-matching black and white. When the awards were announced, I was not sure how we would do, and I was a little surprised when we were announced *1st Place*! The kids were so excited, feeling as if they had conquered vocal jazz *without even understanding it*! But, the truth of the matter came out in the score sheets. *Every adjudicator* noted that our Silhouette Singers were *not a real vocal jazz ensemble*! They scored us according to the score sheets, however, and we won on points, regardless! The next division was for Advanced Show Choirs, and once again, Chamber Singers and Dream Street were competing against each other! However, this year a group from San Gabriel (near Arcadia) was entered in their division, and after watching them perform, I was very impressed with their singing, and therefore *not quite as confident,* regarding our chances of winning! Interestingly, our kids in both Chamber and Dream Street felt the same way about San Gabriel, even though I had not shared a single word about my feelings. At this point, as always, the outcome of this division depended entirely upon impressing the judges! Dream Street performed, and was flawless, a crowd favorite! Next came Chamber Singers' turn to perform. They performed with more energy than I had ever seen from them and their rendition of the ballad, *Memory*, from *Cats*, was very moving! Finally, we reached the end of the competition, and announcement of the awards for the Advanced Division! When they were about to announce the top three, all of our kids, from all of our groups, instinctively held hands and waited with anticipation. They announced,

"In Third Place, San Gabriel Chamber Singers!"

Now our kids held hands tighter, with even more anticipation.

"In Second Place, Nogales High School Dream Street Singers!"

Everyone cheered from Nogales, but the Chamber Singers cheered the loudest, as they expected to hear their name next, officially beating Dream Street, the only group to beat them at Monrovia!

"In First Place, Nogales High School Chamber Singers!"

The room went wild! What an exciting day! I read all of our score sheets, as I always do, and I noticed that one adjudicator said that he gave *one handclap* for our Chamber Singers' choreography, but only *half a clap for their singing*. Win or not, this was the second straight competition where we had *not won* musicianship! So, I knew *exactly* what Chamber Singers would work on, come Monday!

I felt that there was a little lull in our competition schedule, so I entered Chamber and Dream Street into a *Heritage Festival* being held at Universal Studios! The kids were very excited about this one! As we arrived, we were immediately taken to a secluded area where the *Universal Tram* begins, and were herded toward an outdoor stage that had been constructed exclusively for this event! When I call this area *secluded*, I mean that it was away from the Universal Studios guests, and none of the participating students from the competing groups, were allowed to leave this area, all day, because they had to remain in costume! Well, I was disappointed for our kids, but tried to make the best of it, by encouraging them to watch the other groups and learn from things they did. I was so proud of our students' mature demeanor that day, as they graciously watched the other competing groups, including the Burroughs Chamber Choir, who we often saw in competition. The day was slow and hot, as we were outside the entire time. I think the kids had a snack bar and bathrooms available to them, but other than those, it felt like we were in quarantine! When Dream Street and Chamber Singers went on, toward the end of the competition, both groups were a little hot and tired from sitting around in the heat so long. So we "*pizzazzed*" a lot in warm-up, and I think both performances came off as best they could, considering we were performing on an outdoor stage. Both shows were actually very good, and even our sound, through an outdoor sound system, sounded okay. Before the Awards Ceremony, the kids were all allowed to take the famous Universal Studios Backstage Tour. This was a real highlight, and allowed the students to *act like kids* for twenty minutes! When the Awards Ceremony began, just like at Cuesta, I was not sure how we had been scored? This festival gave Gold (90-100), Silver (80-89) and Bronze (70-79) awards to each group, depending on their overall score. When the awards were announced, our kids went crazy, because our two groups were the only ones to earn *Gold Awards!* In addition, Dream Street won the *Best Music Award* of the competition, while Chamber Singers earned *Best Showmanship*, with special individual awards being presented to *Lori Halopoff, David Kater and Jaime Zavala* for being *Outstanding Soloists*! The wonderful day was only marred for Chamber Singers, by the fact that they had not won Musicianship all year, while Dream Street had already won it twice! As successful as our Chamber Singers were, this was really beginning to feel like *Dream Street's year*!

Chamber Singers still had four competitions left! What A busy year! First, the *Fullerton College Jazz Festival* resulted in a *1st Place* (advanced division) for Chamber, *2nd Place* (right behind Chamber) for Dream Street, *1st Place* (novice division) for Renegade and *6th Place* for Silhouette Singers in their second attempt at competing in the novice vocal jazz division. Unfortunately, these vocal jazz adjudicators weren't as impressed with Silhouette's jazz singing, as the adjudicators at Cuesta, had been! Oh well. Overall, another great effort for Nogales at Fullerton!

Next, we competed at the *Colton Competition*, hosted by fellow University of Redlands graduate, *Doug Newton*. We brought three groups to compete in the festival, while everyone else brought only one. The results were a little embarrassing, as Chamber Singers took *1st Place*, Dream Street took *3rd Place* and

Renegade took *5th Place* amongst the five placements. Unfortunately, as a result, we *nearly* got into a *rumble*! At the end of the festival, I was in the theatre lobby, speaking with Doug Newton, our host, when one of my students burst inside and told me about a big fight outside, between our groups and some other school! I immediately rushed outside! There, in the parking lot, was a mob of angry kids from another school viciously attempting to stare down a large group of choir members from Nogales! The temporary peace, between them, felt very fragile, as if it would break at any moment. Looking around, I sought, and finally found their director. We spoke, for a good five minutes, in front of all the students… and somehow, we talked our way out of a fight, and both sides peacefully boarded their buses, without a punch being thrown. After we were safely on the bus, headed for home, I thought about what had "*almost*" happened? I got the distinct feeling, *quite strongly*, in fact, that this director felt as if *we had cheated*, by entering *three different groups into the competition*! But the truth was that the circuit needed to add women's and men's divisions to their festivals, so that we could all compete separately. A mixed division to accommodate all types of groups was no longer working, as evidenced by what *nearly happened tonight*! Numerous schools now competed with women's and even men's groups. The circuit was overdue for a major change in adding separate competing divisions for those groups, and thankfully, *those changes would come before too long*! I didn't fancy getting my choir involved in another midnight standoff, any time soon!

Chamber Singers was nearing the end of their competition year, when they traveled to *Burroughs High School* for their annual event! The kids went all out, as usual, and the result was *1st Place* with both the *Best Showmanship* and *Best Musicianship* plaques! This was a major confidence builder as once again they beat the always powerful, *Bonita Vista Music Machine,* along with every other major player in the Southern California circuit! Burroughs seemed to always be our *go-to* festival during those years.

Chamber Singers felt very confident as they arrived at their final competition of the year, along with Dream Street… *Tops 'n*

Pops! This exciting annual San Diego event was hosted by Chula Vista High School. Well, both Chamber and Dream Street gave exceptional performances! But, the results almost mirrored those from Monrovia, months before when we first began the competition season. Dream Street took 1st *Place* along with both the *Best Showmanship* and *Best Musicianship* plaques, while our Chamber Singers earned *2nd Place*. As I mentioned earlier, no offense to the wonderful year Chamber Singers had, *but this had definitely been Dream Street's year!* Shockingly, when we returned from this overnight trip, *Don Hofer*, our young *student teacher* from Azusa Pacific University, discovered that his car had been stolen, right off the Nogales High School Parking Lot! We all felt just terrible, because even though he had insurance, the deductible was probably more than he could afford! Well, the next week, the kids and their families raised, about $700.00 to help him with his deductible. When we presented it to him, in class, he was so grateful, that I don't think I can ever remember that day without smiling. For the 1989-90 school year, Leonel Diaz was president of Concert Choir, while Sergio Mejia was vice-president, Betty Gardea was secretary and Veronica Bruny was treasurer. In Dream Street, Veronica Bruny was president and Erin Drake Garcia was vice president. Both they, and the other choir officers, including Lori Halopoff, Jaime Zavala and Heather Tjaden, did a wonderful job that year!

One other important accomplishment of 1990 was teaming with drama and producing the musical, *You're A Good Man Charlie Brown*. It featured a very small cast, only six kids, and the three girls' roles were all double cast. The entire cast included:

1990 Cast List of "*You're A Good Man Charlie Brown!*"

Charlie Brown..................*Jose Burciaga*
Schroeder...............................*Fred Dew*
Linus...*Leonel Diaz*
Lucy..........................*Suzan Hernandez/ Nancy Han*
Patty............................*Julpha Maniquis/ Francy Young*
Snoopy...........................*Heather Tjaden/ Lori Halopoff*

This was the first of three musicals that we would successfully put on with drama and their directors, *Lee Oldham, Michael Dalton and John Smithson* over the next nine years.

It was the summer of 1990, and once again, our accompanist resigned, but we were fortunate enough to hire Don Cloud, *whose piano skills were simply off the charts*, to replace her! So, now the band consisted of Don, Bo, Dwayne and Keith. Doug and Della, were also still on board. Due to increased paperwork, we also hired our outstanding 1989 graduate, *Carrie Acosta*, to serve as the choir secretary for the year.

Chamber Singers 1990-91
Colors: *Red & White*
Competition Set
Dreams Are For Today
Heart Of America
Too Darn Hot
Over The Rainbow
Day-o
Johnny B. Goode
Shout

Silhouette Singers 1990-91
Colors: *Gold & Black*
Competition Set
A Nightingale Sang
Steam Heat
Birdland
Starmaker
I Return To Music
O Happy Day

Dream Street Singers 1990-91
Costume Colors:
Blue & White
Competition Set
I Got The Music In Me
Boy From New York City
Respect
Shenandoah
Always On My Mind
Big Spender
Devil With The Blue Dress

Renegade 1990-91
Costume Colors:
Silver Jacket
Competition Set
Shakedown
Macho Medley
Bring Him Home
Duke of Earl
R.O.C.K. in the U.S.A.

With more groups from Nogales competing and having *already competed* with show choirs for the past ten years, it became more and more difficult for us *not* to repeat songs! But with multiple groups we learned to *pass songs around*, so one group's *brand new song* was actually another one of our group's *hand-me-downs*. This year, however, we went with mostly new material for every group. We had a very strong senior class, who were freshmen, when we began our winning ways in 1988. For that reason, we wanted to make these shows exceptional, new and special to everyone!

As luck would have it, John Jacobson, the founder of America Sings, gave me a call in early September. He wanted me, and my groups, to host a local version of *America Sings* in a large park area of Long Beach, in March. His plan was for us to sing, *Just Love Me*, again on an outdoor stage, to open the festivities. We chose talented senior, *Jaime Zavala*, to sing the passionate solo part that LuAnne Ponce had sung in 1989, in Washington DC. Following that, my students would lead each group to the stage, to perform, based on the schedule, supplied. Our groups would also be scheduled to perform. I discussed this with my students and they were all instantly excited! So, it was decided that Chamber Singers, Dream Street Singers and Silhouette Singers would stay overnight in Long Beach and host the event together! Meanwhile, in early February, we were preparing for our first competition at Monrovia!

Chamber Singers and Dream Street arrived at the *Monrovia High School* Auditorium, in late afternoon. As was the custom in those days, that every group got to warm-up on the stage for fifteen minutes, during a block of time prior to the competition. After both of our groups had finished warming up, I just stood there and smiled. Win or lose, these kids performed their shows just the way Doug and I had envisioned them! A few hours later, our groups took the stage, performed and returned to the house to sit down. They were proud of their performances… I could tell! Now it was just a matter of waiting to find out what the judges thought. At the end of the night, Dream Street came in *2nd Place* while Chamber Singers came in *1st* with the plaques for *Best Showmanship* and *Best Musicianship*! A great way to begin the year!

Our next competition took place at *Hart High School* in Newhall. Because the school was located about two hours from Nogales High School, I didn't always choose to go to this one. But, this year, the kids wanted to go everywhere we could! So, here we were! This was also a competition that *did not offer a separate girls division*, so, as usual, Dream Street competed in the Advanced Mixed Division! The atmosphere here was very relaxed and nice. There was no talk of overtime penalties, like at the Aztec Sing, so I sat back and hoped for the best. About 11:00 pm, after everyone had performed, the results were announced. It was a déjà vu from two weeks earlier at Monrovia; Dream Street placed *2nd* and Chamber Singers placed *1st* winning both plaques for *Best Showmanship* and *Best Musicianship*! From the look of things, Chamber Singers had retaken the top spot in their battle with Dream Street! Curiously, this had been one of their major goals of the year! Dream Street's success against Chamber Singers, last year, had really lit a fire under them!

Our next competition was the *Fullerton College Jazz Festival*, where we decided to take everyone. This festival was very popular this year, so all of our divisions ended up being quite large. Renegade's show was short, lasting *under* 10 minutes, which was the festival's *minimum performance time*. So, before we went on, we instructed the boys to *introduce themselves* in the beginning of the show *to add some time* and to crawl slowly off the stage, at the end of the show, *repeatedly reciting, "water,"* while Dwayne played *Stairway to Heaven*, on his guitar just to make sure we went over 10 minutes! It worked like a charm as Doug and I were cracking up, off stage! In the end, Renegade placed *2nd* in the Novice Mixed Division, Silhouette Singers came in *1st* in the Novice Vocal Jazz Division, Dream Street came in *3rd* in the Advanced Mixed Division, while Chamber Singers placed *2nd* in the same division! I don't have access to the other groups' scores in this competition, but I'll bet it was the *Bonita Vista Music Machine*, that came in *1st* that day! We had been beating them for a while, and they had really prepared for this! Nothing like a little personal rivalry to bring the best out of a group! Following this, we began preparing for *America Sings*!

We arrived at our hotel on Friday afternoon, received our special *America Sings* tee shirts and met with John Jacobson and Mac Huff to prepare for the Saturday event! We had nearly 100 students there from Nogales, representing three of our groups, Chamber Singers, Dream Street Singers and Silhouette Singers. After an exciting evening of swimming in the pool, everyone, as far as I know, went to bed! The next morning, we rode our buses to the park, and proceeded to prepare for the onslaught of groups! It was a large turnout, but nothing like the ten thousand in Washington DC in 1989. Everything went well, until it came our turn to perform. Silhouette Singers were on stage, *frozen in place*, as are all of our groups, right before the lights come up and the music begins to start a show. Well, the only problem was that the band never started playing! I looked at Dwayne, our guitar player, and he threw up his arms in frustration? The scene stayed like this for a good ten minutes. *But no one on stage had yet moved a muscle*! Finally, I motioned for them to relax, and walk off stage. They did and everyone started applauding. This entire sequence of events had been so amazing to watch! The culprit had been an unplugged power cord to the stage. The situation was quickly remedied and my groups performed! I'll tell you what, I enjoyed all of the different groups' performances and my students' wonderful job of hosting… but nothing was so memorable as when the Silhouette Singers held a pose for *ten minutes* without moving, under the hot sun and then only breaking their pose when I directed it, and exiting the stage so professionally! I was as proud of those kids, as I have ever been!

Chamber Singers went right back to competition mode, and prepared to compete at *Burroughs High School*. As we warmed up on the stage, I suddenly saw the students from Bonita Vista High School rush through the doors of the auditorium, to watch us. Following our warm-up, I found Ron Bolles, the Bonita Vista director, and asked him, why his kids had rushed in to see us warm-up? He had a big smile on his face, as he replied, "To check out our competition." He seemed very confident. Immediately, I had a *bad feeling* about this. The evening's performances came and went. We performed a fun and passionate show, as usual, and Bonita Vista presented a new updated set that included colorful props and a whole lot of energy! When the awards were announced, Bonita Vista earned *First Place* honors, while our Chamber Singers placed *2nd*! There was a time, not too far in the past, when Chamber Singers would have been more than satisfied with *2nd Place*… but not anymore.

Well, for Chamber Singers, they had only one more competition left. That would be Doug Newton's *Colton Competition*. We had done well there in the past, so that gave us some confidence. Bonita Vista was not competing in that one, so we had to accept, that after beating us twice, in so far as our personal rivalry was concerned… *this year belonged to them*! But, it had still been a very successful year for Chamber Singers, as they had previously won twice and come in second twice! Dream Street was also competing at Colton, in a year of mostly seconds… and they were very inspired to win! Both of our groups performed, that night, as if the survival of the world depended upon it! At the conclusion of the competition, Chamber Singers earned *1st Place* and both plaques for *Best Musicianship* and *Best Showmanship*, while Dream Street earned yet another *2nd Place*! The problem with having two very good show choirs competing in the same division, as we had found in past years, was that *only one of them could win*! This was a good problem, of course, but a problem just the same. As I have mentioned, we needed divisions at every competition! Not only divisions to accommodate different levels of mixed performing groups (novice, intermediate and advanced), which we had already been doing at the NDSCC since 1983, and Fullerton College had been doing for several years now, but divisions to accommodate *all girls* groups and in time, *men's* groups! Next year, we would host our first all-girls show choir event at Citrus College! To my knowledge, *it was the first of its kind in Southern California*!

The remainder of the 1991 competition year consisted of two events. First, Dream Street competed at *Tops 'n Pops*, in San Diego. They gave a wonderful performance, and ultimately placed 2nd behind… Who else? *The Bonita Vista Music Machine*! For the year, Dream Street had accumulated four *2nd Place* awards! Very admirable… but they went into the summer feeling unsatisfied, nonetheless. The final competition of the year was at *Magic Mountain*, with Renegade, Madrigal Singers and the Uptown Singers! We decided to let Madrigal Singers and Uptown Singers compete, after all. I don't have the results, but I'm pretty certain that we all came home with trophies and a lot of happy memories! Many of us, also traveled to San Francisco at the end of the year. It was a great trip, which included a stop in Monterey to see their world class Aquarium! 1991 was a great year. *Debbie Bailey* and *Erin Drake Garcia* were the president and vice-president of Dream Street. They and the other choir officers, including *Lori Halopoff* and *Davina Gaither*, were simply terrific! I would like to honor all of the great kids in Chamber Singers and Dream Street from 1991, for their undying dedication, and for all that they accomplished!

1990-91 Chamber Singers

Kim Abernathy • Paul Alley • Carlos Arias • Michelle Bain
Christina Basurto • Matt Blackstone • Denise Bruny
Jose Burciaga • Reuben Chan • Erin Drake • Alfred Flores
Rika Grier • Antonio Guerrero • Lori Halopoff • Ana Paez
Ellen Lindsay • Julpha Maniquis • Lilia Martinez
Lenna Morales • Juan Ochoa • Stephanie Ponte • Jesse Yee
Deana Acosta • Gabriella Ambriz • Debbie Bailey
Lorna Barrangan • Jenifer Bayless • Mike Blackstone
Jenni Buitrago • Marlo Caguin • Kuilane Cheun
Mildred Fabros • Lenitra Friend • Ric Guerra • David Kater
Ryan Gunchin • Tiffanie Kelly • Patricia Marquez
Mauricio Moet • Angel Munoz • Paula Orozco
Eddie Partida • Allison Tjaden • Christie Young
Jaime Zavala • Francy Young

1990-91 Dream Street Singers

Kim Abernathy • Corina Arambula • Christina Basurto
Jenifer Bayless • Jenni Buitrago • Kuimeuy Cheun
Erin Drake • Rika Grier • Tassa Hampton • Emiko Isa
Yvette Hernandez • Jennifer Jett • Ellen Lindsay
Dornetta Longaway • Lenna Morales • Rebecca North
Stephanie Ponte • Tammie Spivey • Shipra Verma
Deana Acosta • Gabriella Ambriz • Debbie Bailey
Denise Bruny • Kuilane Cheun • Laura Diaz • Lenitra Friend
Lori Halopoff • Maria Hernandez • Nancy Jovel
Tiffanie Kelly • Melissa Martinez • Yvonne Morales
Paula Orozco • Dawn Schlatter • Elizabeth Velez
Courtney Young

As the 1991-92 school year began, we already had a couple of big ideas! We seriously considered taking Chamber Singers on an overnight trip to San Diego, to compete in *Tops 'n Pops*, and we planned to stay at the beautiful Catamaran Resort on Mission Bay, by Sea World! Secondly, we were all set to host the *"Nogales All-Girls Spectacular,"* at Citrus College this year, to give the girls groups of the circuit, a *special* place to go. Dream

Street and the Silhouette Singers (which was now made up of all girls) would host it, and they were all very excited! There were also a couple of band changes, as Steve Farr played bass for part of the year, instead of Keith and Alan Waddington was our drummer for part of the year, instead of Bo. Don and Dwayne were thankfully, still with us. Doug made former student, Sergio Mejia, his assistant choreographer, and Della Long, continued to fill in all the cracks. Our competition sets, for the 1991-92 school year included:

Chamber Singers 1991-92
Costume Colors:
Red & White
Competition Set
Brother Love's
This Joint is Jumpin'
Heatwave
Vespers
Rock 'n Roll Classics
Run To The River

Dream Street Singers 91-92
Costume Colors:
Blue & White
Competition Set
Someone To Watch Over Me
I've Got The Music In Me
It's In His Kiss
Roll With It
Count Your Blessings
My Heart Belongs To Daddy
Great Balls of Fire

Silhouette Singers 1991-92
Costume Colors:
Pink, Black, White
Competition Set
Wooly Bully
Lullaby of Broadway
Puttin' On The Ritz
My Special Angel
Three Little Fishes
Sea Cruise

Madrijazz Singers 91-92
Costume Colors:
Gold & Black
Competition Set
Snap To It
Blue Moon
Great Feelin'

Uptown Singers 1991-92
Costume Colors:
Black & White
Competition Set
Johnny B. Goode
Beauty and the Beast
Rock'n Roll Is Here To Stay

Since most Southern California competitions had *not yet gone with divisions*, Doug and I decided to *split-up* some of the competitions so that Chamber and Dream Street would not have to compete against each other so often. Both of these groups had proven multiple times that they were very capable of beating the other, so that novelty was gone. They both wanted more chances to win! This made for fewer competitions for both groups, but they understood why.

The competition year began, unassumingly enough, with Chamber Singers opening their year with the *Hart High School Competition*! Our group was well prepared and performed like it. But, something didn't feel right? When the awards were announced, Chamber Singers had placed *2nd*. I was okay with that until I found that *we had actually won* and been penalized, and placed second, for going 10 seconds overtime! Ya know? As often as *"time penalty"* reared its ugly head for Chamber Singers, I would never get used to it! In my own festival, we told people they were under or overtime, but *we never penalized them.* I always wanted *the adjudicators' results to mean something*! Strict penalties and creative endeavors just do not mix, in my mind. Oh well…

Next, both Chamber and Dream Street found themselves competing against each other at the *Monrovia event*, which I didn't know yet, but would be the final year that they would be hosting this competition. The reason being, that their director, my sister, *Linda Atherton*, was resigning from that position at the end of the year, citing too much time away from her kids. We performed well, as did Dream Street, but all eyes were on a newcomer… *the Upland High School Chamber Singers*, directed by Bruce Rogers, who had competed last year, for the experience, but seemed much more serious, this year. Their vocals were clean and their choreography was unique, with a touch of ballet! When the results were announced, Dream Street had earned *3rd Place;* Chamber Singers had earned *2nd Place,* and the plaque for *Best Showmanship* while Upland High School had earned *First Place,* with the plaque for *Best Musicianship*. Upland had beaten us by one single point! Although I had only known of them for the past two years, I knew then, that *Upland would immediately be a major force to contend with*!

Riverside City College (RCC) hosted a new competition, with Roger Duffer, the former director of Redlands High School, in charge. I was initially concerned about this one, because Mr. Duffer's attitude toward show choir had always seemed to be that it should be predominantly scored on singing, *with just a little consideration for the show…* and Nogales always sang well, but *really excelled in the performance categories*! However, I was impressed with how he designed his awards to give separate first through thirds in music, in show, and then overall! This was the same award system that had been used in 1986 for the Young Americans National Show Choir Festival, except they had gone with five places! I liked it, because it allowed a group to be excellent in only music or show and still get an award. However, the system was strongly designed to *favor the best singing groups for the overall awards*. Another good thing about this festival was that it offered separate divisions for mixed and women, as well as novice and advanced. So, Dream Street and Chamber Singers jumped head first into the maiden voyage of the RCC event, and only time would tell how it would go for them. That night was like a *Who's Who* of show choir events. *Everyone was there*! In both the advanced mixed and advanced women divisions, they featured groups from *Bonita Vista, Upland, Arcadia and Nogales*, to name a few. Well, the competition began, and both Dream Street and Chamber Singers sang and performed well. I don't think we sang as well as several of our competitors, but our shows rocked! The awards for the women's divisions were read first, and Dream Street earned *2nd Place*, behind either Upland or Arcadia. Alex was just a toddler at that time, and he was having fun, playing with Bruce Rogers' daughters, who were also very young, as we waited for the awards. Bruce Rogers' groups from Upland had had a *wonderful year*, to this point, and he seemed very excited. He walked over to me and we waited for the announcement of the mixed awards together. First, the awards for Best Showmanship were announced. Bonita Vista placed *3rd*, Upland placed *2nd* and Nogales placed *1st*. Next, the awards for Best Musicianship (singing) were announced. Nogales placed *3rd*, Arcadia placed *2nd* and Upland placed *1st*. I was pretty certain that we would get 2nd place overall, unless Arcadia had scored close to us in show, in which case we could possibly get 3rd. Margaret kept telling me that there was a slim chance we would win if our show scores were high enough! A part of me hoped that she was right! At last, the Best Overall awards were read by the low baritone voice of Roger Duffer, "In third place, Arcadia High School Chanteurs." Bruce and I looked at each other. Then Roger Duffer continued, "In second place, Upland High School Chamber Singers." Bruce kept it together, but he looked a little rattled. Finally, Duffer announced, "In first place, *Nogales High School Chamber Singers*!" I kept my cool, but *I was so excited about that win*! We had simultaneously beaten Bonita Vista and Upland! When I saw the score sheets, I discovered that we had beaten Upland by only one single point, due entirely to *our exceptionally high score in Showmanship*! Well, they had beaten us by one point at Monrovia, so I guess turnabout is fair play! Roger Duffer seemed especially upset by the results, however, believing that a group's showmanship score *should not* be such a strong factor in winning a competition (although that's exactly what West Covina did back in the early eighties!). Once again, *Nogales made history*!

The next few competitions were a blur. First, Chamber Singers competed at *Burroughs*. The result was not as good as it had been the past few years, but it was a good performance! They earned *3rd Place* and won the *Best Showmanship* plaque. I think either Upland or Bonita Vista won that one.

On to Fullerton College. We took everyone there, except for Renegade, which I am not even sure even existed in 1992. In Novice, the Uptown Girls placed *7th*. However, on their behalf, *only about ten of the twenty girls in the group made it to that performance*, so I believe they should have been awarded a trophy just for that! Madrijazz had replaced the Silhouette Singers as our vocal jazz group, this year. They placed *3rd* in *Advanced Mixed Vocal Jazz*! Maybe I *did* know something about vocal jazz, but I just didn't know it? Silhouette Singers and Dream Street Singers competed together in one of two Advanced Divisions, with Silhouette placing *3rd*, while Dream Street took

1st! What was so impressive about this win, was that it was in a mixed choir division! Finally, Chamber Singers, competing in the Advanced Division A, placed *2nd*, behind Tony Atienza's *Chula Vista*!

Our next competition for Chamber Singers was a *National Competition in Anaheim* that had been set up by a travel company. When we arrived, at our destination, it was just a big room with a portable stage. I can't even remember how we had gotten into this? Our adjudicator was Ed Lojeski, the famous choral arranger, whom I had met at several prior events, including the Young Americans National Show Choir Festival, where he was also an adjudicator. In addition, I had spoken to him in 1986, at length, about choral arranging. Surprisingly, *there were only a total of two groups there*! First, there were the Nogales Chamber Singers… and second, there was a young group from Arizona or Utah. They performed first. They were good, albeit not at an *advanced competition level*. Next it was our turn. But Don Cloud, our accompanist, wasn't there yet? However, moments later… he burst into the room. Initially, Doug and I sighed with relief, until Don told us that he had *forgotten his music!* Of course, there are those piano players, like Doug or myself, who memorize their parts so if something like this should happen… it is not a calamity. Unfortunately, *Don was not one of those people*! He really *did need* his music! He was an excellent sight-reader and player… *but only with his music*! Well, it was too late to go back for it, so I gave him a pep talk and we performed our show. I personally thought the piano parts he interjected throughout the show were interesting, if not *downright hilarious*, and although he wasn't used to performing without his music, I could tell that he was giving this his *absolute best effort*! The kids were aware of the problem, but to their credit, they did not allow the accompanying cacophony that Don and the band created to deter them! When our performance was over, the other group politely clapped, I guess they imagined that they had just heard a modern take on *show choir by the father of Avant-garde American music, John Cage*! I explained to Mr. Lojeski that Don had forgotten his music, and he politely responded that he could hardly tell. Then, without score sheets of any kind, he proclaimed

Nogales the winner, and we all went home. I don't even think we got a trophy? Maybe that was for the best?

Dream Street and Silhouette Singers also competed at *Upland High School*, for the first year of their competition! Silhouette competed novice, this time and did not place but did win the plaque for *Best Showmanship*! Dream Street competed in the Advanced Division, and placed *2nd*!

For their final competition of the year, Dream Street went out to *Colton High School*, facing all mixed opponents, including the Arcadia Chanteurs! They performed, probably, their best show of the year! When the awards were announced, they were rewarded with *1st Place* and both plaques for *Best Showmanship* and *Best Musicianship*! Our girls screamed for joy, for about ten minutes!

Chamber Singers final competition of the year was scheduled to be *Tops 'n Pops* in San Diego. The kids had each raised the money to stay overnight at the beautiful Catamaran Hotel in Mission Bay, they had packed their suntan lotion, and the bus was off! It was Friday, May 1st, 1992, the third day after *the police officers had been acquitted in the Rodney King beating trial*... and riots had been going-on, in and around Los Angeles, ever since. No one from Nogales High School or from the Rowland Unified School District had told me to cancel the trip, so here we were. About an hour out, our bus driver *suddenly* pulled off the road and got back on the freeway going the other way! I asked as gently as I could, why she had turned back? She said she had received instructions from the Superintendent to do so. Something about the *Rodney King riots*. Well, the drive back was the most disheartening bus ride I had ever taken! The kids, of course, knew what was going on, just as soon as I asked the bus driver. When we arrived back at Nogales High School, I asked everyone to stay in the choir room until I found out what exactly would happen to our trip? The Superintendent arrived, and we had a heated discussion in my office. Finally, she gave us permission to *drive to San Diego, compete, and come back. No overnight at the Catamaran*! I knew that this was the best compromise we were going to get, so I took it. I shared the news with the kids and they allowed themselves to be *begrudgingly* happy, although they were understandably very disappointed at losing their overnight trip. At least they would get to compete, one last time this year! The Catamaran was very kind, and accepted our late cancellation with no penalty. Tony Santorufo, the assistant Superintendent, also assured me that the school district would help pay back parents for their contributions if the choir ran short. So, I have to admit, they made this potentially painful moment as *painless as possible*! Soon, we were headed back to San Diego, on our way to our final competition of the year! This story is already too long, so let me just say that there were other schools *not allowed to compete that night* (including Bonita Vista), but we faced six, mostly San Diego based, groups. We had a very passionate and exciting performance, that night, which I believe would have beaten anyone! When the evening's results were read, Chamber Singers took *1st Place* and both the *Best Showmanship* and *Best Musicianship* plaques! This was one competition none of us would ever forget! My thanks go to the wonderful work by the choir officers, including Kramer Ison, Joanna Miranda and Regina Conley for making this year so memorable!

Now I'd like to talk about the *Nogales All-Girls Spectacular*! On Thursday, February 13th, 1992, at Citrus College, Dream Street and Silhouette Singers hosted *the very first all girls show choir competition in Southern California*! There were ten girls groups participating, many of whom had never competed before. These ten groups included *Anaheim High School Goodtime Singers, La Puente High School Dream Singers, Redlands High School Chanteuse Ensemble, Workman High School Simply Supreme, Rincon Junior High School Rhythm Sensations, Apple Valley High School Vocal Motion, Bonita Vista Sound Unlimited, Burroughs High School Sound Sensations, Helix High School Ladies First*, and *Upland High School Melody 'N Motion.* I have no record of who won that night… but it really doesn't matter. It was so exciting for our two girls groups to host a festival *only for other girls groups*! It was a first step in getting girls groups to be respected as much as the mixed! We didn't make any money on this one, but we all agreed that… *it just didn't matter*!

Although I can't recall the exact year, I think it was 1992 that I experienced my first choir robbery, when the choir had money stolen from the choir office, regardless of the fact that I had it locked up! The thieves, whoever they were, *were kind enough* to leave all of the checks behind, and take only the cash. The administration told me that it sounded like an inside job, probably a student or possibly a temporary custodian, but it was never solved and the money was never recovered. Due to this event, *I never again left money at school*! As a teacher, we want to trust the students and staff to have our best interests at heart, but unfortunately, too often we learn the hard way, *that there are always going to be untrustworthy exceptions*. For me, it was a very hard lesson to learn… that some students and school staff are actually capable of *robbing their own choir…* but I learned it!

Another important development, was that *Lawrence Fitz*, a 1989 Nogales graduate, with the help of his Nogales choir alumni, created *Tournament of Champions*, in 1992, a high school show choir festival, originally designed to earn money for the Nogales program. This festival ended up running for 16 years! Lawrence also developed his own competing show choir through an ROP program, he called, *Celebration*! The group also lasted many years. Another one of our illustrious alumni, *Sergio Mejia*, handled much of the choreography for Lawrence's groups, and also went on to choreograph groups and events all over the world!

When summer ended and the 1992-93 school year began, Doug and I were excited! Last year had turned out so well, and we could not help but think we were living in the *golden age of Nogales High School Choirs*, right now! But then again, *every year at Nogales had felt successful for one reason or another*! So, what would we do, this year? Keith Fort officially resigned his position as bass player, after a nine-year run, but Bo Eder was back as our full time drummer, Dwayne Ganier continued on as our guitar player, while Don Cloud remained as our accompanist. We still felt that we had the *tightest and the most exciting band in the circuit*, as we had for many years now. Wingston Morales and

Tiffany Kelly, two recent graduates, joined us as assistant choreographers! Our 1992-93 competition sets are below:

Chamber Singers 1992-93
Costume Colors:
Red & White
Competition Set
Masquerade
On My Own
Witch Doctor
Cockles and Mussels
Marian the Librarian
Proud Mary
Gimme Some Lovin'
Operator

Silhouette Singers 1992-93
Costume Colors:
White
Competition Set
Why Do Fools Fall
One Fine Day
Sincerely
Fever
Johnny Angel
Do You Wanna Dance?

Dream Street 1992-93
Costume Colors:
Silver & Blue
Competition Set
Get Ready
Eyes of Love
Shuffle Off To Buffalo
Roll With It
Turn Around
Lola
Devil With The Blue Dress

Madrijazz Singers 92-93
Costume Colors:
Gold
Competition Set
Java Jive
This Joint Is Jumpin'
Up On The Roof
Show Me The Way
Go Tell It On The Mountain

Florida Honor Choir 1992-93
Costume Colors: *T-Shirt*
Non-Competition Set
Shine Down
Shut De Doh
Happy Folk
Old Joe Clark
Let Me Be Your Friend
Bless This House

As you can clearly see, every group had a very interesting show this year! We added the use of a *synthesizer* instead of a piano for accompaniment, and we never looked back! We weren't the only group to evolve in this way, but many groups still used the piano. We decided that we needed a strong accompaniment to match our strong vocalists. We also learned the trick of keeping the synthesizer *soft while the group sang* and *loud during dance breaks*. We had actually learned this from listening to *Bonita Vista's band*, when they performed with their groups. Chamber Singers even performed a song, *Masquerade,* from *Phantom of the Opera*, to recorded synthesizer, which allowed us to layer the instrumentation. This was long before some competitions outlawed singing to recorded music in any form.

In the summer of 1992, my wife and I were in the process of buying a house. Strangely, the housing people *insisted* that we had to report to the models every day between 9 am and 5 pm, to keep *dibs* on the house we had selected, since that sale was *contingent* on the sale of our current home in Diamond Bar. Well, between ourselves and friends and former students, such as Wingston Giovanni Morales, Doug Kuhl and Della Long, we were indeed able to *house sit*, until our Diamond Bar House sold. Soon thereafter, we were finally able to move into our new Brea home, that we continue to live in today! That time was special to me, because Della, Wingston and Doug were wonderful for spending all of that time to help us out, and because I remember Doug, painstakingly painting the *Witch Doctor* shields, and the large cut-out of the *Witch Doctor* (to be used in the Chamber Singers show), in the parking lot of the model homes, *for weeks*, while he took his turn waiting there. Anyone who knows Doug, knows that no matter what… *he's always working on the shows*!

When we began the year, a lot of the kids decided that they wanted to go to *Orlando to see the Disney Parks*! Well, the only way the school board would approve a trip like this was if we included performances. That's the *Honor Choir* songs I listed. We had a little trouble raising the money, but in the end, we did go! I'll talk about that later, in more detail.

When competition season rolled around, we actually began the year by sending both Chamber Singers and Dream Street to compete at the *Upland Competition*. Both of our groups sang and performed well, and the new synthesizer added another dimension to our shows, which seemed to make them even more exciting! When the results were announced, Dream Street took *1st Place* and both the *Best Showmanship* and *Best Musicianship* plaques in the Women's Division. Chamber Singers did exactly the same thing in the Mixed Division! *It was a Nogales sweep*!

Next, we went to the *Fullerton College Jazz Festival*, and brought Chamber Singers, Dream Street, Silhouette Singers and Madrijazz with us. I would like to report that all of our groups won that day… but I can't, because sadly, it didn't happen! It was very crowded that day with so many groups competing in so many divisions. However, by the end of the day, I believe all of our groups felt confident about their performances! Fullerton College decided to hold the Awards Ceremony in Plummer Auditorium, across the street from the college. During the clamber of students and teachers rushing inside to get a seat, one of the student ushers purportedly called one of my students, "*a black bitch*!" This was immediately shared with me by her best friend and then confirmed by her. She was not angry, but seemed terribly shocked by the whole ordeal. *I was angry*! I found Terry Blackley, the head of Fine Arts at Fullerton, explained what had happened and demanded an apology to the girl! He agreed, quickly found the usher, *who, while very embarrassed, admitted that he had said it*, and then quickly, and meaningfully apologized to the girl. She graciously accepted his apology, and we continued on to the awards ceremony. I seldom had things like this happen on fieldtrips, or at least I was seldom *told about them*. But this event really shocked me! I still can't fathom that it happened! I guess *you can't ever really be safe from the world's ugliness when it feels like rearing its head*! In any case, the awards were announced. Chamber Singers won *2nd Place* in the Advanced Mixed Division, Dream Street won *6th Place* in the Advanced Women's Division, Madrijazz also earned *6th Place* in the Advanced Vocal Jazz Division and Silhouette Singers took home our only *1st Place*, for the day in the Novice Women's

Division! The biggest question was, what happened to Dream Street? I would guess the adjudicators may have been offended by the synthesizer or the raucous nature of their show, because Silhouette Singers performed a traditional 50s and 60s girls group show, and won? And Madrijazz... as I keep telling you, *I don't really know anything about vocal jazz*, so when scoring like this happens, I guess the adjudicators *really do know* what they're talking about! What about Chamber Singers coming in *2nd*? Well, everybody was improving, and even if they weren't, show choir competitions are always a little bit of a horse race... and the favorite does not always win!

We licked our wounds (except for Silhouette, who had bragging rights for a week), and moved on to *Riverside City College*, (RCC), where we also took all four of our competing groups. Chamber Singers had won, last year, but this year, as he had promised he would, Roger Duffer had revised his score sheets so that showmanship and choreography only counted for 24% of the overall score, down from 30%, by multiplying each of the three show scores by .8, but not doing the same to the music scores. Aside from this, everything felt comfortable when we arrived at RCC. The competition began and each of our groups sang and performed well. When the results were announced, Chamber placed 4th in the Advanced Mixed Division, Dream Street placed *1st* with the *Best Showmanship*, in the Advanced Women's Division, Silhouette Singers placed *3rd* in the Novice Women's Division, and Madrijazz won *Showmanship,* in the Novice Vocal Jazz Division. Not too bad. We had done better last year, of course, but oh well. On to the next one! A wise man, in talking about the *Lakers recent demise*, told me that 'as a Lakers fan, I had to have empathy for fans of *other teams*, because they had spent years eating the Lakers' dust. So, maybe it was their turn to win now, and the Lakers' turn to struggle? I understood his logic and empathy here... but a competitive person is a competitive person through and through. All I could really think about after the awards were announced... *was doing better at the next competition!* Without that drive, I figured that none of my groups would ever win again!

Our next competition was at *Hart High School*, where our Chamber Singers were the only Nogales group going. I remembered last year, *when we had actually won*, but been penalized and placed second due to a ten second overtime. This year, however, we had carefully timed the show and the time necessary to set up and tear down, and we still had a minute to spare. We figured there was no sense taking chances as soon as we realized that their timing was so strict, at the awards last year. The competition began and the new synthesizer-led Chamber Singers went on to win *1st Place* and *Best Showmanship, without being penalized this time*! What a difference a year makes!

The *Pasadena* competition was next! I'm really not sure who hosted it, but I think it may have been *Burroughs High School*, putting on their *competition* there, because they were unable to use their own theatre that year. I'm not certain of this, but it's a good guess anyway. They only offered one category for everyone to compete in, so we decided to take both Chamber Singers and Dream Street. It was fun competing in the Pasadena Civic Auditorium again. This was the very same venue we had performed in for the *Young Americans National Show Choir Competition*, in 1986! Of course, no one was left in our groups from that time, but both Doug and I had to smile as we entered it and recounted the plethora of happy memories we had all accumulated, due to performing here! Both of our groups performed extremely well, and some time later, they were ready to announce the award winners! Dream Street came in *2nd Place*, while Chamber Singers earned *1st Place* and both plaques for *Best Showmanship* and *Best Musicianship!* It was yet another Nogales sweep!

Now with every other group done competing, Chamber Singers prepared for their final one. A trip to San Diego, to compete in *Tops 'n Pops*! Except for coming in *4th* at RCC, this year had been very kind to Chamber Singers, earning them three *1st Places*, and a single *2nd Place* award, thus far! Chamber Singers ended up placing *2nd* at *Tops 'n Pops* that year. It had been a good year for the choral program, with only a few competitions that didn't break our way. I didn't know it then, but 1993 would mark the end of the *"Golden Age"* of the Nogales

High School show choirs, or more accurately, the end of our *six year long* winning streak! Beginning in 1988, we had experienced great growth in our program, which resulted in many wins, many trophies and many competing groups… but it ended after 1993. That is not to say that Nogales would no longer win competitions or have multiple competing groups… but the big surge in students coming to the school, reversed direction, beginning with the 1993-94 school year, and our choral program had to work *much harder*, as a result.

We ended this amazingly busy year with a trip to Orlando for about 25 kids in the program who were willing to raise the money. I had never been to Orlando before, so I made the mistake of using a travel agency, who booked us in a motel *outside* the Disney properties. This caused a little inconvenience at times, as we had to wait for our bus… but once we got inside the parks, we were just fine! In order to get the School Board to pass this trip, we had to guarantee that we would perform. So we did. *We performed at the airport, at the hotel, at dinner and even (unofficially) at the parks.* We presented a slide show of all our adventures in Orlando at the Spring Concert!

I'd be leaving out a very important fact, if I also did not mention the incredible impact that one of my students, *Kramer Ison*, had on Chamber Singers for the past two years! Kramer enrolled in Concert Choir in September of 1991, as a junior. Shortly, after discovering how talented he was, Doug and I convinced him to join Chamber Singers. He was musical, could sing anything, played multiple instruments, was extremely likeable and a quick study on choreography! He ate up pizzazz like Cheerios for Breakfast! Needless to say, he led *a weaker boys section* than we had had for many years, and made them so much better! He sang a solo in the Chamber show both years he was in the group in 92 and 93, and by example, he made everyone who worked with him, realize that they could do better! After graduation he became a regular part of our band, playing keyboard and guitar with an occasional visit to the drums, for many years.

My final memories from 1992-93, involve the festivals we hosted annually, the NDSCC for the mixed groups and the

Nogales All-Girls Spectacular for the girls groups. Both events had their dates reserved at Citrus College, same as last year, but I received a distressing call from the theatre manager in September of 1992. She told me that due to rehearsal needs for a show that they had booked, they would have to cancel our dates this year. I tried to protest, but she assured me that it was a *done deal*, and there would be no point arguing it. She did say, however, that Citrus would take a thousand dollars off of our bill *next year* to make up for this inconvenience. I hadn't realized before, that they had the *right to cancel a date that was already booked*? But, I suppose we learn something new everyday! Since there seemed to be no other options left to me, I got to work right away, looking for and finding another venue! The first thing I did was to check the availability of all the local theatres I had ever rented before or competed in. My investigation was fruitless and eventually felt hopeless. Even the local high school theatres, like Brea and Diamond Bar were booked for late January and early February! Finally, on a whim, based on a half-serious suggestion from Doug, I called Knott's Berry Farm and asked about the availability of their Goodtime Theatre. Thankfully, they had two open dates on Thursday, February 18th and Friday, February 19th! These dates were a week later than normal, but who was I to quibble! We signed the contracts and immediately sent out our festival information to all of the show choirs in the circuit who might be interested, noting that our venue for this year was to be the *Knott's Good Time Theatre*! We had eleven competing groups each night and two Sold Out Audiences! Well, I know that this sounds like the fairy tale that ends, "and they lived happily ever after," but *what we see is not always what we get*! To make a long story much longer, when we arrived at the theatre, on Thursday, to set-up for the *Nogales All Girls Spectacular*, the techs had already wired up the piano with microphones and placed it in an immovable spot in the *middle of the stage!* I quickly explained to them that in show choir everyone used or didn't use the piano differently, so it would be best to keep the piano unhampered with cords. The techs seemed very confused but graciously removed the wires from the piano, anyway. Then, later, as the show began, we had a major problem in the house! You see, as always, we had sold reserved seats to everybody, and the ushers, apparently unaware, had told the people entering the house to sit wherever they wanted to! This had a lot of people who had bought *good seats*, and were now stuck in the back, furious! So, we had to take about ten minutes at the start of Thursday's event, to *insist* that everyone move to his or her correctly ticketed seats! After that, the All Girls Spectacular went okay. Whew! *But then came Friday.* We arrived at the theatre, about 3:00 pm to set up for our mixed event, the *Nogales Divisional Show Choir Competition*! About 4 pm, when groups were scheduled to begin arriving for their warm-ups, we heard a *crash* outside, from inside the theatre. Apparently, Upland's prop truck had backed up into a wall, near the theatre, and caused some damage for both it and the truck! I rushed out and talked to Bruce Rogers, Upland's director, who seemed to already have matters under control with the Knott's security people. As every group arrived, they asked us what was going on, and we, of course, had to tell them. All afternoon, there was more interest on the broken wall outside, than the groups who were rehearsing on stage! I should have taken that as a bad omen for the evening, but I chose to think that "these things happen," instead. The competition was about to begin and *the audience was seated in their correctly ticketed seats* when all eyes in the house went to the ceiling! It had started to rain outside and unbeknownst to me… *the ceiling of the theatre leaked!* Soon, the theatre staff was wildly running throughout the house, placing plastic pails on the floor to catch the rain! The evening went so slowly that night as the rain continued to drip and splatter into the house all night. Finally, one of the last competing groups of the night took the stage, it was either Los Altos or Brea, and just before they began, the top of the stage proscenium (the fancy woodwork making a frame for the audience at the front of the stage), *crashed to the floor*! Luckily, the curtain had not opened yet, so some techs quickly removed the heavy wood beam, and the show continued to the end. I can't remember if we got a special price for all of the problems we encountered or if we were just happy that we all made it out alive! In any case, I never rented the *Good Time Theatre* again! That's because that second night, it seemed less like a theatre and more like the *haunted shack*!

As I mentioned earlier, 1992-93 marked the end of our "*historical*," six-year "*golden age*," where Chamber and Dream Street were consistently *winning competitions*, beginning in 1987-88! We did win again… but not in 1993-94. Here are the members of Chamber Singers and Dream Street Singers from 1992-93. A special thanks to *Patty Marquez*, president of Chamber Singers, *Kramer Ison*, vice-president of Chamber Singers, and to the wonderful work of all the officers!

1992-93 Chamber Singers

Kim Abernathy • Donna Bailey • Matt Blackstone
Monica Brenes • Jeanne Chang • Mildred Fabros
Livia Gee • Michelle Gurola • Jamie Hammonds
Michelle Hoguin • Kramer Ison • Katie Kwak
Jason Lofthouse • Luis Mejia • Paula Orozco • Jesse Yee
Christa Peterson • Tanya Russel • Selina Soriano
Theresa Tulud • Megan Young • Shante Abram • Peggy Poon
Alice Ballantyne • Mike Blackstone • Jenni Buitrago
Dion De Rosas • Brian Gaither • Rika Grier • Kurt Schlatter
Alex Gutierrez • Tassa Hampton • Heather Holmes
Jennifer Jamison • Celena Lares • Patty Marquez
Tonnette Mouton • Eddie Partida • Allison Tjaden

1992-93 Dream Street Singers

Kim Abernathy • Donna Bailey • Barbara Blackmon
Regina Castaneda • Yesenia Collazo • Mildred Fabros
Bernadette Gonzales • Tassa Hampton • Yamilia Ibanez
Uyen Mai • Becky Mantanic • Hazel Miguel • Paula Orozco
Paula Mosqueda • Helen Palomo • Melanie Piercy
Jennifer Rey • Angela Shoals • Tammy Spivey • Rika Grier
Yvonne Velasco • Germany Bactista • Melissa Black
Jenni Buitrago • Bonnie Chacon • Ana Enriquez
Joanna Gallagher • Yvette Hernandez • Dee Dee Longaway
Cherry Mandani • Patty Marquez • Misty Moritts
Roxanne Myer • Claudia Palomo • Lily Pastrana
Liz Ramirez • Heidi Sheldon • Andrea Silva • Loraine Tulud

CHAPTER 6

Nogales High School... 1993-98... Rebuilding The Greatness!

At the end of the 1992-93 school year, we auditioned students, as always, for next year's groups. We had already lost a lot of seniors, but even so, we were surprised and a *bit shaken* by the historically low turnout? To be honest, the choirs really began getting a little smaller after 1991. But the 1993-94 choir auditions looked to be the *smallest and youngest* we had had in years! We knew that our day of reckoning would come eventually, but the idea of *rebuilding* was not a popular one for either Doug or I. So, we entered the year, planning to make a few tweaks to the program, which would hopefully make it easier for us to maintain our winning groups. First, we combined the NDSCC and the Nogales All Girls Spectacular into one festival, (six girls groups and six mixed) to save us double rental at Citrus College. Secondly, although we continued to order the Chamber Singers outfits from Hollywood Babe, I ordered a *much more inexpensive dress* through the mail (the first time I have ever done that) from a show choir catalogue, for Dream Street. I didn't know if Dream Street's flood of new members, *would pay for their dresses*, so I wanted to take some of the pressure off of the choir having to raise the money for them. Third, we gave our groups easier material to match the newer level of singers and performers that we had just auditioned into the groups. Our talented 1993 graduate, Kramer Ison, joined Don, Bo, and Dwayne as the second keyboardist in our band! The competition sets for our groups included:

Chamber Singers 1993-94
Costume Colors: *Red & White*
Competition Set
Free Ride
Hernando's Hideaway
Doctor Looney
Sing A Rainbow
Tears In Heaven
I Got Rhythm

Silhouette Singers 1993-94
Costume Colors: *White*
Competition Set
Mister Sandman
Sweet Talkin' Guy
You Made Me Love You
Your Mama Don't Dance

Dream Street Singers 93-94
Costume Colors: *Blue*
Competition Set
Gimme Some Lovin'
Soon It's Gonna Rain
Three Little Fishes
Old Friends
Cabaret
R.O.C.K. in the U.S.A.

Madrijazz 1993-94
Costume Colors: *Gold*
Competition Set
All That Jazz
Imagine
One

The Chamber Singers show was quite an *eclectic collection of songs*. From the hard rocking *Free Ride* (a song I had also used during my first year at Norco), to the theatrical, *Hernando's Hideaway* (from *Pajama Game*), to *Doctor Looney*, a popular children's song from Parachute Express, to Andy William's sweet song, *Sing A Rainbow*, serving as their a cappella, to Eric Clapton's heartfelt *Tears In Heaven* and ending with George Gershwin's popular *I Got Rhythm*. It was designed specifically for this group, which lacked a lot of experienced members, so each song had a *built-in personality*, which made extensive individual interpretation by the students, somewhat moot. I must confess that *Sing A Rainbow* and *Doctor Looney* were two of my young son, Alex's favorite songs (he was just two years old), and that knowledge may have led me to include them in the show!

The Dream Street Singers show ended up looking like hard driving Dream Street of the present coupled with the sweet Dream Street of the past. Their show began with the exciting

Gimme Some Lovin,' to the lovely ballad from the *Fantastiks*, *Soon It's Gonna Rain*, To the Andrews Sisters 1940s hit, *Three Little Fishes*, To one of my favorite Simon and Garfunkel tunes, *Old Friends*, serving as their a cappella, to *Cabaret* from the show *Cabaret* and ending with John Cougar's *R.O.C.K. in the U.S.A.*!

Before discussing our competition year, I would like explain what happened with Dream Street's mail-order costumes. As I said, I ordered their dresses through a mail-order catalogue, to save money. However, when they arrived, *flat in boxes*, made of very thin fabric, with absolutely no body to them, *I felt like the stupidest man alive*! I immediately gave them to Doug and Margaret (my resident problem solvers), who found a way to make them look better by adding a pink scarf and doing something to the skirt. Thank goodness. I would suggest that *no one order costumes from a catalogue unless you know exactly what you are getting*! This mishap has taught me two things. First, leave the costumes to the professionals and second, *use Hollywood Babe for everything*! And we did, thereafter!

Well, as luck would have it, our first public performance was at our own competition, the *NDSCC*, where we would be scored, but no one else would know how we did! Sounded good! The night arrived, and Dream Street, as the host of the Girls Division, was the very first group to perform. Just as soon as the curtain opened, and they started singing, I knew that we were in trouble! There were audible gasps from students in the audience, who could not believe that what they were seeing and hearing was *the famous Dream Street*? When it came time to sing our a cappella, *Old Friends*, I went up to direct it, but they were so nervous that they couldn't keep in tune. Poor girls. But this moment made me clearly remember *why I had not given Dream Street an a cappella to sing in prior years*! In hindsight, the arrangement was just too difficult for them, when combined with their intense case of nerves. The show ended and I am not sure how anything else looked or sounded in their show, because *I was so upset about the a cappella sounding so bad*! Well, the damage was done. We had a lot of hard work to do when we got back to school on Monday! Meanwhile, Chamber Singers were the first group to perform for the Mixed Division. Their performance didn't fall apart, the way that Dream Street's did, but the best way I can explain what I saw and heard on stage was by saying that *it was not bad in the technical sense, just a little dull and uninspired.* Most of the kids in both groups were young and inexperienced, but Doug and I had thought that they would rise to the occasion… well, *they hadn't!* So, *the cat was out of the bag*, so to speak, and now that *everyone knew* that Nogales was in rebuilding mode, we decided that *we might as well rebuild*!

I'm sure that through the way I'm describing it, this year must sound, to you, like it's already lost! I mean, after the uninspired NDSCC performances of Chamber Singers and Dream Street… *but nothing could be farther from the truth*! Thanks to the NDSCC performances, Doug and I knew exactly where each group was both musically and performance-wise. Now, it was time for us to find out how *much they both could improve in one year!* We had experienced *an eerily similar year, to this one, ten years before, in 1984*, when Chamber Singers had lost most of their members following the group's first award winning campaign, the year before… and consequently, after an initial win, started the rest of the year off a little shaky. But that group came back, and by 1985, the very next year, *Chamber Singers had won and beaten West Covina twice*! So, these rebuilding years, although *not always a lot of fun*, are far from the end of the world.

I don't want to miss talking about Silhouette Singers and Madrijazz, but as far as I know, they only competed once, during the 1994 competition season. Both groups competed in the novice girls division of Fullerton College! I think Silhouette Singers placed *3rd* and Madrijazz did not place at all. They too had a lot of young members, and the experience they received from going to Fullerton was going to drastically help each student in the future. To tell you the truth, I really enjoyed both of their performances that year, whether they had won or not! Doug and I agreed, that we had a great nucleus for both groups, next year!

We had a week to rebuild the Chamber and Dream Street shows before we began competing. I'm not sure if all of these changes were made during this week or if a few of them were added later. But, in any case... both shows were *drastically changed*, salvaging any songs that the groups performed effectively and dumping the rest. The new *versions* of the Chamber and Dream Street competition shows became the following:

Chamber Singers Show Updated

We Will Rock You/ Free Ride
Hernando's Hideaway
Sing A Rainbow
Tears In Heaven
I Got Rhythm
Devil With The Blue Dress On

Dream Street Singers Show Updated

Rain Medley
Get Ready
Cabaret
Gimme Some Lovin'

The Chamber Singers Show only changed nominally, with the addition of *We Will Rock You* at the beginning and *Devil With The Blue Dress* added to the end. *Doctor Looney* was the only song dropped from the set. To be honest, *it really never should have been put into the show in the first place*, because the vocal parts and the beat of the song itself did not lend themselves to traditional show choir! Don't worry, though. "Doctor Looney" was used often, in the future, in the wacky *Notorious* show at Diamond Bar and the outrageous *Thunder Cats* show, at Brea Olinda High School! Dream Street added *Singin' In The Rain*, as part of the *Rain Medley*, coupled with *Soon It's Gonna Rain,* to start the show. *Get Ready* was also added and *Gimme Some Lovin'* was moved from the opener to the ender. Three of the songs from their original show were dropped. These included *Three Little Fishes, Old Friends* and *R.O.C. K. in the U.S.A. Three Little Fishes* was a dud in this show, *Old Friends* was much too difficult for them to sing and R.O.C.K. was dull, because their vocal sound was too light. So, the changes for both shows seemed to be intelligent things to do. We realized that both of our top groups had *fallen off a cliff*, compared to last year! But, due to our immediate steps to rebuild the shows, we strongly believed, at the very least, they would both have a better chance of placing!

Our first official competition for both Chamber Singers and Dream Street was the *Upland Festival*! This had always been an odd one for us, ever since it had started, several years before. The reason being that Bruce Rogers didn't want the "typical" adjudicators to work his event… he appeared to want judges who were not necessarily involved in show choir and had never seen any of us before at any other competition! I admired his attempt at being fair for everyone, but the results had been mixed for us, at best! We never really knew how to prepare for this event, since we did not know the judges from other show choir events. The same was probably true for our competitors as well, often making the results of this competition *a real head scratcher*! Chamber Singers and Dream Street arrived at the event early, so we had the opportunity to watch some of the other groups warming up. I'll be honest. *Our competitors looked pretty darn good*! Still, I tried to keep both groups positive, as we entered the house, and prepared for the competition to begin! When Dream Street took the stage, they were so much better than they had been the week before at the NDSCC, but they still seemed a bit young. Upland had both the mixed and all girls divisions, but they only offered them in advanced. So, even if I had logically decided to compete Dream Street or Chamber in an intermediate division… I couldn't! Chamber Singers took the stage before too long. Their performance was good, but they too seemed young. It remained to be seen whether this "*youthful quality*" would undermine our competition season. Bruce Rogers approached me about ten minutes after our Chamber Singers had completed their performance. He informed me that Chamber Singers had been clocked *going about fifteen seconds overtime*, and he wasn't sure if he was going to disqualify us yet. He would let me know. Great! *I so loved overtime penalties!* Well, about an hour later, just before the awards were announced, Bruce Rodgers sought me out again. This time, he "sadly," almost "apologetically" told me that he would *not be penalizing Chamber Singers for going overtime, after all*. It was very strange. Even for show choir! Soon, Bruce was on the stage, announcing the awards! Dream Street, with their mail order dresses and newly revamped show, actually earned *2nd Place,* in the *All-Girls Division*! That was certainly a *nice* surprise! But, when the mixed awards were announced… Chamber Singers' name was *never called*! That was a *terrible* surprise! Nogales Chamber Singers had spent most of the past decade *placing or winning* at every competition they had entered! This was certainly a new experience for any of these kids who had been in the group, in years past! *It was also very humbling*. I had forgotten how *not placing* felt, but it didn't take long for me to remember… *and it didn't feel good*! So, we would accept our new status as a group that did not always place, and try to win something at our next event. Have you ever read Mark Twain's *The Prince and the Pauper?* We all definitely felt like *the pauper* right now!

Well, what a difference a year makes! We were no longer considered one of the major players of the show choir circuit, but let's be fair, here… the Nogales groups had spent a lot of years playing that role, and maybe now it was some other school's turn? *Nope. Wrong answer*! We just had to reinvent ourselves, that's all. Like Doug's old saying, that he shared with the groups when they seemed unmotivated, "*If you believe you are Miss America, then you are*!" It was right after this, that I received an invitation from Showstoppers, the national show choir festival company of the time, who asked us to compete at Disneyland, on the Tomorrowland stage, against other excellent show choirs from all over the country! Wow! This could be it? Our reinvention? The entry fee was not too bad, and the date fit our calendar. But, was I actually considering taking these young groups to national competition? *You're darn right I was*! Doug, Margaret and the kids loved the idea! I saw *that special spark* return to the kids' eyes! You know what? We would make this trip extra special by staying overnight at the *Disneyland Hotel!* Now everyone got really excited! I would deal with the costs later. For now, our groups had an exciting national competition to look forward to!

Our next competition was *Tournament of Champions*, or TOC. If you remember, a 1989 graduate of mine, Lawrence Fitz, assembled a group of alumni to run this festival to raise money for the Nogales choirs. I don't recall receiving any money, but over the years, this competition was good for everyone in the show choir community! As I recall, only Chamber Singers competed there. The list of groups competing in 1994 featured many, whom I had never heard of before, since they didn't compete regularly in the Southern California circuit. For this reason, I thought that Chamber Singers' experience would give us a good chance to win here. However, at the awards ceremony, a show choir from Canyon High School, in Anaheim Hills, featuring a fantastic soloist named *Eden Espinosa*, who went on, years later, to play *Elphaba,* in *Wicked,* on Broadway… won instead! We actually took *2nd or 3rd Place*, I believe. Getting beat by a future Broadway star seems just fine now, but at the time, we were disappointed, but still *relieved* to rejoin the ranks of the *show choirs who had placed*, once again!

There were other festivals we attended that year, such as the *Fullerton College Jazz Festival* where I think both Chamber Singers and Dream Street placed *4th*, and *Colton*, where Erica Atchue, Chamber Singer's lead soprano, was unable to attend, so we fell apart during the a cappella (*Sing A Rainbow*), and ended up placing *9th* out of 10, and *Tops 'n Pops*, where Dream Street was doing great, and then they *fell apart at the end of Gimme Some Lovin,'* at the end of their show, and ended up not placing. But I prefer talking about what happened to us at the *Showstoppers Disneyland National Show Choir Competition*! This was the final competition of the year for Chamber Singers and Dream Street, competing together in separate divisions!

After school, one Friday, in April, we took a school bus to the Disneyland Hotel, where we checked into our assigned rooms. Next, we had fun swimming in the pool and discovering the other amenities the Disneyland Hotel offered! We certainly enjoyed being at the hotel during the short time we were there! Bright and early, on Saturday morning, inside Disneyland, the competition began! Erica Atchue, our lead soprano, made the trip, but she had a broken leg, in a cast, so she was pretty much limited to solos and simple, upper-body-only, choreography. Regardless, at the end of the competition, Dream Street earned *1st Runner-Up* (in the Women's Division) and Chamber Singers earned *2nd Runner-Up* (in the Mixed Division)! This was quite a feat, when you considered that we were competing against some of the strongest show choirs in the country! We definitely had our best performances of the year, as Chamber and Dream Street successfully *rose* to the occasion!

To end the year with a fun event, Chamber Singers entered the *Magic Mountain Show Choir Competition*! There were a number of high profile groups there, and we hoped we would at least beat some of them! Actually, we finished in *3rd Place*, ahead of Burroughs Chamber Choir, who had performed a medley from *Cats*! In any case, it was a fun way to end the year! A special thanks to Eddie Partida, the president of Chamber Singers, Uyen Mai, president of Dream Street, Roselani Hockenhull and Mary Anne Garcia, the president and vice president of Madrijazz and to all of the other choir officers for their outstanding leadership during this challenging year!

The summer of 1994 was a big one for Doug and I. We had to put this, arguably *successful, rebuilding year* behind us, and let all of our competitors know that Nogales was back… by dreaming up competition shows that would rock! Our veteran kids were a year older and the new kids we had auditioned for both Chamber and Dream Street, held a lot of potential, so, we decided to go for a home run! Neither the students nor the staff wanted to experience that difficult time, of the past year, again, any time soon! The only major change in our band was that Dwayne Ganier, after playing guitar for us, so well, for the past ten years, had decided to move on, leaving only Don, Bo and Kramer in the band. We knew that we had to drastically change our look, in order to grab people's attention, after last year, so, we ordered a *complete set of risers*, from Wengar, and Chamber Singers immediately began rehearsing with them! To the best of my knowledge, all of our other groups continued to perform with boxes, as they had since 1988. We began to feel the effects of the school's declining enrollment, as we were forced to drop

Madrijazz Singers, due to a lack of people. Our competition shows for the 1995 competition season, were as follows:

Chamber Singers 1994-95
Costume Colors: *Gold & White*
Competition Set
Songs of the South
By The Sea
Moonglow
Classic Rock
You'll Never Walk Alone

Silhouette Singers 1994-95
Costume Colors: *White*
Competition Set
Downtown
My First Love
It Had To Be You
Material Girl
Who Put The Bomp
Sea Cruise

Dream Street Singers 94-95
Costume Colors:
Green & White
Competition Set
A Dream Is A Wish
Dream Street Theme
Broadway Surprise
Unchained Melody
For Rockers Only

Renegade 1994-95
Costume Colors:
Black & White
Competition Set
Shakedown
Brown Eyed Squirrel
River of Dreams
Calendar Girl
Proud Mary

I feel a need to explain these shows in detail, so that you will understand how truly *revolutionary* they were at this time! First of all, the Chamber Singers show was *not* a collection of *good, but random songs*, as many of our previous shows had been. This year, each song was especially selected, to make the show *impressive from beginning to end*! We opened with *Songs of the South*, a medley of minstrel songs featuring lit tambourines, which we had used a number of years ago, including the powerful a cappella, *In The Hills of Shilo*! Followed that with *By The Sea*, a medley of turn of the 19th century tunes including *A Bicycle Built For Two*. Then the show went to a cool vocal jazz tune, *Moonglow*. Next, we had a really fun collection of 1980s hits called *Classic Rock*, including *Centerfold*. We finished off the show with a very powerful arrangement of *You'll Never Walk Alone*, which never failed to bring the house down!

To be honest, at the beginning of the year, we had *Classic Rock* ending our show. But, we very quickly found that *nothing* can follow *You'll Never Walk Alone*, when you have an effective soloist... and it just so happened, that we did, and her name was Erica Atchue! We recreated Dream Street in the model of everything that had been effective for them over the years. By this time, girls groups were required to sing an a cappella ballad in the Advanced Division, so we opened their show with Disney's *A Dream Is A Wish Your Hear Makes.* The next song, we wrote just for them, to make them stand out as being special and unique. This song was called *The Dream Street Theme*! Next, to spice things up, they sang *Broadway Surprise*, a collection of upbeat Broadway tunes, complete with the colorful props! Then we featured their power ballad, *Unchained Melody*, with dynamic background vocals encasing a beautiful solo voice. And Finally, we ended with *For Rockers Only*, a collection of 1960s rock songs! Our Silhouette Singers were all girls this year, competing in the intermediate women's division. Hence, their show was loaded with lightweight pop songs of the fifties and sixties to entertain audiences with a big dose of *musical nostalgia*! Renegade was back, after a three-year absence, and as usual, focused their show on *fun with lots of testosterone!*

Chamber Singers' first competition was the *Aztec Sing*, which we had not competed in since 1989! Sadly, this year, we didn't do much better than the last time we'd competed there! Show choir is like Hollywood. Once you put out a mediocre show, as it was perceived we did last year, especially when it was compared to what we had done in the past, your star tarnishes, and it takes a while, *and a lot of effort to get your shine back*! Aztec Sing took pride in always having the same judges, some of whom may have watched us compete last year, at other competitions! In any case, Chamber Singers earned *6th Place*, one point out of fifth, and so, we did not receive a trophy nor have our name called, and we couldn't blame it on being disqualified due to an overtime penalty, this time, either! The kids were very disappointed, but this reminded each and every one of us, of just *how hard we would have to work to return to show choir relevancy*!

Next, Chamber Singers competed at the Brea competition, *Festival 95*, held at Citrus College, for advanced mixed groups. I remember Chamber Singers trying really hard, after they had been shutout at the Aztec Sing, but since these were basically the same adjudicators we had seen there, I didn't feel too confident. However, when the awards were announced, I was *pleasantly surprised*, as Chamber Singers earned *2nd Place*, right behind Upland, I think! Thank goodness! We really needed that!

Following this, Dream Street traveled to Brea Olinda High School for the *Ladies First* competition, in the advanced women's division! They had a very energized performance (as usual) and everyone felt good about their show, when they came off stage. When the awards were announced, Dream Street earned *1st Place* along with both plaques for *Best Showmanship* and *Best Musicianship*! It felt just like old times!

The *Upland High School* competition was next. Both Chamber Singers and Dream Street participated, since we were a little short on competitions for both groups, this year. Each group gave a very passionate performance that received huge audience applause. When the awards were announced, Chamber Singers had earned *3rd Place*, in the Advanced Mixed Division, while Dream Street had earned *2nd Place,* in the Advanced Women's Division. These results were actually pretty good, especially when you considered that both Burroughs and Bonita Vista were there as well. Both groups went home happy… if not satisfied.

We then moved on to Arcadia High School's *Big Pow Wow*. As usual, only our Chamber Singers participated, as there were no divisions to accommodate our girls' groups. Chamber Singers gave a very explosive performance, as they always did at Arcadia, and then waited for the results. When the awards were announced, they had earned *3rd Place,* while Upland was 1st and Burroughs came in 2nd. Upland, Burroughs, Arcadia, Brea and Bonita Vista were now the groups to beat at every competition. We were working hard to reach their level just as fast as we could, and this was certainly a big step forward… *but our kids were still frustrated.*

Finally, the date of the *Fullerton College Jazz Festival* arrived. Our kids always liked this one, because we tended to do well and it was a fun Friday, away from school! This year, we brought Chamber Singers, Dream Street Singers, Silhouette Singers and Renegade to compete. I received the competition results for this one from a variety of dependable former students, who were there, almost *twenty-five years ago*, at the time of this writing in 2018. The only thing *they could not agree on*, was where Renegade had placed? So, I will go with the most popular memory. Again, every performance seemed to go perfectly! Each group's performance had reached a consistency, by this point in the year that made both Doug and I very happy. When the awards were announced, we were literally blown away! Silhouette Singers earned *1st Place* in the Intermediate Mixed Division, Renegade also earned *1st Place,* in the Men's Division, Dream Street earned *1st Place* in the Advanced Women's Division… and Chamber Singers earned 1st Place in the Advanced Mixed Division! Four wins for four Nogales groups! That was a very proud day for our kids. Best of all, Chamber and Dream Street felt that they were finally back, after not winning for all of last year!

We moved on to the *Riverside City College* (RCC) competition. We took Chamber Singers, Dream Street and Silhouette Singers. If you recall, at this time, RCC was much more of a vocal competition than a show one. Doug's choreography scores didn't count here *nearly as much* as they did in almost every other competition, so we had worked extra hard on our vocals, in preparation. The big day arrived, and all three of our groups performed well. However, there were a lot of tough competitors here… I believe almost every top group was there! Well, when the awards were announced, Chamber Singers had been shut out! There were four trophies given in the Advanced Mixed Division, and they went to: 1st place, Bonita Vista, 2nd place, Arcadia, 3rd place, Upland and 4th place, Brea. Chamber Singers had experienced this very disappointing outcome a number of times, last year, so it didn't hurt quite as much… but it still wasn't pleasant. Solitaire, meanwhile, fared much better, as they took home *2nd Place*. Silhouette Singers also won a trophy, earning *4th Place*. This was such a tough day to follow the exuberance of winning four divisions at Fullerton, just one week before. But, I explained to the kids that RCC was primarily a vocal competition, and with all of our movement, our singing probably did not come through as well as some of the other groups' had. Chamber and Dream Street only had one competition left! That competition would be in Chula Vista… *and they vowed to be ready*!

Tops 'n Pops arrived, quickly and our kids were more than ready. Dream Street performed first. They were a hit! A spontaneous cheer went up, after their performance that went on for a while! Chamber Singers performed, soon after them. The group was good, as always, and just as they had told me… *tonight they were going all out*! Their vocals sounded richer and their choreography looked sharper. This was Chamber Singers' best performance of the year! When they were set to announce the awards, our kids were excited, but not afraid. Maybe they just knew how good they were tonight, regardless of what the adjudicators said? In any case, Dream Street earned *2nd Place* in the Advanced Women's Division while Chamber Singers earned *3rd Place* (just one point out of second) in the Advanced Mixed Division. Chamber Singers also tied Bonita Vista (the winner) for the Best Musicianship plaque! Burroughs placed second. It wasn't what the kids had hoped for… but it was enough to keep them motivated until next year! How could Chamber Singers have had such an inconsistent competition record year, earning a sixth, a fifth, three thirds, a second and a first? While Dream Street had a much more consistent competition record, compiling three seconds and two firsts? My belief is that we really can't explain *subjective results in a logical manner*. There are just too many variables. In theory, I think that when each group does their best and accepts their results… everyone is a lot happier. But, of course, that seldom happens because we are so competitive. But, I also believe that when you have a great show idea that both you and the students are excited about… *it is your responsibility to see that show come to life, whether the adjudicators end up liking it or not!* After all, in show choir, our first allegiance should always be to the *art we are creating*, while *placing*, only represents someone else's reaction to that art and needs to be recognized as such. A special thanks to Kurt Schlatter, the president of Chamber Singers, Uyen Mai, the president of Dream Street, and to all of the other choir officers, including, Becky Mantanic, and Mei Ning, for their great work during the 1994-05 school year!

With the emergence of Burroughs, Bonita Vista, Brea, Upland and Arcadia, as the schools to beat, we still remained strong competitors. The kids in the 1995 Nogales groups were dedicated and brought us back to respectability. Once again… what a difference a year makes! On a very sad note, this was the year that one of our talented and well-liked Chamber Singer members, *Carol de Guzman*, was tragically killed in an auto accident! Many of us attended her funeral, and I can tell you, I've never experienced anything sadder and more pointless than her death. She was and will continue to be greatly missed.

I'm sorry to admit that 1995-96 was a year that was difficult to find our competition results. If I'd known, forty years ago, that I would be writing a book about this someday, I would most certainly have saved a list of our competition accomplishments *every year…* but alas, I didn't. On the other hand, I do know that we had a great year, from the few results that I was able to find! Our band was still composed of Don, Bo and Kramer, with a guest appearance by Jason Freese, later, at Showstoppers. Della Long had now worked as an integral part of the program for her *13th straight year!* And best of all… the Madrijazz Singers began to compete again! The groups we had in 1996 until I left after the 1998 school year were made up of some of the *hardest working and most dedicated kids we had ever had*, as confirmed by the excellent show scores we would routinely receive from our competitions! We were also blessed each of those years with multiple soloists of the highest degree! We sang very well too, although we never seemed to have enough male voices to create that "fuller" sound that many of our competitors were blessed with. In any case, our groups took what they had and always gave it their best! Our competition shows included:

Chamber Singers 1995-96
Costume Colors:
Yellow & Blue
Competition Set
Volcano/ Too Darn Hot
Weekend In New England
By The Sea/ Fins
Someone's Waiting For You
Roll Over Beethoven/ Shout
You'll Never Walk Alone

Silhouette Singers 1995-96
Costume Colors:
White
Competition Set
As If We Never Said
Guys And Dolls
Farmer Tan

Dream Street Singers 95-96
Costume Colors: *Pink & White*
Competition Set
I've Got The Music In Me
Shuffle Off To Buffalo
Bad Boys
Dream Street Theme
Baby Mine
Hard Hearted Hannah
Colors Of The Wind
Heartbreaker

Madrijazz Singers 95-96
Costume Colors: *Unknown*
Competition Set
Stop! In The Name of Love
Imagine
Do You Wanna Dance?

When you glance over these shows, you will probably notice that Silhouette Singers had gone back to being a mixed group while Madrijazz had become a beginning girls' show choir. Nogales High School was continuing to experience a sharp decline in enrollment, and it was really affecting the size of our younger choir groups… but Chamber and Dream Street remained fine… for now. Many of their members had started out with us as freshmen in 1994 or 95. Thankfully, the groups they were in, just seemed to get better and better!

We hadn't returned to Show Stoppers at Disneyland, in 1995, because the Fullerton College Jazz Festival fell on the exact same date! After thinking about it, we decided that it would be much more beneficial to the choral program to take *all four of our groups* to Fullerton than taking only Chamber and Dream Street to Showstoppers. With all of that winning at Fullerton, we are very happy that we did! But this year, we had planned from summer, to go back and really test our groups against national competitors! That explains why the Chamber Singer show includes a very effective song that we had used in their competition set last year… *You'll Never Walk Alone!* The idea of using the *same ending song*, although not a common practice in show choir, served a purpose this year… since we hadn't gone to Showstoppers last year, those judges *had never seen or heard it!* We were fortunate once again to have a super soloist to sing it, named *Dorothy Nacita*! The Chamber show also used multiple colorful surfboards in a redo of the *By The Sea* medley, which now featured Jimmy Buffet's *Fins*! To ensure that this was an impressive show from beginning to end, we opened with another Jimmy Buffet song, *Volcano*, which featured fire extinguishers blowing steam! Very fun! Dream Street was also packed to the gills in fun! Their show opened with *I've Got The Music In Me,* an infectious rock song by Kiki Dee, from 1974, and then immediately followed that with *Shuffle Off To Buffalo*, from 42nd Street, complete with props and colors of the 1930s! Soon, they returned with the *Dream Street Theme*, since none of the Showstoppers judges had heard it last year, and any group with its own theme song was obviously special! Next, Dream Street sang their a cappella ballad, *Baby Mine*, from Disney's *Dumbo.* This led to *Colors Of The Wind,* from Disney's *Pocahontas*, which would take advantage of our Disneyland performance site, with a beautiful ballad from a Disney show! And the show ended with one of the strongest songs I have ever used, *Heartbreaker*, by Pat Benatar! Yet another rock song from the seventies! So, both Chamber Singers and Dream Street were ready to go!

Chamber Singers' first competition was The *Aztec Sing*. We had placed sixth here last year, but I felt encouraged enough by our continued improvement, to bring them back for a second consecutive year! We felt that win or lose, Chamber Singers could use this event to get feedback on their vocals, in preparation for Showstoppers, through the comments they would receive from the adjudicators. Well, with Upland, Burroughs, Bonita Vista, Brea and Arcadia competing, we knew this would be a tough one. When the awards were announced, if memory serves, we had placed *3rd*! The adjudicators loved hearing *You'll Never Walk Alone*, again, and they found our entire show to be very musical and fun! This was a huge relief!

The only festival that Silhouette Singers and Madrijazz Singers competed in, all year, joined by Chamber and Dream Street, I believe, was at the *Fullerton College Jazz Festival*. If memory serves, Silhouette placed *3rd*, while Madrijazz did not place, Dream Street placed 1st and Chamber Singers earned a *2nd Place*! Not as sensational as some years for everyone… but certainly a lot better than 1994's rough outing. If I had learned anything in my 20 years of show choir competitions, it was to *appreciate everything you get*, because what you *wanted* to get… *was always far from guaranteed*!

We competed at other festivals throughout the year, with Chamber Singers generally earning *3rd Place* awards and Dream Street either winning or coming in second, everywhere they went! I loved the Chamber show, but we did not have the depth of the vocal sound that the other top contenders had, so more and more, we had to rely on our show, our energy and our soloists to impress judges. Dream Street, on the other hand, had the whole package. Everyone seemed to love them!

The Final competition of the year for both Chamber and Dream Street was the *Disneyland Showstoppers National Show Choir Competition*! By this time, both Doug and I had already been working for Disneyland in the Guest Talent Division, since late 1995. I had to make sure that there was no potential conflict of interest with my groups competing there. Thankfully, I found that there was none, because Disneyland had nothing to do with this event. In reality, Showstoppers, *rented* the Tomorrowland Stage and the necessary technicians and ushers to help run their event. In an effort to bolster our band, we learned that *Jason Freese*, the son of then, Disneyland Band Director, Stan Freese, was an excellent sax and clarinet player, who took on gigs like this one, so I got his number, called him, and he agreed to do it! As I recall, Jason only needed to rehearse with us once, and all of the parts that he played were improvised! But he added greatly to the band! Jason went on to perform with many famous bands, including, *Green Day*!

The morning of the event began with auditions for the outstanding soloists, within the competing choirs. I think each school could enter three students. These students would then, take turns competing on the stage in the Golden Horseshoe Saloon, while their group was not performing on stage. After everyone had auditioned, at some point, the top five were announced, and asked to perform their songs in front of the show choir judges that night to select the ultimate winner! In 1996, we had three extremely qualified soloists, in *Dorothy Nacita, Michael Washington* and *Margaux Yap*. When they announced the finalists for the Solo Competition, a few hours later… I believe that *all three of our entrants* had made the final five!

Meanwhile, Dream Street performed for the audience and adjudicators and received a long period of applause. Honestly? They were dynamic, sweet when they needed to be and hard rocking when *that* was called for! Everything seemed to go according to plan. Soon it was Chamber Singers turn! They could not have worked any harder! Their vocal sound was full and their choreography was oh so clean! They too received a long period of applause. Before the awards were presented, the five finalists in the solo competition sang their songs. All five of them were terrific, and I knew that this would be a close contest. The soloists were presented their awards first. They presented 4th runner up through the Winner. I can't recall the exact order of finish, but a male soloist from some other school was the ultimate winner. I remember feeling so very proud of our three finalists for sincerely smiling and congratulating him. They were learning to accept whatever they received, *graciously* and since this situation called for it… *to lose gracefully*. Next came the awards for the Women's Division.

Third Runner-Up… It was not us.
Second Runner-Up… It was not us.
First Runner-Up… It was not us.
Grand Champion…
The Nogales High School Dream Street Singers!

The Dream Street Singers went crazy with joy! They were so excited! They had never earned such a high honor in competition, as this one, before! They felt like *Olympic Champions*! Next, came the awards honoring the Mixed Division.

Fifth Runner-Up… It was not us.
Fourth Runner-Up… It was not us.
Third Runner-Up… It was not us.
Second Runner-Up… It was not us.
First Runner-Up…
The Nogales High School Chamber Singers!

I think the Chamber Singers were very excited, but a little disappointed that they did not win! However, the mixed group that won Grand Champion was from Wisconsin, I believe, and like us, they had given a *phenomenal performance*! This left it up to the judges. As I recall they only won by a point or two. So, we learned to be thankful but not satisfied with second place. We would try again next year. However, this second place finish in a national competition was the highest a Nogales High School mixed show choir had ever earned before, as was the *win* for Dream Street in women's competition! I was so proud of both Dream Street and Chamber's monumental achievements! A special thanks goes to Dahlia Hamza, the president of Chamber Singers, Becky Mantanic, the president of Dream Street and to all of the other choir officers, including Dorothy Nacita and Margaux Yap, from the 1995-96 school year. You guys were the best!

The final accomplishment from 1996 that I would like to mention, was when we teamed with drama and put on *Godspell*! I remember that lead director, Lee Oldham, was originally not crazy about this choice, but I was adamant about doing it, so he eventually agreed. This was one of the *most moving musicals* I have ever been a part of! Kenny Bednar and Mark Buenaluz, worked with the techs, while the performers are listed on the following page:

1996 Cast List for "*Godspell*"

Jesus: *Mitchell Asa*
John/ Judas: *David Bradley*

Disciples

Lisette Hoyos • Bryant Jimenez • Laura Kettle Dorothy Nacita • Eddie Rojas • Sarah Solorio Michael Washington • Margaux Yap

Chorus

Adrian De Guzman • Mary Anne Garcia • Natalie Mauk Don Ning • Lily Talavera • Lindsay Mallari Rowena Macatiag • Arlene Dayoan

The band, for these performances, which was really effective in a rock'n roll sort of way, was made up of Don Cloud, Kramer Ison and Lisa Kettle. Everyone in the cast and the audience thoroughly enjoyed this wonderful production!

The summer of 1996 arrived, and Doug and I were right back at it, designing the shows for next year's groups! After auditions, we retained a lot of this year's students in the groups, but also added some talented newcomers. We were always hoping for slightly larger groups to fill-out our choral sound, which had grown a bit lighter since 1993, but we were excited about what we had, just the same! The one sad change in our program was the loss of Della Long, as our choir secretary, stage manager and magical accomplisher of whatever the choirs needed, since 1984! She had moved on to her own teaching career, and did not have the time to share her magic with us anymore! We could never replace her. Her dedication to the kids, the staff and the program, was second to none! She would be missed greatly! Our competition shows were:

Chamber Singers 97
Costume Colors:
Red & White
Competition Set
On Broadway/ Celebrate
On My Own
Witch Doctor
Vespers
Marian The Librarian
Sixties Medley
The Bridge

Dream Street Singers 97
Costume Colors:
Fuchsia & White
Competition Set
Roll With It
Mister Sandman
Whatever Lola Wants
America
Send In The Clowns
Don't Cry Out Loud
Great Balls of Fire
Good Lovin'

Although Madrijazz and Silhouette Singers were alive and well at Nogales High School, as classes, I can find absolutely *no records that they competed at all in 1997*! Silhouette Singers did perform songs from, *Les Miserables* at the end of the NDSCC, and both groups joined Chamber and Dream Street at our home concerts, but for whatever reasons, they don't seem to show up anywhere with competition results. Ruben Dario Hoyos Marin did tell me that he remembers Silhouette competing their "*Les Miz*" show at Upland in 1997… but not placing. That's all we've got on them!

You may have noticed that in this year's shows, Chamber and Dream Street were singing more *repeats,* or songs we have competed with before. Well, this was our 18th year at Nogales, and by this time we had a pretty good idea of which songs these choirs could sing most effectively. Chamber Singers, did have *Marian The Librarian* and *The Bridge*, which were completely new to Nogales High School. *Marian The Librarian* was a cute song from the Broadway show, *The Music Man.* Doug wanted the song to take place in a library, like in the original, but we needed *forty matching, hardback books* that were in good shape, to make the choreography work! The school's books were far too worn looking, even if they had let us use them. So, I got lucky, one day at Ralph's supermarket. They were running a promotion, where if you bought the first book of an encyclopedia collection *for one dollar*, you had the option of buying each subsequent encyclopedia book for the discounted price of ten dollars, when they were offered each month. I told the checker that I wanted forty copies of the first book for one dollar each! He gave me a funny look. But, after I explained that they were for a school... *he sold them to me*. Those books looked great on stage, all year! The Bridge is actually the combination of two gospel-styled songs, *Bridge Over Troubled Water* and *Lead Me, Precious Lord,* superbly performed by *Michael Washington* and *Margaux Yap*. It was one of the *greatest crowd pleasers our Chamber Singers ever performed*! Sadly, we never attempted to perform this dynamic medley again due to the *incredibly high bar* that Michael and Margaux had set for the soloists! Dream Street's show, also contained a lot of previously performed material, but that's because those songs fit the concept of their Broadway/American Pop show so perfectly. We have learned, over the years, to never mess with perfection!

Our first competition was the *Tournament of Champions (TOC)*. They offered separate divisions for mixed and women's groups, so we took both Chamber and Dream Street. Chamber Singers earned *2nd Place* in the Advanced Mixed Division while Dream Street earned *1st Place* and the *Showmanship* plaque in the Advanced Women's Division! This was a great way to start the year, and it gave us hope for the remainder of the season.

Our next competition was the Brea's *Festival 1997,* their advanced mixed event, at Citrus College. This event was always well stocked with the best show choirs around, so Chamber Singers really had to give their best! Their performance was very fun, throughout and they received a hearty round of applause when they left the stage. When the awards were announced, Chamber Singers earned *3rd Place*! They were very happy... but they would not be satisfied until they won.

Soon after that, Dream Street traveled to Brea Olinda High School for their women's event, *Ladies First*. They were excited, and gave a great performance to prove it! Ultimately, Dream Street earned *1st Place* with the *Showmanship* plaque in the Advanced Women's Division. Ever since they had won *Grand Champion* at Showstoppers, last year, their level of confidence had been on fire, as if no one could stop them!

Next, Chamber Singers went to Arcadia's *Big Pow Wow*. This festival was always very competitive, using a similar score sheet to that used at the Aztec Sing, with the addition of one additional performance category. So, singing counted for about 70% of each group's final score. I don't remember who won, that night, but I do remember that several of the adjudicators were very impressed with the group's performance of *The Bridge*! That's probably why we earned *3rd Place*, instead of our usual fourth place! Coming in third, was really quite an achievement for us at the *Big Pow Wow*! I remember the kids celebrating on the bus ride home as if we'd won!

Before we knew it, we were back at *Disneyland Showstoppers National Show Choir Competition*! This year, the event had grown with more groups entering from California and likewise, from out of state. With so many strong competitors, everyone in Chamber and Dream Street felt excited and a little nervous at the same time. I'm sure all of our competitors felt the same way. They had the soloist competition, as usual, and our very own, Margaux Yap, made it to the final five. Our group performances went great. The vocals sounded very good, especially considering we were in an outdoor venue, with limited microphones. I was very proud of our kids, and the exceptional energy they put forth throughout their shows. When it came time for the awards, all of us waited anxiously, in the Tomorrowland Theatre, as they were announced. First the awards for the final five soloists were announced. The *Best Soloist Award* went to *Margaux Yap*! Everyone from Nogales was so happy for her! Next they announced the Women's Division awards. We really thought that Dream Street would win Showstoppers twice in a row, but they earned *1st Runner-Up*, instead. Still, it was a great achievement. Finally, the Mixed Awards. We knew our show was terrific, but the adjudicators' scores would of course… have the last word. Chamber Singers earned *3rd Runner-Up*, and beat a good number of their competitors! A little disappointing compared to last year, but still a fine achievement!

A few years back, Tony Atienza, a young director, who had spent four years as a member of the Bonita Vista show choirs, emerged as the new choir director of Chula Vista High School.

One of his first moves was to change their show choir competition's name, from *Tops 'n Pops* to *The Southern California Performance Show-Choir Invitational…* nicknamed *So Cal*. This was a much more dynamic title, and it successfully endured beyond after I left teaching in 2016. Chamber Singers and Dream Street decided to end their competition season there, and make it part of an overnight tour! When the Saturday competition arrived, it was a very long day, by any stretch of the imagination! But, at the end of it, both of our groups placed! Masquerade earned *3rd Place* in the Advanced Mixed Division and Dream Street earned *4th Place* in the Advanced Women's Division. Not the best we had done in competition, this year, but not the worst, either. In any case, we returned to the Catamaran, the beautiful hotel we were staying at, in Mission Bay, and had a marvelous weekend!

1997 was much more than just a competition season! We also raised the money to spend 5 days in Orlando, Florida, visiting all of the Disney Parks! In the end, about 40 kids went on this trip, which we referred to as, *Operation Orlando*! We even had tee shirts made! It was a great trip in almost every detail. The one activity that we could have done without *was the very thing we were required to do*, in order to get school board's approval for this trip. During one of our evenings, we had to spend *four precious hours* participating in a poorly put together, Disney Workshop. It was supposed to be a workshop on performing, but as I remember, our facilitators spent most of their effort on teaching us how to correctly *put on stage make-up*! Since Doug and I both gave student workshops at California Disneyland, we knew that the workshops *always* lasted exactly 90 minutes. Our Orlando hosts told us that we were fortunate, because we were selected to try a brand new *four-hour* workshop that they had only just developed! Oh, the rides and attractions we missed! But, aside from that… everything about our Orlando 1997 trip was awesome! My greatest memory of this trip was watching Alex, who I believe was five years old at the time, dancing with the "*roaming gypsies*" one night in EPCOT, trying hard to master their learned routine, with complete abandon! That was incredible to watch!

The final memory I would like to share about 1997, was our *very special Spring Concert*! For many years now, Doug and I had been privately complaining that we had to perform all of our concerts in our gym, on a makeshift stage! Although we were thankful for that, we felt that our kids and their families deserved a spring concert on a big stage in a real theatre! Well, I knew that Citrus College was way too expensive, so I looked into the closest possibilities, Diamond Bar High School, Brea Olinda High School and Mt. SAC. Of the three, only Brea Olinda was available on our desired date. So, I signed the contract, and we were off! Since we had to add the costs of buses to get the students there, we raised the price of the tickets to $8.00 (up from $6.00) and only included *Chamber Singers* and *Dream Street Singers* in this concert. Madrijazz and Silhouette had their separate Spring Concert planned in the Nogales Little Theatre. The day of the Brea Olinda event arrived! After school, we bused everyone from Nogales to Brea Olinda. We had a quick two-hour tech rehearsal, fed the kids individual pizzas from Round Table for dinner, and presented, *"In Concert" 1997*, to about 200 people (the theatre seats 400). It seemed like a blur, as the show quickly ran from group to group, separated by a few student acts. But I loved it! I think the kids did too! As I watched the kids ending the concert singing, *Never Walk Alone*, I wished that someday I could have a theatre, just like this one, for my choirs to perform in! It seems kind of funny now, but eight years later, I *was* hired as the new choir director of Brea Olinda High School! Thanks go to *Margaux Yap Cruz*, Chamber Singers president, *Sara Bach Lydiard*, Dream Street President and to all of our other choir officers from the 1996-7 school year, for doing such an incredible job!

The summer of 1997 arrived and Doug and I had to face the fact that Nogales High School was continuing to face *declining enrollment*. With the strong possibility of smaller groups, we got busy designing shows that would be effective with less vocal sound. The truth is, when a group is lucky enough to have an abundance of good singers and performers, it's not too difficult to build a show around them, because *almost anything will look and sound good*! But, when you don't have that luxury, and in fact you have some obvious shortcomings, you really have to get creative if you are trying to win! Our groups coming in had *good vocal talent and attitudes*, but *limited performing experience* and *a weaker overall vocal sound than last year*. But, we had some exceptional soloists, dancers and leaders, so we knew that we were actually in pretty good shape! Another plus was the fact that we still had a *great band*, the same one as last year, so, we were very encouraged! To best describe the Chamber Singers' show, I would call it an *eclectic collection of some of my favorite arrangements from the sixties, seventies and eighties*! It fit the group well. The Dream Street show was likewise a collection of vintage arrangements, albeit a bit less driving, but a good fit for them, just the same! The groups' competition sets for the 1998 season, were as follows:

Chamber Singers 1997-98
Costume Colors: Costume
Lime Green & Rainbow
Competition Set
Psychedelic Sixties
It's A Miracle
Vincent
The Impossible Dream
Respect/ Heartbreaker

Silhouette Singers 1997-98
Colors:
Black
Competition Set
Masquerade
God Help The Outcasts
Love Is A Wonderful Thing
Mony Mony

Dream Street Singers 97-98
Costume Colors: *Pink*
Competition Set
Fever/Steam Heat
Summertime Fifties
Someone To Watch Over Me
Over The Rainbow
Get Ready/Gimme Some Lovin'

Madrijazz Singers 97-98
Costume Colors: *Unknown*
Competition Set
Rock and Roll Is Here
Stop! In The Name of Love
Lean On Me
Who Put The Bomp

With smaller and less experienced groups, this year, we focused the shows more on the tried and true. Both the Chamber and Dream Street shows featured soft centers (where the a cappella is immediately followed by the power ballad) because we thought this would give each group the opportunity to showoff their singing prowess. Although the choreography was active and exciting for both shows, as always, Doug was *very careful to choreograph both groups* so as not interfere with their singing. We were actually very excited about all four of our shows.

For the 1998 competition season, Chamber Singers and Dream Street again shared the same first competition at *Tournament of Champions* (TOC). Chamber Singers had a great day and earned *1st Place* and both plaques, *Best Showmanship* and *Best Musicianship.* Dream Street, did likewise, in the Women's Division, by winning *1st Place* and the *Best Musicianship* plaque. What an awesome way to begin the competition year!

Next, both groups traveled to *Upland High School*, along with Silhouette Singers. After our stellar beginning at TOC, we hoped for a similar outcome here. Our performances were all good, but, as usual, we didn't know any of the adjudicators, which can sometimes be a bad sign. We hoped that this time would be the exception. At the awards, after Silhouette was announced *4th Place* in the Intermediate Mixed Division and Dream Street was announced *3rd Place*, in the Women's Advanced Division, Masquerade waited patiently, holding hands. The host had already announced fifth place through second places *without* calling their name, so our kids were all set for the big finish! *But it never came*, as they announced another school, and our kids, shocked, walked slowly to the bus. Over the years, we had certainly been through this *disappointing scenario* before, as most groups have… but the TOC sweep, seemed to give us a false sense of confidence. In truth, the only times that I have seen a group win back to backs, are when there are no other strong competitors in the competition, when the *same judges* had them winning at the last competition or when the judges, for some reason, had a stake in the outcome. It was very important for my kids to understand this truism, in order to know that winning and losing did not always reflect how good a group's performance was. Understanding this, although possibly helpful, was of little solace to our Chamber Singers, however.

Chamber Singer's next competition was Brea's *Festival 98*, held at Citrus College. Throughout the years, they had always placed here, I think, but now their seemed to be more "big groups" to contend with. Chamber Singers had a very good performance, bringing the house down with their dynamic performance of *Heartbreaker*! Soon, Mark Henson, the host of the event, strode to the microphone to announce the winners. Chamber Singers were announced coming in *3rd Place*! The Chamber Singers and their parents cheered loudly! It was evident that day, that my Chamber Singers had learned something. *Although you can't always get what you want, learn to appreciate what you get!* Yep. I think my kids realized that it was a lot more fun to feel happy than to always be in a state of morose disappointment about not winning!

About two weeks later, Solitaire traveled to Brea Olinda High School to compete in *Ladies First*, their women's event. They performed better than anyone, which I think, was usually the case, and came off stage tired, but *so happy*! When the awards for the Advanced Women's Division, were announced, Dream Street earned *1st Place* with the *Showmanship* plaque! Those girls were on a roll!

Now, it was time for the Chamber Singers to compete at a couple of competitions, by themselves. Our first event was the Arcadia *Big Pow Wow*! No real surprises here. We were very good that night, and received a lot of applause. But, the adjudicators scored us in *4th Place*. That actually had become our normal placing at Arcadia, these days. That didn't bother the kids nearly as much as the fact that Diamond Bar had placed third, in front of them! This marked the first time, in recent memory that *Diamond Bar had ever beaten us*! But, we had placed, we were still in the game, and for that, we were thankful. Now the Chamber Singers were more driven than ever to do better at their next competition!

The second competition that Chamber Singers journeyed to without the Dream Street Singers was the *Gladstone Review*! Rob Hodo, another former member of the Bonita Vista Music

Machine, was our host, and instantly made us feel welcome. That night, without a doubt, we had our best performance of the year, so far! When the awards were announced, we were given 2nd *Place* along with the plaque for *Best Showmanship*! We hadn't won, but boy did those awards feel good! Now Chamber Singers had earned a *1st*,a *2nd*, a *3rd* and a *4th* place award this year! There were not many competing groups out there who could claim the same level of success in advanced show choir competitions! I think our kids were experiencing the joy of appreciating every achievement, instead of throwing out everything but firsts! This group had a wonderful attitude!

Well, Chamber, Dream Street and Silhouette Singers traveled together, on to the *Fullerton College Jazz Festival*, where they all did very well. Chamber Singers earned *3rd Place*, in the Advanced Mixed Division, while Silhouette Singers earned 1st Place in the Novice Mixed Division, and Dream Street tied for *1st Place, in the Advanced Women's Division*! This marked the end of the 1998 competition season, with the exception of Showstoppers!

Disneyland Showstoppers National Show Choir Competition was very much like it had been in previous years, but with a lot more groups competing. In the vocal competition, we had at least one of our singers selected, for the finals, *Michael Washington*, and I believe *Lisette Hoyos*, was selected, as well. Well, both Dream Street and Chamber Singers, once again gave excellent performances, and felt very confident when it came time for the awards. In the soloist competition, *Michael Washington, was Showstoppers Disneyland's 1998's top winner!* Everyone felt very proud of him! He had worked so very hard for this! Dream Street, earned *1st Runner-Up* honors in the Women's Division, for the second year in a row, while Chamber Singers earned *3rd Runner Up* in the Mixed Division. I can't say that everyone was satisfied, because these Nogales kids were so competitive in those days, but they had placed in a national competition for the *fifth time in five years* competing at both the Young Americans event and Showstoppers! That was an exceptional record! The kids went home that night, feeling like they always felt after a competition… appreciative of placing, but counting down the days, until the next time they could compete! Unfortunately for them, it would not be until next year. But they would still have the thrill of learning a new show in the fall! A special thanks goes to *Melanie Sanchez*, the president of Chamber Singers, *Amie Pomeroy*, the president of Dream Street and to all of the other choir officers from the 1997-98 school year, for doing such an awesome job, by never giving up and never allowing our groups to give up, either!

Earlier in the year, the choir, once again, combined with the drama department to present the musical, *The Music Man. Mitchell Asa* superbly performed the title character, Harold Hill, and *Lisette Hoyos* made a great Marian Paroo. We were especially proud of the fact that more choir members participated in this production than in any musical we had combined with the drama department to put on, so far! There were 24 choir students in the cast! The entire cast for *The Music Man* is listed below:

1998 Cast List for "*The Music Man*"

Harold Hill: *Mitchell Asa* **Marion Paroo:** *Lisette Hoyos*
Mayor Shinn: *Ian Goulet* **Mrs. Shinn:** *Nicole Seeber*
Zaneeta: *Abigail Yap* **Gracie:** *Tricey Davis*
Marcellus: *Tony Palacios* **Tommy:** *Robert Valadez*
Mrs. Paroo: *Amanda Burnham* **Winthrop:** *Cliff Banagal*
Ethel: *Samantha Ames* **Mrs. Squires:** *Michelle Sandoval*
Mrs. Dunlop: *Elizabeth Mason* **Amaryllis:** *Ivory Gutierrez*
Quartet: *Michael Trompeta • Ruben Hoyos • Romeo Cervas & Brian Mason*
Alma Hix: *Linda Pitts* **Conductor/Constable:** *Tim Duffy*
Charlie: *Eddie Rojas*
Pick-a-little Ladies: *Hoda Aboulwafa • Liza Reyes & Kristine Protacio*
Townspeople: *Isaac Arevalo, Michelle Racho, Grace Caballos, Lisa Fonseca, Letty Gomez, Marla Gonzalez, Aumier Harris, Julie Anne Ines, Christine McFarland, Wendy Mei, Orlando Patterson, Albert Reyes, Brent Sanchez, Melanie Sanchez, Radhika Sharma, Sarah Jane Wunsch, Amie Pomeroy & Brian Jones*

We completed the school year by taking a wonderful trip to San Francisco, Monterey and Carmel. About forty kids participated, and they had the time of their lives, sightseeing and exploring Northern California! I had a lot of fun too, as did Margaret, Doug and Alex… who was now six years old.

In the next chapter, I will briefly explain *why I left Nogales High School*, but not how much I appreciated the Nogales kids and their non-stop determination, for 19 years, *no matter what the obstacles,* to always put on a winning performance, whether we won or not! I loved my Nogales students as if they were my own kids! We didn't just work well together… sometimes I felt that the kids and me along with Doug and Margaret, were all *connected at the hip*! Needless to say, I felt terrible about leaving. But, I have never forgotten all of the *life-changing singing and performance experiences* that we shared, leading to concepts that shaped the rest of my career! Things like *how to work harder than you ever have before, how to sing and perform from the heart* and *understanding that the power of winning is not just found in the individual, but in the group working cohesively together*! We started with dreams, back in the early years. Through 19 wonderful years of singing, dancing, and learning, just as hard as we could, *we made a lot of those dreams come true*! Thank you so much for everything. *I will never forget any of you*!

CHAPTER 7

Diamond Bar High School... 1998-2001... Instant Success!

In May of 1998, Kathy Whitescarver Milner, a former student and accompanist of mine at Norco High School, called me on the phone. She told me that she was leaving Diamond Bar High School, and wondered if I was interested in her job? I took a long moment, before replying. In truth, I was *very happy* with my program at Nogales High School, but *I had never had a real auditorium* to perform my shows in. *Diamond Bar had one of the nicest ones in the area*! I replied, "Maybe." She told me that applications were being accepted through Friday and that interviews for the finalists would begin next week!

I was presently concluding my twenty-first year of teaching, and for the most part, I was very comfortable at Nogales! So, that night, I believe it was Tuesday, I discussed the ramifications of the job with Margaret, Alex and Doug. It was a very hard choice to make, because *we had built Nogales up into a major show choir power on the west coast* and we absolutely loved the kids! We had just finished competing at *Disneyland Showstoppers*, and had done very well, so the idea of starting over, in a program that historically was *not a major power* in the show choir circuit, sounded like a lot of work! But, we knew that Diamond Bar High School had a nice theatre which neither Doug nor I had had the luxury of having during our entire careers, thus far! In addition, I felt that I wasn't getting any younger, and at some point in my career, I wanted to have a real theatre to work with! I had already spent endless time trying to convince the Rowland district (of which Nogales High School was a part) to build a theatre for the entire district to use! In that way, it would benefit all of the performing arts programs! They responded by giving each high school a portable stage to be set up in the gymnasium for our concerts. The stage was rickety, the acoustics were awful (we were singing in a gym), they provided us with no technicians, so the choir staff had to open and close the curtain and run the lights and sound simultaneously while doing the jobs we were being paid for. The school only provided us with one microphone and stand… while we had to purchase and take care of setting up and taking down the rest! What I perceived as a lack of understanding for my program, and the *virtual impossibility of ever getting a theatre at Nogales*, pretty much made up my mind for me. So, on Friday afternoon, just before the 4 pm deadline, I turned in my hand written application to the Walnut district office. Soon, I was interviewing with the "Fine Arts Dean" of Diamond Bar High School. I also met with the principal and parents before I was finally offered the job. To be honest, I was overwhelmed! Diamond Bar High School seemed so *formal* compared to the breath of fresh air that my program at Nogales High School represented. So, *I agonized over this decision, only because I loved the kids I would be leaving.* But, ultimately, even though I would take a pay cut, since I had been teaching for 21 years, and the district only accepted 10 years of my experience, I decided to make the change. The choir kids and their teacher, Mrs. Milner, even had a *Welcoming Party* for Doug and I during the summer. Recently, I had some *possible cancer growths* removed from my face, so there was a great big bandage across my right cheek all the way to my nose. I looked like I had been in an accident, but the kids were polite enough, not to mention it.

Initially, I felt like a fish out of water. Although the Diamond Bar kids were very nice, I really missed the warmth, humor and energy of the Nogales kids, that only 19 years of working in the same choral program can bring. But, it was really too late to have any second thoughts about this move… so, I embraced it. We hired Don Cloud, Bo Eder and Kramer Ison to come along with us to be our accompanying band. Margaux Yap, a former choir member and 1997 graduate of Nogales High

School, also joined us as Doug's choreography assistant, that first year at Diamond Bar.

Margaret, Doug, Alex and I worked through the summer to organize the room. There was nothing intrinsically wrong with the choir room, except that *I didn't know where anything was*? So, I changed everything around… until I did! Margaret and Doug transformed the room to look welcoming and colorful, we bought a new desk for the choir office, and all too quickly, it was time for the new school year to begin!

It was quickly apparent to me that not *everyone* was happy to see me taking over the choirs, at Diamond Bar High School. In the week before classes started, I read a hideous article in *The Windmill* (the local paper) that basically trashed me both personally and professionally and left no doubt, that the author felt very negatively about my hiring! A number of students were also very standoffish, apparently taking the wait and see approach. *Welcome to Diamond Bar*. On the other hand, there were a lot of students who seemed genuinely glad to see us, and the good changes that we brought with us. Fortunately, they overwhelmed the negativity for me. Doug came into school with me for the entire first week, so that we could audition the kids in each group, together. All five of the classes were moderate sized, and I think the program included 130 different students with *no crossovers*! Apparently, it had not been part of their culture to have students in more than one group. As I recall, the groups were called Encore (mixed show choir), Allegra (women's show choir), Treble Choir, Beginning Choir and a period of Guitar. Diamond Bar had never competed in show choir, with more than two groups, for as long as I had followed them, with previous directors, *Larry Cline, Essie Fisher or Kathy Milner*. So, the first thing we did was to *increase the number of competing show choirs!* This was something I had learned to do at Nogales High School and was *immediately applying to Diamond Bar*. As soon as we did this, most students in our Diamond Bar show choir classes seemed to feel an instant sense of excitement, fun and direction! We hoped that this would quickly evolve into a determined work ethic! But, what this new restructuring *really meant*, was that every member of show choir would be encouraged to *pay a fee* to cover the costs of their costume and weekly choreography! I think the fee we suggested, was on average, about four hundred dollars per student. I waited with anticipation, for the angry parent phone calls and administrative *visits*, telling me that I could *not charge my students a fee*! But, I think because the fees *were not mandatory to be in show choir, only suggested…* I got through that initial time with a minimum of parent phone calls or complaints.

As far as student officers were concerned, I believe they already had officers elected for "the choral department," who all also happened to be members of their top mixed group, *Encore*. So, I immediately changed these elected officers into just *Encore officers* and directed all of the other choirs to vote for their own leaders. I always liked this method far better than having one set of officers from the top mixed group leading all of the other groups! In this case, my proclamation immediately created buzz throughout all of the Diamond Bar choirs!

Next, we wanted to continue the choral department's makeover by changing the group names to ones that would be *immediately identifiable with Diamond Bar High School*. The word, *diamond* (from *Diamond Bar*), lent itself, so well, to a plethora of names, all sounding classy! So, we began. Encore became *Marquis* (which is a fancy diamond cut), Allegra became *Solitaire* (which is a single diamond) and Treble Choir became *Dazzle.* We had wanted to name the group, *Diamond Girls*, but the new Dean of Fine Arts, blocked it, saying that every choral group we offered had to be open to boys and girls, if not in reality, by name, or we'd be breaking some law. Okay. If I learned nothing else from my administrators, I have learned to adapt. The Beginning Choir classes became the *Diamond Bar Singers.* We started with one section of this, and by second semester, I had dropped the guitar class, giving us *two sections*! For now, these two sections would compete together as one group!

There was so much that we had developed in our Nogales program that perfectly paralleled the progress in our new program at Diamond Bar! For example, we had called the Christmas concert, *Holiday Magic* for the last few years at

Nogales and we immediately adopted it for Diamond Bar. In addition, our Nogales tradition of taking a trip to *Disneyland* every year, to perform, compete or participate in a workshop, plugged right into the Diamond Bar program. However, we also kept an exciting element, *inherent in the previous program at Diamond Bar* that we did not have at Nogales… *a summer music program*! I had attended Diamond Bar's summer music performance of *You're A Good Man Charlie Brown,* in the summer, and immediately began to dream of what *I would do* with that in a real live theatre! We would call this summer program, *Summer Magic*! We held a Summer Magic program (including a performance) during the summers of 1999 through 2005. We then did the exact same thing at Brea Olinda High School, during the summers of 2006 through 2016. Curiously, Doug and I were both working at Disneyland on weekends, as part of *Magic Music Days*, the Guest Talent Department, in the late 1990s and early 2000s. I think the word, "*magic*," just popped up one day as a great name for our concerts! By the time we got to Brea in 2005-06, *every concert* we put on… ended with the word, *Magic*!

When the 1998-99 school year rolled around, at Diamond Bar High School, Doug and I had already selected the songs for the competition shows of the entire program. Every group would also sing and perform *traditional choral music* at festivals and/or home concerts to keep their music education balanced. I had called this my *pyramid concept*! One third of the energy of each of my choir classes focuses on show choir, one third focuses on traditional singing and one third focuses on the individual musical and performance development of each student! I was a little bit concerned about the "*classical*" part of this program, because although I had taken choirs to "*stand-up*" festivals before, at both Norco and Nogales high schools, my emphasis at both schools had been developing a well-balanced *show choir program* first. I decided right away, that I was going to have to put *more emphasis* on my groups' classical singing, from the get go! Our competition sets for 1999 were as follows:

Marquis 1998-99
Costume Colors:
Gold & White & Purple
Competition Set
Dixieland
The Hills of Shilo
Broadway Twenties
Marquis A-Go-Go
Let It Be Me

Dazzle 1998-99
Costume Colors:
White & Red
Competition Set
Downtown
Why Do Fools Fall
Mister Sandman
I Can't Help Falling
Great Balls of Fire

Solitaire 1998-99
Costume Colors:
Red
Competition Set
Solitaire Theme
Hit Me With Your Best Shot
Soon It's Gonna Rain
Singing In The Rain
Always On My Mind
My Heart Belongs To Daddy
Johnny B. Goode/Shout

DB Singers 1998-99
Costume Colors:
Off-White & Gold
Competition Set
Walkin' On Sunshine
My First Love
Do You Wanna Dance?

Many of the songs we used for both Solitaire and the Dazzle, were also songs we had used at Nogales, which we could order from a publisher, mostly nostalgic fifties and sixties songs. I complemented these sets with songs I had composed or arranged. Solitaire looked like a Dream Street's "*Greatest Hits,*" except that their theme song was brand new! Marquis was also similar to Chamber Singers, with their *Minstrel Medley,* renamed, *Dixieland,* and The *Hills Of Shilo*, but after that, both *Broadway Twenties* and *Marquis A-Go-Go* were basically new material that *we had not used before*. We lit-up the tambourines for *Dixieland*, as we had at Nogales, to give our opening a little more pop! *I absolutely cannot deny the influence of Nogales on Diamond Bar, especially during that first year…* but Doug and I hoped that these groups would become winners immediately, so we figured that this was the best way to go about doing it!

We decided not to use risers with the Diamond Bar groups, since they would be too expensive to order at the start of school, when we had no money. We opted, instead, to make a set of boxes, similar to the Nogales boxes, except for the fact that these would have a bright gold *DB* printed across each one, and they would be painted white, instead of black!

It's unfortunate that we don't have a comprehensive list of the competition results for our show choirs, from that first year at Diamond Bar, so, I will just say that I am about 75% sure that the results I am about to report, *are accurate*. But I can say with *100% accuracy*, that our groups did great in competition, and even won our share, during that first year!

As I remember, the first competition for both Marquis and Solitaire was the *Tournament of Champions* (TOC). This was held at Whittier Union High School. I recall two very energetic and passionate performances that night! In any case, after every group was done competing, and the awards were announced, Solitaire had won *1st Place*, in the Women's Division, by one point over Burbank's group. Marquis earned *2nd Place*, right behind Burbank's mixed group! Our kids were so excited! They were not used to doing so well in competitions! The bus ride home was reminiscent of the bus ride home with the Nogales Chamber Singers after they had won their first trophy (*5th Place*), in 1983! It was all laughter and cheers!

Marquis and Solitaire's second competition was the *Gladstone Review*. This one took place at Citrus College. Rob Hodo was the host. Our kids were still pumped-up about doing so well at TOC, and seemed to exude a lot more confidence this time around! I felt it during warm-up for both groups, as the kids took what we were doing *very seriously,* understanding, that their *determined attitudes* would help them to win! Both of our performances were outstanding, even better than at TOC! When it came time to announce the awards, Rob Hodo stood in the middle of the stage with the results. In the Women's Division, Solitaire earned *2nd Place*, while in the Mixed Division Marquis earned *1st Place*! *Marquis' very first win*! Whereas Solitaire was excited about the results, *Marquis was exuberant*! The results for our two groups were turned around from what they had been at

TOC, where Solitaire had won and Marquis had placed second. This was already shaping up to be a very exciting year for both of them!

By this time, the choir members, parents and school were growing very excited about our achievements in show choir this year! We didn't have a formal booster club, but our parents were very good at helping out and working Diamond Bar High School Bingo, to raise money for the choirs. We even had a parent or two ride the buses to festivals as chaperones. In a nutshell, I was pleased by the helpfulness of these parents!

Our next competition took Marquis to the Arcadia *Big Pow Wow*! The line-up of competitors was steep, but we ultimately placed *3rd!* Although we had just won at Gladstone, the kids were very happy with the result. On the bus ride home, I recall, everyone chatting excitedly about their just past performance, for the entire trip! I think they were beginning to understand that *consistently placing at competitions* was really much more realistic of a goal than *always winning*. But this *understanding* would certainly not stop them from trying!

Glendora High School hosted a competition at Citrus College, and we took both Marquis and Solitaire to participate. Once the smoke had cleared, Solitaire had placed *2nd* in the Advanced Women's Division, while Marquis, earned *their second 1st Place of the year*! It felt as if we could do nothing wrong, at this time. We felt just a little bit *invincible!*

Our next competition was *The Nogales Divisional Show Choir Competition.* I really didn't want to go there, seeing as it was hosted by my former school, because a lot of the kids there were understandably, *still angry with Doug and I for leaving*, but I finally agreed to take only Marquis. Unlike holding the event at Citrus College, as we had done in past years, the new director, who was originally from the mid-west, held it at Plummer Auditorium, in Fullerton, and flew all of his judges out from the mid-west circuit, to adjudicate. Immediately, after arriving, we were asked to delay our performance start time by an hour, so the judges would have time to get dinner. I told our host, in no uncertain terms, that some of my students had another event tonight, so we would have to perform close to our assigned time, or not at all. He was angry, but told me that the judges would eat fast! Well, they returned in about forty-five minutes, and we performed. But then out of nowhere, came some unexpected drama. Our group was seated in the balcony. Apparently, some of the Burbank kids, who were also seated there, complained to the festival host, that *the Diamond Bar kids had been harassing them*. After speaking to our kids in the balcony, they didn't seem to have a clue what Burbank was talking about? I then spoke with their director and assured her that I was certain this was not the case. To be honest with you, aside from this year, I had not heard of any competing Burbank show choir for years! I had absolutely *no idea* why our kids would even think to harass them? But I did learn that their director was a graduate of Burbank's *Burroughs High School*. Perhaps our two schools had a rivalry that I didn't know about? Oh well. I believe there were only *three awards* given out in the Advanced Mixed Division... and we did not receive any of them! If memory serves, after I had a chance to look over our score sheets, *we had finished dead last*! So much for feeling *invincible*! At the time I attributed this result to a possible three reasons:

1) *When a group competes first in a division, if the judges don't know you, and these judges did not, then they tend to often hold back points.*

2) *These judges were all adjudicators from the mid-west where large accompanying bands are the stars of the show. If the judges did not understand our style of show, including a big pause in the action, to sing an a cappella ballad, which they do not do in the mid-west, then that could account for our low scores.*

3) *This competition was rigged from the very beginning, so that we would do poorly, no matter what, for some unknown reason?*

Now, why don't you guess which reason most of the kids in Marquis chose? But, at the end of the day, it was just another competition, wasn't it? I think our kids learned that they probably wouldn't please everyone who adjudicated them at every competition they entered, but as long as they felt proud of themselves and the group… that's really all that mattered! But the whole experience still left a bitter taste in our mouths.

Our final competition of the year was the *Fullerton College Jazz Festival*. Dazzle, our intermediate girls group, joined Marquis and Solitaire to compete for the first time ever! It was a long and exciting day as our groups joined the exciting madhouse that was the Fullerton Festival! When the awards were announced, Dazzle had earned *3rd Place* in the Intermediate Women's Division, Solitaire had earned *1st Place,* in the Advanced Women's Division while Marquis had also earned *1st Place* in the Advanced Mixed Division. I won't lie. The winning felt good!

Even with the disappointing outcome at the Nogales festival, by anyone's standards, the Diamond Bar show choirs had a very successful competition season! But, competing was certainly not all that we did in choir. We also hosted the First Annual *Diamond Bar Spectacular*, a show choir competition, at Citrus College, and we participated with the other performing arts groups at DBHS in presenting *An Evening of the Arts*. We put on a myriad of *sold out* home concerts, hosted Bingo two or three times a year, with our parents, and we traveled twice a year to Disneyland, either to participate in a workshop or to perform! Doug and I were still working at Disneyland at this time, but the fact that my schedule at DBHS was so much busier than it had been at Nogales, led me to quit my Disneyland job, at the beginning of 2000, not because I didn't love it, but for lack of available time. One other event that the choir and I were involved with was the all school musical, put on mostly by the drama department with help from choir, dance and band. "*Joseph and the Amazing Technicolor Dreamcoat*" was 1999's entry, and it proved to be a lot of fun for everyone! Believe it or not, I had never worked on this show before. So, I was able to learn a lot of fun new songs as a result of serving as the music director. Although I don't have a cast list, I do know that a lot of choir kids were involved in the show, including *Lauren Bishop*, who played the narrator, *JoDel Clark, who* played Potiphar's wife, *Pete Buccola*, who played Potiphar, and *Jessie Davis Brown*, who played the Baker! This was the first of seven musicals I collaborated on with the other performing arts teachers at Diamond Bar High School. I really wish I had a copy of this program, to share the entire cast with you… but unfortunately I don't!

The hardworking slate of ***1998-99 student officers*** for each group included:

Marquis
President: *Jude Lopez*
Vice-President: *Nick Yanez*
Sec/ Treas: *Terri Hopper*
Social Chairman: *Ron Im*
Historian: *Tiffanie White*
I.O.C. Rep: *Evelyn Khalemsky*
Special Projects: *Pete Buccola*

Dazzle
President: *Diana Pianalto*
Vice-Pres: *Marissa Rosen*
Secretary: *Kim Forkner*
Treasurer: *Jenny Page*
Historian: *Kristin Hilliard*

Solitaire
President: *Janna Piper*
Vice-President/ Historian: *Mindy Hyman*
Secretary/Treasurer: *Kelly Donnellan*

DB Singers Period 1
President: *Ritika Bhavadwaj*
Vice-Pres: *Kristi Parenti*
Secretary: *Valerie Gero*
Treasurer: *Jennifer Chang*
Historian: *Bethany Franco*

DB Singers Period 6
President: *Jill Hollenbach*
Vice-Pres: *Valerie Banks*
Secretary: *Andrea Brown*
Treasurer: *Lizett Moreira*
Historian: *Jackie Urenia*

The summer of 1999 came quickly. Doug and I spent a long time discussing what we should do next, to improve these groups, after working with them for a year? We ultimately decided to implement a single row of risers at the back of the Marquis show, to help our stage pictures appear bigger. We also agreed to shake things up by using boxes for them at times, and to continue using boxes for all of our other groups. Sadly, Kramer Ison, resigned his position as second keyboardist in our band, a position he'd filled perfectly, for the past six years, due to his other activities. We replaced him with the very talented and experienced, *Alan Devries*. Also, a talented member of Marquis, who had graduated in 1999, *Melissa Quigley*, became Doug's new assistant choreographer. We took away one of the two periods of the *Diamond Bar Singers* and added another girls' group, which we decided would compete novice. To stay consistent, we kept the word, *diamond,* in their name. We *creatively* called them, the *Diamondaires.* None of my choral programs at any other high school had ever had their group names so *themed* before. But, when you have a high school named, *Diamond* Bar… the group names are *screaming to be themed*! The competition sets for our show choirs in the year 2000, were:

Marquis 1999-2000
Costume Colors:
Gold & Black
Competition Set
Once Upon A Time
Broadway Celebration
Pop Goes Marquis
Candle On The Water
Summertime Fifties

Dazzle 1999-2000
Costume Colors:
Pink
Competition Set
Gimme Some Lovin'
Stop! In The Name of Love
I Can't Help Falling

Solitaire 1999-2000
Costume Colors: *White, Gold, Yellow Blue & Pink*
Competition Set
My Guy
I Will
Hard Hearted Hannah
I Could Have Danced
Colors Of The Wind
Heartbreaker

Diamondaires 1999-2000
Costume Colors:
Black w/ multicolor specks
Competition Set
Masquerade
Hernando's Hideaway
A Dream Is A Wish
Show Me The Way
Brand New Day

Notorious 1999-2000
Costume Colors: *Hawaiian Shirts*
Competition Set
Johnny B. Goode/ Pretty Woman
Duke of Earl/ Ghost Riders
R.O C. K. in the U.S.A.

Once again, the *Tournament of Champions* (TOC) was Marquis and Solitaire's first competition. Although they both sang and performed well, when the awards were announced, Solitaire earned *2nd Place*, in the Advanced Women's Division, while Marquis earned *3rd Place* in the Advanced Mixed Division. Both groups, by this time, performed to win, and this outcome, although good, and they appreciated the trophies… *was a bit unsatisfying*.

The next competition for Marquis and Solitaire was the *Glendora High School* event at Citrus College. There were plenty of other competitors for us to contend with, but I noted that by this point, both Marquis and Solitaire felt very confident and did not seem intimidated. After our performances, which were both outstanding, we waited, for the awards ceremony. When the awards were announced, Solitaire picked up another *2nd Place*, with the plaque for *Best Showmanship* while Marquis earned their first, *1st Place* trophy, of the year, and also won the *Best Showmanship* plaque! These performances were definitely stronger than their shows at TOC, last week. But, I got the feeling that neither group was done improving.

The Arcadia *Big Pow Wow* was the third competition for us. Since they still did not offer a women's division, Marquis, was once again, our sole participant. Arcadia, has always been one of the tougher competitions for Doug and my groups to win, due to their music-heavy score sheet. We had won their showmanship plaque a number of times, but had never done better than a second place finish there, and that was only once, by the Nogales Chamber Singers! We had considered that, when we had put this year's competition show together. One of Marquis' strongest points was their well-balanced and tone-filled choral sound. With that in mind, we opened the show with several beautiful songs from Cinderella, which were designed to leave no doubt that this was a quality vocal ensemble! That night, we sang and performed extremely well, and we really stressed to the kids that *they had to be singers first*, performers second. Soon, the awards were announced. Marquis earned *1st Place* and the plaque for *Best Showmanship*! Wow! For these kids, this was only their second season with Doug and I, so they were just excited for another win. But for Doug and I, we had faithfully been bringing groups here for over ten years, and it felt so good to finally be able to say, "*We won at Arcadia*!"

Our next competition was at *Riverside City College* (RCC). I had not brought groups here lately, due to their policy of multiplying every group's showmanship score by .8, to make sure that those show points didn't count too much in the group's final score. The host once threatened to have his adjudicators sit backwards during all of the performances, of the competition, so that they would not be influenced by *what they saw*, only by *what they heard*! The truth is, I greatly admired the director of RCC for *standing behind his beliefs*. But, being a performer myself, in musical theatre, I just did not agree with his assessment of the value of the show. After all, isn't this *show* choir? Well, this year, I brought our newest group, the Diamondaires, to compete, since they needed a place to go. The girls were very nervous as they entered the warm-up room. I told them to just sing and perform like they had been practicing! Their songs and choreography were the perfect level for these young novice performers. The problem was, of course, they had *very little experience competing*. In any case, they went out there and did a nice job. I congratulated them as they stepped off stage. They were still, terribly nervous as they waited for the awards to be announced. In the end, in the Novice Women's Division, Diamondaires placed *3rd*! You would have thought they had *won*, by their uncontrollable screaming, after the announcement! You see? Show choir results are *so relative*! For a new group, like Diamondaires, just having their name called, was enough. To me, that seemed very healthy!

Next, we participated in the *Gladstone Review*! As usual, Rob Hodo was a perfect host, and every competitor there, seemed to be very relaxed. Our kids in Solitaire and in Marquis were more than ready to perform once their times finally came! There is nothing like being relaxed before a competition performance. Some directors swear that you've got to *rile your group up during warm-up*, prior to their performance, in order to focus their energy. But I disagree. I did that for a number of years, and I think it wasted my group's energy for the stage, resulting in less passionate performances. I had learned, by this point in my career, that festivals like this, which were relaxed, led to the best performances, *if your students remained quietly focused.* Just to prove that point, *both groups had outstanding performances that night!* When the awards were announced Solitaire earned *2nd Place for the third consecutive competition* and were awarded the *Best Showmanship* plaque in the Advanced Women's Division. Marquis, meanwhile, earned their *third consecutive 1st Place* trophy and the plaque for *Best Showmanship* in the Advanced Mixed Division! If Marquis had one goal, which they had not achieved yet, it was to win the *Musicianship plaque*, one of these days. If Solitaire had one goal, it was to figure out why they apparently always came up a little short in competitions this year? *Three, 2nd place finishes in a row*, was very nice, but unfortunately, *"very nice"* was not their goal!

Our next festival was at *Upland High School*. Diamond Bar hadn't attended this one yet, because when we had competed there with Nogales, we sometimes felt that the adjudication was unreliable, and therefore *we never knew exactly how to prepare for it*? But, this was a new year, and Dazzle needed someplace to go! So, they went by themselves to compete at Upland. When we arrived, it was very busy on campus, with groups coming and going. Dazzle was to compete in the Intermediate Women's Division. Some of the girls in this group had competed last year at Fullerton College and placed third. In warm-up, they shared with the other girls some tips concerning what they should do to control their excitement and fear while on stage for the best possible experience! Before long, Dazzle entered the stage and performed their show very well! Their singing was a little young sounding, but they were very musical. When the awards were announced, they had won *4th Place*! Just like Diamondaires, at RCC, they were all very excited, relieved and satisfied! It was a pleasant ride home!

The biggest competition of the year was the *Fullerton College Jazz Festival*! This year, we had four groups entered to compete in all different divisions! Marquis was competing in the Advanced Mixed, Division, Solitaire was competing in the Advanced Women's Division, Diamondaires was competing in the Novice Women's Division and our all boys group, Notorious, was competing in the Men's Division! We had a very busy and exciting day at Fullerton College as we jumped from one performance location to another, which has always been the Fullerton way. After we had all performed, everyone gathered on the large lawn outside the music building, to accommodate the hundreds of show choir kids who were there. In the Novice Women's Division, the Diamondaires were awarded *4th Place*. In the Men's Division, *in their first competition*, Notorious was awarded *1st Place*! In the Advanced Women's Division, Solitaire was awarded *1st Place*! Finally! In the Advanced Mixed Division, Marquis was awarded *2nd Place*! This was a great effort by everyone, resulting in *all four of our groups earning awards*! It's really hard to take show choir awards too seriously, since they are always somewhat subjective. In other words, sometimes you end up receiving or not receiving an award partially because of how the adjudicators felt about you, separate from the score sheet. That's only human. So, I have learned that whether you do poorly or well, you should never overthink the result… *just enjoy the positives inherent in the moment*!

Our final competition of the year, for Marquis and Solitaire, was *The Southern California Show Choir Performance Invitational…* called *So Cal*, for short. Doug and I had last participated in 1997, with our Nogales Chamber Singers and Dream Street Singers. But, since the students in both Marquis and Solitaire wanted to go, as part of a San Diego tour, we decided to do just that! On the day of the festival, we arrived at the event in a large convention hall, with a portable stage set-up at the end. We performed during the day, at our allotted times. Our performances were all good, but a portable stage equipped with a portable sound system, in a huge hall is never going to compare to the facilities in a real theatre. Just the same, our kids worked very hard that day, and in the early evening, gathered together with the other groups, for the announcement of the awards! In the Women's Division, Solitaire received, *4th Place*! In the Mixed Division, Marquis received *2nd Place* with the plaque for *Best Showmanship*! Not bad for our first time! So ended our very successful 2000, competition season, as we returned to the Catamaran Hotel to get on with our choir tour!

We ended the school year by taking a trip to Orlando, for any choir kids who chose to go. I think our group numbered about forty kids, as usual. We, of course, had a great time. My son Alex, who was eight, at the time, also went along. One of his favorite pastimes was teasing some of the girls on the trip. I think that Janae Nafziger and Alyssa Cossey were two of his favorite targets!

Our school musical for the year was *Grease*! *Greg Buccola* played Danny Zucko, *Christine Nelson* played Rizzo, *JoDel Clark* was a Pink Lady, *Jessie Davis Brown* played Jan while *Lauren Bishop Borgogna*, *Jean Bostic* and *Ricky Nelson* were also in the production! Everyone in the cast was very good performing their roles, and this show proved to be great fun! Unfortunately, I do not have the cast list for this one.

Our esteemed student officers for the **1999-2000** school year, included:

Diamond Bar Singers
President: *Angela Perez*
Vice-Pres: *Yolanda Cortez*
Sec/Treas: *Joanna Gonzalez*
Historian: *Mindy Lukens*

Dazzle
President: *Kristy Parenti*
Vice-Pres: *Julia Haager*
Sec/Treas: *Bethany Franco*
Historian: *Noelle Brown & Cynthia Mercado*

Solitaire
President: *Katrina Herrera*
Vice-Pres: *Jessie Davis & Emily Haager*
Secretary: *Natalie Heaton*
Treasurer: *Lillian Chung*
Historian: *Lindsay Farmer, Kim Forkner, Rynicia Wilson & Kris Hilliard*

Marquis
President: *Matt Adams*
Vice-Pres: *Lauren Bishop & Ron Im*
Secretary: *Tiffany White*
Treasurer: *Heidi Hill*
Historian: *Gina Chang*
Spec Proj: *Pete Buccola*
I.O.C. Reps: *Evelyn Khalemsky & Greg Buccola*
Social Chairman: *Ron Im*
Tech: *Stephen Garber*

<u>Diamondaires</u>
President: *Jenny Page*
Vice-President: *Andrea Brown*
Secretary/ Treasurer: *Elysia Collins*
Historian: *Cathy Larson*
Special Projects: *Jill Hollenbach & Michelle McMillan*

At the end of the 1999-2000, school year, our choral program had grown so much in size, at Diamond Bar High School, that the school agreed to add a sixth period for 2000-2001! Our program now consisted of the advanced show choirs *Marquis* and *Solitaire*, intermediate show choirs *Dazzle* and *Diamondaires*, beginning mixed or women's choir, the *Diamond Bar Singers* and the brand new novice women's show choir, called the *Diamondettes*! This was going to be a very special year for us, for yet another reason. Many of the most passionate members of Marquis and Spellbound, as well as our strongest leaders, had been sophomores when Doug and I had first arrived at Diamond Bar, and were now seniors. They were generally *very supportive* of everything we tried to do in the name of improving the program! So, we really wanted to pay them back for their trust, and end their tenure at DBHS in style! *Don Cloud* resigned that summer, to accept the position of choral director at Rowland High School. We knew that we would miss him, but we wished him well. We replaced his position with a young and talented pianist named, *Eric Hendrickson*. We also added an excellent guitar player named *Buddy McMillan*. In that same year, we were fortunate enough to gain two students who played piano very well; *Jeff Tsu*, who was also a member of Marquis, and accompanied the show, in class, when necessary and *Hannah Nam*, a senior, who became our daily accompanist in the Diamond Bar Singers, as well as playing piano alongside Eric, at competitions for Masquerade. Melissa Quigley returned for her second year, serving as Doug's assistant choreographer. Life at Diamond Bar was feeling very good! Each of our talented groups looked eager to learn their shows, and Doug and I were able to do so many different things with our own theatre. Although we had always been blessed with very talented kids wherever we went, we had *never experienced* this type of peripheral support before! The competition sets for the 2001 season included:

Marquis 2000-01
Costume Colors:
Black, Blue & Gold
Competition Set
Marquis In Love
Marquis By The Sea
Marquis Country

Diamondaires 2000-01
Costume Colors:
Black with Rainbow Dots
Competition Set
Magic To Do
Roll With It/ Moonglow
Too Darn Hot
God Help The Outcasts
The Wiz

Solitaire 2000-01
Costume Colors:
Green & Orange
Competition Set
Solitaire Follies
A Chorus Line
Solitaire Sixties

Diamond Bar Singers 2000-01
Costume Colors:
Purple w/ Diamonds
Competition Set
Consider Yourself
Mister Sandman
My Favorite Things
Puttin' On The Ritz
Johnny B. Goode

Dazzle 2000-01
Costume Colors:
Hot Pink w/ Silver
Competition Set
Get Ready
Build Me Up Buttercup
I'm A Woman
A Dream Is A Wish
Reflections
Great Balls of Fire

Diamondettes 2000-01
Costume Colors:
Black w/ Rainbow Dots
Competition Set
Lollipop
Count Your Blessings
Why Do Fools Fall In Love?

Notorious 2000-01

Costume Colors:

Multi-Colored Hawaiian Shirts

Competition Set

I Won't Grow Up

Love Potion Number Nine

Brown Eyed Squirrel

Silhouettes

Bye Bye Love/ Good Lovin'

When I peruse these shows, I vividly remember *what a monster, we had created*! With every choral group, now *competing* at Diamond Bar High School, we had *seven* shows to teach the songs, choreography and performance skills! Going back as far as Norco High School, we always had "*after school choreography rehearsals*" for the advanced show choirs… but what about the other ones? Well, Doug came into classes *twice a week*, and that time had to suffice to learn the choreography in the other five groups! Of course that gave me less time to teach their vocals in preparation for the choreography and for non-dancing concerts like our traditional Christmas concerts. So, we adapted by doing some of the same Christmas songs every year so they would be easier and faster to learn! We also decided that just because one group performed a certain song that was no reason why *another group* could not perform the very same song, within the next year or so. When this happened, we usually had a couple of kids remember the vocals and choreography from the other group, and it helped us to teach it quickly! It seems that every one of our groups was always pressed for time. But this helped create a focused and hard working environment! Just a note on the Marquis and Solitaire shows. We began categorizing Marquis' songs into *three specific medleys* and accompanying each of those medleys with a costume change, beginning with the 2000, competition year. This year, that philosophy applied to Solitaire, as well.

Our first competition of the year, was the Nogales *NDSCC*. We were a little leery about going back to it, after we felt we had been treated so rudely in 1999. However, that director had left his position, prior to the end of that first year, and the new director, seemed to be very nice. So, Marquis and Solitaire opened their 2001 competition season at the Nogales NDSCC! Most of the kids at Nogales whom I had taught... had now graduated. Everyone was friendly and consequently we felt very comfortable there. When the awards were announced, Solitaire earned *1st Place* and both the *Best Showmanship* and *Best Musicianship* plaques in the Advanced Women's Division, while Marquis earned *1st Place* and the *Best Showmanship* plaque in the Advanced Mixed Division! Our kids were, of course, *thrilled* with the outcome, and I was *thrilled* to return to a friendly NDSCC, after our unfortunate 1999 experience! Kudos to the Nogales Choir staff and to all of their wonderful students!

Our second competition, took us to Whittier Union High School, where Marquis and Solitaire competed in *Tournament of Champions* (TOC)! As I remember, both of our groups gave pretty flawless performances, which resulted in a lot of applause and cheering at the end of each performance. In any case, as soon as the awards were announced, Solitaire, had earned a solid *2nd Place* in the Women's Division, while Marquis won *1st Place*, as well as the plaques for *Best Showmanship* and *Best Musicianship*, in the Mixed Division. Both groups were excited about their placements, but Marquis was especially excited about winning the plaque for *Best Musicianship*. According to my records, it was the *first time, in their three years of competing, that they had ever won Best Musicianship*!

The *Hart High School* festival was one we had not attended, in my previous two years at Diamond Bar. It was a very long drive, sometimes as much as two hours, and the adjudicators weren't always friendly. But, we really needed places to go, with so many different Diamond Bar groups competing this year! So, we took Marquis and Solitaire, to compete in the advanced divisions and Diamondaires and Dazzle, to compete together in the intermediate women's! We started competing in the afternoon, but it was not time for the awards until almost midnight, which was sadly becoming the norm, at a lot of competitions. But, the results were worth waiting for! In the Intermediate Women's Division, Dazzle earned *2nd Place* while

Diamondaires earned *1st Place*! In the Advanced Women's Division, Solitaire won *1st Place* and the plaque for *Best Musicianship*! Meanwhile, in the Advanced Mixed Division, Marquis earned *2nd Place*! We were all ecstatic about the results! I didn't hear one complaint as we finally arrived back at Diamond Bar High School at 2:30 am!

Next on our list of competitions was *Glendora High School's* event, at Citrus College. Once again, we brought Marquis and Solitaire to the event. We arrived in the afternoon, took our turns at warming up, and then most of the staff ate dinner at *Sizzler*, not far away. The evening came and both Solitaire and Marquis performed. I'm probably a bit biased, but I thought that both performances were probably the best they had done all year! When the awards were announced, it appeared I was correct in my earlier appraisal of my groups' performances. Solitaire earned *1st Place* along with both plaques for *Best Showmanship* and *Best Musicianship* for the Advanced Women's Division. Marquis, meanwhile, took *1st Place* in the Advanced Mixed Division, along with the *Best Showmanship* plaque! At this point in the year, it was very difficult for me to remember a better collection of competition results than we had amassed so far! Our kids were very excited about their awards, and could not wait until their next competition!

Marquis competed next at the Arcadia *Big Pow Wow*! This was always a tough one, although we had won it last year, and this year, the group *knew that they sang the best they had in three years.* For these reasons, they were very confident. They performed, and walked off stage feeling very good! I knew, for one thing, we had *not gone overtime*, and usually that was my biggest fear at this one. When it came time for the awards to be announced, everyone held hands and grew very focused on Rollie Maxson, who was about to announce the awards. In the end, Marquis earned *2nd Place* and the *Best Showmanship* plaque! It was not exactly what they had hoped for… but it was close! We had a jolly bus ride home!

The next competition was the *Fullerton College Jazz Festival*, which had already played such a huge role in the history of all my prior show choirs! This year we opted to take

Diamondaires, who would compete in the intermediate women's division, Diamondettes, who would compete in the novice division, Marquis, who would compete advanced mixed and Notorious who would compete in the novice mixed division. It was odd, not taking the other groups to Fullerton, like we usually did, but at the same time, it was kind of nice bonding with these four groups, without rushing around all day, like we usually did, when we took everybody! Each group performed and was *very well received by their audiences*, judging from their laughter and applause. That evening, at the awards ceremony, Diamondettes earned *2nd Place* in the Novice Women's Division, and Diamondaires also earned *2nd Place* in the Intermediate Women's Division! Notorious, also earned *2nd Place,* in the Novice Mixed Division, and the audience *just loved them*! I had never seen such cheering from our groups, in my life! To say that they were excited doesn't begin to tell the story! It made me glad that we had decided to bring these groups on this special trip! For Marquis, however, it was a different story. We put on a great performance to a cheering crowd of *standing room only* inside the Fullerton College Campus Theatre. But, at the Awards Ceremony, that evening… *Marquis did not place in the top five*! After my initial surprise, I decided to check the scores and find out what we had done wrong? After a brief perusal, I found that one judge, had scored us *just low enough*, that when added to the much higher scores of the other two judges, our combined score, placed us sixth… *just out of trophy range*! Keeping in mind that Marquis had won competitions *a record five times, throughout the year*, also earning most of the plaques for *Best Showmanship* and even a *Best Musicianship plaque*, I was anxious to read this adjudicator's comments, and find out why, in fact, they had seen fit to give us such low scores? To put it in a nutshell, this person assessed the show as being *glitzy*, with *wonderful costumes, good singing* and *fun choreography… but entirely without a soul!* They accused our kids of performing *without feeling anything*, and Doug and I of *selling out*! They said quite a bit more, but this was their gist. I actually saved those score sheets and posted them in my office for quite some time, until Doug asked me to throw them away. He claimed they gave the office bad *feng shui*! Well,

I complained that next week to the dean of fine arts at Fullerton College. I gave him a copy of the score sheets and told him that the adjudicator had *not* scored us according to the categories on the score sheet, as they were supposed to, but had been *entirely subjective* with their scores and comments instead, to the point where they were insulting! The dean apologized, and told me that he would take care of it! That whole experience left a bad taste in everyone's mouth, but *a day gone is a day gone*, whether you win or you lose… so, after addressing the problem, it felt time to move on.

Next, the *Southern California Vocal Association*, or SCVA, for short, hosted their show choir competition. I didn't take my groups to this one very often, because it came so late in the year, but this year, with so many groups to find competitions for, I kind of needed it! It was an all-afternoon competition on a Saturday, and we entered Diamondaires into the intermediate women's division along with Dazzle, while the Diamond Bar Singers and Diamondettes were entered into the novice women's division. I remember spending many hours taking my groups on and off stage, and then watching all of their other competitors perform. I really did not know what to expect, because SCVA is really about singing, while hosting show choir festivals was a *relatively recent development for them.* I was impressed by the demeanor of all the kids in the audience, however, because unlike most show choir competitions I had witnessed throughout the year, the kids from *these groups* seemed to be *very well behaved*! When it came time for the awards, all of our girls, excitedly held hands. In the Novice Women's Division, the Diamond Bar Singers earned *4th Place*, while Diamondettes earned *1st Place*! In the Intermediate Women's Division, Dazzle earned *3rd Place*, and Diamondaires earned *2nd Place*! The girls were happy with their awards, *especially Diamondettes*, and I was happy that we had all competed together, and bonded! Just as a side note, it was kind of fun to have won a *1st*, *2nd*, *3rd* and a *4th* at the very same competition! You don't see that everyday!

Now, as we neared the end of the festival season, Marquis and Solitaire participated in a new competition in Ramona, California, called the *Ramona Jamboree*, hosted by Ramona's new director, (formerly of Gladstone HS), *Rob Hodo*! My groups, back at Nogales had competed a few times against Ramona, when we used to compete in San Diego nearly every year. However, I couldn't tell you where Ramona was located… *and apparently, neither could our bus drivers?* So, under a dense fog, with pitch-black skies, we drove through rural fields, *forever it seemed*, until we finally saw a sign that told us which way to turn, to get to the high school. The trip there, took us well over two hours, and we were barely on time! But, the competition was well worth attending, as Marquis earned *1st Place* as well as both plaques for *Best Musicianship* and *Best Showmanship*, and Solitaire earned *2nd Place*, right behind them, in the same division! Marquis and Solitaire's performances were relaxed and yet passionate at the same time! It was a thrill for me to watch them, and also for our supportive band of parents who had come along as chaperones. Luckily, we found a freeway, on the way back, close to Ramona High School, and we got home in just over an hour! Sometimes the most unlikely competitions can actually turn out to be some of your most memorable!

Our final competition of 2001, took us to a brand new event at Disneyland, which I believe was called the *Disneyland Show Choir Spectacular*! This competition, was actually set-up more like the mid-west events, with the awards ranging from *Fourth Runner Up to First Runner Up*, and with the top score getter, among *all of the competitors* in both the mixed and the women's division, being crowned *Grand Champion.* I had always thought these award placement titles made an event seem just a little bit more exciting for all of the competitors, although I have never used this system for any of my own competitions. The best part is they always make you sound as if you came in *one place higher* than you actually did. For example, *First Runner Up* is actually Second Place… but your award title has *first* in it, which tends to make everyone involved feel better! As an aside, during my first two years at Diamond Bar High School, our principal had never permitted the choirs to have an end of the year banquet *off-campus*, as we had been doing for years, at Nogales. This "reward" was only given to sports teams who were champions of their league! Several choir leaders argued with the principal that show choir didn't have a *definitive league to win…* so he relented. His deal was that if we won this final competition at Disneyland, we could hold our banquets off-campus! How's that for instant motivation! Well, both Marquis and Solitaire did, in fact, perform very well, on the Tomorrowland Stage, earning hearty applause from the audience. There were a lot of quality groups competing at Disneyland, but one particular mixed group, from San Diego, had me a little concerned. They sang pretty well, but their Pirate themed show was complete with a lot of *very impressive physical movement*, mostly using poles. The audience went crazy for them, and there was absolutely nothing we could do about it. It seemed funny to me, really. My groups of the past had won plenty of competitions without being scored the best singing group in the room, based on our energetic performances. That night, I realized that we would probably score higher than them on vocals, but based on the audience's reaction to their performance… we would most likely be *beaten by their show*! I think they call that, *what goes around, comes around*! Sure enough, Solitaire and Marquis each *won* their respective divisions, resulting in *1st Runner-Up* awards, while the single *Grand Champion* of the competition was Vista High School, from San Diego! Aside from obviously being a little disappointed at our final rankings in the competition, luckily, being the *First Runner-Ups*, proved to be just enough to hold our banquet off-campus! The students showed the principal the word *first,* engraved on both of their trophies, and explained that they had both come in *first in their divisions*, or league… and he gladly granted our request! The mid-west style of awards, had indeed, presented us with an unlikely gift! We held our first off-campus banquet for Marquis and Solitaire at Kellogg West, on the campus of Cal Poly, Pomona. The other Diamond Bar choral groups, continued to hold their banquet in the school's Performing Arts Center, as they always had!

Our school musical, for the year was *Crazy For You*, which is definitely my favorite musical we'd put on during my seven years at Diamond Bar! Peter Bland directed, Doug Kuhl choreographed while I taught the music. In the story, two of the male leads need to be similar enough in body shape, facial features and height to both play the *same role*, one, as the real character (Mr. Zangler), while the other is the imposter (Bobby). We were *lucky* enough to have fraternal twins, *Greg and Pete Buccola*, in choir and drama... and they executed those two roles perfectly! *Lauren Bishop*, another choir member, played Polly, the female lead, a sassy but likeable "cowgirl" to a tee! Come to think of it, there were a lot of choir kids in that show, and they were all great! The multi-talented *Janae Nafziger West* was cast as Mitzy, the lead tap dancer. We added two solos to her part, and they were both terrific! Anyway, we had so much fun watching this show every night that I don't believe that any of us on the staff, ever wanted the show to end! I was fortunate enough to get the cast list from *Spike Abeyta*! It's listed below:

2001 Cast List for *"Crazy For You!"*

Bobby Child: *Pete Buccola*
Bela Zangler: *Greg Buccola*
Lank Hawkins: *Ricky Nelson*
Everett Baker: *Kyle Roberts*
Polly Baker: *Lauren Bishop*
Irene Roth: *Christine Nelson*
Eugene Fodor: *Joe Janesin*
Patricia Fodor: *Jean Bostic*
Mother: *Marissa Rosen* **Tess:** *Veronica Fitzgerald*
Moose: *Jason Meeks* **Wyatt:** *Kris Gunawan*
Custus: *Mike Merola* **Billy:** *Nick Cervantes*
Patsy: *Deanna Badosa* **Perkins:** *Heather Calmes*
Chaffeur: *Tyson Tagaloa* **Pete:** *Charles Trinidad*
Jimmy: *Tyson Tagaloa*

Follies Girls

Ashley Benson • Kelly Brashear • Jenna D'Abusco
Shannon Gidley • Janae Nafziger • Jacque Nelson,
Jeanne Myers • Jill Ramos • Dana Siemsen

Cowgirls

Alice Chiu • Alyssa Cossey • Katie Rockwood
Kristine Songco

Cowboys

Nick Cervantes • Kris Gunawan • Jason Meeks
Mike Merola

Chorus

Jillian Avery, Zahir Bazra, Sarah Brander, Heather Calmes, Megan Carey, Jenny Chen, Sherry Chen, Alice Chu, Brianna Fidel, Laci Flinders, Tracy Holmes, Erica Louie, Chris Love, Michelle McMillan, Natasha Menta, Mike Merola, Whitney Miller, Heather O'Shea, Ogonna Owu, Wes Paul, Angelica Petris, Lisa Ralls, Ashley Rush, Edwin Salveron, Charles Trinidad, Tara Vorkink, Rachel Weiss, Rynicia Wilson, Mona Yakak, Laney Zhao

In the spring of 2001, the seniors, from one of the most successful show choir years in Diamond Bar High School history, *graduated.* It wasn't just the trophies they'd won, or their positive attitudes, or their leadership skills, or their terrific energy, or even their drive to succeed that made them so special. It was their *willingness to follow Doug and I,* even when they didn't really know where we were taking them… *it was their trust*! I wish I could have found rosters for Marquis and Solitaire from this school year, to let both groups, but especially the seniors, know how much Doug and I appreciated sharing our first three years at Diamond Bar High School with them. It was amazing what we accomplished together! When I think about it, these first three years could have been tumultuous with infighting and consequently led us to getting less done in rehearsals with far less success in competitions! But thankfully, it didn't go that way. It takes a special group of kids to blindly trust their new directors, and these graduating seniors led the way! Thank you!

Our illustrious student officers for **2000-01** were:

Diamondaires
President: *Melanie Dilger*
Vice-Pres: *Andrea Brown, Latanya Banks & Marissa Flores*
Sec/Treas: *Jill Hollenbach*
Hist/Lib: *Valerie Banks & Elysia Collins*

Dazzle
President: *Letty Garcia*
Vice-Pres: *Alanna Flores, Jennifer Kumala & Cynthia Mercado*
Sec/Treas: *Jill Hollenbach*
Hist/Lib: *Toni Kelley*

Marquis
President: *Lauren Bishop*
Vice-Pres: *Pete Buccola, Janae Nafziger, Greg Buccola & Alyssa Cossey*
Sec/Treas: *Amanda Neufeld*
Hist/Lib: *Jenny Layton*
Tech Master: *Nick Gagner*
I.O.C. Rep: *Harmony Hill*

Solitaire
Pres: *Christine Lamorena*
Asst. Pres: *Marisa Rosen*
Vice-Pres: *Kristen Hilliard, Jenny Layton & Emily Haager*
Sec/Treas: *Zehra Seyed*
Hist/Lib: *Rynicia Wilson*
Tech Master: *Alice Chiu*

Diamond Bar Singers
President: *Jennifer Devera*
Sec/Treas: *Samantha Quimpo*
Hist/Lib: *Mona Yamak*

Diamondettes
President: *Lizett Moreira*
VP: *Nicole Rubalcaba*
Secretary/Treasurer: *Felicia Hernandez*
Historian/Librarian: *Stephanie Ramos*

CHAPTER 8

Diamond Bar High School... 2001-2005... Surprise Rebuilding!

The 2001-2002 school year represented our fourth year at Diamond Bar High School! We had very high expectations, due to all of the seniors we were fortunate enough to have in Marquis and Solitaire, whom had spent the *past three years in choir with us*! This was to be *our greatest year at Diamond Bar, yet*! However, before the year began, several of our strongest girls from Marquis, suddenly *quit*, citing 'scheduling conflicts' as the reason for dropping choir. I recalled that the very same thing had happened years ago when I had taught at Norco High School, and what had followed was a *very tough year*! Well, I scratched my head and realized that there was probably something going on, but I figured that making a *national case* out of it would only make things worse! So, I opted not to worry about it, but to patiently wait, instead, to find out if anything serious unfolded. Our band continued to evolve, as due to Eric Hendrickson's surprise resignation, just after the school year began, *Hannah Num*, now became our everyday accompanist! Hannah was joined by Bo Eder on the drums, the return of Kramer Ison on second keyboard, student Jeff Hsu, on keyboard bass, and the talented Buddy McMillan, returning for a second year, on guitar. Melissa Quigley also returned for her third year as Doug's assistant choreographer, assisted by Kris Hilliard. We once again revamped our family of choirs. We introduced a new intermediate mixed show choir (which doubled as a concert choir) called *Diamondtones*. We felt that we had too many women's groups competing, so we dropped Dazzle, and kept the other groups intact. Doug and I had prepared competition sets for Marquis and Solitaire, over the summer that once again, featured *very different segments*, with a dramatic costume change for each one! The competition sets for all of the groups, included:

Marquis 2001-02
Costume Colors:
Yellow & Blue
Competition Set
Shall We Dance
Hollywood Medley
I'm A Believer

Notorious 2001-02
Costume Colors:
Hawaiian Shirts
Competition Set
Get Ready
Right Here Waiting For You
Doctor Looney
Centerfold

Solitaire 2001-02
Costume Colors:
Unknown
Competition Set
Nostalgic Solitaire
Classic Solitaire

Diamondettes 2001-02
Costume Colors:
Pink with White Polka Dots
Competition Set
My Guy
Heatwave
Tears In Heaven
Good Golly Miss Molly

Diamondaires 2001-02
Costume Colors:
Black
Competition Set
Volcano
Too Darn Hot
My Funny Valentine
Respect
Over The Rainbow
Shout

Diamond Bar Singers 2001-02
Costume Colors:
Unknown
Competition Set
There Is A New Day A-Comin'
Lullaby of Broadway
Starmaker
Joseph and The Dreamcoat

<u>Diamondtones 2001-02</u>

Costume Colors: *Hot Pink w/ Music Notes*

<u>Competition Set</u>

Yesterday Once More
Rock Around The Clock
Crazy Little Thing Called Love
Dust In The Wind
Mony Mony

As Marquis rehearsed, during the fall of 2001, in preparation for the 2002 competition season, Doug and I quickly noticed two *concerning behaviors* about them, that may have been tied-in to the mystery of the several kids dropping?

1) *They lacked the drive of the past three seasons, as their focus during rehearsals tended to wane.*

2) *The group seemed a bit more immature, and opinionated, going so far as openly complaining about the Gershwin songs in our opening medley, because they had never heard of them?*

This was definitely a younger group than last year's, with a lot of new faces, but… we attributed these two "*concerns*" to the *additional time it always requires to train a new group*, and moved on. Our other groups seemed to be on target, if you didn't factor in the slower rehearsals, due in large part to the substantial number of new members they also had.

Marquis' first competition was hosted by Brea, *Festival 2002*, at Citrus College for advanced mixed groups. Our show was good, but unfortunately, flawed. We had lost a lot of strong singers at the end of the past year, and we were still developing this year's sound. Our a cappella ballad, *Their Hearts Were Full Of Spring*, was simply too difficult for this group to handle, and our performance of it demonstrated that! Still, we walked out of the Brea festival having earned *2nd Place* and the plaque for *Best Showmanship*! However, singers from other groups, who were already active on social media, claimed that *we did not deserve 2nd Place*! This upset our young group, so Doug and I immediately got busy strengthening the show's problems. We substituted *The Search*, a nice a cappella, that was not too difficult, for our previous one, *Their Hearts Were Full Of Spring*. We hoped that would do the trick!

Our next competition, the *Ramona Jamboree*, was one we had *dominated* last year. Once again, Marquis and Solitaire went as a team, competing in the festival's only division. Both groups performed well, only maybe not as well as last year. When the awards were announced, Marquis had earned *2nd Place* and won the *Best Showmanship* plaque, while Solitaire earned *3rd Place*, right behind them. I can't recall the name of the school that beat us... but we were definitely getting the feeling that this year's performances were *not quite as impressive* to the adjudicators, as they had been last year. So, in preparation for our third competition, Doug and I decided to add the power ballad, *Never Walk Alone*, to the end of Marquis' second medley, to add some *pizzazz* to the show! We had several possible soloists in our group, for this, and had found this song to be very moving when we had performed it previously at Nogales. It was pretty rhythmic toward the end, and as we found in rehearsal, *rhythm was definitely not one of Marquis' strong points!*

Our third competition was a big one! We were taking five groups, including Marquis and Solitaire, to the festival at *Riverside City College* (RCC), now run by a *new director*. As soon as I had heard about RCC having a new director, I called her, and explained our problem with the RCC score sheets to her (multiplying each group's showmanship score by .8 to make it less) and she agreed with me that it did not accurately reflect the judges' evaluations! As a result of our conversation... she removed that rule from the scoring. *I finally felt vindicated*, after going round and round with the former director, about how unfair this rule really was! We arrived in early afternoon, and began competing almost immediately. The Diamondettes were first. They were young and scared, but pulled off a very enjoyable performance in novice women. Diamondaires were next, and they likewise did well in the intermediate women's division. Then followed the brand new, Diamondtones who were very fun to watch in the intermediate mixed division. Solitaire was next. There were a lot of strong competitors in their division, including Arcadia New Spirit, who always did well here, but Solitaire, although not dominant, did very well. Finally, it was time for Marquis to perform. They took the stage, and everything seemed great… until, *Never Walk Alone* reached that rhythmic ending. I'm not sure what happened, whether the drums sped up or the kids did, but for about thirty excruciating seconds, *there was chaos on the stage*, as the kids fought to get back on beat. The most disturbing part was witnessing a number of the kids visibly and audibly *breaking character*, on the stage, by beginning to laugh. We finished the show, and I had the terrible feeling that with so many great competitors, any group that made a major flaw like that, was unlikely to place. When the competition ended and the awards were announced, our groups had placed, as follows. The Diamondettes earned *2nd Place* in the Novice Women's Division, the Diamondaires earned *2nd Place* in the Intermediate Women's Division, the Diamondtones earned *2nd* Place in the Intermediate Mixed Division, Solitaire earned *3rd Place* in the Advanced Women's Division and Marquis earned *3rd Place* in the Advanced Mixed Division, but was penalized, and ultimately placed 4th due to a *performance overtime of 25 seconds*! Well, as much as I hated getting another overtime penalty, the results here had been pretty good. Although none of our groups had won, we had all been very close. I'm afraid that our days of dominating our competitors were probably over, *at least for now*. This year was turning out to be a classic *rebuilding year…* but in spite of that, our young kids were doing *just fine in competition*! The question now, was whether or not any of our groups could finish the year with at least *one win*?

It just so happened that the former choir director of Burbank High School, now worked at *Azusa Pacific University*, and decided to host a show choir competition in Pasadena, during her first year there! While Marquis did not participate, we sent Solitaire to compete in the Advanced Women's Division! The APU event, took place in the beautiful, vintage *Pasadena Civic Auditorium*, where Doug and I had taken a few groups to perform in the past. Solitaire was slated to perform last. They entered the stage and began their performance. It was a really good performance, that night, easily their best. All of a sudden, something fell from above, and landed with a crash, on the stage!

As I remember, it was a *very heavy Fresnel light*. During its drop, it had fallen between several girls on stage, even grazing one of their heads! But not a performer on that stage flinched or missed one beat of the choreography! It was amazing to watch and I was so very proud of all of those girls! Afterwards, I checked on the one girl who had been hit in the head, one of our seniors, *Alyssa Cossey*. She was lying down on the floor of the lobby, when I found her, complaining of a headache, with a wet cloth, on her head but otherwise, seemed to be okay. Solitaire had experienced an unexpected problem tonight, as Marquis had at RCC… *but they had handled it decidedly better*! Perhaps Solitaire was the more advanced of the two groups, this year? That question was soon answered as the awards were announced. Solitaire had earned *1st Place* and both plaques for *Best Showmanship* and *Best Musicianship*!

Next came the *Fullerton College Jazz Festival*. We decided to take five of our groups this year, Marquis, Diamondaires, Diamondtones, Notorious and Diamondettes. It was one of those hectic days we had grown accustomed to, at the Fullerton festival, but, every group performed well, and the kids had a lot of fun *playing hooky* from school! When the awards were announced, Diamondettes earned *4th Place* in the Novice Women Division, Diamondtones earned *5th Place* in the Intermediate Mixed Division, Diamondaires earned *2nd Place* in the Intermediate Women's Division, Notorious, in their first outing of the year, earned *4th Place* in the Men's Division, and Marquis earned *3rd Place* in the Advanced Mixed Division. Every one of our groups placed, but aside from Diamondaires who had placed *2nd* at RCC and *2nd* at Fullerton, and Marquis, who had placed *3rd* at RCC and 3rd at Fullerton, every other group of ours, that was at RCC, *placed lower at Fullerton*! This was just one of those years where the spirit of each of our groups wanted to win, but unfortunately, *we still had a ways to go* until we became more *consistent in competition*! In any case, I told the kids how proud I was of them, and that Diamondettes, Diamondtones and Diamondaires still had the SCVA Competition to try to add to their awards, in just two weeks! Notorious was done competing for the year, while Marquis still had one more with Solitaire.

The *Tournament of Champions* (TOC) was next for Marquis and Solitaire. But, while Solitaire had come on strong toward the end of the season, winning impressively at the Azusa Pacific University event in Pasadena, Marquis had settled for two seconds and two thirds. I don't mean to sound arrogant, like we automatically deserved to win everywhere we went, but Marquis had pretty much dominated much of their competition from 1999-2001. This Marquis squad, *which struggled a bit in competition*, was new and unpredictable to all of us! At rehearsal, on Monday, I told the kids in Marquis that we were changing our power ballad from *Never Walk Alone* to *Don't Cry Out Loud,* a dependable arrangement that I had used since 1980, for my very first Nogales Chamber Singers. I don't think that even one person was disappointed with that decision. Our competitors at TOC were tough, and the way I figured it, we needed a strong performance *just to earn 3rd place*! Since *Never Walk Alone* always seemed to have problems, replacing it with *Don't Cry Out Loud*, almost seemed like a no-brainer! The night of TOC arrived. The event, for some reason, was being held at Citrus College, for the first time! Solitaire took the stage first. Their show could not have gone better! After a while, Marquis took the stage. Their performance was easily the best of the year, with *Don't Cry Out Loud* earning them a standing ovation! When the awards were read, Solitaire had earned *1st Place* in the Women's Division. Everyone cheered. In a difficult year, Solitaire had now won twice! Meanwhile, Marquis earned *3rd Place*! Pandemonium! The cheering was deafening as our entire Marquis group rushed the stage, trying to accept the award (this had been planned)! It was the perfect ending to both Solitaire and Marquis' competition year. Solitaire continued their winning ways… and the third place trophy earned by Marquis… *was their most meaningful trophy of the year!*

But wait! The competition year was not completely over yet! Diamondaires, Diamondtones, Diamondettes and the Diamond Bar Singers (their only competition of the year) still had the *SCVA* (Southern California Vocal Association) Competition to give it their one last try! It had been a lot of fun last year, taking these choirs out to this competition. But this year, our groups *seemed a lot more serious*, with another year's experience under their belts! I believe they had *come here to compete*! Each of our groups performed on the stage, and at the end of each show, I was so proud, and it showed! People around me must have thought I was crazy. I didn't care. I told each of our groups how well I thought they had sung and performed. I told them not to get too hung-up on what trophies they would win or not win, because their trophy, no matter what it was, didn't compare to my thrill of watching them in performance today! I was trying to prepare them for anything. Soon it was time for the awards ceremony. Diamondettes earned *3rd Place* with the plaque for *Best Showmanship* in the Novice Women's Division, Diamond Bar Singers, in that same Novice Women's Division, earned *2nd Place,* in the Intermediate Mixed Division, Diamondtones earned *1st Place* and both plaques for *Best Showmanship* and *Best Musicianship*, Diamondaires, in the Intermediate Women's Division, *also earned 1st Place* and both plaques for *Best Showmanship* and *Best Musicianship*! Wow!

I learned more from the 2002 competition year, than I had from all three of my other years at Diamond Bar High School, *combined*! I'm afraid that earlier in the year, I had gotten too involved in the *trials and tribulations* of a rebuilding Marquis to notice something very important… Spellbound, Diamondaires and Diamondtones had *won* competitions this year, while Notorious, Diamondettes and Diamond Bar Singers were close behind. Marquis had a very good rebuilding year, and I was very proud of them, especially at the end. But, it took me a while to notice that our other groups were already competitive! When you are given the role of leader, it's very important to keep tabs on the growth of *everyone*, instead of spending most of your energy fixating on the troubles of one. Well, we're never too old to learn, I guess!

Our school musical for 2002 was *The Music Man*! Doug Kuhl continued serving in the role of choreographer. This show was double cast, and both sets of leads (Alyssa Cossey/Nick Cervantes and Shayne Stephen/Ricky Nelson) were terrific! As with all of the school musicals, the kids in choir were well represented throughout the cast! The entire cast for this outstanding production, directed by *Peter Bland*, choreographed by *Doug Kuhl* and musically directed by yours truly, is listed in its entirety on the next page. Where two names are listed for one role, the role has been double cast.

The 2002 Cast List for *"The Music Man"*

Charlie Cowell: *Ryan Satin/ Edwin Salveron*
Conductor: *Ray Ayers*
Harold Hill: *Ricky T. Nelson/ Nick Cervantes*
Mayor Shin: *Kyle Roberts*
The Quartet:
Ewart Dunlop: *Kris Gunawan*
Oliver Hix: *Spike Abeyta*
Jacey Squire: *Tyson Tagaloa*
Olin Britt: *Chase Rebensdorf*
Marcellus Washburn: *Robert Waters/ Joe Janesin*
Tommy Djilas: *John Venti/ Jeff Buccola*
Marian Paroo: *Shayne Stephen/ Alyssa Cossey*
Mrs Paroo: *Sarah Weiss/ Sally Jacob*
Amaryllis: *Jayci Stephen/ Chelsea Burton*
Winthrop Paroo: *Levi Flinders/ J.J. Burton*
Eulalie Shinn: *Rachel Weiss/ Kristin Lindemulder*
Zaneeta Shinn: *Gloria Cheng/ Jessica Hessom*
Gracie Shinn: *Jaydin Stephen*
Alma Hix: *Michelle McMillan*
Maud Dunlop: *Deanna Badosa*
Ethel Toffelmier: *Heather O'Shea*
Mrs. Squires: *Katie Rockwood*
Constable Locke: *Joshua Ard*

Pick-A-Little Ladies

Jill Avery • Deanna Badosa • Amanda Burton
Heather Calmes • Megan Carey • Laci Flinders
Becca Guiza • Kimberly Horcher • Kayla Keel
Michelle McMillan • Natasha Mehta • Heather O'Shea,
Katie Rockwood • Vienna Valdez • Mutiara Williams

Ensemble (Townspeople)

Ray Ayers, Aleece Arnold, Sarah Batistelli, Ashley Benison, Sarah Brander, Aleese Carlson, Linda Chang, Shana Dahlin, Jenna D'Abusco, Lauren Davis, Megan Dong, Cheyenne Flinders, Stefanie Garcia, Shannon Gidley, Kimi Gortner, Jaclyn Lindemulder, Shawn Reyes, Kelsi Roberts, Shae Saldana, Katrina Stevens, Tina Thomas, Claire Tratnyek, Lesley Wu

Our outstanding student officers for choir in **2001-02** were:

Diamondaires
President: *Melanie Dilger*
Vice-Pres: *Andrea Brown & Samantha Quimpo*
Sec/Treas: *Jennifer Devera*
Historian: *Steph Delarosa & Felicia Hernandez*

Diamondtones
President: *Sheri Vernon*
Vice-Pres: *Alyssa Cossey & Jackie Wissman*
Sec/Pres: *Aleece Arnold*
Hist: *Stephanie Ramos, Ashley Alvarez & Natasha Tomovich*

Diamond Bar Singers
President: *Stephanie Carver*
Vice-Pres: *Michelle Smith & Sabrina Jangda*
Sec/Treas: *Kandace Moore*
Historian: *Leann Saplan*

Notorious
President: *Rick Nelson*
VP: *Joe Janesin*

Marquis
President: *Alyssa Cossey*
Vice-Pres: *Rick Nelson, Amanda Neufeld & Angela Reimer*
Sec/Treas: *Katie Rockwood & Shayne Stephen*
I.O.C. Rep: *Kris Gunawan*

Solitaire
President: *Kim Forkner*
Vice-Pres: *Katie Allen, Jessie Davis & Brianna Fidel*
Secretary: *Zehra Seyed*
Treas: *Michelle McMillan*
Historian: *Kristine Songco*

<u>Diamondettes</u>
President: *Sarah Batistelli*
Vice-President: *Caroline Yenydunyeyan*
Secretary/Treasurer: *Christine Le*
Historian: *Erica Hanson*

The 2002-2003 school year came upon us in no time, and Doug and I were ready! We had spent a lot of time designing and arranging our groups' new shows. What was great was that we had almost 20 years worth of songs from our Nogales days, as well as a lot of new ones, we had already used at Diamond Bar, to choose from. Yes, if you go through all of our competition sets, for all of our groups, you will find a number of repeats, some titles even appear in shows often! But, as you already know, Doug and I believed that just because a song had been performed before, by one of our groups, *it didn't mean we should not use it again*! Sometimes, a particular song just makes a set complete! Melissa Quigley was back for her fourth year as assistant choreographer, assisted by 2002 graduate, Alyssa Cossey. Buddy McMillan had moved on, as our guitar player, but the rest of the band, Hannah Nam, Bo Eder, Kramer Ison and Jeff Hsu, was still intact. The program was continuing to grow, but the Diamond Bar Singers stopped being a show choir, and morphed into a traditional Chamber Singers group. The competition sets we chose for each show choir included:

<u>Marquis 2002-03</u>
Costume Colors: *Rainbow, Pink & Red*
<u>Competition Set</u>
Children of the Revolution- Part One (Beatles songs)
Children of the Revolution- Part Two (songs from the film, Moulin Rouge)

Solitaire 2002-03
Costume Colors:
Unknown
Competition Set
Solitaire Country
Solitaire Broadway
Solitaire 80s

Notorious 2002-03
Costume Colors:
Hawaiian Shirt
Competition Set
Day-o
Sea Cruise
Farmer Tan
Beach Boys
My Heart Will Go On
Fins

Diamondaires 2002-03
Costume Colors:
Blue
Competition Set
Turn Around
Diamondaires Theme
Fever
Too Darn Hot
Colors of the Wind
Devil With The Blue Dress

Diamondtones 2002-03
Costume Colors:
Unknown
Competition Set
Twinkle Twinkle Little Star
Trickle Trickle
Let's Hear It For The Boy
Blue Moon
Teenager In Love
We Go Together

Diamondettes 2002-03
Costume Colors: *Unknown*
Competition Set
Please Mister Postman
Movin' On
When Will I Be Loved
Great Balls Of Fire

Marquis was reloaded with both talent and experience, and we had high expectations for them. On a special note, *Kelsey South*, our next-door neighbor in Diamond Bar, until 1993, when we moved to Brea, was a very talented athlete and an exceptional student, but to my knowledge, had never shown a desire to perform. Surprisingly, she *auditioned at the end of 2002* and was accepted into Marquis, for 2002-03, her senior year! She was really good, too! Such energy! Doug and I both enjoyed working with her throughout the year. Marquis really seemed destined for something great! The only group that we were concerned about, at all, was Diamondtones. They were a mixed group, but the boys sang very softly. So, since they were required to sing an a cappella piece within their set, we quickly arranged, *Twinkle, Twinkle, Little Star,* with the girls singing the melody and harmony, while the boys generally made *non-musical sound effects*. Believe it or not, it worked, and the group went on to place everywhere they went!

Marquis' first competition of the year was Brea's *Festival 2003,* their advanced mixed competition, with all of the other "big boys," at Citrus College in Glendora. Marquis sang and performed well… in fact, they sang and performed almost perfectly! Doug and I were so proud of that show. But, when the awards were announced, Marquis had earned *3rd Place* and the plaque for *Best Showmanship*! Burroughs *Powerhouse* (formerly called Chamber Choir) was the winner! I can honestly say that I thought Marquis' singing was impressive, along with their show… but apparently the adjudicators weren't quite as impressed as I was. So, we all cheered and appreciated what we had gotten, and Doug and I spent the weekend trying to figure out exactly where Marquis had gone wrong? Third place is certainly not bad, but we just felt that, perhaps, their performance had deserved better?

Since Brea's women's festival, *Ladies First*, was divided up into different divisions, and was held locally at Brea Olinda High School, we decided to bring Diamondaires along to compete in its intermediate division, while Solitaire competed advanced. The afternoon of the competition arrived and Diamondaires performed first. They were very good, exhibiting a whole lot of energy! Next, it was Solitaire's turn. They were also excellent. Their three-segment show, really worked for them! When it came time for the awards, Diamondaires, at Brea for the first time, was especially excited! In the Intermediate Women's Division, Diamondaires earned *1st Place* along with both plaques for *Best Showmanship* and *Best Musicianship*! In the Advanced Women's Division, Solitaire *also* earned *1st Place* and both plaques for *Best*

Showmanship and *Best Musicianship*! Now that's how we like to start the year!

Our next competition, took Marquis to *Hart High School in Newhall*. Although we didn't drive this far to compete, very often, since *everyone* was there, we wanted to find out *exactly how well we stacked up against our competitors*. Marquis took the stage and almost immediately began to hear cheering from the audience, as they ran through their show. When the kids were done, and had come off stage, they were out of breath and about to faint… a very good sign for show choir! The awards were announced, and Marquis earned *2nd Place* in the Advanced Mixed Division. That was very good, considering how tough our competitors were! Winning for the second straight time, however, was Burroughs *Powerhouse*, who had definitely "*come into their own,*" by this time! But, they had only beaten us *by a few points*, so we were encouraged that we *could* eventually beat them.

For our next competition, we took Diamondaires and Diamondtones to *El Modena High School*. Although Diamondaires was ready to compete, Diamondtones, as mentioned, suffered greatly from a lack of male sound, which made them sound weak, especially in the ballad. So, several boys from Marquis volunteered to help them out, by joining the group and then learning to sing their ballads, since they probably wouldn't have time to learn any of the choreography. The way I had it figured, on paper, Travis Ranch Middle School's *Encore* and us would probably be fighting it out for third place. Travis Ranch *wasn't technically qualified to compete in a high school festival*, but since they had been dominating their middle school competitions, the host had agreed to let them in. Diamondaires, performed pretty early in the women's division and they were great! Diamondtones was the last scheduled group to perform, as I remember it. So, we saw most of our competitors' performances, before we took the stage. Travis Ranch was very good. I could see why they had been allowed into this festival. In the warm-up room, I told the Diamondtones that placing here (there were only three awards) was possible, but in order to make it *probable*, they had to pump out their best show of the year! The kids hit the stage and did exactly that! I still was not certain that

Travis Ranch would not beat us, but at least we had a fighting chance. When the awards were announced, they began with the Intermediate Women's Division. Diamondaires earned *2nd Place* and the plaque for *Best Showmanship*! Everyone cheered. Now it was time to announce the awards for the Intermediate Mixed Division. All of our kids were holding hands and hoping for a trophy. Ultimately… Diamondtones earned *3rd Place*, only three points ahead of Travis Ranch! Diamondtones began screaming like they had just won the Nationals! That was one of the few times we had almost gotten beat by a middle school choir! I did say, *almost*!

The Arcadia *Big Pow Wow,* was next. Marquis had done very well here, over the past four years, even *winning it in 2000*! The evening was always fun, because the competition was held in the beautiful, and I do mean *beautiful* San Gabriel Mission Playhouse! To describe it, this theatre uses nineteenth century Spanish architecture on the outside, while the inside is glorious, with paintings and ornate woodwork on the ceiling and private boxes lining both sides of the theatre. Sitting in a box with my family, at this competition, was great… it usually helped *numb the pain of not winning*. Doug and I both believed that this year's show and group, *made-up one of the best, mixed show choirs we'd ever had*! It was contemporary (*Moulin Rouge*- the movie and the *Beatles*) and extremely energetic and very musical. Marquis had *not won* a competition, the year before, or during this entire year, so believe me… *they were hungry*! Well the evening came, we performed, and the awards were announced. Marquis ended up earning a close *3rd Place* with the plaque for *Best Showmanship*! Everyone in the group was happy with those awards… but I'm told that they quietly wondered if they would *ever win a competition this year*? That was a valid question, that I'm afraid… *I really had no answer for.*

While Marquis was flirting with winning competitions, Solitaire had already won at Brea! Next, our two advanced groups traveled together to the *Tournament of Champions* (TOC), Marquis hoping for a win and Solitaire hoping to add *another win* to their trophy case! Our two performances were fantastic! Everyone in both groups, felt wonderful when they came off stage. At the end of the night, when Lawrence Fitz announced the trophy winners, Solitaire had earned *1st Place* with the plaque for *Best Showmanship*, in the Women's Division, while Marquis, had earned *2nd Place*, in the Mixed Division, as Burroughs *Powerhouse* swept, once again! Now, we all knew that Burroughs was having one great year, but we had been thinking, that we could beat them! After the third time of being beaten by them I think everyone in Marquis, finally threw in the towel, and felt that we would *probably end the year with a second place showing, behind Burroughs*, as had been the case at TOC. So, the officers and I decided to have tee shirts made for our entire group, which said, **WE'RE NUMBER TWO!** This was our *not so very subtle* way of dealing with the inevitable! Everyone in the group was united behind this slogan!

Next, Solitaire went out to San Diego to compete in the Bonita Vista women's event, *For Ladies Only,* at Eastlake High School. We did not go to San Diego often, but Solitaire really wanted to go this year! There were a number of groups there, whom we had never seen before... all residing in San Diego. The atmosphere was pleasant as everyone cheered for everyone else's performance. In the end, Solitaire earned *2nd Place*, but it felt like a win. That was because, the group that won, was very good and also quite friendly. I don't remember what their name was, but I do remember what a good time Solitaire had!

Marquis' final competition of the year was the *Fullerton College Jazz Festival.* In fact, all six of our competing groups participated. Marquis arrived at Fullerton, wearing their **WE'RE NUMBER TWO** tee shirts. These produced more than a few questioning stares, but the kids were determined to wear them. All of our groups placed their garment bags in an open grassy area, and scattered all over campus to watch some of the other competing groups in one of six show choir venues! Over the next eight hours, each of our groups got their garment bag, changed into their costume, and competed. Just before the awards were announced, many of my almost three hundred kids, held hands, and hoped together. In their only competition of the year, Diamondettes earned *3rd Place,* in the Novice Women's Division, Diamondtones, fresh off their third place finish at El Modena, earned *1st Place*, in the Intermediate Mixed Division, Diamondaires earned *2nd Place* in the Intermediate Women's Division, Notorious, in their sole competition effort, earned *4th Place* in the Men's Division, Solitaire continued their winning ways, by earning *1st Place* in the Advanced Women's Division.... and Marquis... just as they had all suspected... earned *2nd Place* in the Advanced Mixed Division! Very good results for everyone... but believe it or not... I think Marquis was the most, smug. *They had correctly predicted their 2nd Place finish!*

SCVA (Southern California Vocal Association) hosted our final competition of the year. Solitaire, Diamondaires and Diamondtones were all participating. I think I have mentioned before, that this festival was scored heavily (70%) on each group's singing with only about 30% of the points scored on their show. So, we never quite knew how we would do there, although we had done well there, in the past! Once again, the atmosphere was nice. It was conducive to presenting all of the kids involved, with a pleasant day of show choir competition, minus the anger and theatrics of some of the other festivals we had been to, over the years. This was just a fun day that also happened to be a competition! When the awards were announced, Diamondtones had earned *3rd Place,* in the Intermediate Mixed Division, Diamondaires had earned *2nd Place* as well as the plaque for *Best Showmanship*, in the Intermediate Women's Division, and finally, Solitaire had earned *2nd Place* with the plaque for *Best Showmanship*, in the Advanced Women's Division! Not a bad way to end the year, at all. For the year, in competition, our six groups had jointly earned one *4th Place*, six *3rd Places*, seven *2nd Places* and five *1st Places*! They had also won one plaque for *Best Musicianship* and five plaques for *Best Showmanship*! Regardless of Marquis' not winning for the second year in a row... as a *competing show choir program*, Diamond Bar had done *exceptionally well*, in 2003!

Our school musical, in 2003, was *Oklahoma*! It was a good old-fashioned show that ended up being a real crowd pleaser! The choir kids, who participated, included *Chase Rebensdorf, Shayne Stephen, Kelsi Christ, Jessica Watts, Joe Janesin, Kelsi Roberts,*

Caroline Yenydunyeyan and *Robert Waters*. This was the final musical that Doug Kuhl choreographed for the school, with that duty, then returning back to the dance teacher, who had choreographed all of the school's musicals before him. Sadly, we do not have a cast list to share for this one.

Our hard working choir officers for **2002-03** included:

Diamondaires
President: *Samantha Quimpo*
Vice-Pres: *Cassie Pereyra, Ashley Rush & Brittany Schmidt*
Secretary: *Stephanie Hughes*
Treasurer: *Dana Avelar*
Historian: *Steph Delarosas & Felicia Hernandez*

Diamond Bar Singers
President: *Mona Yamak*
Vice-Pres: Chantel Carter
Sec/Treas: *Jill Tsai*
Historian: *Anastassia Moynihan*

Diamondtones
President: *Kandace Moore*
VP: *Brenda Coronado*
Sec/Treas: *Denise Hills*
Historian: *Yesenia Aldrete*

Solitaire
President: *Jessica Hessom*
Vice-Pres: *Katie Allen, Megan Dong, Aimee Eller, Julia Haager, Sheri Vernon, Courtney Walborn, Jacqueline Wissman & Joanna Zirbes*
Secretary: *Erica Louie*
Treasurer: *Gloria Cheng*
Historian: *Kelsey Roberts*

Marquis
President: *Shayne Stephen*
Vice-Pres: *Spike Abeyta, Karen Baral, Jeff Buccola, Megan Lomeli, Brittany Pettus, Kevin Ramirez, Chase Rebensdorf & Chase Saldana*
Secretary: *Alice Vijjeswarapu*
Treasurer: *Ashlee Gilespie, Holly Kreuger, Erin Mearns & Kristine Songco*
Special Projects: *Joe Janesin & Robert Waters*
Assistant Director: *Jeff Hsu*

Notorious
(Both Self-Proclaimed)
President: *Robert Waters*
Vice-Pres: *Joe Janesin*

Diamondettes
President: *Carolina Altamirano*
Vice-President: *Mona Yamak*
Secretary/Treasurer: *Darlene Silva*
Historian: *Kelly West*

The summer of 2003, arrived, and Doug and I, had big plans for the 2004 school year! We decided to take Marquis to a *national competition, hosted by FAME, in Branson*! I had heard about this event for years now, but hadn't considered going, until now. We both felt that Marquis needed something big to prepare for, in order to break their two-year curse of not winning. I believe, in that time, there were plenty of competitions we participated in, that they *could have won*, if luck had been on our side. But, frustratingly, although I am not really complaining, coming in *second or third* seemed to be their new normal. 2003-4 marked the official beginning of our new group, the *Chamber Singers*. But unlike the show choir, of the same name, at Nogales, this one was strictly a traditional choir that traveled to local non-competitive festivals and sang for home concerts. Our accompanying band lost Jeff Hsu, who graduated and entered college, but still remained at four, as guitarist, Charm Park joined Hannah, Bo and Kramer. Both Melissa Quigley and Alyssa Cossey resigned as assistant choreographers, due to their other commitments.

To break down the Marquis set by *song*, they were performing *A Lovely Night, O My Luve's Like A Red Red Rose, Ten Minutes Ago, Come Along With Me, Ring Ring The Banjo, Don't Cry Out Loud* and *Livin' La Vida Loca.* Marquis was making plans, as previously mentioned, to participate in a national competition at Branson, in the spring! Doug and I decided that they would have the best chance of doing well, if their songs represented *Marquis' "Greatest Hits*!" That's *exactly* what we called the set, too! We basically included the most successful competition songs that Marquis had ever performed! Meanwhile, Solitaire had a colorful montage of jazz songs, songs from the fifties and songs from the sixties, complete with effective costume changes. Diamondaires, Diamondtones and

Diamondettes had more traditional shows, most of their songs being stock arrangements. Although Notorious did not compete, Kramer Ison agreed to teach them their show, and serve as their director, this year, as I was very busy with Branson. Finally, *Zirconia,* was a group made up of the boys in Diamondtones, headed up by senior, Spike Abeyta. He told me that since they were not a real Diamond Bar group, he named them after a fake diamond, hence, *Zirconia*! They didn't compete this year, either, but they did perform at our two Spring Magic concerts!

Our groups' competition sets included:

Marquis 2003-04
Costume Colors:
Blue, Gold & Black
Competition Set
Once Upon A Time
Songs of the South
Pop Goes Marquis

Diamondaires 2003-04
Costume Colors:
Unknown
Competition Set
A Dream Is A Wish
Singin' In The Rain
Roll With It
Over The Rainbow
Ease On Down The Road

Solitaire 2003-04
Costume Colors:
Black, Red, Multicolored
Competition Set
Solitaire Jazz
Solitaire Fifties
Solitaire Sixties

Notorious 2003-04
Costume Colors:
Hawaiian Shirts
Non-Competition Set
(Directed by Kramer Ison)
America
Silhouette
S'wonderful
You Don't Love Me
Gimme Some Lovin

Diamondettes 2003-04
Costume Colors: *Unknown*
Competition Set
Twinkle Twinkle Little Star
Lollipop
My First Love
Puttin' On The Ritz

Diamondtones 2003-04
Costume Colors: *Red*
Competition Set
The Heart of America
I'll Be There For You
Show Me The Way
Footloose

<u>Zirconia 2003-04</u>
Costume Colors: *Unknown*
<u>Non-Competition Set</u>
(Directed by Spike Abeyta)
I Won't Grow Up
Seize The Day

Marquis began their competition year at Brea's *Festival 2004*, their advanced mixed event at Citrus College. The kids were anxious to find out how their "Greatest Hits" would be received? To be perfectly honest, this set was a *troublesome one*, as it not only represented the most successful parts of their shows, of the past five years… but also some of the most *difficult* ones! They weren't quite ready by early February, but we had to start sometime. When the awards were announced, Marquis had earned *5th Place* with the plaque for *Best Showmanship,* in the Advanced Mixed Division! I know that fifth place doesn't sound too impressive, but against the likes of Burroughs, Bonita Vista, Burbank, Arcadia and Upland, and winning best show, to boot, it felt like a very good way to start. The kids were happy with their awards, but they certainly weren't satisfied!

Meanwhile, Solitaire, Diamondettes and Diamondaires traveled to Brea Olinda High School a couple of weeks later, to compete in the Brea Women's Event, *Ladies First!* Solitaire hoped that these judges would like their jazz, 50s and 60s show as much as they had liked last year's effort, when they had swept all of their top awards. Diamondaires, who had won here, last year, as well, wondered if they could do it again? Diamondettes… well, they were just happy to be there! All three groups gave super performances, and now they just had to wait for the awards. When the awards were announced, Diamondettes earned *1st Place* in the Novice Women's Division, Diamondaires earned *1st Place* in the Intermediate Women's Division and Solitaire, once again, swept all of the top awards in the Advanced Women's Division, earning *1st Place* and both plaques for *Best Showmanship* and *Best Musicianship!* That was a day everyone in our groups would have just loved to repeat!

Next, Solitaire returned to the Bonita Vista women's festival, *For Ladies Only*, and hoped to beat last year's second place finish. By this time, Solitaire had become one of the most successful girls' show choirs around! So, the kids and I truly believed that they had a good chance of winning! Well, we shouldn't have worried, I guess, because when the results were announced, Solitaire had earned *1st Place* and both plaques for *Best Showmanship* and *Best Musicianship*. In other words, they had *swept* the top awards for the second consecutive time this year!

Our next outing, took Marquis and Solitaire to the *Hart Festival in Newhall*. Although both of our groups gave very passionate performances, we noticed that our groups seemed *far different from the other groups there*. Mostly, they seemed to have bigger bands and they used risers! This was, of course, the influence of the mid-west show choirs. Nothing wrong with it, but I still preferred the freedom of a full stage, instead of binding the kids to riser formations. When the awards were announced, Marquis had earned *3rd Place* in the Advanced Mixed Division while Solitaire had also earned *3rd Place* in the Advanced Women's Division. It seems funny that a group, like Solitaire can sweep the awards at their first two competitions and follow that with a third place at their next one? But that's why I learned to choose my competitions carefully. Some embrace the old California free-style, some reward more singing, some favor more dancing, some embrace the mid-west style… it all depends on the score sheets and the judges. There is little reason to believe that if a certain judge doesn't like your style at one competition, he or she will score you any higher at the next competition! All directors have their favorite judges, of course. Mine were former *successful* show choir directors and show producers… *who appreciated what we were doing*!

Our next competition took Marquis back, once again, to the Arcadia High School, *Big Pow Wow*! We thought of this performance as an important tune-up before Branson. As usual, our performance was passionate, and we didn't expect any overtime penalties either. When the awards were finally announced, Marquis had not only earned *3rd Place*, but they had taken the *Best Showmanship* plaque as well! The kids were very happy, especially about earning the Showmanship award! Things were looking up!

Now it was time for our Diamondtones and Diamondaires to compete at the *Glendora High School* competition. I believe that 2004 was the final year for this event. As usual, it was held at Citrus College, and these divisions were held in late morning and early afternoon. Our competitors were pretty tough, but we felt that both groups would have a fair shot at placing. If memory serves, there were only three trophies in each division, that year. Diamondaires performed first and was good, as usual. Diamondtones was a little weak in the men, as usual, but their energetic performance made up for it. When the awards were announced, Diamondaires had earned *2nd Place* in the Intermediate Women's Division while our Diamondtones earned *3rd Place* in the Intermediate Mixed Division. It was a fun and worthwhile afternoon.

Speaking of Citrus College, our next competition, for Marquis and Solitaire was hosted by *Burroughs High School*. But, since their own theatre was not available, they had rented the Citrus College Auditorium, for this year only. Solitaire was looking for another first place at this competition. They were having another solid year, and most of the girls believed that they had a great chance of winning this one! Marquis, on the other hand, *had not won in three straight seasons* (this being their third) and they too, were looking for a win! Three years of not winning, is a long time, to a group that formerly dominated. Many of Marquis' members probably didn't even know what *winning felt like*? The competition began, and soon Solitaire hit the stage. At the risk of sounding redundant, they sang and performed, as they always did… *like winners*! Later, during Marquis' warm-up, someone asked the group what it would mean to them to win this competition? Different choir members, especially the older ones, expressed their frustration at not winning for nearly three years! Some of them, almost in tears, urged everyone to make it happen! So, we hit the stage, maybe a little emotional, but entirely united. The Marquis show, like the Solitaire show, ran smoothly, and I could feel the fire in every student's performance! Later, as they were about to announce the awards, everyone took hands, as was our custom, and looked determined to accept whatever the results were... *together.* In the Advanced Women's Division, Solitaire earned *1st Place* and the plaque for *Best Showmanship.* The girls cheered loudly and hugged each other. In the Advanced Mixed Division, Marquis also earned *1st Place* and the plaque for *Best Showmanship*! Those kids immediately began screaming, for what seemed like half an hour (although it was probably closer to *five minutes*). They were so excited! *The curse had finally been broken!* Marquis had won their first competition since 2001! I actually went backstage and thanked Mary Rago, Burroughs' director, for hosting this event, that saw fit to *making us winners after almost a three year drought*!

Now it was time for *Riverside City College's* (RCC) competition. Because Marquis and Solitaire competed in so many more events, this trip was limited to Diamondaires, Diamondtones and Diamondettes. This would be the final competition of the year, for them, so everyone was excited. Throughout the afternoon, each of our groups performed well on the stage. But, we had not forgotten that the score sheet was tipped heavily toward the vocals, so logically, all three groups knew that it would be tough to win, considering they had *so much active choreography*! It didn't matter, though. They tried hard on their choreography, anyway! When the awards were announced, Diamondtones earned *3rd Place*, in the Intermediate Mixed Division, Diamondaires earned *2nd Place* and the plaque for *Best Showmanship*, in the Intermediate Women's Division and Diamondettes earned *1st Place* (their second one of the year) and the plaque for *Best Musicianship*, in the Novice Women's Division! All of the groups were grateful for their awards... but especially the young Diamondettes, who were treated like rock stars because they had not only won their division but had also earned the plaque for Best Musicianship... *at the music heavy RCC*!

Before we knew it, it was time for Marquis to travel to Branson to compete in the much-anticipated *FAME Nationals*! This was very exciting, as we had never competed in a national competition with any Diamond Bar group, before. I'd heard about Branson for years, now, and finally, *we were going*! The flight had a stopover, and that was followed by a four-hour bus ride. So, although we left LAX, early in the morning, with the time change, we arrived at our hotel, after dark (we did stop for dinner en route), about 8:30 pm. The hotel was very modest, and somewhat run-down, but the kids were fine with it. They were in *Branson, Missouri*! The next day our truck arrived with all of our costumes and props and band equipment. We traveled to the selected Branson Theatre, and excitedly waited our turn to perform. There were a zillion groups there (actually about 23) and if memory serves, we were all scheduled to compete together today, and later tonight they would announce the fifteen finalists, who would compete for trophies tomorrow! When it came our turn to perform, the kids gave it all they had! In fact, they showed a little bit of swagger, as they came off the stage, which seemed ideal for a national competition. Next, we were ushered into a private room, where one of the FAME reps, proceeded to tell us what the judges felt we needed to work on. She began by saying that singing an a cappella piece slows down the show, especially when it's directed. She went on to say that we needed to incorporate the risers more. I was calm when I responded to her that show choirs in California were required to perform a cappella numbers and that we *chose* not to embrace full risers in order to accommodate our show. She just nodded, uncomfortably, and left the room. I took the next ten minutes explaining to our kids that we were who we were, and we had to be proud of that! I told them that *I believed* they would make the finals tomorrow, with the show they had just performed. I also told them that I would let them know, *for sure,* as soon as I was informed. That night, about 10 pm, I received news that *Marquis* was not only in the finals, but that they had earned *5th Place* in the preliminary competition! Our kids were so jazzed that night; I'm surprised any of them got any sleep! The next day, at the Finals, we performed relatively early, and then watched every other group perform. It was a lot of fun, because we had never seen *any* of these groups before! Every other group used the risers and sang an accompanied ballad, as the FAME rep told us the judges wanted us to do! I thought that our uniqueness might actually be a positive, when it came to the adjudicators' scoring. After a very long day and into the evening… the awards were announced. Only four schools were announced as trophy winners, and *Diamond Bar was not among them*. The kids and I were a little disappointed but not crushed since only four schools placed here out of 23. Of course, once I got my score sheets, my feelings changed dramatically! The same judges who had placed us 5th the day before… had us placed *next to last in the Finals*! They didn't say much, but their scores were impossibly low! I was tempted to go "speak" with the judges, right then, but I took a deep breath to calm myself down… and I walked away, knowing that my complaining to the judges… *wouldn't change a thing*. So, we took a fun dinner cruise, returned to our hotel, and flew back home the next day. On Monday I phoned the FAME people and told them, in no uncertain terms, of *my displeasure with their judges*! How could we have gotten so much worse, according to the same judges, in just one day? I don't really know what happened, but my personal theory is that once the judges had caught wind of the fact that we *weren't going to change our show to fit their mold*, as the FAME rep probably reported to them, they *killed us*… metaphorically speaking... to teach us a lesson. The FAME people apologized and promised to look into it. About a week later, a *5th Place* trophy arrived from FAME with a congratulatory note, on our wonderful *preliminary performance*, apologizing for our distressful Finals experience and promising to be more careful in hiring judges. I laughed. This trophy really didn't mean anything to me… but at least FAME had tried. And actually, now the kids from Marquis had a trophy to represent their first trip to the Show Choir Nationals! This experience was the *beginning* of my feeling that some mid-west show choir judges treated any group that varied from their basic model (big band, risers, no a cappella song), *as being wrong*. I'm sure they weren't all like this, at that time, but that FAME competition left me, as a free spirited Southern California show choir director, *with a bad taste in my mouth*, just the same.

Chula Vista High School's, *So Cal Competition*, represented our final festival of the year! We took Marquis and Solitaire, and as I remember, we made a nice tour out of it, by staying at the Catamaran Resort, on Mission Bay. The atmosphere was fun, and although once again, the stage was of the temporary variety, at the convention hall, where this event was being held, the kids really didn't mind. Solitaire went first and dazzled the audience with their energy and good clean singing! Marquis was on stage a while later and impressed the audience with *Marquis' Greatest Hits*, from the past five years of competing. They really had a good time on the stage, I could tell. In the end, Marquis earned *3rd Place* in the Advanced Mixed Division while Solitaire earned *2nd Place* in the Advanced Women's Division. Over the years of competing, I had learned, that no matter how good your group is you *can't always win*. Now, I think the kids were beginning to understand the unpredictability of show choir competition a little bit better, and thus felt the same way. Sometimes just presenting a couple of *kickass* shows is enough… but the second and third place trophies were nice too!

Our school musical for 2004 was *Damn Yankees,* directed by Peter Bland, choreographed by Janna Lindenberg, and musically directed by me. Although this was not well known by our audiences, like all of our Diamond Bar shows, it ended up having a great run! Thanks to *Spike Abeyta,* I have a cast list to share for this one!

2004 Cast List for *"Damn Yankees!"*

Joe Boyd: *Chris Penticoff*
Meg Boyd: *Erica Louie*
Applegate: *Edwin Salveron*
Sister: *Melissa Mendoza*
Doris: *Kayla Keel*
Joe Hardy: *Chase Rebensdorf*
Smokey: *Ray Ayers*
Vernon: *Kevin Lee*
Van Buren: *Jeff Buccola*
Rocky: *Spike Abeyta*
Gloria: *Anjie Petris*
Welch: *Jeff Fong*
Henry/ Postmaster: *David Anis*
Lola: *Jeanette Devera/ Jamie Garza*
Sohovik/ Commissioner: *Shawn Reyes*
Lynch/ Guard: *Ryan Farabee*
Harry, Sullivan & Bryant: *Erik Hsiao*
Bouley, Strand & Gilbert: *Anthony Smith*

Bubba & Mickey: *Sherwin Querubin*
Miss Weston: *Anna Gutierrez*

The All-Star Team: *Spike Abeyta, Ray Ayers, Jeff Buccola, Jeanette Devera, Jeff Fong, Jamie Garza, Kayla Keel, Kevin Lee, Anjie Petris, Erica Louie, Melissa Mendoza, Chris Penticoff, Chase Rebensdorf, Edwin Salveron, Tina Thomas, Jennifer Anderson, Melody Ciria, Lauren Davis, Jean Kim, Esther Joe, Vanessa Babida, Jessica Jann, Samantha Herrick, Alexandra Santiago, Anna Gutierrez, Ryan Farabee, Erik Hsiao, David Anis, Sherwin Querubin, Shawn Reyes, Anthony Smith, Kelsey Roberts, Danae Rebensdorf, Priscilla Sosa, Emily Bischof, Sarah Batistelli, Gloria Cheng, Stephanie Yang, Shana Dahlen, Amy O'Shea, Jayme Elliott, Caroline Yenydunyeyan, Stefanie Garcia, Jennifer Apea, Elizabeth Hessom, Kayla Dimmick, Chelsea Johnson-Long, Karina Stevens, Stefany Mandap, Amanda Mandelcorn*

I couldn't find listings of any of the Marquis officers, but the fantastic **2003-04** choir officers, *I was able to find*, included:

Diamondettes
President: *Jeanette Devera*
Vice-Pres: *Sarah Hall*
Sec/Treas: *Esther Kim*
Historian: *Cassie Pereyra*

Zirconia
President: *Spike Abeyta*

Marquis *(best guesses)*
President: *Jeff Buccola*
Vice-Pres: *Erica Louie*

Diamondtones
President: *Wendy Barclay*
VP:*Natasha Tomovich*
Secretary/Treasurer:
Romeo Francisco & Judy Chen

Notorious
President: *Joey Dimauro*

Diamondaires
President: *Cassie Pereyra*
Vice-Pres: *Mercedes Hart*
Sec/Treas: *Yesenia Aldrete & Lauren Byrum*
Hist: *Stephanie Ramos & Kristen Ingoglia*

<u>Solitaire</u>
President: *Kelsey Christ*
Vice-Pres: *Tracy Wynne, Jennifer Devera, Sheri Vernon & Leah Benavides*
Sec/Treas: *Jeanette Devera*
Dance Capt: *Courtney Walborn*

One other thing I would like to mention is a special concert we put on in January called, "*An Evening With Solitaire*." Honestly, I don't know what prompted this special Solitaire concert, but I would guess it was because Marquis got to travel to Branson that year to compete. The concert was a lot of fun, featuring skits, songs and maybe even a *Beauty Pageant*! In any case, here are the talented girls who put that concert on!

<u>An Evening With Solitaire</u>
<u>Cast List- January 27th, 2004</u>

Brittany Summers • Kelsey Christ • Denise Hills
Linda Kang • Heather Bolhuis • Erica Hansen
Leah Benavides • Nicole Schwartzlander • Medina Rudianto
Rachel Kim • Kelley Milligan • Vivian Chen • Becky Mang
Esther Kim • Tracy Christ • Toni Kelley • Ashley Rush
Kandice Moore • Elizabeth Hessom • Sherry Vernon
Joyce Kao • Jillian Rockwood • Mary Wunder
Brigette Reimer • Tiffany Ya • Carolina Altamirano
Courtney Walborn • Ashley Benison • Jennifer Kim
Kelley Malm • Kayla Dimmick • Jennifer Apea
Sarah Meastas • Kayla Keel • Deborah Lee
Sabrina Jangda • Cassie Pereyra • Kristina Faeldan
Candace Vassalle • Jeanette Devera • Shannon Gidley
Wendy Barclay • Tracey Wynne • Jennifer Devera
Kim Miyakawa • Chelsea Johnson-Long • Dana Avelar
Kelly Miyakawa • Georgette Delgado • Danielle Parmentier

The summer of 2004 came around, and Doug and I were anxiously putting together the groups' competition shows for the upcoming 2005 season. Surprisingly, the school took away my 6th period (extra period), after four years, claiming that they were taking away everybody's… but I found out that wasn't true. *The real reason*, as I gathered from the fine arts dean, was because *I had refused to make my classes smaller, thus allowing the other electives to grow*. As it turned out, they were playing hardball with me. So, not wishing to lose our Chamber Singers/Diamond Bar Singers, the traditional choir in our program, we were forced to say goodbye to the *Diamondettes*, our novice girls show choir, which had been so very successful over the years. Surprisingly, that still left us with six competing show choirs if you include *Notorious*, which rehearsed on Saturdays. That's because of the addition of "Prestige." *Prestige* was actually the all-girl Chamber Singers that we had, who also wanted compete show choir this year. There was one change to our staff as Charm Park left as our guitar player, but Hannah, Bo, and Kramer still remained, making up our band and for the second year in a row, Doug was working without a dance assistant. Solitaire and Diamondaires were scheduled to host their very first women's competition called, *Girls Night Out*, in late February. They couldn't wait! The big news for Marquis was that *they would be going to compete nationally again…* in *New York City* in the spring! The company hosting this event was *Showstoppers*, who Doug and I had had very positive experiences with, while we were at Nogales, when they had hosted the *Disneyland Showstoppers* event. The reason we were competing in a national competition for the *second year in a row*, was because we felt that Marquis deserved a *better national competition experience* than last year's, and besides, I had not visited New York City since 1986! At that time, I traveled there with Margaret to watch one of my former students, *LuAnne Ponce*, perform the role of *Little Red Riding Hood,* in Stephen Sondheim's *Into The Woods*! There was plenty in NYC for all of us to see, especially, the musicals on Broadway! The competition sets for 2005 included:

Marquis 2004-05
Costume Colors:
Black, white & Fuchsia
Competition Set
West Side Story
Thoroughly Modern Marquis
Sweet American Heartbreaker

Solitaire 2004-05
Costume Colors:
Pink & Red
Competition Set
Solitaire Broadway
Solitaire ABBA
Solitaire Country

Notorious 2004-05
Costume Colors:
Hawaiian Shirt
Competition Set
Get Ready
Jump Down Spin Around
Doctor Looney
Bring Him Home
Centerfold

Prestige 2004-05
Costume Colors:
Black
Competition Set
Cantate Domino
La Speranza Ballet
Chatanooga Choo Choo
Though Philomela Lost
Hello Girls
Heatwave

Diamondtones 2004-05
Costume Colors:
Unknown
Competition Set
Magic To Do
Steam Heat
Joseph and the Dreamcoat

Diamondaires 2004-05
Costume Colors:
Unknown
Competition Set
Spinning Wheel
Too Darn Hot
Lullaby
On My Own
Roll Over Beethoven

Competition season began, as it always *used to*, with the *Aztec Sing*. The only change was, the old director, John Wilson, had retired a few years back, and *Leslie Clutterham* had taken over. So, Marquis returned to the competition where my Nogales Chamber Singers *had won their first trophy, ever*, in 1983! My groups had a lot of history here, over the years. That night, when it became our turn to perform, my kids took the stage like they owned it! Their performance was very good, and they left the stage, feeling giddy, as a result. When they announced the awards, Marquis had earned *4th Place,* as well as the plaque for *Best Showmanship*! The kids cheered, especially for the showmanship plaque. Our scores were all good… this had just been a very competitive festival.

Marquis, as usual, competed in *Festival 2005*, Brea's advanced mixed event at Citrus College. We really wanted to get a little bit sharper at each of our competitions, in preparation for the national Showstoppers competition in New York City, in April! Our performance, that night was very strong. When the awards were announced, we had earned *3rd Place* and the plaque for *Best Showmanship*! Again, our scores were good, but our outstanding competitors had made this a very tight contest!

A couple of weeks later, Solitaire, Diamondaires and Prestige competed in the women's competition, *Ladies First*, at Brea Olinda High School. The number of groups in each division was about four or five. Throughout the day, all three of our entrants did very well, singing and performing their hearts out. When it came time for the awards, Prestige earned *1st Place* in the Novice Women's Division, Diamondaires earned *1st Place* in the Intermediate Women's Division while Solitaire earned *2nd Place*, in the Advanced Women's Division. Although Solitaire was getting used to winning a lot, they appreciated their second place too. All in all, it had been a great day.

The next competition was a trip for Solitaire to Bonita Vista's *For Ladies Only*. They faced a lot of competing choirs that night, and they made a resolve to win. They went on stage and they were electric! *From Broadway to ABBA to Country…* they rocked the house! When it came time to announce the awards, Solitaire had earned *1st Place* and both plaques for *Best Showmanship* and *Best Musicianship*! There. Now that's more like it.

The *Riverside City College* competition or RCC, as we preferred to call it, was upon us before we knew it. We took every competing group except for *Prestige*, including, Marquis, Solitaire, Diamondaires, Diamondtones and Notorious. This was to be a very long day. In actuality, RCC announced the winners of each division, as they competed, but for our purposes, I will announce all of our groups' competition results, at the end.

Diamondaires went on first. Their performance was so moving during their beautiful a cappella, *Lullaby*, and yet so exciting at the end, when they performed the *Roll Over Beethoven/Shout* medley! They looked and sounded sensational! Diamondtones was next. We had been a little concerned about the boys' lack of sound (a normal problem), but they really came through today. Their rendition of *Joseph and the Amazing Technicolor Dreamcoat*, at the end of their show, was nothing short of spectacular! Now, it was Notorious' turn to perform. They had not rehearsed for this nearly enough, since they did not meet as a class, but I could see, during their performance, that they were really trying to win! The group only had about 20 guys, but man did they work! I think their funniest song, as far as audience reaction, had to be their ender, *Centerfold*. Solitaire went on next. They were pretty much flawless. So entertaining and so energetic in addition to singing very well! Our final group to go on was Marquis. To my knowledge, *they had never won at RCC*. This year, in preparation for Showstoppers, to a person, they were committed to giving it their best! Well, the show began, and I was blown away by how rich their vocals sounded. Their choreography was also clean and sharp. When they finished their show, everyone in the group was dripping in sweat and looked like they were about to faint, they were so tired! But everyone also felt that they had just given a *great performance*! Soon it came time for the awards to be announced. Diamondaires, competing in the Intermediate Women's Division, earned *1st Place* with both plaques for *Best Showmanship* and *Best Musicianship*, Diamondtones, competing in the Intermediate Mixed Division, also earned *1st Place* with both plaques for *Best Showmanship* and *Best Musicianship*, Notorious, competing in the Men's Division, earned *2nd Place* and the plaque for *Best Showmanship*, Solitaire, competing in the Advanced Women's Division, earned *1st Place* along with both plaques for *Best Showmanship* and *Best Musicianship*, and Marquis, competing in the Advanced Mixed Division, *earned 1st Place at RCC, for the very first time, as well as the plaque for Best Showmanship!* That day could not have gone much better!

Next, Marquis and Solitaire traveled to the *Burroughs Competition*. As I recall, everyone was there, and the festival was very competitive. Solitaire had another wonderful performance, as we had become accustomed to. Marquis was also very solid vocally and passionate throughout. When the awards were announced, Solitaire earned *1st Place* along with the plaque for *Best Showmanship*! They were ecstatic! Marquis, meanwhile, earned *2nd Place*, and they too were very happy!

Now came time for the big day of competing at the *Fullerton College Jazz Festival*. This was the one event where we took all six of our show choirs, including *Prestige*, who was again taking the place of Diamondettes, at least for this year. It was a very fun, but busy day for everyone. Like always, when coming to Fullerton, we had a *home base* (a vacant patch of lawn or patio) where the kids from all of our groups, kept their garment bags. We also had a very accurate time schedule for when kids needed to change. Many of these kids were in two or three different groups! We also had a schedule telling us what time; certain students were assigned to watch our home base area, making sure that people were always there, so nothing would be stolen. To my knowledge, nothing ever was. Our first group to perform was *Prestige*, who competed in the Novice Women's Division. They were a very small group, about twenty girls, I think, but they sang so very well! I could see the judges' faces. They were definitely impressed! Our next group to perform was *Diamondtones*, in the Intermediate Mixed Division. They took the stage an immediately began performing in *Magic To Do,* and finishing things off with *Joseph and his Amazing Technicolor Dreamcoat!* Bravo! Great performance! The *Diamondaires* performed next, in the Intermediate Women's Division. They were made up of a pretty large number of girls who filled out the stage nicely. Beginning with *Spinning Wheel*, and all the way to the end of their show, they kept their energized singing and performing going strong! Wow! Our all boys group, *Notorious*, was next, competing in the Men's Division. What can I say? They were charming, daring, silly and endearing. The crowd loved them! It was now *Solitaire's* turn to compete, in the Advanced Women's Division. As always, they were wonderful, and a whole lot of fun to watch! Finally, *Marquis* took the stage, in the Advanced Mixed Division. Their show really came alive here, as it often did in the Campus Theatre at Fullerton College. I remember, we were the last to perform, and the theatre was packed with screaming teenagers! It was great! Not too long, following Marquis' performance, the awards were announced. In the Novice Women's Division, Prestige earned *1st Place,* in the Intermediate Mixed Division, Diamondtones earned *1st Place,* in the Intermediate Women's Division, Diamondaires earned *1st Place,* in the Men's Division, Notorious earned *2nd Place,* in the Advanced Women's Division, Solitaire earned *3rd Place* and in the Advanced Mixed Division, Marquis earned *1st Place*! Needless to say, all of our kids were very happy at the results! Since this marked the final competition for Diamondtones, Diamondaires and Prestige… I would like to *proudly mention* that this trio of groups competed a total of *seven times* this year and *won 1st Place seven times!* I don't recall ever having two, *much less three groups* who went through the entire season undefeated! *This was historical and one for the record books!*

Finally, it was time for Marquis to travel to New York City to compete in *Showstoppers*! No one drove a prop truck all that way, as we had done last year. No, as I recall, we shipped whatever props we could not carry, to the *Marriott Marquis*, where we were staying and competing. We had made a deal with Showstoppers to arrange for our kids to see *three Broadway shows*, instead of the customary, two. The two shows they had originally selected for us were *Mamma Mia and Phantom of the Opera.* We added *Wicked,* only one year after it had premiered! Because the show was *very nearly sold out*, our tickets ended up being singles, twos and threes, *scattered all over the theatre…* but no one in our group complained. We were lucky to get any seats for *Wicked,* at all! In addition, there was plenty of time for sightseeing, and everyone did exactly that. The competition, itself, was held in a ballroom, of the beautiful Marriott Marquis Hotel. Of course the acoustics were flat, so no group's vocals sounded as good as they should have, but, every group I saw, from across the states, looked very good. Marquis had a solid performance, full of energy… but, unfortunately, they did not place in the top three, which were the only places that received trophies. Actually, we came in a very respectable *5th Place!* Bo Eder, our drummer/photographer, took a really nice picture of the group in Time Square, out in front of the Marriot Marquis, where they were advertising their current show, which just happened to be, *Thoroughly Modern Millie!* That was so meaningful to us, because a number of songs from that show were featured in the second of three sections, of our competition show! I have that picture hanging up at home, representing one of the *greatest experiences we had*, while I taught at Diamond Bar High School.

Our final competition of the year, took us back to Chula Vista High School's *"SoCal" Competition!* We took Marquis, Solitaire and Notorious. To this point, all three groups had competed very well, this year. Notorious, had a pair of Second Places, they had earned at RCC and Fullerton. Solitaire had accumulated three First Places from Bonita Vista, RCC and Burroughs, as well as a Second Place from Brea and a Third Place from Fullerton. Marquis had a pair of First Places from RCC and Fullerton, a Second Place from Burroughs, a Third Place from Brea, a pair of Fourth Places from the Aztec Sing and Arcadia and a Fifth Place from Showstoppers NYC! So, they all felt confident that *they would at least be competitive*, as they had been all year. We were once again staying at the upscale Catamaran Resort in Mission Bay, and we spent Friday night, before the competition, resting and relaxing in style! On Saturday morning, we arrived at the festival, held in a convention center in downtown San Diego. Throughout the day, each of our three groups performed. Their performances were very good, but the *sound system was not*, and they once again, performed on a portable stage… in Marquis' case… *all 70 kids!* By far, we had the largest group there, and the stage was very crowded. When it came time for the awards to be announced, our kids waited, expectantly, along with all of the other groups. Well, Notorious earned *5th Place*. But this was not really a surprise, since our competitors were all much larger groups, and most of them had a class every day… they didn't just throw their shows together over a few Saturdays, like we did. The boys seemed okay with their award. Next Solitaire was announced *4th Place!* Considering they had *beaten most of these groups* in competition earlier this year, this came as a complete surprise. They didn't win a plaque, either, which was very unusual for Solitaire. But, the girls cheered, and were excellent sports about it. Finally, the awards for the Advanced Mixed Division were announced. Marquis was announced in *4th Place*. After Notorious and Solitaire's awards, I assumed that Marquis would *not do well here*. So, their placement, although a bit disappointing, was something I took it stride. When I got a hold of the score sheets, it became crystal clear that *none of the judges had really enjoyed our shows*. I guess they liked the styles of Burroughs, Burbank and Bonita Vista, better, since *they had mostly placed ahead of us*. This scenario happens in competing, from time to time, no matter what school and group you are or how many previous competitions you may have won. *It's not fun*, but I believe that it's just part of the game. Soon our buses were loaded, and we prepared to depart. I found Marquis' fourth place trophy *awkwardly stuffed* in a bush by the sidewalk, in front of the theatre. I started to retrieve it, but members of Marquis, blatantly told me that *they did not want it*! So, I left it up to them. I found out later, that they had, indeed, *left the trophy behind*. Tony Atienza, of Chula Vista High School, later told me that he thought this was very rude of them. I told him that this was the kids' way of dealing with their disappointment, and their belief that they had not been scored accurately… and since they *technically* earned that trophy, if they really felt like leaving it behind… I thought they had that right. A lot of directors would have probably handled that situation differently, but I respected the wishes of my kids. I also agreed with them, that the numbers on their score sheets seemed to be *uncharacteristically low*. Of course, I didn't like the idea of insulting our host, Chula Vista High School, at all. I have never had a group leave a trophy behind, either before or after this event. So in that sense, I find this action to be *uniquely memorable…* in an *odd* sort of way! To top things off, this turned to be *my final competition* with Diamond Bar High School.

Our Outstanding choir officers for **2004-05** included:

Chamber Singers/ Prestige
President: *Courtney Walborn*
Vice-Pres: *Dana Avelar*
Sec/Treas: *Vivian Chen*
Historian: *Dana Avelar*

Diamondtones
President: *Kim Miyakawa*
Vice-Pres: *Dominic Truong*
S/T: *Dominic Tibayan*
Historian: *Judy Chen*

Marquis
President: *Kelsi Roberts*
Vice-Pres: *Courtney Walborn, Sarah Batistelli & Cheryl Vijjeswarapu*
Secretary: *Nathan Sangalang*
Treasurer: *Paul Leonor*
Historian: *David Rusackus, Danny Rusackus & Phillip Francisco*
Special Proj: *Rob Lamorena*

Solitaire
President: *Jeanette Devera*
VP: *Courtney Walborn, Erica Hansen & Kandace Moore*
Secretary: *Joyce Kao*
Treasurer: *Linda Kang*
Hist: *Courtney Walborn, Erica Hansen & Tracey Christ*

Diamondaires
President: *Jasmine Arora*
Vice-Pres: *Sarah Monte*
Sec/Treas: *Marissa Collins*
Historian: *Judy Chen*

Notorious (?)
Pres: *Robert Lamorena*
Vice-Pres: *Whoever*
Sec/Treas: *Knot Likely*
Historian: *Good Luck*

The final musical that Diamond Bar High School put on, while I was the music director, was *The Wizard of Oz*. This one had some *great technical achievements* in it, to make it truer to the original, and overall, we were all very proud of it! The choir kids who participated in *The Wizard of Oz*, included, *Sarah Batistelli, Katelyn Vorkink, Kelsi Roberts, Emily Bischof, Alice Vijjeswarapu, Cheryl Vijjeswarapu and Anna Gutierrez.* With that, Doug's and my time at Diamond Bar High School… came to a close.

Our entire choir staff *loved the kids and the program* at Diamond Bar High School. Leaving had nothing to do with either one of them. It was just one of those very difficult decisions that we all face at multiple points in our lives. My wife, Margaret and I lived in Diamond Bar for ten years, from 1983 to 1993, and we thought we had died and gone to heaven! My son, Alex, was even born there, in 1991! It's a wonderful community, a perfect place to build a show choir. We won there, starting with that first year, and we won big! That was a *special experience* I have never had at any other school I have taught at! In addition to the choir concerts, competitions and trips, some of my fondest memories involve having lots of fun running the Summer Magic program in June and July, every year, with a lot of very sweet and hard working students! This was a *magical* time for creating hilarious skits, Broadway scenes and songs that always *brought the house down*! There were so many wonderfully talented and hard working members of our Diamond Bar choirs over our seven years, and I wish I could list them all, to honor them! But sadly, all of my *Diamond Bar group rosters* became permanently lost as the result of my computer crash! Aside from a Solitaire roster from 2004, which I already shared in this book, the only group rosters, from Diamond Bar, I have on my computer, are the members for 2005-06 Marquis and Solitaire… *the last Diamond Bar advanced groups Doug and I auditioned…* but unfortunately, never had the opportunity to direct, due to our move to Brea. So, in honor of all my wonderful Diamond Bar students, I will now list those talented kids, who started up Patty Breitag's excellent show choir program, the very next year after Doug and I left, in 2005-06!

The Final Advanced Diamond Bar Show Choirs That Doug & I Auditioned!

Marquis 2005-06

Emily Bischof • Katelyn Vorkink • Jade Harb • Tracey Christ
Julianne Coronado • Danae Rebensdorf • Elizabeth Hessom
Kelley Malm • Kara Wang • Jillian Rockwood • Paul Kim
Jayna Gavieres • Stefany Mandap • Deborah Lee
Scott Yoshimoto • George Franco • Timothy Wang
Keith Yamashita • Dominic Tibayan • Danny Rusackus
Daniel Jung • Patrick Ayers • Michael Dee • Kyei Ko
Andrea Schwartzlander • April Morton • Robert Silva
Amanda Mandelcorn • Carolyn Kaiser • Samantha Herrick
Kayla Dimmick • Jennifer Apea • Brittany Cortez • Heath Hill
Priscilla Sosa • Brigette Reimer • Nicole Valencia • Kyle Furuya
David Rusackus • Dominic Truong • Shereef Abdou
Andrew de la Santos, Parker Rebensdorf • Clinton Arnold
Jeremy Beeman • Chris Kaiser • Chelsea Johnson-Long

Solitaire 2005-06

April Morton • Kelley Milligan • Ashley Rogers • Irene Tang
Julie Luber • Christine Hamel • Julie Cho • Jasmine Querubin
Kristin Ingoglia • Melanie McMillan • Jenny Soo Hoo • Jenni Yi
Abby Clark • Sharon Lee • Deborah Lee • Aida Solomon
Carol Park • Claudia Chin • Christina Lawson • Anna Wunder
Helen Lin • Priscilla Sosa • Carolyn Kaiser • Tracey Christ
Jessica Sunderland • Denise Hills • Jasmine Arora • Ellen Kim
Corina Moynihan • Lindsey Robertson • Joanne Choi
Sheina Bawa • Tiffany Wang • Katherine Kim • Marissa Collins
Jayna Gavieres • Dinithi Ketagoda • Jessica Leonor
Hannah Batistelli • Lauren Rodriguez • Amanda Godinez
Sandy Huang • Rachel Wes

CHAPTER 9

Brea Olinda High School... 2005-2006... Rebuilding The Program!

So, Doug and I were breezing along at Diamond Bar High School! Our groups were good, the home concerts were always *sold-out*, bills were paid, money was fundraised, and people were making plenty of donations! What wasn't to like? Well, let's just say that *the school administration and I did not agree on some very important things*. For one, as I mentioned in the last chapter, they strongly suggested to me that as my choirs grew to nearly 300 students, other electives were shrinking as a result. They "*asked*" me **not** to accept as many kids into choir to alleviate the problem. *I refused.* I explained to them that I always, as a rule, accepted every interested student who auditioned and placed them somewhere within the program. So they took my extra (6th) period away, leaving me with five choir classes as large as 70 kids apiece, not to mention that my personal income was cut by 17%! They hinted that I *could get the choir period back* if I did as they asked. Then, after an unpleasant, but unrelated meeting with the principal, I ended up in *Emergency*, complaining of chest pains… luckily it was not a heart attack. I could go on, but I think you get the idea. *I was very stressed and unhappy.*

During the summer of 2005, I learned that Mark Henson, the talented choir director at Brea Olinda High School, was leaving after 13 years! I had been really looking forward to my son, Alex, joining his program that next fall, so as a choir director, I was very concerned! I immediately called the principal of Brea Olinda High School, *Jerry Halpin.* After introducing myself, I told him about my concerns and asked if I could sit in on the hiring committee? He agreed to allow me to do that, and then out of the blue, he asked me if I would like to apply for the position, myself? I was blindsided, as I had never even considered the possibility? Politely, I told him that I would think about it and let him know. Doug really enjoyed choreographing at Diamond Bar *a lot,* but told me he would, of course, join me at Brea Olinda if I took the job. My wife, Margaret and son, Alex, were very supportive and asked me to do whatever I decided was best for me. Actually, the *best thing* for me was that if I took this job, *I would be Alex's choir teacher for four years!* The next day, I received a call from Mark Henson, who asked if Doug and I would meet him for lunch, to discuss the opening at Brea. We met, Mark encouraged me to apply for the job… *and I did.* I was ultimately offered the job, an hour after my interview, and of course, I accepted it. I helped to advertise my now, open position at Diamond Bar High School, but everyone I knew who taught choir, was happy with their jobs. Finally, they hired *Janae Nafziger*, a talented 2001 choir graduate of mine, straight out of college, to temporarily fill the position. By October, *Patty Breitag*, Brea Olinda High School's former accompanist, was hired as Diamond Bar's new vocal music director. Consequently, Hannah Nam, resigned her accompanist position at Diamond Bar and came over to Brea Olinda, where she joined Kramer Ison and Bo Eder in the band. I spent most of the summer reorganizing the music library, as I had done at every school prior, so I would be familiar with the contents. The Brea Olinda choir room was *by far* the tiniest room I have ever been asked to teach in, so, we had to get creative. Doug painted the entire room, we reorganized the furniture, getting rid of most of it, creating more precious space to sing and dance in. When it was time to start school, in the fall, the room looked great, but we had no idea what we had gotten ourselves into!

The first day of school was very telling. While Mark Henson was here, he had built a very fine choral program, including show choir. But, a few years before he left, the school, and subsequently, the choir, suffered from *declining enrollment*. There hadn't been any choir at Brea's lone middle school, Brea

Junior High, for a few years, until Mark took it upon himself to teach one junior high choir class (my son, Alex, was in it, in seventh grade), for the past two years, to eventually act as a feeder for his struggling high school choirs! I'm telling you this to prepare you for the shock that Doug and I felt upon first meeting our students. My schedule consisted of four classes at the high school, Wildcat Choir, Silver Note Singers, Chamber Choir and Music Appreciation, and then one class, Concert Choir, at the junior high. There were a grand total of only *63 kids in the three choirs at the high school,* and absolutely no one was taking more than one choir class! *It was like starting all over again*! But luckily, Brea had a *strong history of show choir*, and because Doug and I had transformed the choirs at Nogales and Diamond Bar, into *show choir powers,* we saw no reason why we could not do the same thing here... although it might take a while. As part of our "*plan,*" we decided to bring those things into the program that had *defined us wherever we went*. For example, although Brea did not have a history of doing this, we hooked them up with the "*traveling to Disneyland every year, to perform, compete or participate in a backstage workshop tradition*." It did not take long for this to become one of our kids' favorite choir activities! Aside from occasionally performing there, *we traveled to Disneyland every year* to participate in a ninety-minute dance or singing workshop as a "*choir bonding activity*!" The year just wouldn't have felt right, without that trip in November or December of each year!

The first day of school arrived and Alex and I drove together. That was a good thing! Brea Olinda High School was only ten minutes away from my house. That was also a good thing! The principal, Jerry Halpin, was very supportive, and encouraged me to build up this depleted program. That was a good thing, too! So, Alex and I (and I believe that Doug was there, too) arrived about 7:45 am, on the first day of school, and I felt both happy and excited. My first period, I believe, was Wildcat Choir. It was actually a group of about eighteen kids with varying degrees of talent and attitude, who *didn't say a word*, as we walked in. This strangely reminded me of my first day at Nogales High School, 28 years before. My second period was Silver Note Singers. This served as the girls group at BOHS, which under Mark Henson, sometimes competed as a show choir. They mainly competed and placed in the intermediate divisions, once in a while, but I don't believe they had ever competed seriously in the advanced division. This class was the largest, with twenty-six girls, mostly freshmen, but again, they lacked any enthusiasm, when we talked to them. Next, came Chamber Choir. This was supposedly *elite*, a select group of twenty, ten girls and ten boys. Over the summer, a few guys were able to add some friends from football... otherwise, I believe only four of the boys were returning while Alex and his friends Zach and Harrison represented the only new freshmen boys. The boys seemed modestly talented and certainly able to hold their own parts. The girls were vocally talented too, but not really dancers. As I learned, the attitude in here was very much like my first year of teaching at Norco, where I already felt a strong sense of *muted animosity*, coming primarily from some of the veteran students. Mark Henson, like Chet Farmer, had been a very popular teacher with his kids, and like the principal confirmed, *they did not want anything changed!* As senior, Jenny Eckels Winters recalled, "*All of a sudden, we were changing names, policy, audition process, age restrictions, leadership roles and plans for the year. It was a bit overwhelming, even for those excited for it. We had the old process engrained, and in a sense, changing that process, almost felt disloyal to the work we had put in the previous three years.*" I know that getting a new director and the changes that follow, are always difficult for groups. Although, as I mentioned, I felt animosity from some, many of the kids were trying very hard to make this new situation work! My next class was Music Appreciation. Actually, the class was filled with eighteen boys and one girl, who apparently couldn't care less about music, unless it was *their* music! We learned a potpourri of things about music, that first year... but my plan was to ultimately *replace that class* with another show choir, by the following year.

Based on our observations regarding that first day, Doug and I perceived that in the kids' world, Chamber Choir was the group, *to be in*, while the people in every other group probably suffered from serious *inferiority complexes*! Mark used the same system of student officers as Kathy Milner had embraced at Diamond Bar, before I arrived. In this centralized system, all of the *overall choir officers* were also members of Chamber Choir, while every other group only had a representative, who met with the Chamber officers monthly. *I immediately changed all of the established officers to Chamber Choir officers only, and proceeded to have elections for additional officers in both of the other groups.* I could feel the enthusiasm for this change, coming from Wildcat Choir and Silver Notes… but from Chamber, *the officers were openly miffed*! Some argued that the old system had worked just fine. Maybe it had, I argued, but it was obvious that it didn't work now! Sadly, some of the Chamber Choir members never seemed to accept that Mark Henson was gone, and Doug and I had taken over. In any case, we now had *three independent show choirs*, who each had to learn to self-govern. Our second change involved renaming the groups, at least the show choirs, to make them sound more exciting! Doug came up with the new name for Silver Note Singers... it was *Spellbound.* It sounded strong. I was going to name Chamber Choir, *Magic*, but no one else was blown away by that one. Then one day, Chamber was singing *Masquerade*, from *Phantom of the Opera*, and almost immediately, after I suggested it, *everyone loved it*, as the show choir name most likely to replace Chamber Choir! I did not rename the class altogether, they would still perform at classical festivals as Chamber Choir. Wildcat Choir, had it's name changed to O.C. Premier, just in case we ever decided to compete with them in show choir. My third change, involved moving kids around and teaching them *the joy of being in more than one group*! We added about ten new girls, mostly from Silver Notes, to Chamber Choir, and thankfully, most of them were able to take both classes. This kept us from depleting Silver Notes. A few of the Chamber Choir members were not happy about adding the girls, going so far as calling them *unqualified.* But, Doug needed dancers and I needed more sound, in order to be competitive, so we selected the strongest options we had. The fourth change was convincing the principal and then the school board that the advanced show choirs (Masquerade and Spellbound) *deserved and needed P.E. credit*. I explained to them how other top show choir schools, like Burroughs, Burbank, Bonita Vista and Glendora offered it to their kids, allowing them to forego taking a P.E. class, by *taking a show choir instead.* I further, clarified how *physical we were in rehearsals*, and assured them that we would still make those *P.E. credit kids* take any *mandated state testing* that was required. Finally I emphatically stated that this was the easiest way to build up the choir program! *We had it by the second semester!* The fifth change was installing a choir fee to pay for costumes and Doug's twice weekly in-class choreography sessions. *Brea never embraced this completely*, but usually about 60-70% of the kids participated in the fundraising and donations that accounted for this suggested fee. However, we never kept any student out of a group simply because they could not pay… we never have! Ultimately show choir is about talent and attitude. If they were qualified in both of those areas, even if they couldn't pay, *we embraced them.*

Masquerade and Spellbound had their competition sets completely learned by the middle of December, in order to perform for *An Evening Of The Arts* concerts, where BOHS band, choir, dance and drama, each shared something for the audiences. These two concerts acted as the main tune-up for our competition season, which was only a month away! Our 2005-06 competition sets included:

Masquerade 2005-06
Costume Colors:
Red, Blue, Black
Competition Set
As If We Never Said Goodbye
Masquerade
O My Luv's Like A Red Rose
Toxic
Broadway Baby
Sing, Sing, Sing
Don't Cry Out Loud
Too Darn Hot

Spellbound 2005-06
Costume Colors:
White w/ Blue polka dots
Competition Set
Diamonds Are A Girl's Best
Chattanooga Choo Choo
You Are The New Day
I've Got Rhythm
Your Song
Devil With The Blue Dress

O.C. Premier 2005-06

Costume Colors:

Unknown

Competition Set

Footloose

I Can't Help Falling In Love With You

Why Must I Be A Teenager In Love

Heatwave

Great Balls of Fire

Doug and I tried very hard to preserve part of the *Brea choir feel* that Mark Henson had instilled into the program, over the years, to help make the students feel more comfortable. We achieved this through keeping two of the choir's previous activities, *Brea Idol* and *Singing Valentines,* as part of the choir year. As far as the show choirs go, although we rehearsed the kids very hard, we were not initially able to create one of our typical *Nogales or Diamond Bar type of shows,* due to the fact that *we did not have the dance expertise or hard work ethic instilled in the performers yet. The power of pizzazz was nowhere to be seen*! I think we probably would have fared better, initially competing in the *intermediate division*, but that would not have shown the kids where we were ultimately going. So, we prepared to take our lumps in the advanced division, competing against all of our old adversaries. We also continued Mark Henson's tradition of hosting an advanced mixed competition at Citrus College, but we changed the name to the *Brea Olinda Show Choir Classic*! We also hosted a women's event, on campus, called *Ladies Center Stage*. In addition, Brea Junior High choir hosted their own event, called *Middle School Madness*. We decided to use risers this year, since our groups were so small. We couldn't afford to purchase a set, so a former student of mine, from Diamond Bar High School, *Stephen Garber*, was kind enough to build us a set out of wood, that could be transported by truck. The only problem was that every section was so heavy it took about four kids to carry it! Nevertheless, we hauled them to every competition we went to! At the time of this writing, those wooden risers are *still in use*, located in the Brea Junior High choir classroom, where they have been for over ten years! The show choirs there rehearse on them daily!

Our first competition was the *Aztec Sing*! Since Masquerade's show featured more *traditional show choir singing and dancing*, it lent itself well to the Aztec Sing's *music heavy score sheet*. So, Doug and I agreed, *as our very first competition*, the Aztec Sing was perfect! The veteran kids seemed a bit nervous, as our show and costumes were *very different* from what they were used to. However, the new kids seemed just fine… they didn't have any other shows to compare this to! We performed well, with just a few jitters, and then we waited for the results. When the awards were announced, Masquerade had earned *3rd Place*, in their very first competition! The kids were extremely excited, while Doug and I were… *encouraged.* However, we knew that most festivals had a *much higher percentage of show categories on their score sheets*, than the Aztec Sing, so third place or not, *we had better get right back to work*!

If there was ever talk of *TOC* (Tournament of Champions) being in our back pocket, because Lawrence Fitz, the host, was a former choir member of mine, the following competition results, *completely obliterate that possibility*! Masquerade and Spellbound took their turns competing, and both groups, were pretty good. Masquerade performed with more confidence than they had at the Aztec Sing. Spellbound, however, was a little nervous, although I don't think anyone could tell. When the awards were announced… *neither of our groups' names were called.* We actually both came in *5th Place*, but trophies, at that time, were only awarded to the top three finishers! We had not experienced two of our groups being shutout, in the same competition, in quite a while, but, unfortunately, I had an ominous feeling that this year was going to be *full of surprises like that*! The most bizarre insult of the night was when one adjudicator asked me, on the score sheet, if I had written our ballad, *The Song That Goes Like This*, from *Spamalot*, because he had never heard it before? After that, we replaced *The Song That Goes Like This,* with another ballad that was tried and true, that even he, had probably heard of, called *Don't Cry Out Loud.* We never had a question *like that* asked, from any adjudicator for the remainder of the year… or *for the remainder of my career*, for that matter!

The next competition Spellbound attended was Bonita Vista's *For Lady's Only*. This festival gave out five trophies, so our girls had some hope of placing! The uncomfortable thing for me was that Diamond Bar's Solitaire, was also attending the competition, with their *new director, Patty Breitag*. As luck would have it, *they were seated right next to us in the theatre*! A couple of the Solitaire girls said "hi," to me, but the majority of them just looked on, with no expression. It must have been just as difficult for them as it was for me. We performed first, and did a better job than we had at TOC. They went on next, and performed a Michael Jackson medley, full of energy and pizzazz! I hoped our Brea girls were watching them… and they certainly were. When the awards were announced, Diamond Bar's Solitaire came in third while Brea's Spellbound earned *4th Place*, right behind them. *Hey a trophy is a trophy*… and this one, *was Spellbound's first*! Our girls were pretty excited. Mark Henson, was one of our adjudicators, so I asked him if he wanted to say, "hi" to the girls? He did, and that made this event even more special for the group. The most important thing our kids gained from this competition, in my opinion, was seeing first hand, *what pizzazz looks like on stage*, from Diamond Bar! I fully expected Spellbound to perform even better at their next competition, because of it!

Masquerade and O.C. Premier headed for the Los Alamitos High School competition, *Xtravaganza*, next. I believe this was my first time attending it. I didn't know what to expect, but it was a very long day. The theatre at Los Alamitos was small, but so were our groups, so we fit on the stage perfectly! O.C. Premiere performed first. They were still learning to perform on stage, but I thought they did well, considering that this was their first time out! Masquerade went next. They sang well, but I still wished that *everyone would commit to the choreography*! It was a good performance, but not a great one. When the awards were announced, once again, *neither of our groups' names were called*! How do you like that? *Another double shut out*! O.C. Premier actually came in seventh in the Intermediate Mixed Division, while Masquerade came in sixth in the Advanced Mixed Division. Not much to cheer about here, but both groups did get some much-needed experience!

Next, Masquerade, Spellbound and O.C. Premier attended the *Burroughs High School* festival. Masquerade and O.C. Premier were already depressed over their results from Los Alamitos, but I hoped that bad feeling would drive them to be more *energetic* as they competed. All of the "heavy hitters" were attending, as usual, so Doug and I saw this competition as more of a *learning experience* for our groups, although we never told them that. This was another *all-day event*, and each of us and about fifty zillion other groups took our turns performing. The festival was simply a long blur, but I was proud of our groups. Even O.C. Premier had sung and danced well. But honestly, *all of our groups were too small* to put out much sound, and that made it difficult to compete with the other groups, especially in the advanced divisions! The awards were finally announced, about midnight. O.C. Premier earned a *5th Place* in the Intermediate Mixed Division and Spellbound earned a *5th Place* in the Advanced Women's Division, while Masquerade *just missed placing*, by coming in sixth, in the Advanced Mixed Division. Not bad. Every Brea group had put out a good effort! I really felt like we were improving!

O.C. Premier was done competing for the year, but they had earned a trophy! I knew that this would motivate them all the more next year. Spellbound, however, had one competition left! It was, of all festivals, the Diamond Bar *Girls Night Out* competition! It was being held, just as it had been last year, during its first year, in the *Diamond Bar High School campus theatre*! I wasn't looking forward to returning to that campus, so soon after leaving, but I bit the bullet, and we went. Actually, it was fine, once we got there. All of my former students were friendly, and they were very nice to my Spellbound girls. Then my phone rang. *Jennie Eckels*, our senior soloist, had been in a car accident and was banged up, so she couldn't dance tonight's show! I asked if she could at least sing her ballad solo, and she told me that she would try to get to Diamond Bar High School before Spellbound had performed! Here was the big deal. If memory serves, there were six or seven groups competing, and they were only giving awards to the top three. Two of the groups, I can't remember who they were, but *they were going to beat us tonight*, just as they had all year! But that third place… *was up for grabs*. Jenny was an excellent singer and she gave Spellbound something special, when she sang the ballad, *Your Song*. In the end, she arrived in the nick of time, and did indeed sing the ballad with as much passion as she always did. When the awards were announced, Spellbound had earned *3rd Place* in the Advanced Women's Division! The girls were ecstatic, as were our parents who had come along to watch. So, Spellbound successfully accomplished what they had set out to do. I was so proud!

Next, it was Masquerade's turn to experience their final competition of the year! They traveled to Arcadia's, *Big Pow Wow*, held at the beautiful San Gabriel Mission Playhouse! Tonight was their last chance to place, again. They had already placed once, at the *Aztec Sing*, but had come up short at every competition since! The adjudicators were almost the same ones that had adjudicated the Aztec Sing and the score sheet was very similar, but the list of competing groups, for tonight, was truly impressive! So, when it came our turn to compete, the kids *gave-it-their-all* and made us proud! But would that be enough to place? We would find out in a couple of hours. When the awards were finally announced, Masquerade earned a solid *3rd Place*! This year had been tough for so many reasons. But placing tonight, had made us forget all about them, and instead, *had allowed us to feel hopeful for next year*!

Now, let me add that we did much more than simply compete in 2005-06. We put on a host of home concerts, performed for the community, and were responsible for putting on a musical, in March, toward the end of competition season! We selected, *Cinderella*, because it was a family show… and because it did not require a lot of solo-caliber boys, which we were *a little short on*. When it came time for the auditions, only a few boys tried out. Ultimately, *Drew Olvey* was cast as the King while *Alex Willert,* was cast as the Prince. Both boys performed well. All of the other male parts were much less vocally demanding, so thankfully, we were able to fill them. Joe Bartell, Brea Olinda's band director, led a select group, made-up of his students, and a few ringers, to accompany all of our performances, as was the tradition (started last year) at Brea. Our informal booster leader, Janet Youngblood, even organized a wonderful carnival, for the kids to attend, prior to the show. We also gave a *free performance for select students of the Brea elementary schools*, just to get word of the show out there! This turned out to be a full house of excitement! The performers loved it! In addition, we rented a professional set, and costumes, from Stagelight Productions. Doug and a number of students worked many hours making it look perfect! But, unfortunately, the BOHS theatre was only booked for a week, *so we had to close after only 4 performances*. Needless to say, the ticket sales we needed, in order to break-even... *never materialized.* So, we lost about five thousand dollars! I learned a lot by putting on that show. Number one, *we never used the school band again*, to accompany us, because, although they played well, they tended to play too loudly, and they required too much rehearsal time. All future shows were either done with a *live combo*, or *on tape*. Number two... I extended every other musical we did, at Brea, to *two weeks*! We needed that time, in order to sell enough tickets to break even. We actually made a profit on every show *since*!

2006 Cast List for "*Cinderella*"

Cinderella: *Jenny Eckles* **Prince:** *Alex Willert*
Stepmother: *Chrystin Galentine*
Olga: *Amy Sargent* **Petunia:** *Charlotte Larcabal*
King: *Drew Olvey* **Queen:** *Caitlin Sampson*
Herald: *Jeremy Parodi* **Godmother:** *Marisa Cabraloff*
Fairies: *Emily Veling & Lauren Ward*
Chef: *Zach Youngblood* **Steward:** *Nathan Carey*
Footman: *Ryan Clark* **Coachman:** *Sean Juarez*
Mice: *Shawnee Magliocchi • Kristin Webster*
Kristi Im • Stella Kim • Tiffany Nunez • Ashley Diskin
Horses: *Krysta Kurz • Kayla Luedke • Holly McMorris*
Melissa Hankins

Royal Chorus (High School)

Kalynne Allers • Yara Almouradi • Lenore Ayers
Michele Barnes • Adrian Berrner • Brandyna Bishop
Carissa Brinckerhoff • Lauren Brinckerhoff • Linette Choi
Kelly Faxon • Jessica Garcia • Jordyn Georgianna
Greta Goellrich • Ligia Gonzalez • Jamie Holman
Katie Horton • Elizabeth Irvine • Mariel Lising
Elsa Macedo, Kaitlin McKnight, Brianna Ortman
Emily Reed • Rory Rodriguez • Vivian Rodriguez • Liz Saenz
Sarah Schendon • Faye Tatonera • Jazmine Titular
Emily Visenger

Royal Children (Junior High)

Laura Bradburn • Kayla Camacho • Trish Crow
Julia Dwyer • Heather Freshour • Gabriela Hirsh
Kate Hocking • Hailey Holman • Alison Iles
Shelby Johnson • Justin Lovell • Hailey Markman
Sarah Morgigno • Alex Olvey • Crystal Perez
Lydia Prochman • Erin Purdom • Jill Purdom
Jessica Raine • Ruth Ramirez • Holly Ramsey
Sadie Reeves • Angelica Rodriguez • Valerie Schrepferman
Tana Schwarz • Kevin Siazon • Kaylie Simec
Brittany Slater-Shew • Melissa Strom • Alexa Vandermeer

We ended the year by taking a *four-night trip to New York City*! This was only the third time I had been to that great city, but the Diamond Bar trip, the year before, convinced me that this was a place that offered so much, musicals, history, shopping and sightseeing, that maybe we'd come back here every other year? This was not a competition trip, but purely sightseeing. The trip's group consisted of the choir staff, about thirty kids and parents, and *Marti Repp* and *Rita Jones*, who both worked at the school. They just asked me one day if they could come along? It was very refreshing, actually! Marti, in fact, continued to go with us on every major trip we took, until I retired in 2016. By the way, the trip was great! We saw four musicals, as a group, *Wicked, The Phantom of the Opera, Beauty And The Beast or Avenue Q* and *Spamalot.* Some people saw two additional shows during their free time! Yes. I decided, after that trip, *we would be returning soon!*

The final thing I would like to mention about the 2005-06 school year was that although it had been rife with upheaval, change and a new direction, by the end of the year, Doug and I strongly felt that most of the students *had bought into the new United Choirs of Brea*! I want to thank all of those kids who gave our changes a chance. Aside from the seniors, such as *Jenny Eckels*, who had been such a major part of this first year's success… it was the underclassmen, who were providing the bulk of the support! Doug and I both had the feeling that next year, this support would pay major dividends!

Our excellent student officers for the **2005-06** school year, are listed on the next page:

Masquerade/ Chamber
President: *Drew Olvey*
Asst. Pres: *Jennifer Eckles & Stella Kim*
Vice-Pres: *Caitlyn Grant*
Dance Capt: *Amy Sargent & Kristy Im*
Secretary: *Amy Sargent*
Treasurer: *Jeremy Parodi*
Publicist: *Greta Goellrich*

Spellbound/ Silver Notes
President: *Ashley Johnson*
Asst. Pres: *Hollie McMorris*
Vice-Pres: *Melissa Hankins*
Dance Captain *Kaitlyn McKnight*
Sec/Treas: *Jocelyn Green*
Historian: *Krysta Kurtz*

O.C. Premier/ Wildcat Choir
President: *Ligia Gonzalez*
Assistant President: *Faye Tajonera & Ashley Johnson*
Vice-President: *Ryan Pflug & Carly Novoa*
Dance Captain: *Jacqueline Quijano*
Secretary/Treasurer: *Megan Fero*
Historian: *Lauren Kent*

CHAPTER 10

Brea Olinda High School... 2006-2009... Brea Rises Again!

Remember the *three long years of waiting*, before a Nogales show choir ever won a trophy? Well, Doug and I were older and wiser now, and did not have the *patience* to wait that long again, before one of our show choirs at Brea *won a competition*! We had high hopes for Masquerade and Spellbound, following their rebuilding years in 2005-06. Unfortunately, half of the boys in Masquerade, realizing after a year, that they were not really *cut out to be choir kids*, after all… *quit*! Nonetheless, including the boys we had added, I believe we still had 14 boys and 26 girls. This was still a bit on the small side, but Doug designed the show to make it work! Spellbound, had a healthy 42 girls, which was also very workable. Talking about miracles… California had an "arts fund" they gave to each public school, that year, to *buy necessary equipment. That was a completely unexpected godsend*, as I was now able to purchase a *complete set of risers for the choirs, along with a synthesizer and a lot of choral music*! This marked the only time, spanning my entire career, that California had offered that! Great timing! Our choir band changed a bit, as *Bo Eder* resigned and was replaced on drums by *Drew Hemwall*. We also added two new guitarists, *Jon Collier* and *Anthony Arcos*. Happily, Hannah and Kramer were still there to anchor the band. Our competition sets, for the 2006-07 school year included:

Masquerade 2006-07
Costume Colors:
Silver, Black
Competition Set
I Got Rhythm
By The Sea
Summer In The City

O.C. Premier 2006-07
Costume Colors:
Unknown
Competition Set
Tear Them Down
Seasons of Love
Crazy
Hit Me With A Hot Note

Spellbound 2006-07
Costume Colors:
Pink, Black
Competition Set
Anything Goes
Country Girls
Heartbreaker

Thunder Cats 2006-07
Costume Colors:
Unknown
Competition Set
R.O.C.K. In The U.S.A.
Brown Eyed Squirrel
Duke of Earl
Centerfold

Chamber Choir 2006-07
Costume Colors: *Black*
Competition Set (Vocal Jazz)
Trickle Trickle
Moonglow
A Quiet Place
I Return To Music

In this, my second year at Brea, I was able to drop *Music Appreciation*, and split the Chamber Choir/ Masquerade class, I had had last year, in half! Chamber Choir, was deemed our new classical and vocal jazz group. So, now there was no confusion about the name of Brea's *top mixed show choir…* it was *Masquerade*! We also added *Thunder Cats*, our all boys group, following in the footsteps of *Renegade* (Nogales) and *Notorious* (Diamond Bar) before them. I have no record of Thunder Cats competing all year, so I am guessing that they only performed at the *Spring Magic* concerts, at the end of the year. One more thing, Spellbound decided to enter a national Showstoppers competition in Orlando, Florida, which was being held at *Disney's Epcot Park.* Our girls were *very excited to be the only Brea group, going*!

Masquerade began their competition season, by traveling to The *Aztec Sing*, at Citrus College. The times had changed, and it was no longer everyone's first competition. Many groups had stopped competing there, altogether, I believe, for three basic reasons:

1. *Because of the stringent time limits, which did not allow them the necessary time to set-up and tear down their "stage sets."*
2. *Because it came in January, which was pretty early for most groups to have their shows learned and prepared for competition.*
3. *Because of the vocal-heavy score sheet, at a time when most groups were greatly expanding every aspect of their shows!*

But we went. When it was time for Masquerade to hit the stage, they were ready. We actually had a great show that night. When the awards were announced, we had earned *2nd Place* along with the plaque for *Best Showmanship*! We hadn't won, *but we sure came close*! Everyone was hoping that this was *an omen of even better things to come*!

The very next week, Masquerade attended the *Diamond Bar Spectacular.* It was also held at Citrus College. Our competitors were tougher here than at the Aztec Sing, as more groups were now ready to compete. The competition was a blur of good show choirs performing. When the awards were announced, we had earned *4th Place*! Masquerade still had a ways to go, in order to become an elite show choir, like the *Brea Chamber Choir*, was in the past, *but we did place*! Masquerade had already earned two trophies this year, which was our *grand total* for all of last year. We felt empowered!

Next, Masquerade and Spellbound, traveled to the *Burroughs High School* competition. This one had been good to us, over the years, but this year looked to be very competitive. With every performance, Masquerade was getting stronger. Soon, we felt, that strength would naturally morph into a win! Spellbound was competing for the first time this year. They were just a little bit nervous. Both of our groups looked and sounded good in their performances. When the awards were announced, Spellbound earned *4th Place*, in the Advanced Women's Division, while Masquerade had tied with Hart for *4th Place*, in the Advanced Mixed Division. I won't lie. Our kids were disappointed. Yes, both groups had placed, but they had expected to do better! Both groups were obviously much stronger than they were last year, but apparently, as the results had confirmed, *we were not where we needed to be, yet*!

For both Masquerade and Spellbound, their next destination was Whittier Union High School, to compete in *TOC* (Tournament of Champions). The results here had always been unpredictable, because usually the judges were not from the normal pool of adjudicators that many local competitions used. This was good, because it made every group feel like they had a chance, and bad, because it was tough to prepare for. For the Masquerade show, we had purchased a portable, but professional grade, *strobe light*, which I operated from the orchestra pit, to add another dimension to a select part of their show. I believe that we had also used it at Burroughs. Spellbound hit the stage and the crowd loved them! That seemed very promising. When it came Masquerade's turn to perform, they received a similar reaction. The crowd really cheered for the strobe light effect, which made me glad that I had purchased it! When the awards were announced, Spellbound had earned *1st Place* along with both plaques for *Best Showmanship* and *Best Musicianship*, while Masquerade… *did not place!* They had earned their *first shutout*, of the year! I remember, senior, Drew Olvey asking me, what had happened? To this day, I don't really know? Their performance seemed to be solid! But, when it comes right down to it, every competition is a turkey shoot, especially when you don't have any idea what the adjudicators like? On the other hand, the sweep for Spellbound was a *huge confidence booster*!

The Los Alamitos High School competition, *Xtravaganza*, was next. We had not done much there, last year, but both Marquis and Spellbound were ready to prove that they were now groups to be reckoned with. The advanced competition ran most of the afternoon and into the night. Spellbound performed first. I recall the stage being a bit small, but their performance was spot on! Before Masquerade performed, while in the warm-up room, we talked about *proving how good we were by giving a totally electric performance*! The kids shared that they didn't really care where they placed, as long as their show was perfect! I was proud of their attitude, as they entered the stage. Their performance *was* electric, and garnered a lot of applause from the audience. When the kids came off stage, I could see that they were proud! Well, when the awards were announced, Spellbound had earned *3rd Place* in the Advanced Women's Division. This was a definite improvement over their 5th place finish last year, so they were happy. In the Advanced Mixed Division, it was very exiting as they slowly announced the top four. In *4th place* was *Burroughs Powerhouse*, in *3rd place* was *Burbank's In Sync*, in *2nd place*, with the *Best Musicianship* plaque were *Arcadia's Chanteurs* and in *1st Place* with the *Best Showmanship* plaque... was *Brea Olinda's Masquerade*! The theatre went nuts! Apparently, we *weren't supposed to win*? A few directors and choreographers were shouting their displeasure outside while I witnessed one director almost break into tears as he yelled at the host director for his group's poor showing. The only people who congratulated us were our own parents. *This entire reaction felt totally surreal*! But, this also opened my eyes. In the old days, show choir competitions were judged by, presumably impartial experts, who tried to be fair. Today, I'm not so sure that's true, at least for some competitions? Why did these directors get so angry when they did not win? They certainly were not setting a good example for their kids? Arcadia, predominantly a vocal group, came in second and had won the plaque for Best Musicianship, which they often did, so that came as no surprise. The only thing amiss, to these directors... *was that they had not won!* Their brand of show choir, where it's *only about winning*... does not sound fun to me, on the days when they lose... *from the looks of things*!

O.C. Premier (novice) and Chamber Choir (advanced), competed at the *Fullerton College Jazz Festival*, which no longer hosted show choirs. So, they both entered their competitions as vocal jazz groups, which they were truthfully… *not.* But, this gave them a place to go. I don't need to tell you that although they sang very well… *they did not come close to placing on that day.* But we had a fun bonding experience. None of the kids really seemed upset. After all, *their director knew very little about the vocal jazz style*, and they all *knew* this would probably happen, going in.

It was finally time for Spellbound, to get ready for their big trip to Orlando, Florida, to compete in *Showstoppers*! Sadly, only about half of the girls in the group (23) had ultimately decided to go, due to the cost. I believe each kid paid about $800.00, which was inclusive of everything. Doug and I, and probably the group, knew that we would not win this, at half strength… but since there were three trophies and only three girls groups competing… *we were guaranteed a trophy in a national competition*! How do you like those odds? We arrived in Orlando, got to our Disney hotel, and I found that I already had a message, at the front desk to call Showstoppers. I called them, and they asked me where my permission slips were? I asked if they meant medical forms (which I had), and they told me, no, we had to have signed parent permission slips from every participant… *Disney rules.* Apparently, I'd missed that part of the instructions. No problem. We contacted Brea Olinda High School, and they took care of getting all of those permission slips signed and overnighted to Showstoppers, the next day. That night was supposed to be the traditional pre-competition meeting with Showstoppers, the adjudicators and the directors. It happened to storm that night, and besides, I was tired, so, *I decided not to go*. The next day, at stage warm-ups, at Epcot, the Showstoppers people acted a little miffed at our decision not to attend. But, I figured the worst they could do to us was to place us last… but since that was 3rd place… I fully expected to get that anyway! Well, our tiny group of predominantly freshmen and sophomores performed their hearts out, but the other two groups were bigger, older and more experienced, so I knew what was coming. When the awards were announced, Spellbound, as predicted, had earned *3rd Place* at Showstoppers Epcot! Our girls screamed with joy at the third place trophy they had won, while the group who had come in second was visibly crying. Show choir results are always better when you can look at a *non-win, with a positive spin*!

Our final competition of the year was the *Hart High School* festival, in Newhall. I knew that we would not be scored well there, because the judges were all from the mid-west, and from experience, I'd found that they generally seemed to like *the big band style,* while we had a *small combo* and *were just a different animal to them.* That night, Spellbound and Masquerade performed very well, *but I had warned the kids, during warm-ups, that these adjudicators would probably not like our style.* When the awards were announced, Spellbound earned *3rd Place* in the Advanced Women's Division while Masquerade, in the Advanced Mixed Division, was *shutout,* for a second time, this year. But, to a kid, both groups thought that these had been their best shows of the year, and trophy or not, *no one could take away that memory*! For the season, Spellbound had earned a first, two thirds, a fourth and a fifth, and had placed at every competition they had attended. Masquerade had earned a first, a second and two fourths. They also *did not* place at two of their competitions. This competition record was far superior to last year, and *both groups had a nice win under their belts*! With so many talented kids, experienced one or two years with us, we felt that our breakout year was definitely appearing on the horizon, in 2007-08! However, I feel that since this was the first year that Spellbound and Masquerade had *won,* since Doug and I had been at Brea, these talented and hard-working students should be acknowledged:

Our First Advanced BOHS Show Choirs To Win A Competition!

Masquerade 2006-07

Emily Reed • Melissa Hankins • Madison Reeves
Elizabeth Stark • Jocelyn Green • Kaylin Woolard
Charlotte Larcabal • Stella Kim • Greta Goellrich
Shawnee Magliocchi • Brooke Fuller • Tracie Miller
Jordyn Georgianna • Hollie McMorris • Alex Willert
Justin Lovell • Kevin Siazon • Ryan Clark • Sam Rood
Zack Youngblood • Rory Rodriguez • Cezar Hernandez
Kristen Webster • Kaitlyn McKnight • Emily Veling
Shannon Eastman • Hailey Markman • Krysta Kurz
Elizabeth Irvine • Kelly Faxon • Lauren Ward
Caitlyn Grant • Amy Sargent • Marisa Cabraloff
Chrystin Galentine • Drew Olvey • Alex Olvey
Harrison Schultz • John Paul Wilson • Jon Baker
Ryan Pflug • Anthony Arcos • Josh Rood

Spellbound 2006-07

Shannon Eastman • Kaitlyn McKnight • Kalyanne Allers
Kailey Van Voris • Kaitlyn April • Jill Purdom
Tiffany Nunez • Hanna Coonis • Elizabeth Garcia
Brittany Slater-Shew • Jacquie Quijano • Hollie McMorris
Kaylin Woolard • Jamie Holman • Dani Gomez
Kayla Camacho • Erin Purdom • Kayla Luedke
Ashley Diskin • Alina Rotariu • Lisa Bales • Amy Sargent
Laura Bradburn • Heather La Carra • Jordyn Georgianna
Katie Horton • Emily Morgigno • Shelby Johnson
Emily Visinger • Marisa Cabraloff • Sarah Schenden
Elizabeth Irvine • Valerie Schrepferman

The final event I would like to mention about the 2006-07 school year was that the choir successfully put on the musical, *Grease,* for two weeks! We made a nice profit, and the kids that performed in it, really enjoyed it! Our show choir band, including Hannah, Drew and Kramer, played live for all of the performances, which was especially nice! Putting on a musical was fast becoming many of our students' *favorite activities of the year*! The entire cast list for *Grease* is listed below:

2007 Cast List for "*Grease*"

Miss Lynch: *Marti Repp*
Patty Simcox: *Kaitlin McKnight*
Eugene: *Alex Olvey*
Fred: *Kevin Siazon*
Jan: *Stella Kim*
Marty: *Shea Nichols*
Rizzo: *Chrystin Galentine*
Doodie: *Jared Toves*
Roger: *Mark Leyva*
Kenicke: *Drew Olvey*
Sonny: *Zack Youngblood*
Frenchy: *Madison Reeves*
Sandy: *Brooke Fuller*
Danny: *Alex Willert*
Tom The Jock: *John Paul Wilson*
Vince Fontaine: *Gary Stein*
Scorpion Leader: *Mike Cabraloff*
Cha Cha: *Emily Veling*
Teen Angel: *Drew Olvey*
T.V. Director: *Anthony Arcos*
Camera Man: *Chris Mosqueda*
Johnny Casino: *Kevin Siazon*

The Johnny Angels

Amy Sargent • Kristen Webster • Marisa Cabraloff
Greta Goellrich • Jordyn Georgianna • Hollie McMorris
Stephanie Warshaw • Kayla Camacho

The Scorpions

Carissa Brinckerhoft • Teya Delancey • Anna Chi
Chris Mosqueda • Harrison Schultz

The Cheerleaders

Elizabeth Irvine • Lauren Ward • Ashley Diskin
Erin Purdom • Jill Purdom • Brittney Slater-Shew
Kelly Faxon • Shannon Eastman • Emily Veling
Kaylee Dysart

The Grease Ensemble

Wade Beach • Mallorie Flowers • Jumana Salameh
Heather Freshour • Kimberly Mendez • Elizabeth Garcia
Lauren Kent • Julia Dwyer • Tara Mazeika • Sadie Reeves-Rios
Sarah Morgigno • Kate Hocking • Monique Amin •Allison Rigsby
Danielle Santos • Jezebel Durado • Dayna Booth
Katie Horton • Stacey Agrelius • Kaitlyn Nichols
Melissa Strom • Lydia Prochman • Tana Schwarz
Jessica Raine • Emily Malotte • Beckie Clark
Savannah Maske • Hailey Holman • Shelby Johnson
Adrienne Carey • Alexa Vandermeer • Gabriel Navarro
Emmalee Wetzel • Emily Elias • Gabie Hirsh • Baylee Heagle

This was the first year since I had been at Brea Olinda, that we *began the school year* with multiple and individual officers for each group! The students were beginning to learn what "*autonomous*" meant, as for the second year, every group thought for itself!

Our wonderful student officers for the **2006-07** school year, included:

Chamber Choir
President: *Stella Kim*
Vice-Pres: *Alex Willert*
Sec/Treas: *Kaitlin McKnight*
Hist/Lib: *Amy Sargent*

O.C. Premier
President: *Megan Fero*
Vice-Pres: *Nikki Gonzalez*
S/T: *Heather Freshour*
Hist/Lib: *Lauren Kent*

Masquerade
President: *Amy Sargent*
Asst. President: *Drew Olvey*
Vice-Pres: *Marissa Cabraloff & Charlotte Larcabal*
Sec/Treas: *Kaitlin McKnight*
Hist/Lib: *Greta Goellrich*
Dance Captain: *Madison Reeves*

Spellbound
Pres: *Kaitlin McKnight*
VP: *Shannon Eastman*
Ashley Diskin
Sec/Treas: *Sarah Schenden*
Hist/L: *Jordyn Georgianna & Melissa Hankins*
Dance Captain: *Amy Sargent*

Thunder Cats
President: *Drew Olvey*

The summer of 2007 arrived and Doug and I quickly got to work, trying to figure out what songs to give Masquerade and Spellbound? We knew that this was going to be a breakout year for them, so we took our time, and selected a little vintage stuff, and some brand new arrangements, as well. This was also the first year of *Tiffany's,* an intermediate women's group that we created mostly to train the incoming freshman girls. *O.C. Premier* was dropped, as a result. Chamber Choir, unofficially, changed its name to *Chamber Singers*, for no better reason, than *I liked it better*. Chamber Singers remained our traditional choir, but they also got into the show choir competing act, developing a show to compete in the intermediate mixed division, for the first time! We planned a trip back to New York City in May, for anyone, in choir, who wanted to go! All they had to do was *pay fifteen hundred dollars*, covering, air travel, hotel (Marriott Marquis), tickets to 4 Broadway shows, a daily food stipend, all bus travel and travelers insurance (mandatory per the district). Our competition sets included:

Spellbound 2007-8
Costume Colors:
Black & Pink
Competition Set
The Time of the Season
You Ought To Be In Pictures
Hit Me With Your Best Shot

Chamber Singers 2007-08
Costume Colors:
Unknown
Costume Set
Hold Me Rock Me
Hand Jive/ Day-o
Show Me The Way
Do You Love Me?

Masquerade 2007-08
Costume Colors:
White, Pink, Blue
Competition Set
In The Hills of Shilo
Songs of the South
The Corny Collins Show
Supercalifragilistic

Tiffany's 2007-08
Costume Colors:
White & Blue
Competition Set
Tiffany's Theme
Soon It's Gonna Rain
Don't Rain On My
My First Love
Big Spender
Too Darn Hot

<u>Thunder Cats 2007-08</u>

Costume Colors: *White w/ Hawaiian Shirts*

<u>Competition Sets</u>

Takin' Care of Business
Sixteen Tons
Hair
Blackbird
Respect
My Heart Will Go On
Centerfold

This was such a big year for us! In all, we now had five competing groups, at Brea Olinda, that all competed in either the advanced or intermediate show choir divisions! I just wanted to mention that Tiffany's had a theme song, that we ended up using, almost every year, in their shows, *because the girls liked it.* At the Fall Magic concerts, every year, we even asked all of the *Tiffany's alumni*, to come up on the stage, to dance and sing the Tiffany's Theme, with the current group! We also spent a lot of years ending their show with, *Too Darn Hot.* It's traditions, like these, that seem to endear former members to the group. Thunder Cats also ended their show, most years, with J. Geils' *Centerfold.* Again, that's because *all of the boys liked it*! In Masquerade, we added a Corny Collins set to the show, because *Hairspray* was popular, at the time. We also arranged a medley of Mary Poppins songs to end the show. Doug envisioned chimney sweeps, brooms, and ferocious dancing. It all sounded great to me!

Masquerade began their 2008 competition season by competing at the *Aztec Sing*! As I mentioned, not all advanced mixed groups attended this one anymore. Still, if I remember right, there were about nine groups participating. When Masquerade hit the stage, they weren't just good… they were great! *The Hills of Shilo* is such an effective a cappella and *Mary Poppins*, as it turned out, *was a fabulous ender*. When the awards were announced, Masquerade had earned *1st Place* along with both plaques, for *Best Showmanship* and *Best Musicianship*! This was the very first time that a group of mine had *won* the Aztec

Sing, since we began competing, in 1978, *a span of over thirty years*!

Next, Masquerade competed at the *Diamond Bar Spectacular*. The lineup of competitors was tough, but the kids felt pretty confident they would do well, after sweeping at the Aztec Sing, the week before. The time came, and Masquerade once again performed very well, receiving spontaneous applause throughout the show. When the awards were announced, Masquerade had earned *2nd Place*. Not as exciting as a sweep, but very good, just the same.

Masquerade, then traveled to San Diego, to compete in *Bonita Vista's* new competition for mixed groups! They had not competed here previously, and were pleasantly surprised at how friendly everyone was. There were two divisions at this festival with Masquerade competing in the advanced. The stage was a little small, but Masquerade had another exciting performance. When the awards were announced they had earned *1st Place* and the plaque for *Best Showmanship*. The group was so excited! They had just collected their second win, in the advanced mixed division, in their first three competitions!

Our next competition took place at Diamond Bar High School, called, *Girls Night Out!* They offered divisions, so we took Spellbound (advanced) and Tiffany's (intermediate). It began in the late afternoon and continued through the evening. There was a full house competing, and some very good groups among them. Tiffany's went first! The adjudicators looked charmed, as they all smiled throughout their performance. It was a very good performance, especially when you considered that this was *Tiffany's very first competition... ever*! Spellbound competed a bit later, and was also very good, although their set was *completely different* from Tiffany's, consisting of a lot of rock 'n roll, which the adjudicators were not as visibly taken with it. When the awards were announced, Tiffany's earned *1st Place* and both plaques for *Best Showmanship* and *Best Musicianship*, in the Intermediate Division, while Spellbound, earned *2nd Place* and the plaque for *Best Showmanship*, in the Advanced! They were beaten by a wonderfully vocally blended, *Arcadia New Spirit*! Overall it was a very successful outing!

Tiffany's went off to compete at a festival I had never been to, before, *the Alta Loma High School Show Choir Competition*! It was especially designed to accommodate, *only*, *intermediate level show choirs*. So, I thought this might be the perfect place to bring Tiffany's, following their win at Diamond Bar. It was actually a very interesting competition. I don't believe I had ever seen any of the show choirs competing there, at any other competition, this year? But, nonetheless, they were solid young groups. The competition began and it wasn't too long, before we headed backstage to warm-up, before our performance! We experienced a small hiccup, however, during our warm-up, when our girls tried, *unsuccessfully,* to sing their a cappella ballad, *Soon It's Gonna Rain*, in tune! The sopranos seemed to be very nervous, as they kept sharping, even after I brought it to their attention! Finally, their president, *Madison Reeves*, spoke very calmly to them about what they needed to do to win this competition. They responded very positively, although they still sharped on the song in warm-up. If memory serves, the stage was rather small, at the end of a multi-purpose room, where the choirs and audience were seated. But Tiffany's wasn't a very big group, so they fit perfectly. The group was very focused as they sang and danced their first song, *Tiffany's Theme*. At the end of that, I slowly walked to the front of the stage to direct, *Soon It's Gonna Rain*. I was smiling at the girls, but in my head I was saying, "Please don't sharp!" The a cappella ballad began… *and it was beautiful*! They reached the part where they had been sharping so badly in warm-up… and they sang it *perfectly in tune*! The rest of their performance was a blur to me, as I was so excited about their singing in *Soon It's Gonna Rain*! Some would say that I had just witnessed a miracle… but I don't think so. I credit the group's quick turnaround to Madison Reeves. She knew just what to say, and it worked. At the end of the competition, the awards were announced. We were just hoping to make the top three. Tiffany's earned *1st Place* and both plaques for *Best Showmanship* and *Best Musicianship*! Alta Loma proved to be a long bus ride up and a long bus ride back… *but no one complained.*

Our next competition was *TOC* (Tournament of Champions) at Whittier Union High School. TOC only offered two divisions, *advanced mixed* and *advanced women.* So, in order to bring Tiffany's, they had to compete against Spellbound, in the advanced women's division. TOC had not been kind to Masquerade over the past couple of years. But, we were still inventing ourselves then… now, we felt that we could be very competitive *everywhere* we went! Tiffany's competed first. They were every bit as good as they had been during their first two competitions! But, there was a higher level of competition here! Spellbound was our second group to perform. They were tough, filled with so much personality. They were quite literally, *a joy to watch*! Masquerade was next. Everyone in the audience seemed to love their show. I mean, what was not to like? Opening with, *In the Hills of Shilo*, a beautiful a cappella, followed by the impressive choreography in *Songs of the South*, going into a fun medley of Corny Collins (Hairspray) and the Beatles, and ending with *Mary Poppins*! When the awards were announced, Spellbound earned *1st Place* along with both plaques for *Best Showmanship* and *Best Musicianship*, in the Advanced Women's Division. Tiffany's earned *2nd Place*, in that same division. Meanwhile, Masquerade also earned *1st Place* and both plaques for *Best Showmanship* and *Best Musicianship*, in the Advanced Mixed Division! For the year, so far, this marked the *third competition win for Masquerade*! This also marked the first competition win for Spellbound and the first time in three tries that Tiffany's *hadn't* won! *The Brea show choir program was officially back*!

The Los Alamitos High School *Xtravaganza*, was our very next competition. We took all five of our groups there, because it offered different divisions for everyone! It was one short year ago, that Masquerade had won this, *in very dramatic fashion*, and thereby announced their return to the upper ranks of mixed show choirs! Once again, it proved to be *a hideously long day*, as we began competing at nine in the morning, and the competition finally ended about midnight! But, we all got the chance to compete, so that made it worthwhile! At midnight, when they finally announced the trophy winners, Chamber Singers took *2nd*

Place, in the Intermediate Mixed Division, Tiffany's took *1st Place* and both plaques for *Best Showmanship* and *Best Musicianship* in the Intermediate Women's Division, Thunder Cats took *3rd Place* in the Men's Division, Spellbound took *3rd Place* in the Advanced Women's Division, while Masquerade took *3rd Place* in the Advanced Mixed Division. What a great first year Tiffany's was enjoying, by earning their *third first place of the year*, and Chamber Singers proved to be very competitive, earning a second place, in their very first competition! Masquerade, Spellbound and Thunder Cats were happy with their thirds, albeit they were all focused on winning, their next time out! Overall, it ended up being a very productive day!

Since Thunder Cats and Chamber Singers had only been able to compete once, this year, we signed them up to compete in a brand new show choir competition, at Disney's California Adventure. It was called, *Five, Six, Seven, Eight,* and was being held on the outdoor *Monsters Inc.* stage. The day arrived, and we entered California Adventure. Soon we were met by our hosts, escorted backstage, and the students changed into their costumes, which were waiting for them, thanks to a choir mom, who had earlier driven them backstage. Then, we warmed up. Everyone in the groups was happy to be here, especially many of the boys, who were actually in *both groups,* and got to compete twice! As I remember, there were no divisions here, except for mixed, women, middle school and men. So, Chamber Singers were competing against the Arcadia Chanteurs and other formidable competitors! Chamber Singers went on first. Their show was fun and musical, from *Hold Me Rock Me* to *Do You Love Me!* They got a nice round of applause from the audience. A while later, Thunder Cats took the stage. This year, they had a longer show, and a lot of talent! This show also featured the all-male ballet for *Titanic's* love song, *My Heart Will Go On*, as well as the manly *Sixteen Tons*, lead sung by Jon Baker and *Respect,* sung completely in falsetto, by Alex Willert. *Basically, their show was a riot*! They really got the crowd going! Soon the awards were announced. In the mixed division, Chamber Singers earned *3rd Place*, behind the Arcadia Chanteurs, who won the division. In the men's division, Thunder Cats earned *1st Place*! It was a very fun day for all of us!

Thunder Cats, Chamber Singers and Tiffany's were now done competing. They had all experienced very successful campaigns. Solitaire, however, still had one festival left, on their schedule… the *Hart High School* competition. Hart had not been kind to Masquerade, last year, when they didn't even place, but Spellbound wanted to go, anyway. The Hart High School stage was a little small, but it was a good "intimate" size for Spellbound, who was used to rehearsing in the Brea choir room, which was even smaller! Spellbound went on stage in early evening and had to wait until about 11:30 pm, to find out how they had done, because the advanced mixed groups had to perform first. When the trophies were finally announced, Spellbound had earned *3rd Place*. Not bad, but they had acquired a taste for *first,* over the past two seasons, and they were determined to win more than one competition, next year!

Masquerade's final competition of the year was the *Arcadia Big Pow Wow*. As usual, this was one of the *most anticipated competitions of the year*, because although they had never won it, they had always placed! The evening got started as the intermediate groups performed. Not long after they were done, they started the advanced division, and soon it was our turn to go into warm-up. After getting physically and vocally warmed-up, some of the officers began their pep talks. Then it was my turn. I told the kids that they had already grown into one of the top show choirs in California… so not to worry about placement, just have fun! I followed this with several choruses of "pizzazz," before we were finally called to the stage. The show was the best of the year, as it should have been. When the awards were announced, Masquerade earned *3rd Place* in the Advanced Mixed Division. Our kids cheered and hugged. Of course, first place, would have been nice, but they had executed a nearly perfect show and had the time of their lives doing it… and apparently… that was more important to them than the final outcome.

One very important thing that occurred during the 2007-08 school year, was that after years of having to rent trucks to carry our props and sets to competitions, *we bought our very own green prop trailer*! According to longtime choir parent, Andrea Strom, this represented a joint-fundraising effort between two of our choir parents, *Bud Reed* and *Craig Georgianna.* They even personalized the trailer with painted likenesses of the choir staff! This saved us a lot of money on rentals and went on to serve the choir extremely well through the remainder of my tenure and beyond!

Our annual musical was *Crazy For You*, with *Alex Willert* playing the lead role of Bobby and two fellow juniors, *Kristen Webster* and *Lauren Howard* switching off, performing the female lead of Polly. Junior, *Rachael Kuhl* (Doug's niece) was also a lead, playing Bobby's girlfriend, Irene, switching off with senior, *Chrystin Galentine*. *Jeff Howarth*, a senior played Lank, Irene's love interest. I just thought I would mention this casting, because four out of these six leads were *juniors*! We didn't have a large senior class, and it was really the juniors, who were leading the way. I should mention that this year, both Rachael Kuhl and Lauren Howard, had transferred into Brea as juniors, *because they wanted to be a part of the Brea show c*hoirs. This was called an *instant upgrade* for us! Of the six presidents we had, two were seniors and four were juniors. Of the other officers, three were seniors, eight were juniors, five were sophomores and five were freshmen. Just as we'd hoped, each group having their own officers had truly *empowered them*! This was a very fun time to be in the United Choirs of Brea! Oh, by the way, *Crazy For You* was both a critical and financial success! This 2008 production remains one of my favorites, out of all the musicals I have ever been a part of!

2008 Cast List for "*Crazy For You*"

Bobby: *Alex Willert*
Polly: *Lauren Howard/ Kristen Webster*
Zangler: *Josiah Pak/ Justin Lovell*
Lank: *Jeff Howarth*
Irene: *Chrystin Galentine/ Rachael Kuhl*
Patricia: *Liz Irvine/ Jordyn Georgianna*
Eugene: *Christian Villanueva*
Everett: *Harrison Schultz/ Cezar Hernandez*
Mother: *Emily Reed/ Mallorie Flowers*
Perkins: *Chris Mosqueda* **Chauffeur:** *Michael Tirona*
Junior: *Jocelyn Green* **Billy:** *Michael Tirona*
Tess: *Kaylie Dysart* **Sam:** *Kevin Siazon*
Patsy: *Madison Reeves* **Jimmy:** *Melanie Ramsey*
Mitzi: *Ally Catanesi* **Harry:** *Josiah Pak/ Justin Lovell*
Moose: *Jared Toves* **Wyatt:** *Michael Garate*
Pete: *Cezar Hernandez/ Harrison Schultz*
Mingo: *Harry Alegria* **Custus:** *Chris Mosqueda*

Follies Girls

Julia Dwyer • Ashley Schweitzer • Sadie Reeves
Jen Harpster • Kate Hocking • Kayla Camacho
Erin Purdom • Jill Purdom • Kellie Galentine • Allison Iles
Melissa Strom • Chanel Dickson • Jumana Salameh
Hailey Holman • Hollie Ramsey • Becca Harpster
Jordyn Georgianna • Melissa Hankins

Cowboy Chorus

Vanessa Alvarez • Emmalee Wetzel • Rachel Gallegos
Gabie Hirsh • Challoi McCuller • Jessica Raine
Adriana Vonjo • Shelby Johnson • Eunice Yoon
Jezabel Jurado • Justine Garate • Sarah Morgigno
Emily Malotte • Katie Bower • Emily Elias • Megan Miller
Amy Czerwinsky • Allison Rigsby • Beckie Clark
Gabriel Navarro • Devanie Zenzola • Baylee Heagle
Megan Strom • Isi Perez • Madeline Ellingson
Samantha Seyed • Marysa Leite • Olivia Chapman
Jake Flowers • Daniel Cabrera • Alexa Vandermeer

The final thing I would like to mention, regarding 2008, is that we returned to New York City, just as I'd hoped, *two years after our first trip*. As mentioned, the cost increased to $1750.00 per person, but that didn't seem to deter anyone who really wanted to go. We left BOHS and drove to LAX with 46 students, parents and staff, making up our tour group. This time, the Marriot Marquis was not available, so we stayed at the *also beautiful,* Westin Times Square. We attended the musicals *Grease, Legally Blonde, Cry Baby* or *Spring Awakening* and *Young Frankenstein*, among others. We all had a wonderful time, and as usual… looked forward to traveling there again!

Our exceptional student officers, from the **2007-08** school year were:

Masquerade
President: *Chrystin Galentine*
Vice-Pres: *Madison Reeves, Alex Willert & Kevin Siazon*
Secretary: *Melissa Hankins*
Treasurer: *Kayla Camacho*
Historian: *Kristen Webster*

Chamber Choir
President: *Jocelyn Green & Alex Willert*
Vice-President: *Jared Toves*
Sec/Treas: *Chrystin Galentine*
Historian: *Madison Reeves*

Thunder Cats
President: *Jon Baker*
Vice-Pres: *Cezar Hernandez*

Spellbound
Pres: *Jordyn Georgianna*
VP: *Kristen Webster, Kelly Faxon & Kayla Camacho*
Secretary: *Jill Purdom*
Treas: *Melissa Hankins*
Historian: *Madison Reeves*

Tiffany's
President: *Madison Reeves*
Vice-President: *Savannah Maske & Heather Freshour*
Secretary: *Julia Dwyer*
Treasurer: *Alison Iles*
Historian: *Melissa Strom*

2008-09 was bittersweet for me. The show choirs were now built-up and competitive, but, the kids, who had pioneered this wonderful transformation, including my own son, Alex, *were graduating this year*. So, Doug and I, with Alex's help, got to work, right away in summer, planning their sets, which included a medley of songs by the *Plain White Ts*, making Masquerade very happy! Our accompanying band grew larger as we attempted to make them more competitive with the huge bands of the other top show choirs. Bo Eder returned to the band, after being away for a couple of years and sometimes played a second drum set with Drew, but also played percussion, Susan Wetzel played harp, while Cam Malotte and Doug Jones played trumpet. This was our most sophisticated band at Brea, since we had been here! The groups felt stronger than they had last year, as their evolution was continuing, with another great year of experience under their belts! To say that Doug and I felt confident that this would be a very good year… was a *massive understatement*! Our competition sets included:

Masquerade 2008-09
Costume Colors:
Red, Blue, Gold
Competition Set
Once Upon A Time
Our Time Now
The Boy From Oz

Chamber Singers 2008-09
Costume Colors:
Unknown
Competition Set
There Is A New Day
Hold Me Rock Me
Jump Shout Boogie
Come What May
I'm A Believer

Tiffany's 2008-09
Costume Colors:
Blue
Competition Set
Tiffany's Theme
It Don't Mean A Thing
Baby Mine
Heart Belongs To Daddy
Angel of the Morning
Too Darn Hot

Spellbound 2008-09
Costume Colors:
Orange & Purple
Competition Set
Lullaby of Broadway
Gypsies, Tramps & Thieves

<u>Thunder Cats 2008-09</u>

Costume Colors: *Green w/ Black Tights*

<u>Competition Set</u>

Shake Down
Brown Eyed Squirrel
Doctor Looney
Afternoon Delight
I Feel Pretty
Men In Tights
Centerfold

Masquerade began the year by once again, competing at the *Aztec Sing,* at Citrus College! There were a number of strong competitors, but our group felt confident, all the same. Masquerade put on an excellent performance, considering that this was their first competition, of the year. In a close contest, Masquerade earned *2nd Place*, and the plaque for *Best Showmanship*, behind Burbank's *In Sync*, who earned First Place and Musicianship! Our kids weren't too disappointed. In fact, they were actually very excited! What a great way to start the year!

Masquerade's next competition was also held at Citrus College, the very next week! *The Diamond Bar Spectacular* featured the best groups around. Masquerade already had a show under their belt, so they were much less nervous at this one. They performed, working on all cylinders. When the awards were announced, Masquerade earned *2nd Place*, a point or two from winning the Showmanship and Musicianship plaques. The kids were excited, but growing a little impatient about getting, their first win of the year!

Next, Masquerade attended the *Bonita Vista High School* mixed competition, held at Eastlake High School. The stage was a little small, but they made it work. After delivering a great performance, we all waited for the awards to be announced. It was well worth the wait, as Masquerade earned *1st Place* and both plaques for *Best Showmanship* and *Best Musicianship!* Masquerade had won their first competition of the year, after earning two consecutive seconds, and they celebrated in the theatre for ten minutes!

The next day, Spellbound began their competition season at Bonita Vista's *For Ladies Only*. There were six award winning groups competing in the advanced division, but Spellbound knew that they had a great show! The first half featured traditional Broadway tunes, while the second half got gritty, with gypsy tunes, like *Be Italian*! In any case, the audience gave them a standing ovation, and the adjudicators may as well have. Spellbound earned *1st Place* with both plaques for *Best Showmanship* and *Best Musicianship*! Spellbound had earned their first win of the year, at their very first competition!

Our next festival, *TOC* (Tournament of Champions), had become what the Fullerton Jazz Festival had been to Nogales and Diamond Bar… a fun place to take all of our groups to! So, we brought Masquerade, Spellbound, Tiffany's and Chamber Singers. We seemed to be competing all afternoon, and well into the night. Every group did great, but we were a little concerned with one of the judges who had been a choreographer for one of our top competitors, in the past. There was a bit of bad blood between us due to a confrontation we had had years ago. The awards were announced, and Chamber Singers earned *3rd Place* in the Intermediate Mixed Division, Tiffany's earned *1st Place* along with both plaques for *Best Showmanship* and *Best Musicianship* in the Intermediate Women's Division, Spellbound earned *1st Place* along with both plaques for *Best Showmanship* and *Best Musicianship* in the Advanced Women's Division, Masquerade earned *1st Place* along with both plaques for *Best Showmanship* and *Best Musicianship*, in the Advanced Mixed Division, while Alex Willert was awarded *Best Male Soloist* of the competition, by the adjudicators. Remember that judge we were so concerned about? *She loved our shows*! We ended up having a very nice conversation together at the end of the competition. Sometimes ancient grudges *do* work themselves out.

Next, Spellbound and Tiffany's went to Diamond Bar's, *Girls Night Out*, held at Diamond Bar High School. Both Tiffany's and Spellbound gave great performances, although the stage was a little on the small side. When the awards were announced, Tiffany's earned *1st Place* and both plaques for *Best Showmanship* and *Best Musicianship* in the Intermediate Division, while Spellbound earned *2nd Place* and the plaque for *Best Showmanship* in the Advanced Division. Our girls were very happy!

As festivals go, the Los Alamitos High School, *Xtravaganza,* was the big one! It ran for three days and had a place for everyone to compete… even Thunder Cats! So, with five groups entered, we arrived in the morning, about 9 am, and didn't leave until about 1:30 am, the *next* morning! Everyone was there, along with several top groups from the mid-west who decided to try their luck in California. That morning, while driving to school, my car was hit from behind by a BOHS student. Almost immediately, my back muscles tensed up. After completing my drive to school, I felt more intense pain in my back, so I left and drove to Emergency. The doctor confirmed that I had whiplash and prescribed some powerful muscle relaxants and painkillers for me to use while I was at the festival. Well, the competition had already started and I could not possibly make it in time to direct Tiffany's, so Doug agreed to direct their a cappella ballad. I arrived there just as Tiffany's had finished. Doug assured me that everything had gone well with their performance, so it was on to our next group! I will spare you the blow-by-blow description of events that followed, and just tell you that *I was feeling pretty good*! Whatever those pills were, that I was taking for my back pain… *they took all of my pain away*! All of our groups performed well, and now it was time to announce the awards. Chamber Singers earned *2nd Place* and the plaque for *Best Musicianship,* in the Intermediate Mixed Division. Thunder Cats earned *3rd Place,* in the Advanced Men's Division. Tiffany's earned *2nd Place,* in the Intermediate Women's Division. Spellbound earned *4th Place,* in the Advanced Women's Division, while Masquerade earned *5th Place,* in the Advanced Mixed Division. The adjudicators had also chosen *Alex Willert* as the recipient of the *Best Male Soloist* award. In a separate soloist competition that Alex had entered against singers from all the competing schools, he ended up earning *2nd Place*, with a score of 99, only one point behind a talented singer from Burroughs. Strangely enough, Alex and the student from Burroughs, *both attended Chapman University*, and sang together in the choir! These results were pretty good, until I looked at the score sheets and it was like Branson (Diamond Bar) all over again! The judges were all from the mid-west and were evidently looking for *some other kind of show, from ours. We did not fit their mold at all!* I'm telling you this, because this year, the Advanced Mixed Division was being run like a mid-west competition. They took the top five placing groups from the preliminary competition (the one we had just competed in), and all of those groups were scheduled to compete a second time, in the Finals! Well, we had placed fifth, but we were *forty points behind Chula Vista*, who was in fourth place. Every group ahead of us was mid-west style with a big band… I deduced, fairly easily, that we were going to come in *fifth place* no matter what we did! So, in warm-up that night, I borrowed Bill Murray's speech from *Meatballs,* when he's telling his team of misfit campers that *it just doesn't matter* whether they win or they lose! I was feeling a little giddy at that time (probably from my pills), and the kids joined right into my weird moment, chanting, "It just doesn't matter," in regards to ultimately placing fifth! Before we took the stage, the kids were determined to give their best performance, but we decided as a group, after we were announced in fifth place… *we would cheer in unity for five minutes*! Well, the competition ended at 1:30 am, and they quickly announced the awards. The first one they read was fifth place. "In Fifth Place… Brea Masquerade!" Our kids cheered so loudly it was as if they had won! Whoever it was that went up for the trophy, held it up to the group, from the stage, like this trophy represented some *magnificent achievement*. David Moellenkamp, the host director, kept glaring toward our kids, as he rightly wanted to continue with the ceremony, and eventually, we stopped. That was fun, and *that, is how you take a competition lemon… and turn it into lemonade*!

The Arcadia, *Big Pow Wow* was next. Like I have already told you, Masquerade loved the Beautiful San Gabriel Mission Playhouse, where this event was hosted, even though we usually placed third or fourth. We had a great performance… probably the best of the year! When the awards were announced… sure enough… *Masquerade earned 3rd Place*! But they were okay with it. As one girl told me, "Well, it's better than fourth!"

The *Fullerton College Jazz Festival* surprisingly decided to offer show choir in their festival, again, this year. We decided to take only Spellbound and Masquerade, because the advanced divisions were scheduled for the late afternoon, so no students would have to miss any school for this, since I believe, AP testing was going on at this time. However, although Fullerton offered both mixed and women's divisions in their novice and intermediate, since Spellbound was the only group entered in the *advanced* women's division, they combined that division with the advanced mixed division, which included, Masquerade. Both of our groups were excited about this change, because now they would find out, *once and for all*, which group was better this year! The competition day arrived, and I have to say that both groups executed awesome performances! When the awards were announced, Masquerade had received scores of 96, 99 and 98 (out of 100 points), for a total score of 293. Spellbound had received scores of 99, 99 and 96, for a total score of 294! One judge had tied them, one had Masquerade up by two and one judge had Spellbound ahead by three. So, *Spellbound won the competition*, while Masquerade placed second, *one point behind them!* However, that didn't stop the controversy from lasting right up until the end of the school year, at which time Spellbound and Masquerade *finally agreed to disagree*, on which performance was actually better!

Next, Tiffany's, Thunder Cats and Chamber Singers headed to Disney's California Adventure, to compete in the *Five, Six, Seven, Eight* competition. Once again, it was held on the *Monsters Inc.* stage. We arrived in the morning and gradually performed throughout the day. First, Tiffany's performed. The outdoor sound system did not do their singing justice, but their show was very energetic and fun to watch, just the same. Next up, Chamber Singers. They too had a fun performance, which featured some very nice vocals! When Thunder Cats reached the stage, the audience (including a number of our parents and alumni), were already laughing! Needless to say, Thunder Cats once again... were a hit! When the awards were announced, Chamber Singers earned *2nd Place,* in the Mixed Division, Thunder Cats earned *1st Place,* in the Men's Division while Tiffany's earned *2nd Place,* in the Women's Division! This competition was so much fun, it was fast becoming everyone's choice for ending the competition year... *every year*!

Our final competition of the year was Chula Vista's *So Cal,* which we took Masquerade and Spellbound to, and decided to make a mini-tour out of it, with the group staying two nights at our favorite *San Diego mini-tour hotel*, the Catamaran Resort! As a parent, I was thinking that this was going to be Alex's *final* high school show choir competition! I had so enjoyed having him as a member of my show choirs, and also as a part of the Brea choirs' *Renaissance*. I'll bet every parent of a senior choir member felt this same way! I know that in talking to Doug, he felt that way about his niece, Rachael Kuhl, who had spent the past two years in our program, but would be graduating in June! We arrived at downtown San Diego, on Front Street, and entered the convention hall. It was, as always, *massive*! The stage was portable, however, and we knew that with our groups being larger than last year, it would be a tight fit! Spellbound and Masquerade performed, and although the echoed acoustics created by the high ceilings, played havoc with our vocals... every other competing group was in the very same boat. When the awards were announced, Spellbound earned *3rd Place* in the Advanced Women's Division, while Masquerade earned *4th Place* in the Advanced Mixed Division. In addition, Chula Vista's director, Tony Atienza, presented Alex Willert with the plaque for *Best Male Performer*. The kids were a little disappointed that they had not done better, but that did not last long, as we drove back to the Catamaran Resort to continue our tour!

The musical we chose to do, this year, was *All Shook Up*! It was a fun story (very much like *Footloose*), where an Elvis Presley character comes to town on his motorcycle and discovers that the mayor of the town has banned music! All of the songs were Elvis songs and we had lots of main characters in the story learn to be happy and fall in love, through Elvis' inspiration (and his songs). This was a *very talented year*, with plenty of students who could sing solos, dance and act, which is why the challenging vocal harmonies were no problem. This feel-good show, *was an enormous hit*! I think our audiences were sad to see it close, after its two week run. I know I was. We had a live band accompanying this show, including Hannah Nam on synthesizer, Drew Hemwall on percussion, Kramer Ison on guitar and Cody Somerville on saxophone.

2009 Cast List for "*All Shook Up*"

Chad: *Alex Willert* **Natalie:** *Kristen Webster*
Jim: *Harrison Schultz/ Alex Olvey*
Sylvia: *Kayla Camacho/ Emily Reed*
Dennis: *Kevin Siazon/Jared Toves*
Sandra: *Kaylee Dysart & Lauren Howard*
Lorraine: *Jordyn Georgianna & Maddie Reeves*
Barbie: *Jen Harpster & Melissa Hankins*
Dean: *Eitan Weisner & Christian Villanueva*
Matilda: *Jocelyn Green/ Rachael Kuhl*
Grandma: *Julia Dwyer/ Marti Repp*
Earl: *David Snyder/ Mike Garate*
Warden: *Daniel Cabrera* **Bus Driver:** *Mike Tirona*
Fella: *Gabriel Navarro* **Guy One:** *Ryan Savosh*
Guy Two: *Chris Flores* **Henrietta:** *Samantha Seyed*
Joy: *Liz Irvine* **Shoe Salesgirl:** *Sarah Morgigno*
Shoe Fainter: *Abby Ortega*

Bar Flies

Charisse Green • Sophia Valero • Emmalee Wetzel
Melissa Hankins • Jen Harpster

Dancers

Emily Elias • Jumana Salameh • Rebecca Harpster
Elizabeth Garcia • Alyssa Garcia • Baylee Heagle
Kellie Galentine • Ally Catanesi • Hailey Holman
Kate Hocking • Emily Malotte • Melanie Ramsey
Brittany Lovell • Maddie Ellingson • Alina Rotariu
Beckie Clark • Jill Purdom • Erin Purdom
Chanel Dickson • Megan Miller • Brianna Kdeiss
Amy Czerwinsky • Justine Garate • Tara Mazeika

Townspeople

Hannah Flowers • Krista Benedict • Allison Rigsby
Puja Mazumder • Megan Berrocal • Michelle Arno
Olivia Chapman • Evette Rodriguez • Terry Dopson
Haley Russo • Gailyn Tan • Nicole McEntee • Rob Catanesi
Jake Flowers • Hannah Pipes • Devanie Zenzola • Megan Strom
Vanessa Alvarez • Nikki Cuerdo • Aleah Tunuufi
Samantha Mauriss • Harli Paxton • Alexa Walters
Becka Heagle • Isi Perez • Challoi McCuller • Marysa Leite

We returned to New York City, in May! This tour group was a little larger than last year, due to more parents coming along. Once again, we stayed at the beautiful Marriott Marquis. The musicals we watched this trip, included *West Side Story, Avenue Q* or *Wicked, Alter Boyz* or *Phantom Of The Opera* and *Mary Poppins* or *In The Heights* or *Chicago*. We gave the group plenty of choices. But the most exciting thing to happen was that *Green Day* was performing, *free,* in Central Park, on the day after we arrived! Anyone who wanted a spot to see them, had to arrive at Central Park, about five or six in the morning. I, for one, was too jet-lagged to get up, but plenty of our kids, and even some parents attended. They all told me that it was an *"awesome"* experience! All of our trips to New York City have been special, but we really did have a great time watching plays, sightseeing, and seeing and hearing Green Day perform in the park, this year. It was a wonderful way to end the school year!

Our incredible student officers for the 2008-09 school year, included:

Masquerade
President: *Alex Willert*
Vice-Pres: *Madison Reeves, Kristen Webster & Kevin Siazon*
Sec/Treas: *Melanie Ramsey & Christian Villanueva*
Hist/Lib: *Justin Lovell & Rachael Kuhl*
Publicity: *Nathan Carey*

Spellbound
President: *Rachael Kuhl*
VP: *Jordyn Georgianna, Lauren Howard & Madison Reeves*
Sec/Treas: *Kayla Camacho & Mallorie Flowers*
Hist/Lib: *Julia Dwyer & Chanel Dickson*

<u>Chamber Choir</u>
President: *Jocelyn Green*
Vice-President: *Alex Willert*
Sec/Treas: *Ashley Rangel*
Hist/Lib: *Kristen Webster*

<u>Thunder Cats</u>
President: *Eitan Weisner*
Vice-Pres: *Alex Willert*

<u>Tiffany's</u>
President: *Madison Reeves*
Vice-Pres: *Sadie Reeves & Mallorie Flowers*
Sec/Treas: *Gabie Hirsh Rebecca Harpster*
Hist/Lib: *Jezebel Jurado & Megan Miller*

2009, was an incredible year for both Masquerade and Spellbound. They did not go to a national competition, but they both dominated many of their local competitions, by coming in first or second. I believe that these were two of the best singing groups I have ever had the pleasure of working with! These groups were led by the hard work and experience of the seniors, who had spent *all four years of high school*, in choir. They included *Kristen Webster, Jocelyn Green, Emily Reed, Jordyn Georgianna, Elizabeth Irvine, Alex Willert, Harrison Schultz, Melissa Hankins, Madison Reeves and Elizabeth Garcia*. They were my first four-year graduating class from Brea Olinda High School, and it was tough seeing all of these outstanding seniors go. But, the strength of our sophomores and juniors too, many of whom had begun as members of the very successful, first Brea Junior High, *Show Choir Express*, contributed mightily to these groups as well! Even our freshmen contributed to the choirs' success! You see, I had learned through the decades that relying only on a strong senior class to drive your group, guarantees that the year after they graduate will be a *rebuilding year*! But when *every class is contributing, all of the time*, if the senior class is small, ineffective or graduates, this only opens the door for the underclassmen to *step up*, as they have been prepared to do, and lead the groups to success! That's why during the 2007-08 season, even with a very small senior class, our juniors were fully prepared to step up! At this point in my short tenure at Brea Olinda, we had already achieved so much? So the question was, what challenges did we want to take on in the future? Well, we had very talented groups next year, so our first challenges would be the very same as last year; *create perfect shows* and *always strive to win*! *Build that tradition*! I've listed the complete rosters for both of these two remarkable groups, *Masquerade and Spellbound, 2008-09*, below!

Masquerade 2008-09

Kristen Webster • Jocelyn Green • Emily Reed • Jill Purdom
Chanel Dickson • Melissa Strom • Jordyn Georgianna
Melanie Ramsey • Ashley Schweitzer • Brittany Slater-Shew
Kayla Comacho • Kaylee Dysart • Elizabeth Irvine
Allison Iles • Valerie Shrepferman • Shelby Johnson
Alex Willert • Jared Toves • Justin Lovell • Logan Luedke
Austin Dix • Harrison Schultz • Dakota Michaloff
Chris Mosqueda • David Snyder • Joseph Chang
Chris Flores • Rachael Kuhl • Lauren Howard
Melissa Hankins • Kayla Luedke • Julia Dwyer • Alex Olvey
Hailey Markman • Madison Reeves • Kaylie Simec
Savannah Maske • Holly Ramsey • Mallorie Flowers
Ally Catanesi • Ashley Rangel • Erin Purdom
Samantha Syed • Kate Hocking • Kevin Siazon
Christian Villanueva • Eitan Weisner • Daniel Cabrera
Gabriel Navarro • Michael Garate • Michael Tirona
Chad Rabago • Matt Ferrell • Edward Hope

Spellbound 2008-09

Kristen Webster • Madison Reeves • Lauren Howard
Chanel Dickson • Jessica Raine • Emmalee Wetzel
Trisha Bermudez • Rachel Weeks • Sarah Morgigno
Michele McManamy • Kate Hocking • Holly Ramsey
Baylee Heagle • Megan Miller • Justine Garate
Kayla Camacho • Brandi Evans • Ashley Rangel
Jumaneh Salameh • Jen Harpster • Krista Benedict
Emily Elias • Brianna Kdeiss • Tara Mazeika
Rachael Kuhl • Emily Reed • Jocelyn Green
Hannah Coonis • Julia Dwyer • Hailey Holman
Elizabeth Garcia • Madeline Ellingson • Sadie Reeves
Jordyn Georgianna • Savanah Maske • Becca Harpster
Emily Malotte • Lauren Brinckerhoff • Ally Catanesi
Samantha Seyed • Gabie Hirsh • Shelby Johnson
Katie Bower • Kellie Galentine • Tana Schwartz
Danielle Santos • Mallorie Flowers • Alexa Vandermeer

CHAPTER 11

Brea Olinda High School... 2009-2012... Maintaining The Greatness!

No offense intended, but I'd just like to share an observation. The seniors during my fourth year at Diamond Bar High School (2002) *did not seem to have the same drive* they'd shown for the first three years prior, when Diamond Bar was dominating other groups in competition. Yet, in contrast, the 2009 Brea seniors, in their fourth year, *did not lose any of their focus to win*! My best guess is that because Diamond Bar began winning *right from the start*, they may have grown a bit complacent, by that fourth year. On the other hand, Brea had to *work much harder* to become a winner again, taking all of two years to do it! So, I believe those seniors, who had worked so very hard to get where they were, didn't want to be remembered for being anything less than winners!

This year, we still had a great attitude intact, in each group. A lot of the new seniors had been members of that first, *Show Choir Express*, and they were bred to win! Fritz Wienecke, joined our illustrious band as a third trumpet with Cam Malotte and Doug Jones. Otherwise, the band was still the same as last year, Hannah Nam on keyboard, Drew Hemwall and Bo Eder on percussion and Susan Wetzel on harp. We also decided to stop competing Chamber Singers in show choir events, and made them a full time traditional choir, instead. We had lost some very talented and hard working seniors last year, but we still had a lot of great kids remaining, who had competed with last year's groups… So, we went into the 2009-10 school year with some very high expectations! The competition sets for 2009-10 were:

Masquerade 2009-10
Costume Colors:
Blue, Red, White
Competition Show
FUNBOX

1. *Swinging London*
2. *Rendevous In Paris*
3. *The Storm*
4. *The Hope*

Tiffany's 2009-10
Costume Colors:
Gold
Competition Show
Lullaby
Tiffany's Theme
Boy From New York City
America
Whatever Lola Wants
Too Darn Hot

Spellbound 2009-10
Costume Colors:
White, Blue, Red
Competition Show
"Lost In The Moulin Rouge"

Thunder Cats 2009-10
Costume Colors:
Unknown
Competition Show
Thunder Cats Theme
Trickle Trickle
Mighty Mouse
Book Of Love
Annie
Thriller
Centerfold

The Masquerade show was so much fun, that it was appropriately called *FUNBOX*. This set was basically a little bit of everything, including an ending of *You'll Never Walk Alone*, gorgeously sung by senior, *Haley Markman*. She had left us at the beginning of her junior year, after spending her first two years of high school in Masquerade, to enroll in OCHSA (Orange County High School of the Arts). She came back, after her junior year, because she felt that what Brea offered was a far better fit for her musical performance development. She was a senior now, and she came back fully determined to win, just like everybody else in the group!

Masquerade, started their competition year at the *Aztec Sing*. In recent years, the most consistent groups there had been Burbank and Brea… with Burbank usually winning. Our group hoped to turn the tables on them this year! When it came our turn to perform, Masquerade went out there and dazzled the audience for twenty minutes! When the awards were announced, Masquerade had earned *2nd Place* and the plaque for *Best Showmanship*! But once again, Burbank had bested us with their vocals. Still, it marked a good start to our season.

Masquerade's next competition was the *Diamond Bar Spectacular*. More of the tougher groups were there, than at the Aztec Sing, including both Burroughs and Burbank. Masquerade gave another fast and fun-filled performance, but both Burroughs and Burbank were very good, as well. When the awards were announced, this time, Masquerade earned *3rd Place*. There is nothing wrong with that, except they found themselves going in the wrong direction, as far as their competition results, and that had everyone more than a little concerned.

Masquerade's third festival of the year, took us to the *Bonita Vista High School* mixed show choir competition. After a fine performance, they earned *2nd Place* and the plaque for *Best Showmanship*. Los Alamitos won. I won't lie. We took this one very hard. During the ride back, on the bus, Doug and I planned the changes we would make, in order to have a better chance of winning next time. Dropping the underachieving, "*Cuban Pete*" from the show and replacing it with, "*Lucy In The Sky With Diamonds*," seemed like a good first step… but there were still more changes to come. Surprisingly, *we were finding it very tough for Masquerade to win this year*!

Spellbound started their competition year, the next day, at Bonita Vista's *For Ladies Only*. They were excited about their show, which was basically a redo of Diamond Bar Marquis' *Moulin Rouge* show, with a number of songs added to it. The choreography was very active! When Spellbound performed, it was as if they were the headliners in a concert, as the entire audience cheered for them. When the awards were announced, to no one's surprise, they earned *1st Place* and both plaques for *Best Showmanship* and *Best Musicianship*! I loved it whenever that happened!

The next competition on the list was the Los Alamitos High School, *Xtravaganza, which Masquerade very wisely chose to miss, due to their last year's adjudication.* However, we still took Spellbound, Tiffany's and Thunder Cats to compete. It was a very long day, as always, but as I remember, each one of our groups came off the stage happy with their performances. Thunder Cats incorporated *"Brea Juice"* throughout their set to *honor* the video at Hart, a couple of years ago that spoofed Brea's stage energy by saying they took *Brea Juice*. It was sort of an inside joke, but it worked well with the audiences just the same. When it finally came time for awards, everyone was exhausted, but rushed to the theatre to find out how they had done. Thunder Cats earned *3rd Place* in the *Advanced Men's Division*, Spellbound also earned *3rd Place* in the *Advanced Women's Division*, but Tiffany's earned *1st Place* and both plaques for *Best Showmanship* and *Best Musicianship* in the Intermediate Women's Division! *Never underestimate the power of Tiffany's.* Winning, was becoming a habit for them!

Masquerade was in the midst of a highly successful year, armed with a very entertaining show, but in their first three competitions, they only had two seconds and a third to show for it… *no wins*. Something had to be changed or added to their show, if for no other reason, than to excite our own performers! Then, one day, while I was at Brea Junior High, with Doug rehearsing the group, *I suddenly had an epiphany*! I took a piece of paper and wrote out a new section for *Yesterday*, our a cappella. In essence, the group would sing the word, *yesterday*, with staggered entrances, and dissonant chords, as loudly as they could, three times, toward then end of the song, hopefully, resulting in shock and awe, from the audience. When I taught this new part to the Masquerade, and they sang it… *we all went crazy*! The power and dissonance of the moment was simply awesome! *This* would serve *just fine*, as our much needed change.

The next competition for Masquerade was Arcadia High School's *Big Pow Wow*, where we had a long history of coming in third or fourth. However, we hoped to surprise everyone tonight! When it was time for us to perform, our kids couldn't wait to share their newest surprise, with the audience. The song, *Yesterday,* started like normal. Hailey Markman was singing against the choir, gently and beautifully, as our a cappella gradually unfolded. Suddenly, Masquerade began singing the new section, and after the initial "ahs," the audience spontaneously followed that with thunderous applause, until the section ended. I was up front directing, and I could scarcely hide my beaming smile! The kids had just created a *show choir moment* for everyone in that auditorium that would last as long as they lived. *It was electrifying!* The remainder of the Masquerade performance was equally passionate and beautiful. When our kids came off the stage, they were laughing and crying at the same time... *they were so happy*. I really thought we would win, that night, and I'll bet everyone in the audience believed that too! But, when the awards were announced, Masquerade had earned *2nd Place* and the plaque for *Best Showmanship*. They had missed winning, by *one point* to Burroughs! But you know what? *This was the very first time I had ever heard an audience applaud for an a cappella*? I'll take that special moment, the one we created in the a cappella that night, *anytime*, over a mere first place trophy... and I believe the kids in Masquerade felt much the same way!

Next on the agenda, Solitaire and Tiffany's traveled to Diamond Bar High School, to compete in the *Girls Night Out* competition. There were quite a few groups there, which we had already seen throughout the year. This was going to be a very competitive event! Both Solitaire and Tiffany's gave exceptional performances, like always. When the awards were announced, Spellbound earned *2nd Place* and the plaque for *Best Showmanship* in the *Advanced Division*, while Tiffany's, once again, dazzled the judges by earning *1st Place* and both plaques for *Best Showmanship* and *Best Musicianship,* in the *Intermediate Division*! This was a great night for both of our groups!

The final competition of the year, for Masquerade and Spellbound, and the next to the last one for Thunder Cats, was Chula Vista's *So Cal*. We made the trip into a San Diego tour, staying, I believe, at the Catamaran Resort, as we usually did. The competition was once again held in downtown San Diego, at a convention hall, and when we arrived, our kids were very excited! The competition lasted all day, and well into the night. Thunder Cats had prepared a special version of the song, "*Bye Bye Bye,*" by 'NSYNC, including a puppet of Lance Bass, one of NSYNC's members, *who just happened to be a judge* this year, at the competition! Apparently, the video of "*Bye Bye Bye,*" had featured all of the 'NSYNC members, as puppets on strings, so our boys thought their parody would be very funny. It was! Lance Bass laughed during the show and actually signed their puppet at the end of the competition! As always, the Thunder Cat show was a riot! Spellbound gave their best performance of the year, probably because this was their final competition. Masquerade, likewise, gave a great performance, although the a cappella, *Yesterday*, did not receive quite as much audience response as their performance at Arcadia had garnered, probably because a lot of the people here had already heard it. Nonetheless, it was still breathtaking! When the awards were announced, Thunder Cats did not place (but they had Lance Bass's autograph), Masquerade earned *3rd Place* and Spellbound tied Burroughs for 1st, but was ultimately placed *2nd* because Burbank had a higher music score… *which, we were told was how they broke ties.* In any case, everyone was happy. Masquerade had not won a competition all year… but they had a pretty great run! Solitaire also had nothing to complain about. But Thunder Cats still had one more competition… and one final opportunity to win.

Brea's final competition of the year was *Five, Six, Seven, Eight,* once again, being held at Disney's *California Adventure.* Our Thunder Cats and Tiffany's were the only Brea groups participating. There were a lot of groups competing, including the Arcadia Chanteurs, in the mixed division. Thunder Cats went on relatively early, and received a great deal of laughter and applause. They were always a crowd favorite, wherever they went. Tiffany's performed a little bit later, and once again, seemed to *captivate the judges as well as the audience*, through their patented mixture of humor and fun, combined with beautiful singing and passionate performing. I mean really… what's not to like? When the awards were announced, Thunder Cats had won *1st Place* in the *Men's Division*, Tiffany's had won *1st Place* in the *Women's Division* and the Arcadia Chanteurs had won *1st Place* in the *Mixed Division*. Now, came the award for Sweepstakes (highest point score of the day). And the award went to… TIFFANY'S! Wow! *No one had seen that one coming*! This completed Tiffany's perfect season. They had swept at Diamond Bar, at Los Alamitos and now against everyone at *Five, Six, Seven, Eight*! So, although *all of our groups* did well in competition in 2010… This was truly, *Tiffany's year*! I have listed the individual members of the remarkable 2010 Tiffany's group, below:

TIFFANY'S 2010… THEIR FIRST UNDEFEATED YEAR!

Soprano One	**Soprano Two**	**Alto**
Brittany Lovell	*Katrina Ortiz*	*Kaylee Dysart*
Amy Czerwinski	*Kelsey Besch*	*Emily Elias*
Trisha Bermudez	*Amber Dailey*	**Charisse Green*
Puja Muzumder	*Megan Berrocal*	*Alexa Fishman*
Julia Ludwig	*Nicole McEntee*	*Kelsey Garcia*
Hannah Rossell	*Roxanne Clark*	*Moriah Guerrero*
Vanessa Alvarez	*Allison Rigsby*	*Noemi Hernandez*
Saige Lee	*Megan Strom*	*Monica Prochman*
Marysa Leite	*Abby Ortega*	*Evette Rodriguez*
Molly Barba	*Abby Ciencia*	*Hiba Salameh*
Rochelle Atienza	*Sabrina Lee*	*Rachel Gallegos*
Challoi McCuller	*Devanie Zenzola*	*J.R. Villanueva*
	*President: **	*Tara Mazeika*

A special choir memory from 2010 happened at Preview Night. Brian Rigsby had asked me if it would be okay if he sang a song for his wife, Frieda, that night. I agreed, but what happened was unbelievable. He sang to a recorded accompaniment, *with so much warmth and feeling*, that he had every woman in the concert *loudly sighing, and even crying… especially his own wife, Frieda*. The concert was very entertaining from start to finish, and the kids, as always, were wonderful… but nothing came close to the audience reaction that

Brian Rigsby received that night, for his singing, but also for his courage to tell a live audience that *he loved his wife*! Way to go Brian!

In addition to competing, the choirs put on a wonderful production of *Joseph and the Amazing Technicolor Dreamcoat*! We were short boys, so Kaylee Dysart, *graciously volunteered to play one of Joseph's brothers*, and no one was the wiser! Kevin Siazon, played the title role to perfection, and the rest of the cast, was also delightful, including BOHS employee, Marti Repp, who was asked to play Joseph's mother! Again, we performed this to a live band, made up of Hannah Nam, Drew Hemwall and Cody Somerville. This production was a huge hit!

2010 Cast List for "*Joseph and the Amazing Technicolor Dreamcoat*"

Joseph: *Kevin Siazon*

Narrators: *Hailey Markman & Julia Dwyer*

Pharaoh: *Dakota Michaloff*
Mrs. Potiphar: *Kaylee Dysart*
Baker: *Herman Hope*
Rachel: *Marti Repp*
Simeon: *David Snyder*
Naphtali: *Herman Hope*
Dan: *David Dumond*
Asher: *Jared Toves*
Judah: *Chad Rubago*

Potiphar: *Alex Olvey*
Butler: *Ryan Savosh*
Jacob: *Doug Kuhl*
Reuben: *Alex Olvey*
Levi: *Gabriel Navarro*
Issachar: *Brandon Jones*
Zebulon: *Ryan Savosh*
Gad: *Kaylee Dysart*
Benjamin: *Daniel Dwyer*

Ishmaelites

Michelle Arno • Hailey Holman • Vanessa Alvarez
Jake Flowers • Terry Dopson • Isi Perez • Olson Walters
Megan Berrocal

The Wives

Saige Lee • Jill Purdom • Kaylie Simec • Tara Mazeika
Nicole Berkey • Emmalee Wetzel • Dallas Schindler
Rachel Weeks • Krista Benedict • Shelby Johnson
Erin Purdom • Kayla Camacho • Emily Elias

Dance Corp

Marysa Leite • Savannah Maske • Holly Ramsey
Melanie Ramsey • Maddie Ellingson • Becca Harpster
Tana Schwarz • Baylee Heagle • Beckie Clark
Brittany Lovell • Amy Czerwinsky • Julia Ludwig
Michelle Arno • Nicole McEntee • Amanda Crosby
Evette Rodriguez • Ally Catanesi • Megan Miller
Hailey Holman • Hannah Pipes • Julianne Sexton
Hannah Rossell

BOHS Ensemble

Puja Muzumder • Jennifer Cao • Abby Ortega
Terry Dopson • Charlotte Neal • Devanie Zenzola
Vanessa Alvarez • Alyssa Garcia • Isi Perez
Roxanne Clark • Grace Garcia • Proma Mazumder
Vanessa Hurtado • Audrey Marra • Thea O'Dell
Alex Parish • Brandon Soto • Jake Flowers • Becca Clark
Olson Walters • Megan Berrocal

BJH Ensemble

Carrie Bower • Samantha Mauriss • Chrissy Streitz
Paige Garcia • Leena Fritz • Emily Boliver • Maddy Miller
Becka Heagle • Aidan Pipes • Sierra McCoy • Monica Siazon
Ally Behunin

Our wonderful student leaders for the **2009-10** school year included:

Chamber Singers
President: *Hailey Markman*
Vice-President: *Jared Toves*
Secretary: *Alison Iles*
Treasurer: *Kevin Seo*
Historian: *Olivia Chapman*
Librarian: *Brandon Jones*

Tiffany's
President: *Charisse Green*
Vice-Pres: *Megan Berrocal*
Secretary: *Megan Strom*
Treasurer: *Katrina Ortiz*
Historian: *Amy Czerwinsky*
Librarian: *Tara Mazeika*

Masquerade
President: *Alex Olvey & Kevin Siazon*
Vice-Pres: *Ashley Rangel, Kaylee Dysart, Justin Lovell & Christian Villanueva*
Secretary: *Melanie Ramsey*
Treasurer: *Kayla Camacho*
Tech Man: *David Snyder*
Historian: *Melissa Strom & Julia Dwyer*
Librarian: *Chanel Dickson & Shelby Johnson*

Spellbound
President: *Julia Dwyer & Kayla Camacho*
Vice-Pres: *Kaylee Dysart, Ashley Rangel & Melanie Ramsey*
Secretary: *Ally Catanesi*
Treasurer: *Melissa Strom*
Historian: *Beckie Clark*
Librarian: *Kate Hocking*

Thunder Cats
President: *Alex Olvey*
Vice-President: *Christian Villanueva*

During the summer of 2010, Doug and I decided that we wanted to change Masquerade's show in a dramatic way, just for the fun of it! So, we brainstormed, and came up with the idea of *American Idiot* by *Green Day*! Next, Doug and Margaret designed some ultra cool, military influenced uniforms and we were well on our way to our 2011 punk makeover! We decided to pair Mary Poppins with that, to make the *best possible contrast of styles*! Our band was nearly the same as last year except that Bo Eder no longer played with us full time and Fritz Wienecki had left the band when his daughter, Alyssa, had graduated, at the end of last year. This was also the year that we consolidated all three of our hosted competitions, *The Brea Classic, Ladies Center Stage* and *Middle School Madness,* to create one larger event, called *The California Classic*, in order to make it easier for everyone! Our competition sets included:

Masquerade 2010-11
Costume Colors:
Pink, Gold, Green, Black
Competition Set
The New Broadway:
1. Mary Poppins
2. American Idiot!

Spellbound 2010-11
Costume Colors:
Blue, Green, Purple, White
Competition Set
"Gypsy Noir"

Tiffany's 2010-11
Costume Colors:
White, Red, Blue
Competition Set
Tiffany's Theme
Singin' in the Rain
Soon It's Gonna Rain
Don't Rain On My Parade
My First Love
Big Spender
Too Darn Hot

Thunder Cats 2010-11
Costume Colors:
Unknown
Competition Set
I Am A Man Of Constant
Home On The Range
Fever
Centerfold

Masquerade began their festival season competing in the Diamond Bar *Spectacular*. Our group was very large and our show and costumes were *extremely contrasting*, exactly as we'd hoped, as we went from Mary Poppins to American Idiot... but it was very effective! When the awards were announced, Masquerade had earned *1st Place* and the plaque for *Best Showmanship*! The kids really celebrated this win, as they had been unsure, up to this moment how their show would be received by the adjudicators... *but now they knew*!

The next festival attended by Masquerade, was the *Bonita Vista High School* mixed show choir event. Although their show had been scored well at Diamond Bar, there were concerns as we faced San Diego adjudicators, for the first time. We shouldn't really have worried. When the awards were announced, Masquerade had not only swept the event, taking *1st Place*, *Best Showmanship* and *Best Musicianship*... but they also won *Best A*

Cappella, for their singing of Green Day's *Wake Me Up When September Ends.* The night could not have gone better!

Spellbound began their competition season, by attending Diamond Bar's *Girl's Night Out,* at Diamond Bar High School. This was when many groups supported that event, so there was a solid advanced women's line-up, if I recall correctly, including Burroughs, Hart, Arcadia, Brea and Glendora. The Spellbound "*Gypsy Noir*" show was fantastic! It was passionate, dazzling and musical, just as we had imagined it. But, when the awards were announced, they had earned *2nd Place*, behind Burroughs, whom as I recall… swept all of the top awards. Still, it was a good start to the competition season.

Now it was Tiffany's turn to compete at the local *Walnut High School* women's competition. Their show was very sweet, full of traditional musical theatre tunes, which usually had worked well for them in the past. Most of the girls were freshmen, a little green, perhaps, but very excited to compete with Tiffany's for the first time! Their performance went over very well, although their sound was a little light. When the awards were announced, they had placed 2nd, behind Burroughs, I think. A great first competition! The girls had gotten their feet wet, and next time they would enter competition with a lot more confidence.

Our next competition was the *Gladstone Star Reflections*! Janae West, a former student of mine from Diamond Bar High School, was our gracious host. This year, we took Tiffany's, Spellbound and Masquerade there! The memory, I recall the most, is scolding Masquerade, during warm-up, for not working as hard during the *Mary Poppins Medley*, as they did in the *American Idiot Medley*! I told them that *Spellbound could beat them today*, since they were both competing in the same division! There were tears, there was determination, and the rest was in their hands. All three of our groups performed well, with a lot of positive audience reaction as a result. When the awards were announced, Tiffany's had earned *1st Place* and *Best Showmanship* in the Intermediate Women's Division, Spellbound had earned *2nd Place* in the Advanced Women's Division and Masquerade had taken *1st Place* and both plaques for *Best Showmanship* and

Best Musicianship in the Advanced Division. All of our groups did very well, but Masquerade had now quietly won their *third straight competition!*

Next, Masquerade traveled to the Arcadia *Big Pow Wow*. Their history there was to place, but never to win. But this year's show was so different, that anything could happen, right? Right! They gave a wonderful performance that left the audience cheering. When the awards were announced, Masquerade had swept, winning *1st Place*, *Best Showmanship* and *Best Musicianship*! That made it *four wins* for the year, and marked the very first time, that Masquerade had ever won *Arcadia's Big Pow Wow*!

Our next competition was the *Fullerton College Jazz Festival*. They only offered three divisions this year; *Mixed*, where we entered Masquerade, *Women's*, where we entered Spellbound and Tiffany's together, and *Men's*, where we entered Thunder Cats. As hoped, all four of our groups had good performances, but Masquerade and Spellbound had the most audience applause. When the awards were announced, Thunder Cats won *1st Place* in the Men's Division, Spellbound won *1st Place* in the Women's Division, Tiffany's took *2nd Place* in the Women's Division, and Masquerade won *1st Place* in the Mixed Division. For Masquerade, that was a record *five wins for the season!* For everyone else, this was another great competition!

On a whim, I had decided, early in the year, after talking with representatives from FAME on the phone, and being assured that *we would not experience any of the same troubling problems* my Diamond Bar group, *Marquis*, had experienced at Fame Branson, in 2004, to enter *Masquerade* and *Spellbound* into their preliminary competition, *FAME Hollywood*! I say *preliminary*, because FAME had redesigned their format, this year, so that the top three finishers from their preliminary competitions in Hollywood, New York City, Chicago, Branson and Orlando, would compete together, at the end of the year, in the *Show Choir Nationals* in Indianapolis! I, of course had *no plans to do that*, since it would involve too much fundraising to raise the necessary amount of money, in such a short time… so, I saw this festival as being *just another competition*. Well, the festival was held at an old majestic theatre in Hollywood (the name escapes me) and both Masquerade and Spellbound did very well there! In the mixed division, the top five scoring groups from the first round of competing… competed together a second time, for trophy placement. Masquerade placed *first* in the first performance, but dropped to *3rd*, in the final round. However, they also won *Best Vocals* and *Best Performer* (Rebecca Harpster). Spellbound, though, *completely blew the judges away*! They won *Grand Champion* of the Women's Division, and actually *scored the highest of any group*, including the mixed, that competed that day! At the awards ceremony, FAME announced that due to Spellbound's extraordinary performance, effective this year, they were now adding a *Women's Division* to the FAME Nationals! This great showing at FAME, *strongly encouraged* some of our parents, especially *Andrea Strom*, to try to convince me to take the two groups to the Nationals in Indianapolis, which they had both qualified for! Finally, I agreed. I won't spend a long time discussing our fundraising efforts, but everyone worked hard finding parent and friend donations. Per state mandate, we couldn't charge our individual students a fee to go, but *had to raise the money for everyone, as a group*! In the end, we did, and in late April, both groups flew out to Indianapolis for the *FAME National Show Choir Finals*! The Masquerade show's ending, *where they throw toilet paper all over the stage and even into the audience*, in total anarchy, was Doug's favorite show ending ever! It captured the punk feel of the Broadway show, *American Idiot*, which as fate would have it, had several of its cast members here at the Nationals, as judges! When we were done competing, they spoke with a number of our students and told them just how much they enjoyed our performance. One of them, on her adjudication tape, started laughing, saying, "This is rich," when the kissing scene took place, during *Twenty-One Guns.* That was definitely a high point in the year. When the awards were announced, Spellbound earned *1st Runner-Up,* in the Women's Division, while Masquerade earned *4th Runner-Up* in the Mixed Division. Although our kids were a little disappointed, I explained that competing in the Nationals was competing with the *best show choirs in the entire country*... and we had done very well! This was the first time either group had ever competed in a national show choir competition! We were already planning our trip to the FAME Show Choir Nationals, *for the next year*!

In addition to the competitions, 2011 was an exciting year for other reasons too. First of all, this was yet another year that interested members of the choir and their parents journeyed to New York City to see Broadway shows, sightsee and participate in a professional dance workshop with Sergio Mejia and a number of current Broadway performers. The trip was a hit! Once again, we stayed at the beautiful Marriott Marquis Hotel in the middle of Time Square. The Broadway shows we were fortunate enough to see included *Billy Elliott, Anything Goes, Phantom of the Opera* and *How To Succeed In Business Without Really Trying*. Sadly, this marked the end of our school board allowing us to take this trip without *scheduling a competition,* as a mandatory part of it.

The choir also produced Disney's *Beauty and the Beast,* to sold-out crowds and excellent reviews. By this point, I had stopped directing the musicals, and my former directing assistant, *Kurt Nielsen*, took over, working alongside *Doug Kuhl*. Our special thanks go to Janice Kraus and Stagelight Family Productions for renting us the exceptional costumes and set! This was the first time, since I had worked in Brea, that we had chosen to use orchestral "tracks" (recorded music), instead of using live musicians. For this show, it worked perfectly! In watching this outstanding production for six performances, I was especially taken by the incredible talent inherent in our performers! They were believeable, animated and sang beautifully. There is nothing better for a performing arts teacher, than to watch his students singing and performing at such a high level!

"Beauty And The Beast" Cast List for 2011

Beast: *Gabriel Navarro*
Belle: Nicole Berkey/ Julia Dwyer
Gaston: *Herman Hope*
Le Fou: *Chad Rabago/ Daniel Dwyer*
Lumiere: *Brandon Jones*
Cogsworth: *Brandon Allen/ Melissa Strom*
Maurice: *Ryan Savosh/ David Dumond*
Mrs. Potts: *Emmalee Wetzel/ Kaylie Simec*
Wardrobe: *Rachel Weeks/ Justice Bolden*
Mr. D'Arque: *Jake Flowers/ Matt Ferrell*
Mrs. D'Arque: *Michelle Arno/ Julia Ludwig*
Babette: *Becca Harpster/ Charisse Green*
La Cretia D'Arque: *Kim Lopez/ Maddie Ellingson*
Chip: *Gavin Armstrong/ Aidan Pipes*
China: *Caitlyn Gutierrez/ Erica Cline*
Carpet: *Allison Rigsby/ Ally Catanesi*
Footstool: *Ben Veling/ Izzy Perez*
Armor: *Travis Morrill/ Rob Catanesi*
Statue: *Savannah Maske/ Beckie Clark*
Bookseller: *Terry Dopson*

Silly Girls

Nicole McEntee • Tana Schwarz • Uche Ewenike
Hannah Pipes • Sam Mauriss • Sophia Valero
Tara Mazeika • Emily Elias • Emily Malotte
Challoi McCuller • Justine Garate • Julianne Sexton

Dancers

Brianna Clark • Victoria Rivas • Alyssa Alcaraz
Vanessa Alvarez • Hannah Rossell • Baylee Heagle
Becka Heagle • Sierra McCoy • Hailey Holman
Evette Rodriguez • Marysa Leite • Amy Czerwinski
Emelda Rodriguez • Amanda Crosby • Audrey Marra
Megan Berrocal

Ensemble

Courtney Tindal • Sarah Rosner • Chris Serna
Chrissy Streitz • Ben Harpster • Aleah Tunuufi
Mariah Guerrero • Chase Parker • Caity Sampley
Ken Southard • Mika Wheaton • Ruth Lee
Proma Mazumder • Fontini Vega • Elaina Lee
Stephanie Torres • Monica Siazon • Michelle Nunez
Samara Eghterafi • Hailey Hamilton • Sam Cho
Esmeralda Torres • Tristan Brannen • Leena Fritz
Brandon Soto • Tori Stuht • Kelsey Besch
Kelsey Garcia • Hailey Johnson • Caroline Bower
Emily Boliver • Mimi Macias

Because *our very expensive trip to Indianapolis* was planned and fundraised, *through necessity*, in less than two months, the administration of BOHS, *strongly felt*, that due to our projected need for large amounts of money, in order to compete nationally, in the future, *we should have a booster club*. At first, I was *against* having one, because of all the horror stories I had heard, but, Andrea Strom and I discussed it and in the end, I agreed, that it did sound like a good idea. She and Ron Anderson worked with a lawyer to make it legal and by July 14, 2011, our *Brea Olinda Choir Booster Club* was officially born. I don't need to tell you what a *lifesaver it has been to have our boosters working every event and constantly raising money for the choirs!* They have become an integral part of this program! The first Booster Board, included:

President: *Andrea Strom*
VP/Public Relations: *Mary Pipes*
Secretary: *Susan Elias*
Treasurer: *Ron Anderson*
Performance Fundraising: *Becky Czerwinsky*
Performance Fundraising: *Lorraine Dwyer*
Project Fundraising: *Robin Berkey*
Box Office: *Elaine Ellingson*
Box Office: *Shannon Van Malsen*

Once they started, the boosters continued to evolve with new and creative ways to raise money and to help the choirs succeed! Whereas, the first board consisted of nine hardworking parents, by 2017-18 (two years after I had retired), the board had increased to fifteen parents!

Our outstanding *student officers* for the **2010-11** school year included:

Masquerade
President: *Julia Dwyer*
Vice-Pres: *Tana Schwarz, Charisse Green & Ally Catanesi*
Secretary: *Ali Iles*
Treasurer: *Melissa Strom*
Focus Leader: *Herman Hope*
Historian: *Emily Elias & Nicole Berkey*
Librarian: *Brandon Jones*

Spellbound
President: *Ally Catanesi*
VP: *Rebecca Harpste Melissa Strom & Julia Dwyer*
Sec: *Savannah Maske*
Treas: *Emmalee Wetzel*
Focus Leader: *Amanda Crosby*
Historian: *Becky Clark & Megan Miller*
Librarian: *Amanda Crosby*

Chamber Singers
President: *Ali Iles*
Vice-Pres: *Sophia Sarinana*
Secretary: *Kaylie Simec*
Treasurer: *Justine Garate*
Historian: *Terry Dopson & Nicole Berkey*
Librarian: *Matt Ferrell*

Tiffany's
President: *Charisse Green*
VP: *Megan Berrocal, Allison Rigsby & Sarah Morgigno*
Secretary: *Hannah Rossell*
Treas: *Devanie Zenzola*
Historian: *Megan Miller & Hannah Pipes*
Librarian: *Roxanne Clark*

Thunder Cats
President: *Ryan Savosh*
Vice-Pres: *David Dumond*

2011 was a year in choir like we had never known before at Brea. It was the year that *Masquerade* won *five competitions*. It was also the year when *Spellbound's* performance at FAME Hollywood was so good that it forced FAME to *add a Women's Division* to their annual Fame Nationals! Thirdly, it was Doug and my sixth year at Brea Olinda High School, and the program only seemed to be getting better with age! In addition, the Choir Boosters were well on their way to becoming a legal organization this summer, and I could already feel the excitement as the parents were discussing fundraisers and organization charts! Finally, Masquerade and Spellbound were the *first Brea show choirs*, since Doug and I had been there, to compete in a national competition, with *both of them placing*! It is my privilege to honor those talented kids, by posting their names below!

First Time National Competitors In Fame Indianapolis 2011

Masquerade 2010-11

Emmalee Wetzel • Kaylie Simec • Hailey Holman • Saige Lee
Jessica Raine • Justice Bolden • Megan Strom • Sam Cho
Marysa Leite • Sarah Morgigno • Becca Harpster
Holly Ramsey • Savannah Maske • Maddie Ellingson
Allison Rigsby • Emily Elias • Charisse Green
Kate Hocking • Megan Miller • Brianna Kdeiss
Beckie Clark • Rachel Gallegos • Evette Rodriguez
Brittany Lovell • Brandon Jones • David Dumond
Tyler Schwarz • Daniel Dwyer • Kenneth Southard
Chris Serna • Ryan Savosh • Izzi Perez • Jake Flowers
Rob Catanesi • Julia Dwyer • Rachel Weeks • Nicole Berkey
Emily Malotte • Amanda Crosby • Sophia Valero
Erin Maddex • Melissa Strom • Tana Schwarz
Baylee Heagle • Kellie Galentine • Nicole McEntee
Megan Berocal • Julia Ludwig • Justine Garate
Tara Mazeika • Sophia Sarinana • Ally Catanesi
Allison Iles • Michelle Arno • Alyssa Garcia • Jacob Elias
Amy Czerwinsky • Gabriel Navarro • Terry Dopson
Jordan Carey • Joseph Ramsey • Taylor Calas
Herman Hope • Matt Ferrell • Brandon Allen • Tyler Brown

Chad Rabago • Travis Morrill • Daniel Palomar
Cody Fuller • Josh Guerrero • Brandon Soto • Ben Veling

Spellbound 2010-11

Emmalee Wetzel • Rachel Weeks • Jessica Raine
Amanda Crosby • Devanie Zenzola • Hannah Pipes
Marissa Luedke • Carissa Welsh • Asal Nezafati
Alyssa Alcaraz • Melissa Strom • Jennifer Cao
Baylee Heagle • Olivia Chapman • Roxanne Clark
Uche Ewenike • Jessilyn Winberg • Tara Mazeika
Cassidy Winder • Megan Miller • Amy Czerwinski
Tiffany Park • Samara Eghterafi • Johnnie Villanueva
Monica Prochman • Kelsey Besch • Ariana Veltre
Julia Dwyer • Hailey Holman • Justice Bolden
Abby Ortega • Erin Hocking • Samantha Mauriss
Tori Stuht • Erin Maddex • Taylor Schweitzer
Carolyn Lewis • Becca Harpster • Holly Ramsey
Savannah Maske • Maddie Ellingson • Challoi McCuller
Becka Heagle • Emily Elias • Hannah Rossell
Vanessa Alvarez • Ally Catanesi • Beckie Clark
Mariah Guerrero • Rochelle Atienza • Abby Ciencia
Raven Myers • Nicole Yim

The summer of 2011 left Doug and I searching for a way to follow our great successes of the 2011 competition year, with another set of great shows for 2012! The results were another hard-driving show for Spellbound, called, "*From Hero To Heartbreaker*," a cute set for Tiffany's called "*You Ought To Be In Pictures,*" a wacky show that *Alex Willert* dreamed up for Thunder Cats, starring *Daniel Dwyer*, called "*Daniel's Adventures in Thunderland*," and a mega show for Masquerade called "*Nineteenth Century Madness*," with three separate parts, *La Vida Loca*, *Moulin Rouge* and *Alice Through The Doors*. The Alice section was made-up of *completely new material* and featured a lot of exciting songs by *The Doors* set to tell the story of Alice in Wonderland. Unexpectedly, we had to change the original ending for the Alice segment, because it really upset our audience to see *Alice stabbing the Queen of Hearts with a sword*, at our performance on Preview Night! It was probably too violent for such a well-loved children's story. Consequently, we "*softened*" the ending for the competitions, so that now, the audience only saw Alice "*push*" the Red Queen off the stage. Our complete competition sets can be seen below.

Masquerade 2011-12
Costume Colors:
Blue, Yellow, Green
Competition Set
"Nineteenth Century Madness"

1. *La Vida Loca*
2. *Moulin Rouge*
3. *Alice Through The Doors*

Tiffany's 2011-12
Costume Colors:
Gold, Pink
Competition Set
"You Ota Be In Pictures"

Spellbound 2011-12
Costume Colors:
Gold, Black
Competition Set
"From Hero to Heartbreaker"

Thunder Cats 2011-12
Costume Colors:
Black
Competition Set
"Daniel's Adventures In Thunderland"
(Directed by Alex Willert)

As far as the choir band was concerned, Bo Eder moved from percussion to keyboard, specifically to play second keyboard to Hannah's first keyboard. Of the two trumpets we had last year, only Doug Jones remained while Drew Hemwall continued to be our drummer. Besides Doug, our choir staff consisted of *Kurt Nielsen* (acting coach), *Alex Willert* (musical coach) and in her first year, *Julia Dwyer* (performance coach).

In exchange for receiving a discounted rate from FAME this year, Masquerade and Spellbound agreed to perform at the *NAMM Show* (National Association of Music Merchants), held at the Anaheim Convention Center. We essentially demonstrated a lot of their sound equipment, through our performances. To be perfectly honest, *the kids really enjoyed it* and that sound equipment made them sound great! It was a nice rehearsal, before the competition season started. In addition, after we were done performing, I was interviewed by a writer from *Choral Director Magazine,* for a cover story about my *long tenure in show choir.* The story was published in their March 2012, issue. That was fun.

Masquerade's competition season began with the Diamond Bar *Spectacular.* Diamond Bar's director, Patty Breitag, always hosted a welcoming event, and this year was no different. We were, a little nervous about our unusual *Alice* section, but everyone seemed to enjoy it, which was quite a relief. When the awards were announced, Masquerade had swept the top awards including *1st Place, Best Showmanship* and *Best Musicianship.* Everyone felt a lot more confident after that.

Our second competition saw Spellbound and Tiffany's compete at Diamond Bar's *Girls Night Out!* Our two groups competed in separate divisions, and each gave a stellar performance. When the awards were announced, Tiffany's earned *1st Place* in the Intermediate Division while Spellbound swept the Advanced Division, taking *1st Place, Best Showmanship* and *Best Musicianship*! So far, as far as competition results, the year was perfect!

Next, Masquerade participated, once again in *Bonita Vista High School's* mixed show choir event. This year, they had added the award of Sweepstakes for the group with the highest score of the night. Masquerade gave an *electrifying performance*, even better than their last one. When the awards were announced, they were rewarded with *1st Place, Best Showmanship, Best Musicianship, Best Soloist* (Julianne Sexton)… and *Sweepstakes*!

The very next night, Spellbound participated in Bonita Vista's *For Ladies Only.* This festival was usually small and friendly, and featured a panel of experienced and outstanding adjudicators. Spellbound took their *A Game*, as they always did, and gave a very exciting performance. After the awards were announced, they were speechless. Not only had they won *1st Place, Best Showmanship* and *Best Musicianship…* but a few new categories, as well, including *Best Performer* (Justice Bolton), *Best Soloist* (Uche Ewenike) and *Best A Cappella* (Starry, Starry Night).

Next, We took all four of our groups to Rob Hodo's *Murrieta High School* event, in Temecula. If I remember correctly, *we were the only advanced groups in this competition*, but he created categories for us anyway. Masquerade and Spellbound used this as a tune-up for FAME. All of our performances were exciting, but I would have to say that the audience enjoyed Thunder Cats the best! When the awards were announced, Masquerade took *1st Place, Best Showmanship* and *Best Musicianship* in the Advanced Mixed Division, Thunder Cats took *1st Place* and the knowledge that *the crowd loved them* in the Advanced Men's Division, Spellbound took *1st Place* in the Advanced Women's Division, while Tiffany's came in *2nd Place*, right behind them.

So, Masquerade and Spellbound, each armed with three consecutive wins in competitions this year, headed for Thousand Oaks, to compete in *FAME Hollywood*! Our only regular competitor, competing there from California was Los Alamitos. Our other competitors were groups we were not familiar with, mostly from California. When we arrived, the auditorium looked huge and beautiful! As always, the competition was held in two rounds for the mixed groups. Masquerade gave a fun and passionate performance. At the end of the first round, Los Alamitos led Masquerade by less than a point, while everyone else was far back. Spellbound also had a performance in that first round, and was very exciting to watch. At the conclusion of the second round, the awards were announced. In the Women's Division, Spellbound won *FAME Hollywood Grand Champion,* for the second consecutive year! In the Mixed Division, Masquerade earned *1st Runner-Up* behind Los Alamitos, by a very thin margin. But, the *most important thing* was that both Masquerade and Spellbound were now eligible to compete in the FAME Nationals, which were being held in *Chicago* this year! The kids were excited, and could hardly wait!

One of the two "regular" festivals left was *Hart High School*, which we decided to take Masquerade and Thunder Cats to this year. As always, the waiting time between groups was long, as every group had to load in and load out their stage sets through the small stage door... but everyone seemed to be entertaining themselves just fine. When it was Thunder Cats' turn to perform, they went on stage with determination, as they presented their entertaining show, "Daniel In Thunderland!" They received wonderful audience applause at the end, as I knew they would. Finally, it was Masquerade's turn to perform. Their show had gotten very tight by this time and the performance was terrific. They too received a good deal of audience applause. When the awards were announced, about midnight, Thunder Cats had earned *4th Place*, in the Men's Division while Masquerade had also earned *4th Place,* in the Advanced Mixed Division, behind Burroughs, Burbank and Los Alamitos. *Becca Harpster* also received the award for *Best Female Performer*! So, we didn't do too badly at Hart. But most importantly, this festival had served nicely as another tune-up for FAME.

Next, Masquerade went to the Arcadia *Big Pow Wow*. The show was all tuned up and ready. Masquerade performed very well, that night, and now it was just a matter of waiting to find out how much, the adjudicators liked it. When the awards were announced, Masquerade had won *1st Place*, *Best Showmanship*, *Best Musicianship* and *Sweepstakes*, for earning the highest score of the night! Perfect!

At last, the time had finally come for Masquerade and Spellbound to travel to Chicago to compete in the *FAME National Show Choir Finals*! We had quite a healthy number of parents going along, as well. We really had a great time enjoying the tourist area of Chicago… but before we knew it, it was time to compete. The Women's Division went first. When it came time for Spellbound to go on, they hit the stage with the same energy that got them here last year. They gave a great performance, as evidenced by the thunderous applause they received. After a while, the competition moved to the Mixed Division. While I was with Masquerade in warm-up, I went over our a cappella ballad, *Someone's Waiting For You*, and no matter what I did, we could not seem to sing that song in tune! It was frustrating and I remember giving the kids a more passionate/stern pep talk than usual, probably because of that, and then they went on stage to perform. Their performance was actually very good. Those kids were absolutely giving their all!

The performance of our a cappella ballad wasn't perfect… but I think it was pretty close. When it came time for FAME to announce the awards, Spellbound earned *1st Runner* Up behind the Los Alamitos girls group while Masquerade earned *6th Runner-Up,* behind the mixed winner who happened to also be from Los Alamitos. None of our kids were very happy! Spellbound, had placed *first runner-up* in the nationals for the *second consecutive year*, and they were frustrated! By the same token, Masquerade felt that by placing so low, all of those five wins they'd amassed earlier in the year… amounted to *absolutely nothing*! *But that was not true.* To be honest, even in placing sixth runner-up, out of fifteen or so award winning show choirs, Masquerade had beaten a *lot of very successful groups*, from all over America, who probably felt that *they deserved* to do better… just as we did! As for Spellbound, they were currently ranked the second best women's show choir in America! If they wanted to be ranked number one, they would just have to get the courage and determination to *go back to Fame in another year, and try to win it all, once again*! In any case, I was very proud of both of our groups! Our plane flights left early in the morning, and we were home before we knew it.

Besides a full year of competitions, we performed the musical, *Grease*, once again. Only this time we added staff members, student alumni, parents and even our principal, taking turns at each show, playing the cameo role of *Teen Angel*. It was a great success, and everyone had a terrific time. We switched back to a live combo for this one, featuring Hannah Nam on synthesizer, Drew Hemwall on drums and Rene Lopez on guitar! We actually had eight performances of this one (normally we had six) to accommodate all eight of the "guest leads" performing the role of *Teen Angel* and singing *Beauty School Drop-Out*. These eight *incredibly talented* men included, Jerry Halpin, Kurt Nielsen, Darin Sauer, Drew Olvey, Doug Green, Doug Kuhl, Alex Willert… and me! It was funny, because each of these men had their own fan base. But, the loudest by far, were the *North Hills Church* fans, coming especially to see and hear Doug Green perform. Wow! Talk about passion! This show was a whole lot of fun for the cast and audiences, alike. I, personally, *looked forward to every performance*!

2012 Cast List for "*Grease*"

Sandy: *Nicole McEntee/ Julianne Sexton*
Danny: *Brandon Jones*
Rizzo: *Nicole Berkey/ Justice Bolden*
Kenickie: *Travis Morrill/ Herman Hope*
Frenchy: *Tatiana Alvarez/ Marysa Leite*
Doody: *David Dumond*
Marty: *Becca Harpster/ Charisse Green*
Roger: *Daniel Dwyer*
Jan: *Julia Ludwig/ Amy Czerwinski*
Sonny: *Izzy Perez*
Patty Simcox: *Maddie Ellingson/ Beckie Clark*
Cha Cha: *Teresa Martinez/ Megan Miller*
Eugene: *Sam Cho* **Fred:** *Colton Fuller*
Johnny Casino: *Herman Hope & Travis Morrill*
Vince Fontaine: *Terry Dopson*
Scorpion Leader: *Chris Serna* **Selma:** *Amanda Crosby*
Miss Lynch: Marti Repp **Tom:** *Ben Harpster*
Cameramen: *Chase Parker & Nate Thomas*

Teen Angel

Jerry Halpin • Kurt Nielsen • Darin Sauer
Drew Olvey • Doug Green • Doug Kuhl
Alex Willert • Dave Willert

The Scorpion Gang

Anthony Pham • Kenneth Southard • Louie Jota
Aidan Pipes • Hayden Mangum • Kendon Fuller
Andrew Strom • Gavin Armstrong

The Cheerleaders

Proma Muzumder • Courtney Tindall • Hailey Holman
Challoi McCuller • Becka Heagle • Evette Rodriguez
Abby Ciencia • Sierra McCoy • Samantha Mauriss
Hannah Pipes • Tori Stuht

The Johnny Angels

Rachel Gallegos • Nikki Kennedy • Samara Eghterafi
Sarah Rosner • Vanessa Alvarez • Kelsey Besch
Sophia Valero • Leena Fritz • Baylee Heagle,
Devanie Zenzola • Saige Lee • Lirissa Tittle

The Ensemble

Danielle Zenzola • Emily Boliver • Stephanie Torres
Kayla DeLeon • Lacey Currey • Victoria Rivas
Alexandra Roncero • Fotini Vega • Tristan Brannen
Gabrielle Mendiaz • Rebecca Nevarez • Aleah Tunuufi
Jessica Patow • Taylor Diaz • Jaden Johnson
Esmeralda Torres • Hailey Johnson • Taulima Nua
Madi Betz • Audrey Lee • Jennifer Frazier
Kristen Bertoloni • Angela Truesdale • Brandon Soto
Sophia Gastellum • Olivia Chapman • Thalia Reyes
Amber O'Barr • Elaina Lee • Chrissy Streitz
Erica Cline • Amaris Solis • Katie Petri
Monica Siazon • Amanda Dewell • Paris Valdivia
Maddy Miller • Justine Barcelona

Another fun memory from 2011-12 was that we hosted the *first and only performance,* of a *show choir*, especially designed for our choir parents and alumni, to join, appropriately named, *PIZZAZZ*! About seventeen current Brea choir parents and three of Doug and my Diamond Bar High School choir alumni, faithfully came to weekly rehearsals and ultimately danced and sang, *We Go Together*, from *Grease*, to the delight of the audience of Fall Magic! The Brea parents included *Andrea Strom, Rossana Alvarez, Dan and Lorraine Dwyer, Henry and Julie Mauriss, Linda and Elmer Clark, Debbie Miller, Leanne Anderson, Shannon Van Malsen, Susan Elias, Brian Rigsby, Mary Pipes, Robin Berkey, Shawn Stuht and Brenda Green*, while the Diamond Bar High School alumni included *Caroline Yenydunyeyan, Sarah Meastas and Anna Gutierrez*. This group was certainly a *big hit*… but alas, they ultimately decided to *keep their day jobs* and disband following their only performance! Thank goodness we have our memories… along with a DVD of

Fall Magic 2011, to prove that this *parent/alumni* performance *actually* happened!

Sadly, Disneyland's *Carnation Plaza Stage*, where my choral groups had performed, on and off, almost since the *beginning of my teaching career, in the late 1970s*, was closed on April 30th, 2012, to make room for their new *Fantasy Faire*. Tiffany's, was fortunate enough, to be one of the final groups to perform on it, on Wednesday, April 25th, 2012, *just days before it closed*. For me, that performance was bittersweet, as I realized *I would never be bringing groups to perform on that stage, again*! For those of you who were fortunate enough to perform there, at least once, during your time in high school or junior high school, you, like me... will always have those *special and happy memories*!

Our wonderful student officers for the **2011-12** school year included:

Masquerade
President: *Charisse Green*
Vice-Pres: *Brandon Jones, Herman Hope & Rebecca Harpster*
Secretary: *Allison Rigsby*
Treasurer: *Sam Cho*
Historian: *Tara, Amy & Beckie*
Librarian: *Terry Dopson*
Dance Capt: *Rebecca Harpster & Marysa Leite*

Spellbound
Pres: *Rebecca Harpster*
VP: *Maddie Ellingson, Tara Mazeika, Nicole Berkey & Uche Ewenike*
Secretary: *Baylee Heagle*
Treasurer: *Roxanne Clark*
Hist: *Rachel Gallegos & Amy Czerwinski*
Librarian: *Brianna Kdeiss*
Dance Capt *Allison Rigsby & Beckie Clark*

Chamber Singers
President: *Brandon Jones*
Vice-President: *Justine Garate*
Secretary: *Alyssa Garcia*
Treasurer: *David Dumond*
Historian: *Terry Dopson*
Librarian: *Olivia Chapman & Izzy Perez*

Thunder Cats
President: *Daniel Dwyer*
Vice-Pres: *David Dumond*

Tiffany's
President: *Nicole Berkey*
Vice-Pres: *Charisse Green, Hannah Pipes & Megan Strom*
Secretary: *Hannah Rossell*
Treasurer: *Amanda Crosby*
Historian: *Megan Miller*
Librarian: *Teresa Martinez*
Dance Capt: *Beckie Clark, Hannah Rossell & Challoi McCuller*

CHAPTER 12

Brea Olinda High School... May 2012-January 2013... My Stroke!

Well, early in the morning of Sunday, May 13th, something happened to me that significantly changed my life and the lives of everyone around me… *I had a stroke*! I'll explain the details a little later, but as soon as the doctor knew that I was going to live… he explained to me that everything on my right side was very weak… *not paralyzed…* but that he had *no idea* how much of my movement, *if any*, would return. He told me that being patient and having a good attitude would be the best way to treat this. Secretly, he told my wife to prepare a room for me downstairs, because I might *never climb the stairs again.* He also suggested that she quit her job, and stay home with me. I think he thought that I would need a *fulltime caregiver.* I also think that everyone *assumed* I was going to retire… but that definitely *was not the ending I had in mind to this story*! The following article is what I wrote for the *Brea Olinda High School newspaper*, soon after returning to work, in February of 2013. I wanted the kids throughout the school, as well as their parents, to understand exactly what had happened to me and why I had returned to school… a little *different* than before. I wanted them to understand that my getting *back to school* was a major victory for me, and a time of appreciation for being alive.

My adventure began the night of May 12th, 2012. It was late Saturday night, and I went to bed with a stomachache. About 3:00 am, I woke up, and fell out of bed. I was startled to discover that my mind was suddenly very foggy, the entire right side of my body didn't work and I couldn't speak legibly… I could only make sounds! My wife, Margaret, immediately woke up and asked me what had happened? When I wasn't able to respond verbally, she asked me to raise both arms above my head and to smile. I tried, but I was only able to lift my left arm while the right side of my mouth severely drooped. I heard her cry out, "Oh, God!" She called 911, and the fire department arrived soon. I had little sense of time. My mind was completely confused. One of the men calmly spoke to me, asking what had happened? I momentarily regained my mental clarity and began explaining the situation to him. Regrettably, this recovery was short-lived and my mind once again became foggy. I heard him say to the others in the room, "He's going down again."

The firemen carried me down the twisting stairs, of my house, and into the back of the waiting ambulance. My wife, as she told me later, was not allowed to ride in back, so she rode up front with the ambulance driver. When we arrived at St. Jude's Hospital, in Fullerton, I was very groggy and only overheard parts of what people around me were saying. A CAT scan was taken, nothing irregular was found, and I was diagnosed with a probable seizure, causing all of the *stroke-like symptoms*. The doctor suggested that I would probably return to normal within a few days. I was then moved to Intensive Care. But, by the third day, I had not improved, so the doctor ordered an MRI, at my wife's request. It was here they found *the tiny stroke* (blockage of blood flow to the brain) at the base of my skull that had caused so much damage.

The next four and a half weeks were spent in the hospital convalescing and rehabbing from the effects of the stroke. Thankfully, for me, my wife spent almost every day and night with me in the hospital, while my son, Alex and good friend, Doug, were also constant visitors. Aside from them, *I would not allow anyone else to visit me*. I was too self-conscious about the negative effects of the stroke. I had daily physical therapy, occupational (life skills) therapy and speech therapy. The therapists were very hardworking and I found them to be caring, which made this whole shocking experience tolerable. As a result of the therapies, my speech became understandable when I spoke slowly and carefully, I learned to dress myself and get ready in the bathroom without using my right arm… but my abilities to walk and balance were still very weak.

When I left the hospital, 36 days after entering it, I went home, unsure of what my future held in store. I wasn't sure if I would ever teach again and aside from going to therapy three days a week, I really never left the house. The beginning of my emotional and psychological recovery came when my wife and my friend, Doug, began taking me to Disneyland to watch my son, Alex, perform in the parades. It was frightening for me, going out in public. I was acutely aware of the sagging right side of my face and my wheelchair… but no one else seemed to be bothered by them. When I did run into acquaintances there… we actually had some pretty nice conversations. Next we began going to the movies. I was still terribly self-conscious, but it got easier with each trip. By late October of 2012, I began taking driving lessons twice a week, to learn to drive with my left foot. We had my car customized to accommodate this and by December, I was at the Norco DMV, taking my driver's test. Needless to say… *I passed*! I was well on my way to returning to Brea Olinda High School and Brea Junior High as the choir teacher! But something magical had happened prior, which had given me the courage to go back to school and return to my students, in the first place. It was something completely unexpected.

It was the middle of October in 2012, and I hadn't been back to school since attending part of a Summer Magic concert in July, while I was still confined to a wheelchair. At that time, I had gone inside the theatre after the show had started and left before it ended to avoid talking to anyone. I tried a similar strategy for October's concert, Fall Magic, but neglected to leave soon enough. Before I got to my car, parked near the door leading to the choir room, I found myself surrounded by at least 100 excited choir kids… *MY kids*! *I was overcome with emotion*! Simply overwhelmed by this spontaneous and genuine show of caring! I spent the next hour, speaking individually with each child. It was truly amazing to see them patiently waiting their turns to talk with me. The most common question I was asked was, "When are you coming back?" And without even having to think about it, my response was, "Soon!"

That single, magical event suddenly gave me a compelling reason to return to school. I felt loved… and it became my duty to return to my kids as soon as possible! Two weeks later, I was taking driving lessons and by early February of 2013, I returned to my role as choir director at both Brea Olinda High School and Brea Junior High. I will not tell you that returning to school was easy then, or that it is completely easy now… but it's getting easier all of the time. I limp now... but the good news is that I can walk unassisted. My right arm doesn't function well… but it does have movement in it, and it is getting stronger with every bi-weekly visit to the gym. The muscles in the right side of my face are not completely back… but I am thankful that I can speak clearly and smile… two of the most important tools for a teacher. None of this recovery would have been possible without the love and caring of my immediate family and my close friends. A situation like this one will always bring out the best in your loved ones. Half the battle now, is convincing people *not to feel sorry for me, or my handicaps*. The way I see it, I can do everything that was important to me before the stroke by adapting to what I have to work with. The bottom line is, I needed a good challenge in my life anyway. In many ways, dealing with the fallout, caused by this stroke, has made me a better and more understanding **teacher**… and that… after all… is what I am.

According to Andrea Strom, the choirs' Booster President, at the time,

"*I got a text from someone who heard that you were in the hospital. I believe it was the day after your stroke (Sunday) and so I texted Doug, to get some information. He called back, and although he was trying to put a positive spin on things, I could tell that he was upset, worried and heartbroken. I knew by the sound of his voice and some tears he shed, that your stroke was a much bigger deal than his words were expressing. I also knew that strokes are very unpredictable, as far as recovery, so in my communication with the choir parents, Doug and I talked about sharing the news, but being brief and reassuring. I told the choir parents in my weekly email that, Doug and Hannah had things under control, but I didn't make any predictions or commitments on your return. I think I also said that it was a "minor" stroke, but in my heart, I knew that it was a bigger one. We moved forward with the year, including the banquet, which you viewed from your hospital room and "Dave Magic!" I think the time that went into planning that event was a big boost for the kids and the parents. In most situations where you feel helpless, doing something productive is helpful and is good for the soul. Knowing that the kids were putting on a show to honor you, and to give you a cash gift to help you, I think gave them a great outlet for those final weeks in school, before summer. It was a good focus for parents too. As we moved into summer, and you were able to start posting a few things on Facebook, I think that was helpful to the kids and parents. It gave us the hope that you would return. It was just a matter of time. I was asked to be on the selection committee to hire the new interim director, as well as several students, including my son, Andrew. I think it helped parents, knowing that we had a part in the process and that we approved of Miss Deitch! She was the best choice of candidates that applied. I became more involved in the choir because Doug asked me to come in on Tuesdays and Thursdays to help with the financials. I did get some updates from Doug as the weeks progressed and they were all very positive. So, I feel like the fall became about not, "if," but "when" you were coming back. Miss Deitch was a good teacher, but her style was different, so the kids had to adjust. She was good at responding to issues and was not afraid to interact with the parents. As we moved through the fall, I was asked two questions more than I can count ~ "Is Dave returning?" which was always followed by "When is Dave returning?" I think when you attended Fall Magic, in October, everyone was able not just to read what you wrote on Facebook, but able to see you in person! I think that turned hope into expectation. That November we did "America's Got Talent," which was a fun activity that choir had never done. I think the staff, kids and even Mr. Halpin, will remember that as a fun time, and frankly a good distraction. Once we moved into Christmas and the New Year, I think the expectation of your return might have turned into impatience. Competition season was underway, and everyone wanted you at the helm. You returned in February, at the beginning of the new semester. I know everyone was happy you were back. We were all amazed at your determination to come back and fight to do so. I think we all used it as a lesson to share with others."*

As you probably gathered, my choir students had a substitute teacher for all of my classes from mid-May, 2012 all the way until the beginning of February, 2013, when I was finally able to return to work! Luckily, Doug, Hannah, Kurt and Alex were there to assist the substitute at the end of the school year. When the 2012-13 school year began, as Andrea mentioned, the school hired a long-term substitute, *Miss Deitch*, who was effective, with Doug's help. She was there the entire first semester that I was gone. Unfortunately, Hannah (our accompanist) had resigned during the summer, so the kids started out the new school year with a brand new accompanist (Eric Hendrickson) to go along with their brand new substitute teacher (Miss Deitch)! But, I kept in daily contact with the teacher and Doug filled in every void that was apparent… so the first semester, thankfully, went well!

However, what the *kids experienced*, from the time they heard about my stroke to the end of the 2012 school year is something that concerned me, especially since I would not be going back to say goodbye to the seniors. I did not want this to, in any way, ruin the end of their year! I want to thank *Charisse Green Groh*, a wonderful senior and Masquerade president, from 2011-2012, for taking the time and effort to share her honest and heartfelt memories of what she recalls experiencing, during that very difficult time.

"I still remember exactly where I was sitting when Doug told us about your stroke. It was the first period of choir and he came in, sat down under the TV on that stool by the microphone, and started bawling. I honestly thought it was all a joke! Like some weird repeat of Alex Olvey's senior "prank." After about a minute of him crying though is when it really set in- you had a stroke and you were in the hospital. You weren't coming back. There would be no Dave at the banquet. No Dave at graduation. No Dave for the rest of my senior year. I was devastated.

Dave, I hope you know this, but I honestly don't know where I'd be today if it weren't for you. You spoke LIFE into me everyday. You loved me and cared for me like I was your daughter. For some insane reason, you saw something in me that I didn't see in myself. I can honestly say that when I realized fully that you weren't coming back, it was a punch to my gut. I felt personally affected because, in some ways, I felt like I was closer to you than most of the other students. It was truly devastating.

I don't remember quite when, but we suddenly started rolling with the Dave Magic idea. We quickly came up with a list of acts to recycle from the year (both "Boogie Woogie" and "Cellblock Tango" were performed again) and we started prepping for the spur-of-the-moment show! We raised ticket prices and sold it like it was a benefit concert. We sold out both nights. My dad was asked to come pray before both shows and he led us in singing Kumbaya. ("Save our brother, Lord, Kumbaya. Someone's praying, Lord, Kumbaya.") It was emotional. I remember crying both nights. "Dave Magic" was also strange, though. In some ways, we had already "lived" our lasts. Spring Magic was when all the seniors cried through "Friends" and when each group would "give it their all," as they performed Saturday night's "last show." So coming back, a month later, and doing those things all over again resurrected feelings of all things coming to an end. So as a senior, I definitely got a double-whammy of grief over graduating!!

In addition to Dave Magic, choir without you was so, so strange. In a lot of ways, because I felt so isolated my senior year, you became my person. I would come into your office everyday and we'd talk about anything and everything. You just exuded kindness and love to me every day. So not having that suddenly was very hard.

I remember the day when Doug asked me to direct the seniors at graduation. I think I cried all over again. It was another reminder that you weren't going to be there. I felt so sad (and a little angry) that I had waited 4 years for you to "blow us a kiss" at graduation, one last time, and I was cheated on that. I don't say this to make you feel bad, but really the opposite. I loved you so much that it really, truly was so devastating to not have you for those last senior moments.

I wasn't there, obviously, in the years after you came back, but I want to say how truly inspired I am of your strength and joyfulness. You will always be someone to me who never gave up and never let outside circumstances get you down, and that's something I will always treasure about you!"

As Charisse, so eloquently put, "*I can honestly say that when I realized fully that you weren't coming back, it was a punch to my gut*!" My not being able to say, "Congratulations," or "Goodbye," to the seniors, or ask them about their future plans… really messed up the end of the year, *for the seniors and for me, in a big way*… it made it feel incomplete! I felt so sad during May and June, when I was trapped at the hospital, unable to return to school! Every night I dreamed that I was miraculously healed! But as soon as I woke up, I'd immediately realize that I had only been dreaming. Progress for me felt very slow, and most days I didn't feel any progress at all! I always worked my hardest at whatever task the therapists gave me, because I knew that a positive attitude would keep me going! But, a positive attitude *did not* seem to be fixing me any faster… although, according to one of my therapists, it was keeping me away from *serious depression*! No matter how hard I tried to return to normal… it just wasn't happening! I realized before long that I was going to have to adapt to the *new me*… and although I still exercise and pray for a miracle… *I have adapted*!

In my heart, I knew I wanted to be back at school at the end of the school year... stroke or no stroke! I halfheartedly planned my *escape* from St. Jude's Hospital, in Fullerton a number of times! My plan was to wheel myself down to the street (I was in a wheelchair for the first few months), hitchhike home, and have Margaret or Alex take me back to school! *But, no one would assist me with that plan*! So, I stayed in the hospital.

I want to thank the Brea choirs and parents for being so supportive of me, both while I was out with the stroke and after I returned. The thousands of dollars they raised for me, through their "*Dave Magic*" concerts, paid for therapies and equipment not covered by our insurance! *It was truly a godsend*! I also loved reading all of the letters and notes that my students and parents took the time to write, and we especially appreciated all of the truly helpful gift cards, like "*Meals on Wheels*!" We used them all!

Now it's been more than six years since my stroke. I retired from teaching, following the 2015-2016 school year, on my own terms. I feel thankful, lucky and blessed. A stroke or heart attack can happen to anyone at any time… I'm one of the lucky ones, who survived! I want to thank everyone who was there for me in my time of need, and I want you to know that if the situation is ever reversed… *I will be there for you*! Now, back to school!

CHAPTER 13

Brea Olinda High School... February 2013-2016... Back To School!

I can remember my first day back to school, like it happened yesterday. It was the first day of the second semester, in February of 2013. I'd gone out with Margaret on Friday night to Citrus College to watch Masquerade perform, and to watch them ultimately place *second* at the *Diamond Bar Show Choir Spectacular*, their first competition of the year! Although I enjoyed Masquerade's performance very much, I immediately began thinking of ways to make the show even better… *because that's what directors do*! On my first day back, I walked into the PAC, that morning, through the back stage door, because that eliminated me from having to take any stairs, which were quite a problem for me, at the time. I walked with a cane, and that left me no hand to support myself on the handrail. I believe that Masquerade was first period. As soon as the choirs saw me walking toward them, down the hallway, they spontaneously broke into applause, like you sometimes see in the movies. I pretended that they should stop… but actually, the applause made me feel very welcome, and somewhat *broke the ice*, since I had been gone for nine months! I remember immediately working with Masquerade on their a cappella, *The Hills of Shilo,* during that first morning. I added dynamics, just the way I liked them… it sounded good… and I felt great! From that time on, I was handicapped… but I was back!

The choir band, as mentioned earlier, had changed quite drastically. After Hannah Nam had resigned, toward the end of the summer, *Eric Hendrickson*, who had also played for our choirs at Diamond Bar for a year, was hired to take her place. At the same time, *Bo Eder* returned as our full time drummer, replacing Drew Hemwall. That was the extent of our band. The choir staff was still intact with Doug Kuhl, our choreographer, Kurt Nielsen, our acting coach, Alex Willert, our vocal coach and Julia Dwyer, our performance coach. I know that it probably appeared to be a very unstable time for the Brea Olinda choral program, what with a new band and me returning mid-year… but we all worked together and *everything fell pretty much into place*. Another major change in the choral program, was what I like to call, *the Thunder Cats experiment*. We have always had trouble attracting enough boys into the program to balance our girls, especially in Masquerade, so beginning with the 2012-13 school year, I thought we would drop Chamber Singers for a few years and see if having Thunder Cats as an actual class, would draw more boys into the program? I knew how important it was to keep Chamber Singers alive, so we split many of their responsibilities, such as hosting Brea Idol and performing Singing Valentines all day, at school, on Valentine's Day, between Spellbound and Masquerade. This was the first year of *that experiment*. Whether or not this experiment was successful, remained to be seen… but the boys who had enrolled in our brand new Thunder Cats class… were delighted! Our groups' competition sets, were as follows:

Masquerade 2012-13
Costume Colors:
Gold, Green, Red, Blue
Competition Set
Riverboat
The Hills of Shilo
Meet The Beatles
On The Rooftops of London

Spellbound 2012-13
Costume Colors:
Red, Yellow, Pink, White,
Competition Set
Brother Love's
Big Spender
Starry Starry Night
Livin' La Vida Loca
The Boy From Oz

<u>Thunder Cats 2012-13</u>
Costume Colors:
Black & Blue
<u>Competition Set</u>
Farmer Tan
Fins
A,B,C
Ghost Riders in the Sky
Men In Tights
Doctor Looney
Titanic
Centerfold

<u>Tiffany's 2012-13</u>
Costume Colors:
White
<u>Competition Set</u>
Tiffany's Theme
Downtown
Whatever Lola Wants
Vespers
Good Lovin'
Don't Cry Out Loud
Too Darn Hot

The second competition of the season actually came only *five days* after I had returned to school. This was Tiffany's visit to the *Walnut High School* event. As I have said before, Miss Deitch and Doug did a *great job of preparing every Brea choir for competition*, in my absence. My job, therefore, throughout the competition season, was simply to fine-tune the vocals, continue developing the talent of the group and to provide inspirational talks whenever necessary… but especially when we were in warm-up for a competition… *like today*! I remember telling the girls how much I believed in them, and how much I had enjoyed our week of preparation together. Then they went out and performed! The show was excellent, especially the singing in *Vespers* (Christopher Robin) and *Don't Cry Out Loud*. When the awards were announced, Tiffany's had earned *1st Place* and *Best Showmanship*! I have a picture of Hannah Pipes and I discussing the score sheets, after the competition. Seeing this picture helped me to feel more normal! This had been a great way for Tiffany's to open the season.

After Masquerade's impressive *2nd Place* finish along with earning the plaque for *Best Showmanship*, at the *Diamond Bar Spectacular*, they, along with Spellbound, were off to Arcadia to compete at the *Big Pow Wow*, in their brand new auditorium! The director who had replaced Rollie Maxson, Rick England, was actually a classmate of mine, from many years ago, in the

University of Redlands' music department. He made special provisions for me to use the elevator to get to the balcony, where my students were assigned. I always appreciated kindness like that. Spellbound performed in the Advanced Women's Division, which went first. Their show was terrific, as usual, but the stage microphones really picked up their vocals… so they *sounded especially great*! Masquerade performed a few hours later, in the Advanced Mixed Division. Their show was very entertaining, and their a cappella, *The Hills of Shilo*, was especially nice. When the awards were announced, Spellbound had won *1st Place* and *Best Showmanship* in the Advanced Women's Division, while Masquerade had earned *2nd Place* in the Advanced Mixed Division. From what Doug and I had originally feared would be a *rebuilding year…* was far exceeding our expectations, as our groups were doing *every bit as well in competition, as ever*!! Never underestimate the power of a good work ethic, like the one our groups had!

Our next competition took Masquerade to *Bonita Vista High School's* mixed show choir event. Bonita Vista had been expanding their awards, the way they do at FAME, the past couple of years, which gave individuals a chance to be acknowledged! Masquerade was the final group to perform… and their show brought the house down! When the awards were announced, Masquerade had earned a lot! They won *1st Place*, *Best Showmanship*, *Best Musicianship*, *Best Male Soloist* (Daniel Dwyer), *Best Female Soloist* (Julianne Sexton), *Best Female Performer* (Marysa Leite) and *Best Male Performer* (Jacob Elias & Izzy Perez). Wow! That long drive to San Diego certainly proved to be worthwhile! The kids celebrated on the bus, *all the way home*.

The very next night was Spellbound's turn to attend Bonita Vista's show choir competition, aptly called, *For Ladies Only*. There was a full slate of groups competing, that night. But when Spellbound finally hit the stage, it was pure magic! When the awards were announced, they had earned *1st Place*, *Best Showmanship*, *Best Musicianship*, *Best Soloist* (Julianne Sexton), and *Best Performer* (Rachel Gallegos). Spellbound, now had their second consecutive win!

The next week, Spellbound and Tiffany's traveled to Diamond Bar High School to participate in *Girls Night Out*! This year, a lot of schools were represented, including Hart and Burroughs, which promised that this would be a competitive event. The intermediate division performed first. Tiffany's performed another great show, which elicited a great deal of applause. When the advanced division started sometime later, and it was Spellbound's turn to perform, *they took the stage, as if they owned it*! *Brother Love's* and *Livin' La Vida Loca* were especially exciting to watch! When the awards were announced, Tiffany's had placed *2nd* along with getting *Best Showmanship*, in the Intermediate Division, while Spellbound earned *1st Place* with *Best Showmanship* and *Best Musicianship,* in the Advanced Division! It was a terrific bus ride home for the girls.

Cypress Star Reflections was our next competition. Janae West was the director of Cypress High School, and she always made it comfortable and fun for our students. Since this was one of our final events of the year, we took all of our groups to compete. As usual, this event took all day and ran into the evening. Each of our groups performed well, although in some of the advanced divisions, *we were the only group entered!* This festival had not been running for very long, and to this point, mostly intermediate level groups entered. When the awards were announced, Tiffany's had earned *1st Place* with *Best Showmanship* as well as *Best Musicianship* in the Intermediate Women's Division. Thunder Cats, in their first year of being an actual class, also earned *1st Place* along with *Best Showmanship* and *Best Musicianship*, in the Advanced Men's Division. Spellbound, earned *1st Place* with *Best Showmanship* and *Best Musicianship* in the Advanced Women's Division while Masquerade, also earned *1st Place* with *Best Showmanship* and *Best Musicianship*. Although these awards were impressive, I think the kids in our groups longed for a more *advanced slate of competitors*. Our final competition, *So Cal*, hosted by Chula Vista, would definitely offer that!

So, our *So Cal* trip, beginning at the Catamaran Resort, in Mission Bay, fell a little short of the excitement generated from our Chicago trip, last year… but it seemed *just right to me*, because there was *no financial strain* on the kids or on the choir, like out of state trips always brought. We would compete at So Cal tomorrow. The excitement so far on this trip, had been that one of our bus drivers, on the way up, had *scared the parents and students half to death* with her "perceived" unsafe driving. So, I had to call the bus company and have them send out another driver to take her place for the rest of the trip. After that, everyone dispersed to their rooms and enjoyed the hotel. A while later, Kurt and I met with all of the kids on the Catamaran's private beach in front of the bay. It was beautiful. Basically, we had a meditation/ inspiration session, as we sang together, did pizzazz together, and closed our eyes and imagined things together. This session was meant to bond and unite us… but for me… it made me feel a little bit more normal. *This was me… this was what I did*! I think that everyone else felt just a little bit better after that session, as well. The next morning we headed for Chula Vista High School, where the competition was being held this year. As we arrived Mr. Heagle who was pulling the choir trailer, was stopped by a parent from another school, who stood directly in front of him, as he attempted to park the trailer in a vacant parking space. The man indicated that the vacant parking spot was being *saved for the Los Alamitos* truck which was expected to arrive in a couple of hours. I interceded and told the man, whom I had casually known, for years, that we merely wanted to park and unload… and then we would move. He grew tenacious and refused to move. He went so far as to sit, with his arms crossed, in front of Mr. Heagle's truck! We went on, back and forth for five minutes, while everybody anxiously watched, which prompted one of the Chula Vista students, to run inside the theatre to get Tony Atienza to resolve this quickly escalating problem. Izzy Perez, one of my students, later told me that if the man had tried to hit me, he and the other students on the unloading crew, *had my back*! Good to know. Finally, Mr. Heagle just parked the trailer right there in the middle of the theatre parking lot, and the kids unloaded from there. When they were done, he parked the truck about 100 feet away, against a building, so that Los Alamitos' parking spot would be left open for them. My boys appreciated the fact that I had *never backed down* from opposing the man's unreasonable request. I wondered why that *incident* had even happened? Coincidentally, a few years later, at the Arcadia competition, that same man humbly apologized for his *outrageous* behavior that day. He said that the dads, from his school, who had witnessed the whole thing, immediately started laughing at him, and jokingly calling him, "*Little Buddha,*" ever since, for sitting down in the parking lot and crossing his arms! I'm glad we put that *weird experience* behind us, and I greatly appreciated the apology, although I told him it was not necessary. Show choir competitions really do bring out the passion in people... *even in the parking lot*! Well, the competition began with the Women's Division. Spellbound was terrific. But, after a while, our kids, including those in Spellbound, grew very hungry and left the school on one of our buses to find some quick fast food before the Women's Division Awards began. Unfortunately, Tony Atienza moved the Awards Ceremony to an earlier time than announced, so most of the Spellbound girls missed the ceremony. In any case, Spellbound had been tied for first, with Burbank, but were ultimately awarded *2nd Place* with *Best Musicianship*, apparently because the judges voted two to one, against them. This *was not the way* So Cal had broken the tie in 2010, however, a year when Spellbound, had found themselves in the very same situation! At that one, Burroughs was given *1st Place, over Spellbound,* because they had a *higher musicianship score... just like Spellbound did this year*! So, needless to say, a number of students and parents who had been at both events were confused and pretty steamed, when they found out about it. But, only a few of us were there to see the awards, and the frustration, *resulting in a number of emails from Brea parents to Tony Atienza*, did not happen until later. In the meantime, right after the awards, *Eden Espinosa*, one of the adjudicators and a graduate of Canyon High School, *who had recently played the role of Elphaba, in Wicked, on Broadway*, performed a couple of songs from the show with the Chula Vista choir. *It was impressive*! Thunder Cats performed right after the break, and were very well received. Their show garnered plenty of laughter and applause to prove my point! Soon, the advanced mixed division began. While Masquerade was in warm-up, I told them that they had already surpassed all of the staff's expectations… now it was time for them to surpass their own! They went on stage and performed, easily, their best show of the year! When it came time for the awards to be announced, Thunder Cats placed *4th* in the Men's Division while Masquerade placed *3rd* in the Advanced Mixed Division with the added award of *Best Female Performer* (Shay Jarrett). Well done!

The last thing that I would like to mention about 2013 is our very entertaining choir production of the Disney musical, *Aladdin*! With a shortage of traditional male leads to pick from, at the high school, we actually cast a young seventh grader, *Wesley Mathews*, as our Aladdin, and he did an incredible job! In fact, many of our leads were playing large roles in this choir musical for the first time! The cast was very big, predominantly on the younger side, but they all came through, and the show was great! *Aladdin* became an instant classic!

2013 Cast List for "*Aladdin*"

Aladdin: *Wesley Mathews*
Jasmine: *Nicole McEntee/ Rachel Gallegos*
Genie: *Izzy Perez/ Sierra McCoy*
Iago: *Daniel Dwyer/ Marisa Leite*
Sultan: *Sam Cho/ Leena Fritz*
Razoul: *Stephen Gonzales/ Vanessa Alvarez*
Abu: *Jocelyn Abrahamson*
Carpet: *Brianna Clark/ Tatiana Alvarez*
Tassle: *Erica Cline/ Proma Mazumder*
Gazeem: *Izzy Perez/ Stephen Gonzales*
Prince Achmed: *Sam Cho/ Daniel Dwyer*
Old Man: *Daniel Dwyer/ Izzy Perez*
Proprietor: *Izzy Perez/ Stephen Gonzales*
Three Wishes: *Samara Eghterafi • Rhyan Belanger & Becka Heagle*

Narrators

Uche Ewenike • Niki Kennedy • Saige Lee • Julia Ludwig
Samantha Mauriss • Challoi McCuller • Hannah Pipes
Julianne Sexton • Megan Strom • Tori Stuht
Devanie Zenzola

Guards

Gavin Armstrong • Paul Boardwell • Emily Boliver
Hayden Mangum • Alex Nunley • Chase Parker
Aidan Pipes • Kenneth Southard • Nate Thomas

Dancers

Tatiana Alvarez • Rhyan Belanger • Anna Blaho
Brianna Clark • Samara Eghterafi • Becka Heagle
Maddie Miller • Victoria Rivas • Sarah Rosner
Monica Siazon • Chrissy Streitz • Angela Truesdale
Alexa Walters

Ensemble

Brandon Soto • Cori Bourgeois • Jaden Johnson
Natalie Salas • Kendon Fuller • Maya Gutowski
Ishmael Serna • Carrie Bower • Elaina Lee
Hannah Fritz • Katie Petri • Ayla Golshan • Jessica Patow
Taylor Baker • Audrey Lee • Amber O'Barr • Amaris Salas
Valerie Tetreault • Aleah Tunuufi • Nate Nolen • Kara Dietz
Sarah Hill • Stephanie Torres • Fotini Vega • Caity Sampley
Becky Nevarez • Taulima Nua • Jessica Martinez
Tristan Brannen • Imani Keyes • Kristin Camacho
Julian Martinez • Angela Tunuufi • Danielle Zenzola
Taylor Diaz • Michelle Nunez • Amanda Dewell
Emilio Lara • Sierra Thomas • Kristen Bertoloni
Aolynn Saena • Esmeralda Torres

As I mentioned at the beginning of this chapter, our list of choir classes changed dramatically during this school year, because Thunder Cats was now an *actual class*, while Chamber Singers, at least for now, had been removed from our choir family! The students were also younger and the groups were smaller than they had been in the past. My classes also had a substitute teacher and a new accompanist for the entire first semester! But this did not deter our students from having yet another, *very good year*! Our remarkable student leaders for the **2012-13** choir year included:

Masquerade
President: *Julia Ludwig*
Vice-Pres: *Megan Strom & Sam Cho*
Secretary: *Rachel Gallegos*
Treasurer: *Nicole McEntee*
Historian: *Tori Stuht & Hannah Pipes*
Librarian: *Terry Dopson*

Spellbound
President: *Uche Ewenike*
VP: *Rachel Gallegos & Samantha Mauriss*
Sec: *Devanie Zenzola*
Treas: *Proma Mazumder*
Historian: *Saige Lee*
Librarian: *Courtney Tindal*

Thunder Cats
President: *Izzy Perez*
Vice-Pres: *Jacob Elias & Daniel Dwyer*
Secretary: *Brandon Soto*
Treasurer: *Terry Dopson*
Historian: *Terry Dopson & Alex Nunley*
Librarian: *Chase Parker*

Tiffany's
President: *Hannah Pipes*
Vice-Pres: *Marysa Leite & Proma Mazumder*
Secretary: *Leena Fritz*
Treasurer: *Megan Strom*
Historian: *Taylor Diaz*
Librarian: *Ashley Alger*

The 2013-14 school year was here before we knew it. Doug and I spent our summer preparing a couple of exciting but challenging shows for Masquerade and Spellbound. We, of course would discuss going back to FAME with the kids, even just the local event, to generate a little more excitement for the year. But in our minds, both of these shows were going to be exceptional! This year in addition Eric Hendrickson on synthesizer and Bo Eder on drums (backed up by Erick Pipes), we were also able to add Doug Jackson, a professional *rock guitar* player, to our band. We found him, by accident, while Masquerade was performing for The *Orange County Teacher of the Year* celebration, at the Disneyland Hotel, in the fall. We were also able to add talented alumni, *Kaylee Dysart*, to our staff, as a performance coach, joining, the illustrious, Julia Dwyer. Doug, Kurt and Alex, *were of course*, still on the staff. The competition sets for all of the groups are listed below:

Masquerade 2013-14
Costume Colors:
Black, Green, Pink
Competition Set
"Suite Dreams"
1. *Cinderella*
2. *Bacio Zingaro*
3. *Sweet Heartbreaker*
4. *You'll Never Walk Alone*

Spellbound 2013-14
Costume Colors:
Gold, Purple, Red, Black
Competition Set
"Psychedelic Idiot"
1. *Psychedelic Sixties*
2. *American Idiot*

Tiffany's 2013-14
Costume Colors:
Pink
Competition Set
Tiffany's Theme
Gimme Some Lovin'
Someone to Watch Over Me
Don't Rain on My Parade
Angel of the Morning
Devil with the Blue Dress

Thunder Cats 2013-14
Costume Colors:
Black & Gold
Competition Set
Sherry
Get Ready
Duke of Earl
The Old Achoo
Brown Eyed Squirrel
Next To Lovin'
Weekend In New England
R.O.C.K. in the U.S.A.

Masquerade's first competition, took them Citrus College, to compete in the Diamond Bar *Spectacular*! There were fewer groups competing in it, this year, but there were still a good six or seven. Masquerade's performance was delightful, earning them a huge ovation, especially after they completed their ender, *You'll Never Walk Alone*, with junior Julianne Sexton, passionately singing the lead. When the awards were announced, Masquerade earned *2nd Place* with *Best Showmanship*. Once again, this was an excellent start to the competition year.

Masquerade and Spellbound, journeyed to our next competition, which was Arcadia's, *Big Pow Wow*! Participation was so full that the performance schedule was breaking at the seams, as nearly every show choir that competed in Southern California was there! As a result, every division was filled to the max. Spellbound gave a solid performance for their first competition. Masquerade also gave a good performance, although it appeared that our male sound was a little light this year, as it had been last year. When the awards were announced, Spellbound earned *3rd Place* while Masquerade earned *4th Place*. Not ideal, but we had both placed, and received some very good feedback from the judges.

Next, Masquerade went to the *Bonita Vista High School* mixed show choir event. We enjoyed going to this festival, because we had always done well here and because the atmosphere was very friendly. I don't believe I ever remember a group being penalized here for anything? Not even for going overtime! Masquerade's performance was much tighter than it had been at Arcadia, and our male section actually sounded full! When the awards were announced, Masquerade earned *1st Place* along with *Best Showmanship* and *Best Musicianship!*

The next day, Spellbound and Tiffany's went to Bonita Vista's *For Ladies Only*. Like Masquerade, Spellbound had a long history of doing well here, but if I'm not mistaken, I believe this was *Tiffany's first time going*. We wanted to find out how Tiffany's would do, competing in an advanced competition. Well, Tiffany's performed their show with such freshness and spirit, that the audience could not help but fall in love with them, which was very apparent by their applause. Some of the Spellbound girls looked a little nervous, but those nerves quickly transformed into determination in the warm-up room. Spellbound's performance was *absolutely electric!* I had not seen them like that all year. I guess they just needed a little competition from Tiffany's to deliver their best show of the year, so far! When the awards were announced, Spellbound was victorious earning *1st Place*, *Best Showmanship* and *Best Musicianship*! But Tiffany's was only a few points behind them, in *2nd Place*. It was a good thing for Spellbound that they hadn't taken Tiffany's too lightly. Both performances were amazing!

The *FAME Hollywood*, preliminary competition was next. So, on a rainy day, we packed into the buses, and Masquerade and Spellbound headed toward Cal State Los Angeles, where we competed in the *Luckman Theatre*. Doug and I remembered how every other group at our FAME competitions two years before, had very large bands... so we hired our former musicians, Drew Hemwall and Hannah Nam, to join us. We now had a healthy five-piece band, which would certainly help our chances. Spellbound was once again, *electric,* and there was little doubt in my mind that they would win their division, although show choir competition results don't always come out the way you think! Masquerade was also terrific, but our band's sound didn't quite match-up to the gigantic bands of some of our competitors, but it certainly wasn't for lack of trying! When the awards were announced, Spellbound, once again won *Grand Champion* in the Women's Division! They were screaming and going bonkers! Masquerade placed *2nd* along with *Best Vocals*, but *Evolution,* an outstanding group from Utah, won the Mixed Division, along with Best Show and Best Band. Masquerade was excited, but FAME always had a way of disappointing them too. They had *never won a Fame Competition*. But Spellbound, on the other hand, *could hardly be contained*!

When we got back to school on Monday, I began looking through the FAME program, which included the line-ups from every competition FAME had hosted this year. Suddenly it dawned on me that I had *never heard of many of these groups* and the fields, for most of the FAME competitions this year, had been quite small. *A light bulb suddenly turned on in my brain!* Masquerade had placed a close second at FAME Hollywood while Spellbound had won Grand Champion. *We were very good this year*! It appeared that most of the groups, who would be competing in the FAME Finals, would probably be groups that had never won it! Suddenly, I knew that we had to go to Chicago to compete in the FAME Finals again! I convinced the kids that we had to do it, even though it cost a lot of money and we only had a couple of months to raise it! I never heard from the parents, either way, but I suspect that there were a *lot of heated discussions with their kids that night* about going to the Fame Finals on such short notice and having to raise all of that money! But as they say, when opportunity knocks, it's best to answer the door… or go to FAME Chicago! In any case, the kids and parents got behind it, and we prepared to go to Chicago once again.

We had one more competition before the FAME NATIONALS, and that was *Cypress Star Reflections*! We took all of our groups, this year. It was being held at the beautiful Kennedy High School Auditorium, as usual. Spellbound and Tiffany's competed together in the same division. When Tiffany's performed, they pretty much got the same animated reaction from the audience, they had received at Bonita Vista, where they were barely beaten by Spellbound. When Spellbound performed, they were excellent, but *maybe not quite as electric* as they had been at Bonita Vista. Thunder Cats brought down the house! As the only men's group entered, they were *reasonably assured* of winning their division, even before they took the stage. Masquerade was wonderful. They just got better with every performance! When the awards were announced, Thunder Cats took *1st Place in the Men's Division*, Masquerade took *1st Place* in the Mixed Division, Tiffany's took *1st Place* in the Women's Division, and Spellbound earned *2nd Place, only points behind Tiffany's*! Well, Tiffany's had warned them at Bonita Vista that they were to be taken seriously, and today… *they beat Spellbound*! Tiffany's didn't do that very often, but when they did, they gloated about it for weeks! However, this incident seemed to ignite Spellbound's determination *not to let down*, as they felt they had done today, as they prepared for the FAME Finals.

In preparation for the Finals, Doug had one of his dance captains, *Tatiana Alvarez*, teach Masquerade, a short choreography break using "contemporary" dance moves, that she'd seen the other FAME groups use in 2012 and at Fame Hollywood this year. We hoped that this would make our group *a little more competitive* and that it would give them something new to be excited about! We arrived in Chicago, to compete in the *FAME National Show Choir Finals*, more confident than ever, because most of us had been here before, back in 2012, and we knew what the judges were looking for… *more or less*. Spellbound competed first, in the women's division. Their show was great, but all I can think about, is the ending where the girls crowded behind a huge chain-link fence, while *Brianna Clark* stood in front, menacingly cracking a whip, during the American Idiot segment, and then *everyone chanting together*, "It just doesn't matter," over and over again, with an increasingly louder volume! That ending was classic! The audience was simultaneously *shocked and enthralled…* but it was more than apparent, that *they absolutely loved it*! Before I mention Masquerade's performance, I will tell you that we searched for and found a portion of the convention center that was deserted, where I instructed our kids to rehearse their new "hip" dance segment for *over an hour*, under Doug and my watchful eyes, until they had it looking as second nature as the rest of their show! What I also wanted to say is that *not one member of Masquerade complained about that* to me, or to Doug. Masquerade was really bonded by this point. Well, their performance was truly amazing. They sang incredibly well, their dancing was sharp and energized, *and the band rocked*! I was so proud of those kids! When it came time to announce the awards, Spellbound won *National Grand Champion*, in the Women's Division along with *Best Vocals* and *Best Choreography!* They had finally done it! Meanwhile, Masquerade, had earned *4th Runner-Up* in the Mixed Division! *That was not too shabby either*! I think everyone was pretty glad they had come to the Chicago Finals now… *especially Spellbound*, who was met by camera crews from a local television station, when we returned to Brea, for being the newest *Fame National Women's Show Choir Grand Champions*! We even got to keep the huge trophy in the BOHS office for a year, but we had to return it before the next year's Finals. Not to take anything away from Masquerade. They did an amazing job, and placed fifth, out of fifteen of the best show choirs in America, *even though our band only had three people in it and everyone else seemed to have at least twenty!* This was a definite high point in Brea's show choir history!

In May, we took our *once every two years trip* to New York City. The school board had changed the rules, since our last trip two years prior, and now we had to include a *competition*! So we did. We entered a *Heritage Festival* that took place in the beautiful, *Riverside Church*, just outside of *Harlem*. We had a sizeable group going with us, including a large number of chaperones. We were able to stay at the wonderful Marriott Marquis at Time Square. On this trip we saw *Wicked, Cinderella* or *Matilda* or *Jersey Boys, Newsies* and *Pippin*. The shows, shopping and sightseeing were wonderful. As for the festival, our little choir sang very well in that beautiful old church (which felt more like a cathedral). Subsequently, we earned *First Place* and a *Gold Medal*! Many of the kids sang show tunes all the way back to our hotel on the top of our tour bus! Ah, Memories!

Doug and I really took our time in selecting the musical for the year, because we wanted it to fit the kids we had and to give parts to as many students as possible. Surprisingly, we ended up selecting, *Bye Bye Birdie,* which was not a newer, hip show, like *Aladdin*, was last year… but rather a very *old show* from the 1950s! But, this show was also very cute, and had a lot of *catchy songs* in it, which took a big cast to put on correctly! In a word… it was *perfect* for us! We were able to find a fun part for everyone who auditioned, and lead roles for some of the talented younger kids, who probably would not have gotten one in most shows we did. I would like to say that this show was a big success and ran flawlessly for two weeks… *but I can't*. I *will* say that it was fun and successful for a week and one performance of the second week. Toward the end of the second performance of the second week, while Daniel Dwyer was singing, *Baby, Talk To Me,* we experienced a pretty sizeable earthquake that really rattled the theatre and for good measure, sent some small pieces of the ceiling tiles, *down on the audience*! It was pandemonium! The audience was screaming, while they were being told over and over again, by a tech, over the sound system to *exit slowly!* The theatre was immediately *shut down*! Consequently, we rented the local Curtis Theatre, and two Saturdays later we performed a double header, allowing all of the ticket holders from the last two scheduled shows, to see *Bye Bye Birdie*! Did I mention that we were on TV? Well, we were! Someone gave the news a phone video of the event actually happening, and we became a *breaking story on the nightly news*! In addition, at least one late night show host (I think I watched Jimmy Kimmel), aired the footage, and then told his studio audience, something to the effect, "The best thing about this earthquake, was that no one had to watch *Bye Bye Birdie* anymore!" Yes, laughter erupted from everybody!

2014 Cast List for "*Bye Bye Birdie*"

Albert: *Daniel Dwyer*
Rose: *Hannah Pipes/ Tatiana Alvarez*
Hugo: *Aidan Pipes/ Gavin Armstrong*
Kim: *Brianna Clark/ Julianne Sexton*
Conrad: *Hayden Mangum/ Wesley Mathews*
Mae Peterson: *Leena Fritz*
Mr. MacAfee: *Alex Nunley/ Louie Jota*
Mrs. MacAfee: *Tori Stuht/ Sam Mauriss*
Randolph: *Nate Nolen & Garret Murphy*
Little Debbie: *Erica Cline & Jocelyn Abrahamson*
Ursula: *Maddie Miller/ Michelle Nunez*
Alice: *Riley Hahn*
Helen: *Sarah Rosner* **Margie:** *Victoria Rivas*
Nancy: *Leilani Gonzalez* **Penelope:** *Carrie Bower*
Phyllis: *Ashley Alger* **Charity:** *Charlotte Kim*
Suzie: *Chrissie Streitz* **Deborah Sue:** *Thalia Reyes*
Judy: *Audrey Lee* **Donna:** *Amber O'Barr*
Harvey Johnson: *Ben Harpster*
Gloria: *Rhyan Belanger/ Becka Heagle*
Mayor: *Kenneth Southard*
Mayor's Wife: *Taylor Diaz/Alana Ferracioli*
Mr. Johnson: *Julian Martinez* **Mrs. Merkle:** *Katie Petri*
Cameraman: *Kenneth Southard*
Reporter One: *Jessica Patow*
Reporter Three: *Lacey Currey*

Dancers

Ashley Alger • Riley Hahn • Chrissy Streitz
Maya Gutowski • Sarah Rosner • Lacey Currey
Victoria Rivas • Becka Heagle • Rhyan Belanger
Monica Siazon • Julianne Sexton • Brianna Clark
Samantha Mauriss • Tori Stuht • Tatiana Alvarez
Hannah Pipes • Jocelyn Abrahamson • Madi Betz
Jessica Patow • Maddie Miller

Ensemble

Imani Keyes • Catalina Perez • Kara Dietz
Stephanie Torres • Justine Barcelona • Danielle Zenzola
Esmeralda Torres • Amy Ramirez • Hannah Fritz
Kate Root • Jocelyn Jordan • Alyssa Hendrickson
Tristan Brannen • Jessica Martinez • Becky Nevarez
Elaina Lee • Pauline Rejniak • Kaitlyn Serna
Victoria Bell • Ciara Stephens • Erica O'Barr
Kristin Camacho • Isabel Garcia

Fortunately, our *Spring Magic* concerts were performed at the brand new, state-of-the-art *El Dorado High School Auditorium*, as we had no working theatre at Brea-Olinda, due to the earthquake. Both of our concerts went very well, but, as they say, *there's no place like home*. Having to commute to another theatre, made everyone appreciate our own theatre, that much more! There was not really any timeline for when our own theatre would be repaired, either. Apparently, the damage was severe enough to require state inspectors to assess the damage, before our school district could come up with a plan to repair it. I had a feeling we would be using *other schools' theatres* for quite some time! I was correct in feeling that way, as we were not able to use our theatre again, for nine long months, until the *following January*!

In 2014, after a couple of close misses in 2011 and 2012, Spellbound, *finally* became *Fame National Women's Show Choir Grand Champions* in Chicago! This achievement cannot be overstated, as so few show choirs have ever achieved this! While at *Nogales High School*, our *Dream Street Singers* had achieved this honor in 1996 at the Disneyland Showstoppers, but aside from that, no group of mine had ever won a National Championship, until now! Spellbound was obviously very good in order to make this happen, but the student techs also played a major role in making the show go smoothly. Although I don't have a list of them, I think they should be congratulated for this success along with the staff and the band. Listed on the next page, is that special group of Spellbound girls who finally *found a way to get it done, and to win the FAME Nationals*!

Spellbound 2013-14 National Grand Champions!

Julianne Sexton • Sierra Thomas • Elaina Lee
Michelle Nunez • Kristen Bertoloni • Amber O'Barr
Lacy Currey • Cori Bourgeois • Rhyan Belanger
Pauline Rejniak • Mimi Macias • Leena Fritz
Hannah Pipes • Hailey Johnson • Tori Stuht
Samara Eghterafi • Becky Nevarez • Maddie Miller
Charlotte Kim • Victoria Rivas • Amaris Salas
Tatiana Alvarez • Louise Bearzi-Guedes • Ashley Alger
Chrissy Streitz • Elizabeth Garcia • Ayla Golshan
Samantha Mauriss • Taulima Nua • Caitlyn Gutierrez
Briana Clark • Thalia Reyes • Becka Heagle
Lindsey Gutierrez • Carrie Bower • Katie Petri
Monica Siazon • Uche Ewenike • Sarah Rosner
Jessica Patow • Stephanie Cruz • Jocelyn Abrahamson
Audrey Lee • Taylor Diaz • Alana Ferracioli

Our wonderful student leaders for the *highly memorable* **2013-14** school year, included:

<u>Masquerade</u>
President: *Hannah Pipes & Daniel Dwyer*
Vice-Pres: *Tatiana Alvarez & Bonnie Yoon*
Dance Capt: *Brianna Clark & Tatiana Alvarez*
Secretary: *Riley Hahn*
Treasurer: *Samantha Mauriss*
Librarian: *Louie Jota*
Historian: *Uche Ewenike*

<u>Spellbound</u>
President: *Leena Fritz & Uche Ewenike*
VP: *Jocelyn Abrahamson & Tori Stuht*
Dance Captain: *Tatiana Alvarez & Brianna Clark*
Secretary: *Maddie Miller*
Treasurer: *Becka Heagle*
Historian: *Lirissa Tittle*

<u>Thunder Cats</u>
President: *Daniel Dwyer*
Vice-Pres: *Gavin Armstrong, Alex Nunley & Andrew Strom*

<u>Tiffany's</u>
Pres: *Angela Truesdale*
VP: *Leilani Gonzalez & Emily Boliver*
Dance Captain: *Tatiana Alvarez & Ashley Alger*
Secretary: *Julianne Sexton*
Treasurer: *Lauren Smith*
Lib: *Alana Ferracioli*
Historian: *Hannah Keller*

The 2014-15 school year, from the very start, was planned to be a FAME year, where we would participate in the preliminary competition in Orlando, Florida, hopefully qualify, and then fly out to compete in the *National Show Choir Finals* in Chicago. We had announced this at the end of the past school year! In addition, after having Thunder Cats as a class for two years, we felt it was high time to take them along, as well! Our band still consisted of Eric Hendrickson on synthesizer, Bo Eder on drums and Doug Jackson on the guitar. Doug Kuhl and I had just *packed* Masquerade to the gills, at last year's auditions, ending up with a record *70 kids*, at least *28 of which were boys*, in order to become more competitive. I know these numbers sound impressive, but many of these boys were either new this year, or had come straight from the junior high. We had a very challenging show, in mind for them, and we knew we had to all work hard from the very beginning! Spellbound had lost a dynamic core of seniors from last year's *Grand Champion* performance in Chicago, and we hoped the new seniors would be able to pick up the slack. Another "issue" that came up, was that an aggressive company called *Tresona*, was going around contacting all of the high school show choirs, and *threatening to sue them* if they did not comply with the law by "buying" permission from the publishers for each song they chose to arrange themselves. Well, like most high school arrangers, since there was no buying or selling going on, I had always believed that public school music teachers were *entitled* to arrange their own songs, by the education "fair use" clause in the copyright laws. To say that the law is *vague* on this… *is an understatement*! However, *because* the law is vague, like almost every other school, *we paid Tresona*… in our case, over $6000.00 for the rights to *arrange* Masquerade and Spellbound's shows, and to steer clear of a legal battle. This took quite a chunk out of our coffers, but we wanted to remain on the right side of the law, so we paid it. Doug took a real interest in the ballads this year, as we had never performed two of his *all-time favorites*! So, I arranged them at the end of the summer, to his specifications, and two of our groups got brand new ballads in their shows! Spellbound got Harry Nilsson's, *Without You*, while Tiffany's got Tom Jones,' *Without Love*! Both ballads, for your information, turned out beautifully! Our very special competition sets were as follows:

Masquerade 2014-15
Costume Colors:
Red, Blue, Pink
Competition Set
"Masquerade: The Musical"
Yesterday
Winchester Cathedral
Are You Gonna Be My Girl?
Super Freak
Revolution
Broadway Baby
Lullaby of Broadway
Jumpin' Jack Flash
Check Yes Juliet
Hate
Morning Glow
Saturday Night's Alright

Spellbound 2014-15
Costume Colors:
Red, Black, White, Gold
Competition Set
"Get Spellbound"
Hit Me With A Hot Note
The Joint Is Jumpin'
Cellblock Tango
It Don't Mean A Thing
How Do I Make You
Starry Starry Night
Barracuda
Walk This Way
Whip It
Without You
Hero/ Almost Paradise

Thunder Cats 2014-15
Costume Colors:
Black, Blue, Red
Competition Set
"Fresh Step"
I'm A Believer
River of Dreams
Carwash
Be Our Guest
American Idiot
The Impossible Dream
School's Out

Tiffany's 2014-15
Costume Colors:
Blue w/ White Trim
Competition Set
Tiffany's Theme
We're In The Money
Big Spender
Too Darn Hot
You Belong With Me
Desperado
It's So Easy
Without Love
Poor, Poor, Pitiful Me

Merely considering the large number of different songs, in both the Masquerade and Spellbound shows, tells you how much work this year was going to be. To think, that we used to believe, *a good competition show consisted of four or five songs*, for years! I have no idea *what possessed us* to take on so much! In any case, Masquerade was too big and too new to work very fast, and even when they had something learned, a lot of the performers were *underwhelming,* due to their lack of experience. Rehearsals tended to be a little frustrating, early on. Spellbound's show just didn't seem to jell? We moved songs around, but we simply couldn't figure out what *exactly* was wrong? Thunder Cats were competing nationally this year, too, so basically, we gave them mostly up-tempo and driving songs, and tried to move them up to the next level of singing and performing, by getting a lot more serious. Tiffany's was Tiffany's. They were especially excited, because this year they got to perform a popular Taylor Swift song in their show, for the first time, called *You Belong With Me*! Tiffany's was always a breath of fresh air in our program, but especially this year, because they were our only group, *not feeling the pressure of competing nationally.*

Masquerade's first competition, took them to the Diamond Bar *Spectacular*. To Doug and I, this competition would tell us pretty quickly, whether or not Masquerade was *competition-ready*. The competition was held at Diamond Bar High School, instead of Citrus College, so we wondered how our gigantic group was going to fit on their much smaller stage? Well, we were about to find out! Actually the show went great. Masquerade won *1st Place*, *Best Showmanship* and *Best Musicianship*. Our band had been a little loud, but it was a fine first competition. However, after hearing the video, I sensed that the band was not playing down when the group sang. I spoke to our drummer, Bo Eder. To make a long story short, I think my bluntness may have insulted him, and *he politely retired from the band*. Wow! Well, we had the Arcadia competition coming up, on the following week, *so I was frantic to find a good drummer*! Fortunately for us, *Drew Hemwall*, our drummer before my stroke, offered to come back… and we welcomed him with open arms!

We rehearsed the band together, with Drew, our new drummer, for a couple of rehearsals, but I knew that it would be *impossible* for him to learn the Masquerade, Spellbound, and Tiffany's shows so quickly, so we talked to Drew, *all day at* Arcadia's *Big Pow Wow*, before each of our groups performed. Due to his skill and professionalism… he was able to pull it off! I really didn't pay too much attention to our group's performances, as I was too busy monitoring the band. When the awards were announced, Tiffany's earned *3rd Place* in the Advanced Women's Division, while Spellbound earned *4th Place*, with *Best Showmanship... behind Tiffany's!* Masquerade earned *4th Place,* because as one of the adjudicators shared with me after the competition, '*You were just too darn loud, and you did everything on stage, I have spent my entire career fighting against*!' Well, *that was certainly not a compliment*! However, in the first place, we *never did very well* at Arcadia, anymore, ever since they had moved the competition to their own high school. In the second place, Masquerade and Spellbound's shows were designed to be competitive at FAME, by being "rock shows," and Arcadia's score sheet didn't have nearly as many show categories to appreciate that! And in the third place... *our shows were still not working the way we wanted them to,* and like the adjudicator had shared earlier, *our band was still too loud!* We would try to solve these problems at rehearsal on Monday.

As we prepared for the *Bonita Vista Festivals*, at rehearsal, I also discussed a major problem that had reared its ugly head. Many of our Masquerade, Spellbound and Thunder Cat members *had not raised the necessary money for their upcoming trip to Orlando, which was scheduled to happen, in just over a month*! This trip had been *planned since the end of last year*! But with so many new members, there was apparently, *little determination within the groups to get this trip paid for*! So, the Boosters stepped in, and President, Andrea Strom and her crew somehow got the money raised. This was no small feat, as we needed to raise money for 120 students plus the staff! I will be eternally grateful to Andrea and the parents for *finding a way* to raise enough money to make this trip happen!

This year, Bonita Vista changed the name of their competition to *San Diego Sings,* and they ran both the *women's* and the *mixed* divisions, on a single day. So, we took everyone, and competed at the school all day. When the awards were announced, Spellbound placed *1st* and Tiffany's placed *2nd* in the Advanced Women's Division, Thunder Cats placed *1st*, in the Men's Division and Masquerade placed *1st* in the Mixed

Division. Everyone in each of our groups was excited for their awards, but Doug and I feared the new kids would think winning was easy, since this competition was. Our competitors at FAME Orlando this year, were going to be *very tough*! We needed to make the new kids understand *just how tough…* and we only had one competition left to do that.

Our final non-FAME competition of the year was the *Cypress Star Reflections*. This one, like most of the competitions we had participated in, so far this year, was *not particularly full of advanced groups*. Still, it was our final competition tune-up before FAME Orlando, and the adjudicator comments could be beneficial. All four of our groups performed well, each in their own way. When the awards were announced, Thunder Cats had placed *1st* in the Advanced Men's Division, Masquerade had placed *1st* in the Advanced Mixed Division along with earning *Best Showmanship* and *Best Musicianship*, Spellbound had placed *2nd* in the Advanced Women's Division, and Tiffany's had *swept* the Advanced Women's Division winning *1st Place*, *Best Showmanship* and *Best Musicianship*! They had surprised Spellbound, by beating them once again! *This made it twice on the year*!

Based on the outcomes of the past four festivals, we decided that we had to make some *song* and/or *song order* changes for each group in order to keep their sets from being too long and losing steam, as some adjudicators had pointed out. In Masquerade, we hesitantly cut *Revolution* and *Check Yes Juliet*, leaving us with the show performed at the first FAME:

***Masquerade's* First Fame Show**

"Masquerade: The Musical"
Yesterday
Winchester Cathedral
Are You Gonna Be My Girl?
Super Freak
Broadway Baby/Lullaby of Broadway
Jumpin' Jack Flash
Hate/ Morning Glow
Saturday Night's Alright

Spellbound's show was hardly changed at all, this time around. We simply cut *Whip It,* because it didn't seem to go anywhere. Their "new" show for the first FAME consisted of:

***Spellbound's* First Fame Show**
"Get Spellbound"
Hit Me With A Hot Note
The Joint Is Jumpin'
Cellblock Tango
It Don't Mean A Thing
How Do I Make You
Starry, Starry Night
Barracuda
Walk This Way
Without You
Hero
Almost Paradise

Thunder Cats were going into the FAME competition with exactly the same show they had been performing all year. Their show for the first FAME was:

***Thunder Cats'* First Fame Show**
"Fresh Step"
I'm A Believer
River Of Dreams
Carwash
Be Our Guest
American Idiot
The Impossible Dream
School's Out

Soon it was time to fly out to Florida, to compete in *FAME Orlando*! We arrived in Orlando and were soon transported by a Disney Shuttle to a nice Disney hotel. The kids visited one of the Disney parks, for a short time, if they chose to, or just hung around the hotel, that first day and night. The next day, we spent most of the day at Universal Studios, visiting *The Wizarding World of Harry Potter*. Then, the following day was the FAME competition! Spellbound and Thunder Cats had very good performances. But what I remember most about Masquerade was their "unfocused" warm-up, *before* their performance. Westside High School's *Amazing Technicolor Show Choir* preceded us in the warm-up room and *they were excited*! I mean, *that room was rocking and rolling from their warm ups…* whatever they were doing? But my point is, *they were very energetic*! When it came our turn to warm-up, the kids wandered in, listless and tired, I assumed, from spending so much time in the parks. So, I tried to get everyone pumped up, but it just didn't happen this time. We reminded the kids what they had to do, and they performed! It was a fine show, but… like I've been saying for this entire chapter, *something was missing*? Before I announce the awards, I want to explain that in the Mixed Division, only the *top three finishers* were invited to compete in the National Finals in Chicago. In the Single-Gender Division (formerly called the Women's Division), where only three groups were competing, Spellbound, Thunder Cats and Hart High School's Hartbreakers, only the *top two finishers* would be extended an invitation. That meant that unless Thunder Cats placed first or second, *they could kiss their Thunder Cat dreams of being the first men's group to compete in the Finals... goodbye*! When the Single-Gender awards were announced, Spellbound had earned *Grand Champion of Fame Orlando* in the Women's Division! Thunder Cats had placed *second,* qualifying for the finals, in the process! Spellbound and Thunder Cats were screaming and hugging each other, they were so excited! But, when the Mixed Choir awards were announced, Masquerade had placed *fifth*, a few points behind The Amazing Technicolor Show Choir, who had placed fourth. Then, after a short delay, the festival host announced that *Attache,* the group from Mississippi, who had won, had chosen *not to go to the Finals*, and one of the FAME preliminary festivals had been canceled this year, so… they were inviting the *top four groups* from the mixed division, instead of the usual three. Have you been paying attention? That meant that Masquerade had somehow *backed into a competing spot in the*

Finals! The kids were so confused by now, that when I told them they were being invited to the Finals after all… *they all looked a little shell-shocked!* Anyway, all three of our groups had qualified to compete in the National Finals, but after coming in fifth in the preliminaries, *granted, it was a very competitive one*, I just wondered if the Masquerade kids were up to spending the next month, doing whatever it would take, to fix our show and our group to be more competitive? After a little problem coordinating the Disney buses that were taking us to the airport, we flew home that next day.

Monday morning, *I issued the kids an ultimatum*! Since all money collected by the choir, had to fall under the category of *non-mandatory donations*, I told them to discuss the FAME Finals with their parents. If 80% of the kids brought checks in for $800.00, on Wednesday, *we would go.* But that would be the *absolute deadline,* since the Finals were less than a month away! I wasn't sure if $800.00 would actually be enough, but I knew that our Boosters had some money put away that I figured they would be *happy to share* for this good cause. Wednesday morning arrived… *and happily, I was inundated with checks all morning*! Approximately 78% of the kids had come through with the challenge, which to be honest, really impressed me! If these kids wanted a chance to do well in the FAME Finals, and their parents supported them… *then Doug and I were going to go full-out, to try to make that happen*! The first thing we did was to analyze every show by the previous FAME festival score sheets. Although Thunder Cats would change a few things, Spellbound and especially Masquerade, *would get some serious makeovers*!

Beginning with Thunder Cats. They had a great performance in Orlando, but the song, *Carwash*, as much as the group liked it, had rather sloppy execution of the choreography, so, it was pulled from their show. Their new FAME show looked like this:

***Thunder Cats'* Second Fame Show**

"Fresh Step"
I'm A Believer
River Of Dreams
Be Our Guest
American Idiot
The Impossible Dream
School's Out

As for Spellbound, they already had a very good show, but Doug and I decided to make it even *more exciting* than it already was! First, we put *Cellblock Tango* and *The Joint is Jumpin,'* second and third, instead of the other way around. Next we cut *It Don't Mean A Thing*, because it was too similar to *The Joint is Jumpin'* and replaced it with *I Walk Alone,* sung solo by Lirissa Tittle, while the other girls were changing clothes. This was common practice in mid-west-styled shows. Then we went right into *Barracuda*, followed by *How Do I Make You.* We then sang *Starry Starry Night*, and followed that with a medley of *Walk This Way* and the newly added *Respect.* The show ended as it did before with *Without You* followed by the ender, *Hero/ Almost Paradise*. Their *newly altered* competition set is listed below:

***Spellbound's* Second Fame Show**

"Get Spellbound"
Hit Me With A Hot Note
Cellblock Tango
The Joint is Jumpin'
I Walk Alone (Lirissa Tittle)
Barracuda/ How Do I Make You
Starry Starry Night
Walk This Way/ Respect
Without You
Hero/ Almost Paradise

Masquerade had much bigger problems. According to the FAME score sheets, their show was *too much the same, throughout, and very frantic*. They also mentioned that the choreography wasn't sharp enough. One judge went so far as saying that he grew *bored* watching our show! Let me preface this by saying that Doug and I *did not necessarily agree with these judges*, but, they were *FAME* judges and we were going back to a *FAME* competition, so, we did the smart thing, and quickly got to work dramatically changing the show! To begin with, since the judges perceived the choreography as *not being sharp enough*, we decided to change to *couples* for this show. So, we put twenty-five boys and twenty-five girls into each dance number, while the remaining 20 people sat out. We auditioned every song judiciously, being certain we had enough strong singers, as well as dancers in the mix. Everyone in the group would still perform the new a cappella, the ballad and the ender. Next we very hesitantly cu*t Lullaby of Broadway,* the song the group *had spent the most time learning and perfecting*, full of color and fun. The problem was, *we didn't perform it accurately enough*, and it never seemed to get any better. The next change was with the song, *Yesterday*. This a cappella had worked the whole year… *except at FAME*, where they generally didn't appreciate a full length a cappella song and thought it slowed down the show (they also said this in comments). So, we turned it into a solo for Julianne, while the group changed clothes. As I mentioned, for Spellbound, who was doing the same "solo" thing, this was a very popular practice in the mid-west-styled shows we had previously watched. We ended up also using our "cool" middle section of *Yesterday*, as the *opening of our show*, so that it would not be wasted. We also extended *Jumpin' Jack Flash* with a lengthy dance break, and brought back *Check Yes Juliet*. But the biggest changes involved adding a new "rock" a cappella, *Hey There Delilah*, and dropping *Morning Glow* for a more exciting power ballad, *Your Song/Come What May*, while also dropping *Hate* and adding a little novelty number… *The Fox*! Their complete *altered show* is listed below:

***Masquerade's* Second Fame Show**
"Masquerade: The Musical"
Yesterday
Are You Gonna Be My Girl
Winchester Cathedral
Super Freak
Yesterday (reprise) (solo by Julianne Sexton)
Jumpin' Jack Flash
Hey There, Delilah
The Fox/ Check Yes Juliet
Your Song/ Come What May
Saturday Night's Alright For Fighting

I imagine all of these changes must sound like they took an awful lot of time and effort to execute, and I agree, *they did*! But I was so excited about making our shows *right,* as well as being so proud of our kids for taking the initial action, by bringing in their *Finals checks* at the deadline, that in a word… I felt *empowered*! And it did not take me long to see that all of the kids were feeling that way too! It felt as if our destiny was to go to FAME Finals this year… whether we did well or not was secondary to the fact that we were doing everything we could to become more competitive!

The *FAME National Show Choir Finals* were being held in the beautiful old Genesee Theatre in Waukegan, Illinois, about fifty miles outside of Chicago. Unfortunately, the prior location in Chicago was not available, so FAME scrambled to find this theatre at the last minute. Although the theatre was charming, the town was *run-down, depressed and desolate…* a far cry from bustling Chicago. But, we hadn't come here for sightseeing *we had come here to compete*! The day of the competition was busy. There were seven unisex groups competing (Thunder Cats was the only men's group), and *eighteen* mixed groups! Although this competition only gave out *three* trophies, they did acknowledge the top ten scorers, in the Mixed Division, as being "The Top Ten Show Choirs of 2015!" The Unisex groups started competing pretty early in the morning. Thunder Cats were very well received, as they performed with energy, musicality and professionalism. It would have been difficult, *not* to be proud of them! Spellbound gave a sensational performance of their *new show*, that felt every bit as polished as last year, when they had won Grand Champion! Masquerade's show was the most different, with the addition of four new songs, which they had *not competed* with in Orlando. But they had rehearsed them so much, that it looked and felt as if they had performed this show all year! When Masquerade got to, *The Fox*, a former Internet sensation by the Ylvis brothers from Norway, the crowd laughed in surprise, but they sure enjoyed it. Just like last year, we had included a "mid-west-styled" dance break in the song, which brought the house down! At the end of all of our shows, the staff hung out in a local restaurant/bar down the street to wait for the awards ceremony to come… *and to keep warm*! Finally, we returned to the Genesee Theatre. When the awards were announced, Spellbound was the *2nd Runner-Up*, with *Best Costumes* and *Best Stage Presence*, behind Los Alamitos and Carroll. In the same division, Thunder Cats was the *6th Runner-Up*. Masquerade, meanwhile, in the Mixed Division, was the *8th Runner-Up*, and was announced as one of the *Top Ten Mixed Show Choirs of 2015!* I don't know about the kids, but *I was so proud and so excited*! In Orlando, Masquerade had placed fifth out of six. But here, against eighteen *top three* finishing groups, from six different FAME preliminary competitions, competing together in this one, we placed in the *top ten*, beating the *Amazing Technicolor Show Choir*, who had previously beat us at Orlando! Most of all, *we had all worked together to make this possible*! Spellbound and Thunder Cats had also *dramatically improved their shows*, and they had displayed it on stage! Bravo! Because of the heart and determination of these groups at Waukegan, I would have to say that this was one of my *favorite competition years* at Brea!

In 2015, the *Brea Thunder Cats* became the very first all-men's group to *ever* compete in the Fame preliminary competitions, and to also qualify and compete in the Fame Nationals! This was no small feat, for a group that had been famous, for years, for their simple costumes, moderately rehearsed but highly entertaining show and spontaneous attitude to become *really competitive...* but they certainly accomplished it! Listed below is that historical group!

Thunder Cats- First All-Male Show Choir to Compete in Fame and Fame Nationals

History Making "Thunder Cats" 2014-15

Vinchy Jota • Ben Harpster • Wesley Mathews
Erick Flores • Garret Murphy •Josiah Madrigal
Nate Nolen • Emilio Lares • Hayden Mangum
Aidan Pipes • Ishmael Serna • Justen Baker
Kramer Southard • Andrew Strom • Alex Nunley
Edward Kwon • Gavin Armstrong • Luis Contreras
Jacob Morton • Stephen Gonzales • Julian Martinez
Travis Miller • Jake Drake • Alex Macedo
Matt Bryan • Mitchell Slife • Lorenzo Casas

Sadly, this would turn out to be the final year that Thunder Cats would be offered as a class period. The three-year "*experiment*" had created some pretty awesome Thunder Cat shows, but it *had not significantly drawn in boys from outside the choir program*, as we'd hoped. So, the next year, Thunder Cats returned to being an after school group, and we re-introduced *Chamber Singers*, the traditional stand-up choir, back into the program.

The only other thing I would like to mention about 2015 was our exciting choir musical, *Thoroughly Modern Millie*! We had never produced this show before, but Tatiana Alvarez *pleaded with us* to select that show every year! So, we finally did! What a *perfect show* for our talented kids to put on! It proved to be a hit, and since Tatiana Alvarez and Brianna Clark were so good at *performing both of the two female leading roles*, Mrs. Meers and Millie, we had them *switch parts after the first week*! This was also Julianne Sexton's senior year, and her final Brea Olinda musical! She had built a brilliant soloist career at Brea, and she certainly did not disappoint here! Colton Fuller was the musical director of "Muzzy's Boys," and he did a marvelous job teaching them all of the difficult jazz harmonies! Bravo! *Julianne, Tatiana, Brianna, Wesley, Travis, Leena, Carrie, Colton, Aidan, Andrew, Alex, Maddy* and all the rest of this very talented cast put on a delightful presentation that our audiences raved about for weeks after the show was over! The entire cast is listed below:

2015 Cast List for "Thoroughly Modern Millie"

MILLIE: *Brianna Clark /Tatiana Alvarez*
MRS. MEERS: *Tatiana Alvarez / Brianna Clark*
JIMMY: *Wesley Mathews*
MISS DOROTHY: *Julianne Sexton*
TREVOR GRAYDON: *Travis Miller*
MUZZY: *Leena Fritz*
MISS FLANNERY: *Carrie Bowers*
BUN FOO: *Andrew Strom* **CHIN HO:** *Aidan Pipes*
FENG SHUI: *Alex Nunley* **GLORIA:** *Maddy Miller*
RUTH: *Jocelyn Abrahamson* **ALICE** *Jenny Jung*
ETHEL: *Taylor Diaz* **CORA:** *Victoria Rivas*
HAZEL: *Taulima Nua* **LUCILLE:** *Chrissy Streitz*
RITA: *Jessica Patow* **SISSY:** *Audrey Lee*
CLARA: *Kasey Jacques* **DAPHNE:** *Amanda Cox*
DOROTHY PARKER: *Jessica Martinez*
MATHILDE: *Kristin Bertoloni*
KENNETH: *Colton Fuller* **DEXTER:** *Alex Macedo*
RODNEY: *Ben Harpster* **NEW MODERN:** *Lindsey Morrill*

MUZZY'S BOYS (Directed by *Colton Fuller*)
Colton Fuller • Stephen Gonzalez • Ben Harpster
Vinchy Jota • Hayden Mangum • Julian Martinez

MUZZY'S DANCERS
Monica Siazon • Maya Gutowski • Amber O'Barr
Thalia Reyes • Cori Bourgeois • Lindsey Morrill
Kristin Camacho

TAPPERS
Maddy Miller • Jocelyn Abrahamson • Chrissy Streitz

Jenny Jun • Kristin Camacho • Jenna Norseth

ENSEMBLE

Justen Baker • Victoria Bell • Tristan Brannen • Kara Dietz
Hannah Fritz • Claire Manson • Carmen Martinez
Madyson Miguel • Garret Murphy • Becky Nevarez
Nate Nolen • Erica O'Barr • Ashton Ogden • Catalina Perez
Pauline Rejniak • Kate Root • Berenice Rosales
Elizabeth Sanchez • Naomi Santiago • Clara Stephens
Jaymi Wilson

Our wonderful student officers for the **2014-15** school year, included:

Masquerade
President: *Colton Fuller, Andrew Strom, Brianna Clark, Tatiana Alvarez & Angela Truesdale*
Dance Capt: *Tatiana Alvarez, Gavin Armstrong, Brianna Clark, Maddie Miller, Ben Harpster, & Jenny Jung*
Secretary: *Michelle Nunez*
Treasurer: *Taulima Nua*
Librarian: *Lirissa Tittle*
Historian: *Vinchy Jota*

Spellbound
President: *Rhyan Belanger, Maddie Miller, Leena Fritz, Brianna Clark, Jenny Jung & Tatiana Alvarez*
Dance Captain: *Brianna Clark, Jenny Jung, Tatiana Alvarez, & Maddie Miller*
Secretary: *Chrissy Streitz*
Treasurer: *Monica Siazon*
Hist/Lib: *Lacey Currey*

Thunder Cats
President: *Alex Nunley, Ben Harpster, Andrew Strom & Gavin Armstrong*
Dance Capt: *Gavin Armstrong & Ben Harpster*
Secretary: *Hayden Mangum*
Treasurer: *Stephen Gonzalez*
Librarian: *Vinchy Jota*
Historian: *Emilio Lara*

Tiffany's
President: *Julianne Sexton, Taylor Diaz & Carrie Bower*
Dance Captain: *Tatiana Alvarez & Maddie Miller*
Secretary: *Allie Mayer*
Treasurer: *Hailey Johnson*
Librarian: *Maddie Miller*
Historian: *Maya Gutowski*

The 2015-16 school year, which would prove to be my last year of teaching, started out with smaller groups, especially Masquerade, which had gone from 70 students last year to only 46 this year. Spellbound was our largest group, at 49 while Tiffany's held its own, at 42. Seeing our number of boys in Masquerade reduced from nearly 30 last year to only 15 this year, presented us with some very *serious* vocal and choreography challenges to think about, due to the large discrepancy in numbers, between the boys and the girls in the group. As for our band, Eric Hendrickson and Drew Hemwall returned and Eric Abrahamson, a professional "Disneyland" pianist, joined us as the second keyboard player. Unfortunately, we lost Doug Jackson, our former guitar player. Our staff of Doug Kuhl, Kurt Nielsen, Alex Willert and Kaylee Dysart, remained intact. Ever since I had returned to choir, from my stroke, it seemed that we had been dealing with *"rebuilding"* issues every year! So, this year, to make things a bit easier on the students, we limited each group to only *one costume, apiece*. This would make the amount we needed to fundraise, much less (unlike the nightmares of last year), and costume changes would *not* need to be built-in to the choreography. We gave each show a title that would encompass every song that we had selected for it. Masquerade's show was a full-length version of the twelve-minute homage to Alice in Wonderland we had competed with in 2012, called "*Return To Wonderland.*" This new version had some great new songs added like *Welcome To Wonderland*, *Stairway To Heaven*, *O My Luve's Like A Red Red Rose*, *Shut Up and Dance With Me* and *Heartbreaker*, in addition to all of the Door's songs found in the original. Spellbound had a fun homage to Elvis Presley, called "*Viva Spellbound.*" In an effort to increase our male choir population, our all-girls group, *Tiffany's*, became the *new mixed group*, *Tiffany's & Company*, whose show was called, "*Steamboats and Southern Charm.*" *Thunder Cats*, who now rehearsed after school and on Saturdays, had a fun set, made up of a plethora of things, titled, *"Yesterday and Today."* Most importantly, we decided *not* to have our groups compete nationally, this year, since last year had been such a trying, albeit *successful*, experience for everyone. Our competition sets were as follows:

Masquerade 2015-16
Costume Colors:
Red & Silver
Competition Set
"Return To Wonderland"

Tiffany's and Co. 2015-16
Costume Colors:
Blue
Competition Set
"Steamboats and Southern Charm"

Spellbound 2015-16
Costume Colors:
Gold & White
Competition Set
"Viva Spellbound"

Thunder Cats 2015-16
Costume Colors:
Brown & White
Competition Set
"Yesterday and Today"

For their first festival of the year, *Masquerade* and *Tiffany's & Company*, competed at the *Diamond Bar Spectacular*, held at Diamond Bar High School. The line-up was very small, this year, as including *Masquerade* and *Tiffany's & Company;* there were only *three total competing groups!* There had been a *gradual decline* in the number of groups competing at the Diamond Bar Spectacular, over the past few years. This fact *seemed to be foretelling* the end of this competition, if something drastic didn't change in the future. It saddened me to think this, as Doug and I had *started this competition*, when we had first arrived at Diamond Bar High School, back in 1998. The festival was short and sweet. Tiffany's & Company, was very entertaining and Masquerade was fast paced and very musical. When the awards were announced, Tiffany's & Company placed *2nd* while Masquerade swept, winning *1st Place*, *Best Showmanship* and *Best Musicianship*. Not a bad way to start the year!

Our second competition, took us to the Arcadia, *Big Pow Wow*. We had not done very well here for the past several years, but regardless, it was a good tune-up for our future competitions. Since we were not attending many festivals this year… we took everyone! I won't leave you in suspense. All of our groups, including Thunder Cats, had good solid performances. When it came time to announce the awards, Thunder Cats earned *2nd Place* in the Men's Division, Spellbound earned *3rd Place* and *Best Showmanship*, but was penalized and placed *4th* for going overtime, in the Advanced Women's Division, Tiffany's and Company, earned *2nd Place*, in the Intermediate Mixed Division, only a few points behind Burbank, while Masquerade earned *3rd Place*, in the Advanced Mixed Division. We didn't win any divisions, but these placements were *definitely* better than they had been last year at this festival!

Next, Masquerade and Spellbound went to the Bonita Vista competition, *San Diego Sings*! This year, it was held at Lincoln High School in San Diego. To be honest, I enjoyed the competition much more during all of the years it was held at *Eastlake High School* in Chula Vista. Win or lose, the Eastlake High School location made the festival feel very friendly and enjoyable. The mood of *this* event, at Lincoln High School, *seemed rather cold in comparison*. But, I realized that Bonita Vista was *trying to attract more groups by using a larger facility*, and I supported that. In similar circumstances, I may have done the very same thing! Spellbound had a *terrific performance*… although it was without a drummer… due to Drew arriving a little late. However, they performed like pros, and filled the void! When it came time for Masquerade to perform, they too, were very good. Everything seemed to go right. When it came time to announce the awards, Spellbound swept, taking *1st Place*, *Best Showmanship* and *Best Musicianship* in the Advanced Women's Division, while Masquerade earned *1st Place*, in the Advanced Mixed Division, but the plaques went to Carlsbad and Hart, who were competing in the Intermediate Division. Spellbound felt redeemed, after their poor showing at Arcadia, but Masquerade felt… *a little confused*?

Our next competition was Rob Hodo's *Chaparral Showcase*. This was the first year he was able to accommodate all of our choirs. He did this by forming *one Advanced Division* for three of our mixed and men's groups, as well as Carlsbad's mixed group. Spellbound, meanwhile, competed in the open women's division. So, we were able to bring everyone to this event! On the day of the festival, it was actually a lot of fun. All of our groups performed brilliantly! When the awards were announced, Spellbound won the Open Women's Division, while in the Advanced Division, Thunder Cats placed *4th*, Tiffany's and

Company placed *3rd*, Carlsbad placed *2nd* and Masquerade placed *1st*! Unfortunately, like always, I observed a director or two complaining very passionately to Rob about the results. I know it's tough to not win when you are so competitive, but I learned a long time ago, that *win or lose, at any competition*, it's much healthier to let *the results speak for themselves*, and move on.

Our final competition of the year was *So Cal*, hosted by Chula Vista High School. This year, it was held in a different convention hall, than usual, in San Diego. Once again, because Tiffany's and Company and Thunder Cats had not competed as much as normal, *we took everybody*! It was a very long day, and unfortunately, there was no food sold in the hall or nearby, so most of us spent a lot of the day hungry. There were two large rooms, which all of the groups could have used as *changing rooms*, but unfortunately for the rest of us, according to Tony Atienza, they had already been reserved for Burroughs and Los Alamitos, because they had asked first. So, our kids, along with many of the others who were competing, changed clothes in the bathrooms. Our group performances all seemed to go well, until we were about an hour out, before Masquerade performed. Tony Atienza sought me out and apologetically told me that the riser change we had asked for… *and he had approved… could not be done* today, after all, because the union stage hands had just told him *they were not allowed to move any of the risers at all*! Wow! We had performed with this riser set-up all year! This formation created an *open middle*, where we pushed the *wheeled ladder* through, students held *hedge flats* in formation, we set our *a cappella formation* in and an endless array of other choreography took place in… but today, it *would not be set-up*? It would have been very easy to get mad about this and refuse to perform… but Doug and I opted to go forward as planned. There was certainly no time, at this point, to re-choreograph, so we pulled the kids together, explained the situation… and encouraged them to give it their all, regardless! They were truly bummed, but what could we do? On stage, they gave an energized and musical show, which from my perspective, was very enjoyable to watch. But, Doug's well-thought-out and rehearsed staging and choreography had to be spontaneously adapted to account for *the risers being set-up right in the middle of the stage, where our group had formerly danced*! At the end of their performance, Masquerade departed the stage knowing that they had done the best they could, under the circumstances. When the awards were announced, Thunder Cats earned *2nd Place* in the Men's Division, Spellbound earned *3rd Place* in the Advanced Women's Division while Masquerade earned *6th Place* and Tiffany's & Company earned *7th Place* in the Advanced Mixed Division. This was the final competition of my career, and I had to smile. At the end of the day, the final rankings *were not the most important thing* that happened... as they *never had been*. No, it was the way that each of our groups battled, showing heart and integrity, *no matter what obstacles were thrown at them*! I was proud of all of my groups today, but especially Masquerade, for *performing their hearts out*, knowing that it was probably for a lost cause! If I were a Texan, I'd say, "Remember the Alamo!" Yes… *their courage left me in awe*!

Once again, many of us traveled to New York City on a five-day, four-night trip in late May. We stayed at the beautiful Hyatt Times Square, and spent much of our time sightseeing throughout that great city. Our 35 students, who made up the Honor Choir, once again, competed at the Riverside Church, near Harlem, at a Heritage Festival, as a traditional a cappella chamber choir. However, since we only had *8 boys* going on this trip, with 27 girls, we decided to have all of the boys sing bass while our altos sang tenor and our second sopranos sang alto. It actually worked out perfectly that our final group had 8 or 9 singers in each of our four vocal sections, for a very balanced ensemble, and a *very balanced* sound! Honor Choir ended up earning a *1st Place* trophy and a *Silver Medal*, just missing a Gold by a point! We also saw four wonderful Broadway shows, on this trip, including *An American In Paris*, *Les Miserables*, *Something Rotten* and *School of Rock*! We got *extra-special orchestra seats* for *"School of Rock,"* because a good "Disney" friend of Kurt's was in the show, and helped us to acquire them! Visiting New York, once again with my students, was a perfect way to end my teaching career. Like my students, I simply *love New York City*, especially

Broadway and all of the wonderful shows to see! For lack of a better description, to me, Broadway is a kind of *show choir Disneyland, which I never grow tired of visiting*!

Our musical this year was one of my all-time favorites… *Crazy For You*! We double-cast most of the lead roles, and were very successful with both groups! This was a *repeat* show, first performed at Brea in 2008. That production was classic, so obviously Doug and I were pretty excited about doing it again! Nothing really changed between the older and the newer productions, *except for the casts*. I don't know of a single person who didn't *love* this show! Initially, after losing so many talented students, last year, to graduation, Doug, Kurt and I were not sure that we would have the *particular talent* needed to put this on? But, we of course, we did! In fact, we were overjoyed to find that we had *two bonified leading men*, Hayden Mangum and Wesley Mathews, to play Bobby! We also had a number of very qualified girls that we considered for Polly, but we ultimately decided on Rhyan Belanger and Brianna Clark, who both auditioned as if they were up for a role on Broadway! That kind of determination never fails! Need I say it? This show was a *great success*, both critically and at the box office. This was the *perfect musical* to end my teaching career with, especially considering that it was my *all-time favorite show*! The entire cast is listed on the following page.

2016 Cast List for *"CRAZY FOR YOU"*

Bobby Child: *Hayden Mangum/ Wesley Mathews*
Pete: *Wesley Mathews/ Hayden Mangum*
Bela Zangler: *Andrew Strom/Jacob Morton*
Eugene Fodor/ Jimmy: *Jacob Morton/ Andrew Strom*
Lank Hawkins: *Travis Miller*
Everett Baker: *Aidan Pipes*
Polly Baker: *Rhyan Belanger/ Brianna Clark*
Flo: *Brianna Clark/ Rhyan Belanger*
Irene Roth: *Kristin Camacho/ Amber O'Barr*
Greta: *Amber O'Barr/ Kristin Camacho*
Mother: *Becky Nevarez/ Pauline Rejniak*
Cowgirl: *Pauline Rejniak/ Becky Nevarez*
Perkins/ Chauffer/ Lola: *Jaymi Wilson*
Patricia Fodor: *Erica Cline/ Jocelyn Abrahamson*
Maxine: *Jocelyn Abrahamson/ Erica Cline*
Moose: *Ben Harpster*
Mingo: *Justen Baker*
Sam: *Nate Nolen*
Custus: *Blake Farfan*
Harry (bartender): *Edward Kwon*

Tess: *Cori Bourgeois*
Dee Dee: *Lindsey Morrill*
Trixie: *Jessica Patow*
Susie: *Allie Mayer*
Patsy: *Audrey Lee*
Fran: *Lacey Currey*
Mitzy: *Jenna Norseth*

FOLLIES GIRLS

Elaine: *Lauren Patrick*
Louise: *Hannah Fritz*
Evelyn: *Jade McClinton*
Eve: *Esther Min*
Jilly: *Jaylene Hernandez*
Ginger: *Ashton Ogden*
Marilyn: *Shalis Danayan*
Betsy: *Maya Gutowski*
Vera: *Claire Manson*
Lilly: *Emilie Daedler*
Margie: *Ayla Golshan*
Rita: *Amaris Salas*
Dottie: *Erica O'Barr*
Loretta: *Jessica Martinez*
Lola: *Jaymi Wilson*

COWBOY AND COWGIRL CHORUS

Tristan Brannen • Patrick Kim • Ana Contreras
Amaya Llanes • Madyson Miguel • Kara Dietz
Ashley Munson • Elyse Wilson • Valerie Tetreault
Sarah Turner • Berenice Rosales • Brandon Nyuyen
Leia Sanchez • Jacob Godges • Kayla Dewberry
Elizabeth Sanchez • Megan Coday • Reghan Hall
Paige Legendre • Kaitlyn Serna • Jaylene Gonzales
Naomi Santiago • Garret Murphy • Rachel Ramil
Elizabeth Garcia

One of the most *unique* and *exciting* projects that my choirs have ever had the privilege of participating in was recording the choral backgrounds for the *ending titles* in the film, *Krampus!* The whole thing began innocently enough, in October of 2015, when *Douglas Pipes*, the uncle of two of my former students, Aidan and Hannah Pipes, asked, me if I would be interested in having a few select kids sing his arrangements for the ending titles, of the upcoming film, *Krampus*? Apparently, the choir that he had been using was not available and *Krampus* was due to be released to the theatres in only *one short month*! In other words, this project had to be completed right away! I learned then that Douglas Pipes was a professional composer/ arranger, who had already worked on an impressive list of films, including composing the scores for the films *Trick 'r Treat* and *Monster House*. He offered to pay us, as well, which was a bonus, but I would have agreed to do it for free! He wanted eight or nine girls in total to sing soprano and alto, and three or four boys to sing the baritone. We had a lot of good singers in our groups, but I finally chose the following students, based on their individual musicality and ability to blend! The list included, *Jocelyn Abrahamson, Kristin Camacho, Audrey Lee and Allie Mayer* on alto. On soprano we had *Brianna Clark, Rhyan Belanger, Cori Bourgeois, Hannah Fritz and Lindsey Morrill*. Finally, our baritones included, *Ben Harpster, Wesley Mathews, Aidan Pipes and Andrew Strom*. Douglas Pipes soon delivered the sheet music for the choir to learn and the recorded music for us to rehearse with. If memory serves, we had two or three very intense rehearsals, over a couple of days, until I felt confident that the kids could sing through the material flawlessly. I don't think the total time between when we were first invited to sing and the recording date spanned more than four days in total! Quickly, the recording date arrived, and everyone showed up after school at the Curtis Theatre, in downtown Brea, the site Mr. Pipes had selected for the recording session. Doug Kuhl and I arrived, just to watch the whole process, when Mr. Pipes informed me that *I was the one who would be directing the kids on this recording*! Huh? I had believed, over the past few days, that I was only *preparing the kids to* be *directed by him on the recording*? But, I quickly changed gears, and we had a very *exciting albeit grueling* recording session! I think we were there together, about two and a half hours. At the end, I was exhausted, as I know the kids were also, but we all felt that our ending product was great! According to Douglas Pipes, the composer, this is what *actually happened* to put the Brea singers into position to record for the film, *Krampus*:

"In the summer of 2015, I was composing the score to the horror/comedy film Krampus. In early September, the score was recorded in New Zealand with The New Zealand Symphony Orchestra, with an additional session featuring The Tudor Consort Choristers of Wellington Cathedral. We had a very limited window of time to schedule the sessions with the NZSO and had already recorded the score and were back in Los Angeles in the final weeks of post-production when the call came to create a song for the end credits. The idea for the song was to create a cautionary tale warning children about the perils of losing the spirit of Christmas and how doing so would unleash the wrath of Krampus, a folkloric creature that punishes children who misbehave! I wrote the song, but by this time the Tudor Consort Choristers were no longer available schedule-wise. I was in a crunch. I immediately thought of the Brea Olinda High School Choir, having seen my niece and nephew perform in their outstanding show choir productions. I had attended several of their concerts and knew that they were a very talented group of singers, and I always noted how the choir director, Dave Willert, brought out fantastic performances from his singers! Time was tight and I wanted to get them on board. I reached out to my

brother and sister-in-law, Erick and Mary Pipes, to immediately coordinate with Dave, the school, and even a stage where we could quickly coordinate and record the session. I contacted the studio and all involved on my end and very quickly, we got the session scheduled! The enthusiasm and energy Dave and the singers brought to the session was incredible! Dave had such a wonderful bond with his singers and he absolutely brought out the perfect performance for the song. He helped capture the perfect blend of musical performance while conveying the intensity of the lyrics. We got it recorded and mixed into the movie as the final warning to all who just watched to keep the Christmas spirit alive, or else you might get a visit from Krampus! I was so excited for how this turned out, and hearing the Brea Olinda High School Choir perform this cautionary tale, sends chills up my spine every time I hear it!"

About a month later, when *Krampus* hit the theatres, it was such a kick to hear our kids sing during the credits and to watch *The Brea Olinda High School Singers directed by Dave Willert*, scroll down the screen, crediting us with singing the ending titles! During my forty years in education, I had never directed a choir to sing for a film, prior to this. It was so much fun! For most of us, this was our first experience "performing" on the silver screen! But for a few of the kids… I'll bet it won't be their last! One of our singers on the project, *Cori Bourgeois*, had this to say, "*It was such an amazing experience to be a part of! I couldn't believe that as a high schooler, I was getting to sing in an actual movie! Watching the movie and staying until the end credits to see Brea Olinda High School Singers and hearing our voices during the credits was surreal and I'm so thankful I had the opportunity to be a part of it!*"

My final Masquerade and Spellbound groups, who worked *tirelessly* during the 2016 competition year, should definitely be recognized, for the outstanding shows they consistently put on! I guess you could say they were even a little *extra special* to me... for being my *final advanced show choirs*, after all of these years. Some of the songs that both groups sang, as part of their 2016 competition shows, were sung by my choirs for the very *first time in my career*! I suppose, I might have had a small "inkling" over the summer, that this might be my final year. So, this was my last chance to hear my choirs sing, *Stairway To Heaven*, and all of those Elvis Presley tunes, that I always wanted my groups to perform! Here are those terrific kids who made up my final two advanced show choirs:

The Final Two Advanced High School Show Choirs Of My Career!

Masquerade 2015-16

Brianna Clark • Cori Bourgeois • Hannah Fritz
Claire Manson • Madison McWhirter • Carrie Bower
Kasey Jacques • Jessica Patow • Lauren Patrick
Jocelyn Abrahamson • Audrey Lee • Leia Sanchez
Emilie Daedler • Jaymi Wilson • Shalis Danayan
Ben Harpster • Aaron Menezes • Nate Nolen
Lukas Drake • Andrew Strom • Travis Miller
Blake Farfan • Rhyan Belanger • Amber O'Barr
Lindsey Morrill • Ashton Ogden • Erica O'Barr
Allie Mayer • Maya Gutowski • Lauren Pease
Alyssa Hendrickson • Micah Munet • Carren Penuliar
Janae Escarez • Kristin Camacho • Catalina Perez
Esther Min • Wesley Mathews • Justen Baker
Jeremy Alcaraz • Erick Flores • Aidan Pipes
Jacob Morton • Edward Kwon

Spellbound 2015-16

Brianna Clark • Jenna Norseth • Lacey Currey
Erica Cline • Amy Ramirez • Paris Valdivia
Kate Root • Madison McWhirter • Kara Dietz
Jessica Patow • Kaitlyn Rigsby • Valerie Tetreault
Jocelyn Jordan • Trinity Key • Lauren Patrick
Becky Nevarez • Iliana Rodriguez • Kristin Camacho
Alex Weiss • Sabrina Liu • Dunya Golshan
Jessica Martinez • Carmen Martinez • Lyndsey Gutierrez
Rhyan Belanger • Lindsey Morrill • Elizabeth Garcia
Amber O'Barr • Ashton Ogden • Kassie McCanless
Kaitlyn Serna • Sierra West • Ayla Golshan
Maya Gutowski • Charlotte Kim • Pauline Rejniak
Arli Bianco • Naomi Santiago • Esmeralda Torres
Jaylene Hernandez • Jocelyn Abrahamson • Rachel Ramil
Jaymi Wilson • Mia Dalgleish • Leia Sanchez
Shanelle Gorospe • Luna Robinson • Jade McClinton
Elyse Wilson

The roles of the student officers in our program, changed a lot during my final few years. I believed that we had too many officers, at one point, who *didn't know exactly what their jobs were*? So, in my final two years, I made multiple presidents in each group, *all with different duties*. After the kids got over their initial shock of the change, that system worked pretty well. In some cases, I gave them a *daily job*, like taking roll, to keep them even more involved! I just like to constantly evolve for the better, and the officers each year have proven to be very adaptable! Our incredible student officers for the **2015-16** school year, included:

Masquerade
Pres/ Treas: *Andrew Strom*
Pres/ Lib: *Rhyan Belanger*
Pres/ Oper: *Cori Bourgeois*
Pres/ Oper: *Joc Abrahamson*
Pres/ Sec: *Audrey Lee*
Dance Capt: *Brianna Clark & Ben Harpster*
Soprano 1 Section Leader: *Brianna Clark*
Soprano 2 Section Leader: *Allie Mayer*
Alto Section Leader: *Jocelyn Abrahamson*
Tenor Section Leader: *Wesley Mathews*
Bass Section Leader: *Travis Miller*

Chamber Singers
President: *Carrie Bower*
Vice-Pres/Lib: *Andrew Strom*
Sec/Treas: *Audrey Lee*
Soprano 1 Section Leader: *Erica Cline*
Soprano 2 Section Leader: *Carrie Bower*
Alto Section Leader: *Valerie Tetreault*
Tenor Section Leader: *Ben Harpster*
Bass Section Leader: *Jacob Morton*

Thunder Cats
President: *Andrew Strom, Ben Harpster, Jacob Morton & Erick Flores*

Spellbound
Pres/ Treas: *Amber O'Barr*
Pres/ *Lib*: *Lindsey Morrill*
Pres/ Oper: *Brianna Clark*
Pres/ Oper: *Jessica Patow*
Pres/ Sec: *Ayla Golshan*
Dance Captain: *Maya Gutowski & Brianna Clark*
Soprano 1 Section Leader: *Rhyan Belanger*
Soprano 2 Section Leader: *Jessica Patow*
Alto Section Leader: *Kristin Camacho*

Tiffany's & Company
Pres/ Treas: *Allie Mayer*
Pres/ Lib: *Becky Nevarez*
Pres/ Op: *Hayden Mangum*
Pres/ Secretary: *Cassie McCanless*
Dance Captain: *Maya Gutowski & Lindsey Gutierrez*
Soprano 1 Section Leader: *Cori Bourgeois*
Soprano 2 Section Leader: *Esmeralda Torres*
Alto Section Leader: *Jessica Martinez*
Baritone Section Leader: *Hayden Mangum*

Finally, It was very difficult for me to say, goodbye, to my wonderful Brea Olinda High School choir students for the last time, at our annual Awards Banquet at the Brea Embassy Suites, in June of 2016. The kids sang a special song for me, we all hugged, and I received some very thoughtful gifts. Like Nogales, the kids at Brea had to learn to become winners through hard work, dedication and determination. I cannot say enough about the incredible rehearsals and performances we all shared over eleven terrific years that reflected those very qualities! The fact that Brea show choirs have continued to shine in competition, *after I retired*, makes me feel so very proud! I know that the hard work, dedication and determination these kids have *learned, and also demonstrated* in performance after performance… *will follow them throughout their lives*! Many of these performers, like some of the kids from both Nogales and Diamond Bar high schools, ended up as featured performers at Disneyland, or at local theatres or on cruise ships! A real testament to both their talent and their desire! I was fortunate enough to work with this abundance of talent at Brea Olinda High School, for eleven wonderful years, and as their retired director… I will always be very thankful for *all of those unforgettable experiences* we achieved together!

CHAPTER 14

Brea Junior High... 2005-2016... Show Choir Anyone?

There were really only two things I did not want to do in education, number one, be an *administrator*, and number two, *teach at a junior high*! When I took the job at Brea Olinda High School, I also accepted the job at Brea Junior High, as part of the *total package*! I accepted this, fully understanding that I would have to create two sets of trips, two sets of bus requests, two newsletters, two rehearsal schedules, two performance schedules, two sets of fieldtrips, two fundraising campaigns and two sets of music and choreography! I tried to merge the two programs together, especially in the years after my stroke, in 2013-2016, by putting our home concerts together. This, ultimately made things a lot easier! Having Doug come in twice a week, as he did for the high school choir, also made the job more manageable, as I now had two days a week to complete the *mountains of paper work*, I seemed to always have.

In reality, my dread at the thought of teaching junior high choir, did not really apply to Brea Junior. When we arrived in the fall of 2005, the kids welcomed Doug and I with smiles, a passion for show choir and a good hard work ethic. This was in direct contrast to Brea Olinda High School, where many of the leaders and some of the veterans seemed to meet us with a *guarded contempt* and not much excitement about the changes Doug and I brought to their program. The junior high was a welcomed change from the animosity and lack of passion we were met with at the high school. I actually looked forward to going over there at the end of every day, to work with such likeable students! Certainly that positive attitude, going along with their good base of talent, had a lot to do with their quick success.

Through eleven exciting years, Doug and I taught most of our *eventual high school students* at Brea Junior High, first. Every year was successful in competition, although, some more than others. Our biggest adversary for most of those years was **Travis Ranch Middle School!** However, by the end of my tenure, I think that **Burbank Middle School** may have taken over that role… or perhaps it was both of them? On another topic, I had to learn, and it was a very hard lesson, that many of the strongest leaders, dancers and athletes in choir at the junior high, *did not necessarily continue on* with choir at the high school, but branched off instead into ASB, athletics, drama, dance or no activity at all. I found the boys in junior high choir to be especially prone to this. But, I also learned not to take it too personally, as I know that high school is a great time to try-out different activities. From that respect, I know that all of the junior high school choir members who *chose to stay in choir all the way through their senior years of high school… were very valuable to us*! Without a doubt, I believe that *they* had a lot to do with our successes at both schools!

The competition sets, listed in this chapter, from 2005 through 2016, represent *every song* performed by Show Choir Express or Dream Street Singers in competition, while I was the director. Through looking at all of the trophies earned by Show Choir Express, that were sitting in the choir room, I was able to piece together *most* of the competitions we competed in. But, then finding a stash of competition scores from my past eleven years at BJH, hidden in a drawer… *thoroughly completed the information I needed.* So, sit back and join me, as we briefly re-experience 2005-2016 with *Show Choir Express* and special guest star, the *Dream Street Singers*!

In the fall of 2005, when I first walked into the band room (where we rehearsed), at Brea Junior High to greet my new students, I asked my lone choir class, if they wanted to be a show choir? "What's a show choir," they asked? I told them, and they excitedly replied, "Yes!" The name, *Show Choir Express*, was meant to be a temporary placeholder, until we came up with a better name. But, since we competed in our first festival using that name, and did pretty well... it *kinda* stuck! Doug and I devised the following show, to introduce them to show choir:

Show Choir Express 2005-06

Costume Colors: *Red*

Competition Set

Celebrate America
How Merrily We Live
Hernando's Hideaway
Over The Rainbow
We Go Together

The choir kids at Brea Junior High, unlike a lot of the choir kids at Brea Olinda High School, in 2005, were fun and welcoming. They took to our exercise of *pizzazz*, right away. They diligently practiced all of their singing and dancing, every day, as if the world depended on it. When we finally began competing, at the *Tournament of Champions* competition (TOC), in February of 2006, I was just *hoping to place*! I told the kids in warm-up, that they should pay close attention to all of the other, *more experienced groups*, and try not to be too concerned about where they placed. After all, this was their *very first show choir competition*. Good advice, huh? When the awards were announced, Show Choir Express had won *1st Place*, along with *Best Showmanship* and *Best Musicianship*! They had even beat Travis Ranch, the perennial winner, *until today*, of all middle school show choir competitions! In fact, they beat Travis Ranch by over 20 points! I was so shocked I didn't know what to say for several seconds! *These kids had no experience at all in show choir*... but never underestimate what a great attitude mixed with a good base of talent can do. This group also competed at Los Alamitos High School's *Xtravaganza*, a little later in the year, where they won *1st Place* along with *Best Showmanship* and *Best Musicianship*, for the second time in a row! So, Show Choir Express was born, and their birth was something to behold!

These kids also participated in the high school's production of *Cinderella*, with *almost every member of Show Choir Express, participating*! To top things off, we started *Middle School Madness,* an annual show choir competition for middle schools, and it was hosted, very professionally, by Show Choir Express. Here are the student officers, for that historical first year:

Show Choir Express Officers 2005-06
President: *Hailey Markman*
Vice-President: *Kevin Siazon & Alex Olvey*
& Valerie Schrepferman
Dance Captain: *Brittney Slater-Shew & Tana Schwarz*
Secretary/ Treasurer: *Justin Lovell*
Historian: *Heather Freshour*

The Original, Award Winning Show Choir Express 2005-06
Julia Dwyer • Kayla Camacho • Sadie Reeves
Valerie Schrepferman • Kevin Siazon •Trisha Bermudez
Lydia Prochman • Justin Lovell • Allison Iles • Ruth Ramire
Sarah Morgigno • Jessica Raine • Kaylie Simec • Alex Olvey
Melissa Strom • Shelby Johnson • Gabi Hirsch • Trish Crow
Markie Stella • Hailey Markman • Holly Ramsey
Laura Bradburn • Kate Hocking • Brittany Slater-Shew
Heather Freshour • Jill Purdom • Tana Schwartz
Hailey Holman • Erin Purdom • Holly Ramsey
Alexa Vandermeer • Crystal Perez • Ruth Ramirez
Angelica Rodriguez

The original group is listed above. I apologize if I missed anyone. *We had no list…* but pieced the names together using several very good memories, and a picture!

The 2006-07 year started off, much like our first year, with everyone very excited and looking forward to everything we did in class. Although we had lost a terrific bunch of eighth graders, from last year, to the high school, our new group of seventh graders, looked to be pretty talented, while our new eighth graders seemed ready to work, from the start! We selected the following competition set for them:

Show Choir Express 2006-07

Costume Colors: *Red*

Competition Set

Ease On Down The Road
Steam Heat
A Dream Is A Wish Your Heart Makes
Witch Doctor
Show Me The Way
Johnny B Goode/ Shout

This set included handheld shields for the song, "*Witch Doctor*" to make the show just a little more special. Their first competition of the year was *Tournament of Champions*, better known as TOC, where we had experienced our surprise win, in our very first competition, last year. Show Choir Express performed very well, but this time, they earned *2nd Place, behind* Travis Ranch! Well, *you win some and you lose some*! But, our kids were more frustrated than disappointed. They wanted to win this year, and they were determined! Our second competition was at Los Alamitos High School's *Xtravaganza*! Once again, we were competing against our *archrival*, Travis Ranch. It was very close, but when the awards were announced, Travis Ranch beat us in Music by one point, we beat them in Showmanship by three points, so ultimately *we won the competition by two points*! Our third competition was called *ENCORE*, after the name of the host show choir, from Travis Ranch Middle School, and was held at Valencia High School, in Placentia. The kids, and their feisty president, Julia Dwyer, were more than ready for this one. When the awards were announced, Show Choir Express had won *1st Place*, and both plaques for *Best Showmanship* and *Best Musicianship*! This was a great way to cap off a terrific year! Show Choir Express had now firmly established themselves as one of the top junior high school show choirs in the circuit! Once again, the officers had a lot to do with the group's success!

Show Choir Express Officers 2006-07
President: *Julia Dwyer*
Vice-President: *Kaylie Simec*
Vice-President: *Lydia Prochman*
Secretary/ Treasurer: *Melissa Strom*
Historian: *Alexa Vander Meer/ Sadie Reeves*
Dance Captain: *Savannah Maske/ Ally Catanesi*

The following year, in 2007-08, the group was so large we had to split it into two sections. We called both of these sections, Show Choir Express, because they performed together as one group… but we separated each class, by grade level. This year, I experienced a few problems in the eighth grade class, involving soloists, I selected, that a few other kids disagreed with. But after I told them that they were free to disagree, but I would not be changing anything… most of the trouble stopped. The competition set was fun and highly energetic… just like our group!

Show Choir Express 2007-08

Costume Colors: *Magenta*

Competition Set

I've Got The Music In Me
Singin' In The Rain
Pure Imagination
Roll With It
God Help The Outcasts
Great Balls Of Fire

Our competition year began at Los Alamitos High School's *Xtravaganza*. Our group was by far the *largest group competing in our division*, but due to a lack of rehearsing the seventh and eighth grade groups together, Doug and I were a little concerned with what they would look like together, on stage! My fears were alleviated just as soon as we performed! Show Choir Express was great! I honestly looked forward to the awards ceremony. When the awards were announced, we had earned *2nd Place* and the plaque for *Best Showmanship…* while Travis Ranch had won first place! I have to admit, *I was actually surprised.* I had really thought Show Choir Express would win this one! Our kids seemed a little disappointed as they left the theatre, but that quickly dissipated as they took pictures with their trophies and headed toward the bus. I always read the judges scores and comments just as soon as I received them, following each competition, and this time was no exception. However, when I read them, I could not believe my eyes? According to the recap sheet… *we had actually won*! I quickly sought out the host director to see if these scores were correct. After only a few seconds, they apologized to me for the error and promised to send us a new *1st Place* trophy in the mail. I hurried to the bus and told the kids that they had actually won! Some of them immediately wanted to *find Travis Ranch to exchange trophies with them*! But, I explained that our first place trophy would be coming in the mail, and there was no sense in spoiling Travis Ranch's day. We had actually won, but everyone on the bus felt a little depressed, since they had missed *that magical moment when your group is announced first place*, in front of the entire audience! I only hoped that they would get that same chance again, at their next competition! Their next and final competition of the year was the Travis Ranch *Encore* event at Valencia High School! We were so ready for this one. We had rehearsed very hard every day, in preparation. Our warm-up went great, I went out to the house, took my seat in the first row, and waited impatiently for the curtain to open. But, when it did, I was aghast! Our group was so large they had obviously had a difficult time fitting on that tiny stage. The riser rows were over to the left side, by a good six feet, causing the front view of the show to be visibly *off center*! We had worked so hard, that the mere *possibility* of this faulty setting costing us the win *was very upsetting to me*! I couldn't even focus on the performance. I didn't stay in the theatre for the awards, choosing instead, to wait outside. When people began to file out of the theatre, I knew the awards had been announced. Finally our kids came out. But I couldn't tell if they were happy or not? So I asked one of our kids how they did. She turned to me and screamed, "We swept!" And so they had. According to the score sheets, they had won *Best Showmanship* and *Best Musicianship* by sizeable margins, easily taking *1st Place!* And not a single adjudicator had even commented on their faulty setting! So, there you go. Another perfect end to the competition year! I've listed our hard working officers, below:

Show Choir Express Officers 2007-8

Seventh Grade Officers
President: *Alexa Fishman*
Vice-Pres: *Challoi McCuller*
Secretary: *Samantha Blair*
Historian: *Devanie Zenzola & Melanie Chieng*
Soprano Section Leader: *Megan Strom*
Alto Section Leader: *Rachel Gallegos*

Eighth Grade Officers
President: *Gabriel Navarro & Emily Malotte*
Vice-Pres: *Emily Davis*
Sec: *Maddy Ellingson*
Hist: *Sophia Valero*
Soprano Section Leader: *Rebecca Harpster & Rachel Weeks*
Alto Section Leader: *Emily Malotte & Emily Elias*

For the 2008-2009, school year, Doug and I decided to split Show Choir Express into two different show choirs, instead of both classes being part of the same group. In theory, this would alleviate the need for any *after-school practices*, to rehearse the two sections of Show Choir Express together. In truth, these joint rehearsals had created quite a problem last year, especially with attendance! Although breaking our kids into two different choirs may have sounded like a good decision at the time… in actuality, *it significantly weakened* both Show Choir Express and our new group, by reducing each one's size to 30 members! Last year's Show Choir Express had competed very successfully, with sixty kids! Another important fact was that a large number of the kids from last year's group, had been eighth graders, and we had *very few returning members*, even without the split. Well, live and learn. In those days, we didn't hold an audition, so anyone who wanted to join, could simply sign-up for choir at BJH. We named the new group, *The Dream Street Singers*, after a very successful girls' group that Doug and I had directed at Nogales High School, many years before. I've listed both Show Choir Express and Dream Street's competition sets below:

Show Choir Express 2008-9
Costume Colors:
Blue & Green
Competition Set
Celebrate America
Rockin' Pneumonia
Varsity Drag
Show Me The Way
Shout

Dream St. Singers 2008-09
Costume Colors:
Blue & Green
Competition Set
Dream Street Theme
Three Little Fishes
Puttin' On The Ritz
Always On My Mind
Proud Mary
Gimme Some Lovin'

Our first competition, took us to Temecula, where Rob Hodo hosted an event, with Margarita Middle School, called *The Mustang Showcase*. We, of course, took both groups. We knew that Dream Street performed like a younger group, so we entered them in the intermediate category. But, even though Show Choir Express was a lot smaller than last year, Doug and I both wanted to see them compete in the advanced division. My strongest memory of this competition is that Dream Street had no major problems during their warm-up or performance, but that during Show Choir Express' warm-up, whether it was nerves or a lack of confidence, *they simply could not sing their a cappella, I Will, in tune, if their lives had depended on it*! So, we had to cut the song, and hope for the best. Their performance showed a lot of effort, but without the larger size, we usually had, the vocals sounded a bit weak. When the awards were announced, Dream Street had earned *3rd Place* in the Intermediate Division while Show Choir Express also earned *3rd Place* and the plaque for *Best Showmanship* in the Advanced Division. Both of those thirds represented *last place* in each of their respective divisions! Dream Street was celebrating on the bus, as most of them had never competed before. Show Choir Express, in marked contrast, was very quiet. That third place trophy represented the *lowest award Show Choir Express had won in four years*! As I explained earlier, this situation was really my fault for splitting the group in two… but it didn't matter, the entire group would have to work together to figure out a way to do better in their next competition! By the way, our next competition was the Los Alamitos *Xtravaganza*. In preparation for this one, Doug had borrowed some colorful flats from the high school, to set-up behind Show Choir Express to add more pizzazz to their show. He also added some steam (fire extinguishers) to be blown at the end. Dream Street's show was also improved, as far as their dancing and singing, *but not theatrically*. When we arrived at the Los Alamitos competition, we immediately looked over the groups in our division. Including both of our groups, there were six. This was one of the toughest line-ups we'd competed against here. The groups competing with us included Travis Ranch, Tuffree, and two strong groups from the Los Alamitos school district. There were only four trophies in this one, so for both Dream Street and Show Choir Express to place, we would have to sing and perform the best we had done all year! The competition began, and Dream Street hit the stage. They were good. They received a lot of applause for their efforts, too! When Show Choir Express was in warm-up, they were excited and could not wait to show off their new show! This was a complete turnaround from their jitters at Temecula. In any case, their show was a hit! Everyone in the audience loved the steam, the signs in back and the group's energy. We even *sang* better than last time! When the awards were announced, Dream Street earned *4th Place* in this advanced division, while Show Choir Express earned *2nd Place,* only three points ahead of Tuffree, *but over twenty points behind Travis Ranch, the winner*. We didn't win, this time… but it sure felt like we did! Oh, I almost forgot. Both groups ended their competition season by competing in the *Five, Six, Seven, Eight* show choir competition at Disney's California Adventure, on the Monster's Inc. Stage. To make a long story short, neither group placed very well at this event, but Dream Street actually *placed higher* than did Show Choir Express! Still, they each earned a *beautiful glass plate* with their ranking engraved on it. On the Monday, following this event, some members of Dream Street *teased Show Choir Express* about beating them. The next thing I knew, someone had *accidentally broken* Dream Street's plate! The next day, as soon as Dream Street caught wind of this, someone *accidentally broke* Show Choir Express' plate! To be honest, both groups scored so low, I doubt that either group really cared about the destruction of their plates. I think they rather enjoyed the whole episode! Anyway, until this happened, I had no idea that our two groups felt any kind of playful rivalry with one another. But, now I knew. Listed below are the hardworking officers from both award-winning groups:

Show Choir Express Officers 2008-09
President: *Megan Strom*
Vice-President: *Rob Catanesi*
Secretary/Treasurer: *Alexa Fishman*
Secretary/Treasurer: *Hannah Pipes*
Historian/Librarian: *Marysa Leite*

Dream Street Singers Officers 2008-09
President: *Harli Paxton*
Vice-President: *Taylor Sweitzer*
Secretary/Treasurer: *Charity Comer*
Secretary/Treasurer: *Aleah Tuunufi*
Historian/Librarian: *Ashley Alger*

For the 2009-2010 school year, Doug and I decided to continue competing with two different groups. This year, however, due to the *larger number of boys* who auditioned for choir, we decided to make both *Show Choir Express* (advanced) and *Dream Street Singers* (intermediate), *mixed groups*! We had originally wanted our second group to be a *traditional concert choir*, but the kids in the group successfully convinced us to keep them a show choir. Their competition sets were as follows:

Show Choir Express 2009-10
Costume Colors: *Royal Blue*
Competition Set
The Psychedelic Sixties
By The Sea
Reflections

Dream St. Singers 2009-10
Costume Colors: *Unknown*
Competition Set
Joseph and the Dreamcoat
Count Your Blessings
We Go Together

Great Balls of Fire

We began our competition season, as we usually did, in Temecula, at the *Mustang Showcase*. I don't have any competition results for Dream Street Singers, except at *Five, Six, Seven, Eight* so I will not be mentioning them for a while. Show Choir Express had a very entertaining show that really pleased the judges. When the awards were announced, they had *Placed 1st* with the plaque for *Best Showmanship*! Quite an improvement over their last place finish, at this same competition, only one year before! Next, they participated in the Los Alamitos *Xtravaganza*. They had placed second here last year, but the group was really hoping to improve that placing this year. As soon as they hit the stage it was obvious, that this was going to be a great performance! When the awards were read, Show Choir Express had *swept*! They had earned *First Place*, *Best Showmanship* and *Best Musicianship.* I have a picture of the president, *Hannah Pipes* and other students celebrating this win at Los Alamitos. It still makes me smile, as soon as I remember just how hard they all worked for this! Our third competition of the year was the Travis Ranch *Encore* event. Although we put on a great show, I believe that Burbank beat us, while we came in a very close *2nd Place*, along with the plaque for *Best Showmanship*. We reached the end of the year, and many, *but not all* of the kids in Show Choir Express and Dream Street, decided to once again participate in the *Five Six, Seven, Eight* competition at Disney's California Adventure. The only problem was that certain solos and key spots in the choreography, *vacated by those students who were not going*, had to be covered by new people, without much practice. But as a teacher, I knew that this experience would be good for them. So, we filled those open spots with other talented kids! Both of our performances were good, albeit, a little shaky at times, probably due to all of the changes in spots and solos. When the awards were announced, Dream Street earned *7th Place* while Show Choir Express took home *4th Place*. Not our best achievements of the year, but I thought the new soloists and dancers in both groups did a terrific job! Our officers for these groups were:

Show Choir Express Officers 2009-10

President: *Hannah Pipes*
Vice-President: *Uche Ewenike, Paige Garcia & Nikki Cuerdo*
Secretary: *Marissa Luedke & Becka Heagle*
Treasurer: *Samara Eghterafi*
Historian: *Alexa Walters & Samantha Mauriss*
Librarian: *Rob Catanesi*

Dream Street Singers Officers 2009-10

President: *Sandra Salazar*
Vice-President: *Brittany Lervold and Leilani Gonzales*
Secretary: *Daniella Serna*
Treasurer: *Mark Bautista*
Historian: *Kayla Deleon*
Librarian: *Chase Parker*

At the beginning of the 2010-11 school year, in addition to Show Choir Express, we had a small second group that *unenthusiastically* decided to become a show choir. They even voted on a name, *Magical Melody*! We had tee shirts made with that name on them, to prove it! But, the group's interest in show choir soon waned, and after performing with Show Choir Express at the Holiday Magic concerts, the class spent the remainder of the year as a *non-performing music appreciation class*, while the few kids *who still wanted to be in show choir*, added to Show Choir Express for the second semester. So, the Brea Junior High Show Choir Department… once again, returned to one competing choir… *Show Choir Express*. Their competition set was terrific and they were equipped with exceptionally talented soloists. They entered the 2011 competition season, ready for anything! By the way, this group was one of my personal favorites, due to their strong work ethic and their desire to win!

Show Choir Express 2010-11

Costume Colors: *Pink*

Competition Set

Celebrate America
Ease On Down The Road
Hernando's Hideaway
Witch Doctor
God Help The Outcasts
Johnny B Goode/ Shout

We began the competition season at Margarita Middle School's *Mustang Showcase*. Our top competitors there included Travis Ranch and Tuffree, but as I said before, our group was very good, and we were ready for anything. In their performance at Margarita, Show Choir Express sang and performed great. It was truly amazing to see how this group had come together so quickly. When the awards were announced, Show Choir Express had won *1st Place* and both plaques for *Best Showmanship* and *Best Musicianship*, beating Travis Ranch, who placed second, by over fifty points! But, I knew that we could *lose* by fifty points at our next competition, if we got cocky… so, we enjoyed the moment, but continued to work hard. Our next, and final competition was the Travis Ranch *Encore* event. Generally, we did well here, but we did not always win, as Burbank had recently challenged us for first place! Show Choir Express gave a wonderful performance… but so did everyone else in the division! When it finally came time to announce the awards, however, Show Choir Express had won *First Place* and the plaque for *Best Showmanship*! We may have also won best soloist or performer, but I don't have any record of that, just my memory. Two wins in two outings! We didn't do that very often… but this group was phenomenal! Disappointingly, a large percentage of kids from this group *did not continue on with choir at the high school*. I guess this was just a special group that came together for only one year… but I'm still thankful for that!

<u>Show Choir Express Officers 2010-11</u>
President- *Summer Wagner*
Vice-President- *Sierra McCoy*
Vice-President- *Julianne Sexton*
Vice-President- *Riley Hahn*
Secretary- *Jennifer Jung*
Treasurer- *Hayley Mazeika*
Librarian- *Maddy Miller*
Historian- *Caitlyn Gutierrez & Lirissa Tittle*

For the 2011-12 school year, Doug and I decided that the idea of *two choirs was not working out anymore* at BJH, as evidenced by *Magical Melody*, last year. So, I started an academic class, *Performing Arts Appreciation Class* (PAAC) in which interested students on campus could learn about music, drama, dance and show business, through an interactive and fast paced class! Sounds good, right? Well, I had prepared units all summer for this class, including, the Beatles, musicals, acting, movies, making a movie, classical music, rock music, movement, dance and mime, creating an original television show, debate, singing, song writing, careers, writing resumes and we even took a field trip to Disneyland to work with the head of entertainment casting there! The problem was that in that first semester, the counselors had filled my class with lower achieving (I had a number of kids with all F's in their other classes) and disrespectful students, mixed in with some wonderful kids who really wanted to learn! The result was a grind of daily discipline problems throughout the class. Still I stuck to the course syllabus, and we eventually finished the semester. Second semester was smaller, and the counselors, *at my request, omitted any known "problem students"* from my class roster. We officially moved, from the choir room to the room next door, which was vacant, so the students would not "*mess*" with the choir equipment, as some of them had been doing during that tumultuous first semester. I found this arrangement to be satisfactory for note taking lectures, but we migrated back into the choir room often, for activities that required the synthesizer or television. As a side note, a few kids from the PAAC class joined choir either that second semester or the following year, and proved to be *some of our most talented and devoted choir members*!

Show Choir Express, meanwhile, looked very healthy, on paper! It boasted over fifty members and had eight boys! Hopefully, that was a sign of good things to come. Their competition set, this year, was a fun, mixture of fifties and sixties tunes that always has seemed to work for them.

Show Choir Express 2011-12

Costume Colors: *Pink*

Competition Set

Rockin' With The Oldies

We began our competition season at the *Murrieta Show Choir Showcase*. Their director, Rob Hodo, had changed schools, and his former event was called the Mustang Showcase, the one, we had usually begun each season with. Once again, Travis Ranch was our main competition. As in past years, whichever one of us beat the other in the first competition usually went on to beat them all year. So, our kids were ready to compete! Our performance was very polished and passionate. But the Travis Ranch show was very entertaining, as well. Everyone in our group was on pins and needles as the awards were announced. In the end, Show Choir Express… swept! They earned *1st Place* and both plaques for *Best Showmanship* and *Best Musicianship*! Wow! It was a great way to start out the competition year! Our next and final competition for the year was the Los Alamitos *Xtravaganza*. This one was truly the toughest line-up I had ever seen here! We were competing with both Travis Ranch and Burbank in the advanced division! All three of these groups were used to winning! That competition was both incredible and awful at the same time. Incredible, because all three groups were so good and so entertaining and awful, because… *only one group could win*! When it came time for the awards to be announced, the kids from Travis Ranch, Burbank and Show Choir Express looked overwrought with worry. I could totally understand their feelings. When the placements were finally unveiled, Show Choir

Express had earned *2nd Place*, five points behind Burbank and three points ahead of Travis Ranch. Burbank had also won Best Showmanship by five points over us, while Travis Ranch won Best Musicianship by one point ahead of Burbank and us, who were both tied for second! Wow! As I told the kids at the time, it could have been worse. We did earn *2nd Place*! So we ended the year on a tough note, but not a bad note. It's so difficult to win back-to-back competitions with so many good groups out there. In any case… we came very close. Although every year was special at Brea Junior High, many of the eighth graders in this group were destined to "graduate" with me in 2016, and the seventh graders were destined to build a wonderful first year in 2017, for their new director, my son, Alex. For these reasons, I am very grateful. So, I would like to honor all of these kids by listing their names:

Show Choir Express 2011-12

Hailey Jenson • Brianna Clark • Ben Harpster
Carrie Bower • Kaitlyn Rigsby • Carrie Bower
Rhyan Belanger • Gavin Armstrong • Sophia Lincoln
Paris Valdivia • Katryna Wallace • Hayden Mangum
Hannah Roark • Katherine Schloss • Cori Bourgeois
Aiden Pipes • Jessica Patow • Jocelyn Jordan
Lyndsey Gutierrez • Andrew Strom • Jocelyn Abrahamson
Emily Muntean • Emily Lopez • Nick Carillo • Ayla Golshan
Sierra Chaffin • Rebecca Nevarrez • Jeremy Alcaraz
Jaden Johnson • Corinne Sanchez • Sierra Leal
Kendan Fuller • Esmeralda Torres • Jennifer Erich
AOLynne Saena • Audrey Lee • Amanda Dewell
Katie Sampley • Pauline Rejniak • Amber O'Barr
Sara Chee • Erica Cline • Lauren Patrick • Maya Gutowski
Sirena Orti • Kassie McCanless • Jessica Martinez
Sabrina Liu • Micah Munet • Elizabeth Garcia
Jada Gutierrez

Unfortunately, I suffered a major stroke in May of 2012, which I explained in detail in Chapter 12, of this book. This could have thrown the choir programs at BOHS and Brea Junior High into chaos, but thanks to Doug, Kurt, Alex, Hannah, the choir officers and the parents… *this did not happen*! So, the fall of 2012-13 came around and a very good substitute teacher, *Miss Dietch*, was in place for all of my classes until I returned. Doug and I had worked out each group's competition set, over the summer, and I emailed my lesson plans to Miss Dietch every day, as well as asking her how everything was going? This year's show was a lot of fun and very energetic, as usual.

Show Choir Express 2012-13

Costume Colors: *Pink & Black*

Competition Set

Great Balls of Fire
Under The Boardwalk
Who Put The Bomp
When You Wish Upon A Star
Somewhere Over The Rainbow
Johnny B Goode
Shout

I remember it well. That first weekend, after I came back to school (in the beginning of February), we were entered in a competition at *Walnut High School*! I had only worked with this group for a week, and didn't really know half of them, but Doug and Miss Deitch had done a beautiful job of getting them ready for this, so I spent most of my time during warm-up, just trying to prepare them mentally. Once again, Travis Ranch was there. We performed well and won *Best Showmanship*, but we still ended up coming in *2nd*, behind Travis Ranch. Our next competition was the Travis Ranch *Encore* event. Burbank was there, as usual. Our kids were blown away by their performance, as they sang a *four part a cappella in Latin*! Needless to say, we placed *2nd*, with the plaque for *Best Showmanship*, behind Burbank. Our final competition of the year was the *Cypress Star Reflections*. I was still getting to know these kids, but one thing I knew for sure, we seemed to always win *Best Showmanship* while not winning the competition! So, *we needed to tighten up our vocals*! We did just that, spending the next two weeks working tirelessly on our vocal tone, accuracy, blend, diction and dynamics. It sounds like a lot of work, and it was… but by diving into this head first, the kids and I *finally* had a real chance to work together and get to know one another. The day of Star Reflections arrived, and for the first time, this year, I really felt as if Show Choir Express was *my* group, again! They went on stage and dazzled the audience as usual, with their performing, but this time, *also with their singing*! When the awards were announced… Show Choir Express had swept, winning *1st Place*, *Best Showmanship* and *Best Musicianship*! I don't know which other groups competed in that festival, and to tell you the truth, I don't really care! *This was Show Choir Express' first win of the year…* and it came at exactly the right time. I couldn't find a list of the officers, but I did find a list of the section leaders!

Show Choir Express Section Leaders 2012-13

Soprano Section Leaders

Katherine Schloss & Amber O'Barr

Alto Section Leaders

Cori Bourgeois & Micah Munet

Tenor Section Leaders

Aidan Pipes & Hayden Mangum

During the summer of 2013, Doug and I carefully planned out the 2014 competition set for Show Choir Express. We needed to sing a beautiful a cappella ballad to match-up better with Burbank, and we had to have a great power ballad to set us apart from every other group. We settled on *A Dream Is A Wish Your Heart Makes*, for our "a cappella" and *The Impossible Dream*, for our power ballad. The rest of the show showcased our usual high energy and fun

Show Choir Express 2013-14

Costume Colors: *Blue*

Competition Set

Celebrate America
Ease On Down The Road
A Dream Is A Wish
Witch Doctor
The Impossible Dream
Sixties Fun

Our first competition was the *Chaparral Show Choir Showcase*. There were a total of seven groups competing in our division, but our kids didn't seem to be worried. Actually, they seemed as ready as ever! Our performance was very good, but a lot of our competitors, were also good! When the awards were announced, we had *swept*, taking *1st Place*, *Best Showmanship* and *Best Musicianship*! That was a great first outing, but we still had *plenty of things to work on*, and I think we all knew it. Our second competition took us to the Travis Ranch *Encore* event. We had worked very hard for this one! When the awards were announced, we had come in *2nd Place…* while Burbank had swept! We were very disappointed, but it just meant getting back to work. Our third and final competition of the year, took us back to *Cypress Star Reflections*. We had won it last year, so the kids felt pretty confident. However, when the awards were announced, not only had we placed *2nd* behind *Oak Middle School* (from Los Alamitos), but even though we had tied with Oak for Best Showmanship, the festival had made an unfortunate mistake and given the award to another school. The host director *apologized profusely* for the error, but what can you do? So, for the second year in a row we ended the year on a tough note… *but not a bad note*! Just because we didn't always win, *we had not placed lower than second*, for quite some time, now. So, it was on to next year! Our esteemed officers included:

Show Choir Express Officers 2013-14
President: *Wesley Mathews*
Vice-President: *Kristin Camacho*
Activities: *Valerie Tetreault*
Pizzazz Leader: *Imani Keyes*
Secretary: *Natalie Salas*
Treasurer: *Jessica Santucci & Lindsey Morrill*
Librarian: *Natalia Villa & Katie Southard*

Going into the 2014-15 school year, we had one giant question to answer, specifically, *how do we beat Burbank?* The past couple of years had been frustrating for us, as we had seen ourselves working harder and harder, yet still coming up just a little short in head to head competition with them. Of course, we had beaten them before… but none of these kids were around then! Anyway, we designed another fast paced show. We chose *I See The Light*, from Tangled, as our a cappella, and pulled out *a can't miss,* power ballad, called "*Don't Cry Out Loud*." We even added *Mary Poppins*, with the same choreography as we had used, when we performed it with Masquerade! We knew that on paper, this show was a winner. The question was, whether or not this group was ready to give it their all, since we believed that's what it would take to beat Burbank! Hannah Fritz was President, and I believed from the very beginning that she and the staff were on the same wavelength. Beat Burbank!

Show Choir Express 2014-15

Costume Colors: *Purple*

Competition Set

Proud Mary/ Great Balls of Fire
I See The Light
Freeze Frame
Don't Cry Out Loud
Mary Poppins

Because I was so busy in 2015, with two trips for the high school, to Orlando and Chicago, we only competed twice this year. Our first competition took us back to the Chaparral *Show Choir Showcase*. Again, we were competing with our old friend, Travis Ranch. We performed very well, but in all honesty, so did they. When the awards were announced, either we had edged Travis for *1st Place* or they had edged us… *I have conflicting information.* But, we *definitely* earned the plaque for *Best Showmanship,* while they earned the plaque for Best Musicianship! We were beginning to think that every competition from now on was going to be close. It did make for a lot of excitement, however! Our final competition of the year was *Cypress Star Reflections*. Burbank was there, but this time, we hoped to be ready for them! We sang and performed as hard as we could. I don't think we could have tried any harder! But, when the awards were announced… we had once again earned *2nd Place* behind Burbank, who earned 1st Place and both plaques for Best Showmanship and Best Musicianship! On the positive side, we did fight as hard as we could, and although we didn't win, we showed a lot of group integrity! I could feel a determination rising-up from the seventh graders that *they would find a way* to beat Burbank next year! I was right there with them! Their two top officers were:

Show Choir Express Officers 2014-15
President: *Hannah Fritz*
Vice-President: *Kate Root*

The 2015-16 school year rolled around, and almost from the first week of school, I could feel the enthusiasm from the kids, to immediately start working on the competition show! *They could not wait to get out there and compete*! It was fueled, of course, from the frustrated eighth graders who *had not ended their year with a loss* against Burbank, as seventh graders. But, the new seventh graders gladly joined in, and we were instantly on a mission! The show that Doug and I chose for them was simply, "*Let's Go To The Fifties*," full of fun fifties dance songs and ballads! In my estimation, *this was a very talented group*, with a lot of excellent eighth graders and a whole slew of vocal and dance talent coming into the group from the seventh grade class!

<u>Show Choir Express 2015-16</u>

Costume Colors: *Pink and Silver*

<u>Competition Set</u>

"Let's Go To The Fifties!"

Our first competition was the *Chaparral Showcase*, in Temecula. We were competing this year, in a division of eight advanced show choirs, including Travis Ranch. But there was something special about this version of Show Choir Express! I could feel it all year. These students were talented musically and with performance skills… *and they had the confidence to prove it*! Our performance at Chaparral was terrific! Our competitors looked good too, but I just felt that maybe we were *a notch better*, that day. When the awards were announced, sure enough, Show Choir Express swept all of the top awards, earning *1st Place, Best Showmanship* and *Best Musicianship*! Our next competition was at the Los Alamitos *Xtravaganza*. Two years ago, we had fought it out with Travis Ranch and Burbank and had ultimately come in second, behind Burbank, earning no plaques. But, as I said, this year felt different. We took the stage, and our performance looked and sounded amazing! I don't honestly remember how many or which groups we competed against, but I think Travis Ranch was there, and I know that Burbank wasn't. When the awards were announced, Show Choir Express had once again won the competition and earned both plaques for *Best Showmanship* and *Best Musicianship*! Now they had won *two straight competitions*! Of course, a couple of our groups, through the years, had already done that. But *none* of our groups had ever won *three in a row*! Our next and final competition was *The Travis Ranch Illusion* competition (they had recently changed the name of their festival from *Encore*). This was going to be, yet another match-up with Burbank. Over the past eleven years I think we had beaten them *only once*, and that had been quite a while ago! But, our group believed in themselves, and I knew that win or lose, this was going to be their best performance of the year! When we took the stage, I could instantly feel their energy filling the auditorium. Their performance was flawless, and the applause at the end, was unbelievable! I didn't see Burbank perform, but I hear that they too, were incredible. I was loading the car with props, with Doug, when the people began to stream out of the auditorium. Soon Doug received a phone call from one of the parents. He repeated out loud, what the parent told him, so that I could also hear it. We had lost the Best Musicianship plaque to Burbank by one point, but we had won the *Best Showmanship* plaque… *and we had ultimately won the competition by six* points! All of our kids and parents were going crazy! After all, it wasn't often that we beat Burbank or that *we won three consecutive competitions during the same year*! Wow! By this point, I knew that I would be retiring next year, so *this was the nicest present the kids could have possibly given me*!

You know, in revisiting this eleven-year adventure with Show Choir Express, by moving quickly through the years (even though half of the kids changed, after every year*)*, the program stayed essentially the same, with a steadfast passion for excellence and a never-ending drive to win! It's fun to win… a lot more fun than losing! But every loss brought our group solidly together, as they sought to find a way to improve! What I loved about Show Choir Express was how *quickly they would get behind every "new" change to the show*, whether it was a song or choreography, in our continued quest to win competitions! I wonder if Travis Ranch and Burbank *know just how much we used them to motivate our groups*? Think of how boring show choir would have been for our junior high choir students *without* Travis Ranch, Burbank or *the real possibility of losing*, to drive us to higher and higher heights? I would like to thank all of the kids and parents who spent a year or two in the Brea Junior High choir program with me. I hope it was as much fun for you as it was for me! I've listed the entire *2015-16* group below, to honor them, for their wonderful competition achievements, but also because they were *my final Brea Junior High show choir*!

Show Choir Express 2015-16
Winner of Three Consecutive Competitions!

Madyson Miguel • Megan Coday • Reghan Hall • Sara Scott
Jaylene Gonzalez • Chloe Stoddard • Jillian Parker
Nate Mathews • Natalie Murphy • Zhiarrizely Rosimo
Anika Escarez • John Root • Kaitlyn Ho • Emily Flores
Makenna Tompkins • Jazmine Serna • Jacob Hendrickson
Lauren Skinner • Patti Hazlett • Joshua Suc • Adam Cruze
Anthony Sanchez • Austin Fuller • Emma Wood
Amanda Galvez • Jillian Pearson • Kurtis Camacho
Evan Dalgleish • Sophia Hobby • Madison Tukuloff
Tisha Dinh • Ashley Munson • Paige Legendre • Emily Stroh
Gabby Calmelat • Ana Contreras • Macy Pease • Haley Villa
Martisse Watkins • Shaila Ramirez • Samantha Warren
Anessa Lajoie • Mckenna Jackman • Trinity Stinson
Amaya Llanes • Sophia Todorov • Ellie Witt • Carly Noller
Emma Grammell • Kailey Johnson • Malaya Mitchell
Tessa Clements • Sydney Noller • Malena Weiseth
Kathy Cazares • Karina Prieto • Kayla Dewberry
Gianna Reyno • Alexa Hauser • Elizabeth Sanchez
Sadie Dedrick • Gisselle Rifenburg • Zoe Tschumper

I'll never forget when Show Choir Express, so beautifully sang, *For Good*, from *Wicked,* at our Awards Banquet, and dedicated it to me. Afterwards *every single choir member gave me a big hug*! That was one of the sweetest moments I have ever experienced in teaching. Also, I want to thank every member of a Brea Junior High choir from 2005-2016, for changing my mind about working with middle school kids. I would not trade those eleven glorious years with all of you, for anything! My Brea junior high choir kids were *full of energy, creativity and heart*! What's not to like? You impressed a *beautiful memory*, forever on my heart. Thank you!

CHAPTER 15

Memories From Norco High School's New Generation 1977-1979

Norco High School, I hardly knew you, spending only my first two years of teaching there! But, New Generation was *my very first show choir*, and the Norco students gave me the chance to learn my craft. Many of the students were also very talented and dedicated, and we produced some very entertaining shows and concerts together. Following are a number of my former Norco student's memories. Enjoy!

How fun to be your student at the start of your career. I wasn't happy at first. Boy, you know it's hard to be the "next" high school director. You were fantastic from the start. I enjoyed playing piano for you at Nogales when I was at CSUF. I started teaching music in 1989 in Jurupa, before moving to MVSD. I'm starting my 28th year, teaching choir, piano and music. So blessed!

Kathleen Scott Kay

Hi Mr. Willert. Had a good time in your class. It was great finding new ways to hide in your classroom, and not be found by you, in order to ditch other classes!

Laura Aldrich Berger

I have only fond memories of high school. The choir room was always home base, and Bonnie and I were small enough to hide just about anywhere without being discovered by you. Farmer had found all of our hideouts, but you were easy to hide from. So, I would say we liked you at first because you were easy to deceive, then we got to know you and liked you for real! Sounds terrible, but it was high school in the crazy seventies! I do remember that a lot of New Gen members were unhappy with you for changing our rock and roll image more into a show choir by adding music from Pippin. Chris Breyer was right. We were cultish, but most of the leaders graduated in 76 and 77, and it was changing anyways.

Annette Ambrose Schumann

Hi! Mr. Willert, being in New Gen was the most fun I had in high school! I met some great friends at Norco in the music classes. Some of my favorite memories were us going to San Francisco on tour. The Pink and Blue Poof's ha ha, and watching Mary and Ron sing the Grease songs. We had so many great memories.

Gwen Benner Marotte

First of all: Dave, you were very easy to tease. It was fun.
My story--
We (by that I mean, me and a few other choir members, don't remember who else. Can I have some help here?) stole or found Dave's wallet. This was only for the purpose to see what was in it. During this prank we found out that his nickname was "Big Dave." We thought that was hilarious! After that, the wallet was returned with all its contents intact.

Cheri Hale Patterson

Hi Mr. Willert. I didn't make it into New Generation my first year, because you said I had too much country twang, lol! But when you judged at the Norco Fair Talent Show that year, I won 2nd Place with my, "Poor, Poor Pitiful Me!" I was in Concert Choir with you and the Girls (overflow) Choir. You had way too many girls who wanted to be in New Gen. I was in New Gen my junior and senior years. Anyway, thank you for your part in my long love of singing. I am now a worship leader at my church. My daughters, who later, also were in Norco High's choirs, are or have been worship leaders in church. I have fond memories of choir and I made some lifelong friends. Choir, the music and the people were the most important part of my school years. I loved singing the harmonies and dancing. I can say that choir helped me feel accepted in my years of adolescent awkwardness.

Karen Smith Gladu

Now, as you know, I was new to the music department. I came from being a varsity baseball player… and class president. I basically came to the music department because of all the girls! Imagine that? But although I was pretty shy about performing and such, because of you and others around me, I got really involved in New Gen, and before the year was over, I had several choir classes, was involved in several different performing groups, became an officer in the music department, made lifelong friends… and when you named me "Most Improved" at the Awards Banquet, it was a surprise… and remains one of my fondest memories of high school. Thank you for that fond memory! I also remember being both excited and nervous before the Azusa Aztec Sing. I was new to New Gen, and we were all nervous about the expectations for us to do as well as the previous year's group. Even though we still did some 'rock' we had changed quite a bit from previous years… and of course some of the groups were very polished, awesome to watch. I remember being very excited at the other groups' response and applause for us, I even think we won Best Showmanship! It's one of my most fond memories from the group. The most surprising thing I learned in choir was that I actually liked to sing, and in New Gen, I liked to dance!

Guy Wessell

We were all devastated to find Farmer gone when we came back to school. Mr. Willert, you sure stepped into a firestorm and from what I remember, you managed quite well. We were afraid we would lose New Gen as part of the transition. But, no, everything worked out for us. I remember feeling intimidated by the competition because our style was so different. But I learned to love the competition for the love of being there. The trip to San Diego was a brilliant idea. Gave us a positive goal and it was very healing. This is a weird one, but it is one of my big memories. I loved the after show trips to Bob's Big Boy (or JB's? Can't remember). A bunch of us would gather around a couple of tables pulled together, or squeeze into a booth, and eat and talk and smoke. Or in my case, I would breathe through my glass of water because I didn't smoke, and I didn't like breathing smoke. But I didn't care because I loved being a part of the gang. I remember the group camaraderie much more than the performances. (I eventually developed an allergy to cigarette smoke. That's probably why I remember the after dinners so well.) Happy memories.

Kathy Briggs Van Wagoner

Hey Chief! Of course there is the epic concert in the gymnasium when the flash-pots got accidentally over-loaded. And then there was the polish target pistol John Dettmore and I used during the Jingle-Bell Travelogue! I actually tried to make things easier for you. The New Kid always has it tougher, I just thought I would try something different on you. Despite the explosions and occasional fires… I think overall… it was a pretty good time!

Chris Breyer

Well, it was the beginning of my junior year at Norco High School, and my second year in New Generation, and Mr. Farmer was nowhere to be found? We were all shocked, and hurt. Farmer was, we thought, our friend and he didn't even have the nerve tell us he was leaving! In walks Mr. Dave Willert, the poor new guy on the block, and we were out for blood, and were so mean to him. But we all soon learned what a great guy Dave was and that he was fun to work with. We ended up doing a lot of things that we probably would never have done because they were out of our comfort zones and I think we all learned a lot! Thank for helping us grow! Also, I remember doing Comedy Tonight, in the little theater. It was so much fun revolving that huge set! One night we lost control of it, pushing Lyle Allen out into the audience, but he kept on singing. As he sang out the last note on "Tonight," he spit out his false tooth into the second row of the audience! Talk about funny!

Jeff Crawford

We stayed at the Yerba Buena in San Francisco. I don't recall where we stayed in Solvang. One of my most memorable memories was a group dinner at the San Franciscan at Fisherman's Wharf – and then our visit to Hearst Castle. I fondly recall this time, every time I visit San Francisco.

Tim Steele

I have so many happy memories of my time in New Gen, so many long lasting friendships that I have to this day. I grew in my love of music and singing, which has continued on, in the form of being on a worship team and singing every Sunday! I play the bass or guitar, occasionally and always sing harmony. So thank you so much, Mr. Willert, for encouraging me in school. It has lasted a lifetime, for sure! When we went to San Francisco, I had the time of my life! My mom, Dee Hall, came along as well and that made it all the more fun! I became great friends with Steve Hauser on that trip and pulled some pranks that we still laugh about, to this day. Then there were the pink and blue poofs, as well... you know who you are! I met my late husband, through Kevin Hauser, Steve Hauser and Karen Gladu, after I graduated. I had two sons, one of which married Steve and Paula Hauser's daughter, Ashley. I am so very blessed! My life was altered through being a part of New Gen, in so many ways... that last to this day. Thank you, thank you, thank you!

Jonnie Hall Mount

The school year was 1978-79, and I was a junior at Norco High School when I decided that I wanted to join the New Generation show choir. I was also a cheerleader and the experience of being a part of two different and some thought, opposing groups, helped shape who I am today. My athlete friends, many of whom I had gone to elementary and junior high with, would say, "I can't believe you want to hang out with 'those' people. They're a bunch of gay singing geeks!" Some of my new show choir friends would say, "Why do you like any of those dumb jocks?" When I first watched the television show Glee, you can imagine my reaction. It immediately transported me back to a time where I was being stereotyped, prejudged and constantly questioned about my identity and choices to coexist within diverse cultures. Although this time was confusing, as soon as I walked through the doors into my choir class, I felt safe. Mr. Willert made this space safe with his big smile, warm heart, calm direction and ability to make me feel like I belonged. I belonged with "those" people who quickly welcomed me into their world of music, laughter and friendship. We didn't win any competitions and were never judged "the best" by others, but we were always encouraged to be our best selves. We wore ugly brown polyester costumes while others wore costumes that were bright and sparkled, but we still did our best to shine. While others may have been singing showstoppers, we sang a Randy Newman medley, which included "Short People" so at only 4'11, I was front and center and learned to laugh at myself. You never know when a moment in time will turn into a life-changing experience that will impact your character and life's work. I've spent my adult life working with youth to empower them to be inclusive, kind and compassionate. I encourage them to strengthen relationships by building bridges of understanding and provide them a safe place to find their confidence and their voice. Just like Mr. Willert did thirty-eight years ago for me. Our big finale song was always "Celebrate" by Three Dog Night, which to this day when I hear it, I smile and my eyes well up with happy tears, because we were given the opportunity to "Celebrate and dance to the music."

Lysa Gamboa-Levy

CHAPTER 16

Memories From The Nogales High School Show Choirs 1979-1998

I owe Nogales High School, so very much. It was here that Doug and I created ourselves and honed our skills in producing, choreographing and directing show choirs that served us well throughout our long careers! Many thanks, to all of the principals and staff members who were so supportive, throughout my nineteen-year stay. Assistant Superintendent, *Tony Santorufo*, will always stand out in my heart as the one who always had my back and supported everything the choir did. Thank you, Tony! I had some marvelous kids at Nogales High, to work with for 19 years, who loved music and performing as much as Doug and I loved teaching it! Here are some of their memories.

Being in choir was one of my best high school experiences. I came in my sophomore year, not knowing a single person. Being in Chamber Singers/ Dream Street, I was immediately accepted. I consider everyone family forever!

Nancy Mendoza Sams

Hi Dave. I was in Chamber singers from 90-94. I still have the ovation guitar that you gave me. It now belongs to my daughter who learned to play with it!

Eddie Partida

I keep thinking about my one special memory, but the truth is I have so many! But, the strongest memory I have was you telling us we were professionals and treating us so... we believed it! We were! The wonderful experiences gave us confidence, optimism and the desire to dream and make those dreams come true. A few times a year I embrace my "Inner Mr. Willert" and take my students on a special "show choir journey" that inspires, entertains and brings smiles to our school during our Winter and Spring Shows. Do you realize how many people you've touched through me? That's just one person! I've shared the magic I learned from you in the 20 years of my teaching. Everybody should be so lucky to know you or know about you. Soooo the most specialist memory I have is that you made each one of us feel empowered, positive and most definitely special. Can't ever thank you enough! In retrospect, I learned that we had the power to make our little corner of the world a happy, and safe place. As an adult I realize how the lessons you taught us went beyond musical notes, and performances. You taught us life lessons (that I believe everybody should be privy to know.) I learned that work ethics, determination, commitment and a positive attitude are the factors that make this world a better place for everyone. You taught us we have the power and the responsibility! We soar, because you taught us it was ok to dream... to fly!

Betty Gardea

I learned to work hard, practice, practice, practice, and to realize that family isn't always blood. I also learned to let my guard down and trust my family, in creating memories for a lifetime. But most of all, to have fun and enjoy the moments! The best times!!!

Marylen Ayash-Borgen

Two things that stick out as "big moments" for me were:

1. Finally Beating West Covina. Unfortunately, I don't remember the year (someone help me out here) or the comp. (1985 at Fullerton Competition) It was so amazing to finally beat them after always preparing for 2nd place. I can still see us jumping up and down in the auditorium after our name was announced. I think it was at Fullerton JC.

2. When Dream Street beat Chamber at the Act One competition in 1988! It was a small comp at the Fullerton college theater. CS and DSS were in the same division, which rarely happened. I remember as a "double duty" performer, I was really torn. On one hand I wanted to be elated that DSS won (and bested Chamber), but on the other hand, Chamber was really upset. I think that was the beginning of the "it just doesn't matter" era.

Also, the principal who hired me for my first teaching job had a license plate that said, "pzazzzz." I felt it was fate.

Jennifer Dunigan-Zamora

The choir room was my "Safe Haven." My home life was abusive, crazy and chaotic. Even when I screwed up during my junior year, you welcomed me back, my senior year and gave me a second chance. I am forever grateful to you for doing that. You were one of only 3 good male role models I had in my life (you, my grandfather and Lynn Hurd's dad). You were an angel sent from Heaven to help me through a difficult time in my life, and gave me something to look forward to everyday. Thank you! A memory. No matter where we were going for an event, you always knew where a McDonald's was! And this was before smartphones and Google Maps!!!

Mary Grubb Hinojos

I have a few favorite memories from 1981. Remember, when we all got hooked on Rocky Horror? Or the time you decided we should play softball, but we were all horrible at it, and our 1st baseman, Doug, was busy tap dancing on the base, and the balls just rolled by him when someone got a hit! I thought it was funny! Or the time when about 5 of us ditched class to go to the beach? My parents were in Las Vegas, so no one could get a hold of them. It was Mary, Keith, me and a couple of others. And we might have gotten away with it, but when you asked, where everyone was, a girl named Susan started singing clues to you; "everybody's gone surfin'!" Well, it's one of my fondest memories, anyway. I have one other special memory from 1981, when we went to a Nogales feeder school to perform for the kids. One little girl loved us so much she drew a picture of our performance that was so cute. I recognized that she drew me! I was shorter than the others, but she drew it so much like me, that I still remember it. I was touched by that, and from then on I knew how we could influence future performers with our performances.

Eleanora "El Riggers" Hackworth

I'm Ana's younger sister, Gracie Enriquez. I was at Nogales your last years as well. I was there from 95/96 through 97/98. You left my senior year! I was in Dream Street. Those were the best years, as we had placed 1st at almost every competition and had many sweeps! That includes placing 1st in the Nation at Showstoppers! Choir was our life at Nogales... it truly was the reason that many of us even went to school, the passion we had for our group ran deep within us. We wore those t-shirts, like they were a badge of honor! Thank you for putting this book together, I can't wait to buy one!

Gracie Enriquez

Omigosh, I was a runner for the judges at NDSCC in '91, and could not BELIEVE I got to meet Nia Peeples! She was everything back in the day! Thanks for that! I was in Nogales choir from '88-'92! DSS in '88-'89, then Chamber the rest of the years. Best time ever! I was talking to a friend of a friend recently, and she had been in choir in her high school years as well. We were reminiscing about show choirs in general, when she asked me where I went to HS. When I told here, Nogales, she freaked and said we were her high school's ultimate! It feels like forever ago, yet we STILL have fangirls and fanboys! You created something so special in those musical groups, and I will forever be grateful that I played a small part in it. Thank you, Mr. Willert, from the bottom of my heart.

Julpha Chamina Maniquis-Dormitorio

1989! I never felt so defeated like I did at the Aztec competition. We worked so hard and had so much to prove. We felt so much joy and happiness after the performance because we had nailed it. Then the Awards Ceremony came and we never got called! 24 seconds over our time got us disqualified! I remember looking around confused and in shock! We all cried uncontrollably, as we walked to the bus and just held one another. Our poor parents trying to make us all feel better, but they couldn't. We sat on the bus and Mr. Willert gave us the most uplifting speech and explained that sometimes the game is not fair. He read our scores and comments and told us to FOCUS on all the positives that we achieved, and that he was so proud of us. So, we didn't get a trophy, but we made you proud, and that was important to all of us.

Giovanni Wingston Morales

The 1997 Showstoppers at Disneyland. I was so honored to win the title of Grand National Champion for the Solo division. I believe Dream Street won the Woman's Division and Chamber Singers got 4th place? Regardless of where we placed... this was one of my fondest memories!

Margaux Yap Cruz

I felt so proud to belong to show choir. You were the first teacher that made me feel like I was worth something. The experience definitely made me a better person and I feel it gave me a confidence that I carry with me throughout my life. At that time, in my life, my family was falling apart. I met a new kind of family. High school would have been unbearable had it not been for Choir. One of my most memorable and exciting times was when we went to the Young Americans competition. I so enjoyed meeting new people, learning new dances and all the camaraderie that was shared while we were at the workshops. I remember feeling very honored and proud to be a part of it. I'll take that with me forever!

Gloria Hernandez Romero

Hello everyone... I'm from Nogales High School, 97 or 98 Dream Street! A song that I still sing to myself every now and then is... well I don't remember the name of it... but it started off with... "Brothers and sisters, sisters and brothers. Don't you know we love one another? Put your hand in mine. Everything is fine! (The Dream Street Theme) That's just the one that still, until this day, I think about! Mr. Willert, thank you for providing those memories. That made my whole high school experience. It was a blast! I still tell people how we were unbeatable! That helped me to be more confident with myself, my voice, and is the reason I still sing today! You were an awesome teacher! I will never forget you or the years I sang in your choirs! A former Dream Street Singer!

Crystal Garcia

Being so proud to wear my hair in rollers to school on performance days. Drying my hair under the hand dryer in a school bathroom after a swim meet and before driving myself to the choir competition. Choir was family, fun, silly, serious. I always smile thinking about when Drea, Uyen and I performed our "Dream Street Rejects" act at our senior Spring Concert. I got a "C" in cheerleading because I chose choir practices over cheerleading at basketball games. Oh, and I lip synced quite a bit my first year (sophomore) when I was soprano because I couldn't hit those high notes, I think my big hair got me in? By senior year, I could actually sing (alto) and even had a solo in Dream Street. It's really some of my best high school memories!

Jamie Drinville Lesnever

Choir is what made school worth going to. To be honest, I don't remember much about high school other than being involved in the choral department. I know I had other teachers/classes... and maybe even a few friends that weren't in show choir... but I really don't remember many. My world revolved around being in show choir. One funny thing is it took me years to stop raising my eyebrows when smiling! I couldn't figure out why I always looked crazy in pictures... then I realized it was because I was raising my eyebrows... that full-on show choir smile/face... can we say PIZZAZZ! I'm not sure if anyone will remember, but my house burned down three days before I was to graduate from NHS... 6/16/86. We lost everything that was upstairs (all the bedrooms). I pretty much lost everything I owned... including my cap and gown, graduation dress... plus my beloved DSS and CS dresses and not to mention the trophies I had just received at the banquet. I visited the school/choir room, the day before graduation and Mr. Willert handed me an envelope with over $200.00 in it... it had been collected from the choral department. It meant the world to me. He also told me that they had reordered my trophies. The choral department was more than school... it was family. I am so happy to see all of these pictures, because I had nothing, they were all pretty much lost in the fire... and now I do!

Colleen Ory Caron

One of my best memories and worst memories was in 1980, when we performed for the nursing home and I got over-heated and passed out. I ended up with seven stitches in the back of my head. Other than that, you and Doug made it fun to be in Choir. I remember just loving to be there. We were a big family that took care of each other. To this day, I am still friends with a lot of them, and they are still my family.

Lynn Romanofsky Hurd

The highlight of my high school life was being in Chamber Singers from 1985 to 1988. From dancing and singing together with my friends to learning choreography and competing against other choirs to traveling to places like Hotel Del in San Diego and San Francisco too. I loved every minute of it. My only regret is that I didn't join the group in my freshmen year in 84. Oh yes, I still have a sequin vest that we wore for competition, from back in the day. Every once in a while I'll put it on and dance around the house singing, "This joint is jumpin!" Jk lol. Who remembers that song?

Shun L. Griffin

Although I'd been performing most of my life and been on stage before, the first time I was on stage with the Chamber Singers, the curtain opened and I saw the light booth at Citrus College! I froze, but knew I had to keep going, and as soon as it was over... I was hooked, and couldn't wait to be on stage the next time! It felt like family. It was the best time, I think, I ever had! It was a chance for me to be as crazy as I wanted, and no one really cared... because we were all oddballs... and we loved every minute of it!

Troy Peace

Let me see... I was in Concert Choir at Nogales in 1982, I think. We wore those hideous green robes with gold overlay. It was the Christmas season and we were singing in the little theatre. I guess I locked my knees (huge mistake when singing on stage, especially on choral risers), and I fainted! The next thing I knew, I was sitting down with drinking water and Willert called a time-out during the performance. I auditioned for Chamber, but because I couldn't smile (hence the name Vulture Face), I didn't make it right away. Singing, smiling and liking what I was doing, were hard to do all at once. My brother, Vince, was with me for one year, in 82/83, and without him, I couldn't join, because my mom thought show choir was sinful! Anywho, I was a member of Dream Street and Chamber for two years, and still Concert Choir. I remember we sang in the gym during a pep rally and NOBODY paid attention, in 1983. We were the true "rainbow coalition" of choirs. We were from the wrong side of the tracks. I got my hair braided just before a competition, and I had iridescent beads. Doug and Dave flipped because we had to be uniform! In 1985, Disneyland wasn't as popular for choirs, and it was freezing. About ten people watched us. We sang, "Texas has an uh-oh in it." I got flipped and kicked in the head. Gabriel Lomeli, said I was too heavy! I only weighed 115 lbs... but he weighed 100 lbs! Best partner ever! I was the only girl allowed to wear a hat during "Hot Note," because I was fierce! I think the greatest choir highlight, for me, was when we finally beat Bonita Vista, Rowland and West Covina. Our struggle was very real, because we were the "Bad News Bears" of choir... but we did it! My most surprising memory about choir was that I actually loved being there. I thought show choir was for weird people. As it turned out... it is!

Laura Ann Washington-Franklin

Dream Street from 1994-95 was the very first year I have ever performed in a show choir group, even though I have been singing since I was a toddler. It was the most awkward thing I have ever done, but Doug and Dave were so gracious and merciful and patient with me! I remember how intimidating all the dancers were, because I had never danced in my entire life. I wasn't allowed to, where I came from! The Fullerton competition was the most nerve-racking competition ever! But, Dream Street got through it! My second and last year in show choir was my senior year and best year! Dream Street and Chamber were busy, busy, busy! Sorry, I can't remember the dates, but Showstoppers was definitely the highlight of that year! I love how the officers made special things for us members. Mr. Willert always had a smile on his face. I don't think I have ever seen him not smiling? One of the most hilarious things I remember is practicing to smile at the focus point, and holding it as long as we could, until our muscles hurt! But still, our faces held-up, showing our teeth. Our faces looked so awkwardly hilarious! I so wish someone took a picture of it! I'll bet every year had this experience!

Dorothy Nacita Swayne

I felt that I was part of a family. We did a lot of activities together, like the summer potlucks at Schabarum Park, to parties for holidays, and working as hard as we could for practice to place in shows. I loved having people giving you the confidence you needed to improve and having close bonds with each other.

Davina Gaither De La Cruz

Silhouette Singers began during the 1987-1988 school year. It was another show choir group, besides the Dream Street Singers 1984-85 school year launch, that I was able to participate in during its launching. There was no Renegade group that 1987-1988 school year, so that group had to have been launched after those of us from the class of 1988 had already graduated. There were Chamber Singers, Dream Street Singers, Silhouette Singers and Uptown Girls during our Class of 1988's final (1987-1988) school year. The Silhouette Singers' first song set was: "Tear Them Down," "I Dreamed A Dream" and "Bye, Bye Love!" Wow, there was a Concert Choir and then a Varsity Concert Choir before Silhouette Singers and Uptown Girls. So many different new named groups emerged between the late 1980s to the early-mid 1990s, it seems!

During my NHS Show Choir Years of 1984-1988, I enjoyed all the musical trips we took to the Grand Dinner Theatre in Anaheim, back when the Grand Dinner Theatre was still open, still existed. We were able to have dinners and watch musicals like this one: "Sugar Babies" we got to see it when it first premiered there! We saw "A Chorus Line," and others. Some of us even got souvenir glasses during each musical show too.

Jeanette Zapata

Being in choir was AMAZING! I remember the nerves and then the exhilaration of being on stage. And I remember sitting together during the awards, sometimes at 11 pm, and sweeping every competition. There were long hours of practice, learning choreography and remembering that it was a crime to touch your face or adjust your dress while on stage. I also mastered the skill of changing from one outfit (regular clothes) to another (choir dress) without showing a single secret. It's been a life skill, honestly. I can change fast, in limited space and 100% discretely. I remember, "You practice the way you perform!" I also remember wearing curlers in my hair all day at school, so I'd have beautiful curls for the show. I wouldn't trade a minute. Mr. Willert, what you and Doug (and everyone else who contributed to our shows) did was absolutely remarkable! The arts are crucial to the development of a well-rounded individual and you provided an above average experience for every group you've worked with. We didn't just sing and dance to compete... we did it to belong. We all had different and varying levels of talent. I always say I was in Chamber Singers because I did great stage face, I had amazing hair, and my singing ability came in third, but you always made me feel like I had tremendous talent and value. You treated us with patience and kindness and everyday you were an extraordinary example to us. You were generous with praise and excellent at your job, but you always made clear your expectations that we be good people, good competitors and good friends. Always. Thank you, wholeheartedly and sincerely for being such a wonderful and positive teacher and influence. I will always be immeasurably grateful for the time I spent as your student and the memories I will always cherish. Thank you!

Vanessa Gonzalez Saavedra

The first time I saw the Chamber Singers was when they came to perform at Giano Jr. High. They wore beautiful sparkly dresses, they sang so powerfully and danced their way into my heart! I was smitten and awed by this group of shiny happy people!! In that moment I knew I NEEDED to be a part of this. When the auditions came I was so nervous! The choir room was filled to the brim with students anxious to be a part of the Show Choirs. I looked around and saw so many talented people. The choreography was taught at a quick pace and all the older kids seemed to catch on right away. I felt intimidated, yet still determined to make the cut. The singing portion was even more nerve-racking. I was called into the small room where Mr. Willert sat. I scrubbed my sweaty palms on my jeans, took a deep breath & sang, Edelweiss, from the Sound of Music. Mr. Willert's kind eyes & gentle smile helped me relax. A few days later my friend Megan & I eagerly awaited the results. We were thrilled beyond belief that we both made it into Chamber our freshman year! That was the beginning of four years, filled with amazing performances & friendships that I will always be grateful for. Many people will say that they hated their high school experience. I can honestly say, I loved my experience, and it's due in large part to the awesome program developed by Mr. Dave Willert and Doug. Thank you so much!!!

Ana Enriquez Chico

In choir, I was surprised to learn that I had a "some kind of rhythm!" I tried!! I was also surprised that I could have the confidence to perform in front of audiences!

Aisha Salgado Guillen

Thank you, Mr. Willert, for giving us kids the love and respect we have for music and friends and fond memories to last us a lifetime. Because of you, I was able to break out of my shyness and go on to pursue a singing career. I lasted many years singing in Mexican clubs and formed my own band for 12 years called, "Caravan," along with endless charity events. I did so much on TV and radio but due to me getting hit with thyroid cancer, 7 years ago, I'm unable to sing the way I used to... but, I wouldn't trade those years for anything in the world, and it was all because of my experience and the musical confidence and education you gave us kids! You were the best! Thank you and blessings always. Pizzazz!

Yolanda Ruiz Rodriguez

So I have a memory that is "interesting" and wasn't my favorite, but has been one that has always stuck out the most. The time we were at Tops 'n Pops in San Diego in 1988, and after my friends from my former school, Bonita Vista had performed, I gave them a standing ovation. When we went to the green room to warm up, you let me have it for standing up for BV and told me that standing up for our competition was the same as handing them the trophy. We went on to win Tops 'n Pops. I must say, I would not be where I am today if not for the amazing training I got during my years in the choir department. Show choir taught me so much, especially how to be prepared. I would do it all over again. The love and work everyone put into the program is unlike any other. I have the phrase, "Success Finds A Way, Failure Finds An Excuse" on the wall of my rehearsal room here in Argentina. I think that phrase has stuck with me the most.

Sergio Mejia

Being in Choir was a truly special time. Friends from that time are now family to me today. My kids call Lawrence Fitz, Uncle Lawrence (AKA Aunti Lo Lo). My younger daughter even performs in a program created by Lawrence for ROP. Jennifer Dunigan sang for both my Grandmother and Mother's funerals. Mike Gash is Godfather to my younger daughter. The Chamber Singers performed at the reception for my marriage to my best friend and Dream Streeter, Lupe. I'm not sure you fully realize what an impact your program made on so many young lives, Mr. Willert. The work ethic you instilled in us, and the camaraderie you created amongst us. My life would not be quite as full if it had not been for my time with Chamber.

Dale G. Hersh Jr.

We swept at Fullerton. I still think back to that moment of pure joy, knowing that it was the fruits of all our hard work. Years later, I realized that I learned the importance of working as a group to accomplish things much greater than I could ever accomplish alone. Thank you for those life lessons. I also remember you conducting one competition with giant Mickey Mouse gloves! You taught generations of teenagers that they can be a part of something bigger than themselves and that it is a worthwhile endeavor! I was also surprised to learn that I was outgoing!

Natalie Mauk Ridley

Choir memories. Way too many to list, but I'll rattle off what I think of first…

**Pizzazz.*
**Living On Dream Street, the musical.*
**Being in charge of props, and so dedicated that looking back, I was a bit of a fanatic.*
**Love in Any Language.*
**Jaime Zavala solos.*
**Orozco sisters and solos.*
**I won a 1st place trophy for a solo at the Universal Studios show choir competition.*
**You and Doug, whispering back and forth, during auditions and rehearsals.*
**You never raised your voice, yet you could scold a child with a smile on your face.*
**You got mad at seniors for going on "senior ditch day" in 1991.*
**Trip to Washington, D.C.*
**Trips up north, near San Francisco.*
**Trips down south to San Diego.*
**High school drama, usually about who liked who and so on.*
**You posted stuff in class, up on the wall, that made sense, but I'm not sure I remember the right phrases. Something like, "Success Finds A Way, Failure Finds an Excuse."*
**David Kater solos.*
**Jennifer Dunigan solos.*
**Heather Tjaden Jefferson and her beautiful everything… face, hair, voice, etc.*
**The songs you wrote like, "Just Love Me."*
**The John Jacobson event, America Sings, that helped raise money for the homeless.*
**Bo on drums, Francine on piano, Don on piano, Dwayne on guitar.*
**Lots of hair, Lots of sequins, Lots of curls, Lots of practice.*
**Warm up exercises such as "pizzazz."*
**In the Hills of Shilo.*
**Carlos Morales and his cool hair.*

**Singing, "Always" with Ric Guerra.*
**Kevin Pinedo's loud laugh.*
**Lawrence Fitz humor.*
**Keisha singing, "Just take a hold of your soul," during Footloose.*
**Singing, "Prisoner of Love" with Rika and Tassa.*
**Hip hop dance with Jesse Yee, and there were supposed to be two other dancers!*
**Props, boxes and more props.*
**The unexpected marriage unions that developed:*
Lizsa and Kevin
Dale and Lupe
Keith and Tracy
Lila and Brad
**Singing, "watermelon," when you forget the words or don't know them at all.*
**Feeling cool at the time, but later in life realizing I was a choir nerd... but no shame!*

One of my favorite memories was helping the guys group in 1990-91. I helped with the choreography, as needed, when Doug was unavailable. Then at Magic Mountain, we were short too many guys that day, so you put me in as "one of the guys!" When I think of choir, I think of big hair, rollers, hairspray, sparkles, glitter, shiny silver heel dance shoes, fun, laughter, friendships, drama, love of music, and the idea that music sees no color.

I also wanted to mention the brilliance and innovation and humor of Doug Kuhl. He is a phenomenal choreographer and teacher.

Lori Halopoff Fenelon

A memory that stands out to me is a competition to which we wore our brand new black satin 50's style jackets. We thought we looked awesome. A choral director from a competing school thought otherwise. I remember this director walking up to Dave and asking, "Are your kids carrying knives in those jackets?" His contempt and racism dripped from every word. Dave, without a moment's hesitation, casually looked at him and said, "Why yes, they are."

As a teenager, I giggled and walked away but the moment stayed with me. Later, I came to recognize it as the support and validation that Dave always showed us.

Micki Burciaga

1982-83, my first year in Chamber Singers – my first competition was the Aztec Sing. We placed 5th. It was our first competition when we ever placed. I remember Keith, Chrissie, ET Al (the Seniors) were so excited. Over the next four years, we placed or won at nearly every competition. Secondly, winning 1st place at the Johnny Mann competition, at the beginning of the 1984 season. It was our very first, 1st place – ever. Some of the most exciting times in my life were being in choir and Chamber Singers at Nogales.

Glen S. Jimenez

Most important part of those years was meeting my husband Paul, we've been married 23 years this year. The music and performance skills I learned in these groups have served me well throughout my life. From being comfortable training, teaching and holding meetings at work to now being an active member of a competitive Sweet Adeline's chorus.

Kim Abernathy Alley

If Mr. Willert asked me to be in other groups, I would say, yes, so basically I was in all of his groups from 93-96. That one moment when Dream Street won Nationals at Disneyland in 1996 will live in my heart and memories forever. All the girls in that group used all the tools you gave us, Mr. Willert and definitely executed them to the fullest. I still to this day use what you showed us as a teacher, friend, counselor etc. in life today. I would give anything to be able to perform again. Thank you!

Becky Mantanic

I think I was in all the groups, with the exception of Renegade, from 1989-1992. Absolute best years of my life! Dave and Doug not only taught singing and dancing, but life lessons! I am forever grateful for my experience. Helped me become a Disney performer!! Huge thanks to the both of them!! I have huge respect for both of you!!

Deana Acosta Fetty

I was in Nogales HS Dream Street Singers (94-96) and in Chamber Singers (96-97).... some of the most wonderful years of my life! Mr. Willert.... you as well as my fellow choir members helped me find and express myself as a person through music... and I thank you all for that, Mr. Willert ... you truly taught us all the universal language!

Hazel Vargas

Thank you! You really brought out the voice in me and I truly appreciate that! I've taken everything I was taught into my adulthood. You not only taught music, you prepared us for real life through it. Focus, hard work, determination and teamwork! You always kept it cool, even when we were being teenagers! When you said, "Dag nab it," WE KNEW YOU MEANT BUSINESS! THANK YOU FOR ALL YOU INSTILLED IN US! Truly the best of my teenage years!

Jenevieve M. Fuentes

I was proud to be part of such winning and unique groups. From NorCal all the way down to SD, people knew who we were. At other schools, we may have been "choir nerds," but at Nogales, we were kinda cool and very respected. The best part was how close we all were. There were always different combinations of kids together at any given time, always laughing and having fun. Drama was minimal. We just loved being around each other. I definitely learned the art of being poised... to greet people with a smile.... to stand up tall and confident.... to be welcoming. My mom had pointed that out to me about myself years back, and I've noticed it's true! Being part of these groups made my HS years so much fun! All of the competitions, trips to SF and DC, and the most amazing friends who are still in my life all these years later. I've been able to apply so much of what I learned in show choir with you, Dave Willert, to how I live my life, even to this day. (And I'm glad I had that special time with Alex when he was little, too!)

Erin Drake Garcia

During a family camping trip this last weekend, Debbie and I reminisced about show choir. What group sang what songs, who was the soloist, we may have even done a few signature Doug dance moves. Our choir stories are always filled with such passion. It wasn't easy for me to come into choir being "Debbie's little sister." She was the singer, and I was the dancer, both of us equally happy with our own talents. We wore curlers to class, made funny expressions while we sang and worked our butts off during practice. We practically lived in the choir room, by our own choice. I'm not sure if anyone outside of choir will ever really understand just how amazing this experience was. The impact YOU have made on Debbie's and my lives... we will always hold dear to our hearts. I know Debbie would agree 100%!

Donna Bailey

Our competitions, especially our trip to Washington DC for America Sings, were some of my best high school memories. When our lighted tambourines lit up during a performance, it was like magic. "Swanee, how I love you, how I love you..." Show choir was one of my best experiences and I wish I hadn't left Chamber Singers! I felt like I was part of something big and important. It didn't seem like work, at all, since I was having so much fun! It was a wonderful part of high school, I love to remember and share!

Vangie Rustia Obrero

In choir, I was part of a family that understood me. I was able to be myself, do what I loved, with people I loved. I felt like I could do anything I set my heart on. And even with all of my flaws, I was loved. Confidence, energy, and a desire to be better, followed me all four years that I was a part of this wonderful group. While not a stupid kid, I wasn't academically gifted, so school was about whom I met and doing what I loved. Dave Willert and Doug Kuhl captured the strengths in all of us and helped turn our weaknesses into something better. It's been over three decades and I am still eternally grateful for being part of such a family of talented people! Mr. Willert, you indeed were a father figure to so many of us. After my dad died, there were no male role models in my life. Then, freshman year came along, and you were kind, sincere and invested in kids like me. You turned Chamber Singers around, but never at the cost of hurting anyone – only building up. Even when I left CS for a short while during my Young Americans time, you encouraged and welcomed me back to the fold. How grateful I will always be for that. Thank you for being you!

Chrissie Casey Brockman

To me, choir was a lifesaver. It kept me out of the trouble that I was in so much during junior high in Pomona. Even though I was asked to play football at Pomona High, I am so glad that I did not go, but got to meet you, as well as many great people during our years of performing.

Matt Blackstone

Show choir and your direction helped me to get comfortable coming back to school. Many didn't know or don't remember, but I had to do home studies my freshman year due to being pregnant. I had zero clue where I would fit-in when I came back my sophomore year. Deciding to tryout for Dream Street was the best decision I could have ever made. I wasn't the greatest singer, but I sure could dance and had facials for days. You found a place for me and encouraged me to continue on. I was not judged and it gave me the opportunity to make lifelong friends and to have something to look forward to. I don't know if you remember Dave, but you also hired me on to work for you the year after I graduated and it was amazing being able to help out. I will forever be grateful for what you offered and taught me. You provided an atmosphere that helped insecure students know they belonged. Making Chamber, my junior year, was amazing. You were so good at reinforcing that you didn't have to be the best at everything, because everyone served a purpose in your choirs. We learned how to lose gracefully and to strive to be the best. We learned that hard work and lots of practice could get you to the top. We never gave up, because you never gave up. We also learned amazing time management lol. We spent so much time practicing, but our grades were important too. I absolutely attribute a lot of who I am to you and Doug. Just ask my daughter... she will tell you that I don't care how tired she is after two hours of practice, three days a week. We were in the choir room every day during class and almost every night for practices. I constantly tell her how important it is for her facials to be big... so the people in the very back rows can see them!

Carrie Acosta-Edwon

I admired Chamber Singers the moment I saw them perform. At that time, I never would have imagined I'd be part of such an amazing group. When Mr. Willert asked me to audition, I thought he was crazy. The dress, the shoes, the hair... my life changed forever. The experience and memories will last forever. I loved watching the transformation from September to the competition season, from learning individual parts to full-on harmony. Practicing on a dance floor that barely had enough space for us, not to mention props and transition, to performing a flawless program on the big stage. Those boxes that we stood on kept getting modified until they became multi-taskers, and got a lot heavier! I loved Doug! I just get all sentimental thinking about what show choir has done for me. I still refer to my experience and use the skills I learned when I'm teaching music or when I choreograph. It shaped the way I coach young performers every year in my school talent show. I still consider myself fairly shy, and it was Mr. Willert who first called me "gregarious." I love oldies, musicals, and show tunes because of Mr. Willert. Gosh, I get teary just thinking about the experience. How to form vowels, diction, soprano, alto, breathing through your diaphragm, lifting eyebrows, look, I think it's the sun! 1, 2, 3, pizzazz! I discovered Sandi Patti through show choir, believe it or not. I can go on and on. I can't wait for the book to come out! Mr. Willert, you taught me that there is no such thing as, "I can't sing." Anyone can improve with hard work and encouragement. You and Doug taught me to strive for excellence. Most importantly, you taught me to connect the music to the audience, a skill I use regularly when I lead worship, sing in choir, or teach music. I can say that show choir changed my life, but it's really you, Mr. Willert and Doug, who've changed my life.

Kuilane Cheun Garrido

I think 87-88 was one of the classiest shows Nogales had done, up to that point. Singin' in the Rain was timeless and the umbrella "kick line," unforgettable. The 88-89 show was the most innovative show up to that point, with the lighted tambourines in Songs of the South. Dave said that we had to "out BV, Bonita Vista," and we did just that!

In addition, a group of Nogales choral members started the Nogales Choirs Alumni Association (NCAA) around 1990, to provide support and raise money for the choral department. After team-building retreats and regular meetings, the NCAA debuted the Tournament of Champions Invitational (TOCI), which was actually formed as a fundraiser to support the Nogales choirs. After humble beginnings at Pasadena College in 1992 and subsequent moves to Chaffey and Whittier High School Auditoriums, the re-branded Tournament of Champions Show Choir Invitational grew to become one of the most highly anticipated premier events in the California show choir circuit. Who would have ever imagined that a group of Dave's kids from the barrios of La Puente, could create such an event, that would last for 17 years and would impact so very many show choir kids from throughout the state?!

Lawrence Vondrake Fitz

Hi everyone! I'm Megan Young, sister of Christie M. Young Pisapia, who was also in Chamber Singers at Nogales. I'm the class of 95 and I was in Chamber Singers from 91-95. I had Doug, Mr. Willert, Bo and Don Cloud. I couldn't have asked for better mentors. Bo encouraged and helped me when I was interested in drums, Mr. Willert was always there and a steadfast supporter. Doug taught amazing choreography. Don Cloud, I cannot say enough great things about you, from high school when you would bring in music for Jaime Alley, Ana K Chico and I to sing, to being blessed to call you my friend and choir mate when we were at Cal Poly together. You were always kind, helpful and encouraging. Heaven called you back too soon.

Megan Elizabeth Sander

What an exciting project you are working on, Dave. A while back, you asked something about letting you know how being involved with choir, affected our lives? I wanted to tell you that the one event that affected me in a very positive way was the senior letter that you wrote To Me, as I was graduating from high school. In that letter, you stated how proud you were of me for paying my debt off in full, all by myself, and you encouraged me to stay involved in a choir, whether it be Church or College. You said that I had a good voice and that I would be an asset to any choir. Well, I have continued to be in Church choirs all of my adult life, and have even built the confidence to sing solos, so thank you for believing in me!

Ellen Murray Herrick

So, I have a VHS copy of "Living on Dream Street." It is one of my very special possessions. The summer of 1986 was life changing for me. I had to leave my NHS Chamber Singer family. I missed a lot by not getting to graduate from NHS, and the loss of that group has stayed with me for 31 years. On the flip side, met my soul mate very early in life so that was kind of great. Thanks for sharing all these memories. You may not know why, Mr. Willert, I didn't get to graduate with some of my fellow Chamber Singers. I ran away from home, from an emotionally and physically abusive stepparent who took advantage of the fact my father was always working (love my Dad, he just didn't see it). There are two reasons I didn't leave sooner... my little brothers and my Chamber Singer family. I don't think you truly realize the impact your (and Doug's and even Margaret's) time and attention impacted my life. Don't know if anyone ever noticed, but my family never attended an event, with the exception of my father's attendance at Living On Dream Street. My world could have turned out VERY differently, without the support of you and those groups. The ability to join another similar and much younger show choir group was probably the only reason I finished high school. Anyway, you wanted to know... stronger for it. I have also gone on to support the arts in school through my son and my daughter. Giving back has been great therapy.

Lori Strait Gartland

It was the best of times, it was the worst of times (to quote Dickens). It was the late nineteen eighties, and I, like a lot of fourteen year old girls, felt like a fish out of water. I had very few friends, lots of responsibilities at home and a weight problem. My time spent in the Nogales High School Chamber Singers saved me from a debilitating depression. I was suddenly part of a community of performers that lifted my spirits and gave me something to look forward to. I was the youngest member of the group, and being the oldest child in my home, I enjoyed being "the baby." My Chamber Singers family must have sensed that because they nicknamed me "Baby Lu." I received oceans of support and validation from my choir director, who entrusted me with many solos. Each one stretched my vocal range and challenged my performance skills. I am always impressed with how impactful my time in show choir was. During my sophomore year of high school I was cast by Stephen Sondheim, himself, to play Little Red Riding Hood in a new musical he was developing called "Into The Woods," a role that I later went on to play on Broadway. I know that my time in the Nogales High School Chamber Singers, though brief, gave me the belief in myself that I needed to embrace that life changing opportunity. I will always cherish the time that I spent in the choir room, with my childhood friends and my very special choir teacher, Dave Willert.

LuAnne Ponce Montilla

I received my first stitches, ever, at our senior Spring Concert (1997). I forget the song, something about Eugene and being nerds? (Eli's Coming) But there was one part where I was supposed to be fake tripping down, but I miscalculated, because I tripped on top of the lowest riser and went chin first, into the ground. I was so high on adrenaline, that I didn't feel any pain, just "buzzing" from the area. I only knew I had any injury because when I went back stage after, Marissa mentioned that I was bleeding. Parents took me to the hospital before the concert ended, where they said the gash was deep enough to require 3-4 stitches.

Ken Bednar

When I saw Nogales choir at rehearsal for the very first time I knew this was for me! We were a small close-knit group of misfits, but we bonded more and more each day. This was my family for the next 3 1/2 years. The Choir room became our home. I remember after the great success we accomplished at the Young Americans Invitational, Chamber President Tracy Fair and I (VP) set out to create a letter for the Choir Dept., in hopes of becoming eligible for letters. I'm not sure how many were made for '87?

Gabriel Lomeli

Every day in choir was a great memory, but my first and favorite one would be my first competition. We won first place in all categories... it was just amazing! I think those were my best and most fun times in high school. Thank you for being you. I couldn't have had a better teacher and person in my life at that time. Choir kept me grounded.

Amanda Carr Smith

My "famous" big sister, Heather Tjaden Jefferson, had been a star in choir for three years when I entered high school. As a freshman, she was a senior. I was frequently referred to as "Heather's little sister." Though I definitely did not share the talent my sister had, I enjoyed singing and dancing and decided to try out. I made it to Chamber Singers my freshman year (though I must admit, I always wonder if it was because I was "Heather's little sister"). My sister took me under her wing, showed me the "ropes" of Nogales, allowed me to hang out with her friends at times, and we had an incredible year together in

Chamber Singers. Being the shortest, smallest, and youngest looking in the group, I was instructed by Doug to wear my hair in pigtails for competitions and shows. I was not one to rebel, so I obeyed, though I definitely didn't like it. Through the encouragement of Mr. Willert and Doug, throughout the years I grew in my confidence and I grew as my own person. The choir room itself was a safe haven for me in high school. Afraid of things that would go on outside of the choir room at Nogales, I was grateful that Mr. Willert always opened up his room and his heart for us. Being in Chamber Singers definitely defined my high school experience. It was where friendships were made and strengthened, lots of laughter shared, new experiences and places visited, and a love for doing our best was created (as well as a deep desire to win). High school is not an easy season in a young person's life. I would like to express my gratitude to Mr. Willert and Doug for the time and effort you put into helping me grow and creating an experience through choir, which allowed me to shine in my own way. I am now a mother of about 15 children (gave birth to only two of those in case you were wondering) and I pray that I will give my children this same room to shine in their own ways.

Allison Tjaden Tarus

I'd like to share two very special memories. 1. My time as Linus in the musical, "You're A Good Man Charlie Brown." I remember that time very, very fondly. I was pushed so far out of my comfort zone. I was a shy kid and didn't have much experience acting or singing. I was just thinking over and over, "What am I doing here?" The rest of the cast was so experienced and far better singers. The encouragement you had for me was just amazing. I truly felt like a star during the performances. So many friends and family members came to see the show and I loved all the attention. I still cannot speak in public to this day, so, I am so very amazed I was able to get on a stage and sing and dance songs with an amazing cast. I even had a solo with "My Blanket And Me," where I sang and danced by myself. I have a copy of that performance, but I have yet to see it. I'm afraid my performance will not do the memory justice. But I thank both of you for those precious memories and the amazing encouragement of a shy kid. 2. The Cuesta trip. So many great things came out of this trip. Being able to perform with Renegade for the first time, performing in Chamber Singers. But what I loved the most was exploring the quaint little city of Solvang with my group of friends. These are friends I have kept now for 25 years. We still talk everyday. I am the Godfather to some and others have become Godmothers and Godfather to my own daughter. These friendships were given the freedom to explore and blossom because of the Nogales Choir Department and I am truly grateful and thankful to have been a small part of its run. I was surprised to learn, that in choir, I could be myself and people would still love me. It was a time of great change in my life. My friends accepted who I was and I accepted who I was. I found out how lucky I was to find a group of friends who accepted me. Thank you.

Leonel Diaz

You and Doug taught me a valuable lesson that has stuck with me through the years: no matter what, the show must go on! In 1991, I was standing on top of a box, singing the opening of, Respect, when the mic cord fell, clattering to the floor, no vocals to be heard! I was mortified! I think Lori Halopoff Fenelon grabbed the cord and helped me put it back together, all while singing and continuing choreography. During our final competition, in 1993 (Tops n Pops?), my microphone was completely out, for the opening number, Masquerade! I just pushed through and projected as best I could. So many countless mishaps backstage, only to run onstage with the pizzazz smile. It has helped me in countless performances over the years! I almost forgot! Do you remember in 1993, that you both gave me the inspiration to start a show choir group at Rincon Junior High, that year? I choreographed and Mrs. Estes chose the music. We competed that year at the Fullerton Jazz Festival, and Dave, you lent me your conducting gloves for the a cappella. Alex was but a wee and adorable little lad. We won first place! Doug, I may have stolen some moves from you, but thank you both! It really meant a lot to those awesome kids and me! Being in choir was a magical time that I hold dear to my heart, even these many years later. Lifelong friendships and many valuable lessons learned. Dave, you were a great father figure to many of us and taught me the rewards of hard work, discipline and focus. There were times that we didn't get what we wanted (first place)! But we learned from our mistakes and kept a positive attitude to go back and try again and again... and the best part was... it paid off! I can only hope my son has an opportunity to experience such a wonderful high school chapter with a great teacher. But it seems like capturing lightening in a bottle. Thank you!

Tassa Hampton-Varga

I believe that over the years we can all agree, we had an extremely remarkable choir director who led us on a path of great High School memories... from the first tryouts finding our names on a list of groups we made it on from Uptown Singers, Madrigals, Madrijazz, Silhouette, Dream Street, and Chamber Singers. Experiencing the try-on outfits to actually performing with them on. The rigorous practices, bumping into each other to make to our spots on time. Hitting that perfect face while singing. Getting rid of props on time and hitting those notes, the famous curling of the hair and getting it down perfectly. Experiencing each competition with the Mickey mittens on....

Joanna Gallagher-Miranda

I remember when my brother, Dwayne, was in Chamber Singers and I would go to his performances, wishing I was up on the stage with them. When I finally got the chance, I was so excited, and of course, nervous, because I couldn't sing! I still can't sing to this day! Lol Dave and Doug still gave me the opportunity to perform with all of these talented students, who would become family. In choir, I was surprised to learn that I wasn't as shy as I thought I was! After I graduated, I still came back to watch rehearsals, chaperoned a Washington D.C. trip and had the honor of becoming Alex's babysitter, during the first year of his life. I love that we have been reunited again.

Sabrina Ganier Cope

I remember that in 1997, there were challenges regarding attitude, since we didn't get 1st place consistently like BV (Bonita Vista) did. I always thought we had a more entertaining show than BV, but we were always ranked 2nd, right behind them. But I remember Mr. Willert lecturing us that our attitude had to change, and that we had to be grateful, not to mention the fact that Chamber Singers wasn't always focused during rehearsals, before competition season. I really believe that we get what we practice. Finally, at the Chula Vista competition, we competed with all of our heart, and we got the biggest standing ovations from the audience in San Diego, alongside Burroughs, whom also had an exiting show. When we got our 3rd Place, we were proud of it. The lesson: Winning isn't always everything... but attitude is! Speaking of time limits, I remember in 1997 Chamber went overtime at the Arcadia competition. With the actual scoring, we would have gotten 2nd place behind Brea but someone at the competition did not properly keep track of the time and we went overtime. That would have gotten us 6th place. Instead, as a compromise, Rollie Maxson deducted 5-10 points giving us 3rd place. We still got the Showmanship award. I have to add that in 1998, whenever we got a 4th Place trophy, I wouldn't be happy. After you left, when Dream Street got a 4th Place trophy at the Glendora competition, I was happy! I think Chamber and Dream Street took awards for granted.

Ruben D. Hoyos

I have witnessed how Music truly moves and heals souls! With God's grace, Music has driven me to grow stronger in my Faith and has led me to meet some incredible people and build life-long friendships, I would have never imagined... Forever grateful, blessed and humbled by your inspiration! I thought being involved in Music would only be a hobby, but somehow it turned out to be my career! Something I love to do and can never get tired of.

Mary Anne Garcia

Being in choir was the best time and experience of my high school life! Loved the high of performing and being and meeting new friends, and how good it felt to perform on stage was so awesome. Wish I had a time machine to go back, cuz I loved it so much!

Jill Myer Wirz

You will never know how much me being a part of Dream Street Singers (84-87) and Chamber Singers (85-87) helped to make my high school years memorable! It was so wonderful to be friends with such cool & talented people. We were family. Inside the choir room was my safe haven!!! I loved every competition we ever competed in! My first trips to Disneyland & Knott's Berry Farm were with DSS & CS! I fondly remember the trips to San Francisco, San Diego & Del Coronado!! The patience that you and Doug had with us was simply amazing! Before there was Glee, there was Nogales Chamber Singers!

Rosa Grimes

Although I had been in choir from the time I was in elementary school, I never felt the way I did on stage, in front of my peers, wanting nothing more than to hear our name called for the first time ever. Nogales had yet to win at any competition. I remember the fear of not remembering what to do as I walked on the stage that first competition. Nerves raw and heart racing, I had the voice of Mr. Willert swirling in my head to smile, breathe and enjoy. I took that fear and turned it into one of the most exciting times in my life. We did not win at that competition, but we did win later in the year. All of the sweat, hard work, envy and faith in ourselves, was worth that moment Nogales was called up to the stage! Being in Chamber and Dream Street was an experience like no other. When I entered the choir room, I always knew I was with family. I could be who I really was, without judgment. OK, it was not always perfect as sometimes we fought like siblings, but the love was always there to get us through. No matter what was happening outside of school, I always had the comfort of knowing Mr. Willert was there to catch me if I fell. He was like a dad to me. He taught me how to deal with the many personalities that stepped through the door of our choir room. He gave me the opportunity to be a leader and a teacher. He also built-up every one of us, before we competed, and never let us be "spoiled sports," when we did not place (and that was more often than not). Mr. Willert taught us the value of having a good work ethic and the ability to see our mistakes as opportunities to learn and grow. I learned to take chances especially singing solos. I also learned to smile and let outside worries melt away when on stage. I use both of these skills in my classroom. They make me be present with my students and try things I think may work.

I am a teacher because I wanted to emulate him in the classroom. I work hard to instill in my students and daughter the value of hard work and the joy of being part of a community. So many lessons I learned from Mr. Willert... and for that, he will always hold a special place in my heart! I think at Nogales, Mr. Willert and choir were a lifeline for many of us. So many had the not ideal home situations, whether it was due to divorce, absent parents, little money, or other instabilities. Many others felt like they did not belong anywhere at school. With Mr. Willert and choir, we had stability, expectations, hard work, and fun. He gave many of us a safe place, father figure, and family we craved. Perhaps, Nogales was a place with many needy kids or it was the perfect combination of different kids from different backgrounds that needed guidance. However, I like to think of choir as being the perfect storm with the perfect leader, a place of love and acceptance. I cannot imagine that Mr. Willert would have found that at any other school... but I am slightly biased!

Teresa Cimino

Choir was amazing. I was very surprised to learn that I liked to sing, and how to be a leader. Wish I didn't have to move, but 'cause of you, Mr. Willert, we are all still friends, more than 30 years later! Where do you think a lot of us kids would be if it weren't for the guidance and love you gave us? In the time that we all needed support, you were there and we were all one big close family! Thank you, Dave... for being there for us.

Greg Wells

It's not just about the lessons you taught us at competitions. It's the life lessons too. Whenever my now, 10 year old daughter, wanted to give up on something important to her, I reminded her to focus. When she would start giving excuses on why she can't do something, I always tell her that, "Success finds a way, failure finds an excuse." I don't think she quite understood what I meant until I was working with an older Girl Scout Troop member of mine, who had just stopped trying, and was making excuses as to why she wasn't completing her Silver Award Project (the highest award for the level). I led a lesson for all my girls about finding their way to success, to always try their hardest, to problem solve, keep your cool, etcetera. Then, I showed them the few old pictures from high school, I had left, and they saw that quote on the choir room wall. It was like a switch was flipped, and they understood, it takes hard work, and working together to accomplish some of the hardest goals. (Yes, that older girl expanded her team to include more than just her family to complete her project, and my 10 year old, well, let's just say, she's focused). I honestly don't know if I would have my work ethic without that quote, or having learned teamwork in the dynamics that were present in the Dream Street, Chamber, or Silhouette Singer groups I was in.

Melissa Siaotong

Choir gave me a place that was like home and a safe place from everything I had to deal with in high school.

Nadia Stone

I have so many memories from 1984-88, when I was fortunate enough to be in choir. One memory was being a part of the Fullerton College Jazz Soloist Competition, my senior year, where I had the opportunity to sing for Richard Carpenter. That was awesome. But I think just being a part of a group, that I was able to grow and feel safe and learn with, was the best thing ever. My parents were divorced and being one of seven kids, it was hard for my single mother to make ends meet so home life wasn't always easy. Show choir at Nogales was a place to be where I was supported, where I had people around me that were so different in all the best ways, yet we were the same, as well. We were loved and encouraged and we were happy. It's where I learned how to work hard and see the reward that came from that hard work. I also met my husband, Brad Salsman there. Brad joined the group in 1987 and was only in the group his senior year. He loved it so much and he has always regretted not being a part of the group before that year. One of his best memories, he says, is when he was asked to "play" the green guitar as a solo spot in our La Bamba act. Brad and I owe a lot to Dave and Margaret Willert, not just because of all the love and support we received from them in our show choir classes, but because Brad asked me to Senior Prom, that year, but I didn't say yes, right away, because I couldn't afford a dress. Dave talked with me and said he and Margaret would love to help me out. So, Margaret Willert, took me shopping, and bought me my prom dress. Thinking about it now, I still get teary eyed. What a selfless thing for them to do. It remains my second favorite dress, to this day, the first, being the wedding gown I wore the day Brad and I were married. We've been married 25 years now, I sometimes wonder what would have happened if I hadn't been able to go to prom with him that year?

Lila (Orozco) Salsman & Brad Salsman

I started in Chamber Singers at Nogales, as the only freshman girl who made it into the group. I learned so much being a 2nd soprano, especially never knowing how to harmonize or read music before. I was honored and part of a group that won awards, and the moments where our harmonies would hit just the right notes, I still remember the goose-bumps I could feel when we were all in sync. I loved going to Florida and WDW for the very first time, singing "Operator" at the pool, and then loving every Disney moment. I remember going backstage and how much I enjoyed seeing behind the scenes of WDW and DLR when we also competed in Showstoppers. I remember going to Showstoppers, just the year before, when I was still in Jr. High, to support my sister, Margaux, and how special it felt to then be a part of the group, instead of just watching from the crowd. We also got to perform, "Never Walk Alone" that year, a few times, and the emotion, power, feeling when the entire group sang that song, was just pure magic. I remember my sister was once home, sick, and you forced me to substitute in, for her "Never Walk Alone" solo during class one day, and it was TERRIFYING, but also ignited my love for singing that song. While I didn't hold a candle to my sister's singing skills, you and Doug gave everyone the opportunity to shine. I remember holding our end pose for nearly ten minutes, one day, and how important it was to hold until the curtain went down. How important it was for these little details, when putting on a show, would later come into play in my career as a Video Producer in Hollywood. The following year, I was a sophomore and also in Chamber Singers. Everything was psychedelic and I wasn't comfortable in my skin, but the more I performed, the stronger I felt. I remember how much heart the group also had, as we struggled to fill a talent gap, with a lot of the major singers/dancers leaving, the year prior. Michael Washington really gave our group that spark, and the heart, with "The Impossible Dream" was inspiring. The following year, was a big heartbreak. I remember over the summer learning that you would not return. I felt like I was broken up with. We all understood that you had to go to a better environment, but I remember feeling like I wanted to change high schools, to be with you and Doug again. I remember, it was especially hard knowing that my sister and Kramer were both going to help out at Diamond Bar, and it was hard to understand. I also remember making really great friends with a lot of the DB kids, as well, and watching them sing songs that were meant to be "ours," and also rooting for them. That year, we were hopeful that we could have something that resembled what we used to have with you and Doug, but our director didn't pull through. And my senior year, my heart was just not into it. Although I became the president in 1999-2000, I rarely committed to practices fully, the director did not have enough show choir knowledge, that I felt I had to consult him on what little I knew, and to be honest, I had lost my passion for it by then, and I didn't even bother to remember all the words for the solo I had in our show. All in all, I only consider my time in show choir valuable, where I learned from you and Doug, what true showmanship really means. I've also met quite a few co-workers at Disney, that were in competing show choirs, like John Burroughs, and it's something we bond over. Other things I remember, holding my smile for what seemed like hours, and that my facial muscles would hurt. I want to thank you for my experience, as it's been invaluable in shaping who I am today. It's powerful to see that an educator can evoke that kind of passion within a team, and then as an adult, we utilize those same skills of pizzazz, and focus throughout our life and career. You have truly shaped who I am today, even if I was only honored with two years in your choir. Thank you to you and Doug for turning what, at the time, would be considered a poor high school, and making it look and feel like a billion bucks! You are an exceptional person.

Abigail Yap Su

My confidence and self-esteem was low and I cared what others thought. I wanted to be like all the other girls. I ditched school, changed schedules, just to be in the chorus room... What I was taught and learned... Dorothy Nacita Swayne, and I would play with the scales during practice and laughed at ourselves as we made our pun staff. Remember that, Dorothy? Genevieve, Becky and a girl named Jennifer, I believe, encouraged me to smile, make expressions and come out of my comfort zone, to be the best I could be. I was finally able to be proud of myself, and what I did on stage. It also brought people like, my Grassy Knoll friend and Mary Ann Garcia, into my life, who accepted me for exactly who I was. This being said, I did experience a bad situation the following years that could have brought me into a Great Depression... honestly, I remember making that smile and having those friends and deciding to be the people I admired so much in chorus.

Maria Block

1984-1988 Chamber Singers; 1985-1988 Dream Street (Great memories and people!)

All of these years later, I still get to sing in a choir or do a solo every now and then. I'm still in China most of the time. We are looking forward to being back, this summer for a family wedding, and my parents' 50th anniversary. I have a daughter who is a sophomore in college! Time passes too quickly.

Michele Maxwell Appleby

This is just a general memory about being in choir for the first time: sitting on the bus on our way to the Burroughs competition and I remember sitting next to someone in our traveling clothes, only to arrive at the show in performance clothes. It was like turning into a super hero when the call was needed! That skill became useful in college performances too! Apparently my first year was supposed to be a "rebuilding" year, having lost so many seniors from the previous year. I don't remember how many shows we won, but I definitely had a blast in show choir. I don't know if you and Doug remember, but I didn't even want to audition for Chamber at first... you guys convinced me, that it would be fun! And it was! Your choir was where I learned what it took to create a complete show. It was more than learning the songs and choreography. It was staging, costumes, props, musical arrangements and special effects! It truly changed the course of my life. Here's what I learned from you through the choir. You can bring greatness out of someone by showing them how much you truly believe in their potential with the addition of their hard work! Being in Chamber Singers gave me a family in a new land. I moved to Nogales as a junior and it was definitely culture shock for me. Getting into choir helped me to find my kindred spirits. I suppose that not every memory we have of choir is "candy canes and unicorns," so here's a memory I would like to call "The Ghost of Chucky." "Chucky" is the name I'm using because number one, I don't want to defame a person's name and number two, I don't actually remember the name of the person this is about. So, it was my junior year/1st year in choir and I was playing 2nd keyboard for Dream Street. We were about to go on stage to perform. Kurt Schlatter was there with us as he was our chief tech guy, but he was a freshman. Chucky was there as well. He was a senior and had been a band crewmember before. As we were checking that the keyboards were ready to go, Don Cloud, our main keyboard player, plugged in all the cables and got our keyboards working. We had sound and gave the thumbs up to Dave and Doug. When the curtains opened and it was time to count off... there was no sound from the main keyboard. NO SOUND! The lights were on, but NOTHING!!! Don, quickly jumped into action and ran off stage and pushed a grand piano that was off on the wings back onto the stage! Thanks to him the show went on! At the end of the show, it was the first time I had ever seen Dave so upset! He was still composed and professional but it was different. He was definitely steaming. He asked us what had happened? Obviously, we would not have given the thumbs up from the band if we were not ready to go. What Kurt witnessed was that as the curtains were opening, Chucky decided that Don had connected the "incorrect" cable and decided to "fix" it for us. By doing this, he basically disconnected the main keyboard from our amps, rendering it soundless! From that moment, Chucky was banned from the band crew and Kurt became the main guy for the rest of his high school career. Also, anytime we ever had a tech mishap, we would attribute it to the Ghost of Chucky! Good thing bad details fade over time and just become funny. Right? Fun times!

Kramer Kurtz Ison

I loved everything about Show Choir - Competitions, holiday shows, wearing curlers to school, overwhelming McDonalds when we'd all rush in for a quick bite before a competition. I'll also never forget my senior year when I got the chance to play the piano for the holiday show, with the encouragement of Don.

Bonnie Chacon Hooes

After you and Doug left, in 1998, I had years of therapy, so now I can finally talk about it! Just kidding. I was a junior and I did feel a little cheated when you two left. Three years with you two, and on my year to lead, you left! I understood why, but it was my year as president and the replacement director was a joke. So, my senior year turned into being a choir director for the whole choir department. However, the lesson was invaluable and helped my leadership skills. I did win the Branson Jubilee National Invitational Top Male Soloist Award that year, so I made lemonade with a few sour lemons. We couldn't have done it without the help of great friends such as Ruben Dario Hoyos Marin, Abigail Yap Su, Clifford Banagale, Antonio Palacios and many more. We all came together that year. Looking back, I have to say... we were the talk of the town my freshman year when we decided to wear two different colors between the boys and girls. We looked sharp that year and took Showstoppers by storm!

Mitchell Asa

The choir was more than just a choir. It was a family. I learned from both you and Margaret how to nurture, to teach, to support and how to kick someone in the butt when needed. Margaret, you taught me how to be an independent woman while letting your artistic husband do his thing. One clear and concise memory I have is Teresa's and my nicknames. Mine was Butt and Teresa's was Boob. My mother even got necklace charms made for us that said that!

Tracy Fair Fort

It's been said that, with learning, more is "caught than from what's taught." From Dave Willert, I "caught" composure. In my choir years, I never saw Dave lose his composure (my perception). He was always cool under pressure. When things got tense or chaotic; he didn't react by going ballistic or "losing it," he remained calm yet stern. That composure is what I strive to emulate still today, to the best of my abilities. For example, at a Chamber competition in Newhall, it was clear that our show was going to slightly exceed the time limit. Dave had informed the host prior, and the host said it was no big deal. Yet when the results were announced, we came in second! Oddly, in the announcements, the host felt the need to explain, that we would've won if we hadn't exceeded the time limit. The host had caved at protest from the other competitors about our shows length. After awards were handed out, Dave had a 'chat' with the host backstage. I was in the area packing equipment, and 'eavesdropped' on the chat. The host was apologizing to Dave, and explaining how she was getting flack from the other competitors. With composure intact, he said something like; her words lacked integrity & backbone because she caved to the protest, after granting us the grace in time limit. Monday comes around, and it was announced that the competition results changed from us getting second to becoming tied for first.

Dion De Rosas

A memory came to mind I wanted to share with you. It was the end of my junior year of high school, so about May 1994. I was the president of Dream Street. You had asked the class members to sign up if they were interested in continuing choir and noticed I didn't sign up. You could have let that be. But instead, you pulled me aside. You wondered what was going on. No one knew at school, including my best friends. I remember being deeply sad, maybe a little hopeless, because my dad had received a pink slip. It was a notice that he would be laid off from the Department of Water and Power unless others with more seniority decided to retire or voluntarily leave. I was just trying to save every penny I could in case my dad lost his job. Choir wasn't expensive, but dresses and shoes and other expenses added up. I loved choir – there's so much joy in the creativity and expression and camaraderie. It's where I felt at home. The idea of losing one of my favorite activities in the world was heartbreaking, so I started crying those halting sobs where you just can't catch your breath. Your eyes were wide and you smiled. You offered a support program that provided for a dress because of the costume charge. And then all of a sudden I got to keep a little bit of the joy I needed. I scraped together enough money to spray paint my old shoes into the right color. And in the end, enough people retired for my dad to keep his job. But I'll always remember how much relief I felt knowing I got to keep participating in show choir. It gave me an outlet to be a part of something fun and exciting when times weren't so great at home. So thank you, Mr. Willert, for noticing when I didn't sign up and doing something about it. I wish all students had someone like that in their life.

Uyen Mai

I was in A cappella, my freshman year with Mrs. Patterson. I took that class because I loved to sing, and figured it would be an easy A. Then Mr. Willert became our director, my sophomore year. That was 1979... and that year he changed my life. When he told us that he wanted to put together a show choir... one to compete against other schools, I was so excited! We were the beginning... the foundation of what is now an outstanding competition choir ranked among the best. With homemade dresses and tons of heart, we gave our all to Mr. Willert and his dream. We received no trophies, but we all felt like we were the best! Dave's encouraging words and positive attitude kept us going, striving to be the best we could. I had some issues, personally, and Mr. Willert always had faith in me when no one else did. When I was in that choir room, nothing else mattered to me. I could be "me," and that was amazing. Being a soloist presented some challenges... I remember that I would always lose my voice on the way to comp. At first, Mr. Willert and Doug were stressed, but Dave soon realized it was my nerves, and he was prepared for me... with honey and lemon! Lol. I would have no voice, but the second I walked out, on to the stage... my voice was there! His advice, understanding and comforting words were lifesavers to me. He pushed me and always had faith in me. My dream was to join Young Americans, and I auditioned my senior year. What a dream! Sadly, I was involved in a bad car accident after graduation, that left me in traction for six months, and my dream faded. But I auditioned, which, to me, was enough! Without the encouragement from Dave, that would have always been just a dream. What he has done for so many kids, over the years, warms my heart. You are an angel to many, Dave, and we all love and respect you more than you'll ever imagine. God bless you!

Kim Benton Frederick

I still remember when our Nogales group, in 1985, got to tour NBC studios, and my mom, Maryanne Polite Brazil, chaperoned. We all got to experience the taping of the game show, Card Sharks! You were and are a huge inspiration to all of your students, kind caring and firm when needed. I also want to say thank you, for creating lasting friendships with students who might have never been friends if not for the bond that was created through your choral groups. Thank you from the bottom of my heart for making high school so much fun. I greatly look forward to reading your book once it's published. I know it will be amazing!

Amy Wells

Just like to say thank you to Dave Willert, Doug Kuhl, Della Long and Margaret Willert for giving us your time and place to call our second home and family. You guys made such a positive impact on my life. I'm sure many more students would agree too!

Lisa Castilleja Rosas

I learned not to be afraid of taking chances. To sing with passion and to perform your heart out, and love every second of it! I remember standing on stage before the lights went up... and the hum of the crowd just before we began... taking a deep breath... just as we began... to bring the house down, of course!

Brent Sanchez

I went To Nogales High from 1983 thru 1987. In Junior HS the Chamber Singers came to perform and I could not wait to tryout, I was so amazed. My freshman year I tried out. Now I do not have the best voice but I think Dave let me in because I wanted it so much. The group kept me on the straight and narrow life along with the peer pressures I had no time for because he kept us too busy! And we were all like family. Dave and Doug you have given up your own family time to make sure we were the best. I sincerely thank you for all the sacrifices and dedication you and your families made. I am a better person because of both of you! I hope you enjoy your retirement.

Nanette Varela

Tricey was in choir with you going into her junior year, when we found out you were leaving. We were heart broken, devastated, and all those other adjectives. It was like being a product of divorce. There was a lot of anger. On top of that, we got a, I don't know, can't really call him a teacher. Parents were really voting for Lawrence to get the job, as a replacement, but knowing you could not be replaced. I know and understand why you left, but it still took some time to get over. I was so happy when Tricey decided to go into choir and you were still there because I knew she was getting the best choir teacher ever! And I am glad she at least got you for two years. Big shout out to the parents that helped pick up the pieces; Cheryl Pomeroy, Norma Palacios and I know I'm forgetting a few so I'm sorry. Love you Mr. Willert and all the memories that you gave to me, and my daughter.

Norma Jeffries

I work in a before and after school care program for elementary aged children and they have many times asked me why I always have music on? The kids even did a dance to the song Barbara Ann and I had them do some choreography to the song. It shocked the parents that even little kinders were able to participate along with my older kids! I think that's the best family night we ever had! My daughter, to this day asks me why I know the words to so many songs? She now is in the 4th grade and just loves music in general. The impact show choir had on me is great as I made many friends even though I was shy and not very outgoing. I remember the trips to San Luis Obispo and Cuesta College, and changing in a moving bus. Choir gave me a small place where I felt I belonged.

Catherine Pinard Rhodes

I enjoyed all the fun... from going to San Francisco to Phantom of the Opera and of course your son's baby shower! Such amazing memories I made in such a short time with you, Doug, Bo and Mrs. Willert... you planted a seed that blossomed into confidence that I needed as I stepped into adulthood! You challenged me as well as always pushed for us to step outside of our comfort zones... my first and only solo for Spring Concert my first year was a wonderful experience... forever grateful!

Nancy Jovel Penman

Hi, Mr. Willert...sorry it has taken me a bit to chime in, but I honestly feel at a loss for adequate words to encapsulate what being a member of your Nogales Choirs from 1986-1990 meant to me!! I was in Chamber Singers for all four High School years and loved every moment! Dream Street Singers '87-'90 and any other choir that needed support in those years!! Living On Dream Street" was definitely a highlight, being cast as Snoopy in "You're A Good Man, Charlie Brown" challenged & stretched me in new ways! In my choir years, I learned teamwork and to always push myself to excellence... deep relationships through hard work and dedication were formed and to add "pizzazz" to every aspect of my life! Due to your influence, I went on to study music at UCLA & got my BA in music education... I have taught music in elementary schools & directed countless children's musicals... teaching them all the essence of "pizzazz" & love for music... you believed in me, poured courage into me, and drew out the gifts placed within me! I am forever grateful for you, esteem you highly, and love you so very much!

Heather Tjaden Jefferson

I can honestly say that I was excited and couldn't wait to get to Concert Choir every single day! Choir class was a safe, super fun and nourishing environment. The teaching style we were given helped me to not feel so self-conscious in participating during class. What a blessing Concert Choir was to my life, to my heart. Thank you Mr.Willert for treating us all so kindly and gently, while teaching us, so we could sing freely and to our greatest abilities. Thank you, Mr. Willert, from the bottom of my heart!

Patricia Mountain Romero

I was an amazingly shy girl, with thick glasses, who lived music. I never thought I was good enough, because I didn't make junior high choir. My neighbor, Troy Peace, encouraged me to tryout. He loved the group. So, I mustered all the strength to tryout and made it into Dream Street for my first two years (85, 86). I really wanted to be in Chamber, but that came later. I did both groups for my final two years. I just want to thank you for the opportunity and all the fun times that made high school so much fun.

Initially, our bond was music. Then we came to love you, and yes, Doug. Then we began to love ourselves, and then each other. For many, choir was the family they didn't have, while for others, an enhancement of our real family. We found lifelong friends, with a bond that has been tough to break. We had so much fun. We had love drama and regular personal issues. A few choir couples even lasted all this time! Of course, Kevin and I connected years later and have been married 11 years and counting! You were the one who created that atmosphere. You welcomed everyone and gave everyone a chance. You showed Christ's love, even when we didn't realize that's what it was. Now I know without a doubt, that's what it was, whether intentional or not.

As for specific memories, how we placed was apparently not my focus, cuz I don't remember from one to the next, like some others! I remember changing on the bus. Looking forward to more time together outside of school, whether extra practice, fun at someone's house or fieldtrips and weekends away. I remember getting in trouble in San Francisco, because the girls' room had an adjoining room next to the boys, and we hung out. It was all innocent, but man was it scary to have to come back and give an account to Mr. Baker! I remember being chosen to be a first or second soprano section leader. I was also picked as a backup for 'Singing in the Rain,' with Lila. I remember wearing rags in my hair to make curls on competition days. I also remember being chosen to record your songs. I know I have that tape somewhere!

You obviously made an impression, because hundreds still choose to support and follow you. People think that I am crazy, when I mention I have friends that are still my closest, since the age of five! They are even more impressed that we keep in touch with a teacher that made an impact! That's you, Dave. We are your legacy. Like in Harry Potter, we are your, horcrux!

When we heard of your stroke, it shook our family, as we knew exactly how you and your family were going to be impacted, on many levels, as our mom, a supporter of all of us, also survived a stroke. But, as usual, you handled it with grace and probably even a little pride! You pulled through and you haven't let it stop you. I can't be anything but proud of you for your fighting spirit and tenacity.

All that, to really just say, thank you Dave! Although, Mr. Willert, is how you'll always be remembered... out of respect.

Lizsa Halopoff Pinedo and Kevin Pinedo

SO MANY MEMORIES

- *Being somewhat forced to audition for choir (totally insecure and shy) at the end of my freshman year. I think I sang a song from "Annie." Then seeing my name on that list for Chamber Singers... I had no idea what I was getting myself into, but I also knew I was doing exactly what I was meant to do. That first year I did choir and drill team. I dropped drill team mid year. My heart had found a new home.*
- *Leaving choir period dripping with sweat... And they still made us take P.E.?!!*
- *Curling my hair in the back of the choir room and the leg of my chair slipped off the step. I fell backwards and I remember laughing so hard we were crying. Didn't help the makeup situation!*
- *Hanging out in Mr. Willert's office during lunch. The choir room was our favorite place to lunch and it was open for us every day.*
- *At Cuesta, singing "In the Hills of Shiloh" outside as a warm up and to get into the zone. The hills were green, the fog was thick and it was almost eerie. But beautiful.*
- *My first year was a rebuild year. Learned quickly what the term "green" meant.*
- *Sweeping at Burroughs. I think it was my Junior year on my birthday. That's the one win I remember the most. We worked hard for it.*
- *Simultaneously discovering my love for photography, by using my choir friends as subjects. Historian was my favorite gig!*
- *My ears were not pierced before choir and I had to wear clip-ons. Sometimes during performances they would fly off. I finally convinced my dad to let me pierce my ears just for choir. As an adult, I never wear earrings. Go figure!*
- *The anticipation of a performance. Setting up backstage. Waiting in the dark. Heart pounding. Clearing*

my throat. Over and over again. Hearing our name be announced. The crowd going wild... And those curtains going up. What an absolute thrill. Every. Single. Time.

- *My mom would cry watching me perform. She was so proud of me. I'm a mom now. I understand those tears. I'm thankful she had those moments too.*
- *Singing solos. There were bigger and better soloists than me, but I'll always remember the rush.*
- *Mr. Willert and Doug were so protective of me... Boyfriends, friends, they never hesitated to tell me what they really thought.*
- *I will always remember the feeling of wishing Mr. Willert was my dad. (I had dad issues.) Mr. Willert made me feel like I was his daughter. He treated me as such. It was genuine. It was real.*
- *Going to Washington D.C. my sophomore year. My mom and sister went too. "Just Love Me." The sea of people on that field during the big event. The cherry blossom trees.*
- *Scatting. It was NOT my thing. I cringed every time we had to.*
- *Pizzazz! and Focus!*
- *Friends. Working hard next to them. Day after day. Failing. Winning. Crying. Laughing. Lots and lots of laughing. Loving them. Feeling deeply connected.*
- *I can't imagine not having those three years of choir. It gave me purpose and confidence. Choir is still so much a part of me; so much a part of how I became ME. It's not just one memory or story... It's all of it!*

Debbie Bailey Lee

CHAPTER 17

Memories From The Diamond Bar High School Show Choirs 1998-2005

I spent enough time at Diamond Bar High School, *seven years*, to make a beautiful potpourri of wonderful memories! My former students, of course, have their own special memories, which I would like to share here.

I remember all of those times when we won Showmanship and Brea Olinda won Musicianship and everyone said if you lose musicianship, you get 2nd place, but our musicianship score was high enough to get 1st place! The big shocker was that one Arcadia competition, where musicianship was weighted higher than showmanship, and we actually won 1st place! What I remember most about that time was that everyone cared about the choruses and in a way, about each other. I got sad around April, because I knew there would be no more competitions. Pretty soon we'd do the spring concerts, then it was graduation. Honestly though, my time in Show Choir greatly influenced my academic and career path. And I do value my time at DBHS.

Tsar Agus

I was there for your first year at DBHS, which I believe was 98? And then I was there for my junior year, through 2000, I believe, and then left choir when I went on independent study. I am so happy that you came into my life when you did. You made me believe that I had a special gift. You gave me confidence in my singing that I never had before. With your encouragement, I pursued my dream and that dream has become a reality for me. I am incredibly blessed to be touring the country, doing what I love for a living. We, unfortunately, lost many of my childhood photos, including those from high school choir. I'll never forget the fabulous costumes, though! My favorite was the white dress, kind of a sailor cut, with a red bow and rainbow sequins. I'll never forget traveling in the school buses, hair up in sponge curls, putting our stage makeup on, and all of the "pizazz!"

Daniella Dalli

I can say without question, my experiences of show choir were some of the best in my life. I met some of the most amazing people and traveled to places I probably would never have gone otherwise. To this day, when I look back and think of high school, I can't help but smile. I'm truly thankful for all I learned; not just about music... but about life!

Priscilla Sosa Vela

In regards to my favorite show, I'd say 2002-2003 in Marquis. I loved the mash-up of the Beatles and Moulin Rouge. I remember getting goosebumps every time we sang, "Yesterday," a cappella. It was such a dramatic and unexpected opening, because it started the show so quiet and grew louder, as the show went on.

Julia Brooke Haager-Devin

We had no idea what we were in store for! The biggest improvement was learning showmanship. We got our pizzazz! Finally, choreography! Excitement! It was so much fun once you and Doug came into town. I just remember that you took our group to the next level. Better costumes, better dance routines, first place after first place trophies! It was amazing, and we got group names that suited our school, from Allegra to Solitaire and Encore to Marquis. One random memory is when we were practicing and you wanted us to keep smiling, no matter what. You told us a story of a girl who got bit by a spider on stage, but kept smiling through it!

Lauren Nicole Poling

Fifth period was my favorite time of day at school. It meant that I got to sing and dance alongside some of the most talented people I had ever come across and we were a community! Looking back now, as an adult, with two kids of my own and one of them growing an interest in choir and theatre, I am realizing how pivotal it was to my growing in confidence and in doing what I loved to do: sing and dance and perform! You and the team made it all come alive for us! It was so fun and I still talk about it, so much so that my husband can probably recite the stories (and he did not attend DB!)

Tiffany Rush Harper

"Fun zone," best describes my high school years! They were years when I had to deal with my parents split and divorce. Since then, I've always liked to find ways of escape like reading and singing. Show choir was a fun escape from all the craziness of my life. I learned the power of positivity in choir! You were the first teacher that came into my life, who was always happy, and always smiling, and you wanted us to be the same! Since then, I walk around always happy and smiling. I try to make the most of every day. Also, you taught me you can work hard, yet still have fun doing it!

Ruby Minori

I remember having a day once a month when whoever wanted to, would sing for the class, anything we wanted to sing. When you would give us our new song and once we learned it, you would be so proud when we sang in concert. We were family and you made sure that's what we felt. The choir award night in 2001 was a fun night.

Erica Schneider

Our shows were like Disneyland shows! They left people in awe, smiling from ear to ear. They always had a special flow, and an almost over the top euphoric sense. We had lots of good times in choir in those days. Especially before 9-11, when the world was a different place and money was more easily raised for such fun shenanigans!

Jessica Marvin-Jones

I want to let you know that I really learned a lot from my experience in show choir when you taught at DBHS. Show choir, to me, wasn't just a place where I went to perform, but it was a place where I learned about life, friendships and the ability of music to cure any situation I was faced with. I met my lifelong friends in choir. Choir was always a safe place I could go to forget about anything that was difficult in life. I always knew that once I walked through those doors, you would have us doing some goofy activity to help us break out of our comfort zones and to truly be in the moment. I want to say, I know I wasn't always the most focused student and could easily be distracted. However, despite that fact, I never once took my experience for granted. High school would not have been the same had I not been in show choir, under your direction. This experience is one I will never forget! I often think back on my time in choir with such joy and happiness. The friendships and bonds I made while in the choir program are things that cannot be duplicated. You taught us the importance of focus, determination, unity and truly enjoying life and living the moment. I am forever grateful to you for my experience in show choir! Please know that my words cannot ever fully convey what those four years meant to me. I know, without a doubt, that being in show choir shaped me into the strong, caring, loving and hardworking individual I am today. It is at this time that I am awaiting bar results to hopefully become a licensed California attorney. I will always carry the lessons you taught us, with me into the future. When things get tough, I have never failed to recall the words placed on the choir walls, during my time at DBHS, "Success Finds A Way and Failure Finds An Excuse!"

Tiffany Yanez Gruenberg

My favorite memory would have to be my senior year and being part of two choirs, which were Diamondettes and Diamondtones. I had so much fun being in two choirs and learning all the different dances for each song. Every time I hear a song we sang that year, like "Yesterday Once More," "My Guy" or "Crazy Little Thing Called Love," it brings me back to my days in choir, where you could just have fun, enjoy your love for singing and dancing and being part of an awesome show once all the hard work was done. I remember, I was also an aide for Solitaire that year and you thanked me for being part of Diamondettes and showing the younger choir members, or kids as you called us, all that I had learned in four years. I was in choir and working hard, plus I learned from doing, Pizzazz, that it was important to have fun, not caring what others think, as long as you're having fun. Keep your face up, be positive and never let anyone know you made a mistake, just keep on going. I still use that today, how to just be myself. I also remember my Grandma coming to my choir concert that year and loving it so much that is all she talked about for months! Being in choir my four years of high school was the best experience I had from high school.

Katrina Gonzales

I learned leadership in choir. Being a choir officer really boosted my public confidence. During my senior year, when I was president of Solitaire, and you were out for all of those weeks, healing from your injury, I ***Really*** *learned leadership, controlling dozens of same aged teenage girls, for weeks on my own! That was a real trial by fire, growing experience that I have carried with me into my personal life and in my career as a scientist, in business.*

Jessica Hessom Watts

Anytime I feel intimidated going into a situation, I remind myself that, "If you think you're Miss America, then you are." I thought that was the silliest thing at the time... but it has truly become an essential tool in my adult life.

Kimberly Forkner Mitchell

Honestly – focus. Everything goes back to it. If I'm stressed about something, I step back and try to focus on what I need to do first. If I'm at a fun event, I try to focus on making it a great memory. If something bad is happening, I try to focus on how to turn things around or look for a positive growth opportunity.

Christine Criss Lamorena Lopez

Being in choir, made my love for music anywhere and everywhere, blossom! Positivity, posture and breathing, everyday!

Leticia Garcia

In choir, I learned confidence! If you can sing in front of people, you can do just about anything!

Alyssa Layton Greusel

You used to have a quote on the wall, "Success finds a way, Failure, finds an excuse!" That one always stuck with me!
Alyson Behrend Ripa

If I hadn't found choir, I would have never graduated! I struggled to keep a passing grade, so I could stay in choir and perform. If I didn't have that to fight for, I think I would have given-up. There are a few memories I have that have always stuck with me, but the one I think hit the hardest was singing "Trashin' the Camp," from Tarzan. We were practicing the scat improvisation and you would point at us randomly. You pointed at me and I froze! I couldn't come up with anything. I felt like I had let you down, being a senior in three groups, with a few solo parts in the shows. I broke down crying. You pulled me aside and let me know that it was all right. We all have bad days. I went home and practiced scatting, and a few days later I was pointed at again, and went with it! You taught me to never give up on myself and always be ready to try new things outside my comfort zone. I also enjoyed doing a workshop at Disneyland, then going into the park. I remember Aleece, Teresa and I standing in line for the Country Bear show, singing Christmas songs! Senior year (2000), we hosted our own competition at DBHS, and we had to come up with a script for the show. If I remember, it was a pretty bad script... but it was a lot of fun!
Catherine Larson

The most surprising thing I learned in show choir was to be myself. It wasn't until I was an adult that I really realized that a lot of people walk around trying to be people they are not and are unhappy with the person they are. Show choir and Pizzazz taught me at a young age to break out of my shell, embrace my inner weirdo and be happy with myself. Like I said, I didn't realize the lesson I had learned until years after I had taken my final bow, but I am grateful for the direction it set my life in.
Ray Ayers

Having been in choir in addition to sports, allows me to connect with my students who are also involved in the arts. It helped develop a love for music, which I play every day in my classroom. Because of choir and being in musicals, I make an effort to attend as many concerts and plays/musicals as possible, to support my students and colleagues. The experience of being on stage, allows me to get up in front of my class each day and not be afraid to make a fool of myself sometimes, and to go over the top just to help them have fun while learning Spanish or make a student's day better when they are feeling down. Just a few things... I found choir to be empowering, supportive and a refuge.

Spike Abeyta

I remember when you guys took over. We had a new sound and great moves and even better costumes. The best years of my life!

A'Chauntae (Jasmine) Hall

Show choir was a highlight of my high school years. I still frequently have memories of songs we performed. My greatest memories include bus rides, Disney Magic Music Days, all day curlers, fake eyelashes and Wednesday night choreography practices. I will always remember Marquis' trip to New York City, where we stayed in Times Square and toured the city. On that trip we saw musicals, performed against other show choirs from around the country, and participated in a workshop with a Broadway cast. I appreciate Dave and Doug and the service they provided to DBHS. Thanks for all the fun times!

Jill Rockwood

I actually did not love show choir until you all showed up. I remember sitting in the choir room my freshman year and mostly talking with other students while the teacher was in her office or working with a select group that didn't include me. Then, I remember showing up to performances and still being unsure of what to do on stage, because the rehearsals had been so short and frantic! Show choir was an odd combination of boring and terrifying. Then you and Doug arrived. At first, it took a little time to get used to your methods. I remember you had us audition for solos in front of everyone, which the previous teacher did NOT do. I was so nervous to audition, but ultimately respected the process much more. It felt fair and we were able to see that the soloists, you selected, really were the best in auditions. I remember being impressed that we started working on our show from day one, and we rehearsed that show, until we could do it seamlessly. The rehearsal process was much more intense, but that made it so much more fun on stage. We could hit the stage with confidence! You told us to keep our show and costumes secret, until we were on stage. It made us that much more impressive once we performed. No one knew what to expect! And I felt excited (even a little smug, perhaps?) to display what a great show we had together. Finally, I remember the last day of school, the last day of my senior year, every other class was spent chatting and signing yearbooks. Everyone had mentally checked out. When I arrived in show choir, you said some farewells to students and then said, "Alright, everyone into their places. We are going to run the show." I was shocked! Weren't we just supposed to hang out? But you had us run our show from beginning to end, and it really was a great way to finish our time in show choir.

Rachel Lents Maurer

Hi everybody! I was in Diamondaires my freshman year, then Marquis the other three years. We had Mr. Willert and Doug in person for two years and then they moved to Brea, so we had them in our hearts for the next two. Kramer played keyboard for us but mostly was just there to laugh at my jokes. My sophomore year and last year with Mr. Willert and Doug, we had 72 members in Marquis and it was a BLAST. In addition, both of my brothers were in Marquis while they were in high school. I also participated in the musicals all four years and Mr. Willert directed the music for two of my years. I think Doug choreographed Damn Yankees my freshman year.

I still have all of Burroughs' shows memorized, and I still sing all my parts to everything, especially the "Hear my story..." song. My brothers and I still sing that together. If I just sing the first line, "Hear my story," out of nowhere, they will come in with their parts. And sorry Mr. Willert, but I stole the music to Candelight Carol because I wanted to keep it forever. Let There Be Praise could still make me cry and feel like I'm saying goodbye to seniors. I feel like you can all tell by my long post that my heart found its place in show choir. Even just thinking about it makes me beam with happiness. Mr. Willert and Doug, I am eternally grateful for the gift that you guys gave me, and all my friends. Choir was a place to belong, have so much fun, open up our souls with music, and have something to work for every single year. I wish I could go back and visit those days just to have all that fun all over again. I always loved my choir friends and to this day, they all have a special place in my heart.

Danae Rebensdorf

I went to Diamond Bar High School from 2001-2005. Honestly, if you knew me, you know that show choir was my life. My parents were both very supportive and helped out whenever they could, in addition to attending every single show and competition. Show choir memories are some of the best memories I have. I met great people, got to sing and dance all day long, and loved every minute. Thank you to everyone who impacted my life during those years! Special thanks, to Dave and Doug for being so supportive of me. Those were some of the best years of my life! I have so many great memories from my four years in choir at DBHS, including when that overhead microphone fell on Solitaire and not even one of us moved or flinched! I was a member of both Marquis and Solitaire for all four years, and I also did Chamber Singers my final two years. I was that student who spent every lunch in the choir room, too. I loved every minute and I was very active and passionate about every show and rehearsal. Competitions were such a rush of adrenaline and emotion, and it was really wonderful to be able to sing and dance for two hours or more every day! I'm pretty sure we can all remember those after school practices. We worked so hard, but we wanted to. You could feel the energy in the room. It was a really neat feeling to be a part of something that we were all so enthusiastic about. We shared every high and low together, and eventually had to laugh about competitions that didn't go quite as planned (Branson, anyone?). Solitaire did really well in competitions, and I was always proud to be a part of such a strong and talented group of girls. I loved getting to share in the experiences of both groups, as they were quite different, but equally rewarding. What stands out to me the most now, however, is how important and meaningful the relationships we built were. I felt like "choir people" were my family. What made my time at DBHS so special wasn't just the performing and the costumes and the competitions... it was the people I shared those wonderful experiences with.

Courtney Walborn

The biggest lesson I learned in choir, under Dave Willert, was positive personal outlook. I never saw that man have a bad day, every single day he was happy, very positive and always smiling. Choir was my happy and safe place! There were times when Doug would get upset that we were talking too much during an evening rehearsal and would leave, closing the office door behind him. It was at that point we knew we had to get our act together, stop talking and focus! Dave was quite the encourager and motivator... he has quite a gift! I always thought if I could inspire even half as much he has inspired me... then I'd be living a good life!

Janae Nafziger West

I was in NYC over the holidays and was reminded of the many wonderful memories of being there with Marquis in 2005, and performing on Broadway! We met a real Rockette, and saw Phantom of the Opera and Wicked. It was such an amazing experience, I'm forever grateful for!

Sarah Batistelli Moran

When the news broke that the choir director from Nogales was coming to Diamond Bar High School, the show choir students gasped—partly stunned that a cross-town rival director was taking over, and partly exuberant about the possibilities with the notorious (no pun intended) program and what that could mean for our school. Of course, it was easy to criticize Nogales: they were...the most entertaining and they had fun on stage at the Azusa competition, and oh that boy who conducts with Dad...!

We all gathered in the DBHS theatre to meet Mr. Willert, Doug, and his entourage—I believe Margaret was there, with Don Cloud (RIP) and Bo Eder. Those who entered that meeting with disdain, left the meeting knowing that big change was coming and that the bar was now much higher—and, "how dare he come in here..." The vast majority of the rest of us were giddy, perhaps not as giddy as Dave's infectious energy, for what this team could produce out of what was historically a mediocre program. I distinctly remember asking myself, "Why did they choose us in Diamond Bar? How did we get so lucky?"

Those who were disdainful were right: big changes came. Rehearsals were longer, the music and choreography told a story, and Dave and Doug (with Margaret behind the scenes, and the band in tote), worked so cohesively that there was no time for drama... just lots of rehearsals, sequins, new music, and HIGH ENERGY. My favorite Dave and Doug impact tricks were the audience-favorite lighted tambourines, and the canons Doug shot off at the end of the show.

Mr. Willert and Doug taught us how to truly entertain in a way that changed the audience as much as the performers. By doing Pizzazz exercises, it had a physical and psychological impact on us performers, no matter how late in the evening! The props, sets, band flourishes, and perfectly timed choreography all had a purpose to provide the highest caliber show possible for the audience. The hard work was not only fun... but it was rewarding.

Dave and Doug left an indelible mark on thousands of students and the arts program. They played lead director roles in the supremely quality annual school-wide musicals. Mr. Willert encouraged students of all backgrounds, regardless of their baseline talent, to join one of the choirs he formed, as long as you 1) loved music and performing, and 2) were willing to work to improve. They grew the Show Choir program in to a major operation spanning all cross-sections of the student body. And, we won competitions to boot... lots of them! I think I can take credit for two contributions to the choir program: introducing accompanist Erick Hendrickson to Dave, and for spoiling our rendition of "Livin' La Vida Loca" by playing the part of the least suave Ricky Martin! My kids will never believe me!

On a personal note, I am indebted to Dave and Doug for what they did to shape my work ethic for a high-caliber work product; foster a passion for music that lives with me today; and, for launching my post-high school life at Disney, which was the start of a path that has led me to many career and personal highs.

Dave, Margaret, and Doug: thank you for choosing Diamond Bar High School in 1998-1999 and for bringing your unmatched talent, humor, guidance, selflessness, encouragement, and high-class to us, your students. You continue your legacy, even now through Alex, and in each of us today. We have many VHS tapes to watch and reminisce!

With gratitude, and my deep affection!

Pete Buccola

Things that I'll always remember from Show Choir:

1.) **Choir books: As much as I never have been one to take pictures, those books made the choir special.*
2.) **Diet Dr. Peppers.*
3.) **Smiling and holding a pose, until you were finished telling us about a story or announcement.*
4.) **The stories you would tell to help us add to our animation. (You went from swimming and laughing with Nemo to Nemo is dead). The facial expressions were real at that point. Till this day, my facial expressionsare super exciting!*
5.) **2004-2005 New York Trip (singing, "Masquerade," with the cast of Phantom, dancing with the Rockettes, seeing Wicked and Mama Mia as well, competing).*
6.) **2003-2004 Branson Trip (Bread rolls were thrown at us when we ate atLambert's).*
7.) **Auditions (the most nerve-racking thing in the world, but you always had that smile on your face, no matter what).*
8.) **Success finds a way, Failure, finds an excuse... There wasn't a Diamond Bar Choir Room without that saying.*
9.) **My dad starting the Jingle Bells trend with his keys during Holiday Magic. Also singing Silent Night with the audience.*
10.) **I did four years of Summer Magic and it was a blast. Even when I was a terrified little eighth grader singing, "Prepare Ye" with two choir goddesses.*
11.) **Sequins (This is probably why I still think glitter is life).*

12.) *Learning the hard way to not hairspray near vinyl 50s dresses in the 90-degree heat, because it will melt together.

13.) *Endless opportunities to be in choirs. I know I did three, my senior year.

14.) *Overall life lessons. Leaving problems at the door, hard work, dedication, always doing your best, being there for your team... All of these are skills or ways I still live by.

15.) *The end of the year sight-reading and skits.

16.) *Watching the videos from competitions or shows and being proud and always learning how to get better.

17.) *Being able to perform songs you wrote, like "Just Love Me" and "The Search."

18.) *Designing Choir Shirts and Jackets! (I still have them all!)

My years in choir meant more to me than anything, and it's funny how it still shows. At the same time, I was able to take one really important thing away from choir, and that was the power of positivity. Everyday you greeted us with a smile. You showed us how to believe in ourselves and find those good things in our lives. I think of that everyday, when I step into my classroom, and when I talk with my students. What was also special for me were all the lessons we learned that had nothing to do with music or performing.

It was learning the meaning of work ethic and honesty, always doing your best, even when no one was watching and putting problems aside, and creating a positive environment. At the same time, I knew Choir was my world, because I had been in it since second grade. But, I didn't know how much it affected me, until I graduated. It was and always will be my happy place. Thank you for all the fond memories, Dave, and cheers to your new book! Funny story. This is my second year at school, where I get to direct musicals, dance and theatre. I had two weeks to put together a show, and one of the first catch phrases, next to pizzazz, of course, was, "Hold the focus!" It's been 13 years, since I've really been a part of anything related to performing, but it made me laugh, because it came out naturally... without even thinking about it. As I watched the show, I saw a lot of Doug and you in it, especially when I was directing the a cappella solo. I remembered, at that moment that you would always blow us a kiss when it was over. I went for thumbs up!

Anyway, for a long time, I really missed choir. So many people told me that I needed to let the past go and move on, but in my heart, I always knew I'd find my way back to it. I couldn't be happier doing it in a different light now and I'm grateful for everything I learned from you, over the years. Honestly, my greatest accomplishment was a leg hold. My dream as a kid was to become a ballerina. I was never a trained dancer, so everything I learned about Dance was through choir. Also, choir was the one thing that my parents did not take me out of because of injuries. Anyway, I just remember the amount of hours my friends and I would spend trying to become more flexible. If only you were able to see that process. We did not know what we were doing, but we definitely were committed to making it happen. I remember auditioning for Marquis in 2003 and being stoked that I held my leg up. I'm pretty sure Anna and I celebrated for a long time.

Caroline Yenydunyeyan

CHAPTER 18

Memories From Brea Junior High's Show Choirs

I originally came to Brea Olinda High School for three simple reasons. Number one, my son, Alex would be attending there, and I wanted to spend more time with him. Number two, I already lived in Brea, and it would make for an easy commute. Number three, the school had a wonderful theatre to use. I knew that the former Brea choir director, a good friend of mine for many years, Mark Henson, had experienced declining choir enrollment for several years now, and as a result had begun teaching a period of choir at Brea Junior High. As soon as I accepted the job, the low numbers at the high school confirmed that a junior high feeder was completely necessary. At first, I had misgivings about teaching junior high again after nearly thirty years. I had a rather rough time when I taught for a year at Auburndale Junior High in 1978-79, in the Corona-Norco district… but I soon discovered that it was far different this time around. The principal was very supportive, I had an accompanist, and my first order of business was to make that single choir class into a show choir. Voila! *Show Choir Express* was born! Here are the memories of some of the kids who passed through this *very special program*!

I learned that choir could be more than just singing. When I first joined choir, I thought it was a concert/chamber choir and I was so wrong. I went to auditions and we had to dance and I almost cried, not even kidding, like I couldn't dance! It was awful! But as the year went on, I got better at dancing and singing and I found out I could do both, which made me feel better about a show choir. From this beginning show choir, it made me learn that choirs can be more than just a singing performance. They can be a triple threat performance and it made me continue into the high school program to continue my performing career.

Kara Dietz

The importance of dependability became engrained in me during junior high school. There were some members of choir who were not dedicated, and I remember that was a big issue that came up in class. It is so important to follow through on your commitments and be fully committed. If you're going to half commit, then don't bother. That stuck with me all through high school and is still a major value of mine today.

Terry Dopson

I have a story for how the choir kids were treated by the other students on campus. Unfortunately some of the non-choir students weren't the nicest and did not say very nice things about SCE. When we had to perform for the students going into 7th grade, we wore our costumes. When I was walking back to the choir room I heard non-choir students saying rude comments on our appearance. But the bond our choir had overpowered the negative comments and we realized that if we liked how we looked, no one else's opinions mattered.

Trinity Stinson

Show Choir Express members tend to always have fun, no matter what they are doing! That always leads to the group being very bonded and strong! Their positive attitude and determination, never fails them, no matter what happens. I admire that a lot, in that group. SCE is like the high school choir's little sister that is always looking to be the best they can be. That mindset always seems to lead them to their goal, no matter how high it is! The group may be young, but they are mighty!

Madyson Miguel

I auditioned for Show Choir Express, for the fact that it was better than PAAC (I'm kidding), but I made some close friends who were in choir when I was in PAAC, and when they talked about choir, it sounded like so much fun, and I already loved singing, so I decided to join! I have never regretted it!

Allie Mayer

OK, I remember this day clearly (Travis Ranch Festival in 2016). We were all getting on the bus and like telling each other not to get our hopes up. We got there and we were all so nervous, and then we saw everyone perform and we got more nervous! We went on stage and gave it everything we had. During awards, we just held hands and quietly thought to ourselves, "Please be us, please be us, please be us!" They called second and it wasn't us, and we all freaked out! I don't think I have ever been so proud of myself or of my friends.

Zoe Tschumper

Ah! I remember everyone grabbing hands (at the Travis Ranch Festival in 2016), and waiting for them to announce who got what. The anticipation was incredibly intense! They announced 5th place and so forth, until they finally got to 2nd place. Everyone was expecting second place, but they called Burbank, and all you could hear was a huge gasp and cheering that ended the second it started. We all held everything in until they finally called us for 1st place and at that moment, we erupted into the loudest cheering and screaming I've ever heard from a group of people! I have the moment on video and it's always nice to look back on our victories and remember all of our hard work!

Amaya Llanes

A memory came up. I think it was 2009 BJH was having a competition and the school bus broke down on the way... Do you remember? We were going to be late... panic. My husband, Nick and one other parent went to the stranded bus and collectively brought all the kids to the competition 5 to 8 trips. We managed to sweep the competition, taking all of the awards. Whew! What an experience, but had so much fun getting the kids to the competition!

Denise Catanesi

I really loved my 8th grade year's costumes! They were the purple dresses and jackets with gold, black and silver sequins. They were very pretty. For the worst costume, I don't really think they were horrible, but they definitely presented some problems: The royal blue sequin dresses with the red petticoats and gold buttons. They had a choker collar with Velcro, that often caught our hair in it and the sequins were pretty uncomfortable. I have a funny story about those dresses, actually. When we were performing for the 6th graders in my 7th grade year, the stage was super small! The left side of my skirt looped around and attached to the side of Ashton Ogden's dress. We were completely stuck and were tugging at the sequins, trying to dis-attach ourselves, while trying to smile and sing! We eventually got unstuck, but that happened a lot!

Sarah Turner

I remember before a competition, we would have the most inspirational speeches from Dave. It was the only thing that would get us focused and ready to perform our best! He would somehow know the right things to say, to get out our preshow jitters and of course, he would always throw in a surprise PIZZAZZ, to make sure we were ready for anything!

Becca Harpster Edginton

What made me audition for Show Choir Express? I was way too shy in 7th grade to do it. But with some peer pressure from Erica O'Barr and Nate Nolen, as well as a little push from my mom, I was convinced to join in 8th grade. Now I want to make singing my lifelong career!

Claire Manson

My favorite BJH choir experience was watching my daughter "find her people" the first week of school. Love how much of a family it was and still is!

Katie Moore

*I just remembered. The best memories for me are the ways we got ourselves to be quiet and listen! My favorite was, "Hey, ho, *clap *clap shh!"*

Ayla Golshan

Show Choir Express is the choir to learn the ropes of competitive show choir. I remember going to my first competition back in 2014 at Walnut High School and seeing all the different choirs. I saw who our rivals were, how to behave and look professional... compared to the other choirs, and what a competition is really all about. The thing that really stuck out to me the most, was our first warm-up room rally where we were told to go out, do the best show ever, and most importantly have fun. At the time everything was so new and exciting especially because we won our first comp of the year! Now after graduating and having been in choir for 5 years, I look back at that time and remember that's where everything started. That's where my love for show choir began and it was all thanks to Show Choir Express.

Mia Dalgleish

I have been in choir for three years now, from 7th to now 9th grade and Dave Willert made my first year a delight! One of my favorite choir memories, by far, was his legendary pizzazz. Dave had no ordinary pizzazz. He was able to get me out of my elementary school shell by saying "one, two, three!" However, he would say it with great enthusiasm, encouraging you to overpower him with your, "Pizzazz!" This led me to learning new skills and techniques in a fun way. Everyday I looked forward to coming into choir and being attentive while learning new skills that would be useful later in life. He made my transition from elementary school to junior high a complete breeze, while giving me an amazing first year of choir. As my teacher, Dave Willert taught me so much that will stick with me forever!

Chloe Simone Stoddard

I was ecstatic (when you started a show choir at BJH). Thrilled! What was great was we had some really talented kids that first year, but so many didn't know what to expect... but they knew that their friends were thrilled, so they became excited. So a talented group started with a great attitude. And so many didn't know how good the other groups were, but knew there was one middle school that dominated the competitions, winning every single one! So every rehearsal, we were questioned if we were really working hard enough to beat THAT group? So, a talented group had a great attitude and subsequently, a fantastic work ethic. And not KNOWING who /the other groups were, all we ever did was push to be better! Then, when we finally competed, we ***swept the competition and swept every competition after.*** *Attitude and commitment. We usually fall short of our goals, so it's important to aim high, and not knowing how good the other groups were and always questioning us at rehearsals, if we were working hard enough to defeat this AMAZING group, that really only existed in our imaginations, really only forced us to compare our effort to our own ability. It forced us to not be the best of the other groups, but to be our best selves! Goal setting is such an important part of our lives and we typically fall short, so trying to be your best self every day, is a great motivator! If the sky is the limit, then how are there footprints on the moon? A great, great year at BJH when Dave got there and it helped foment an attitude that would lead into high school... a group that would become such natural leaders a few years later.*

Alex Olvey

We were super on board with show choir from the get-go (which was not the case at the high school) and we won all of our competitions our first year. We always had to be corrected during "Celebrate America," because it sounded like we were saying, "Salivate America," and we had a lot of fun with flashlights in "Hernando's Hideaway." "Somewhere Over The Rainbow/" was our big showstopper. I want to say Tuffree, was our biggest competition, because they had risers and a lot of boys, while we had boxes and three boys. I'm pretty sure Kevin, Alex O. and I were the only three original members from 2004 that were in choir every year, without a break, and participated in every musical for six years!

Kayla Camacho

I was in your show choir (Show Choir Express) at Brea Junior High in 2007-2008. Being in show choir at that time with you was what made me truly discover my love for performing and being on stage. However, once I graduated 8th grade, I wasn't allowed to attend Brea Olinda to continue show choir and had to go to La Habra High instead, and I was devastated. During high school, I actually ended up doing very little performing arts, even though I loved it so much, because I always made-up excuses or was too discouraged to audition.

Fast-forward to just a few months ago - I'm now 22 years old and I was loving my job working with kids with special needs. Singing and dancing and performing was pretty much in my past and I accepted that it was a dream I had to let go of; I was happy with the career path I'd chosen. But recently, completely on a whim, I went to a Sculpted Character audition for Disneyland and I got cast! Today was my last day of training to be a Chipmunk! I know it's not quite the same as performing in a show on stage, but being chosen at that audition, amongst all the people that were there, made me think that maybe, with a lot of hard work, I can try to achieve those dreams of being in shows and doing musical theatre. Now, as an adult, I'm a bit more self-confident, and I've decided that if I don't end up performing like I want to, it won't be for lack of trying! I'm starting to take vocal and dance lessons again, and I'm hoping that with my foot in the door at Disneyland, I can work my way up to being in shows.

I know this is really completely out of the blue, but I wanted to share this with you because you were the one to help me discover my passion for the performing arts, and the first person to believe in my horribly awkward 11-12 year-old self. Thank you for everything you've done for me personally and countless others. I've heard you retired and I hope life is treating you very well.

Gailyn Amber Tan

CHAPTER 19

Memories From The United Choirs of Brea 2005-2016

The final choral program I had the privilege to lead was Brea Olinda High School. This program, like all of the other ones, was unique. In my 11 years here, we produced some phenomenal memories, including *competing in the FAME Show Choir National Finals four times* and on top of our busy performing schedule, producing a successful musical every year! Following are the thoughts and memories that selected students and parents wished to share.

Your arrangement of "Never Walk Alone," was one of my absolute favorites; I am still baffled that Masquerade never won in the 2010 competition season! I also loved: 21 Guns, because it was so powerful (and I got to hit a high note at the end, haha); "Memory," because I had memories (ha) of watching "Cats," on VHS as a child and loved that song, and I was chosen as one of the soloists; and "Be Italian," because it was fun and intense, with a killer dance break- who doesn't like dancing on chairs? I wish I had been in Spellbound in 2010 (the only year I wasn't), because they did "Don't Cry Out Loud," which was very moving! And the classic closer, "Livin' La Vida Loca." Nothing like ending a show with a yell!

Emmalee Wetzel

4 years of concessions, serving a lot of hot coffee, hot cocoa, sodas and snickers bars at the shows for concessions made for a lot of happy memories and lifetime friendships!! How many baskets did we raffle off and the fun putting them together for the sake of choir? You want my favorite memory? I have so many, Dave. Watching my daughter as Spellbound President bring Spellbound to the ultimate level at Fame Hollywood to create a new division for Fame for Women's Division, to compete nationally as they scored so high.... Tears... Joy! "Christmas Fudge" song which I play every year... You guys performed that song about Grandma's Christmas Fudge just shortly after my mother died, Ally and Rob's Grandma. That song still has a special place in my heart... I still love to watch my daughter's dance solos – You and Doug encouraged her dancing and choreo giving her the confidence in life... Most of all, Show Choir was such a positive experience for my kids in high school. Broadway tunes, shows, life friendships, curlers in the hair, makeup on the face, hugs, smiles and tears. Loved every minute, every year! Also, once again I sat down and watched Holiday Magic 2010. I always enjoy watching it so much, each year, even getting emotional when I watch Breath Of Heaven and The Hallelujah Chorus. I thank you so much for these memories!

Denise Catanesi

I was able to get a couple of memories to share: Question: What's your favorite choir memory? Louis Jota – "Performing 21 Guns at Nationals senior year." (2014); Hannah Pipes – "Winning Nationals with Spellbound senior year." (2014) For me, there are so many favorites, far too many to express succinctly. Of course, the best times were whenever my two kids (Hannah and Aidan) were on stage together, whether it was Masquerade (2013-2014) or in any of the musicals (they both did them every year, Aidan starting in 5th grade). Fond memories of the choir kids (and parents) in general – we were always told we had the nicest group, and it was true! I enjoyed how the kids always said hello and greeted me warmly and they were just a huge pleasure to be around at competitions and on field trips. I felt like we were just one big choir family! I started going to competitions with Hannah, before she was even in choir, she wanted to support her older friends. I remember so many amazing sets over the years. Every year it just felt like a huge buildup to the big reveal of Spring Magic! It was always such an exciting night. I think Hannah's freshman year of Spellbound (2011), the set was just perfect from top to bottom and the girls all executed it so well. A HUGE memory was when they won the best/top score at Fame Hollywood that year. It beat all the scores in every category (even the mixed groups) by something like 45 points! It was an unheard of win but even more, a stellar performance. And it was always just fun to be sitting at any competition and hear other groups or parents say things about Brea, when they didn't know you were listening. Examples – Los Alamitos 2010, Show Choir Express performs and Travis Ranch kids, sitting behind me: Kid One: "Well they have a lot of energy." Kid Two: "Well, it's Brea!" Haha, yes, of course, it's the Pizzazz! And at one of the last competitions I went to, Aidan's senior year, 2017, a Chula Vista parent is explaining choir to a novice parent – "This next group, Brea, is so good. For some reason, they don't always win, but they are always the most entertaining." That hit the nail on the head! That's how I felt! We treasure all of our memories and we are so thankful for such a wonderful program for all of my family to be involved in. Thank you to the creative team, Dave, Doug, Kurt and of course, Alex for 2016-2017, as well as the musicians, Eric Hendrickson, Drew Hemwall, Hannah Nam and more! You made it all spectacular!

Mary Wentsel Pipes

My favorite Brea group was probably Masquerade 2009. Probably because it was my senior year, so it was obviously very special to me. I loved "Hey There Delilah," "Hate Is a Strong Word," that whole medley. My favorite musical was "Crazy For You." I love that story and the music is amazing! A close second would be "All Shook Up," because who doesn't love Elvis? The first couple of years were full of so much change (good change) and I remember, as a freshman, how many of the juniors and seniors were against it. They didn't understand the pizzazz and the energy you were trying to bring to Brea. I was brand new, so I didn't know any different. I remember the first day when we got our new costumes for Spellbound; everyone thought they were SO ugly! Looking back, I think it's funny, because now the costumes seem so normal, the sequins, the bright colors, the fluffy sleeves, etcetera! I never had the chance to do Orlando or Chicago, but the New York trips were the best experience. Six shows in five days? Can't get any better than that. I am so grateful to have had the opportunity to go two times – once in 2008 and once in 2009! I will never forget those trips!

Kristen Webster

I loved rehearsals! I remember sometimes when my mom would get home early from work, she'd rush me home after school, so I could shower and put my hair up half-up-half-down and throw some red lipstick on... and then rush me back before 3:30 rolled around. Yes, sometimes the Mondays seemed a bit longer than usual, just because you tried to balance everything else, as far as homework goes. But I really loved rehearsals and I always loved getting my costumes and I'd rush home and show them to my mom and grandma and try them on. Now I get to have them as Halloween costumes. I'm still trying to find my husband an attire that matches them, but he loves it too because show choir was the highlight of my high school years, and he loves seeing me light up when I talk about it. Favorite Group: loved all of them, but my absolute fave would be Masquerade, junior year, 2014, where we did the Cinderella set in the pretty ball gowns.

You can imagine how I was when Doug first showed us those and then transitioning into the Gypsy set, then Heartbreaker, and then finishing it off with, "Never Walk Alone."

Julianne Sexton Hunt

For me, memories of choir are unforgettable. I feel I should've been more lighted up instead of being serious and focusing too much on my studies. Chamber Singers of 2007-2010 are very everlasting in my heart as I think about it when I feel depressed.

Kevin Seo

When I was about 7 or 8, my mom decided to give a piano back to my aunt. It was in the garage for a couple years and she decided to take it out herself. Where I live, there's a hill on my street, so as my mom took it out, it rolled down the hill and to stop it she threw her body over it, making it fall over. As she was trying to come up the hill, some people stopped to help and those people were Dave, Alex, and Margaret. My mom found out that he was the new director at the HS and JHS and was humiliated. Then 5 or 6 years later when I joined SCE, my mom went up to him at the banquet and said "Hi, I don't know if you remember me but I rolled a piano down the street and you helped me get it back," and Dave's eyes widened and said "That was you?" And that's how I met Dave, my neighbor and my future director.

Kara Dietz

You invited my daughter, Taylor and I to a competition in May of 2011. We were interested in having Taylor go to Brea, starting in the fall of 2011. I remember sitting with you and having you ask Taylor all kinds of questions. She was so shy and reserved in answering your questions. Well, that little wallflower blossomed into such a talented performer and lovely adult. She enjoyed her time in the choir department, and I think it brought us closer as a family because I was able to be a member of the board. We enjoyed traveling together. I never missed my daughter on stage, and I cherish watching the moments that made her the fine adult she is today!

Leonel Diaz

I remember picking my daughter up from Masquerade practice, her freshman year. It was always evident that she had worked the entire time and had gone all-out in rehearsal. She was frustrated with some of the older kids, who were formerly in the top groups, before you arrived and it moved into a show choir format. She witnessed their work ethic and thought it did not match their placement front and center. She thought they might feel entitled because they were juniors and seniors. I remember her talking about the practice and how she worked so hard to do her best and move her position. Slowly but surely, she and the other three freshmen were placed here and there, and highlighted. I know she always felt it did not matter where you were during rehearsal, but focus on your performance. Doug recognized her talent, even if she was in the back row learning the dance and perfecting it. To her, it was about going all-out, all the time, every time she practiced. My favorite group was Thunder Cats, and it's hard to pick a favorite year, so I'll go with 2015, because they got to go to FAME.

Andrea Strom

Auditioning for choir for the first time began as one of my most terrifying experiences... but ended up being one of my most rewarding! Initially, I walked into a room full of unfamiliar faces and felt extremely nervous. But, after completing the audition, I felt a rush of relief and gratitude. Overall, this experience prepared me for future auditions and helped shape me into the performer I am today!

Emilie Daedler

Brea Olinda, 2013 (I think?). I was a Thunder Kitty, and in the middle of a Thunder Cats competition performance, as the boys were doing their ballad or a cappella number (I can't exactly remember). I was standing in the wings, and noticed the projector screen coming down. I thought, "This is bad! Why would they randomly put down a projector screen, now? They need to get it together." The boys were trying to stay in character, as they ducked and moved away from the screen. I then looked over, and saw a PA motioning to me to move away, by flailing his hands! I turn around, to find that I am leaning on the projector screen button! Hahaha! I was so embarrassed, but also couldn't help thinking, how hilarious this all was! It's much funnier to look back on now. Choir has given me some wonderful memories!

Nicole McEntee

Better late than never. Here's a shout out to all the siblings in choir. There was something so special about being able to support your brother or sister in show choir, whether it be by watching them perform or singing and dancing alongside them. It was a privilege to be able to share the stage with my sister, Hannah! We did everything in our power to sing with each other as often as possible and thanks to Dave we could. As an alumni watching choir shows still and seeing your sibling continue to do what you loved is such a special and sentimental feeling. From auditioning for acts, to attacking each other at Choir Carwashes to doing each other's hair at competitions our choir siblings were always there to lift us up. Thanks for letting our families become a part of the choir family.

Leena Fritz

Choir was honestly some of the best years of my life. I grew so much as a performer and a person and I'll be forever grateful for the opportunity to be a part of such an amazing program. The staff were/are all such incredible directors, choreographers and coaches, and a lot of what they taught me, I apply to my everyday life. I'm currently not performing anymore (and I don't know if or when I'll perform again) so having the chance to perform on stage was a blessing, and doing it with people I love and admire made the whole experience even better. I remember walking into Tiffany's my Freshman year, and being completely surprised at how much different it was from Show Choir Express, but I knew I could tackle whatever was in store for us. I think of Tiffany's as my "baby" that I got to see grow throughout all four years. Getting the privilege of being a president of that group not once, but twice was such a huge honor. I loved leading the group that was mostly freshmen, and instructing them on how to succeed in UCB, performing and life in general. The hardest group for me to let go of when I graduated was Tiffany's even though I had been in Masquerade and Spellbound, as well. When I realized I would never be part of my first and favorite group at BOHS again, I completely broke down. However, I know that they will succeed continually as long as they put their minds to it. UCB has been such an incredible experience for me to be a part of. I'm so thankful for every experience I had in the program because they all helped shape me into who I am today. A few great memories I have are how Tiffany's went from "sad to rad" and beat Spellbound twice in 2014-15; Tiffany's & Company's only year was in 2015-16 and Masquerade was SO bonded when we did the Wonderland set in 2015-16. I learned how to let go of my fear of what others think of me and just let everything go, while I'm on stage. I gained SO much confidence and discovered that I have great leadership abilities, as well!

Allie Mayer

Apart from singing, choir is where I learned to be a fair leader, how to work in a team, and how to stand-up for myself. My favorite memories surround the countless hours I spent in the choir room or theatre, choreographing with Doug and Kurt. One time, Doug even called me at 10 at night, to meet him at Walmart, to try-on boots for our 2010 set! We did all of the choreography in Walmart, made quick changes, in the shoe section, and did pirouettes down the aisles to make sure they were perfect for competitions. Robby was a huge part, as well, and learned a lot about integrity and commitments through his years at BJH and BOHS. Rob and I will still jam out to Green Day on the radio (singing alto and bass parts, appropriately) and I'll still chant, "It just doesn't matter!" when I'm in a bad place at work. Choir was a huge part of the Catanesi family, and we'll always have mostly fond memories to look back on!

Ally Catanesi

The best thing that happened to Madison in high school was when she joined choir in her freshman year. She truly found her tribe and made lifelong friends. I'm still amazed when I look back at all the talent and different personalities that blended so well! We know that choir kids are special, but their compassion and sharing with each other was something I was so happy to be around. I was thrilled to chaperone this group of crazy and creative kids from time to time and will always value that time spent with the group! One special memory that I love is the competition where Maddie fell on stage, but popped back up and kept going. She was later carried to the stage by Drew Olvey (he ran with her) to collect a special award since she had turned her ankle so badly. I loved that moment. Drew made me laugh! I also loved the friendships I made with the adults. We're all still friends, you, Doug, Margaret and Kurt and so many of the kids' parents! That was a very special time in our family's lives. Another great memory is how special the holidays were with "Holiday Magic" to look forward to! I'm thrilled that my parents were also so invested in the kids and the program. A highlight was when a group came to my dad's office to sing for his workmates. I always got chills when the alumni got on stage for the always amazing, "Let There Be Praise!" Equally wonderful was the last show of the year, when the seniors sang their song together. It was always magic!

Sherry Nobles Reeves

I attended choir in the years 2009-2012. Attending choir was my favorite part of the day, and although hating to admit it, I'd even skip my normal classes to sit in on choirs I wasn't in, just to watch! I had the opportunity, multiple times, to assist Doug and be a part of the magic making backstage, as dance captain. I would help choreograph for competitions as well as for our concerts. Being a part of something so important, the choir took a lot of hard work and dedication from not only myself, but also from the choir as a whole. Remembering the moments of crossing our hands right over left in the audience during award ceremonies for good luck to something so minimal as the Mickey band aids, that were always in our director, Dave's, desk, is so Brea choir. Everything in that little dungeon was nothing short of wonderful! Being an adolescent teenager, I was a handful, and at the time, I did not appreciate what I had. But, looking back, those years are what made my high school experience great! Award winning show choir, the whole time I was there, if I remember correctly, we only lost, maybe a handful of times... even so, we were always in the top 3! Our competition warm-ups included chants, such as, "it just doesn't matter" and "pizzazz" to get our blood flowing. I remember all of the times we would get weird looks from other schools. But looking back at it, we weren't weird... we were just ahead of our time! Being so proud in 2012, that we were still winning first place, without having to use any technology, like Burbank and Los Alamitos. Instead, we had imagination, using props such as a giant moving ladder, fire extinguishers and a great amount of toilet paper, during our set of Green Day, in 2011! My family became quite involved with choir, during my junior year, when Masquerade was doing Green Day. Between my grandpa, Elmer Clark, coming in once a week to fix the golden gates, we used as props, to my sister joining the Chamber Singers on stage, to play the new owners of the toys in Dave's new version of "A Chorus Line," The United Choirs of Brea really became a unity! There was always a time where any one of us could have walked into the choir office (the door was literally always open) and ask any of the staff, Dave, Doug, Kurt, Hannah or even Drew a question. We became so involved that other departments at our school were calling us a "cult" in the year 2011! (I remember that one becoming quite the joke!) The school office was unappreciative of our achievements, all except one... Marti Repp! I remember Marti being the bright face you'd see the minute you stepped into the front office. She even participated in our musicals! In Grease, 2012, she played the principal of the school, while I played her favorite student, Patty Simcox, which made it all, the better! 2012 was an interesting year. A lot happened good... and bad. It was my favorite year, not because I was a senior or because I played a major part in our competition... I think it was my favorite because it made a giant group of kids fully understand that all of those years prior were way too important to take for granted! Choir at Brea Olinda included all of the kids who weren't sure what their purpose was in high school... and gave them one! Choir taught us the valuable lessons of friendship and good sportsmanship. It taught us that we could survive a full school day, as well as a full six-hour rehearsal, and then wake up the next morning and head to a competition! Storage boxes were purchased each year to hold all of our costumes and fabreeze was always available. Our choir was for sure, controlled chaos, that not many people understood... or had the privilege to experience.

Beckie Clark

I always enjoyed helping out with sets, costumes and making feather fans at my house (and still finding feathers floating months later). Another top memory was hosting sectionals at our home, which was always a delight! To have such beautiful music in my living room was magical and I never minded supplying cookies, drinks and snacks for the kids (or that they broke my couch or stained my carpet). Carpets can be replaced and stains lifted, but I will never forget the sweet kids and their amazing voices filling my home! Another favorite memory is chaperoning for the many competitions... even across the country in Chicago, Florida and New York. It was a pleasure to be a surrogate parent to many kids whose parents were never able to attend a competition. Some of the best days I spent including sitting for hours with kids and other parents watching choir performances...

some good, some bad, and some just out of this world, like Masquerade performing their Cinderella set! Some of my best friends today were found through choir!

Debbie Clark

I indeed have a bunch of memories to share. Here is one that I will share today. It was my senior year when we did the Cinderella medley and "Hey There Delilah," as our a cappella. It was the Bonita Vista competition, I believe. I ended up missing school that day, on a Friday, because I was feeling super-sick, like I had the flu or something. I ended up feeling better, and decided to go to the competition. The bus ride wasn't too bad. We ended up getting there and went to our usual spots to get some food, before we went up the street, to the school. I remember, after eating, I just felt so sick, and had chills and body aches like you couldn't believe. I remember telling you and Doug that I couldn't compete, because I felt so awful. So, I don't think too many people knew, but when the guys were getting ready, quite a few of them had forgotten important pieces to their costumes; jackets, vest or even their boots. I had already determined it was not worth me competing, feeling this way, so I gave out the bits and pieces needed to those individuals, so they could perform and go on stage. I remember sitting in the audience with Maddy Reeves' grandparents and parents as well as Marcia Holman and Andrea Thompson Strom. It was so different, actually seeing the show from the audience point of view, since I was usually on the stage, performing it! I so wanted to perform and be on stage, even though I was sick as I was. I still wanted to go out there and give it my all, but I thought it would be better to lose out on one member rather than 5 or 6... so I did this for my team. I have always thought about whether or not I should have gone on and I regret not being able to perform... but I don't regret helping out my fellow choir family!

Daniel Cabrera

This is one of the reasons I loved Tiffany's so much. Yes, we didn't always have the most experienced people, but for the most part, those girls were kind and they were full of life. I never quite remember feeling "drained" in Tiffany's. Our air was never toxic. I loved this breath of naivety, of youth. It consistently brought me back to my freshman year, where I started out without knowledge or skill, and reminded me of why and how I first fell in love with show choir. ☺

This is such a terrible memory, but it's so funny I still remember it! At the first competition of the season, I didn't realize that in the warm-up room was when we all grabbed our "props." That year we only had the feather dusters for the Beauty and the Beast medley, but I completely forgot to get one. It wasn't until we were JUST ABOUT TO GO ON that I realized I didn't have one. I think I thought the world was going to end, Dave. I was so, so stressed about "ruining the show" and I considered not going on at all during that segment because of the missing duster! Luckily, I pulled my act together and just did all the moves as if I had a duster. Obviously, probably very few people noticed, but I never forgot that memory! I learned from it though, which is probably for the better! I also remember "Yesterday," those five or so bars that changed in the "Yesterday, day, ayy, ayy, ayyyyy" (x3) will forever go down in history! WHAT A PART! Man, that a cappella still gives me chills! "Yesterday," along with "Never Walk Alone," were two POWERFUL songs! I loved them!! Another great memory was when the choir bought Hannah and Drew a washer and dryer for their wedding gift! I think I remember Hannah crying.

Charisse Green Groh

I came into show choir, not truly knowing what it was. All my life I had performed on stage in musicals and plays, and I knew I wanted to continue to perform in high school. I was originally planning on attending the Orange County High School of the Performing Arts, also known as OCHSA, and was accepted into their musical theatre conservatory. However, I had a teacher/mentor in junior high who went to Brea Olinda and was a part of their show choir. She told me I should consider show choir as an option. I had no real knowledge of what show choir was, besides what I picked up from the television show, Glee, but I was most definitely interested. I attended the California Classic in early February (the show choir competition Brea Olinda hosts at their own campus theatre), and after watching five or six groups compete, I was very much intrigued. The competition ended with the host group performing, which was 2010-11, Masquerade. I had never seen anything like it! Jumping from Mary Poppins to Green Day, so seamlessly, with amazing full vocals, and the energy was absolutely electric. Nothing could compare to what I had watched. Once their twenty-minute set was over, and I had experienced a rollercoaster of emotions, I knew I wanted to be a part of that. Which led me to audition in early spring. That next year, I was one of two freshman girls to have made Masquerade (the top group), and no freshman girl had made Masquerade over the past four years. So it was a very big deal! I was also a district transfer, so no one had any idea who I was. I was just a little freshman who loved to perform and who made it into one of the top show choir groups in the nation. I was overjoyed to say the least. Thus started my journey as a Brea Olinda show choir member for four years. I was the first person ever to be a member of Tiffany's, Spellbound and Masquerade all four years of high school, and I took on a lot of responsibilities in each group. I had the privilege of being a Tiffany's President, Spellbound President and Masquerade Vice-President in 2014, and Masquerade President in 2015. I was also dance captain for all three groups, and section leader. I worked closely with Dave, Doug and Kurt to lead these groups into victory! My favorite year, by far, as a matter of fact, was the 2014. Masquerade Cinderella/Gypsy/Heartbreaker set and the Spellbound Seventies/Green Day set. Each kid had passion for the group and performing, and always wanted to work hard. Our diligence, work ethic and dedication, led Spellbound to become National Champions at FAME Nationals, and Masquerade to earn 4th Runner-Up. That year, I also accomplished my personal goals, and I was awarded, Best Female Stage Presence, for my Gypsy performance at FAME Hollywood, and was also awarded Best

Female Stage Presence for my performance in Spellbound at FAME Nationals in Chicago. It was an absolute dream come true! Show choir taught me so much about performing and pushed me everyday to become a better singer, dancer and performer. I also gained musician skills and choreography skills I did not have before. But most importantly, show choir made me a better all around person. Those groups became your family. You are with them day in and day out, whether it may be at rehearsals or traveling across the country with them, there is nothing that compares to being surrounded by people every day, that make you want to be better. Of course we had our fair share of drama and problems, like any family, but that is exactly what we were, a family. I knew I could always come into that choir room and feel at home. Because of show choir, I became way more confident with myself, and who I was as a person. I met some of the most amazing people, who have turned into my best friends. Through all the glitter, pizzazz and hair flips, I truly found my home, and I wouldn't change my experience for the world. I really do believe that being a part of Brea Olinda's show choir was one of the best decisions I have ever made!

Tatiana Alvarez

During the competition, I would always love, when it came time for the a cappella. My adrenaline would always be so high from trying to perform my best, because ironically, the song right before the a cappella was the most upbeat and choreographically challenging one in our set! Imagine trying to calm down your heart and catch your breath, before a beautifully arranged slow song... it's very hard! It was always so rewarding to see Dave walk up, with his huge smile, kind of like how a proud parent looks at their child. It was the best way to start the song! At the end of the piece, he would always blow us a two handed kiss, and at that point... I would always feel ready to perform my best, for the rest of the set.

Becca Harpster Edginton

To me, a great memory was when the guy sitting next to me on the plane ride to Orlando, got really drunk, kept a few choir members up all night, and then at the end of the flight, yelled and demanded that we all sing!

Jake Drake

Chicago and New York were so fun. Seeing "Jersey Boys" in Chicago and "How To Succeed in Business" in New York and meeting DanRan with Ally Catanesi was the Best!

Justine Elaina Garate

When I came to BOHS as a freshman in 2005, I knew I wanted to be part of the choral department. My mom was a music teacher, I loved to sing, and I thought it would be a great way to make new friends. I had no idea then, that what I would be joining would become some of my best memories of high school. I'm so thankful to the leadership and vision of Dave Willert, because he really created something special and unique at BOHS that quite frankly other schools in the area didn't have to offer. Not only did I have the chance to be involved in the top Chamber Choir, but also got to be a part of the advanced mixed show choir, Masquerade. Chamber Choir exposed me to rich, classical choral music that was often a challenge to learn. It taught me discipline and helped me work on my sight singing. I believe that what I learned in this class helped me to have the skill set to audition and get into the top choir at the college I went to. On the other hand, Masquerade opened up a whole other world of musical theatre for me. It was like I was a character in Glee, but didn't even know it. I appreciate the excellence that Dave and Doug brought to the table and their creativity to come up with beautiful shows full of singing, dancing, costumes and sets. I loved going to competitions and feeling proud of the show we had worked so hard on. I'm certainly glad I got to be a part of both of these choirs! Pizzazz!

Jocelyn Marie Green

I remember how tired we all were going into "West Side Story," the first night in New York 2009. We all came out during intermission to get candy because it was hard to beat the time change! I fell asleep. I remember waking up during "I Want To Be In America!"

Brianna Kdeiss

2010: Freshman Year: Tiffany's did amazing that year as I recall. I think we were undefeated! Charisse Green was a wonderful and inspiring president. I remember that Dave called us "young" the first few months (and it's very possible we weren't very good at first) but boy did we improve after Preview Night! At the first competition of the year, Hannah Nam, our fabulous accompanist, accidentally started the set with the Tiffany's Theme Song. We had changed the show to start with the a cappella, Goodnight My Angel, the week prior, but she must have forgotten, in the moment. We all leaped up from our positions and started dancing. We handled it like pros. I also had my first solo in our song, "America." That was an exciting start to my show choir career!

2011: Sophomore Year: I feel like this year was a game changer. We were very lucky to get brand new music that Dave had arranged for the Green Day part of the set. The Green Day portion caused waves of awe and excitement in the show choir community. This was the first year that Brea competed in FAME competitions. We first competed in LA, and then moved on as a finalist in Indianapolis, where some of the cast of American Idiot watched our set! We placed 5th and I couldn't be happier. Groups still talk about that set and the toilet paper ending. It's one of our most watched Brea choir videos on YouTube!

2012 Junior Year: This was a solid group in spite of some hardships. The talent was there, but we needed more men to fill-out the group sound. There was a lot of pressure from Dave to do well in competitions that year. Dave had started posting a list of the top choir students every week. Students would be upset if they didn't make it on the list. I don't think the a cappella really clicked for this group. However, the Livin La Vida Loca and

Moulin Rouge parts of the show were fabulous! We felt better about the Alice section, once we added, "Hate," into the set.

2013 Senior Year: This year was the most challenging year for me. I not only had the honor of serving as president of Masquerade and a section leader for two groups, but I also served as the head drum major of the band. The only problem was that Dave was still out and Joe Bartell, the band director, was out serving the government for 3 months. Here I was, two groups—both teachers out! I felt part of my duty was to keep morale up and carry on our traditions as best as possible. THANK GOODNESS FOR DOUG KUHL! Hannah had left this year, so we had a new accompanist, as well. I think my involvement in band and choir had become a full time job, emailing members and coordinating events for both programs (while applying to colleges and doing normal classwork). Despite the stress, I am grateful for the leadership experience I received. This wasn't the most talented group of my four years with Brea choirs, but we had a lot of heart and guts. We fought for Dave and for the Brea legacy. We couldn't let Dave down when he returned from his stroke recovery. In fact, he did return for the second semester! We came out okay in the end. We went to the SoCal competition in San Diego, which was a lot of fun. Dave directed us while we sang on the waterside one evening. It was peaceful and beautiful. That year a group of us made "Brea Juice" and brought it to the competition for a little Brea spirit! I remember that we had to send the group back to the hotel because the buses couldn't stay out past a certain time, so the officers stuck around for awards and Sam Cho had to go up to accept the Best Female Soloist award. HAHAHA. A mom drove us back to the hotel, where we delivered the news to the rest of the group. Dave let me conduct the song, "I See the Light" at graduation, which I will always cherish.

Julia Ludwig

Without my stint through Masquerade and Thunder Cats, as part of the graduating class of '08, I don't think I would have ever learned the tricks to come out of the shell I'd built for myself throughout high school. From shyly stating that I had not been given a spot in that year's main show (I'd joined, several weeks into the school year), to striking that final pose in the final show of the year, I'd never grown more, than I did in show choir. Thank you for that, thank you. Favorite memory: drawing a large crowd during our Thunder Cats routine at Disney's California Adventure's, Five, Six, Seven, Eight show, even people who weren't there to see the competition! T-Cats may never have been the most technically accurate show, but we were certainly the most fun and entertaining!

Sean Barba

My girls, Jamie and Hailey, had the best years of their Jr. High and High School lives, because of the Choir Experience with you! You helped shape their lives into the women they are today, with core values, respect and a hard workmanship ability to make their dreams come true! Thank you, Dave, For All Our Wonderful Memories that have enriched our lives! You Are The Best!

Marcia Holman

A great memory was when we made our Viet Nam veteran, Superintendent, cry, when we performed at the OC Teachers of the Year Awards!

Alex Olvey

I have a few favorite memories from choir. Our trip to San Diego for the So Cal competition my junior year was amazing. The shows turned out great and I even got closer to my friends. I also loved our trip to NYC my senior year. I'm, still best friends with a lot of the people who were on that trip. I also enjoyed performing acts with Melissa Strom. We usually threw something ridiculous together at the last minute, but it was always a blast. Perhaps my fondest memory is the time I sang, "Stand By Me" with Daniel at my final Spring Magic. I am giving my Master's recital tonight. Can't wait to see what the future holds!

Julia Dwyer

One of my favorite memories in my six years of show choir was when we came home from Chicago in 2014. Spellbound had just become National Champions and Masquerade placed high, as well. After an exciting and fun week in Chicago, we returned to Brea as Winners! Not only that, but we were welcomed home with cheering families and friends! A news channel was also waiting to take an interview from us and we were on TV later that night! I love this memory because show choir was one big family and seeing the signs and posters welcoming us home was so special to everyone who had returned. I know, even now that I am out of the UCB family, I can always come back, be greeted with open arms and always have their support.

Brianna Clark

Songs can really make or break a set and I thoroughly enjoyed the songs that were performed in Spellbound's 2014-15, set! Some of my favorite songs, that we performed, came out of that set. It varied from obscure songs, such as, "Whip It," to heart wrenching songs like, "Without You."

Mia Dalgleish

Dave, when you came to Brea, Jan and I had two grandchildren in your first year of Show Choir. Kyle, a senior and Madison, a freshman. Fortunately both had made Masquerade, which still is the name of your top competition team. Kyle was a carryover and Maddie was fortunate to have made it as a freshman. Not an easy thing to do then or now. In the first performance of this group, we saw an amazing performance of the Masquerade number from Phantom of the Opera with both grandkids in it. As you know I still consider that performance as one of your very finest and still like to think you repeated it once ***just for me****! Okay maybe not just for me… but anyway the original will always be a great memory for us. That was the only year for Kyle, but Maddie went on to complete four years in Masquerade as well as Spellbound and Tiffany's. We were hooked and became such fans that we continued to come to the shows all during your tenure there. Now, we are lucky to have Alex and hope to be able to continue to be entertained as we were in all your years. Will always be grateful for our years with you and look forward to "One Two Three Pizzazz!"*

Gene & Jan Nobles

My favorite choir memory happened on a mundane Thursday, during Spellbound's class, when competition season had ended and graduation was just days away. Everyone was buzzing with excitement, anxious for the start of summer, and not really focused on tests or lessons. Thursday would have been a day to work on choreography, but with no new sets to learn, we spent the first few moments of class chatting about summer vacations and university plans. Then Dave told us to stand up – we would be dancing today! Everyone was confused? Doug wasn't on campus? We had no shows to work on? What were we doing? Nevertheless, we assumed our regular competition set positions and awaited instruction. We only danced to 2 minutes of our opening competition number that day, but those 2 minutes taught me a profound lesson that I have utilized throughout many aspects of my life. Before dancing, Dave asked us to run through our opening number and give the dance 100%. So we did. But after a minute of dancing, he stopped us. "That was great," he said. "Now take that 100% and go even farther. Even if you think there is no farther, give it more energy, more sharpness!" We all looked at one another, baffled? Give it more than 100%? We gave this show our all during the year? What more could we do? I'll never forget the feeling of what happened next. The music started, we hit our first few moves, and BAM! It felt like an electric current had enveloped us in the choir room! Everyone stopped for a collective, "Whoa!" The increase in energy was palatable, and our moves were the sharpest we'd ever seen! Even our dance captain remarked how much sharper and more energized she felt! Now, the excited pre-class summer chatter turned into excited whispers about next year's set and competition. Of all my memories of show choir, this dance practice is the most prominent. I thought I had been giving choir my all, but I discovered that you can always dig deeper and give even more. This really helped me succeed after high school, whether it was college, personal relationships, even my career now. When I feel like I'm exhausting my efforts and giving 100%, I take a step back and say, "I can give this more energy. I can give this more!" It's helped me from becoming complacent and comfortable, and, although I may not be dancing anymore, it allows me to continually innovate and consider fresh perspectives that make my work more "well-rounded" and complete. Show choir isn't just about learning choreography and medleys... it taught me valuable lessons about success and hard work that has permeated into my daily life.

Rachael Kuhl

I always knew that the skills I learned in choir would help me when I became a teacher. I am currently substitute teaching in a lot of different schools and whenever I read to my students, I pretend that I am on a Broadway stage: doing voices, using different vocal tones and just going for it 100%! My students just stare up at me as I read and are so engaged in the story because I read like that. My master teacher even complimented me on this when I was student teaching. So, I just wanted to say thank you for helping with those acting skills. Even though I'm not performing on stage, I perform for my students everyday, and it helps them to love reading!

Marysa Leite Grondin

Choir for me was a huge part of my life and to be honest if I never was in choir I never would be where I was today. It made me completely come out of my comfort zone. Even though I was a cheerleader for most of my years, it was nothing compared to being in the choir department. I remember being stressed and almost like I felt unwanted when I went to cheer practice or even just fitting in with those girls. Unlike when I joined the UCB teams I felt like I was a part of a family, and created friendships that will last a lifetime. I finally felt at home when I joined. There are so many memories from choir, but I would have to say one of my favorites would be my senior year in Spellbound at the San Diego competition. It was our last time performing for the year and for me... ever! It was during "Don't Cry Out Loud" and I will never forget the feeling we put into it, the tears that were rolling down our faces, and how tight we were grabbing each other's hands! It was a sisterhood that could never be broken! The performance was astounding! The opportunities you gave us as teachers, coaches, parents, and role models is something I never took for granted. Because of you, I have traveled all around the world performing for the Disneyland Company and have met people along the way who cannot believe my performance skills. I always tell them it's because of the program I grew up in and how hard you pushed us only to become that much better! Thank you from the bottom of my heart!

Kaylee Kristine Dysart

My favorite memories, in no particular order, are when we went to New York and got to meet Fran Drescher on Broadway and all of our New York trips in general, where we got to spend time together with all of our friends. I remember a very special day for me was your first day back in class, after the stroke. I was so excited that you were back. I remember singing in the car on the way to school! I also really enjoyed when we went to Disneyland every year and got to go backstage. The funniest moment was during "Grease," when I got on the table to shake my butt, and the table fell over, spilling food all over the stage! Also, another funny moment was when I sang that song about Moses or something for the musical your friend wrote, and we all thought it was so bad! My biggest memory is of the earthquake during Bye Bye Birdie and all the drama that happened around it. I remember when we performed the show at the Curtis Theatre and during the same part where I was singing the song when the earthquake happened, my microphone went out and made a bunch of really loud sounds, and I started freaking out, and everyone was laughing! Also, there were too many great memories to name from all the Summer Magic, improvisation groups. That was probably my favorite part of choir, because we got to be so creative! Overall, choir was the best high school experience I could have possibly dreamed up, and I am so grateful for getting to be a part of it. Also, on a more personal note, I loved working on the sets and staying at school until midnight or 1:00 am with Paul, Kurt and Doug. We had some great times!

Daniel Dwyer

It's funny how good things, great things, even, are overshadowed by fear. I, and many of my classmates had spent three years under the direction of our original choir director. We followed the rules, worked hard, and learned the ropes. Those ropes became the foundation of what we all knew as the vocal music department. Then the announcement came. Our choir director was retiring and we had no idea what that meant for our program! This program was our safe space, we knew what to expect, and suddenly in my senior year... that was all about to change! In comes a man who was known by many, but not all, who was the previous director from our "rival," who decides to teach us rounds and harmony of "Row, Row, Row Your Boat" in his audition for the role of BOHS choir director!

For me, it was even more fun, because he had also been my next-door neighbor from the age of four. We have a bunch of great memories, like the time I saved his son, Alex, from drowning in the pool... although Dave may remember it as the time I walked Alex into the pool, or the time I really wanted to include Alex in our water gun fight, although I was not quite old enough to understand the ramifications of soaking my younger neighbor... who also happened to be in an arm cast.

I was elated that Dave was chosen for the role. This could be great! He would lead the Chamber Choir to an amazing season... but I can't speak for everyone. There were many bumps along the road and not everyone took to the change gracefully. All of a sudden, we were changing names, policy, audition process, age restrictions, leadership roles and plans for the year. It was a bit overwhelming, even for those excited for it. We had the old process engrained, and in a sense, changing that process, almost felt disloyal to the work we had put in the previous three years.

I think that upheaval turned around when we watched Dave and Doug's passion for the stage in every single class; in every rehearsal, in every move, in every breath. While the change was scary and seemed bigger from the mind of a high-schooler, this was about to be life changing. Dave's experience and true love for the job was invigorating. All of a sudden, I was spending as much time as possible in the program. I participated in every single choir he offered at the time, and I found a confidence in performance, I had never had before!

One of my fondest memories with UCB was getting the chance to help lead the group. I remember sitting in the auditorium with our choir, holding a camera. We would take turns performing our numbers and then watch them back. Not only were Dave and Doug providing feedback, but they also asked me and another student to do the same! We both felt great that they wanted to hear our opinions too! Dave and Doug told us that the best way to improve is to see yourself do it. There are so many applications of this theory that that I've carried with me through life.

Thank you, Dave, for the wonderful memories from ages four through seventeen. I can't imagine a better way to end my time in high school, than as a member of the United Choirs of Brea!

Jennifer Eckels Winters

Get inspired- be inspiring! Those are the words that I remember most, about Brea Olinda show choir. I joined show choir in my senior year of high school. The memories I made while a part of Mr. Willert's show choir are the best ones I made in my high school experience; from making new friends to performing on stages with my long-time friends, and traveling all across the country to compete for our school. While all of these memories are great, they aren't the reasons show choir was great... that honor goes to Mr. Willert. Mr. Willert is one of the most inspirational teachers I've met; he takes challenges head on, dares to be different and treats everyone with kindness. When I first joined the Masquerade group, I had asked Mr. Willert if he could help me improve my voice, and he agreed. So, every Wednesday, before school started, he taught me how to improve my voice and how to read sheet music. I was inspired by Mr. Willert everyday to give everything I had into our set, whether we were performing at FAME or just practice. I owe all my appreciation for music, theater, and show choir to Mr. Willert.

Alex Macedo

I remember walking off stage at a competition with a look of defeat because I knew we hadn't had a very good run, but Dave told me something I never forgot. "Don't look so down, you haven't lost yet. Keep a smile on your face and they'll never know it wasn't your best show." We ended up winning that competition. I also learned that "practice makes permanent" and "perfect practice makes perfect."

Melanie Ramsey Blankenship

Choir was an absolutely amazing experience for me. It really shaped who I am as a person today. There's truly nothing like it. I look back on my years performing on stage and competing and singing and dancing with my groups as hard as we could, so fondly. My absolute favorite memory would have to be leading Spellbound 2014 to victory at Nationals, as vice-president of the group. That group of girls was so bonded and it was such an amazing set. To have all of our hard work and dedication pay off was amazing! I also really loved my senior year of choir, when I was a president of Masquerade (2016). The "Alice" set was an absolute joy to perform! Getting lost in that story and the character, Dormouse, and pouring my heart into it is a feeling that I don't think I will soon replicate. The group, again, was very close, which always made for all the more magic of the show. Being the "stand-in" warm-up player and part-time teacher, is also a fond memory of mine.

Jocelyn Abrahamson

There are some feelings that simply cannot be replicated, nor ever truly relived, despite being composed of seemingly everyday senses: the thick scent of hairspray, the sticky taste of bright red lipstick, the shuffle and clacking of heels on character shoes as they make their way across the stage. There's an air of anticipation, a tickle in your belly, a wave of thrill, a slowly beating drum within your chest preparing you to keep tempo before the music ever even begins, because you know that, after many intense months of practice and preparation, the music now lives within you even in moments of complete silence.

Silence! Hush, whispers, heavy breathing...and the curtains rise, the heat of the lights above growing hotter, charging you like a battery. And it begins.

You sing with every molecule of your being, and as you sing you feel your part—be it alto, soprano, bass, or tenor—locking into place with the others and vibrating across a packed auditorium.

There are some feelings that simply cannot be replicated, nor ever truly relived; and though I do feel I treasured every moment on that stage, I also know that no number of competitions, annual musicals, or seasonal, "magical" performances could ever have been enough. I always yearned for one more, one more. Show choir was my life, and it will forever live within me, dancing inside me with the music that guided me and so many others through those grueling and awkward high school years.

We were the weirdos, the eccentric types. We never missed an opportunity to dazzle and entertain, for any room of any group could be a potential audience. Our parties were always costume parties, our conversations always dominated by the reciting of lyrics and lines from our current favorite musical.

I remember the first time I unveiled my character, "Joy"—my own unique and peculiar addition to our production of "Grease" my sophomore year. It had started as a joke, a passive aggressive act by my angst-y teenage self who had so badly wanted the role of Rizzo and was bitter about being cast as "just a cheerleader."

We cheerleaders had been tasked with writing our own scenes to perform during breaks between some of the more familiar moments in the musical. At our first practice, we introduced our creations in a scene involving roll call: every cheerleader, each peppier than the last, jumped up or posed and stated their name. We went down the line, across the stage, until, finally reaching me, my face unsmiling, my arms crossed.

"Joy," I said, keeping my voice completely monotone. I was the "goth" cheerleader—a perfect compromise between my love for performing and my chosen label as a bit of an "outcast" in my life beyond the stage.

"Joy."

Laughter erupted in the small crowd. I could see the shadows of Dave, Doug, and Kurt sitting in the center of the auditorium, bent over, chortling, trying to contain themselves. I was surprised, to say the least, when they not only allowed me to keep this character I had created as a joke, but also expressed their excitement and pride in my work, and encouraged me to continue developing her. Joy became my favorite version of myself, the identity I clung to as I navigated through the remainder of my high school career. I remember my last day as a senior, saying my goodbyes to our office staff, when the administrative assistant hugged me and said, "I'll miss you, Joy!"

Then, after my first year away at college, I experienced a wonderful, surreal moment as I watched a new "Joy" on stage. I had returned home to discover that Dave and Doug had included the role in their next production of "Grease." I had started a tradition!

Knowing I had made my directors proud and our audiences entertained with a creation of my very own is, to this day, one of the most rewarding experiences of my life. Knowing that my years in Show Choir helped to shape the friend, coworker, spouse, educator, and performer that I am today has made me, as an adult, wish more than anything that every young person could have those same magical experiences. There are some feelings that simply cannot be replicated, and there is nothing quite like Show Choir!

Elizabeth Irvine-Madrid

I first joined in my seventh grade year at Brea Junior High School. Coming from elementary school, I was rather timid and scared. I was leaving a school where I had no friends, and entering a new frontier with so many possibilities and opportunities. I knew I enjoyed singing from participating in my church's choir every Sunday. So my mom recommended choir, as a prospect to make new friends and develop a love and passion for something outside the traditional curriculum. But I truly did not know what I was signing up for, when I check marked the box next to 'Choir' as my daily elective. I entered choir hoping to create friendships, and instead I gained a family.

My experience in Show Choir is the reason I pursue performing today. I graduated California State University, Fullerton with my Bachelor of Fine Arts Degree in Musical Theatre in 2016. Show Choir opened a whole new world to me that I had no idea even existed or was even a possibility for me. And now, I am pursuing performing as a career.

I try to stir up important memories of my time with the Brea Choirs, but the fact is, it was not just crucial moments that impacted my future but rather the experience as a whole. I remember the Monday night rehearsals, the many competitions (including San Diego, Chicago, and Indianapolis), the many lectures (in the class room, on the stage, and even on the side of the ocean shore), going through a musical number over and over again, the Pizzazz, the sequence, the after-school sessions working on props and scenery, the weekend workouts getting in shape for competition season, and most of all the people who lead the whole crazy lot of us: Dave, Doug, Hannah, Drew, and Kurt. From all this, I developed a focus, a love, a drive for more. My teachers longed for their students not to settle, but to work for something greater. I learned nothing is handed to me on a silver platter for I have to work for what I want to earn. And on top of that, I need to stay focused with determination and tenacity to continue to develop my craft. I thank my teacher, Dave Willert, for introducing this concentration and motivation to me. That is what Pizzazz did for me.

Madeline Ellingson

I was a part of show choir, all four years of high school with Dave and Doug. I had the time of my life those years! Every part of it was just joyful. I started off in one show choir, as a freshman, Masquerade, which was pretty awesome because in the past, freshman were not allowed to be in this choir. It gave me a chance to have one year to perform with my older brother Kyle. It was an awesome year and was really my introduction into this special place Dave created for all of us. When I say, "special place," I really mean the choir room was a magical place for me. It started off as one room where I had my required elective, but soon turned into my home. By my senior year I was in all four choirs, so I spent more time in the choir room then really anywhere else! If I could go back, I wouldn't change a thing. I wanted to be around "choir kids" all the time! I finally felt I had a place where I could be myself. It was awesome! Dave was so welcoming to everyone. He and I shared the same extremely high energy and random sense of humor. I wanted to learn anything and everything I could from him. I was very lucky, because I was also very close friends with his son, Alex, so I have so many memories from choir both during school hours and outside of school. The friendships that we all had were so incredibly special to me. We all had so much fun every single day. I met a lot of my lifelong friends, Galentine, Webby, Lauren, just to name a few. We had a blast having the opportunity to sing dance and act for several hours a day.

I think my favorite "performing" memories of choir would be doing all the Magic shows where we would do our show sets, a fun new set for each group, and of course all of the acts! I always loved being in so many things that I would literally have to quick change in 15 seconds and go back out on stage!! It was exhilarating and I loved it so much. I also loved our bus rides to competitions. They were always a great time with great people. Whether or not we would win, we would have such an amazing time at the competitions. I am so thankful for every experience I had during this time and will miss those years.

Outside of school, I have a few funny memories. Most of them involving the members of the infamous Thunder Cats! One was a day I came home from school and I had a few of the girls in choir with me also. We went into my room where I always had two very large teddy bears sitting on the floor. Little did we know there were now "three" sitting there! We start talking and all of a sudden one of the "bears" starts also talking and begins to move toward us! We all get so scared, Ally jumped over a doggy gate and made a run for it and didn't look back! By the time the rest of us were able to get out of the room, my closet doors were also opening and three other boys came out of it! It was Alex, Alex, and Christian, and it was Eitan, inside of the stuffed bear! Now, this was not for a special occasion, this was a random occurrence. This was just done for fun and things like this happened all the time, both in and out of class. It is why I loved everyone and everything about choir. Another day I had a big group over to my house again and when I came outside to my backyard, most of the boys were on my trampoline, wearing my shirts and all matching... it was hysterical! I always loved the look on my dad's face when he would come out to check on me and my crazy friends... it was priceless!

Back to a more serious note, Dave had our backs, no matter what... and that's what I remember. He was a teacher and an adult besides my parents, who I could trust and respect 100%. I knew I could always come to him for anything and he would have a positive outlook, and a solution. I really appreciated having that kind of support and encouragement. I always liked performing, but it wasn't until I did the show choir program that I really found my true love for it. Dave and Doug gave me so many opportunities to perform with singing dancing and acting that I truly fell in love with it. To this day, I have the same love for performing and am forever grateful for that. All I can say is that I feel truly honored to have been a part of the choir program and I will always cherish all my memories from that time. Thank you to Dave and everyone who made it all happen. My life was changed in such a positive way... I will never forget it!

Madison Reeves Berkaw

CHAPTER 20

Memories from My Show Choir Associates 1977-2016

My choir associates were everyone from staff to fellow directors. They shared part of my exciting show choir journey with me, and made it so much better! Here are just a few of their thoughts!

Well, I first became aware of you in high school, because of the competitions I was in. I was a member of the Bonita Vista Music Machine, from 1985-88. I went to observe you at Nogales High School, during my student teaching year, from 1993-94. I have, of course, sought your ideas and advice over all these years. My first year teaching was 1994-95, at Monte Vista High School. The next year, I moved to Gladstone High School, in the Azusa school district. While I was at Gladstone, I began to talk with you more often, and that is when Doug came over to help me out, from 1996-2000. I have learned a lot from you and your program!

Rob Hodo

I just want to express how much fun and excitement I had when doing the four plays I did with choir, Miss Lynch in "Grease"- 2007 & 2012, Grandma in "All Shook Up"- 2009 and Rachel in "Joseph and the Amazing Technicolor Dreamcoat"- 2010, at BOHS. I had never performed in plays like that before, but had always wanted to, and you gave me the opportunity to do this! I can't thank you enough!

I was in choir at Brea Junior High and then Brea Olinda High School from 7th through 11th grade. Girls always wore white blouses and black skirts. (Costumes have definitely changed!) As a freshman, I was in the 'Girls Chorus,' then I was in Silvernotes my sophomore year. I was promoted to the main group my junior year. There were only 3 choir groups at that time; the boys' group (now called Thunder Cats), the all girls group, Silvernotes (now called Tiffany's) and the main choir (which I guess would be Masquerade).

Thank you for allowing me to take part in all the choir activities for eleven years! It was my pleasure and honor to be a part of choir and your staff. I loved doing copying, faxing and any other tasks you asked me to do! I hope your book of memories is successful. You truly are an artist/musician/author, plus a wonderful teacher and friend, and as far as I can see a wonderful husband, father, brother and uncle. You will also make a wonderful father-in-law and grandpa when the time comes in your near future! It's been wonderful to know you and your family!

Martha Eileen Repp (aka Marti Repp)

I first met Dave Willert during the 1982 competition show choir season. I was just starting at Arcadia High School and he had been at Nogales for a couple of years. The first thing I noticed was, that although my groups sang quite well, they looked like emotionless statues on stage compared to the kids from Nogales. They just looked like they were having a lot of fun and always, and I mean always, had remarkable facial expression and energy. When he started his competition in 1983, I took my mixed group, Chanteurs, and my girls group, New Spirit. Since no other all-girl groups had ever competed, and as far as I know, didn't even exist, they had to go against intermediate mixed groups. They did well, including winning the outstanding musicianship award given to the highest music scores for any competing group, including those from the advanced division. Their success was a contributing factor to other schools creating all-girl groups. If Dave had not invited them to his competition, who knows how long it might have been before other girl groups started to compete? So thanks, Dave, for opening the doors.

Dave's groups continued to fare well for twenty years at Nogales, winning awards and leading the way in creativity in their showmanship and show design. They were always a pleasure to watch and I always told my kids to just watch them on stage and observe their facial expression and energy. After a few years, we finally got the message and began to smile more! Dave's groups continued the high level of performance after he moved to Diamond Bar High School in 1999 and later to Brea Olinda High School in 2006. They won a lot of awards and brought enjoyment to those who watched them. Having his friend and choreographer, Doug Kuhl, along for the ride all those years was certainly a big plus; but Dave was the kingpin. His love for his students and his infectious enthusiasm were the guiding factors. He has left an indelible impression on his students and the show choir community.

Rollie Maxson

Participating in show choir competitions was always one of the highlights of the school year. I found that the skills the singers were developing in their traditional choral music were enhanced by simultaneously working on their show choir music, and vice versa. Each year provided a new opportunity for the students to polish a new set of pieces to a professional degree, to offer their best work for adjudication, and to share their efforts with their fellow competitors and the audience.

Competition audiences came to expect a highly polished, exciting, entertaining show whenever Dave Willert's show choirs would take the stage. The performers always demonstrated confidence, professionalism, and passion as they delivered their energetic, well-rehearsed performances. In addition to solid vocals, excellent stage presence, and precise choreography, Dave's groups were dazzling in other ways such as stunning costumes, skilled use of props, and visually impressive set pieces to frame the show with a professional look. Props, set pieces, costume changes, etc. were always well integrated into the performance, and never appeared cumbersome or distracting as they often did with some other groups. The student performers obviously loved what they were doing, and shared their passion and excitement with the audience. Offstage as well, his students, exuded professionalism, love for what they were doing, and a very positive attitude.

Mark Henson

One of my favorite aspects of working with the Brea-Olinda choir students is that several of them have come to work with me at the Disneyland Resort! Lessons they learned during their high school show choir years: professionalism, strength of character, determination, perfecting their talent, grit, along with a little spoonful of sugar of the Disney philosophy has led to over 70 students, over the years, to follow in my footsteps and forge performing careers of their own. One of the best moments in my Brea-Olinda coaching career was standing offstage at the Fame Orlando semi-finals, surrounded by other directors, and hearing that our own motley crew of talented gentlemen, the Thunder

Cats, qualified for the Fame Nationals, beating out several other unisex groups, many very strong competitors, to be the first all-male group to ever compete at Fame! It was quite a moment of wanting to jump for joy and yell out loud, but also trying to be respectful of the other groups that did not qualify, some of which were obviously not thrilled. Judging competitions has led to some interesting revelations. During my early days of judging, I learned some harsh realities, including:

1) *Judges (who were former directors) who held grudges for more than 20 years against former competitors and who would deliberately skew points- and brag about it to the other judges.*
2) *Directors who would stop at nothing to make sure their group performed last, including 'disappearing keyboards' that just happened to be found at the 'last minute,' allowing them to perform last.*
3) *Angry observers who did not like the outcome and would follow us to our cars to confront us.*
4) *Directors getting cranky with me because I scored their band lower than they liked because the band was waaaaaayyy too loud, overpowering the students trying to sing.*
5) *Oh, did I mention they were playing in the band? Check your egos at the stage door, people. This is about the students and not the Directors, Right?*

All of these events (and many more) strengthened my resolve as a judge, striving to be fair and earnest, just like my parents taught me.

Kurt Nielsen

My favorite Nogales Choir memories were always centered around watching and learning the intricacies of creating great show choirs by observing the Nogales Choral Music Team, consisting of Dave, Doug and Margaret. Innovative ideas always seemed to become a distinct possibility. The creativity never stopped; it just kept evolving from one show to the next. Their dedication toward their students, as well as their commitment to excellence, was apparent at every turn. I was so proud to be associated, for a brief moment in time, with these amazing artists and kids. I loved how Dave would let the kids select a lemon drop for additional energy, and focus, before a show. The love and respect that everyone had for Mr. Willert was always abundantly clear by the way they interacted with him. They loved him as both their teacher and friend. Dave was, the best!

Linda Willert Atherton

Way back when Dave Willert was at Nogales High School, we started filming Show Choir Competitions. Our first competition was @ Upland High School. We were there to film Diamond Bar Show Choir for our son who was in the choir. As we were filming, a young man came up and asked us if we could film his group and he would pay us. Well that was maybe 27 years ago and the relationship is still going. We have followed Dave from Nogales to Diamond Bar and then to Brea, the energy this man brings forth for his "Kids" has always amazed me. My most favorite memory, and I've told his classes through the years, is when Alex Willert was a baby, Dave would direct choir holding Alex in his left arm, you could see Dave's hand directing and Alex in his arms would be directing with his little hands. I believe Alex might have been not even a year old. Dave has shared his passion for Music and Pizzazz with thousands of students over the years. I know of some that have gone on to performing on Broadway, or directing their own Choirs at other Schools. It takes a special man to not only believe in himself, but to believe in others. And as Bob Hope always said, "Thanks for The Memories!"

Virgil and Suzanne Lewis

My favorite choir songs were, "Java Jive," "Make Em Laugh," "The Trolley Song," "This Joint Is Jumpin,'" and "Don't Cry Out Loud" (LuAnne was awesome). As a musician, I liked, "Go Tell It On The Mountain" and "Good Lovin.'" But really, I enjoyed them all... and Dave's unique way of explaining what he wanted, "More dar dars on guitar!"

Dwayne Ganier

When Dave Willert became the director at Diamond Bar High School that is when my life changed. I was always a performing arts kid. I started voice lessons at the young age of four. I was in jazz, tap, and ballet at that age as well. I began piano lessons at six. I took acting classes, was in community musical theater and even dabbled in TV shows, commercials, and movie jobs. I was impressed and amazed at how someone could be so positive and so inspiring each and every day. It was always my highlight to be in 5th period show choir and have weekly rehearsals. As a college student, I hated it! No show choir, no happy choral director inspiring me to do my best? So, I struggled a bit. In the first week of college I was kicked out of class for not knowing a minor 6th interval. So, I spent the year lost, changing my major in college over ten times, from music to English to math to psychology. Then I said, "Wait a minute, no! I KNOW! I want to be a music-major, and direct show choirs! I know I can do this! So I decided to transfer schools to a private university where I could be a music major, get the theory and sight singing basics that I needed and still graduate in four years. So I transferred to APU and made that happen. When I graduated from college in 2005, that was the very year Dave told me in the summer that he was transferring to Brea. I applied immediately to Diamond Bar and was accepted as the long-term music sub right away. I found out Friday that I was going to sub for his Diamond Bar choir classes and school started Monday! I was only 20 years old, no teaching credential and no experience whatsoever. It was insane! I was fresh out of college and not quite ready. Luckily, Hannah was still playing piano at Diamond Bar and helped me get started. It was a month later that they hired Patty Breitag. I spent the remainder of the year being the music and "fine arts" teacher at 2 elementary schools in the Walnut District. I then accepted a full time job in Azusa the following year, 2006, and taught at 2 schools, Gladstone High School and Slauson Middle School. I was also in night classes at Azusa Pacific to start and finish my credential. I was lucky because this was the last year the state offered "emergency credentials." Looking back at the student performances in my first couple years teaching, I cringe. They were quite rough. I started with only six students in my last choir class. I was able to double and triple numbers each year I was there until six years later I had large 60 student choirs that competed. We placed first in the novice division at one or two comps a year (only in the novice division), but it was something. I was always in "awe" of Brea's performances and thought, "If only I could get my students to that level," that would be something! Then I transferred to Cypress High, an area where the students had more musical experience. Although we never were at the Brea level, I remember the first time my Cypress students competed and watched Brea perform on stage... their mouths dropped! They were shocked at how a group could be so good! Although I never quite got my groups to that advanced level, it was always something I strived for, to be better than the year before and to be competitive. I feel like I still have so much to learn. Even though I've now finished my 11th year of teaching, and completed my Masters, I don't quite get the sound out of my group that I would like. After taking Cypress to the Chicago Nationals (we got 14th place), I realized that although I love my job very much, Nationals was not "all it was cracked up to be!" At that point, I decided I wanted a life of balance. I downsized and moved to Katella, so I'd have more personal time. I still take my groups to compete but I also get my own space and life as well. Before, my life WAS my job. Spending every day and weekend at school. For many big schools, they have a team of people helping them. Dave had Doug, Kurt and his theatre tech team. For me, well I just had a team of one... me. I decided, I'd rather be a really good intermediate group, than try to compete with the "BIG DOGS." My life would not be what it is now if it weren't for Dave Willert and Doug Kuhl. I definitely am who I am today because of the three short years I was in their class. They inspire, encourage, train and teach their students many lifelong lessons. They give countless hours of their time and dedicate their lives to the art of show choir.

Janae Nafziger West

In the year 1985, I started working with Mr. Willert at Nogales High School, designing and working on dresses for his Choir Department. At that time, my daughter, Regina, was going to school there and she introduced us. It is now the year 2018, thirty-three years later and I'm still working with the Willerts! I have to mention Doug, who I've worked with all these years, who has an amazing vision of what he wants to see on stage! We have worked hand in hand on these projects for all of these years and it has always been fun and challenging! I also had the privilege of watching Alex grow up. We would make matching vests, to match his dad! Thirty years ago, we opened up our company, Hollywood Babe, to sell retail garments to department stores and boutiques. Between all of the hard work, countless hours of design fabrications and trim meetings, I have enjoyed every minute of working with Dave, Margaret, Doug and now Alex!

Yolanda Setoodeh

For decades, the show choirs directed by Dave Willert and choreographed by Doug Kuhl were always a force to be reckoned with by every other choir in any show choir competition. But more importantly they were also a huge source of inspiration to all who witnessed their performances. These two giants in the SoCal competition circuit often set the pace for the rest of us. The relentless energy and power of their ensembles were often matched with incredible dynamic range and musicality that Dave elicited from his students.

Ron: At a time when my choirs were known for singing 'loud and louder,' I was a sonic sponge while listening to Dave's choirs in performance. I learned and relearned about the power and possibility of singing with finesse, refinement and phrasing. His a cappella selections were often sublime as he took the audience on a rollercoaster ride with sudden shifts in volume. My earliest recollection of the show choir scene in Los Angeles was the phenomenal directing and staging by Tom Kessler at West Covina High School in the mid 1970's. I believe Dave was a disciple of Mr. Kessler in the late 1970's. Tom brought show choir to new levels of respectability through his musically perfect and visually stimulating ensembles. I think Dave had the opportunity to learn from the master while serving as a student teacher of Tom's. This led to insights and experiences in quality and creativity that would last throughout Dave's career.

Reina: During the 1980's and 1990's I choreographed for the Music Machine Mixed Show Choir, the Sound Unlimited Girl's Show Choir, and the Barontones Men's Show Choir from Bonita Vista High School in Chula Vista, California. During those years we were almost always in competition with Dave's show choirs from Nogales and Diamond Bar high schools. And yes, COMPETITION it was! Dave's choirs were always outstanding. Creative! Exciting! Energetic! A thrill to watch! The excellence of Dave's groups challenged Ron and me to continually 'up our game' to be a better creative design team for our show choirs. Each year it was fun to see what clever concepts, staging, choreography, costuming, sets, props, and music choices would be in his festival sets.

Ron and Reina: The sheer unbridled energy of the choirs from Nogales taught us how important it was to perform both vocally and visually with precision, passion and projection. Those choirs performed with a 'no regrets,' 'bring it on,' 'own the stage,' 'leave it all on the stage' presence that was always exhilarating. In Dave's years at Diamond Bar, with more resources and more students than we'd ever seen in a show choir, his vision demonstrated that as directors, our show choirs were only limited by our imaginations. The opulent production value of the shows created by the newly renamed and expanded line-up of Diamond Bar ensembles, once again raised the show choir bar to new heights. In the 2000's we saw his choirs less frequently, after we moved on to other career choices. We did marvel at his continued excellence and energy with Brea-Olinda High School, while having the privilege of adjudicating his choirs. We watched him push the envelope of possibility as the program exploded in size and quality. Dave Willert has had a huge impact on the show choir scene for nearly 40 years in Southern California, as he established choral music dynasties at each school where he worked. Those who knew him, will forever fondly remember Dave's artistry, musicianship, arranging and genuine love for his students.

Thank you Dave, for keeping the bar high and for providing wonderful life-long experiences for your performers, as well as for the thousands in the audiences watching your performances. If there were a SoCal Show Choir Director's Hall of Fame, we suspect Dave Willert would certainly be an inaugural nominee!

Ron and Reina Bolles

Pizzazz, (an enthusiasm toward performing expressed through facial expression, vibrancy of singing, and sharp exciting choreography). That was synonymous with Dave and his team. I still remember the first time I saw the Nogales Chamber Singers group. Their performance showed lots of pizzazz, making it impressive and fun. While Nogales was terrific, it was only the start of Dave's showchoir "empire." As time marched on, the shows became increasingly more exciting and spellbinding. Dave managed to take solid singing and added a level of snazzy and creative staging, lighting, backdrops (with a "WOW" factor), and props. To top it all off, there was the incredible choreography and costumes (double "WOW"). The "pizzazzious" elements became more developed until the culminating performances at Brea Olinda, that were nothing short of spectacular - Las Vegas style: completely mesmerizing!

I recall Dave inviting me to work with Marquis at Diamond Bar High School. The singing was terrific, so I had very little work to do. What stands out from the morning was the admiration the kids had for him. Dave has always had a sincere, bigger-than-life and positive attitude that was reflected by his students, creating an impressive synergy. I'm sure that his positivity has had a profound effect on many students to this day.

Doug Newton

Dave inspired students! I learned from his techniques to do the same. Dave groomed future leaders and I love that about the roles I have been in since learning from him. "Treat others like you want to be treated!" I can't remember if it was on the wall in Dave's classroom, but it was in mine. It applied to the students and it applied to me, and anyone who walked in my classroom. Other teachers and administrators were not allowed to disrespect my students in any way. Student's respected Dave. He was able to say, "I've got a job for you..." and they would do it. He didn't have many discipline issues because he and his space were so well respected. Students knew that, while the classroom was their space there were things to be done in the room and there were expectations for all who walked through the doors. I remember in my classroom a few years later, a student was playing some music during lunch, which was typical in my room. A pop song with inappropriate lyrics came on and I asked her to turn the song off. "How do you know what it's saying?" she asked. "Because I know, and that's not what we play in this room. This room is different." The posters and signs around the room made a big impact on me. I believe some of them were "FOCUS" and "ENERGY." I went on to be very intentional about what was on the walls of my room. In my room we spoke in "we's." Teamwork, groups, the common good, were important themes to a successful program. Encouragement was a very necessary component to success. I learned that from Dave. Students need to encourage one another and I could be a facilitator of that. If I noticed a student having a less-than-great day, I would say "I need to hear five good things about Melanie today..." and I did that now and again. They even wanted to do that with me. Dave never took lunch. I guess that's how he stayed thin. His room was always open cause he was always there. I know that was one of the reasons his program grew. His room was a magnet for students. And he would say "no four-letter words here" and "we call our room 'little Disneyland.' " Dave believed it was the happiest place on earth and he showed it by always being in a good mood and always having his signature smile. I have many great memories: "Are we there yet" as we drove to the Central Coast for a festival. Phantom of the Opera, my first musical theater experience ever, competition after competition and the excitement and enthusiasm that went along with it. Dave's remarkable staff, who cared as much as he did. The time the student's took a collection for me when my car had been stolen while away at the competition at the coast. It was a shoebox full of love from them. The memory I will never forget was a typical day in rehearsal that changed my life forever. Dave was conducting the girls choir on an a cappella piece, polishing it for the competition coming up in just days. During class he got a phone call he had to take, so he asked me to step in and conduct and so I continued to work the girls. Mind you, Dave had years of experience and had number one Show Choirs numerous times while I was straight from my Music Education bachelor's program. When Dave came out of his office he stopped the rehearsal and said to all of us, "I've decided that Don will be conducting this number at the competition because you sound better when he's conducting." That confidence changed my life and my music forever. I cannot thank you enough Dave, for all that you and your students poured into me that semester. My life has never been the same. You are the best!

Don Hofer

I came into the program as a transferring junior. My previous school had no music program to speak of... Nogales had an award-winning program. I felt completely out of place. I remember being introduced to you and letting you immediately know, that I had ZERO interest in joining the show choir. I only wanted to stand and sing. In your very Dave Willert way, you convinced me to give it a try and see if I might like it? Long story short, it was the best decision I could have made! From there, you gave me the avenue to stretch myself, not only as a singer, but also as a musician. As a senior, you let me join the band for Dream Street. When I graduated, I bought my first professional keyboard and you brought me aboard as one of your band members. I was able to use my own arrangement ideas (unless you had a specific one) for all of my parts. I played guitar, keyboards and drums at different times in my career with you. I probably played multiple instruments in one show! The experience of playing for your groups, helped me to grow, and I was able to use those skills in my own musical endeavors, after that! I will never forget the feeling of rushing onto the stage to setup (with not much light). Listening to the crowd as they anticipated the award winning performance. Even though I wasn't in the choir at that point, the excitement was the same. I wanted to give my best, so that the kids had the best music for their show. Then the curtain opened and we begin with our signature "4 dings!" Also, I will never forget my synth-string parts that I played for "Never Walk Alone." I remember the first time the melodic line came to me. It was during a dress rehearsal and I knew I had composed something good when my good friend and fellow keyboard player, Don Cloud, looked at me with a nod and a smile. It was moments like those that made me want to stay on the team forever and grow as a musician!

Kramer Kurtz Ison

In 2006, my then girlfriend, Hannah, approached me with the news that your longtime drummer, had suddenly quit! I knew what was coming next:

Hannah: "Do you think you would want to join us at Brea to be OUR drummer?"

Drew: "Nah, thanks, but I don't really do that anymore."

(Cut to next scene)

-There I am playing behind Brea at a competition/ home Magic concert!

Obviously there was some coaxing from you there, too, Dave... but I attribute the career "pallet change" to the influence of romance (Hannah) and the fun, exciting atmosphere of your program. I had ***NEVER*** *experienced that work/playing environment with the other choirs I have accompanied, and I think you could tell, I quickly felt an attachment to the Brea program, you, its goals, the staff (I MISS working with Kramer!!), and of course, the students! All of the people on the staff and many students, I now consider life-long friends! By the way, I think I've mentioned that Hannah and I met backstage, during a competition at the Mission Theater in San Gabriel. I was reticent about talking to her too much, thinking that she might not be long out of high school! We haven't forgotten how show choir, and you, Dave, made it possible for us to be together, and have our wonderful daughter, Keira! Keira was dancing to one of your former choirs, the other night, at the Katella competition! So, Who knows? Maybe she's another one of your Show Choir grand-students!*

Drew Hemwall

Pizzazz! What a perfect title for the electrifying teacher and mentor Dave Willert was to students at Brea Olinda High School for eleven years. When we had a long-time, very much respected and loved vocal music teacher resign, the community was very concerned about finding a qualified replacement. Soon after, I had my first contact with Dave Willert, asking if he could be on the interview panel, because he was the Diamond Bar High School Vocal Music Director and his son (Alex), was going to be starting at BOHS. We had a nice conversation and I began the process of seeing if he might be interested in applying for the position – it would have been a difficult financial decision because he would not be able to count all of his years. I feel like I wore him down, and he applied. He wowed the students on the interview panel with his demonstration lesson, and the rest, as they say, was history.

Dave Willert was a true Pied Piper in leading students and built a tremendous program at BOHS, one of the very best for Show Choir. He gave opportunities for students to shine, who otherwise might never have had that chance. Spellbound, Masquerade, Tiffany's and the Thunder Cats found a place they could call home. As the school Principal, I loved attending shows and competitions, seeing the great things the students did and knowing that they had a positive place to belong. As I told Dave on many occasions, he was one of the best hiring decisions I ever made.

Jerry Halpin

Dave was so supportive and positive even when it was difficult with some of the groups. He soon became a father figure to many of us in choir. The choir room became like a home for me and many other kids. It was a safe place to go before school, at lunch and after school. I loved singing with all the groups that I was a part of. I wasn't a soloist and I loved being behind the scenes. I loved helping Margaret with the tabulation. I learned how to do grades when I was Dave's student assistant. I hadn't planned on going to college, however, with a little encouragement from home and lots of help and support from Dave, Doug and Margaret, I applied to Cal Poly Pomona and was accepted. I worked at Nogales in the choir department and also worked as an instructional assistant with Margaret in the Placentia School District, while taking classes. As a treasurer in many groups, I also learned how to run fundraisers. I have been a teacher now for 27 years, and it is because I had two excellent role models: Winnie Barkley, my first grade teacher, who is still an excellent supporter for me, and Dave Willert. Dave was a wonderful choir director, who never gave up on any student. Dave, Margaret, Doug and Alex have been like family to me for as long as I can remember. When I think about high school, I have good memories, only because of choir. When I go to conferences, as a teacher, these days, I can talk about how these two role models, saw potential in me, to do things outside my comfort zone. These days, that is called a "growth mindset." Most of my other teachers had a "fixed mindset," about me, and they didn't encourage me to do anything beyond the bare minimum. No one in my family went to college, so their thought and mine, at the time, was that I wouldn't either. Dave, Margaret, Doug and Winnie changed that scenario. They all were, and still are, very positive and supportive of me!

Della Long

CHAPTER 21

Alex

When I was young, my dad and my godfather, Doug, used to call me, "The Harry Potter of show choir!" I never really understood what they were talking about, until I got older! It seems as if I have been involved in show choir most of my life. I remember conducting at many concerts and competitions with my dad as a child and going to the rehearsals at both Nogales and Diamond Bar high schools, and then hanging out with the students. When I got to Brea Olinda High School, the first time we won, at the end of my sophomore year was great, after losing so much! I felt like we had really accomplished something! Throughout my high school show choir career, I repeatedly felt that rush that accompanies competition, just so long as we all felt determined to win... even if we did not.

I loved being able to be creative and to make people laugh at the acts my friends and I devised for our home concerts. Just a few of the acts I especially enjoyed creating and then performing with my friends were the Spiderman - Power Rangers battle, humorous Phantom of the Opera in Summer Magic, the Elves at a Press Conference with Alex Olvey at Holiday Magic and Alex and Alex with Alex Olvey at Holiday Magic. It got so we felt that everybody expected us to do something humorous at the concerts... so we usually did. I remember the one serious act I prepared for a concert, had the audience laughing as the curtain opened, simply because they were trained to think this act would be funny! I also loved to audition with acts that intentionally pushed the boundaries of what was appropriate, just to see everyone's reaction. Ah, those were the days!

By watching my directors in both my high school and college choirs, I observed that it is most important for the director of a group to become totally invested in each song the choir sings, before they can expect the same from their choir! Especially when the director is directing a piece, their expressions, style and passion almost create a telepathic connection with their singers! I felt this often in competition when my dad directed. I strive for that same connection with my own students, today!

I have always seen show choir as a means of bringing people together for a common goal. This goal could be perfecting the competition show or achieving something more specific, musically, theatrically, choreographically or even involving attitude. Show choir teaches you a lot of skills you can use throughout your entire life like being goal oriented and working together with a lot of different types of people to create something bigger than yourself! Something that needs everyone determined and involved, working together, to accomplish it! That's what makes show choir so special.

When I became the show choir director at Brea, besides having some big shoes to fill, I soon learned the job was not exactly what I thought it was? In reality, in addition to being a choral director in class everyday, there is a great deal of behind the scenes work to do in order to make what people are supposed to see on the stage, possible. But, between me, Doug and the staff (with a little help from both of my parents), I learned that everything can get done, as long as you don't try to do it all yourself. Sharing the load with staff, boosters and students makes it easier on everyone.

In developing my different show choir themes, I think I like telling a story with my shows, the best. Actually, I like to almost create a mini-Broadway show! I know that a lot of directors build their shows based on an important list of components they expect to see on the competition score sheets, and this probably works well for them. But, I, first and foremost, want my shows to be entertaining! Of course, I want my groups to sing, dance and perform well, but the focus on the stage needs to be on entertaining our audiences!

When it comes right down to it, show choir is just a great way of bringing people together, in this life, with a common passion. It brings the performers together as well as their families and friends in an activity that win or lose... is always a treat to be a part of! My personal experiences, as a child and student, watching, performing and even directing choirs at Nogales, Diamond Bar and Brea Olinda high schools, made for a wonderful childhood! I want to thank my dad, my mom, Doug, Kurt, Hannah and all of the others that shared this special time with me. I suppose doing show choir as a kid, and then becoming a show choir director as an adult, confirms... that I really am Harry Potter!

Alex Willert

CHAPTER 22

Doug

What to say about show choir? It's a lot of work and fun! Putting on shows is a blast... a labor of love. When asked what show choir is, I always say its like taking all the production numbers from a Broadway show and putting them together. Of course it's much broader than that since anything can be brought to stage. And creating is just part of the process. It takes hours of rehearsing and putting it all together. Bring in the performers and then you've got something!

It all started at Norco with New Generation. That was my first exposure to show choir. My first inspiration came from the West Covina Chamber Singers. They were amazing to behold! That was some brilliant work that I still reference to this day. Fortunately, in knowing Tom Kessler, we were able to secure some of their arrangements and choreography, which we've kept alive since. After Tom retired, Dave was ready to take over, but decided to stay at Nogales. That was a great move as Nogales was beginning to take off!

There was a lot of learning at Nogales. Dedication became a key factor in the process of achievement. We spent many long hours rehearsing, but when everyone is working and giving their all, the result was always worth it. Nobody gave as much as the kids from Nogales. I'm so thankful for the video camera, since the shows can still be enjoyed! And really... Nogales kicked some major ass! The performers were alive and talented and giving so much of themselves. You can see and feel the intensity and passion! This is what we still aim for today. We worked so hard and had many laughs along the way. Sure there were flakes and down times but those were way overshadowed by a spirit that wouldn't give up. Nogales will always be an inspiration and was the forerunner of Brea Juice!

Before Brea Juice was Diamond Bar. Diamond Bar was our next adventure. We had a theater and hungry-to-win kids! All transitions are challenging but this one went fairly well! The kids had to adjust to many changes. There wasn't time to waste and to work we went! We brought many new things to the show choir circuit with Diamond Bar and the kids began to understand the work ethic and dedication it takes to create and achieve. There were so many gifts at Diamond Bar and it was exciting to see the ideas visualized. Costume changes, leg holds, sets...this was the beginning of a new era! Like Nogales, so many wonderful people and great times! Unfortunately, the school became a difficult place to work and we were on to Brea.

Dave had to kick me out of Diamond Bar! Brea was a nightmare of a place! The room took two months to get in order! The kids were begrudgingly accepting? As with Diamond Bar, we had a lot of work to do. We worked and struggled but never gave up. We accomplished some great work here and the kids began to understand the work ethic. This was the creation of Brea Juice (thanks Nogales!) Fortunately, most got on board and we've had a lot of good times with a lot of great people!

Show choir has given me such fond memories. Being surrounded by so many wonderful and talented people is certainly a gift! Thanks Dave!

Doug Kuhl

CHAPTER 23

What I Learned About Show Choir Over 40 Years!

It's difficult *not to have learned something* from show choir over forty years of teaching, and in my case, *I have never stopped learning*! Doug and I found, as competing show choir directors that we had to stay alert, because something was *inevitably* always changing! I'm not talking about societal changes or changes in education, because those undoubtedly happened too! I am specifically talking about *intriguing ideas* that were brought to life somewhere in the entertainment field with the power to influence show choir greatly! Things that if adopted, could make our shows *better*, and keep our students *excited*! Things like *new styles of songs*, or *unique costumes*, or *adding new instrumentation to our band* or *connecting our songs with a story*! As both Doug and I learned, *students, who are excited about their shows, make the most motivated singers and performers*! Over my forty years of directing show choirs, after spending a decade, performing on the *stage floor*, we moved to *individual boxes* to elevate the kids for seven years, then we adopted the use of *risers* for four years, then back to boxes for seven, and finally, we returned to risers for my final eleven years. Of course, by the time we decided to shift back to risers, when I was hired by Brea Olinda High School in 2005, *everyone was using them*, and in fact, many festivals made their use *mandatory* for all participants! This encouraged Doug to try-out different formations of the risers, so that we would not look, *just like every other group*! All of our groups needed to look and sound somewhat unique, *in a good way*, in order to be noticed by the audience and the adjudicators, thus making us competitive! Since so many groups, are influenced by the *same things*… after a while, we can all begin to look *generic*, at which point, it behooves us to instigate another face-lift! Show choir can be a very creative activity, if we don't allow *success* to hinder our evolution. By this, I mean that no business that I can think of would last very long without evolving forward, *no matter how successful it initially was*! Show choir, is no different. Finally, the most important thing I learned is that my best choir programs have always been *a healthy marriage among students, staff, parents and administration.* If any one or more of those relationships is strained… *then so is your choir program*! This point is probably the most important, because a teacher who is always feuding with their parents, students or school administration… *will never be truly happy at that school*, no matter how successful their program may appear to be. Therefore, that teacher *probably won't stay* at that school long enough to evolve to their best work! In addition, there's always the danger that the students, reflecting the teacher's unhappiness, will never give 100% and in fact, will routinely sing and perform *uninspired shows*! I have listed *fourteen* additional concepts that I have found, during my own career, to be *most helpful*, to a director or leader in developing strong, healthy competitive show choirs!

1. Rome, Was Not Built in a Day…and Neither Should Your Show Choir Be!

Building a competitive show choir takes *time, training, talent, experience, a vision, of where you are going,* and especially, *positive and excited attitudes from both the staff and students*! The first thing to remember is that, **no matter what**, *you and your group are not failures,* just because you do not win every time you compete! A teacher teaches, and their students *hopefully* learn. *That should be the focus of how you evaluate every competition result*. Is your group improving? Some groups take more time than others. I only stayed at *Norco* for two years and I was a *green, beginning teacher*, so I never really had a chance to dramatically improve *New Generation*. However, we overcame a lot of bad attitudes at the beginning, due, in large part, to the sudden and surprising departure of their former teacher. By the second year, I could already feel the momentum beginning to swing my way. At *Nogales*, we started from the ground up, so it took us a full *four years* before we *placed* in a competition and *five years* before we *won*… but those kids were *always excited about show choir*, so it seemed like we were all on the same page, at all times, win or lose! At *Diamond Bar*, the kids were ready to win almost as soon as we arrived! They had not placed or won a lot, prior to our arrival, so they were hungry, and after they began to trust us, *everything just clicked*! Some members of the *Brea* choirs had negative attitudes, when Doug and I first arrived, because they didn't want their former director to leave. For that reason, we had to fight, and focus mostly on *developing the younger students*, before the groups were truly ready to put in the serious work necessary to win. Although they placed twice in that first year, it took until the end of the second year to win a competition! *Brea Junior High* won immediately, *in their very first competition*, even though *they had never performed as a show choir before*! They were *excited about competing*, and that made them better in every area! I would have to say that a *good attitude*, more than anything else, has the potential to create miracles… or in this case… *terrific show choirs*!

2. The Best Thing to Do in Competitive Show Choir, Is To Win… Or Lose, Trying!

Sometimes it may seem as if your show choir doesn't have the talent or experience to compete at the highest levels anymore. In my opinion, the mistake made by a lot of programs, is to *drop their advanced group* into a lower division, where the director believes they will probably *have a better chance of placing*. I believe, this action *could be detrimental*, because once you take your group out of the highest division your kids may lose their confidence, *believing they can no longer compete with the best*, or at least they'll believe that *you believe that*! Other directors, choirs and adjudicators, may also believe that very same thing, based on your taking that action! So, when you feel that your group needs a shot in the arm and maybe a new direction, bring in your staff and other professionals, who you trust, to help you devise remedies for your group's problems. But for heaven's sake, *continue competing at the highest level*! I believe that the best way for your kids to learn is through competing against the *best show choirs of the day*. I had the legendary super-show-choir, *West Covina Chamber Singers* as my role model, in the late 1970s and early 1980s! We finally beat them, but not until my *eighth year of teaching*! Let everyone in your group know, that they are all taking a giant risk that *they'll lose*, the higher the division is that you decide to compete in. But, by the same token, they should take that risk because they believe in themselves, and they know in their hearts, *that this is where they belong*! I personally believe it's better for the ego to be known as a *competitor against the winners…* than a *winner against the beginners*! That is not to say that entering your groups in the novice or intermediate categories is not a good choice while they are learning how to be a good show choir. But what I *am suggesting*, is that as soon as you begin successfully competing in the advanced division, you should *never allow yourself to drop your group down to a lower division,* simply because you believe you may have a weaker group this year than last. That's a perfect example of *unnecessarily quitting*, as in the saying, "*If the fire's too hot, get out of the kitchen*!" Have patience and exhibit faith in your group, even when they lose. That will pay off enormous dividends in the future! *I promise*!

3. Tailor Your Show to Fit Your Students' Strengths!

I am guessing… *assuming*, I suppose, that every show choir director, who takes this genre seriously, is also an artist, in some way, as a singer, an instrumentalist, an arranger or a composer. As artists we each have our own favorite styles of music, favorite singers, favorite musicals, you get the idea. We should *absolutely* feel free to let our students know what our favorites are, just as the students should be made to feel free to let us know what their favorites are. This, as you well know, is called *mutual sharing,* and is honestly, an essential part of a good teacher-student relationship, no matter *how you may feel* about some of their favorite "music!" But, from experience, I can tell you, that when you build a show, *without considering the talents, likes and experience of your performers…* no matter how great that show is on paper, you will *never* be satisfied with how your students perform it! *Never!* That's because it is probably not a good fit for them! Perhaps a group you have in the future could perform that show more to your liking? But you will only know if you make the effort to learn a little bit about your students first! Also, I advise you *not* to put songs in your show, simply because they're popular right now… because in a few months, when you finally perform them, *they may be old news*. Build your show with the songs that you *know* your group will excel with! This show may end up having a few of your favorite songs, a few that you don't really care for and a few more that you have never heard of before, that were suggested by your choreographer, whom you trust! The students, too, may be helpful when considering song choices… just be aware that their knowledge of musical literature will probably be *severely limited to what is current*. When a song choice obviously doesn't work for your group, *don't keep trying to make it fit… just drop it*, try something else, and move forward. Selecting a winning show is strictly a business. Begin with your students' strengths, and build from there.

4. Keep Learning… Teaching, is a Lifelong Endeavor… Never Stop Evolving!

Teaching, like learning, is a lifelong endeavor, and it's important to never stop growing! Consider all of the changes you see, regardless of whether or not you are personally enthralled with them. The "mid-west" competitive show choir style, which features a traditional big accompanying band (including trumpets and trombones), has been around for decades in the mid-west, but is relatively new to us out here, in California, rearing its head around the year 2000, and becoming popular with a lot of Southern California groups beginning then. It is an exciting style that features a big band that the director usually conducts, leading to powerful accompaniments that the traditional combo can't come close to duplicating. *I admire that part of it*, but I can't afford to hire enough professional arrangers or instrumental performers and the students available to us, are generally not advanced enough to accompany us. I also don't have time to rehearse and direct the band. In addition, I think that if one is not careful, *the instruments can easily blow away the fragile sound of the choir*. So, I acknowledged this change in show choir, *although I did not want to jump head first into it…* but instead, Doug and I *gleaned several important elements from this style*, to up our game.

1) We used risers to let the choir be seen and to strengthen the clarity of the uniform moves.

2) We increased the instrumentation for our accompanying band, usually adding a second keyboard, and a variety of other instruments like harp, guitar, trumpet or extra percussion, whatever each particular show called for.

3) We used the "affected" dynamics that many of these groups used, to enhance our vocal excitement.

In essence, Doug and my groups became *"hybrids" of the free California style and the big band mid-west style!* For us, this was a very doable compromise! This is just one way to keep evolving. There are so many different musical styles that you can use besides pop and musical theatre. Occasionally using an effective arrangement from another genre such as *jazz, classical* or *folk*, will heighten your students' musical awareness and possibly be that "*missing piece*" your show needs to make it a winner!

5. Trophies are Subjective. Learn to Win and Lose With Dignity!

I would love to say that there are *five simple steps to building a winning show choir…* but unfortunately, *there aren't*! In school, we as directors generally have our groups shaped by our available talent, experience and the attitudes of our students. Luck and timing alone, *occasionally* have a lot more to do with a win than the *thousand hours you rehearsed the show* with your group… *but not normally*. Sometimes your group's sound is *not as full* as it should be, due to a shortage of strong singers, but your dancers are terrific! Even if you stress the exceptional dancing in your show, your students will *still not impress with their vocal sound…* so depending upon the score sheet and adjudicators of each competition… sometimes you may find yourself *not placing!* At other times, you may not have strong *dancers* or *singers*! So, you do your magic with their *performance skills…* but again… you may not place at every competition you go to! You may even have a great singing and performing group, *the best you've ever had*, and still wind-up on the wrong side of the trophies! Learning to *lose with dignity* is perhaps the most difficult skill a student can learn. But remember, *they take their cues from you*! You can help them learn to live through a *non-placing event,* by reminding them that anything decided by judges is *subjective*, and perhaps they just didn't see or hear what they were looking for? Or possibly the adjudicators brought up some very valid *key weaknesses* that your group needs to work on? *Losing with dignity* makes *performing,* the more important part of competing… *not the trophies*! Another thing to remember is that it's never a good idea to *blame the adjudicators*, for your losing effort. Even if you secretly believe that a judge or two were *"out to get you"* at the competition… approach this with your students, from the angle that your group probably *"did not give the adjudicators what they were looking for."* This keeps things professional, instead of hateful and emotional. Believe me, it took me a few years to figure this one out! Also, *getting too up about winning*, especially in this age of prominent social media, will label your group to others as being *arrogant*! Learn to win or lose with the same respectful response. That doesn't mean that your kids can't be excited about placing or winning… it means that they should not *gloat about it*! Remember, the old adage, still applies… "*You will pass the same competitors on the way down... as you passed on the way up!"*

6. Stay True to Your Vision… Instead of Trying to Please Everyone Else!

The worst time for any show choir teacher is usually that first year. That's because if they follow a popular teacher, then according to some students, "this year's group *can't possibly be as good as last year's,*" therefore, in their opinions, *the program is going to suck*! For these students, their bias becomes their own *self-fulfilling prophecy*. If the choir turns out to be successful, after all, then those same students may feel stupid, so their *bad attitudes will probably persist* even after the new teacher has established himself, in order to save face! Also, if the teacher has the guts to make significant changes, that they deem necessary to the program, some students, who were close to the former teacher, may take this as an act of disrespect! Again, the bad attitude will probably persist! I personally take the "*no prisoners*," gutsy approach when I have been hired at a new school. I have always been one to *instantly make changes*, which I consider to be better for the program. I hang tough through the plethora of student, parent and administrator complaints, until eventually, *everything falls neatly into place*, and the majority of the kids are happy, while the disgruntled ones normally either quit or graduate. This normally takes a year or two, depending upon how many juniors and seniors are in the program when I first take over, and how popular the last teacher was. What I am trying to say is that I believe every show choir director who is *worth his or her salt* needs to follow their overall vision! This should be true, *regardless* of a few complaints about changing the status quo. In general, very few people like changes, until they are proven to be, *what you knew all along…* better for the program, or they simply get *used* to them! As competing show choir directors, each of us must decide right away, if we are building a show that is a *musical and visual piece of art*, or if we are *merely trying to win*? The answer should be, *both*! Not everyone in your groups may agree with your bold direction, but, even as some students quit, other students who were not in choir before will surely join as soon as they see what a successful and fun place it is to be, in your choir program! The students come and go, from one year to the next, but as long as you are at that school… *your program is what will define you…* so make it your own!

7. If Your Group is Young and Inexperienced... Learn to Develop Talent!

A director does not always have the luxury of *an unlimited supply of ready talent auditioning* for their show choirs. Sometimes, you may find that no one in your group is ready to excel on stage. So what do you do? Well, initially prepare for a few tough outings, but use them *to develop the weak skills in your kids.* Like a sports team using "scrimmages," *expose your kids to the best groups you can,* in competition. Then, assess their skill levels, compared to their competitors, and do whatever is necessary to make them better. Just one *above-average singer* per section, a *soloist* and one *good dancer* will make your well-rehearsed group at least *marginally competitive*! The higher the level of competition you want your group to compete in, the harder you must work them, *and the harder they must work themselves*! Sometimes you may have a potential soloist, who lacks confidence and training, so you work with them every week, and eventually put them out there to sing solo in a performance. As you show more confidence in them, they will surely feel more confidence in themselves! A few more times out there and they will probably be begging you to let them sing solos, *because now that they see themselves as being good at it... it's fun*! When I first began teaching at Nogales High School in 1979, they did not even have a show choir. By 1983, we had already won two trophies, at the highest high school levels for show choir! *It wasn't fun losing competitions during the previous years*, but it was *necessary* for the kids to learn what it took, in order to place as a show choir! Nowadays, with divisions and more competitions, an experienced show choir director and their *modestly skilled, and experienced group,* could probably make the transition from *not placing* to *placing* within the same school year! But the road to success in show choir, for young and inexperienced groups has not changed. You have to first expose your students to *who* and *what* they are trying to beat... *and then go about training them to do exactly that*!

8. Work Just As Hard Preparing Your Women's Groups as Your Mixed!

I observed throughout my decades of directing show choirs, that many schools did not place the same importance on their women's show choirs as their mixed? Tradition is probably the main culprit here, as top mixed show choirs in California generally evolved out of their schools' elite classical mixed chamber singers, *giving them some of the best singers at their school to work with*! To me, women's show choir seems like an obvious thing to add to your program. Most schools offer at least one women's choir, usually more, and in my experience, more girls generally join choir than boys. But, as far as I know, it wasn't until *Rollie Maxson*, of Arcadia High School, unleashed his women's show choir, *New Spirit* on the circuit in the early 1980s, followed by my own Nogales High School *Dream Street Singers*, Bonita Vista's *Sound Unlimited* and Burroughs' *Sound Sensations*... that women's show choirs really began to make a strong impact in competitions, slowly and eventually leading to women's divisions in most major competitions, today! I would have to say that my women's groups, even the younger ones, generally have *amassed better competition records than any of my mixed groups*! I attribute this to many of our competitors' choir programs, *not preparing their women's groups as hard, as they do their mixed groups*. On the other hand, I have always tried to prepare *all of my groups equally hard*. So, when my top mixed group is competing against the best groups out there... sometimes my women's groups have the luxury of competing against less prepared competitors. *This is to take nothing away from the competitive prowess of each of my women's groups.* After all, thcy have been known to *beat some very good mixed groups,* as well, when pitted against them, *including my own*! I suppose I am just saying that until a director considers their women's group as being something more than just a "*secondary*" competitor... *they will be leaving the potential for a lot of show choir success and even more wonderful memories... untapped*!

9. Choose Which Competitions to Attend… Wisely!

There is a time for attending every competition your groups can enter. That would be either when all of your groups are doing incredibly well, or when you are first starting out. If your groups are indeed, *doing incredibly well*, like the Romans did, competing more, allows you to *conquer more*! If you are just starting out, competing more (and generally not placing) shows your students *who* is out their, and *what* it would *theoretically* take, and how *dramatically* they would need to improve… *to beat them*! But if your group falls into the middle category… *where they sometimes place and sometimes don't*, like many groups, it would behoove you to separate those competitions by your group's successes. If you are consistently scored close to last at some competitions, then competing there again and hoping for a different outcome, with all of the same variables… is the *classic definition of insanity*! If your group is stronger this year, and you have added a larger band or extra props and you want to try your show out at that competition again? Do it! If you are still scored low… I would suggest that you take a *hiatus* from there, next year. On the other hand, if you always do well at particular competitions, then obviously those adjudicators like your style, so it would be crazy *not* to keep going there! I hope you are not taking what I am suggesting as *giving up* or *not always trying to improve*. Nothing could be further from the truth! But, having your students *beat-up* by the judges every year, by attending a festival where your group *very obviously does not fit the criteria of what the adjudicators are looking for, is not smart*. You can always go back to that festival, once you figure out what it is your show lacks, according to the judges. Then, maybe you will find some semblance of success for your kids. Bottom line, at the end of the year, it's a lot more fun for your students to say that they placed or *were competitive* almost everywhere they went, than to say, *they were clobbered at a particular competition for the fourth straight year*! Some people say that a little adversity is good for a show choir and I would agree… as long as that adversity *still gives that show choir a chance to win*!

10. Empower Your Students, by Allowing Them to Share in the Responsibility!

Certainly as a director, you know that you usually have the last word, when it comes to your program. But when that word comes *only from you*, your students may feel a lack of *personal responsibility*, leading them to become more like worker ants, *merely following instructions, but never really thinking about why?* Student leaders can be very helpful and responsible, creating another set of voices urging their members to work harder and to get with the program! Many directors I've known, like to consolidate all of their student officers for *every choral group in the entire program... into one class* (their top choir) and then have a *representative* from every other group, attend their officer meetings and report back to their groups, what was discussed. I prefer thinking *of every individual choir as being autonomous*, but still a part of the united choirs of the school. I based this method on the United States, separate, autonomous states, all, but part of the country at large! With five choirs, this means *five different sets of officers*. This method of leadership in my choirs has *empowered* each group to always do the best they can, because they are doing it *for their group* and don't want to let their fellow members down! I believe that everyone works harder and with more drive, when they have a voice and feel a sense of ownership and responsibility. The officers in each individual group will help to personalize everything their choral group does, leading to bonding, and making everyone proud of the group they're in, as well as the choir at large. Other advantages of trusting the students with some of the responsibility, include section leaders teaching parts at lunch, officers setting up "safe" choir parties, leaders designing their choir tee shirts, some of the better dancers assisting the choreographer at rehearsals, officers taking a big part in designing the end of the year banquet, and officers even running an event like a talent show, by themselves! When student leaders are treated as an important part of the leadership team, my experience has been, that they thrive! The key is to make sure that your leaders know you need them! A little trust can go a long way!

11. Don't Try to Do It All by Yourself… Add a Loyal and Competent Staff!

To anyone who has ever run a show choir program, *this one is a no-brainer*. But to anyone who is only *contemplating* directing show choir… let me just enlighten you, as to why adding a loyal and competent staff is so indispensible to being successful over the long haul. Over the years, I have been privileged to work alongside two great talents with loyalty to spare! My wife, Margaret, is a whiz at creating eye-catching programs, beautifully coordinated costumes and efficient score sheets for our festivals and other events. *I don't have those skills*, so as a staff member, she has made my groups better! Doug Kuhl, who has choreographed most of my groups at three different high schools, one junior high and a community college, as well as choreographing almost every musical we have been a part of at Nogales, Diamond Bar and Brea High Schools, from 1980-2016, until I retired, has incredible talent and drive. He also helped Margaret to design the costumes, built props and decorated the choir room! *I don't have Doug's skill set, either*. So, as a staff member, he has made my groups better! My own strengths are arranging music, teaching and directing music, organizing trips and coming up with "*inspirational*" speeches, when I felt the choirs needed one. My skills *complemented* those of Margaret and Doug *hence we became a great team*! I also, almost always had an accompanist. Eventually, however, each one of them quit, and we had to find a new one, hoping that this position would mean *more than just a job to them*. If they did have a problem with our long hours of rehearsal and performances… then their playing was generally *a bit faulty*, probably due to a lack of practice or focus. On the other hand, if they were fully committed to the choirs, then *they were consistently good*, because they *accepted their responsibility*, to the benefit of the entire choir family! Finally, *Fundraising* should be the responsibility of the *parent boosters*, if possible. This gives you, *the director*, more time… *to be just that*!

12. Happy Memories Begin as Positive Experiences!

If you're not careful, over a span of time, repeatedly doing the same things, in the same way… is likely to become rather *boring and monotonous*. In show choir, it's easy to keep things interesting, if you simply vary your shows each year and shake-up the competitions you attend or trips you take, *even just a little*. For example, we would take a choir trip every year, to *Disneyland* to perform or participate in a workshop! The kids would always get very excited about this, even though many of them had Disneyland passes, that allowed them to visit the park *anytime they wanted to*! Why the excitement? Because our choir trip took place on a school day and they were traveling there with all of their friends! In addition, the workshops we participated in *were always a little different each year*. Happy memories? You bet! Another great activity is taking a group of interested students to see a popular *musical* at a professional theatre. I did this mostly while I was teaching at Nogales High School, and I can tell you that not only did the students appreciate it… *but so did their parents*. The most exciting activity, of course, is an *overnight trip*, with or without performing involved, if your school district will allow that choice. I think this type of trip is *always popular* with the kids and parents. From experience, the best places to take your group would include Orlando (stay at a Disney property), New York City (everyone likes to stay at the Marriott Marquis), Chicago (stay in the touristy area) and Washington D.C. (it may be safer to stay in nearby Virginia). If you have previously been to the city your group is traveling to, *don't leave decisions like hotels and flights to a travel agent.* After investigating, select them yourself and have the agent, book them for you, if you like. You will control the trip much better, if there are no *built-in surprises, planned by someone else who probably does not care as much about the trip as you do*. All in all, just keep creating safe, fun and worthwhile activities, and your students will *fondly remember them forever*!

13. Don't Get Frustrated about Collecting Money from Students!

I have always dealt with this "money" issue, but especially since the ACLU sued public school districts, a while back, for charging students fees for costumes, trips or training needed for extracurricular activities (including show choir) when they were guaranteed a *free public education*, by the US government. Every school district, especially in California, quickly changed their wording to abide by this philosophy. Student *fees* became *non-mandatory donations*. Now, I'm hearing that a teacher cannot even tell their students either in writing or verbally exactly *how much money they are being encouraged to donate*! Okay. I get it. Run a major show choir program on donations that are *not mandatory* and *keep the amount that we need secret*? Do these politicians and lawyers ever read what ridiculous things they make performing arts teachers abide by? The state and federal governments certainly don't run on *non-mandatory donations*? If you don't pay your taxes, you get in big trouble, regardless of how poor you are. Do the State Colleges and Universities run on non-mandatory donations? Just try *not paying* your tuition and see how quickly you can say, *kicked out*! The way public schools are treated is completely *ludicrous*! In the old days, choir teachers, like myself, would pay for any students who could not afford something, out of the choir coffers. It worked great and everyone participated. The *current philosophy*, as I understand it, even tells people who *can pay*, that they *don't have to pay*! So, as show choir teachers, our best bet is to gently, because it's for the best, *place the financial responsibility on the participating students and parents*. From experience, my boosters have been such a blessing to the program! I would also host as many concerts as possible and never charge less than the cost of an adult movie ticket. You will make a lot of money. Finally, discuss with your parents and students what type of program they want to have, and if it costs more than they think they can raise, carefully *cut back your program to reflect that lack of financial support.* As teachers, we can come up with all sorts of possibilities for our groups. But the truth is… what we *can* do…

completely depends upon our student and parent financial support!

14. Sell A Lot Of Parent Tickets For Every Local Competition!

I know that this sounds like it belongs on a "*to do*" list, much more than being labeled an essential *choir concept*, but let me explain. Beginning with the 1982 school year and then throughout my career, I have asked my students to buy tickets for *all of their local competitions*, so that we were certain to have a healthy *cheering section*. During my competitions, *prior* to 1982, I don't think I ever *sold any presale tickets*! The thing was, when we had no built-in cheering section, our audience applause was minimal. This resulted in *the adjudicators*, scoring us as if we were an *afterthought*. However, as soon as we began competing with a healthy *cheering section*, our applause improved significantly, and often, the adjudicators seemed to take that into consideration with their scoring, with comments like, "the audience obviously loves you!" This did not guarantee us a trophy, of course, but it made *everybody* notice us. Filling your competitions with your supporters *also* gets your families to appreciate show choir more and builds your choir support! Encouraging them to buy *presale tickets,* pretty much assures you that they will be there! In addition, in the early years, many festivals were generally full by October, because there weren't many competitions out there, to go to! Consequently, every group from the previous year, usually returned to the same competitions and *rushed to buy presale tickets*, so their parents would not be shut out! I was always given *more consideration* to be *accepted into a competition,* when I told the festival host that my group *always bought at least 75 presale tickets* to every local show choir competition that we participated in! This played a major role in getting accepted into both the *Aztec Sing* and the *West Covina* events, while Nogales was just breaking into the show choir circuit, in the early 1980s. Throughout the years, I have noticed that most of the successful groups *always have a healthy support section* at *every competition they go to*! This builds a *climate of success,* where your group *builds off of their supporters* and their thunderous applause at every event they go to! In time, your groups and their supporters will become like *one cohesive entity* that travels from festival to festival *in search of trophies*! When you reach this point… *it becomes a lot of fun for everybody*!

CHAPTER 24

My Final Thoughts

Wow! It's done! This *gargantuan, yet highly enjoyable,* "journey down memory lane," that took me back through forty years of my show choirs' history! I was so driven to write this book, that it feels *absolutely wonderful* to have finally completed it! I fully dedicate, *One, Two, Three, Pizzazz*, to my eclectic and talented show choir *kids*, who graciously shared a few special years of their lives with me, which resulted in the inspiration behind the writing of this book! I hope everyone who was in my show choirs anytime between 1977-2016, can fully appreciate, just how talented, professional and unforgettable, all of you really are! I'm not only talking about the soloists and the leaders… but *every* member of my show choirs had something *very important* to share with their groups, and sometimes you probably didn't even realize that I saw it… *but I always did.* Thank you for your efforts and determination and for the individual skills and passion you shared! As I have read and reread your heartfelt thoughts and memories, it causes me to laugh, tear-up or just smile. In fact, in some ways, reading them makes me feel as if *we were all at school or at a competition, together... once again*! It's as if that time has never ended for any of us!

To be honest though, as much as I loved this process, and all of the reconnections it has led to, I'm a little saddened that I was not able to reconnect with *all of my former students*. I understand how *unlikely,* that scenario was to happen, but just the same, it would have been nice to have everyone at this *party*, to help celebrate our time in show choir together! That being said, I hope to hear from *every one of my former students*, at some point, just to catch up and reminisce about show choir... and then I will finally feel like *this reunion is complete*! In the meantime, a great big **THANK YOU**, to all of my former students, parents and associates who took the time and effort to make this journey more exciting, through the sharing of your memories, thoughts and answers to questions. As a result, no matter how this book turns out... just like our competition shows back in the day... *we created it together*!

Perhaps the one thing I enjoyed most about teaching show choir, was experiencing the process of *creating, building* and *rehearsing* the competition shows. By the time each group was ready to compete, in late January, I just loved watching those *run-throughs of their shows in class every day*! Some of my favorite productions, such as the 1982 Nogales *Chamber Singers* show, the 2003 Diamond Bar *Marquis* show and the 2010 Brea *Masquerade* show... *never won*! In fact, the 1982 Nogales show, *never even placed*! That's why I am so adamant that *trophies aren't really all that important*. Oh, it's awfully fun to win... but over time, just being a part of a *magnificent show*, whether it placed or not, *actually means so much more to everyone involved*, don't you think?

Curiously, through my research, I kept observing a few of my own teaching "*patterns*," that I wasn't really aware of at the time. For example, I was always tinkering with our panel of student officers, especially when I was trying to dramatically improve a group. Most years, we had the traditional *one president per choir*, but there were years where we had as many as *five presidents and no vice-presidents* for one group or *one president and five vice-presidents*! Either way, my thinking was, that each president or vice-president, could individually handle *one different choir need* (daily operations, activities, historian, librarian, treasurer, secretary) and then come together as equals to discuss the general concerns. I also took note (although it was far from a secret) that although I embraced *new technology* insofar as using computers and synthesizers, I remained true to the old "pencil and paper" when it came to arranging songs and I also continued to use "hand-outs" in class instead of telling everyone to *check my website*. In addition, I only used *power point* when I had to! I much preferred the more personal method of spending my time *talking and listening* to the students in my classes. So, in all of these ways, I was apparently, *not evolving* in the normal sense! Instead, I *evolved* to my comfort level with technology, and stayed there for my entire career! But, I do not regret that. Doing things the '*old fashioned*' way somehow just seemed more natural to me. I also liked to "fix" broken shows by adding a tried and true power-ballad, such as *Don't Cry Out Loud* or *Angel of the Morning*, and it always seemed to work, too! More sparingly, I would *add humor* to an a cappella, that needed a boost! A good example would be, *Twinkle, Twinkle Little Star,* where the boys would sing, "Coo Coo, Coo Coo!" Surprisingly, no one in the audience laughed, but we always got a lot of compliments for our *very unusual arrangement*! Finally, I would energize ballads that were too draggy, by adding a *calypso beat*. A good example of this would be *Always On My Mind*. Regardless of what I did, to Doug's credit, *he always made it work with the show*.

An *uncommon* thing that I did with my show choirs, going all the way back to 1977, was to start teaching and rehearsing our competition shows, *beginning in the very first week of school!* I don't think many of the other local choir directors were as focused on show choir as much as I was, because I used to take a little flak from some of them, for doing that. Some of them even suggested that I didn't care about teaching other choral music, or music fundamentals, *only show choir*. At first, this talk bothered me, but after I thought about it, I laughed. *So what, if my show choirs were predominantly focused on show choir music!* After all… *they were show choirs*! In defense of my programs, all of my choirs, including the show choirs, learned some traditional music, every year, to sing at our home concerts, and they became familiar with music fundamentals through learning to sing our competition sets. In addition, all of my groups sang sensitive ballads and/or a cappellas within their shows, chock full of dynamics and well thought-out interpretations. I think I learned, early on, that if I expected my groups to do well in show choir competitions, *I had better grab every possible advantage I could*, because there were always a lot of great competing groups out there that we were trying to beat! Starting rehearsals in September, *always* worked well for my show choirs, and never took away from our traditional singing… *it just made us work a lot harder*! As singer, Rick Nelson said in his song, *Garden Party*, "*You can't please everyone, so you've gotta please yourself!*"

Since we're talking about criticism, not every student or parent or principal, throughout the years, was always happy with my decisions, or for that matter, *with me*! But by the same token, *I did not always agree with their criticisms, either*! Sometimes I think, to make peace, we simply agreed to disagree. Generally I would have to say that most of the criticisms were generated by students or parents being taken out of their *comfort zones* by something I said or *supposedly said,* did *or supposedly did,* or possibly by a misunderstanding. In any case, these complaints *rarely went beyond* a parent conference or a phone call. Eventually we always seemed to get back on the same page. I'll be the first to admit that I can often come across as an *overly focused*, *unpredictable* and *odd* individual. *That's just who I am*! My thanks to all of my students, parents, staff and administrators who put up with me for all of those years, and even joined me in putting on hundreds of *unbelievably exciting performances*! As far as getting along with other choir directors, I didn't really have much trouble, until after my groups became *competitive with theirs*. At one point, I was actually accused of *cheating*, by a particular group of directors, because I allowed my students to be in *multiple groups*! Although I wasn't cheating, *they were absolutely correct*! I have *always encouraged my students* to take more than one choir, for the good of the choral program, and for their own enhanced *singing and performing opportunities*! I believe that if there was *no rule* saying that I *couldn't enter a group into a competition in which some of its members were also in another group,* then exactly how was I cheating? However, when there was a *written rule against this*, on their application forms (as there occasionally was), *I always abided*! Respectfully, I think these directors may have gotten, "*breaking a rule*" confused with "*being creative*." I personally believe that *all show choirs* should never stop improving themselves, and directors often need to be creative in solving any problems or shortcomings their groups may have. *No offense intended to anyone*, but to me, creatively solving problems is a *tremendously important* part of being an effective show choir director. In addition, I believe that any choral director, who *arbitrarily uses rules in the competitions they host* to stop another group from *naturally evolving*, probably does it for one of two reasons:

A) *They fear that without the rule in place, the offending groups may gain an unfair competitive advantage.*
B) *They like things the way they are, and they believe "a rule" will keep the status quo in place!*

In politics, when one party attempts to control *everyone else* through the use of rules, they call this form of government, *fascism*. Again, I truly mean no offense to any other show choir directors, who may hold different opinions from my own. I am well aware that we *need some guidance or rules* in just about everything we do in life, to avoid chaos. But in the *creative arts*, I see arbitrary rules as *stunting the growth* of the imagination. Consider this; freedom of imagination, in time, may evolve show choirs to a place we can't even imagine today! But just because we have the *freedom* to take it there, does *not necessarily* mean that we all have to! Hence, the freedom to NOT all go in the same direction, allowing *diversity* in show choir styles to once again, *be valued*!

In theory, to both Doug and I, show choir was a magical place, where we sought eventual *perfection* (or the closest thing to it) from every student in our show choirs, as far as their *singing, dancing, performing*, and *attitude*. We expected *total dedication*! We believed, for good reason, that this *mindset* would lead a group to become *determined, well rehearsed and united*… and it did, time after time! Most of our problems in show choirs, over the years, did not deal with poor talent but with *poor attitudes*. In show choir, we are always *setting spots* and *auditioning solos*. It seems that no one wanted to be in the back row of a performance and almost everyone wanted a solo! Good for them! However, in the end, *Doug and I would jointly decide* where to place the choir members, and *we would also select* the soloists for each song. Our policy had always been that *all solos and spots are temporary* and may be taken from a student at any time, for the good of the show, by another student, who is *perceived by us* to be performing the spot or singing the solo better! When I was in junior high band, we called this procedure, *challenging someone*! This was a method where, for example, the third chair trumpet could "challenge" the second chair to play a sequence of notes, from one of their band pieces, *better than they could*, in private, in front of the director. The winner would then be awarded *second chair*! Procedures like these are designed to keep everyone working hard *all of the time*, and to allow the hardest working students a chance to improve their situations. But sometimes, every student *did not react well* to the spontaneous changes that Doug and I assessed. When a student appeared to be visibly angry about *not getting what they wanted*, resulting in a poor work ethic, they were usually *invited* to a *private counseling session with me*. If they still did not cease their poor attitude, they ran the risk of *being removed from the show, altogether*! However, this rarely happened. Most disgruntled students eventually got with the program, or quit choir, completely, to find some other activity, better suited to their personal preferences.

During the forty years that I taught show choir, I always felt a tremendous determination to make every group I directed as *perfect as possible*! In theory, I wanted them each to win *every competition they entered*! I was very competitive, and usually, my students were too. For the first twenty-five years, when we did not win, I always studied the adjudicators' score sheets and proceeded to work on all of the problems they mentioned. But, over time, the directors of some of our *previous competitors,* retired, and *became our new adjudicators*! Unfortunately, some of them seemed to always have us pegged for a certain spot, *no matter how we performed.* In all honesty, a number of the adjudicators were always scoring us high, no matter what… while a number of others would always score us lower. Although I honestly refrain from calling anyone a cheater, as I discussed in the *Introduction*, this is when I realized that politics could be playing a part in these competitions, through the adjudicators' incidental preferences. Perhaps they always have? It got so I could call the outcome of every competition we were participating in, based on who the adjudicators were and what style of show choir they preferred, before the competition ever happened! I told my students that life was not always fair, but at the end of the day, win or lose, *they still got to perform their hearts out and thrill the crowds*! This is what they needed to hear, when we sometimes entered competitions that were so contrary to our chances of winning, that we would finish the night in a very uncharacteristic seventh, eighth or ninth place. And of course, we would hopefully follow that competition with a win somewhere else! If competing show choir is nothing else… *it is a roller coaster of emotions that as staff and students, we must learn to navigate… or else we should quit competing altogether*!

Every year, both Doug and I had those *"go to" students*, who would always be there to do whatever was needed. Sometimes, they even stayed on, after graduation, as part of our staff. There were also times when we knew these kids so well, that they almost felt like family! Generally, these students started out as officers and grew into the added responsibility we would give them, at busy times during the year. A special thanks to all of them, and the selfless way they worked to help make the choirs better! A big thank you, also, to all of our *parents and parent boosters*, who have *worked overtime* to help the choirs, whether it was by raising money, riding the bus, selling tickets, sewing costumes, working Bingo, making spaghetti for everyone or a myriad of other things, that ultimately helped our choirs to thrive! I love how the best years in choir have always been those years when *all of us worked so well together*!

You know, I hadn't always planned on spending my entire working life as a teacher. When I got my first teaching job at Norco High School, I vividly recall sharing with a few of my students that I only planned on teaching for five years, or until I found a different career, somewhere in music or entertainment. Toward that end, in addition to teaching, I played guitar and sang at restaurants for a while in groups and as a solo act. I also performed in community theatre musicals in Corona, Glendora and Fontana. But, none of that ever came close to leading me toward a new career, so I basically decided to try something else. Next, I fancied that I wanted to be a professional *choral arranger*. I even met with well-known arranger, Ed Lojeski, and will always be grateful for the excellent arranging advice he gave me. I had groups of my students professionally record the songs, for demos, and then I tried, unsuccessfully, to publish and sell my original songs and arrangements (our company was called DAMAR), for about five years, while I was still teaching at Nogales. Next, I grew interested in teaching at the college level! I got an offer from Mount San Antonio College in Walnut, to teach one single period of show choir, twice a week. Doug and I taught it together, and agreed, after only a month, that *high school choir* was much more fun! So, I only lasted there for one semester. Following this, I got the Disney bug, and wanted to work at Disneyland! This was about 1995. My thought was to go in as a part-time music clinician... but I was hired into the Entertainment Division, as a *guest talent specialist*, instead! My job involved leading visiting groups through workshops, parades and stage concerts on the *Carnation Plaza stage,* mostly during weekends! I owe a lot to Disneyland for giving me that experience. I tried to move up in the company, but it was not in the cards for me. So, I resigned, in 2000, while I was working at Diamond Bar. Next, I tried my hand at directing community musicals! This was not so much as a possible career change, but because my son, Alex, became involved in *Stagelight Productions*, community theatre, in Brea, beginning when he was seven years old. Originally, the owner of Stagelight Productions, *Janice Kraus*, hired me as the music director, but after being paid for *musically directing* my first two shows with Stagelight, I chose to do the same thing for any future shows as a *volunteer*. That's because, for me, I felt that this activity was *mostly about spending time with Alex*, and helping all of the other kids in each cast, as the rest of the parent volunteers were doing... *for free*. Between the years of 1999 to 2011, I often served as music director for a large number of musicals produced by Brea's *Stagelight Productions*. Many times, these musicals were also choreographed and sometimes directed by Doug Kuhl! Besides working with Alex and Doug, the next best thing about my time spent with Stagelight, was that it introduced me to a number of stage musicals which I had never seen before. This experience proved invaluable when we were considering shows to do at both Diamond Bar and Brea Olinda high schools! *Finally*, I rekindled my love for writing prose, in the summer of 2009, and by 2010, while working at Brea, I self-published my first novel, *DIMENSIONS: The Wheat Field*. It actually sold pretty well. The Brea Borders store even had a rack for local authors, where they featured it! In 2011, I self published the sequel, *DIMENSIONS II: The Plethora*. I am sorry to say, this one did not sell as well! I remember buying back twenty copies, for a dollar a book, from Borders, when they closed their stores in May of 2011. *DIMENSIONS III: The Cloud Monsters,* written in 2012, was a story I had begun writing, in the late 1990s, for my son, Alex. It sold all right, but I only had one book signing for it, due to the stroke I incurred, later that year. Finally, the series was completed, when I self-published *DIMENSIONS IV: The Competition*! It turned out to be a pretty fun read, although, I actually wrote it, mostly to make sure that after the stroke… *I was still capable! Mary Pipes*, one of my wonderful choir parents, made a promo for the book, which ran a lot on the Internet. I am so grateful to her, for doing this. The book sold very well… for about a month! You know what? As a result of trying so hard to succeed at all of these *side-careers*, I learned *exactly* what many of my students have learned, through being in choir. I had *tried my hardest to succeed* at every one of these ventures, just as my students have always tried so hard in solo auditions and competitions. Ultimately, I was not always successful, comparable to my students not always getting the solo or winning in competition. But, in actuality, *we were both completely successful at everything we had tried*! That's because of those wonderful experiences we had, with or without the intended payoffs, and the relationships we had made, along the way, which were *beyond incredible*, giving each of us memories that would last a lifetime! You know, that old film, with Richard Dreyfus, *Mr. Holland's Opus*? It was the story of a public school music teacher (Hmm? Sound familiar?), who ended up putting off his dreams of hearing the opus he composed, performed, in order to teach and raise a family. During the last days of his teaching career, before he retired, his former and current students came together to play his opus, enabling him to finally be able to hear it performed, as he directed it! So, his dream came true, after all! Unlike him, however, I was able to chase *all of my dreams*, one at a time, *while* I was a teacher! Even when those adventures ended up being less than what I had hoped for… surprisingly, just having the opportunity to try each of them out… *proved to be completely satisfying!*

A very important truth I learned about show choir, very early, as a matter of fact, is that, *you can't always get what you want, unless you allow yourself to want what you get!* What I mean to say is, understandably, it seems like every competing show choir program wants to win! But winning is not always possible. I learned, first hand, that some years are going to be *lean in the awards categories* for some of your groups, *maybe all of them…* so you adapt the year, putting the emphasis on other things! Perhaps you put on a *musical* or take the group(s) on an *overnight trip* somewhere? Do you see? That year may be a bit disappointing on the competition side, but the entire year does not need to be remembered in that way! Also, there have been many years where my advanced girls group was *way more successful* in competition than my advanced mixed! So, it's important that I ride that *crest of success* with my girls, letting them know that I fully support them, instead of going into *extended mourning* over my mixed group, simply because *they did not reach competition expectations*! I find that the best attitude, when you have multiple show choirs, is to act like a parent with multiple kids. *You love them all*, you support them all, regardless of how talented they are, and in the process, help each one to find their niche! This will give you the best chance of seeing *everything turn out well for everyone*!

I am asked, quite frequently, in fact, what I learned through investigating all of my years of show choir, *with the assistance of my online choir groups*? Well, I actually learned quite a bit, that had *absolutely nothing to do with singing or dancing*! Each of my school choir sites, were very different from one another, just as the choirs I directed at each school, and the time periods they represented, were all very different, and therefore *difficult to compare*. Each site proved to be very unique!

To begin with, the ***Norco*** **(1977-79) site**, with students I had only known for one or two years, *at the very beginning of my career*, was actually quite helpful when I would throw questions at them. Their memories of choir were far different from the other schools, because they didn't have the *backlog of competition experiences* that many of the students from my other programs (where I had taught for a longer time) had. My former students at Norco High School mostly remembered friends and fun, when it came to their *choir experiences.* Specifically, they recalled the two years, when I served as their choir director, as being *tumultuous* in the beginning, but *quite fun*, beyond that! Frankly, I'm surprised they remembered as much as they did. I interviewed them *forty years after the fact*!

The ***Nogales*** **(1979-1998) site** was alert and alive from the very beginning! They came up with answers to questions, almost as quickly as I could ask them! They also remembered costume colors from over thirty years ago! Their posts were heartwarming and honest. Not surprisingly, a larger percentage of my students from Nogales participated in this project than from my other three high schools. Choir somehow seemed to be *more important* to a lot of these kids, and I think that we had a closer relationship, as a result. It was a joy to reconnect with all of that passion and enthusiasm, once again. As many of my former students shared, choir, for them, was a *safe and nurturing family*, where they could find *solace from reality* when they needed to.

The ***Diamond Bar*** **(1998-2005) site** was also very helpful, with a number of former students getting involved! I think most of us agreed that *we achieved some incredible things, over our seven years together at Diamond Bar*! I really enjoyed reading my former students' *memories* and *thoughts* that they posted, because it immediately brought back my own memories of how exciting and fun those seven years at Diamond Bar High School had been! Most of my former students shared memories about the good times they had, and of how choir was *immediately different and successful when Doug and I first arrived*! Their posts were both gracious and thoughtful. Go Brahmas!

The ***Brea Olinda* (2005-2016) site** was different, still. Since I lived in Brea and my son, Alex, was in my program there, this school had a noticeably *unique feel* to me. But, regarding the site, it was active, with a lot of wonderful memories shared! The students who participated gave a great deal of insight into what it was like to be in the choir, at Brea Olinda High School, for each of my eleven years! They remembered a lot of specific things about every competition year! We also had a number of parents help out by answering several difficult *historical* questions, and then posting some beautifully heartfelt memories! Although we always had a number of *very helpful parents* at every school I taught at, with the exception of the Diamond Bar parents graciously coming together *en masse* to work *Bingo, two or three times a year,* my Brea choir parents were *different* from the parents at all of my other schools. That's because from the time I arrived there, they were always *involved and available* to help out in every area. Part of this, I think, was the *tradition of active parents in the Brea Choirs*, which eventually led to a very successful *Choir Booster Club*! A great big *thank you* goes to all of my former Brea students and parents who contributed to the memories we collected! Those terrific memories confirmed, *that we had a great run*!

And finally, the ***Brea Junior High (2005-2016) site, for Show Choir Express***, was a little unusual. The problem was that all of my choir kids from the junior high, when I left teaching in 2016, had already moved on to the high school, by the time I decided to write this book! Furthermore, the majority of my other former BJH choir kids were now *graduated from high school* and *even college*! They were light-years away from their *Show Choir Express* memories! But, the "*kids*" who participated, surprised me with just how much they remembered! Granted, there was not a great deal of activity on the site, but in time, I received *eighteen thoughtful student memories* from our alumni, of all ages... and what they wrote… was *priceless*!

That being said, I am very appreciative of *all the wonderful students and parents, from all of my schools,* who took the time to help me solve a mystery, or to post a special thought or memory from their time in choir. This experience was exactly what I had hoped it would be… *Reconnecting, Remembering and Rejoicing!*

In thinking back, quality *singing, dancing* and *performing* were unquestionably, *terribly important* components in creating a successful show choir. But, I can sum up the *most important ingredient* for success with each of my competing groups, in six words… *Finding the tenacious determination to win! This* was something that each of my students had to individually search for… and *find, within her or himself,* if they ever expected to become a winner! The exercise of *Pizzazz* showcases the energy inherent in *tenacious determination…* but it's certainly no substitute for it. Students, who were successful in their quest, would give a *great effort*, even when others did not. They were always *self-motivated* and in total control of their own performances! These were the kids that Doug and I absolutely *loved working with*, because by their actions, it was clear that they cared as much about each performance, as we did! Kids like that made teaching fun! It was no coincidence that our most successful competition years *always coincided* with united groups that carried *tenacious determination*, into battle!

I remember so many experiences throughout all of my years in show choir that make me smile, but none so much as this. In 1991, my son, Alex, was born! Margaret and I were so excited, and I remember the choir sharing our joy, through throwing a baby shower for us! Well, after his birth, I found myself torn between spending time at school to work with my groups or being home, spending time with Margaret and Alex! Luckily, it proved very doable, as Margaret would often bring Alex to choir rehearsals or performances, so we had the chance to spend more time together, while I was actually working! In the case of competitions, I would sometimes carry baby Alex into the warm-up room with me, and Margaret would then take him, as soon as my group and I headed for the stage. Well, one evening, I think Alex was about one and a half, we were in the warm-up room at Citrus College, with the Nogales High School Chamber Singers, and as we prepared to leave for the stage, Alex began shouting, "Daddy," as he grasped my neck tighter. After repeated unsuccessful attempts, on my part, to transfer him to Margaret, I conceded defeat, and decided to take him out into the theatre house, in the front row, with me. I figured I could direct with one arm while holding him with the other. When the time came for me to direct our a cappella piece, which was *Cockles and Mussels* (an old Irish folk song, that both Margaret and I had often sung to Alex, when we would put him to bed), I rose-up from the chair, holding Alex with my left arm, prepared to direct with my right, as we slowly walked forward, about five steps toward the stage. I began directing the choir. After a few moments, I heard soft, but audible sighs or "ahs" coming from the audience. I had assumed, that they thought Alex was cute, and that had caused the spontaneous reaction. But talking with Margaret after the performance, and watching the video of the performance, later, set me straight. While I was directing *Cockles and Mussels* with my right hand, Alex had actually been *mirroring my movements with his left hand*! *He was directing*! He continued directing with me for a number of years, regardless of the fact that some adjudicators and competing directors complained that *he was an unfair advantage*! Now, twenty-five years later, among other things, Alex has been a choral director, in his own right! Maybe someday his future son or daughter will carry on that same *tradition* with him? I sure hope so!

Well, there *was* show choir *before* I began directing choirs and there *is* still show choir *after I retired.* Show choir did not stop, simply because I did! My forty years of teaching and directing are merely a *speck of dust* in the continuing history of show choirs… but that was a *very special speck of dust for those of us who experienced it together*… and *that's why* this book exists! Look back, through these memory-filled pages, from time to time, at *your show choir history*, and remember it fondly, through the narrative that I've written, in combination with the thoughts and memories that you and your fellow students have contributed. For me, this book represents my final farewell to a life of teaching and competing. All of you "*kids*," who were there with me, even for a year, joined Doug and I and the staff to *create magic*! It was a forty-year adventure that I loved, and I'm so glad that many of you have come back to celebrate it with me!

It just wouldn't have been the same, without you and your wonderful memories! *Thank you*!

Finally, if you should ever come across someone, whom you suspect *may have been in a show choir with me*? There is only *one easy and sure-fire way* to find out. In a very excited manner, quickly *count to three*! If their body *immediately* contorts into an energetic, but awkward looking position and their facial expression looks happier than any face has a right to look… and they yell out a single word, in response to your counting, "Pizzazz!" The odds are… ***they were probably one of mine***!

ACKNOWLEDGEMENTS

My sincerest thanks go to the following individuals. Their contributions of choir memories, costume colors and competition results, without a doubt, made this book more accurate and incredibly enjoyable to read. Their insight and experiences have given this work real *Pizzazz!* Words alone cannot express my gratitude.

With Love and Appreciation,
Dave Willert

CONTRIBUTING PROFESSIONALS

Doug Kuhl (choreographer 1980-2016)
Margaret Willert (costumes and programs 1977-2016)
Alex Willert (vocal coach 2009-16)
Yolanda Romero Setoodeh (choir costumes 1986-2016)
Kurt Nielsen (acting & dance coach 2002-16)
Della Long (choir assistant 1983- 96)
Jerry Halpin (principal 2005-16)
Marti Repp (school/choir secretary 2005-16)
Bo Eder (drummer/ keyboardist 1981-2015)
Don Cloud (keyboardist 1990-2000)
Drew Hemwall (drummer 2005-16)
Dwayne Ganier (guitarist 1986-95)
Eric Hendrickson (keyboardist 2000-01 & 2012-16)
Francine Stewart Martyn (keyboardist 1981-83 & 1987-90)
Hannah Nam Hemwall (keyboardist 1998-2012)
Kathy Keith Boothby (pianist 1984-87)
Kramer Ison (band member 1993-2012)

Keith Fort (bass & drummer 1984-90)
Don Hofer (student teacher 1990)
Doug Newton (show choir associate)
Janae West (show choir associate)
Linda Willert Atherton (show choir associate)
Mark Henson (show choir associate)
Rob Hodo (show choir associate)
Rollie Maxson (show choir associate)
Ron & Reina Bolles (show choir associates)
Showchoir Community (competition results)
Thomas Timm Brucks (theatre arts teacher)
Tom Kessler (show choir associate)
Virgil & Sue Lewis (V and S Video)
Walt Disney (constant inspiration)

CONTRIBUTING WEST COVINA HIGH SCHOOL STUDENTS

Paula (Crowley) Hansen (student 1977)

CONTRIBUTING NORCO HIGH SCHOOL STUDENTS

Annette Ambrose Schumann (student 1977-78)
Becky Kohlenberger Bergsma (student 1977-78)
Carol Mount Feeney (student 1977-78)
Cheri Hale Patterson (student 1977-78)
Chris Breyer (student 1977-78)
Cindy Ellis Crockett (student 1977-78)
Doug Kuhl (student 1978-79)
Guy Wessell (student 1977-78)
Gwen Benner Marotte (student 1978-79)
Jack Homsany (guitar student 1977-78)
Jeff Crawford (student 1977-79)
Jim Thatcher (student 1977-78)
Jonnie Hall Mount (student 1977-79)
Karen Smith Gladu (student 1977-79)
Karen Marion Rupert (student 1977-79)
Kathleen Scott Kay (student 1978-79)
Kathy Griffin Chuck (student 1977-78)
Kathy Briggs Van Wagoner (student 1977-78)
Kevin Heard (student 1977-78)
Laura Aldrich Berger (student 1977-78)
Lysa Gamboa-Levy (student 1977-79)
Mary Leonti (student 1977-79)
Paula Leonti (student 1978-79)
Ron Hughes (student 1977-79)
Scott Chapman (student 1978-79)
Steve Hauser (student 1978-79)
Tami Seaton (student 1977-78)
Tara Sumner-Thornton (student 1977-79)
Teri Mayo (student 1977-79)
Tim Steele (student 1978-79)

CONTRIBUTING NOGALES HIGH SCHOOL STUDENTS

Abigail Yap Su (student 1996-98)
Adrian de Guzman (student)
Adrienne Rochelle Cox (student 1993-97)
Aisha Salgado Guillen (student 1994-95)
Alicia Garcia (student)
Allison Tjaden Tarus (student 1989-93)
Amanda Carr Smith (student 1994-98)
Amanda Vetter (student)
Amy Brazil Wells (student 1984-88)
Ana Enriquez Chico (student 1991-95)
Andrea Bond Ortega (student)
Angel Garcia (student 1994-98)
Anita Burleson (student 1980-82)
Anna Aleman (student 1988-92)
Anna Rosselli (student 1979-83)
Anna Trujillo Jarrell (student 1979-82)
Antonio Guerrero (student 1989-92)
Antonio Palacios (student)
Antrina Mojica (student)
Art Farias (student 1984-88)
Arveta D. Nolan (student)
Ashlee Romero (student)
Barbara Kovacs Minar (student 1984-88)
Barbara Repko (student)
Becky Mantanic (student 1992-96)
Betty Gardea (student 1986-90)
Beverly Boceta Garcia (student 1987-89)
Blandina Vergara Cruz (student 1986-89)
Bonnie Chacon Hooes (student 1991-95)
Brad Salsman (student 1987-88)
Brent Sanchez (student 1994-96)
Brian Gaither (student 1991-95)
Brian Gonzales (student 1995-96)
Brian Nunn (student 1982-86)
Brianne Sheldon (student)

Carlos Morales (student 1987-89)
Carol de Guzman (student 1994-95)
Carrie Acosta Edwon (student 1986-89)
Carrie Shaw (student 1986-1990)
Catherine Pinard Rhodes (student 1987-91)
Cathy Mixco (student 1987-90)
Cathy Valdez (student)
Celeste Wentworth Brown (student 1979-82)
Charmetra Chatmon (student 1987-89)
Cherry Mandani DeCastro (student)
Cheryl St. Amand (student 1986-87)
Chris Diaz (student)
Chris La Mantia (student 1984-87)
Chrissie Casey Brockman (student 1980-84)
Christa Peterson Mitchell (student)
Christie Acevedo Martin (student 1992-94)
Crystal Garcia (student)
Crystal Inman Strelko (student 1986-89)
Claudia Babbette Urrea (student)
Clifford Banagale (student 1996-98)
Colleen Faith Ketner (student)
Colleen Ory Caron (student 1982-86)
Crystal Garcia (student)
Cynthia Joy Blanche (student)
Dahlia Hamza Constantine (student)
Dale Hersh (student 1985-88)
Dan Copeland (student 1979-82)
Davina Gaither-De La Cruz (student 1990-94)
Deana Acosta Fetty (student 1988-92)
Debbie Bailey Lee (student 1988-91)
Dee Mitchell-Gaskin (student 1982-84)
Della Long (student 1979-83)
Denise Pomeroy (student)
Denise Ponce (student)
Dietrich Day (student)
Dion De Rosas (student 1991-93)
Don Ning (student)
Donna Bailey (student 1991-93)

Donna Block (student)
Dorothy Nacita Swayne (student 1994-96)
Drea Silva (student)
Dwayne Ganier (student 1982-85)
Eddie Partida (student 1991-94)
Eleanora El Riggers Hackworth (student 1980-81)
Ellen Murray Herrick (student 1979-81)
Elisa Garcia (student)
Erin Drake Garcia (student 1988-91)
Erin Galvery (student 1995-97)
Erin Lindsey (student)
Ernie Sroka Tovar (student 1981-85)
Gabriel Lomeli (student 1983-87)
Geo Nom Nom (student)
Gerry Miranda (student)
Giovanni "Wingston" Morales (student 1988-92)
Glen Jimenez (student 1982-86)
Gloria Hernandez Romero (student 1984-87)
Gloria Sartiaguin (student)
Gracie Enriquez (student 1995-98)
Greg Wells (student 1983-85)
Hazel Vargas (student 1994-97)
Heather Tjaden Jefferson (student 1986-90)
Hoda Aboulwafa Aguirre (student 1995-98)
Isabel Munoz (student)
Jacqueline Gilbert (student)
Jaime Alley (student 1991-95)
Jaime Zavala (student 1987-91)
James Mills (student 1980-83)
Jamie Drinville Lesnever (student 1992-95)
Jamie Martin (student)
Janet Enriquez (student 1997-98)
Janette Juarez Zelaya (student 1995-98)
Janice Dizon Cruz (student)
Jason Lofthouse (student)
Jeanette Zapata (student 1984-88)
Jeff Crouch (student 1985-87)
Jenevieve Fuentes (student 1993-95)

Jennell Fort (student)
Jenni Buitrago Ikeda (student 1989-93)
Jennifer Dunigan-Zamora (student 1984-88)
Jennifer Keller (student)
Jennifer Rey (student)
Jesse Yee (student)
Jewel Barnes (student 1986-87)
Jill Myer Wirz (student 1994-98)
Jimmy Cunningham (student 1991-95)
Joanna Gallagher-Miranda (student 1989-93)
Jodi Johnson (student 1980-83)
Joelyvette Durousseau (student)
John Sarmiento (student)
Jose Burciaga (student)
Joy Corpuz-Reyes (student)
Jujuan Gailey (student)
Julie Enriquez (student 1997-98)
Julie Anne Ines (student)
Julie Martinez Rodriguez (student 1986-89)
Julpha Maniquis-Dormitorio (student 1988-92)
Keisha Walker Holmes (student 1987-90)
Keith Fort (student 1979-83)
Ken Bednar (student 1993-97)
Kevin Pinedo (student 1984-88)
Kim Abernathy Alley (student 1989-93)
Kim Benton Frederick (student 1979-82)
Kimberly Sue Johnson (student 1980-83)
Kit Downing (student 1979- 83)
Kramer Ison (student 1991-93)
Kristal Garcia (student)
Kuilane Cheun Garrido (student 1987-91)
Kuimeuy Cheun Wang (student 1989-93)
Laura Diaz (student)
Laura Washington Franklin (student 1982-85)
Lawrence Vondrake Fitz (student 1985-89)
Lawrence Lanham (student)
Lenna Morales Nishiyama (student)
Lila Orozco Salsman (student 1984-88)

Leonel Diaz (student 1988-90)
Letty Gomez-Saldivar (student 1995-98)
Linda Dunigan (parent 1984-88)
Lisette Hoyos Marin (student 1994-98)
Lisa Castilleja Rosas (student 1982-1986)
Lisle Menjivar (student)
Lizsa Halopoff Pinedo (student 1984-88)
Loraine Tulud Samonte (student 1992-96)
Loretta Orozco-Vasquez (student)
Lori Strait Gartland (student 1983-86)
Lori Halopoff Fenelon (student 1986-91)
LuAnne Ponce Montilla (student 1983-86)
Lucy Covarrubias Martinez (student 1987-89)
Lupe Baldonado Hersh (student 1985-88)
Luz Barraza (student 1997-98)
Lynn Romanofsky Hurd (student 1979-81)
Manuel Aranda Jr. (student 1980-82)
Margarita Ramirez (student)
Margaux Yap Cruz (student 1993-97)
Maria Block (student)
Maria Pena (student)
Mariana Torres (student)
Marisa Ignacio (student 1993-97)
Maritza Gonzalez Wusstig (student 1984-86)
Mark Buenaluz (student)
Mark Stevens (student)
Mary Anne Garcia (student 1994-97)
Mary Grubb Hinojos (student 1979-83)
Mary Joy Hernandez (student)
Mary Walts (student)
Marylen Ayash-Borgen (student 1982-85)
Matt Blackstone (student 1990-93)
Megan Elizabeth Sander (student 1991-95)
Mei Ning (student)
MeLeah Robinson (student 1991-93)
Melynie Coates Rivers (student)
Melanie Maniquis Manalo (student)
***Melanie* Piercy** (student)

Melissa Black Solomon (student 1991-94)
Melissa Siaotong (student 1990-94)
Mimi Chavez (student 1997-98)
Michael Holguin (student)
Michael Trompeta (student)
Michael Washington (student 1995-98)
Michelle Holguin York (student)
Michelle Maxwell Appleby (student 1984-88)
Michelle Penalber Ahrens (student)
Michelle Alcantara Guray (student)
Michelle Brenes Roselli (student)
Micki Burciaga (student)
Mike Blackstone (student 1990-93)
Mike Anthony Gash (student 1984-87)
Mindy Inman Reichert (student 1985-87)
Misty Morrits (student 1989-93)
Mitchell Asa (student 1995-98)
Moni Grzceszak (student)
Monique Wilson (student 1993-97)
Myisha Morgan (student)
Nadia Stone (student 1991-95)
Nancy Jovel Penman (student 1990-92)
Nancy Mendoza Sams (student 1984-86)
Nanette Varela (student 1983-86)
Natalie Mauk Ridley (student 1994-96)
Nina Lares (student)
Norma Jeffries (student 1979-83)
Patrice Hunt (student)
Patricia Mountain Romero (student 1987-88)
Paul Alley (student 1987-91)
Peter Nguyen (student 1995-98)
Priscilla Lopez (student 1992-96)
Quandeel Davis (student)
Radhika Sharma (student 1996-98)
Ralph Contreras (student)
R.E. Fort (student 1979-80)
Regina Romero Afanador (student)
Ric Guerra (student 1988-91)

Rika Rai Grier-Farley (student 1989-93)
Robert Sanchez (student)
Robyn Price Evarts (student 1983-86)
Ronda Salazar (student)
Rosa *"Rosie" Gastellu* (student 1993-96)
Rosa Grimes (student 1983-87)
Roselani Hockenhull (student 1991-94)
Roxy Myer Rivas (student 1990-94)
Ruben D. Hoyos (student 1996-98)
Ruth Ellis (student)
Sabrina Ganier Cope (student 1984-88)
Sara Bach Lyddiard (student)
Scott Arnold (student 1987-89)
Sergio Mejia (student 1987-90)
Shauna Bragg (student)
Sheila Rantz (student 1981-85)
Shirlene McMurray (student 1982-86)
Shun Griffin (student 1985-88)
Susan Hernandez Burruel (student)
Susan Knox Bensing (student)
Susan Lim See (student)
Tamara Bowles Taz (student)
Tamara Wells (student 1981-84)
Tanya Russell Horsting (student 1990-94)
Tassa Hampton Varga (student 1989-93)
Teresa Cimino (student 1981-85)
Teresa Contreras (student)
Theresa Tulud-Ragasa (student 1991-93)
TJ Murray (student 1981-82)
Tiffanie Rowsell (student)
Tricia Osborn (student)
Tricey Davis (student 1996-98)
Trinette Barnes (student 1987-89)
Troy Peace (student 1982-84)
Uyen Mai (student 1991-95)
Valarie Arguijo (student)
Valerie Greer (student)
Valerie Russel Gerber (student 1996-98)

Vanessa Gonzalez Saavedra (student 1986-89)
Vangie Rustia Obrero (student 1987-89)
Veronica Bruny Anthony (student 1986-90)
Veronica Hilgrimson (student 1979-83)
Victoria Melhuish (student)
Vincent Dacumos (student)
Wallace Ma (student)
Yami Ibanez (student 1991-93)
Yasmeen Hamza-Johnson (student)
Yesenia Collazo Serrano (student 1990-94)
Yolanda Ruiz Rodriguez (student 1986-90)
Yvette Hernandez (student 1989-93)

CONTRIBUTING DIAMOND BAR HIGH SCHOOL STUDENTS/ PARENTS

A'Chauntae (Jasmine) Hall (student 1998-2000)
Aimee Corbin (student)
Alaina Hee (student)
Alanna Flores (student 1998-2001)
Alyson Behrend Ripa (student 1998-2002)
Alyssa Cossey (student 1998-2002)
Alyssa Layton Greusel (student 1998-2000)
Amanda Lampa Monteagudo (student 1998-2001)
Amanda Neufeld Love (student 1998-2000)
Amanda Mandelcorn (student 2003-05)
Amy Junne (student)
Andrea Brown (student 1999-2002)
Andrea Rodriguez (student)
Angela Harju (student)
Anjie Petris (student)
April Morton (student)
Brianna Fidel-Soucy (student 1998-2002)
Brittany Tatarski (student)
Caroline Bird (student)
Caroline Yenydunyeyan (student 2001-05)
Catherine Larson (student)
Chase Rebensdorf (student 2001-04)
Chris Brashear (student)
Christine "Criss" Lamorena Lopez (student 1998-2001)
Christine Miles (student)
Christie Groshong (student)
Christy Boyer (student 1999-2003)
Courtney Walborn (student 2001-05)
Cristin Coleman Toia (student 1999-2003)
Dana Avelar Gardiner (student)
Danae Rebensdorf (student 2003-05)
Daniella Dalli (student 1998-2000)
Diana Pianalto Padilla (student 1998-2000)
Emily Haager (student 1998-2001)
Erica Schneider (student 1998-2001)

Erin Mearns Stensby (student)
Esther Kim (student)
Fak Ang (student)
Georgette Delgado (student)
Giselle Kab (student)
Greg Buccola (student 1999-2002)
Hannah Nam Hemwall (student 2000-01)
Harmony Weber (student)
Hector Chaidez (student)
Jacquelyn Stratford (student)
Jade Harb Johnston (student 2003-05)
Jamie Fiamengo (student 1998-2000)
Janna McRoy (student)
Janae Nafziger West (student 1998-2001)
Jasmine Grady Sosa (student 1998-2000)
Jean Altadel Ruiz (student)
Jeff Buccola (student 2001-05)
Jeff Tsu (student 2000-01)
Jenni Layton Luck (student 1998-2002)
Jennifer McCullough (student)
Jennifer Ocegueda (student)
Jeremy Beeman (student)
Jessica Rae Leonor Michaels (student)
Jessica Marvin-Jones (student 1998-2001)
Jessica Lee (student)
Jessica Hessom Watts (student 1999-2003)
Jessica Sunderland (student)
Jessie Brown (student)
Jill Hollenbach Reeves (student 1998-2001)
Jill Rockwood (student 2003-05)
Joanna Zirbes (student 1999-2003)
JoDel Visser Clark (student 1999-2000)
Joey DiMauro (student)
John & Kathy Walborn (parents 2001-05)
Joseph Janesin (student)
Joe Kim (student 1999-2000)
Julia Brooke Haager-Devin (student 1999-2003)
Julie Luber Weil (student 2003-05)

Katelyn Vorkink Scrimsher (student 2002-05)
Katie Rockwood Price (student 1999-2002)
Katrina Gonzales (student 1998-2002)
Kayla Keel (student)
Keith Yamashita (student)
Kelly Preston (student)
Kelsey Christ Crowder (student 2001-04)
Kelsi Roberts (student 2001-05)
Kersaundra Ke LaRae Williams (student 1998-2001)
Kevin Ramirez (student 2000-04)
Kimberly Forkner Mitchell (student 1998-2002)
Kris Hilliard Doty (student 1998-2001)
Kristen Brittenham Raines (student 1998-2001)
Kristen Mearns (student)
Krystine Daryale (student)
Kyle Roberts (student)
Laura Schamp Isbell (student 1998-2001)
Lauren Bishop Borgogna (student)
Lauren Piper-Poling (student 1998-2000)
Leah Trujillo (student)
Leticia Garcia (student 1998-2001)
Mandy Welch (student 1998-2001)
Matt Adams (student)
Matthew Kaiser (student)
Megan Lomeli (student 2000-04)
Melanie Dilger de la Cantera (student 1998-2002)
Michelle Duenas Johnson (student 1998-2001)
Monique Blair (student 1998-2001)
Nathan Sangalang (student)
Noelle Celene (student)
Nick Cervantes (student 1999-2002)
Parker Rebensdorf (student 2004-05)
Paul Anthony Leonor (student)
Pete Buccola (student 1998-2001)
Priscilla Sosa Vela (student 2002-05)
Rachel Lents Maurer (student 1998-2001)
Ray Ayers (student 2001-04))
Rebecca Guizar-Ward (student)

Rebecca Mayorga (student)
Richard Durazo (student)
Ricky D. Nelson (student)
Robert Lamorena (student 2001-05)
Robert Waters (student)
Ruby Minori (student 1998-2001)
Rynicia Ortiz (student)
Samantha Morvai (student)
Samantha Turgeon (student)
Sarah Batistelli Moran (student)
Sarah Neal (student)
Shae Saldana (student)
Shayne Stephen Dickson (student 1999-2003)
Sheri Vernon (student)
Spike Abeyta (student 2000-04)
Tara Vorkink Flake (student)
Taylor Pedrini Spinogatti (student 1999-2003)
Teri Clemons (student)
Tiffanie Michelle White (student 1998-2000)
Tiffany Rush Harper (student 1998-2000)
Tiffany Yanez Gruenberg (student 2001-05)
Tracey Christ (student)
Tracy Chunchick (student)
Tracy Taylor (student)
Tracy Wynne (student 2000-04)
Tsar Agus (student 1998-2001)

CONTRIBUTING BREA JUNIOR HIGH STUDENTS/ PARENTS

Alex Olvey (student 2005-06)
Ally Catanesi (student 2005-07)
Allie Mayer (student 2012-13)
Alyssa Alcaraz (student)
Alyssa Hendrickson (student 2012-13)
Amanda Galvez (student 2015-16)
Amaris Salas (student 2011-13)
Amaya Llanes (student 2015-16)
Amber O'Barr (student 2012-14)
Andrew Strom (student 2011-12)
Angie Gall (student 2009-10)
Audrey Lee (student 2012-14)
Ayla Golshan (student 2010-12)
Becky Clark (student 2007-08)
Ben Harpster (student 2010-12)
Brianna Clark (student 2010-12)
Bryanna Wallace (student 2009-11)
Caitlyn Gutierrez (student 2009-11)
Carrie Bower (student 2010-12)
Chloe Stoddard (student 2015-16)
Christina Streitz (student 2009-11)
Claire Manson (student 2014-15)
Cori Bourgeois (student 2011-13)
Denise & Nick Catanesi (parents 2005-07)
Derek Miller (parent)
Dienna Catuna (student 2011-13)
Elizabeth Garcia (student 2010-12)
Emily Neva Boliver (student 2009-10)
Emmalee Wetzel (student 2006-07)
Erica Cline (student 2010-12)
Erica O'Barr (student 2013-15)
Gailyn Amber Tan (student 2007-08)
Hailey Summer Holman (student 2005-07)
Hailey Leeann Johnson (student 2010-11)
Hannah Fritz (student 2013-15)

Hayden Mangum (student 2011-13)
Holly Ramsey (student 2005-07)
Jessica Martinez (student 2010-12)
Jessica Patow (student 2009-11)
Jocelyn Abrahamson (student 2010-12)
Jocelyn Jordan (student 2011-13)
Julianne Sexton Hunt (student 2009-11)
Kaitlyn Rigsby (student 2011-13)
Kara Dietz (student 2012-13)
Kathleen Jensen (parent 2009-11)
Katie Moore (parent 2015-16)
Kayla Camacho (student 2005-06)
Kevin Siazon (student 2005-06)
Kristin Camacho (student 2012-14)
Leena Fritz (student 2009-11)
Lyndsey Gutierrez (student 2011-13)
Madeline Ellingson (student 2006-08)
Madyson Miguel (student 2014-16)
Marcia Holman (parent 2005-07)
Maria Carren (student 2012-14)
Marysa (Leite) Grondin (student 2007-09)
Maya Gutowski (student 2011-13)
Megan Strom (student 2007-09)
Melissa Strom (student 2005-07)
Mia Dalgleish (student 2012-13)
Monica Siazon (student 2009-11)
Nicole McEntee (student 2008-09)
Paris Valdivia (student 2011-13)
Pauline Rejniak (student 2010-12)
Rhyan Belanger (student 2010-12)
Sara Scott (student 2015-16)
Sarah Turner (student 2013-15)
Sierra West (student 2011-13)
Terry Dopson (student 2008-09)
Trinity Stinson (student 2015-16)
Zoe Tschumper (student 2015-16)

CONTRIBUTING BREA OLINDA HIGH SCHOOL STUDENTS/ PARENTS

Afsaneh Helali (parent)
Alex Macedo (student 2014-15)
Alex Olvey (student 2006-10)
Alex Willert (student 2005-09)
Alina Rotariu (student)
Allie Mayer (student 2013-16)
Alison Miller Legendre (parent)
Ally Catanesi (student 2007-11)
Amanda Crosby Moh (student 2008-12)
Amy Czerwinski (student 2008-12)
Amy Sargent (student 2005-07)
Andrea Thompson Strom (parent 2007-16)
Andrew Strom (student 2012-16)
Angela Truesdale (student)
Angie Gall (student 2010-14)
Ashley Schweitzer (student)
Ayla Golshan (student 2012-16)
Ashley Rangel (student 2006-10)
Baylee Heagle Grosso (student)
Becca Harpster Edginton (student 2008-12)
Beckie Clark (student 2008-12)
Becky Nevarez (student2012-16)
Ben Harpster (student 2012-16)
Ben Veling (student)
Brandon Allen (student)
Brandon Jones (student 2008-12)
Brianna Clark (student 2012-16)
Brianna Kdeiss (student 2008-12)
Caitlyn Grant Lunceford (student 2005-07)
Carrie Bower (student 2012-16)
Challoi McCuller (student)
Charisse Green Groh (student 2008-12)
Charlotte Kim (student 2012-16)
Charlotte Larcabal (student 2005-07)
Charlotte Martinez (parent)

Chris Flores (student 2008-09)
Christina Cope (parent)
Chrystal Eychaner (parent)
Cindy Hollingshead Fuller (parent)
Claire Manson (student 2015-16)
Claudia Ippel Ludwig (parent 2009-13)
Cori Bourgeois (student 2013-16)
Courtney Tindal (student 2010-13)
Craig Georgianna (parent 2005-09)
Daniel Cabrera (student 2007-09)
Daniel Dwyer (student 2010-14)
Daniel Truesdale (student)
David Dumond (student)
Debbie Clark (parent 2012-16)
Dee Dee Webster (parent 2005-09)
Denise & Nick Catanesi (parents 2005-11)
Denise Potts Dietz (parent 2013-16)
Dolly Jacobson-Boliver (parent 2010-14)
Drew Olvey (student 2005-07)
Ed Heagle (parent)
Elizabeth Garcia (student 2005-09)
Elizabeth Garcia (student 2012-16)
Elizabeth Irvine-Madrid (student 2005-09)
Elmer Clark (parent 2008-2012)
Emilie Daedler (student 2014-16)
Emily Neva Boliver (student 2010-14)
Emily Elias (student 2008-12)
Emily Reed (student 2005-09)
Emily Veling (student)
Emmalee Wetzel (student 2007-11)
Erica Cline (student 2012-2016)
Erica O'Barr (student 2015-16)
Erin Maddex (student)
Esmeralda Torres (student)
Felicia Sophia Torralba-Siazon (parent 2005-16)
Gene & Jan Nobles (super fans 2005-16)
Hailey Johnson (student 2011-15)
Hailey Holman (student 2007-11)

Hannah Fritz (student 2015-16)
Hannah Keller (student)
Harrison Schultz (student 2005-09)
Hayden Mangum (student 2013-16)
Holly Ramsey (student 2007-10)
Jacob Elias (student 2009-13)
Jacob Morton (student 2014-16)
Jake Drake (student 2014-15)
Jamie Holman Bivens (student 2005-07)
Janae Escarez (student)
Jeff Howarth (student)
***Jennifer Eckles* Winters** (student 2005-06)
Jessica Martinez (student 2012-16)
Jessica Patow (student 2011-15)
Jocelyn Abrahamson (student 2012-16)
Jocelyn Green (student 2005-09)
Jon Baker (student 2005-08)
Jordyn Georgianna (student 2005-09)
Josh Guerro (student)
Julia Dwyer (student 2007-11)
Julia Ludwig (student 2009-13)
Julianne Sexton Hunt (student 2011-15)
Julie Bush Heagle (parent)
Justine Eleina Garate (student)
Kaitlyn Rigsby (student 2013-16)
Kalynne Costa (student 2005-06)
Kara Dietz (student 2013-16)
Kassandra McCanless (student 2013-16)
Kathleen Jenson (parent 2011-15)
Katie Petri (student 2011-15)
Kayla Camacho (student 2006-10)
Kaylee Dysart (student 2007-10)
Kaylie Simec Morrill (student)
Kelsey Duhaime (student)
Kevin Seo (student 2007-2010)
Kevin John Siazon (student 2006-10)
Kevin Tukuloff (parent 2014-16)
Kristin Camacho (student 2014-16)

Kristen Webster (student 2005-09)
Lacey Currey (student 2012-16)
Lauren Howard (student 2007-09)
Lauren Patrick (student 2012-16)
Lauren Ward (student)
Leena Fritz (student 2011-15)
Leonel Diaz (parent 2011-15)
Linda Daughtry Clark (parent 2008-12)
Lorenzo Casas (student 2014-15)
Madeline Ellingson (student 2008-12)
Madison Reeves Burkaw (student 2005-09)
Mara Franklin (student 2014-15)
Marcia Holman (parent 2005-11)
Margie Colella Benedict (parent)
Matt Bryan (student 2014-15)
Maureen Nevarez (parent 2012-16)
Mary Wentsel Pipes (parent 2008-17)
Marysa (Leite) Grondin (student 2009-13)
Maya Gutowski (student 2013-16)
Megan Miller (student 2008-12)
Megan Strom (student 2009-13)
Melanie Ramsey Blankenship (student 2006-10)
Melissa Clark-Herbelin (parent)
Melissa Hankins (student 2005-09)
Melissa Strom (student 2007-11)
Melody Drake (parent 2014-16)
Mia Dalgleish (student 2012-16)
Mindy Elorza Verdugo (parent)
Mitchell Slife (student)
Monica Liz Siazon (student)
Nicole McEntee (student 2009-13)
Olson Walters (student)
Paul Bordwell (student 2012-13)
Pauline Rejniak (student 2012-16)
Proma Mazumder (student)
Rachael Kuhl (student 2007-09)
Rachel Gallegos (student)
Rhyan Belanger (student 2012-16)

Rosanna Alvarez (parent 2011-15)
Ryan Savosh (student)
Sophia Lissette (student)
Sarah Morgigno (student)
Sarah Schendon (student 2005-07)
Sean Barba (student 2007-08)
Sherry Nobles Reeves (parent 2005-2009)
Stephen Gonzales (student)
Susan Elias (parent 2008-13)
Susan Youngquist Wetzel (parent 2007-11)
Sylvia Quesada-Cline (parent 2012-16)
Tatiana Alvarez (student 2011-15)
Taylor Norene Diaz (student 2011-15)
Terry Dopson (student 2009-13)
Tracy Dopson (student 2010-13)
Travis Morrill (student)
Trisha Bermudez (student 2007-10)
Tori Stuht (student 2010-14)
Victoria Bower (parent)

If I have inadvertently left any *memory contributors* off of this list, please accept my sincere apologies. But remember, *it's just a list*. You know that you will always remain special to me and to your fellow choir members and parents for your contributions to choir, whether you are listed here or not! Some memories are printed in full, as you shared them, while others were generally used in spirit only. Thank you for your contributions of the past 40 years… *regardless of how big or small they were…* they were all special! I will always appreciate your help on this enormously gratifying project. ☺

One, Two, Three, Pizzazz!

www.ingramcontent.com/pod-product-compliance
Lightning Source LLC
Chambersburg PA
CBHW030939150426
42812CB00064B/3045/J
9781947532717